STANDARD EDITION

THE WEB COLLECTION REVEALED

ADOBE
DREAMWEAVER CS5
FLASH CS5
FIREWORKS CS5

SHERRY BISHOP, JIM SHUMAN & BARBARA M. WAXER

DELMAR
CENGAGE Learning

Australia • Brazil • Japan • Korea • Mexico • Singapore • Spain • United Kingdom • United States

DELMAR
CENGAGE Learning™

The Web Collection Revealed Standard Edition:
Adobe Dreamweaver CS5, Flash CS5, and
Fireworks CS5
Sherry Bishop, Jim Shuman, and
Barbara M. Waxer

Vice President, Career and Professional Editorial:
  Dave Garza

Director of Learning Solutions: Sandy Clark

Senior Acquisitions Editor: Jim Gish

Managing Editor: Larry Main

Product Managers: Jane Hosie-Bounar, Meaghan O'Brien

Editorial Assistant: Sarah Timm

Vice President Marketing, Career and Professional:
  Jennifer Baker

Executive Marketing Manager: Deborah S. Yarnell

Marketing Manager: Erin Brennan

Marketing Coordinator: Erin Deangelo

Production Director: Wendy Troeger

Senior Content Project Manager: Kathryn B. Kucharek

Developmental Editors: Barbara Clemens, Pam Conrad,
  Karen Stevens, Barbara M. Waxer

Technical Editors: John Shanley, Sasha Vodnik,
  Molly Oldfield

Senior Art Director: Joy Kocsis

Cover Design: Joe Villanova

Cover Art: Spitting Images

Cover Photographs:
Wave/surfboard: © istockphoto.com/Reniw Imagery
Sifaka monkey: © istockphoto.com/Life on White

Text Designer: Liz Kingslein

Proofreader: Kim Kosmatka

Indexer: Alexandra Nickerson

Technology Project Manager: Christopher Catalina

For product information and technology assistance,
contact us at **Cengage Learning Customer & Sales
Support, 1-800-354-9706**

For permission to use material from this text or
product, submit all requests online at **www.cengage.
com/permissions**

Further permissions questions can be emailed to
permissionrequest@cengage.com

Library of Congress Control Number: 2010921381

Hardcover edition:
ISBN-13: 978-1-111-13080-0
ISBN-10: 1-111-13080-9

Soft cover edition:
ISBN-13: 978-1-111-13078-7
ISBN-10: 1-111-13078-7

Delmar
5 Maxwell Drive
Clifton Park, NY 12065-2919
USA

Cengage Learning is a leading provider of customized
learning solutions with office locations around the globe,
including Singapore, the United Kingdom, Australia,
Mexico, Brazil, and Japan. Locate your local office at:
international.cengage.com/region

Cengage Learning products are represented in Canada by
Nelson Education, Ltd.

To learn more about Delmar, visit **www.cengage.com/delmar**

Purchase any of our products at your local college store or
at our preferred online store **www.cengagebrain.com**

Notice to the Reader
Publisher does not warrant or guarantee any of the
products described herein or perform any independent
analysis in connection with any of the product information
contained herein. Publisher does not assume, and
expressly disclaims, any obligation to obtain and include
information other than that provided to it by the
manufacturer. The reader is expressly warned to consider
and adopt all safety precautions that might be indicated
by the activities described herein and to avoid all potential
hazards. By following the instructions contained herein,
the reader willingly assumes all risks in connection with
such instructions. The publisher makes no representations
or warranties of any kind, including but not limited
to, the warranties of fitness for particular purpose or
merchantability, nor are any such representations implied
with respect to the material set forth herein, and the
publisher takes no responsibility with respect to such
material. The publisher shall not be liable for any special,
consequential, or exemplary damages resulting, in whole
or part, from the readers' use of, or reliance upon, this
material.

Printed in the United States of America
1 2 3 4 5 6 7 14 13 12 12 10

Revealed Series Vision

The Revealed Series is your guide to today's hottest multimedia applications. These comprehensive books teach the skills behind the application, showing you how to apply smart design principles to multimedia products such as dynamic graphics, animation, websites, software authoring tools, and digital video.

A team of design professionals including multimedia instructors, students, authors, and editors worked together to create this series. We recognized the unique learning environment of the multimedia classroom and created a series that:

- Gives you comprehensive step-by-step instructions
- Offers in-depth explanation of the "Why" behind a skill
- Includes creative projects for additional practice
- Explains concepts clearly using full-color visuals

It was our goal to create a book that speaks directly to the multimedia and design community—one of the most rapidly growing computer fields today. We think we've done just that, with a sophisticated and instructive book design.

—The Revealed Series

New to This Edition

The latest edition of The Web Collection Standard Edition includes many exciting new features, some of which are listed below:

- The new Live view navigation, simplified site setup, and Web 2.0 coverage in Dreamweaver.
- The Text Layout Format and enhanced character animation in Flash.
- Fireworks new features include document templates and presets, the Compound Shape tool, Gradient either control, text flow indicator, custom brushes, and instant access to Photoshop filters.

Authors' Visions

This book will introduce you to three fascinating programs that will hopefully inspire you to create rich and exciting Web sites. Through the work of many talented and creative individuals, this text was created for you. Our Product Manager, Jane Hosie-Bounar, guided and directed the team from start to finish. She is a talented and tireless individual—the ultimate professional and visionary. She is rock solid—someone I can always count on for sage advice and guidance. Barbara Clemens, my Development Editor, is an example of so many things I value: joy, kindness, patience, and determination. Although we live thousands of miles apart, I always feel a void when our working time together is over.

The copyright content was generously provided by my dear friend Barbara Waxer. Additional information on locating media on the Internet and determining its legal use is available in her Revealed Series book *Internet Surf and Turf Revealed: The Essential Guide to Copyright, Fair Use, and Finding Media.*

John Shanley did double duty this time. As the Dreamweaver Technical Editor for both Mac and PC, he carefully tested each step to make sure that the end product was error-free. He gave exceptional feedback as he reviewed each chapter. This part of the publishing process is what truly sets Delmar Cengage Learning apart from other publishers.

Tintu Thomas, Amrin Sahay, and Kathy Kucharek, our Content Product Managers, kept the schedule on track. We thank them for keeping up with the many details and deadlines. The work is beautiful.

Brianna Hawes patiently contacted the websites we used as examples to obtain permission for their inclusion. This component adds much to the content of the book and would not have been possible without her good work. Thank you to each of you that allowed us to use images from your websites.

Kim Kosmatak quietly worked behind the scenes to ensure that my grammatical and punctuation errors were corrected. She also provided valuable insight in regard to the accuracy of content specifics. Paula Melton authored the test banks.

Special thanks go to Jim Gish, Senior Acquisitions Editor, and Sandy Clark, the Director of Learning Solutions. They have embraced the Revealed books with enthusiasm and grace and provided us with such excellent resources to produce products that make us all proud. The book covers and interior design features are spectacular! Joe Villanova did a fantastic job designing new banners and logos for the websites to give them a fresh new look.

The Beach Club in Gulf Shores, Alabama, (www.beachclubal.com) generously allowed us to use several photographs of their beautiful property for The Striped Umbrella Web site. Christie Adams, Executive Assistant, was extremely helpful and gracious.

Typically, your family is the last to be thanked. My husband, Don, supports and encourages me every day, as he has for the last forty years. Our travels with our children and grandchildren provide happy memories for us and content for the Web sites. You will see the faces of my precious grandchildren Jacob, Emma, Thomas, and Caroline peeking out from some of the pages.

—Sherry Bishop

I would like to thank Jane Hosie-Bounar for her leadership in guiding us through this project. A very special thanks to Pam Conrad (for her word wizardry and wit) and to my co-authors Barbara and Sherry. I also want to give a heartfelt thanks to my wife, Barbara, for her patience and support.

—Jim Shuman

Huge thanks to my partner, Lindy, and to a house full of animals who deserve the utmost acknowledgement for their spontaneous contributions that never once bordered on combustion. Special thanks to Jane, who led this complex project perfectly.

—Barbara M. Waxer

Introduction to The Web Collection, Standard Edition

Welcome to *The Web Collection Standard Edition: Adobe Dreamweaver CS5, Flash CS5, and Fireworks CS5—Revealed.* This book offers creative projects, concise instructions, and coverage of basic Dreamweaver, Flash, Fireworks, and Creative Suite integration skills, helping you to create polished, professional-looking websites, animations, and art work. Use this book both in the classroom and as your own reference guide. It also includes many of the new features of CS5.

This text is organized into 16 chapters. In these chapters, you will learn many skills, including how to move amongst the Creative Suite applications, which, in this release, provide familiar functionality from one application to the next.

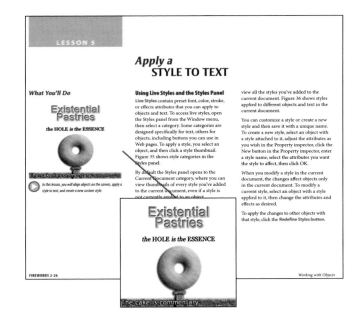

What You'll Do

A What You'll Do figure begins every lesson. This figure gives you an at-a-glance look at what you'll do in the chapter, either by showing you a file from the current project or a tool you'll be using.

Comprehensive Conceptual Lessons

Before jumping into instructions, in-depth conceptual information tells you "why" skills are applied. This book provides the "how" and "why" through the use of professional examples. Also included in the text are tips and sidebars to help you work more efficiently and creatively, or to teach you a bit about the history or design philosophy behind the skill you are using.

Step-by-Step Instructions

This book combines in-depth conceptual information with concise steps to help you learn CS5. Each set of steps guides you through a lesson where you will create, modify, or enhance a CS5 file. Step references to large colorful images and quick step summaries round out the lessons. The Data Files for the steps are provided on the CD at the back of this book.

Projects

This book contains a variety of end-of-chapter materials for additional practice and reinforcement. The Skills Review contains hands-on practice exercises that mirror the progressive nature of the lesson material. The chapter concludes with four projects: two Project Builders, one Design Project, and one Portfolio Project. The Project Builders and the Design Project require you to apply the skills you've learned in the chapter. Portfolio Projects encourage you to address and solve challenges based on the content explored in the chapter in order to create portfolio-quality work.

What Instructor Resources Are Available with This Book?

The Instructor Resources CD-ROM is Delmar's way of putting the resources and information needed to teach and learn effectively into your hands. All the resources are available for both Macintosh and Windows operating systems.

Instructor's Manual

Available as an electronic file, the Instructor's Manual includes chapter overviews and detailed lecture topics for each chapter, with teaching tips. The Instructor's Manual is available on the Instructor Resources CD-ROM.

Sample Syllabus

Available as an electronic file, the Sample Syllabus includes a suggested syllabus for any course that uses this book. The syllabus is available on the Instructor Resources CD-ROM.

PowerPoint Presentations

Each chapter has a corresponding PowerPoint presentation that you can use in lectures, distribute to your students, or customize to suit your course.

Data Files for Students

To complete most of the chapters in this book, your students will need Data Files. The Data Files are available on the CD at the back of this textbook. Instruct students to use the Data Files List at the end of this book. This list gives instructions on organizing files.

Solutions to Exercises

Solution Files are Data Files completed with comprehensive sample answers. Use these files to evaluate your students' work. Or distribute them electronically so students can verify their work. Sample solutions to all lessons and end-of-chapter material are provided with the exception of some portfolio projects.

Test Bank and Test Engine

ExamView is a powerful testing software package that allows instructors to create and administer printed and computer (LAN-based) exams. ExamView includes hundreds of questions that correspond to the topics covered in this text, enabling students to generate detailed study guides that include page references for further review. The computer-based and LAN-based/online testing component allows students to take exams using the EV, Player and also saves the instructor time by grading each exam automatically.

CONTENTS

CHAPTER 1: GETTING STARTED WITH DREAMWEAVER

CHAPTER 3: WORKING WITH TEXT AND CASCADING STYLE SHEETS

Intended Audience

This text is designed for the beginner or intermediate user who wants to learn how to use Dreamweaver CS5, Flash CS5, and Fireworks CS5. The book is designed to provide basic and in-depth material that not only educates, but also encourages you to explore the nuances of these exciting programs. Features new to CS5 and covered in this book are indicated by a New icon.

Approach

The text allows you to work at your own pace through step-by-step tutorials. A concept is presented and the process is explained, followed by the actual steps. To learn the most from the use of the text, you should adopt the following habits:

- Proceed slowly: Accuracy and comprehension are more important than speed.
- Understand what is happening with each step before you continue to the next step.
- After finishing a skill, ask yourself if you could do it on your own, without referring to the steps. If the answer is no, review the steps.

General

Throughout the initial chapters, students are given precise instructions regarding saving their work. Students should feel that they can save their work at any time, not just when instructed to do so.

Icons, Buttons, and Pointers

Symbols for icons, buttons, and pointers are shown in the step each time they are used. Icons may look different in the files panel depending on the file association settings on your computer. Once an icon, button, or pointer has been used on a page, the symbol will be shown for subsequent uses on that page *without* showing its name.

Skills Reference

As a bonus, a Power User Shortcuts table is included at the end of the Dreamweaver chapters. This table contains the quickest method of completing tasks covered in the chapter. It is meant for the more experienced user, or for the user who wants to become more experienced. Tools are shown, not named. Brief directions are given, with no tool or command locations.

Fonts

The Data Files contain a variety of commonly used fonts, but there is no guarantee that these fonts will be available on your computer. In a few cases, fonts other than those common to a PC or a Macintosh are used. If any of the fonts in use is not available on your computer, you can make a substitution, realizing that the results may vary from those in the book.

Windows and Macintosh

Adobe Creative Suite works virtually the same on Windows and Macintosh operating systems. In those cases where there is a significant difference, the abbreviations (Win) and (Mac) are used.

Data Files

To complete the lessons in this book, you need the Data Files on the CD in the back of this book. Your instructor will tell you where to store the files as you work, such as the hard drive, a network server, or a USB storage device. The instructions in the lessons will refer to "the drive and folder where you store your Data Files" when referring to the Data Files for the book.

When you copy the Data Files to your computer, you may see lock icons that indicate that the files are read- only when you view them in the Dreamweaver Files panel. To unlock the files, right-click on the locked file name in the Files panel, then click Turn off Read Only.

Images vs. Graphics

Many times these terms seem to be used interchangeably. For the purposes of the Dreamweaver chapters, the term images is used when referring to pictures on a web page. The term graphics is used as a more encompassing term that refers to non-text items on a web page such as photographs, logos, navigation bars, Flash animations, graphs, background images, and drawings. You may define these terms in a slightly different way, depending on your professional background or business environment.

Preference Settings

The learning process will be much easier if you can see the file extensions for the files you will use in the lessons. To do this in Windows, open Windows Explorer, click Organize, Folder and Search Options, click the View tab, then uncheck the box Hide Extensions for Known File Types. To do this for a Mac, go to the Finder, click the Finder menu, and then click Preferences. Click the Advanced tab, then select the Show all file extensions check box.

To view the Flash content that you will be creating, you must set a preference in your browser to allow active content to run. Otherwise, you will not be able to view objects such as Flash buttons. To set this preference in Internet Explorer, click Tools, Internet Options, Advanced, then check the box Allow active content to run in files on My Computer. Your browser settings may be slightly different, but look for similar wording. When using Windows Internet Explorer 7, you can also click the information bar when prompted to allow blocked content.

Creating a Portfolio

The Portfolio Project and Project Builders allow students to use their creativity to come up with original Dreamweaver, Flash, and Photoshop designs. You might suggest that students create a portfolio in which they can store their original work.

Dreamweaver CS5 System Requirements
For a Windows operating system:

- Intel® Pentium® 4 or AMD Athlon® 64 processor
- Microsoft® Windows® XP with Service Pack 2 (Service Pack 3 recommended) or Windows Vista® Home Premium, Business, Ultimate, or Enterprise with Service Pack 1; or Windows 7

- 512MB of RAM
- 1GB of available hard-disk space for installation; additional free space required during installation (cannot install on removable flash-based storage devices)
- 1280 × 800 display with 16-bit video card
- DVD-ROM drive
- Broadband Internet connection required for online services

For a Macintosh operating system:

- Multicore Intel® processor
- Mac OS X v10.5.7 or v10.6
- 512MB of RAM
- 1.8GB of available hard-disk space for installation; additional free space required during installation (cannot install on a volume that uses a case-sensitive file system or on removable flash-based storage devices)
- 1280 × 800 display with 16-bit video card
- DVD-ROM drive
- Broadband Internet connection required for online services*

Memory Challenges

If, instead of seeing an image on an open page, you see an image placeholder with a large X across it, your RAM is running low. Try closing any other applications that are running to free up memory.

Building a Web site

You will create and develop several Web sites named The Striped Umbrella, Blooms & Bulbs, TripSmart, and Carolyne's Creations in the lesson material and end of unit exercises in this book. Because each chapter builds off of the previous chapter, it is recommended that you work through the chapters in consecutive order.

Web sites Used in Figures

Each time a Web site is used for illustration purposes in a lesson, where necessary, a statement acknowledging that we obtained permission to use the Web site is included, along with the URL of the Web site. Sites whose content is in the public domain, such as federal government Web sites, are acknowledged as a courtesy.

Flash CS5

System Requirements

For a Windows operating system:

- Intel® Pentium® 4 or AMD Athlon® 64 processor
- Microsoft® Windows® XP with Service Pack 2 (Service Pack 3 recommended) or Windows Vista™ Home Premium, Business, Ultimate, or Enterprise with Service Pack 1; or Windows 7
- 1GB of RAM
- 3.5GB of available hard-disk space for installation; additional free space required during installation (cannot install on removable flash-based storage devices)
- 1,024 × 768 display (1280 × 800 recommended) with 16-bit video card
- DVD-ROM drive
- QuickTime 7.6.2 software required for multimedia features

For a Macintosh operating system:

- Multicore Intel processor
- Mac OS X v10.5.7 or v10.6
- 1G of RAM
- 4GB of available hard-disk space for installation; additional free space required during installation (cannot install on a volume that uses a case-sensitive file system or on removable flash-based storage devices)
- 1,024 × 768 display (1,280 × 800 recommended) with 16-bit video card
- DVD-ROM drive
- QuickTime 7.6.2 software required for multimedia features

Projects

Several projects are presented that allow students to apply the skills they have learned in a chapter. Two projects, Ultimate Tours and the Portfolio, build from chapter to chapter. You will need to contact your instructor if you plan to work on these without having completed the previous chapter's project.

Fireworks CS5

System Requirements

For a Windows operating system:

- Intel® Pentium® 4 or AMD Athlon® 64 processor
- Microsoft® Windows® XP with Service Pack 2 (Service Pack 3 recommended)
- or Windows Vista™ Home Premium, Business, Ultimate, or Enterprise with Service Pack 1; or Windows 7

- 512MB of RAM (1GB recommended)
- 1GB of available hard-disk space for installation; additional free space required during installation (cannot install on removable flash-based storage devices)
- 1280 × 1024 with 16-bit video card
- DVD-ROM drive
- QuickTime 7.6.2 software required for multimedia features

For a Macintosh operating system:

- Multicore Intel processor
- Mac OS X v10.5.7 or v10.6
- 512MB of RAM (1GB recommended)

- 1GB of available hard-disk space for installation; additional free space required during installation (cannot install on a volume that uses a case-sensitive file system or on removable flash-based storage devices)
- 1280 × 1024 with 16-bit video card
- DVD-ROM drive
- QuickTime 7.6.2 software required for multimedia features

CHAPTER 1

GETTING STARTED WITH
DREAMWEAVER

1. Explore the Dreamweaver workspace
2. View a web page and use Help
3. Plan and set up a website
4. Add a folder and pages

GETTING STARTED WITH
DREAMWEAVER

Introduction

Adobe Dreamweaver CS5 is a web development tool that lets you create dynamic web pages containing text, images, hyperlinks, animation, sounds, video, and interactive elements. You can use Dreamweaver to create individual web pages or complex websites consisting of many web pages. A **website** is a group of related web pages that are linked together and share a common interface and design. Dreamweaver lets you create design elements such as text, tables, rollover images, and interactive buttons, or import elements from other software programs. You can also save Dreamweaver files in many different file formats, including XHTML, HTML, JavaScript, CSS, or XML, to name a few. **XHTML** is the acronym for eXtensible HyperText Markup Language, the current standard language used to create web pages. You can still use **HTML** (HyperText Markup Language) in Dreamweaver; however, it is no longer considered the standard language. You use a web browser to view your web pages on the Internet. A **web browser** is a program, such as Microsoft Internet Explorer, Google Chrome, Safari, or Mozilla Firefox, which lets you display web pages.

Using Dreamweaver Tools

Creating an excellent website is a complex task. Fortunately, Dreamweaver has an impressive number of tools that can help. Using Dreamweaver design tools, you can create dynamic and interactive web pages without writing a word of code. However, if you prefer to write code, Dreamweaver makes it easy to enter and edit the code directly and see the visual results of the code instantly. Dreamweaver also contains organizational tools that help you work with a team of people to create a website. You can also use the Dreamweaver management tools to help you manage a website. For instance, you can use the **Files panel** to create folders to organize and store the various files for your website, and to add pages to your website.

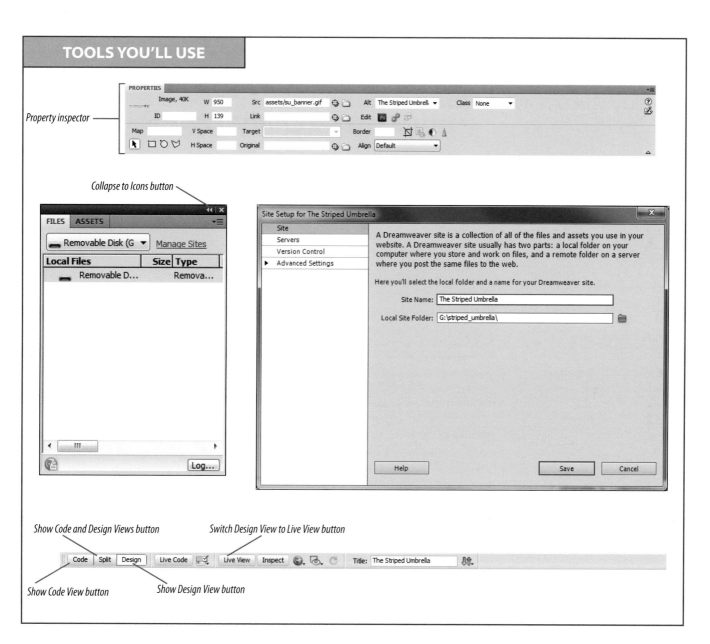

Property inspector

Collapse to Icons button

Show Code and Design Views button

Switch Design View to Live View button

Show Code View button

Show Design View button

Explore the
DREAMWEAVER WORKSPACE

What You'll Do

In this lesson, you will start Dreamweaver, examine the components that make up the Dreamweaver workspace, and change views.

Examining the Dreamweaver Workspace

After you start Dreamweaver, you see the **Dreamweaver workspace**, the screen that includes all of the menus, panels, buttons, inspectors, and panes that you use to create and maintain websites. It is designed to give you easy access to all the tools you need to create web pages. Refer to Figure 1 as you locate the components described below.

The **Document window** is the large area in the Dreamweaver program window where you create and edit web pages. The **Application bar** (Win) or **Menu bar** (Mac), located above the Document window, includes menu names, a Workspace switcher, and other application commands. The Application bar appears on either one bar or two bars, depending on your screen size and resolution. To choose a menu command, click the menu name to open the menu, then click the menu command. The Insert panel appears at the top of the Dreamweaver workspace on the right side of the screen. The **Insert panel**, sometimes called the Insert bar, includes eight categories of buttons displayed through a drop-down menu: Common, Layout,

Forms, Data, Spry, InContext Editing, Text, and Favorites. Clicking a category in the Insert panel displays the buttons and menus for inserting objects associated with that category. For example, if you click the Layout category, you find buttons for using div tags, used for creating blocks of content on pages; Spry buttons for inserting interactive page elements such as buttons or drop-down menus; Table buttons, used for inserting and editing tables; and the Frames button, used for selecting one of 13 different frame layouts.

QUICK TIP

Two additional options are available through the Insert panel drop-down menu. To display the icons in color, click Color Icons, or right-click the Insert panel, then click Color Icons. To hide the button labels, click Hide Labels.

The **Document toolbar** contains buttons and drop-down menus you can use to change the current work mode, check browser compatibility, preview web pages, debug web pages, choose visual aids, and view file-management options.

NEW The **Browser Navigation toolbar**, a new toolbar in Dreamweaver CS5, contains navigation buttons you use when you are following links on your pages in Live view. **Live view** displays an open document as if you were viewing it in a browser, with interactive elements active and functioning.

Two additional toolbars do not appear by default: the Standard toolbar and the Style Rendering toolbar. The **Standard toolbar** contains buttons you can use to execute frequently used commands that are also available on the File and Edit menus. The **Style Rendering toolbar** contains buttons that you can use to display data for different platforms, such as a cell phone. To display or hide the Document, Standard, Browser Navigation, and Style Rendering toolbars, right-click an empty area of an open toolbar, then click the toolbar name you wish to display or hide. You can also use the View, Toolbars menu.

The **Related Files toolbar** is located below an open document's filename tab and displays the names of any related files. **Related files** are files that are linked to a document and are necessary for the document to display and function correctly. An external style sheet, which contains formatting rules that control the appearance of a document, is a good example of a related file. The **Coding toolbar** contains buttons you can use when working

Figure 1 *Dreamweaver CS5 workspace*

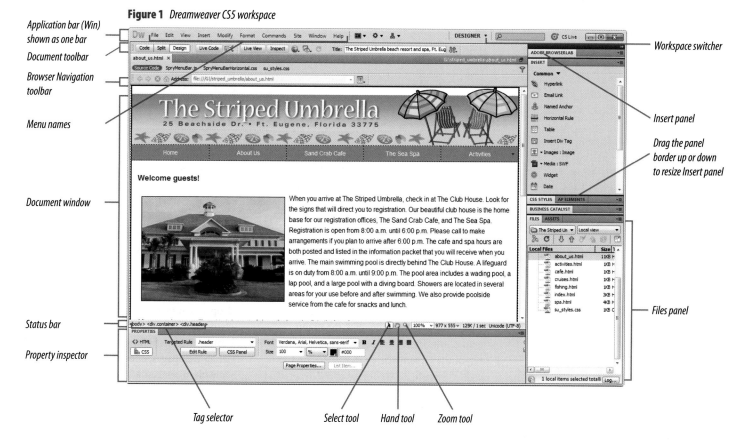

Application bar (Win) shown as one bar

Document toolbar

Browser Navigation toolbar

Menu names

Document window

Status bar

Property inspector

Workspace switcher

Insert panel

Drag the panel border up or down to resize Insert panel

Files panel

Tag selector   Select tool   Hand tool   Zoom tool

directly in the code and is not visible unless you are in Code view. When visible, it appears on the left side of the Document window.

The **Property inspector**, sometimes referred to as the **Properties pane**, located at the bottom of the Dreamweaver window, lets you view and change the properties (characteristics) of a selected object. The Property inspector is context sensitive, which means it changes according to what is selected in the Document window. The **status bar** is located below the Document window. The left side of the status bar displays the **tag selector**, which shows the HTML tags used at the insertion point location. The right side displays the Select tool, used for page editing; the Hand tool, used for panning; the Zoom tool, used for magnifying; and the Set Magnification menu, used to change the percentage of magnification. It also displays the window size and estimated download time for the current page.

A **panel** is a tabbed window that displays information on a particular topic or contains related commands. **Panel groups** are sets of related panels that are grouped together. A collection of panels or panel groups is called a **dock**. To view the contents of a panel in a panel group, click the panel's tab. Panels are docked by default on the right side of the screen. You can undock or "float" them by dragging the panel tab to another screen location. To collapse or expand a panel group, double-click the panel tab or the blank area in the panel title bar, as shown in Figure 2.

NEW When you first start Dreamweaver, the Insert, CSS Styles, AP Elements, Business Catalyst, Files, and Assets panels appear by default. You can open panels using the Window menu commands or the corresponding shortcut keys.

QUICK TIP

The Collapse to Icons button ▶▶ above the top panel lets you collapse all open panels to icons to enlarge the workspace.

Working with Dreamweaver Views

A **view** is a particular way of displaying page content. Dreamweaver has three working views. **Design view** shows the page as it would appear in a browser and is primarily used for designing and creating a web page. **Code view** shows the underlying HTML code for the page; use this view to read or edit the underlying code.

QUICK TIP

You can also split Code view to enable you to work on two different sections of code at once. To change to Split Code view, click View on the Application bar (Win) or Menu bar (Mac), then click Split Code.

Show Code and Design views is a combination of Code view and Design view. Show Code and Design views is the best view for **debugging** or correcting errors because you can immediately see how code modifications change the appearance of the page. The view buttons are located on the Document toolbar.

Figure 2 *Panels in panel group*

Active panel tab

Your drive may differ

Collapse to Icons button

Double-click to collapse or expand panel group

FILES ASSETS

Removable Disk (G ▼   Manage Sites

Local Files   **Size** **Type**
        Removable D...   Remova...

Log...

Figure 3 *Starting Dreamweaver CS5 (Windows)*

Click Adobe
Dreamweaver CS5

Start Dreamweaver (Windows)

1. Click the **Start button** on the taskbar.
2. Point to **All Programs**, then click **Adobe Dreamweaver CS5**, as shown in Figure 3.
3. If the Default Editor dialog box opens, click **OK**.

You started Dreamweaver CS5 for Windows.

Hiding and Displaying Toolbars

To hide or display the Style Rendering, Document, Standard, or Browser Navigation toolbars, click View on the Application bar (Win) or Menu bar (Mac), point to Toolbars, then click Style Rendering, Document, Standard, or Browser Navigation. The Coding toolbar is available only in Code view and the Code window in Split view, and appears vertically in the Document window. By default, the Document and Browser Navigation toolbars appear in the workspace.

Start Dreamweaver (Macintosh)

1. Click **Finder** in the Dock, then click **Applications**.

2. Click the **Adobe Dreamweaver CS5 folder**, then double-click the **Adobe Dreamweaver CS5 application**, as shown in Figure 4.

TIP Once Dreamweaver is running, you can add it to the Dock permanently by [control]-clicking the Dreamweaver icon, clicking Options, then clicking Keep In Dock.

You started Dreamweaver CS5 for Macintosh.

Figure 4 *Starting Dreamweaver CS5 (Macintosh)*

Using Two Monitors for Optimum Workspace Layout

One option you have for workspace layout is Dual Screen layout. **Dual Screen layout** is the layout you would choose when you are using two monitors while working with Dreamweaver. The Document window and Property inspector appear on the first monitor and the panels appear on the second monitor. It is seamless to work between the two monitors and optimizes your workspace by allowing you to have multiple panels open without compromising your Document window space.

Figure 5 *Code view for new document*

Show Code
View button

Show Code and
Design Views button

Show Design
View button

Switch Design View
to Live View button

Application bar may be
displayed as two bars

Coding toolbar

Click to collapse all
panels to icons

Your panel arrangement
may differ depending on
the last placement

1. Click **HTML** in the Create New category on the Dreamweaver Welcome Screen.

   The Dreamweaver Welcome Screen provides shortcuts for opening files and for creating new files or websites.

   TIP If you do not want the Dreamweaver Welcome Screen to appear each time you start Dreamweaver, click the Don't show again check box on the Welcome Screen or remove the check mark next to Show Welcome Screen in the General category in the Preferences dialog box.

2. Click the **Show Code View button** [Code] on the Document toolbar.

   The default code for a new document appears in the Document window, as shown in Figure 5.

   TIP The Coding toolbar is available only in Code view and in the Code window in Split view.

3. Click the **Show Code and Design Views button** [Split] on the Document toolbar.

4. Click the **Show Design View button** [Design] on the Document toolbar.

   TIP If your icons appear in black-and-white and you would like to display them in color, click the Insert panel drop-down menu, then click Color Icons.

   (continued)

5. Click the **Assets panel tab**, then compare your screen to Figure 6.

TIP If the Assets panel is not visible, click Window on the Application bar (Win) or Menu bar (Mac), then click Assets.

6. Click the **Files panel tab** to display the contents of the Files panel.

7. Double-click **Assets** to collapse the panel group.

8. View the contents of the CSS Styles and AP Elements panels.

9. Click and drag the **blank area** next to the AP Elements tab to the middle of the document window.

   The panel group is now in a floating window.

   (continued)

Figure 6 *Displaying a panel group*

Files and Assets panels docked together in one panel group

Drag title bar or blank area next to tabs to undock or "float" panel group

Drag either panel tab to undock or "float" panel separately from group

Choosing a Workspace Layout

The Dreamweaver interface is an integrated workspace, which means that all of the document windows and panels appear in a single application window. Each open document appears as a tab below the document toolbar. (In the Mac OS, documents can either be tabbed together in a single window or displayed in separate windows.) To view a tabbed document, click the tab with the document's filename. The **Workspace switcher**, a drop-down menu in the top right corner on the Application bar, lets you change the workspace layout. The default layout is the Designer workspace layout, where the panels are docked on the right side of the screen and Split view is the default view. Other workplace layouts include App Developer, App Developer Plus, Classic, Coder, Coder Plus, Designer Compact, and Dual Screen. To change the workspace layout, click the Workspace switcher, then click the desired layout. You can also rearrange the workspace using your own choices for panel placement and save the workspace with a unique name using the "New Workspace" and "Manage Workspaces" commands on the Workspace switcher. The Reset 'Current view' option resets the workspace layout to return to the default positions on the screen for the selected view.

Figure 7 *Docking a panel group*

Panel group being docked

INSERT

BUSINESS CATALYST

FILES   ASSETS

(no styles defined)

Blue drop zone appears as a horizontal line

10. Click and drag the **panel title bar** back to its original position, then drop it to dock the panel group below the Insert panel.

Release the mouse only when you see the blue drop zone. The **blue drop zone** is a heavy blue line that appears when the panel is in the correct position to be docked. See Figure 7. If the blue drop zone appears as a box, releasing the button adds the panel to the boxed panel group.

TIP If you have rearranged the panels from their original positions and want to reset them back to their default positions, click the Workspace switcher drop-down menu, then click Reset 'Designer'. You will also have to reset the Color Icons, as color icons are not part of the default Designer workspace.

11. Click **File** on the Application bar (Win) or Menu bar (Mac), then click **Close** to close the open document.

You viewed a new web page using three views, opened panel groups, viewed their contents, then closed panel groups.

Viewing Your Page in Live View

When you view your web pages in Dreamweaver, the page elements appear similar to the way they will appear on the web, but not exactly. To get a better idea of how it will look, you can use the Switch Design View to Live View button on the Document toolbar. This button causes the open document to appear as it would in a browser, with interactive elements active and functioning. Next to the Live View button is the Shows the Live View source in code view button, which displays the code as read-only and cannot be modified without exiting "Shows the Live View source in code view." The code is highlighted in yellow and allows you to see the dynamic changes in the code while you interact with the dynamic content on the page. When the Switch Design View to Live View button is active, the Shows the Live View source in code view button can be toggled on or off. If Live View is not active, selecting the Shows the Live View source in code view button will turn it on. When you click the Live View button the first time, you may see a message that you need to install the Flash plug-in from the Adobe website, www.adobe.com. Download the plug-in and your page can then be viewed using Live View.

View a Web Page
AND USE HELP

What You'll Do

In this lesson, you will open a web page, view several page elements, and access the Help system.

Opening a Web Page

After starting Dreamweaver, you can create a new website, create a new web page, or open an existing website or web page. The first web page that appears when viewers go to a website is called the **home page**. The home page sets the look and feel of the website and directs viewers to the rest of the pages in the site.

Viewing Basic Web Page Elements

There are many elements that make up web pages. Web pages can be very simple and designed primarily with text, or they can be media-rich with images, sound, and movies, creating an enhanced interactive web experience. Figure 8 shows a web page with text and graphics that work together to create a simple and attractive page.

Most information on a web page is presented in the form of text. You can type text directly onto a web page in Dreamweaver or import text created in other programs. You can then use the Property inspector to format text so that it is attractive and easy to read. Text should be short and to the point to engage viewers and prevent them from losing interest and leaving your site.

Hyperlinks, also known as **links**, are images or text elements on a web page that users click to display another location on the page, another web page on the same website, or a web page on a different website.

Images add visual interest to a web page. The saying that "less is more" is certainly true with images, though. Too many images cause the page to load slowly and discourage viewers from waiting for the page to download. Many pages have **banners**, which are images that appear across the top or down the side of the screen that can incorporate a company's logo, contact information, and links to the other pages in the site.

Menu bars, also called navigation bars, are bars that contain multiple links that are usually organized in rows or columns. Sometimes menu bars are used with an image map. An **image map** is an image that has been divided into sections, each of which serves as a link. The way that menu bars and other internal links are used on your pages is referred to as the **navigation structure** of the site.

Rich media content is a comprehensive term that refers to attractive and engaging images, interactive elements, video, or animations.

Some of this content can be created in Dreamweaver, but much of it is created with other programs such as Adobe Flash, Fireworks, Photoshop, or Illustrator.

Getting Help

Dreamweaver has an excellent Help feature that is both comprehensive and easy to use.

When questions or problems arise, you can use the commands on the Help menu to find the answers you need. Clicking the Dreamweaver Help command opens the Dreamweaver Help page that contains a list of topics and subtopics by category. The Help feature in Dreamweaver CS5 **NEW** is now based on Adobe AIR technology. **Adobe AIR** is an Adobe product used for

developing content that can be delivered with a browser or as a desktop application.

The Search text box at the top of the window lets you enter a keyword to search for a specific topic. Context-specific help can be accessed by clicking the Help button on the Property inspector.

Figure 8 *Common web page elements*

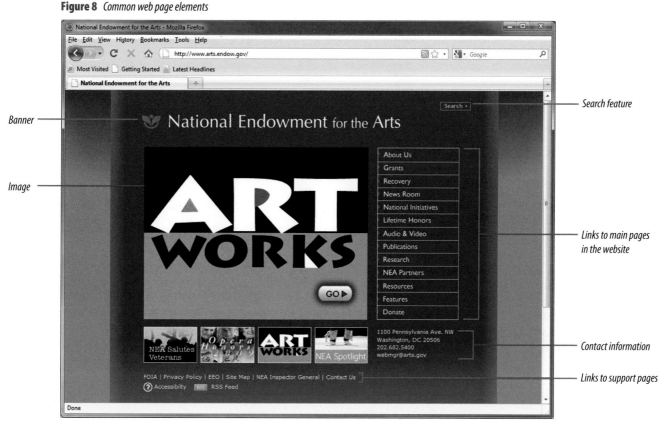

National Endowment for the Arts website – www.arts.endow.gov

Open a web page and view basic page elements

1. Click **File** on the Application bar (Win) or Menu bar (Mac), then click **Open**.

2. Click the **Look in list arrow** (Win), or **navigation list arrow** (Mac), locate the drive and folder where you store your Data Files, then double-click the **chapter_1 folder** (Win), or click the **chapter_1 folder** (Mac).

3. Click **dw1_1.html**, then click **Open**. You may not see the .html file extension if the option for hiding file extensions for known file types is selected on your operating system.

   TIP If you want your screen to match the figures in this book, make sure the Document window is maximized.

4. Click **Window** on the Application bar (Win) or Menu bar (Mac), then click **Hide Panels** to temporarily hide the panels.

   Hiding the panels gives you a larger viewing area for your web pages. You can also press [F4] to show or hide the panels. Note to Mac users: On the newest Mac OS, the F-keys are assigned to system functions. (F1=monitor brightness and F4=widgets) You can change this in your system preferences. Newer keyboards have an "FN" or "fn" key that can be used in conjunction with the F-keys so that they function "normally."

5. Locate each of the web page elements shown in Figure 9.

   TIP Because you are opening a single page that is not in a website with access to the other pages, the links will not work.

   (continued)

Figure 9 *Viewing web page elements (Win)*

Banner   Links to the   Text   Image
          main pages in
          the website

Figure 9 *Viewing web page elements (Mac)*

Banner   Text   Image

Links to the
main pages in
the website

6. Press **[F4]** to show the panels.
7. Click the **Show Code View button** Code to view the code for the page.
8. Scroll down to view all the code, if necessary, then click the **Show Design View button** Design to return to Design view.

TIP To show and highlight the code for a particular page element, select the page element in Design view, then click the Show Code View button.

9. Click **File** on the Application bar (Win) or Menu bar (Mac), then click **Close** to close the open page without saving it.

TIP You can also click the X on the filename tab to close the page.

You opened a web page, located several page elements, viewed the code for the page, then closed the page without saving it.

Use Dreamweaver Help

1. Click **Help** on the Application bar (Win) or Menu bar (Mac), then click **Dreamweaver Help**.

   The Adobe Community Help window opens.

TIP You can also open the Help feature by pressing [F1].

2. Click the **View Help PDF** link in the top right corner of the Adobe Dreamweaver CS5 pane as shown in Figure 10.

TIP If you don't see the link, enlarge or maximize the window.

3. Click the **plus sign** next to Chapter 2: Workspace in the left column, click the **plus sign** next to Working in the Document window, then click **Switch between views in the Document window**.

   The topic opens on the right side of the Help window, as shown in Figure 11.

4. Read the text in the content side of the Help window, then click the **Back button** to return to the opening Help screen.

(continued)

Figure 10 *Dreamweaver Help window*

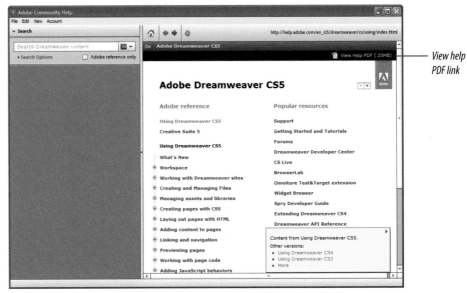

View help PDF link

Figure 11 *Displaying Help content*

Getting Started with Dreamweaver

Figure 12 *Searching for a topic in Help*

5. In the Search pane, type **CSS Property inspector** in the search text box, then press **[Enter]** (Win) or **[Return]** (Mac).

   A list of topics related to the search terms opens in the Search pane, as shown in Figure 12.

6. Click one of the links to read information about one of the topics of your choice.

7. Close the Adobe Community Help window.

You used Adobe Community Help to read information in the Adobe Dreamweaver CS5 documentation and in the Community Help files.

Using Adobe Community Help

When you access the Help feature in Dreamweaver, you have a choice of using offline help (which is similar to searching in a Dreamweaver manual) or using online help. The online help feature is called Adobe Community Help. **Adobe Community Help** is a collection of materials such as tutorials, published articles, or blogs, in addition to the regular help content. All content is monitored and approved by the Adobe Community Expert program.

Plan and Set Up
A WEBSITE

What You'll Do

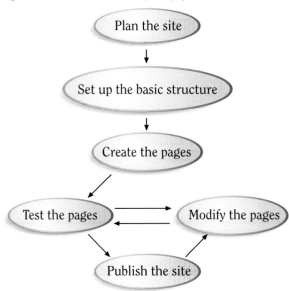

In this lesson, you will review a website plan for The Striped Umbrella, a beach resort and spa. You will also create a local site folder for The Striped Umbrella website, and then set up the website.

Understanding the Website Development Process

Creating a website is a complex process. It can often involve a large team of people working in various roles to ensure that the website contains accurate information, looks good, and works smoothly. Figure 13 illustrates the phases in a website development project.

Planning a Website

Planning is probably the most important part of any successful project. Planning is an essential part of creating a website, and

Figure 13 *Phases of a website development project*

Plan the site

↓

Set up the basic structure

↓

Create the pages

Test the pages ⇄ Modify the pages

Publish the site

is a continuous process that overlaps the subsequent phases. To start planning your website, you need to create a checklist of questions and answers about the site. For example, what are your goals for the site? Who is the audience you want to target? Teenagers? Children? Sports enthusiasts? Senior citizens? How can you design the site to appeal to the target audience? What content is appropriate for the target audience? What content is relevant to the purpose of the website? The more questions you can answer about the site, the more prepared you will be when you begin the developmental phase. Because of the public demand for up-to-date information, your plan should include not just how to get the site up and running, but how to keep it current.

Table 1 lists some of the basic questions you need to answer during the planning phase for almost any type of website. From your checklist, you should create a statement of purpose and scope, a timeline for all due dates, a budget, a task list with work assignments, and a list of resources needed. You should also include a list of deliverables, such as page prototypes and art for approval. The due dates for each deliverable should be included in the timeline.

Plan the Basic Structure

Once you complete the planning phase, you need to determine the structure of the site by creating a wireframe. A **wireframe**, sometimes referred to as a storyboard, is an illustration that represents every page

in a website. Like a flowchart, a wireframe shows the relationship of each page in the site to all the other pages. Wireframes also show how each page element is to be placed on each page. Wireframes are helpful when planning a website, because they allow you to visualize how each page in the site links to others. They are also an important tool to help the client see how the pages will look and work together. Make sure that the client and all other interested stakeholders approve the wireframe before the site construction actually begins. Wireframes range from very simple (known as low-fidelity wireframes) to interactive and multidimensional (known as high-fidelity wireframes).You can create a simple wireframe by using a pencil and

TABLE 1: WEBSITE PLANNING CHECKLIST	
Question	**Examples**
1. Who is the target audience?	Seniors, teens, children
2. How can I tailor the site to reach that audience?	Specify an appropriate reading level, decide the optimal amount of media content, use formal or casual language
3. What are the goals for the site?	Sell a product, provide information
4. How will I gather the information?	Recruit other employees, write it myself, use content from in-house documents
5. What are my sources for media content?	Internal production department, outside production company, my own photographs
6. What is my budget?	Very limited, well financed
7. What is the timeline?	Two weeks, one month, six months
8. Who is on my project team?	Just me, a complete staff of designers
9. How often should the site be updated?	Every 10 minutes, once a month
10. Who will update the site?	Me, other team members

paper or by using a graphics program on a computer, such as Adobe Illustrator, Adobe Fireworks, or Microsoft PowerPoint. To create more complex wireframes that simulate the site navigation and user interaction, use a high-fidelity wireframe program such as OverSite, ProtoShare, Microsoft Visio, or Adobe Flash Catalyst. The basic wireframe shown in Figure 14 shows all the The Striped Umbrella website pages that you will create in this book. The home page appears at the top of the wireframe, and it has four pages linked to it. The home page is called the **parent page**, because it is at a higher level in the web hierarchy and has pages linked to it. The pages linked below it are called **child pages**. The Activities page, which is a child page to the home page, is also a parent page to the Cruises and Fishing pages. You can refer to this wireframe as you create the actual links in Dreamweaver.

More detailed wireframes also include all document names, images, text files, and link information. Use your wireframe as your guide as you develop the site to make sure you follow the planned site structure.

In addition to creating a wireframe for your site, you should also create a folder hierarchy on your computer for all of the files that will be used in the site. Start by creating a folder for the site with a descriptive name, such as the name of the company. This folder, known as the **local site folder**, will store all the pages or HTML files for the site. Traditionally, this folder has been called the **root folder** and many people still use this term; in this book we will call it the local site folder. Then create a subfolder, often called **assets** or **images**, in which you store all of the files that are not pages, such as images and sound files.

QUICK TIP

You should avoid using spaces, special characters, or uppercase characters in your folder names to ensure that all your files can be read and linked successfully on all web servers, whether they are Windows- or UNIX-based.

After you create the local site folder, you need to set up your site. When you **set up** a site, you use the Dreamweaver Site Setup dialog box to assign your site a name and specify the local site folder. After you have set up your site, the site name and any folders and files it contains appear in the **Files panel**, the panel you use to manage your website's files and folders. Using the Files panel to manage your files ensures that the site links work correctly when the website is published. You also use the Files panel to add or delete pages.

Creating the Web Pages and Collecting the Page Content

This is the fun part! After you create your wireframe, obtain approvals, and set up your site, you need to gather the files you'll need to create the pages, including text, images, buttons, video, and animations. You will import some of these pages from other software programs, and some you will create in Dreamweaver. For example, you can create text in a word-processing program and import or paste it into Dreamweaver, or you can create and format text in Dreamweaver.

Images, tables, colors, and horizontal rules all contribute to making a page attractive and interesting, but they can increase file size. In choosing your page elements, carefully

Figure 14 *The Striped Umbrella website wireframe*

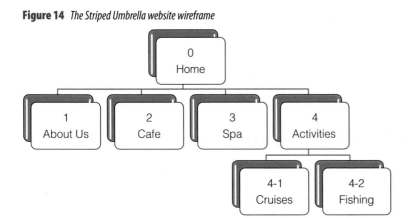

consider the file size of each page. A page with too many graphic elements might take a long time to load, which could cause visitors to leave your site.

Testing the Pages

Once all your pages are completed, you need to test the site to make sure all the links work and that everything looks good. It is important to test your web pages using different browser software. The four most common browsers are Microsoft Internet Explorer, Mozilla Firefox, Google Chrome, and Safari. Test your site using different versions of each browser, because older versions may not support the latest web technology. You should also test your site using a variety of screen sizes. Some viewers may have small monitors, while others may have large, high-resolution monitors. Also consider connection download time. Although more people use cable modems or DSL (digital subscriber line), some still use slower dial-up modems. Testing is a continuous process, for which you should allocate plenty of time.

Modifying the Pages

After you create a website, you'll probably find that you need to keep making changes to it, especially when information on the site needs to be updated. Each time you make a change, such as adding a new button or image to a page, you should test the site again. Modifying and testing pages in a website is an ongoing process.

Publishing the Site

Publishing a website refers to the process of transferring all the files for the site to a **web server**, a computer that is connected to the Internet with an IP (Internet Protocol) address, so that it is available for viewing on the Internet. A website must be published so that Internet users can view it. There are several options for publishing a website. For instance, many **Internet Service Providers (ISPs)** provide space on their servers for customers to publish websites, and some commercial websites provide limited free space for their viewers. Although publishing happens at the end of the process, it's a good idea to set up web server access in the planning phase. Use the Files panel to transfer your files using the Dreamweaver FTP capability. **FTP (File Transfer Protocol)** is the process of uploading and downloading files to and from a remote site.

Managing a Project with a Team

When working with a team, it is essential that you define clear goals for the project and a list of objectives to accomplish those goals. You plan should be finalized after conferring with both the clients and other team members to make sure that the purpose, scope, and objectives are clear to everyone. Establish the **deliverables**, or products that will be provided to the client at the product completion such as new pages or graphic elements created, and a timeline for their delivery. You should present the web pages at strategic times in the development process to your team members and to your clients for feedback and evaluation. Analyze all feedback objectively, incorporating both the positive and the negative comments to help you make improvements to the site and meet the clients' expectations and goals. A common pitfall in team management is **scope creep**. Scope creep means making impromptu changes or additions to a project without corresponding increases in the schedule or budget. Proper project control and communication between team members and clients can minimize scope creep and achieve the successful and timely completion of a project.

Select the location for your website

1. Open or expand the Files panel if necessary to view the contents.
2. Click the **drive or folder** that is currently displayed in the pop-up menu in the Files panel. See Figure 15.
3. Click to select the **drive or folder** (or subfolder) in the list where you will store your folders and files for your websites.

   Dreamweaver will store all of the folders and files you create inside this drive or folder.

You selected the drive or folder where you will create your website.

Figure 15 *Selecting a drive in the Files panel*

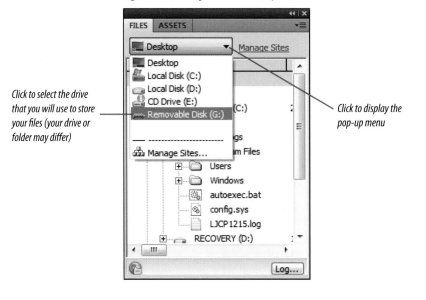

Click to select the drive that you will use to store your files (your drive or folder may differ)

Click to display the pop-up menu

Understanding IP Addresses and Domain Names

To be accessible over the Internet, a website must be published to a web server with a permanent IP address. An **IP address** is an assigned series of numbers, separated by periods, that designates an address on the Internet. To access a web page, you can enter either an IP address or a domain name in the address text box of your browser window. A **domain name** is a web address that is expressed in letters instead of numbers and usually reflects the name of the business represented by the website. For example, the domain name of the Adobe website is www.adobe.com, but the IP address is 192.150.18.200. Because domain names use descriptive text instead of numbers, they are much easier to remember. Compare an IP address to your Social Security number and a domain name to your name. Both your Social Security number and your name are used to refer to you as a person, but your name is much easier for your friends and family to use than your Social Security number. You can type the IP address or the domain name in the address text box of the browser window to access a website. The domain name is also referred to as a **URL** or Uniform Resource Locator.

Getting Started with Dreamweaver

Figure 16 *Creating a local site folder using the Files panel*

Your drive or folder may differ

striped_umbrella folder will become the local site folder after the site is defined (the folder is yellow (Win) or blue (Mac)

If you just see a drive or folder name here, you do not currently have a website open

Figure 17 *Viewing an open website in the Files panel*

striped_umbrella local site folder (the folder is green)

The open website name appears here

If you see the word "Site" here, you do have a website open

Create a local site folder

1. Verify that the drive or folder where you want to store your site is selected in the Files panel, right-click (Windows) or control-click (Macintosh) the **drive or folder**, then click **New Folder**.

2. Type **striped_umbrella** to rename the folder, then press **[Enter]**.

   The folder is renamed striped_umbrella, as shown in Figure 16. You have not created a website yet. You have just created the folder that will serve as the local site folder after you set up the site.

   The folder color is currently yellow (Mac users will see blue folders), but after you set up the site in the next section, it will change to green. Notice the difference between Figure 16 and Figure 17. In Figure 16, you have only created the local site folder, not the website, and the color of the folder is yellow. In Figure 17, The Striped Umbrella website has been created and is open, so the local site folder is green.

You created a new folder to serve as the local site folder for The Striped Umbrella website.

Set up a website

1. Click **Site** on the Application bar (Win) or Menu bar (Mac), then click **New Site**.

2. Click **Site** in the category list in the Site Setup for Unnamed Site dialog box (if necessary), then type **The Striped Umbrella** in the Site name text box.

   TIP You can use uppercase letters and spaces in the site name because it is not the name of a folder or a file.

3. Click the **Browse for folder icon** 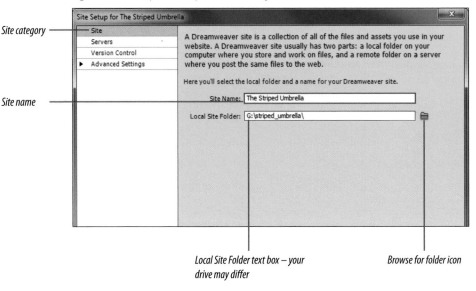 next to the Local Site Folder text box, click the **Select list arrow** (Win) or the **navigation list arrow** (Mac) in the Choose Root folder dialog box, navigate to and click the **drive and folder** where your website files will be stored, then click the **striped_umbrella folder**.

4. Click **Open** (Win) or **Choose** (Mac), then click **Select** (Win). See Figure 18.

   You created a website and set it up with the name The Striped Umbrella. You then told Dreamweaver the folder name and location to use for the local site folder.

Figure 18 *Site Setup for The Striped Umbrella dialog box*

Site category —

Site name —

Local Site Folder text box – your drive may differ

Browse for folder icon

Understanding the Process of Publishing a Website

Before publishing a website so that web viewers can access it, you should first create a local site folder, called the local root folder, to house all the files for your website, as you did on page 1-23. This folder usually resides on your hard drive. Next, you need to gain access to a remote server. A remote server is a web server that hosts websites and is not directly connected to the computer housing the local site. Many Internet Service Providers, or ISPs, provide space for publishing websites on their servers. Once you have access to a remote server, you can then use the Servers category in the Site Setup dialog box to enter information such as the FTP host, host directory, login, and password. After entering this information, you can then use the Put File(s) button in the Files panel to transfer the files to the designated remote server. Once the site is published to a remote server, it is called a remote site.

Figure 19 *Adding a server for Remote Access for the Striped Umbrella website*

Servers category

Add new Server icon

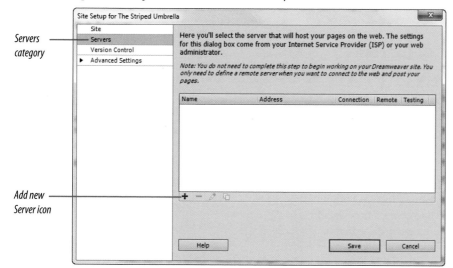

Figure 20 *Entering publishing information for The Striped Umbrella website*

Enter server name here

Choices for publishing a website

Set up web server access

1. Click **Servers** in the Category list, then click the **Add new Server icon** ➕, as shown in Figure 19.

TIP If you do not have the information to publish your website, skip step 2 and continue to step 3. You can specify this information later.

2. Click the **Connect using: list arrow**, choose the method you will use to publish your website, as shown in Figure 20, enter any necessary information in the Site Setup for The Striped Umbrella dialog box based on the setting you chose, then click **Save**.

TIP Your network administrator or web hosting service will give you the necessary information to publish your website.

3. Click **Save** to close the Site Setup dialog box.

You set up the remote access information to prepare you for publishing your website.

Add a Folder
AND PAGES

What You'll Do

In this lesson, you will use the Files panel to create a new folder and new pages for the website.

Adding a Folder to a Website

After setting up a website, you need to create folders to organize the files that will make up the site. Creating a folder called **assets** is a good beginning. There is nothing magic about the word "assets," though. You can name your folder anything that makes sense to you, as long as you follow proper folder naming conventions such as avoiding the use of spaces. You can use the assets folder to store all non-HTML files, such as images or sound files. Many designers name this folder "images" and use additional folders to store other types of supporting files. After you create the assets folder, it is a good idea to set it as the default location to store the website images. This saves a step when you import new images into the website.

DESIGNTIP

Creating An Effective Navigation Structure

When you create a website, it's important to consider how your viewers will navigate from page to page within the site. A menu bar, or navigation bar, is a critical tool for moving around a website, so it's important that all text, buttons, and icons used in a menu bar have a consistent look across all pages. If you use a complex menu bar, such as one that incorporates JavaScript or Flash, it's a good idea to include plain text links in another location on the page for accessibility. Otherwise, viewers might become confused or lost within the site. A navigation structure can include more links than those included in a menu bar, however. For instance, it can contain other sets of links that relate to the content of a specific page and which are placed at the bottom or sides of a page in a different format. No matter which navigation structure you use, make sure that every page includes a link back to the home page. Don't make viewers rely on the Back button on the browser toolbar to find their way back to the home page. It's possible that the viewer's current page might have opened as a result of a search and clicking the Back button will take the viewer out of the website.

Getting Started with Dreamweaver

Creating the Home Page

The **home page** of a website is the first page that viewers see when they visit your site. Most websites contain many other pages that all connect back to the home page. The home page filename usually has the name index.html (.htm), or default.html (.htm).

Adding Pages to a Website

Websites might be as simple as one page or might contain hundreds of pages. When you create a website, you can add all the pages and specify where they should be placed in the website folder structure in the local site folder. Once you add and name all the pages in the website, you can then add the content, such as text and graphics, to each page. One method is to add as many blank pages as you think you will need in the beginning, rather than adding them one at a time with all the content in place. This enables you to set up the navigation structure of the website at the beginning of the development process and view how each page is linked to others. When you are satisfied with the overall structure, you can then add the content to each page. This is strictly a personal preference, however.

You can also choose to add and link pages as you create them, and that will work just fine, too.

You have a choice of several default document types you can generate when you create new HTML pages. The default document type is designated in the Preferences dialog box. XHTML 1.0 Transitional is the default document type when you install Dreamweaver and will be used throughout this book. It's important to understand the terminology—the pages are still called HTML pages and the file extension is still HTML, but the document type will be XHTML 1.0 Transitional.

Using the Files Panel for File Management

You should use the Files panel to add, delete, move, or rename files and folders in a website. It is very important that you perform these file-maintenance tasks in the Files panel rather than in Windows Explorer (Win) or in the Finder (Mac). Working outside of Dreamweaver, such as in Windows Explorer, can cause linking errors. You cannot take advantage of the simple, yet powerful, Dreamweaver site-management features unless you use the Files panel for all file-management activities. You might choose to use Windows Explorer (Win) or the Finder (Mac) only to create the local site folder or to move or copy the local site folder of a website to another location. If you move or copy the local site folder to a new location, you will have to set up the site again in the Files panel, as you did in Lesson 3 of this chapter. Setting up a site is not difficult and will become routine for you after you practice a bit. If you are using Dreamweaver on multiple computers, such as in labs or at home, you will have to set up your sites the first time you change to a different computer.

Add a folder to a website (Windows)

1. Right-click **Site - The Striped Umbrella** in the Files panel, then click **New Folder**.

2. Type **assets** in the folder text box, then press **[Enter]**.

TIP To rename a folder, click the folder name once, pause, click again, then type the new name.

3. Compare your screen to Figure 21.

You used the Files panel to create a new folder in the striped_umbrella folder and named it "assets".

Add a folder to a website (Macintosh)

1. Press and hold **[control]**, click the **striped_umbrella folder**, then click **New Folder**.

2. Type **assets** in the new folder name text box, then press **[return]**.

TIP To rename a folder, click the folder name text box, type the new name, then press **[return]**.

3. Compare your screen to Figure 22.

You used the Files panel to create a new folder in the striped_umbrella folder and named it "assets".

Figure 21 *The Striped Umbrella site in Files panel with assets folder created (Windows)*

New assets folder

Local site folder for The Striped Umbrella website

Figure 22 *The Striped Umbrella site in Files panel with assets folder created (Macintosh)*

Local site folder for The Striped Umbrella website

New assets folder

Getting Started with Dreamweaver

Figure 23 *Site Setup for The Striped Umbrella dialog box with the assets folder set as the default images folder*

Advanced Settings category

Default Images folder text box

Browse for folder icon

Set the default images folder

1. Click the Site pop-up menu in the Files panel, click **Manage Sites**, then click **Edit**.

2. Click **Advanced Settings** in the category list in the Site Setup dialog box, then click **Local Info** if necessary.

3. Click the **Browse for folder icon** 📁 next to the Default Images folder text box.

4. If necessary, navigate to your striped_umbrella folder, double-click the **assets folder** (Win) or click the **assets folder** (Mac) in the Choose Image Folder dialog box, then click **Select** (Win) or **Choose** (Mac).

   Compare your screen to Figure 23.

5. Click **Save**, then click **Done**.

You set the assets folder as the default images folder so that imported images will be automatically saved in it.

Create the home page

1. Open **dw1_2.html** from the drive and folder where you store your Data Files.

   The file has several elements in it, including a banner image.

2. Click **File** on the Application bar (Win) or Menu bar (Mac), click **Save As**, click the **Save in list arrow** (Win) or the **Where list arrow** (Mac), navigate to the striped_umbrella folder, select **dw1_2.html** in the File name text box (Win) or select **dw1_2** in the Save As text box (Mac), then type **index.html**.

   Windows users do not have to type the file extension. It will be added automatically.

3. Click **Save**, then click **No** when asked to update links.

   As shown in Figure 24, the drive where the local site folder is stored, the local site folder name, and the page's filename are displayed to the right of the document tab and in the Address text box in the Browser Navigation toolbar. This information is called the **path**, or location of the open file in relation to other folders in the website.

   The banner image is no longer visible and a gray broken link placeholder appears in its place. This is because although you saved the .html file under a new name in the website's local site folder, you have not yet copied the image file into the website's assets folder. The banner image is still linked to the Data Files folder. You will fix this in the next set of steps.

   You opened a file, then saved it with the filename index.

Figure 24 *index.html placed in the striped_umbrella local site folder*

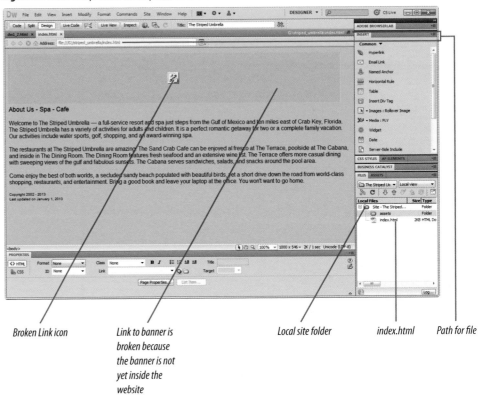

Broken Link icon

Link to banner is broken because the banner is not yet inside the website

Local site folder

index.html

Path for file

Figure 25 *Property inspector showing properties of The Striped Umbrella banner*

The Striped
Umbrella banner

Selection handles

Property inspector
provides details about
the selected image

Src text box

Browse for file icon

Image file has been copied
to the assets folder

Save an image file in the assets folder

1. Click the **broken link placeholder** to select it.

   Small, black selection handles appear around the broken link. To correct the broken link, you must copy the image file from the Data Files folder into the assets folder of your website.

2. Click the **Browse for File icon** 🗁 next to the Src text box in the Property inspector, navigate to the assets folder in your Data Files folder for this chapter, click **su_banner.gif**, click **OK** (Win) or **Choose** (Mac), then click in a blank part of the page. (Click the banner placeholder image again if the banner still doesn't appear.)

   The file for The Striped Umbrella banner, su_banner.gif, is automatically copied to the assets folder of The Striped Umbrella website, the folder that you designated as the default images folder. When the image is selected, the Src text box shows the path of the banner to the assets folder in the website, and the banner image is visible on the page.

   TIP If you do not see the su_banner.gif file listed in the Files panel, click the Refresh button 🔄 on the Files panel toolbar.

3. Select the banner to view the banner properties in the Property inspector, then compare your screen to Figure 25.

   TIP Until you copy an image from an outside folder to your website, the image is not part of the website and will appear as a broken link.

You saved The Striped Umbrella banner in the assets folder.

Add pages to a website (Windows)

1. Click the **plus sign** to the left of the assets folder (if necessary) to open the folder and view its contents, su_banner.gif.

   TIP If you do not see a file listed in the assets folder, click the Refresh button on the Files panel toolbar.

2. Right-click the **striped_umbrella local site folder**, click **New File**, type **about_us.html** to replace untitled.html, then press **[Enter]**.

   Each new file is a page in the website. This page does not have page content or a page title yet.

   TIP If you create a new file in the Files panel, use care to make sure the .html file extension is not deleted or that the file does not end up with a double file extension.

3. Repeat Step 2 to add five more blank pages to The Striped Umbrella website, naming the new files **spa.html**, **cafe.html**, **activities.html**, **cruises.html**, and **fishing.html**.

   TIP Make sure to add the new files to the site folder, not the assets folder. If you accidentally add them to the assets folder, just drag them to the site folder.

4. Click the **Refresh button** on the Files panel to list the files alphabetically, then compare your screen to Figure 26.

5. Click **File**, **Save**, to save the index.html file, if necessary, close both open files, click **File** on the Application bar then click **Exit**.

   TIP If you are prompted to save changes to the dw1_1.html file, click No.

You added the following six pages to The Striped Umbrella website: about_us, activities, cafe, cruises, fishing, and spa.

Figure 26 *New pages added to The Striped Umbrella website (Windows)*

su_banner.gif in the assets folder

New pages added in the striped_umbrella local site folder

DESIGNTIP

Adding Page Titles

When you view a web page in a browser, its page title appears in the browser window title bar. (The page title is different from the filename, the name used to save the page on a computer.) The page title reflects the page content and sets the tone for the page. It is especially important to use words in your page title that are likely to match keywords viewers might enter when using a search engine. Search engines compare the text in page titles to the keywords typed into the search engine. When a title bar displays "Untitled Document," the designer has neglected to give the page a title. This is like giving up free "billboard space" and looks unprofessional.

Figure 27 *New pages added to The Striped Umbrella website (Macintosh)*

New pages added to the striped_umbrella site folder

POWER USER SHORTCUTS	
To do this:	**Use this shortcut:**
Open a file	[Ctrl][O] (Win) or ⌘ [O] (Mac)
Close a file	[Ctrl][W] (Win) or ⌘ [W] (Mac)
Create a new file	[Ctrl][N] (Win) or ⌘ [N] (Mac)
Save a file	[Ctrl][S] (Win) or ⌘ [S] (Mac)
Get Dreamweaver Help	[F1]
Show/Hide panels	[F4]
Switch between Code view and Design view	[Ctrl][`] (Win) or [control] [`] (Mac)

Add pages to a website (Macintosh)

1. Click the **triangle** to the left of the assets folder to open the folder and view its contents.

   TIP If you do not see a file listed in the assets folder, click the Refresh button **C** on the Files panel.

2. [control]-click the **striped_umbrella local site folder**, click **New File**, type **about_us.html** to replace untitled.html, then press **[return]**.

   TIP If you create a new file in the Files panel, use care to make sure the .html file extension is not deleted or that the file does not end up with a double file extension.

3. Repeat Step 2 to add five more blank pages to The Striped Umbrella website, naming the new files **spa.html**, **cafe.html**, **activities.html**, **cruises.html**, and **fishing.html**.

   TIP Make sure to add the new files to the site folder, not the assets folder. If you accidentally add them to the assets folder, just drag them to the site folder.

4. Click the **Refresh button C** to list the files alphabetically, then compare your screen to Figure 27.

5. Click **File**, **Save**, to save the index.html file, then close both open files.

6. Click **Dreamweaver** on the Menu bar, and then click **Quit Dreamweaver**.

   TIP If you are prompted to save changes, click No.

You added six pages to The Striped Umbrella website: about_us, activities, cafe, cruises, fishing, spa.

Explore the Dreamweaver workspace.

1. Start Dreamweaver.
2. Create a new HTML document.
3. Change the view to Code view.
4. Change the view to Code and Design views.
5. Change the view to Design view.
6. Collapse the panels to icons.
7. Expand the panels.
8. Undock the Files panel and float it to the middle of the document window. Dock the Files panel back to its original position.
9. View the Assets panel.
10. Close the page without saving it.

View a web page and use Help.

1. Open the file dw1_3.html from where you store your Data Files.
2. Locate the following page elements: a banner, an image, and text.
3. Change the view to Code view.
4. Change the view to Design view.
5. Use the Dreamweaver Help command to search for information on docking panels.
6. Display and read one of the topics you find.
7. Close the Dreamweaver Help window.
8. Close the page without saving it.

Plan and set up a website.

1. Use the Files panel to select the drive and folder where you store your website files.
2. Create a new local site folder in this folder or drive called **blooms**.
3. Create a new site called **Blooms & Bulbs**.
4. Specify the blooms folder as the local site folder.
5. Use the Remote Info category in the Site Setup for Blooms & Bulbs dialog box to set up web server access. (*Hint*: Skip this step if you do not have the necessary information to set up web server access.)
6. Click Save to close the Site Setup dialog box.

Add a folder and pages.

1. Create a new folder in the blooms local site folder called **assets**.
2. Edit the site to set the assets folder as the default location for the website images.
3. Open the file dw1_4.html from where you store your Data Files, save this file in the blooms local site folder as **index.html**, then click No to updating the links.
4. Select the broken image for the Blooms & Bulbs banner on the page.
5. Use the Property inspector to browse for blooms_banner.jpg, then select it to automatically save it in the assets folder of the Blooms & Bulbs website. (Remember to click off of the banner anywhere else on the page to show the banner as it replaces the broken image if necessary.)
6. Create seven new pages in the Files panel, and name them: **plants.html**, **workshops.html**, **newsletter.html**, **annuals.html**, **perennials.html**, **water_plants.html**, and **tips.html**.
7. Refresh the view to list the new files alphabetically, then compare your screen to Figure 28.
8. Close all open pages.

Figure 28 *Completed Skills Review*

You have been hired to create a website for a travel outfitter called TripSmart. TripSmart specializes in travel products and services. In addition to selling travel products, such as luggage and accessories, they organize trips and offer travel advice. Their clients range from college students to families to vacationing professionals. The owner, Thomas Howard, has requested a dynamic website that conveys the excitement of traveling.

1. Using the information in the preceding paragraph, create a wireframe for this website, using either a pencil and paper or a program such as Microsoft Word. Include the home page with links to four child pages named **catalog.html**, **newsletter.html**, **services.html**, and **tours.html**. Include two child pages under the tours page named **china.html** and **spain.html**.

2. Create a new local site folder named **tripsmart** in the drive and folder where you store your website files.

3. Start Dreamweaver, then create a site with the name **TripSmart**. Set the tripsmart folder as the local site folder for the site.

4. Create an assets folder and set it as the default location for images.

5. Open the file dw1_5.html from where you store your Data Files, then save it in the tripsmart local site folder as **index.html**. (Remember not to update links.)

6. Correct the path for the banner by selecting the banner on the page, browsing to the original source in the Data Files folder, then selecting the file to copy it automatically to your TripSmart assets folder.

7. Create six additional pages for the site, and name them as follows: **catalog.html**, **newsletter.html**, **services.html**, **tours.html**, **china.html**, and **spain.html**. Use your wireframe and Figure 29 as a guide.

8. Refresh the Files panel.

9. Close all open pages.

Figure 29 *Completed Project Builder 1*

Getting Started with Dreamweaver

Your company has been selected to design a website for a catering business called Carolyne's Creations. In addition to catering, Carolyne's services include cooking classes and daily specials available as take-out meals. She also has a retail shop that stocks gourmet treats and kitchen items.

1. Create a wireframe for this website that includes a home page and child pages named **shop.html,** **classes.html, catering.html,** and **recipes.html**. Create two more child pages under the classes.html page called **children.html** and **adults.html**.

2. Create a new local site folder for the site in the drive and folder where you save your website files, then name it **cc**.

3. Create a website with the name **Carolyne's Creations**, using the cc folder for the local site folder.

4. Create an assets folder for the site and set the assets folder as the default location for images.

5. Open dw1_6.html from the where you store your Data Files then save it as **index.html** in the cc folder.

6. Reset the source for the banner to automatically save the cc_banner.jpg file in the assets folder.

7. Using Figure 30 and your wireframe as guides, create the additional pages shown for the website.

8. Refresh the Files panel to sort the files alphabetically.

9. Close all open pages.

Figure 30 *Completed Project Builder 2*

Figure 31 shows the Department of Defense website, a past selection for the Adobe Site of the Day. To visit the current Department of Defense website, connect to the Internet, then go to www.defense.gov. The current page might differ from the figure because dynamic websites are updated frequently to reflect current information. The main navigation structure is under the banner. The page title is The Official Home of the Department of Defense.

Go to the Adobe website at www.adobe.com, click the Customer Showcase link under the Company menu, then click the current Site of the Day. Explore the site and answer the following questions:

1. Do you see page titles for each page you visit?
2. Do the page titles accurately reflect the page content?
3. Is the navigation structure clear?
4. How is the navigation structure organized?
5. Why do you think this site was chosen as a Site of the Day?

Figure 31 *Design Project*

United State Department of Defense website – www.defense.gov

The Portfolio Project will be an ongoing project throughout the book, in which you will plan and create an original website without any Data Files supplied. The focus of the site can be on any topic, organization, sports team, club, or company that you would like. You will build on this site from chapter to chapter, so you must do each Portfolio Project assignment in each chapter to complete your website. When you finish this book, you should have a completed site that would be an excellent addition to a professional portfolio.

1. Decide what type of site you would like to create. It can be a personal site about you, a business site that promotes a fictitious or real company, or an informational site that provides information about a topic, cause, or organization.
2. Write a list of questions and answers about the site you have decided to create.
3. Create a wireframe for your site to include at least four pages. The wireframe should include the home page with at least three child pages under it.
4. Create a local site folder and an assets folder to house the assets, then set up your site using the local site folder as the website local site folder and the assets folder as the default images folder.
5. Create a blank page named **index.html** as a placeholder for the home page.
6. Begin collecting content, such as pictures or text to use in your website. You can use a digital camera to take photos, use a scanner to scan pictures, or create your own graphics using a program such as Adobe Fireworks or Adobe Illustrator. Gather the content in a central location that will be accessible to you as you develop your site.

CHAPTER

DEVELOPING A
WEB PAGE

1. Create head content and set page properties
2. Create, import, and format text
3. Add links to web pages
4. Use the History panel and edit code
5. Modify and test web pages

CHAPTER 2

DEVELOPING A
WEB PAGE

Introduction

The process of developing a web page requires a lot of thought and planning. If the page is a home page, you need to spend some time crafting the head content. The head content contains information search engines use to help viewers find your website. Next, choose the colors for the page background and text. You then need to add the page content, format it attractively, and add links to other pages in the site or to other websites. Finally, to ensure that all links work correctly and are current, you must test them regularly.

Understanding Page Layout

Before you add content to a page, consider the following guidelines for laying out pages:

Use white space effectively. A living room crammed with too much furniture makes it difficult to appreciate the individual pieces. The same is true of a web page. Too many text blocks, links, animations, and images can be distracting. Consider leaving some white space on each page. **White space**, which is not necessarily white, is the area on a page that contains no text or graphics.

Limit media elements. Too many media elements, such as images, video clips, or sounds, can result in a page that takes too long to load. Viewers might leave your site before the entire page finishes loading. Use media elements only if you have a good reason.

Keep it simple. Often the simplest websites are the most appealing and are also the easiest to create and maintain. A simple, well-designed site that works well is far superior to a complex one that contains errors.

Use an intuitive navigation structure. Make sure your site's navigation structure is easy to use. Viewers should always know where they are in the site and be able to easily find their way back to the home page. If viewers get "lost," they might leave the site rather than struggle to find their way around.

Apply a consistent theme. To help give pages in your website a consistent appearance, consider designing your pages using elements that relate to a common theme. Consistency in the use of color and fonts, the placement of the navigation links, and the overall page design gives a website a unified look and promotes greater ease of use and accessibility. Style sheets and pre-developed page layouts called **templates** can make this task much easier.

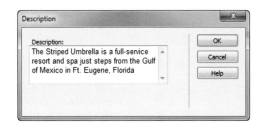

Create Head Content and
SET PAGE PROPERTIES

What You'll Do

In this lesson, you will learn how to enter titles, keywords, and descriptions in the head content section of a web page. You will also change the background color for a web page.

Creating the Head Content

A web page is composed of two distinct sections: the head content and the body. The **head content** includes the page title that appears in the title bar of the browser and some important page elements, called meta tags, that are not visible in the browser.

Meta tags are HTML codes that include information about the page, such as keywords and descriptions. Meta tags are read by screen readers for viewers who have visual impairments. **Keywords** are words that relate to the content of the website. A **description** is a short paragraph that describes the content and features of the website. For instance, the words "beach" and "resort" would be appropriate keywords for The Striped Umbrella website. Search engines find web pages by matching the title, keywords, and description in the head content of web pages with keywords that viewers enter in search engine text boxes. Therefore, it is important to include concise, useful information in the head content. The **body** is the part of the page that appears in a browser window. It contains all the page content that is visible to viewers, such as text, images, and links.

QUICK **TIP**

Don't confuse page titles with filenames, the name used to store each file on the server.

Setting Web Page Properties

When you create a web page, one of the first design decisions that you should make is to choose properties that control the way the page appears in a browser, such as the **background color**, the color that fills the entire page. The background color should complement the colors used for text, links, and images on the page. Often, backgrounds consist of images for either the entire page or a part of the page, such as a table background or Cascading Style Sheet (CSS) layout block. A **CSS layout block** is a section of a web page that is defined and formatted using a Cascading Style Sheet, a set of formatting characteristics you can apply to text, tables, and other page objects. You will learn more about CSS layout blocks in Chapter 6. When you use the Page Properties dialog box to set page properties such as the background color, Dreamweaver automatically creates a style that modifies the body tag to include the properties you added.

A strong contrast between the text color and the background color makes it easier for viewers to read your text. One of the Web Content Accessibility Guidelines (WCAG), Version 2.0, from the World Wide Web Consortium (W3C) states that contrast will "make it easier for users to see content including separating foreground from background." You can choose a light background color with dark text, or a dark background color with light text. A white background with dark text, though not terribly exciting, provides good contrast and is easiest to read for most viewers. Another design decision you need to make is whether to change the **default font** and **default link colors**, which are the colors used by the browser to display text, links, and visited links. The default color for **unvisited links**, or links that the viewer has not clicked yet, is blue. Unvisited links are usually simply called **links**. The default color for **visited links**, or links that have been previously clicked, is purple. You change the background color, text, and link colors using the color picker in the Page Properties dialog box. You can choose colors from one of the five Dreamweaver color palettes, as shown in Figure 1.

Choosing Colors to Convey Information

Before 1994, colors appeared differently on different types of computers. In 1994, Netscape developed the first web-safe color palette, a set of colors that appears consistently in all browsers and on Macintosh, Windows, and UNIX platforms. The evolution of video cards has made this

less relevant today, but use of appropriate colors is an important factor in creating accessible pages. So always consider both web-safe and non-web-safe colors you have used to make sure they are providing good contrast on your pages. Dreamweaver has two web-safe color palettes, Color Cubes and Continuous Tone, each of which contains 216 web-safe colors. Color Cubes is the

default color palette. To choose a different color palette, open the color picker. You can find the color picker on the CSS Property inspector, in various dialog boxes, and in various panels. Click the color picker list arrow, then click the color palette you want. Another WCAG guideline states that color should never be the only visual means of conveying information.

Figure 1 *Color picker showing color palettes*

Click list arrow to choose a color palette

Web-safe palettes

Edit a page title

1. Start Dreamweaver, click the **Site list arrow** on the Files panel, then click **The Striped Umbrella** if necessary.

2. Double-click **index.html** in the Files panel to open The Striped Umbrella home page, click **View** on the Application bar (Win) or Menu bar (Mac), then click **Head Content**.

   The Meta icon , Title icon , and CSS icon are now visible in the head content section. See Figure 2.

3. Click the **Title icon** in the head content section.

   The page title The Striped Umbrella appears in the Title text box in the Property inspector.

4. Click after the end of The Striped Umbrella text in the Title text box in the Property inspector, press **[Spacebar]**, type **beach resort and spa, Ft. Eugene, Florida,** press **[Enter]** (Win) or **[return]** (Mac), then click in the title text box.

   Compare your screen with Figure 3. The new title is better, because it incorporates the words "beach resort" and "spa" and the location of the resort—words that potential customers might use as keywords when using a search engine.

   TIP You can also change the page title using the Title text box on the Document toolbar. To view hidden text in the Title box, click in the title and scroll using the left and right keyboard arrow keys.

You opened The Striped Umbrella website, opened the home page, viewed the head content section, and changed the page title.

Figure 2 *Viewing the head content*

Meta icon   Title icon   CSS icon

Head content section

Title text box on Document toolbar

Figure 3 *Property inspector displaying new page title*

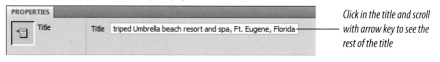

Click in the title and scroll with arrow key to see the rest of the title

DESIGNTIP

Designing Appropriate Content For Your Target Audience

When you begin developing the content for your website, you need to decide what content to include and how to arrange each element on each page. You must design the content with the target audience in mind. What is the age group of your audience? What reading level is appropriate? Should you use a formal or informal tone? Should the pages be simple, consisting mostly of text, or rich with images and media files? Evaluate the font sizes, the number and size of images and animations, the reading level, and the amount of technical expertise necessary to navigate your site, and make sure they fit your audience. Usually, the first page that your audience will see when they visit your site is the home page. Design the home page so that viewers will understand your site's purpose and feel comfortable finding their way around your site's pages.

To ensure that viewers do not get "lost" in your site, design all the pages with a consistent look and feel. You can use templates and Cascading Style Sheets to maintain a common look for each page. **Templates** are web pages that contain the basic layout for each page in the site, including the location of a company logo or a menu of buttons. You'll learn more about Cascading Style Sheets in Lesson 2 and templates in Chapter 12.

Figure 4 *Insert panel displaying the Common category*

Figure 5 *Keywords dialog box*

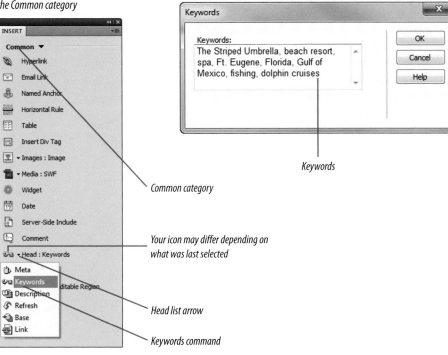

Keywords

Common category

Your icon may differ depending on what was last selected

Head list arrow

Keywords command

Enter keywords

1. Click the **Insert panel list arrow**, then on the dropdown menu, click the **Common category** (if it is not already selected).

2. Click the **Head list arrow**, as shown in Figure 4, then click **Keywords**.

TIP Some buttons on the Insert panel include a list arrow indicating that there is a menu of choices available. The button that you select last will appear on the Insert panel until you select another.

3. Type **The Striped Umbrella**, **beach resort**, **spa**, **Ft. Eugene**, **Florida**, **Gulf of Mexico**, **fishing**, **dolphin cruises** in the Keywords text box, as shown in Figure 5, then click **OK**

The Keywords icon [icon] appears in the head content section, indicating that there are keywords associated with this page. When you click the icon to select it, the keywords appear in the Keywords text box in the Property inspector.

You added keywords relating to the resort to the head content of The Striped Umbrella home page.

DESIGNTIP

Entering Keywords and Descriptions

Search engines use keywords, descriptions, and titles to find pages based on search terms a user enters. Therefore, it is very important to anticipate the search terms your potential customers would use and include these words in the keywords, description, and title. Many search engines display page titles and descriptions in their search results. Some search engines limit the number of keywords that they will index, so make sure you list the most important keywords first. Keep your keywords and descriptions short and concise to ensure that all search engines will include your site. To choose effective keywords, many designers use focus groups to learn which words potential customers or clients might use. A **focus group** is a marketing tool that asks a group of people for feedback about a product, such as the impact of a television ad or the effectiveness of a website design.

Enter a description

1. Click the **Head list arrow** on the Insert panel, then click **Description**.

2. In the Description text box, type **The Striped Umbrella is a full-service resort and spa just steps from the Gulf of Mexico in Ft. Eugene, Florida**.

   Your screen should resemble Figure 6.

3. Click **OK**.

   The description appears in the Description text box in the Property inspector.

4. Click the **Show Code view button** Code on the Document toolbar.

   The title, keywords, and description tags appear in the HTML code in the document window, as shown in Figure 7.

   TIP Your head content line numbers may differ. Also, you can enter and edit the title tag and the meta tags directly in the code in Code view.

5. Click the **Show Design view button** Design to return to Design view.

6. Click **View** on the Application bar (Win) or Menu bar (Mac), then click **Head Content** to close the head content section.

You added a description of The Striped Umbrella resort to the head content of the home page. You then viewed the page in Code view and the head content in the HTML code.

Figure 6 *Description dialog box*

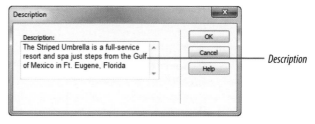

Description

Figure 7 *Head Content displayed in Code view*

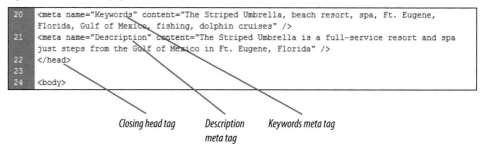

Closing head tag   Description meta tag   Keywords meta tag

Using Descriptions for POWDER Authentication

A website description can be stored in an XML file to provide POWDER authentication. **XML** stands for Extensible Markup Language, a type of file that is used to develop customized tags to store information. **POWDER** is the acronym for **Protocol for Web Description Resources**. This is an evaluation system for web pages developed with the World Wide Web Consortium (W3C) that provides summary information about a website. Examples include the date the site was created, the name of the person or company responsible for the content on the site, and a description of the content. It is designed to help users determine if a site would be considered a trustworthy resource of value and interest. It replaces the previous system called PICS, or Platform for Internet Content Selection.

Developing a Web Page

Figure 8 *Page Properties dialog box*

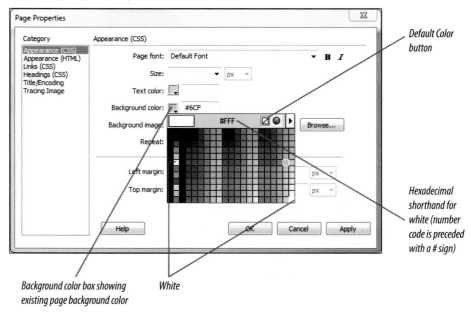

Default Color button

Background color box showing existing page background color

White

Hexadecimal shorthand for white (number code is preceded with a # sign)

Set the page background color

1. Click **Modify** on the Application bar (Win) or Menu bar (Mac), then click **Page Properties** to open the Page Properties dialog box.

2. Click the **Background color box** [ ] to open the color picker, as shown in Figure 8.

   The background color box in the Page Properties dialog box changes color based on the currently selected color. It is now blue, reflecting the current page background color, rather than the default icon color shown in the step instructions.

3. Click the rightmost color in the bottom row (white).

4. Click **Apply**, then click **OK**.

   Clicking Apply lets you see the changes you made to the web page without closing the Page Properties dialog box.

   TIP If you don't like the color you chose, either click the Default Color button [ ] in the color picker to switch to the default color or click a different color. The default page background color is usually white for most browsers. The default text color is usually black.

   The background color of the web page is now white. The black text against the white background provides a nice contrast and makes the text easy to read.

5. Save your work.

You used the Page Properties dialog box to change the background color to white.

Understanding Hexadecimal Values

Each color is assigned a **hexadecimal RGB value**, a value that represents the amount of red, green, and blue present in the color. For example, white, which is made of equal parts of red, green, and blue, has a hexadecimal value of FFFFFF. This is also called an RGB triplet in hexadecimal format (or a **hex triplet**). Each pair of characters in the hexadecimal value represents the red, green, and blue values. The hexadecimal number system is based on 16, rather than 10 in the decimal number system. Because the hexadecimal number system includes only numbers up to 9, values after 9 use the letters of the alphabet. "A" represents the number 10 in the hexadecimal number system. "F" represents the number 15. The hexadecimal values can be entered in the code using a form of shorthand that shortens the six characters to three characters. For instance: FFFFFF become FFF; 0066CC becomes 06C. The number value for a color is preceded by a pound sign (#) in HTML code.

Create, Import,
AND FORMAT TEXT

What You'll Do

In this lesson, you will enter and format text, import text, set text properties, and check the spelling on the Striped Umbrella home page.

Creating and Importing Text

Most information in web pages is presented in the form of text. You can type text directly on a page in Dreamweaver, import, or copy and paste it from another software program. (Macintosh users do not have the option to import text. They must open a text file, copy the text, then paste it into an HTML document.) When using a Windows computer to import text from a Microsoft Word file, it's best to use the Import Word Document command. Not only will the formatting be preserved, but Dreamweaver will generate clean HTML code. **Clean HTML code** is code that does what it is supposed to do without using unnecessary instructions, which take up memory.

When you format text, it is important to keep in mind that visitors to your site must have the same fonts installed on their computers as the fonts you use. Otherwise, the text might appear incorrectly.

QUICK TIP

Some software programs can also convert text into images so that the text retains the same appearance, no matter which fonts are installed. However, text converted into images is no longer editable.

If text does not have a font specified, the default font on the user's computer will be used to display the text. Keep in mind that some fonts might not appear the same on both a Windows and a Macintosh computer. The way fonts are **rendered** (drawn) on the screen differs because Windows and Macintosh computers use different technologies to render them. It is wise to stick to the standard fonts that work well with both systems. Test your pages using both operating systems.

Formatting Text Two Ways: HTML vs. CSS

Because text is more difficult and tiring to read on a computer screen than on a printed page, you should make the text in your website attractive and easy to read. One way to do this is to format text by changing its font, size, and color. Previously web designers used the Property inspector to apply formatting attributes, such as font type, size, color, alignment, and indents. This created HTML tags in the code that directed the way the fonts would appear in a browser. **Tags** are the parts of the code that specify the appearance for all page content when viewed in a browser.

The more accepted method now is to create Cascading Style Sheets (CSS) to format and place web page elements. **Cascading Style Sheets** are sets of formatting attributes that you use to format web pages to provide a consistent presentation for content across the site. Cascading Style Sheets make it easy to separate page content from the page design. The content is placed in the body section on web pages, and the formatting styles are placed in either an external style sheet file or in the page head content. Separating content from design is preferable because editing content and formatting content are really two separate tasks. Since page content is separate from formatting styles, you can update or change the page content without disturbing the page formatting.

You can apply some formatting, without creating styles, using the Bold and Italic HTML tags. You can also use HTML heading tags, which determine the relative size and boldness of text, and which help to show the importance of text relative to the rest of the text on the page.

To apply CSS or HTML formatting, you use the Property inspector, which has a panel for each method: the CSS Property inspector and the HTML Property inspector. You display them by clicking the CSS or the HTML button on the left side of the Property inspector. Some coding options are unique to each one and some coding options are available on both. For instance, HTML heading tags are only available on the HTML Property inspector. Font tags are only available on the CSS Property inspector. The Bold tag is available on both. Regardless of

which Property inspector you use, CSS styles will be created when you format page objects.

Because CSS is a lot to learn when you are just beginning, we are going to begin by using HTML tags for formatting. Although they are not the currently preferred formatting method, it's still a good idea to know about HTML tags because you might "inherit" a web page that contains them. Then in Chapter 3, we will use the preferred method, CSS.

Changing Fonts

You can format your text with different fonts by choosing a font combination, or Font-family, from the Font list in the CSS Property inspector. A **Font-family** is a set of font choices that specify which fonts a browser should use to display the text on your web page. Font-families ensure that if one font is not available, the browser will use the next one specified in the font combination. For example, if text is formatted with the font combination Arial, Helvetica, sans serif, the browser will first look on the viewer's system for Arial. If Arial is not available, then it will look for Helvetica. If Helvetica is not available, then it will look for a sans-serif font to apply to the text. Using fonts within the default settings is wise, because fonts set outside the

default settings might not be available on all viewers' computers.

Changing Font Sizes

There are two ways to change the size of text using the Property inspector. When the CSS option is selected, you can select a numerical value for the size from 9 to 36 pixels (or type a smaller or larger number). Or you can use a size expressed in words from xx-small to larger, which sets the size of selected text relative to other text on the page. On the HTML Property inspector, you do not have font sizes available.

Formatting Paragraphs

The HTML Property inspector displays options to format blocks of text as paragraphs or as different sizes of headings. To format a paragraph as a heading, click anywhere in the paragraph, and then select the heading size you want from the Format list in the HTML Property inspector. The Format list contains six different heading formats. Heading 1 is the largest size, and Heading 6 is the smallest size. Browsers display text formatted as headings in bold, setting them off from paragraphs of text. You can also align paragraphs with the alignment buttons on the CSS Property inspector and indent paragraphs using the Blockquote and Remove Blockquote buttons on the HTML Property inspector.

Enter text

1. Position the insertion point directly after "want to go home." at the end of the paragraph, press **[Enter]** (Win) or **[return]** (Mac), then type **The Striped Umbrella**.

   Pressing [Enter] (Win) or [return] (Mac) creates a new paragraph.

   TIP If the new text does not assume the formatting attributes as the paragraph above it, click the Show Code and Design views button Split, position the cursor right after the period after "home", then go back to the page in Design view and insert a new paragraph.

2. Press and hold **[Shift]**, press **[Enter]** (Win) or **[return]** (Mac), then type **25 Beachside Drive**.

   Pressing and holding [Shift] while you press [Enter] (Win) or [return] (Mac) creates a line break. A **line break** places a new line of text on the next line down without creating a new paragraph. Line breaks are useful when you want to add a new line of text directly below the current line of text and keep the same formatting.

3. Add the following text below the 25 Beachside Drive text, using line breaks after each line:

   Ft. Eugene, Florida 33775

   555-594-9458

4. Compare your screen with Figure 9.

   You entered text for the address and telephone number on the home page.

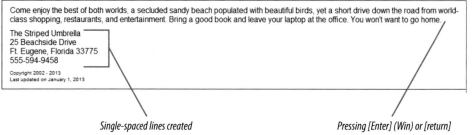

Figure 9 *Entering the address and telephone number on The Striped Umbrella home page*

Come enjoy the best of both worlds, a secluded sandy beach populated with beautiful birds, yet a short drive down the road from world-class shopping, restaurants, and entertainment. Bring a good book and leave your laptop at the office. You won't want to go home.

The Striped Umbrella
25 Beachside Drive
Ft. Eugene, Florida 33775
555-594-9458

Copyright 2002 - 2013
Last updated on January 1, 2013

Single-spaced lines created by using line breaks

Pressing [Enter] (Win) or [return] (Mac) creates a new paragraph

TABLE 1: HTML FORMATTING TAGS	
HTML tag	**Represents**
<p> </p>	Opening and closing paragraph tag
 	Line break tag (does not require a closing tag)
<em> </em>	Opening and closing italic (emphasis) tag
<strong> </strong>	Opening and closing bold tag
<u> </u>	Opening and closing underline tag

Using Keyboard Shortcuts

When working with text, the keyboard shortcuts for Cut, Copy, and Paste are very useful. These are [Ctrl][X] (Win) or ⌘ [X] (Mac) for Cut, [Ctrl][C] (Win) or ⌘ [C] (Mac) for Copy, and [Ctrl][V] (Win) or ⌘ [V] (Mac) for Paste. You can view all Dreamweaver keyboard shortcuts using the Keyboard Shortcuts dialog box, which lets you view existing shortcuts for menu commands, tools, or miscellaneous functions, such as copying HTML or inserting an image. You can also create your own shortcuts or assign shortcuts that you are familiar with from using them in other software programs. To view or modify keyboard shortcuts, click the Keyboard Shortcuts command on the Edit menu (Win) or Dreamweaver menu (Mac), then select the shortcut key set you want. Each chapter in this book includes Power User shortcuts, a list of keyboard shortcuts relevant to that chapter.

Figure 10 *Formatting the address on The Striped Umbrella home page*

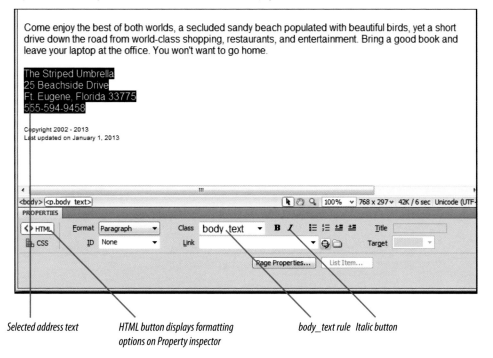

Come enjoy the best of both worlds, a secluded sandy beach populated with beautiful birds, yet a short drive down the road from world-class shopping, restaurants, and entertainment. Bring a good book and leave your laptop at the office. You won't want to go home.

The Striped Umbrella
25 Beachside Drive
Ft. Eugene, Florida 33775
555-594-9458

Copyright 2002 - 2013
Last updated on January 1, 2013

Selected address text   *HTML button displays formatting options on Property inspector*   *body_text rule   Italic button*

Figure 11 *Viewing the HTML code for the address and phone number*

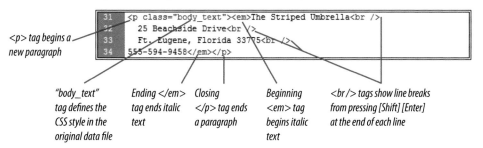

```
31   <p class="body_text"><em>The Striped Umbrella<br />
32       25 Beachside Drive<br />
33       Ft. Eugene, Florida 33775<br />
34   555-594-9458</em></p>
```

<p> tag begins a new paragraph

"body_text" tag defines the CSS style in the original data file   *Ending </em> tag ends italic text*   *Closing </p> tag ends a paragraph*   *Beginning <em> tag begins italic text*   *
 tags show line breaks from pressing [Shift] [Enter] at the end of each line*

Format text

1. Select the entire address and telephone number, then click the **HTML button** <> HTML in the Property inspector (if it is not already selected) to change to the HTML Property inspector, as shown in Figure 10.

2. Click the **Italic button** *I* in the Property inspector to italicize the text, then click after the text to deselect it.

3. Click the **Show Code view button** Code to view the HTML code, as shown in Figure 11.

   It is always helpful to learn what the HTML code means. Refer to Table 1 to locate some basic HTML formatting tags. As you edit and format your pages, read the code to see how it appears for each element. The more familiar you are with the code, the more comfortable you will feel with Dreamweaver and web design. A strong knowledge of HTML is a necessary skill for professional web designers.

4. Click the **Show Design view button** Design to return to Design view.

5. Save your work, then close the page.

You changed the Property inspector options from CSS to HTML, then formatted the address and phone number for The Striped Umbrella by changing the font style to italic.

Save an image file in the assets folder

1. Open dw2_1.html from where you store your Data Files, save it as **spa.html** in the striped_umbrella folder, overwriting the existing file, then click **No** in the Update Links dialog box.

2. Select **The Striped Umbrella** banner.

   Updating links ties the image or hyperlink to the Data Files folder. Because you already copied su_banner.gif to the website, the banner image is visible. Notice that the Src text box shows the link is to the website assets folder, not to the Data Files folder.

3. Click the **sea_spa_logo image broken link placeholder** to select it, click the **Browse for File icon** 🖿 in the Property inspector next to the Src text box, navigate to the chapter_2 assets folder, click **sea_spa_logo.jpg**, then click **OK** (Win) or **Choose** (Mac).

   Because this image was not in the website, it appeared as a broken link. Using the Browse for File icon 🖿 selects the source of the original image file. Dreamweaver automatically copies the file to the assets folder of the website and it is visible on the page. You might have to deselect the new image to see it replace the broken link.

4. Click the **plus sign** (Win) or **expander arrow** (Mac) next to the assets folder in the Files panel, then click the **Refresh button** ⟳ on the Files panel toolbar if you don't see sea_spa_logo.jpg listed.

   A copy of sea_spa_logo.jpg file appears in the assets folder, as shown in Figure 12.

   You opened a new file, saved it as the new spa page, and fixed a broken link by copying the image to the assets folder.

Figure 12 *Image file added to Striped Umbrella assets folder*

Sea Spa image visible and selected on page

Use the Browse for File icon to find the image in the data files assets folder

Refresh button

Expanded assets folder

Figure 13 *Clean Up Word HTML dialog box*

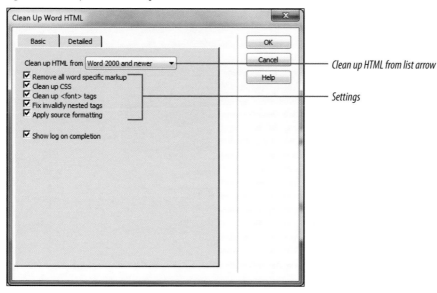

— *Clean up HTML from list arrow*

— *Settings*

Import text

1. Click to place the insertion point to the right of the spa graphic on the spa.html page.

2. Click **File** on the Application bar, point to **Import**, click **Word Document**, double-click the **chapter_2 folder** from where you store your Data Files, then double-click **spa.doc** (Win); or double-click **spa.doc** from where you store your Data Files, select all, copy, close spa.doc, then paste the copied text on the spa page in Dreamweaver (Mac).

3. Click **Commands** on the Application bar (Win) or Menu bar (Mac), then click **Clean Up Word HTML**.

   TIP If a dialog box appears stating that Dreamweaver was unable to determine the version of Word used to generate this document, click OK, click the Clean up HTML from list arrow, then choose the Word 2000 and newer version of Word if it isn't already selected.

4. Make sure each check box in the Clean Up Word HTML dialog box is checked, as shown in Figure 13, click **OK**, then click **OK** again to close the results window.

You imported a Word document, then used the Clean Up Word HTML command.

Choosing Filenames for Web Pages

When you choose a name for a web page, you should use a short, simple descriptive name that reflects the contents of the page. For example, if the page is about your company's products, you could name it products.html. You should also follow some general rules for naming web pages, such as naming the home page index.html. Most file servers look for the file named index.html or default.html to use as the initial page for a website. Do not use spaces, special characters, or punctuation in filenames for files or folders that will you will use in your site. Use underscores rather than spaces for readability; for example: use sea_spa_logo.jpg rather than sea spa logo.jpg. Just to be totally safe for all file servers, use only letters, numbers, or underscores in file or folder names. Many designers also avoid the use of uppercase letters.

Set text properties

1. Select the Common category on the Insert panel if necessary, then scroll up and place the insertion point anywhere within the words "The Sea Spa Services."

2. Click the **Format list arrow** in the HTML Property inspector, then click **Heading 2**.

   The Heading 2 format is applied to the paragraph. Even a single word is considered a paragraph if there is a hard return or paragraph break after it. The HTML code for a Heading 2 tag is <h2>. The tag is then closed with </h2>. For headings, the level of the heading tag follows the h, so the code for a Heading 1 tag is <h1>.

3. Select the text **Massages**, **Facials**, and **Body Treatments**, click the **Format list arrow** in the HTML Property inspector, click **Heading 4**, then click outside the heading to deselect the text.

4. Click after the word "Treatments", insert a line break, click the **Show Code and Design views button** | Split | on the Document toolbar, then compare your screen to Figure 14.

   The word "Massages" after the words "Body Treatments" may be in a different position on your screen. Figure 14 was sized down, so your page will be much wider than the figure shows.

   You applied two heading formats, then viewed the HTML code.

Figure 14 *Viewing the heading tags in Show Code and Design views*

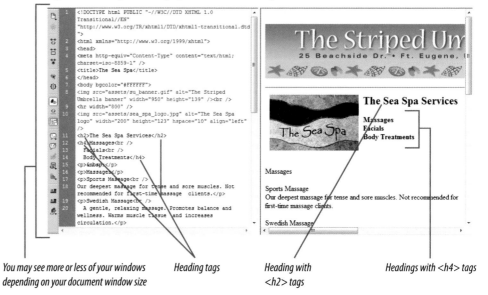

You may see more or less of your windows depending on your document window size

Heading tags

Heading with <h2> tags

Headings with <h4> tags

Importing and Linking Microsoft Office Documents (Windows)

Adobe makes it easy to transfer data between Microsoft Office documents and Dreamweaver web pages. When importing a Word or Excel document, click File on the Application bar, point to Import, then click either Word Document or Excel Document. Select the file you want to import, then click the Formatting list arrow to choose among importing Text only; Text with structure (paragraphs, lists, and tables); Text, structure, basic formatting (bold, italic); or Text, structure, full formatting (bold, italic, styles) before you click Open. The option you choose depends on the importance of the original structure and formatting. Always use the Clean Up Word HTML command after importing a Word file.

You can also create a link to a Word or Excel document on your web page. To do so, browse to locate the Word or Excel document you want to add as a link, then drag the file name to the location on the page where you would like the link to appear. (If the document is located outside the site, you can browse for it using the Site list arrow on the Files panel, Windows Explorer, or Mac Finder.) Next, select the Create a link option button in the Insert Document dialog box, then save the file in your site root folder so it will be uploaded when you publish your site. If it is not uploaded, the link will be broken.

Figure 15 *Check Spelling dialog box*

Facials

Revitalizing Facial
A light massage with a customized essential oil blend that moisturizes the skin and restores circulation.

Gentlemen's Facial
A cleansing facial that restores a healthy glow. Includes a neck and shoulder masage

Milk Mask
A soothing mask that softens and moisturizes the face. Leaves your skin looking

Body Treatments

Salt Glow
Imported sea salts are massaged into the skin, exfoliating and cleansing the pores

Herbal Wrap
Organic lavender blooms create a detoxifying and calming treatment to relieve ac

Seaweed Body Wrap
Seaweed is a natural detoxifying agent that also helps improve circulation.

Call The Sea Spa desk for prices and reservations. Any of our services can be p
until 9:00 p.m. Call 555-594-9458, extension 39

Check Spelling

Word not found in dictionary:
masage.

Change to: massage.
Suggestions:
mas age.
massage.
manage.
message.
masses.
massed.
maser.
messed.

Add to Personal
Ignore
Change
Ignore All
Change All
Close
Help

Misspelled word

Click "Change" to correct spelling

Checking for Spelling Errors

It is very important to check for spelling and grammatical errors before publishing a page. A page that is published with errors will cause the user to immediately judge the site as unprofessional and carelessly made, and the accuracy of the page content will be in question. If you have text in a word processing file that you plan to import into Dreamweaver, check the spelling in the word processor first. Then check the spelling in the imported text again in Dreamweaver. This allows you to add words such as proper names to the Dreamweaver dictionary so the program will not flag them again. Click the Add to Personal button in the Check Spelling dialog box to add a new word to the dictionary. Even though you might have checked a page using the Check Spelling feature, you still must proofread the content yourself to catch usage errors such as "to," "too," and "two." Accuracy in both content and delivery is critical.

Check spelling

1. Click the **Show Design view button** Design to return to Design view.

2. Place the insertion point in front of the text "The Sea Spa Services".

   It is a good idea to start a spelling check at the top of the document because Dreamweaver searches from the insertion point down. If your insertion point is in the middle of the document, you will receive a message asking if you want to check the rest of the document. Starting from the beginning saves time.

3. Click **Commands** on the Application bar (Win) or Menu bar (Mac), then click **Check Spelling**.

   The word "masage" is highlighted on the page as a misspelled word and suggestions are listed to correct it in the Check Spelling dialog box, as shown in Figure 15.

4. Click **massage.** in the Suggestions list if necessary, then click **Change**.

   The word is corrected on the page.

5. Click **OK** to close the Dreamweaver dialog box stating that the Spelling Check is completed.

6. Save and close the spa page, then close the dw2_1.html page.

You checked the page for spelling errors.

Add Links
TO WEB PAGES

What You'll Do

In this lesson, you will open the home page and add links to the menu bar that link to the About Us, Spa, Cafe, and Activities pages. You will then insert an email link at the bottom of the page.

Adding Links to Web Pages

Links, or hyperlinks, provide the real power for web pages. Links make it possible for viewers to navigate all the pages in a website and to connect to other pages anywhere on the web. Users are more likely to return to websites that have a user-friendly navigation structure. Users also enjoy websites that have interesting links to other web pages or other websites.

To add links to a web page, first select the text or image that you want to serve as a link, and then, in the Link text box in the Property inspector, specify a path to the page to which you want to link.

When you create links on a web page, it is important to avoid **broken links**, or links that cannot find their intended destinations. You can accidentally cause a broken link by typing the incorrect address for the link in the Link text box. Broken links can be caused by companies merging, going out of business, or simply moving their website addresses.

In addition to adding links to your pages, you should provide a **point of contact**, or

a place on a web page that provides users with a means of contacting the company. A common point of contact is a **mailto: link**, which is an email address that users with questions or problems can use to contact someone at the company's headquarters.

Using Menu Bars

A **menu bar**, or **navigation bar**, is an area on a web page that contains links to the main pages of a website. Menu bars are usually located at the top or side of the main pages of a website and can be created with text, images, or a combination of the two. Menu bars are the backbone of a website's navigation structure, which includes all navigation aids for moving around a website. You can, however, include additional links to the main pages of the website elsewhere on the page. To make navigating a website as easy as possible, you should place menu bars in the same position on each page. The web page in Figure 16 shows a menu bar that contains a set of main links with additional links that appear as the mouse rolls over each main link. You can create a simple menu bar by typing the names of your website's pages at the top of your web page, formatting the text, and then adding links to each page name. It is always a good idea to provide plain text links for accessibility, regardless of the type of navigation structure you choose to use. For example, if you use Flash for your navigation links, it is a good idea to include a duplicate set of text with links to the same pages.

Following WCAG Accessibility for Navigation

The WCAG Guideline 2.4 lists ways to ensure that all viewers can successfully and easily navigate a website. It states: "Provide ways to help users navigate, find content, and determine where they are." Suggestions include limiting the number of links on a page, using techniques to allow users to quickly access different sections of a page, and making sure that links are readable and easily distinguishable.

Figure 16 *The CIA website*

Central Intelligence Agency website – www.cia.gov

Create a menu bar

1. Open **index.html**.

2. Position the insertion point to the left of "A" in About Us, then drag to select **About Us - Spa - Cafe**.

3. Type **Home - About Us - Spa - Cafe - Activities**, as shown in Figure 17.

   These five text labels will serve as a menu bar. You will add the links later.

You created a new menu bar using text, replacing the original menu bar.

Insert a horizontal rule

1. Click in front of the word "Welcome".

2. Click **Horizontal Rule** in the Common category on the Insert panel to insert a horizontal rule between the menu bar and the first paragraph.

   A horizontal rule is a line used to separate page elements or to organize information on a page.

3. Compare your screen to Figure 18, then save your work.

   TIP An asterisk after the filename in the title bar indicates that you have altered the page since you last saved it. After you save your work, the asterisk does not appear.

You added a horizontal rule to separate the menu bar from the page content.

Figure 17 *Viewing the new menu bar*

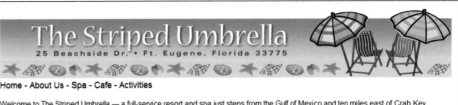

Figure 18 *Inserting a horizontal rule*

Asterisk indicates page has not been saved

Horizontal Rule command

Horizontal rule

Preventing Data Loss

It is always a good idea to save your files frequently. A good practice is to save a file after you have completed a successful edit, before you attempt a difficult edit, and when you have finished working on an open file. It is also a good idea to close a file when you are not working on it. Having unnecessary files open can be a distraction to your work flow. Do not open files from a different website other than the open site in the Files panel, or you might accidentally save them in the wrong folder!

Figure 19 *Selecting text for the Home link*

Selected text

Link text box

Browse for file icon

Figure 20 *Select File dialog box*

Striped Umbrella site root folder

index.html file

Relative to: list arrow

Click OK to set link

Figure 21 *Links added to menu bar*

Menu bar with links added

Add links to web pages

1. Double-click **Home** to select it, as shown in Figure 19.
2. Click the **Browse for File icon** 📁 next to the Link text box in the HTML Property inspector, then navigate to the striped_umbrella local site folder if necessary.
3. Verify that the link is set Relative to Document in the Relative to: list.
4. Click **index.html** as shown in Figure 20, click **OK** (Win) or **Choose** (Mac), then click anywhere on the page to deselect Home.

TIP Your file listing might differ depending on your view settings.

Home now appears in blue with an underline, indicating it is a link. If users click the Home link, a new page will not open, because the link is on the home page. It might seem odd to create a link to the same page on which the link appears, but this will be helpful when you copy the menu bar to other pages in the site. Always provide viewers a link to the home page.

5. Repeat Steps 1–4 to create links for About Us, Spa, Cafe, and Activities to their corresponding pages in the striped_umbrella site folder.
6. When you finish adding the links to the other four pages, deselect all, then compare your screen to Figure 21.

You created a link for each of the five menu bar elements to their respective web pages in The Striped Umbrella website.

Create an email link

1. Place the insertion point after the last digit in the telephone number, then insert a line break.

2. Click **Email Link** in the Common category on the Insert panel to insert an email link.

3. Type **Club Manager** in the Text text box, type **manager@stripedumbrella.com** in the Email text box, as shown in Figure 22, then click **OK** to close the Email Link dialog box.

TIP If the text does not retain the formatting from the previous line use the Edit, Undo command to undo Steps 1–3. Switch to Code view and place the insertion point immediately to the right of the telephone number, then repeat the steps again in Design view.

4. Save your work.

The text "mailto:manager@stripedumbrella.com" appears in the Link text box in the HTML Property inspector. When a viewer clicks this link, a blank email message window opens in the user's default email software, where the user can type a message. See Figure 23.

TIP You must enter the correct email address in the Email text box for the link to work. However, you can enter any descriptive name, such as customer service or Bob Smith in the Text text box. You can also enter the email address as the text if you want to show the actual email address on the web page.

You inserted an email link to serve as a point of contact for The Striped Umbrella.

Figure 22 *Email Link dialog box*

Text for email link on the page (this could also be a person's name or position or the actual email link)

Link information

Figure 23 *mailto: link on the Property inspector*

mailto: link

Figure 24 *The Assets panel URL category*

URLs button

Email link shown as it will appear on the page

Email link on home page

View the email link in the Assets panel

1. Click the **Assets panel tab** to view the Assets panel.

2. Click the **URLs button** to display the URLs in the website.

3. Click the **Refresh button** at the bottom of the Assets panel, if necessary, to view the link, then compare your screen to Figure 24.

   URL stands for Uniform Resource Locator. The URLs listed in the Assets panel show all of the external links, or links pointing outside of the website. An email link is outside the website, so it is an external link. You will learn more about URLs and links in Chapter 5. The links you created to the site pages are internal links (inside the website), and are not listed in the Assets panel.

4. Click the **Files panel tab** to view the Files panel.

You viewed the email link on the home page in the Assets panel.

Use the History PANEL AND EDIT CODE

What You'll Do

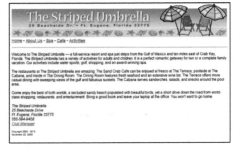

In this lesson, you will use the History panel to undo formatting changes you make to a horizontal rule. You will then use the Code Inspector to view the HTML code for the horizontal rule. You will also insert a date object and then view its code in the Code Inspector.

Using the History Panel

Throughout the process of creating a web page, it's likely that you will make mistakes along the way. Fortunately, you have a tool named the History panel to undo your mistakes. The **History panel** records each editing and formatting task you perform and displays them in a list in the order in which you completed them. Each task listed in the History panel is called a **step**. You can drag the **slider** on the left side of the History panel to undo or redo steps, as shown in Figure 25. You can also click in the bar to the left of a step to undo all steps below it. You click the step to select it. By default, the History panel records 50 steps. You can change the number of steps the History panel records in the General category of the Preferences dialog box. However, keep in mind that setting this number too high might require additional memory and could affect Dreamweaver's performance.

Viewing HTML Code in the Code Inspector

If you enjoy writing code, you occasionally might want to make changes to web pages by entering the code rather than using the panels and tools in Design view. Often it is actually easier to make editing or formatting corrections in the code. You can view the code in Dreamweaver using Code view, Code and Design views, or the Code Inspector. The **Code Inspector**, shown in Figure 26, is a separate window that displays the current page in Code view.

Understanding Other History Panel Features

Dragging the slider up and down in the History panel is a quick way to undo or redo steps. However, the History panel offers much more. It has the capability to "memorize" certain tasks and consolidate them into one command. This is a useful feature for steps that you perform repetitively on web pages. Some Dreamweaver features, such as drag and drop, cannot be recorded in the History panel and are noted by a red "x" placed next to them in the panel. The History panel does not show steps performed in the Files panel.

Developing a Web Page

The advantage of using the Code Inspector is that you can see a full-screen view of your page in Design view while viewing the underlying code in a floating window that you can resize and position wherever you want.

You can add advanced features, such as JavaScript functions, to web pages by copying and pasting code from one page to another in the Code Inspector. A **JavaScript** function is a block of code that adds dynamic content such as rollovers or interactive forms to a web page. A **rollover** is a special effect that changes the appearance of an object when the mouse moves over it.

Figure 25 *The History panel*

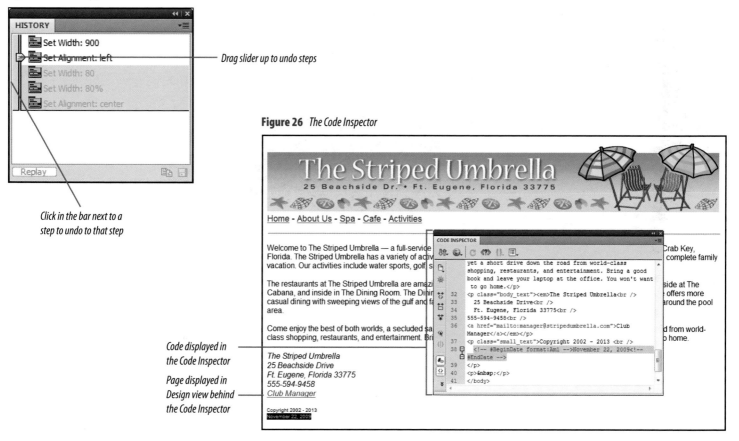

Drag slider up to undo steps

Click in the bar next to a step to undo to that step

Figure 26 *The Code Inspector*

Code displayed in the Code Inspector

Page displayed in Design view behind the Code Inspector

Use the History panel

1. Click **Window** on the Application bar (Win) or Menu bar (Mac), then click **History**.

   The History panel opens and displays steps you have recently performed.

2. Click the **History panel options button**, click **Clear History**, as shown in Figure 27, then click **Yes** to close the warning box.

3. Select the **horizontal rule** on the home page.

   The Property inspector shows the properties of the selected horizontal rule.

4. Click the W text box in the Property inspector, type **900**, click the **Align list arrow**, click **Left**, then compare your Property inspector to Figure 28.

   Horizontal rule widths can be set in pixels or as a percent of the width of the window. If the width is expressed in pixels, the code will only show the number, without the word "pixels". Pixels is understood as the default width setting.

5. Using the Property inspector, change the W text box value to **80**, change the measurement unit to **%**, click the **Align list arrow**, then click **Center**.

6. Drag the **slider** on the History panel up to Set Alignment: left, as shown in Figure 29.

   The bottom three steps in the History panel appear gray, indicating that these steps have been undone.

7. Right-click (Win) or Control-click (Mac) the **History panel title bar**, then click **Close** to close the History panel.

You formatted the horizontal rule, made changes to it, then used the History panel to undo some of the changes.

Figure 27 *Clearing the History panel*

You may see different steps depending on your keystrokes

Panel options button

Clear History command

You will see additional commands if your panel is displayed in a tab group

Figure 28 *Property inspector settings for horizontal rule*

Width set to 900 pixels

Alignment of horizontal rule set to left side of page

Figure 29 *Undoing steps using the History panel*

Slider

Set Alignment: left

Steps that have been undone

Figure 30 *Viewing the Options menu in the Code Inspector*

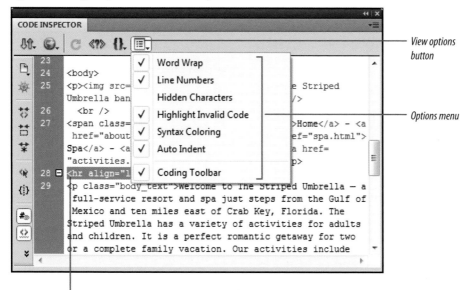

View options button

Options menu

Code for horizontal rule

Use the Code Inspector

1. Click the **horizontal rule** to select it if necessary, click **Window** on the Application bar (Win) or Menu bar (Mac), then click **Code Inspector**.

   Because the horizontal rule on the page is selected, the corresponding code is highlighted in the Code Inspector.

   TIP You can also press [F10](Win) or [fn][option][F10] (Mac) to display the Code Inspector.

2. Click the **View Options button** on the Code Inspector toolbar to display the View Options menu, then if **Word Wrap** is unchecked, click it once to activate it.

   The Word Wrap feature forces text to stay within the confines of the Code Inspector window, allowing you to read without scrolling sideways.

3. Click the **View Options button** , then verify that the Word Wrap, Line Numbers, Highlight Invalid Code, Syntax Coloring, Auto Indent, and Coding Toolbar menu items are checked, as shown in Figure 30. If they are not checked, check them.

4. Select **900** in the horizontal rule width code, type **950**, then click the Refresh button C Refresh in the Property inspector.

You changed the width of the horizontal rule by changing the code in the Code Inspector.

POWER USER SHORTCUTS	
To do this:	**Use this shortcut:**
Select All	[Ctrl][A] (Win) or ⌘ [A] (Mac)
Copy	[Ctrl][C] (Win) or ⌘ [C] (Mac)
Cut	[Ctrl][X] (Win) or ⌘ [X] (Mac)
Paste	[Ctrl][V] (Win) or ⌘ [V] (Mac)
Line Break	[Shift][Enter] (Win) or [Shift][return] (Mac)
Show or hide the Code Inspector	[F10] (Win) or [fn][option][F10] (Mac)
Preview in browser	[F12] (Win) or [fn][option][F12] (Mac)
Check spelling	[Shift][F7] (Win) or [fn][Shift][F7] (Mac)

Use the Reference panel

1. With the horizontal rule still selected, click the **Reference button** <?> on the Code Inspector toolbar, as shown in Figure 31, to open the Results Tab Group below the Property inspector, with the Reference panel visible.

TIP If the horizontal rule is not still selected, you will not see the horizontal rule description in the Reference panel.

2. Read the information about horizontal rules in the Reference panel, as shown in Figure 32, right-click in an empty area of the **Results Tab Group title bar**, then click **Close Tab Group** (Win) or click the **Panel options button** ▼≡ then click **Close Tab Group** (Mac and Win) to close the Results Tab Group.

3. Close the Code Inspector.

You read information about horizontal rule settings in the Reference panel.

Figure 31 *Reference button on the Code Inspector toolbar*

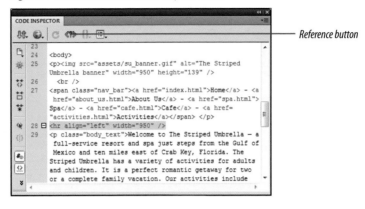

Reference button

Figure 32 *Viewing the Reference panel*

Information on <HR> (horizontal rule tag)

Figure 33 *Insert Date dialog box*

Date formats

Update automatically on save check box

Figure 34 *Viewing the date object code*

Code for date object (your date code may be on a different line number)

```
            >
37    <p class="small_text">Copyright 2002 - 2013 <br />
38    Last updated on
39    <!-- #BeginDate format:Am1 -->May 16, 2010<!-- #EndDate -->
40    </p>
41    <p> </p>
42    </body>
43    </html>
```

Insert a date object

1. Scroll down the page, if necessary, to select **January 1, 2013**, then press **[Delete]** (Win) or **[delete]** (Mac).

2. Click **Date** in the Common category in the Insert panel, then click **March 7, 1974** if necessary in the Date format list.

3. Check the **Update automatically on save check box**, as shown in Figure 33, click **OK**, then deselect the text.

4. Change to Code and Design views.

   The code has changed to reflect the date object, which is set to today's date, as shown in Figure 34. (Your date will be different.) The new code is highlighted with a light yellow background, indicating that it is a date object, automatically coded by Dreamweaver, rather than a date that has been manually typed on the page by the designer.

5. Return to Design view, then save the page.

You inserted a date object that will be updated automatically when you open and save the home page.

Inserting Comments

A handy Dreamweaver feature is the ability to insert comments into HTML code. Comments can provide helpful information describing portions of the code, such as a JavaScript function. You can create comments in any Dreamweaver view, but you must turn on Invisible Elements to see them in Design view. Use the Edit (Win) or Dreamweaver (Mac), Preferences, Invisible Elements, Comments option to enable viewing of comments; then use the View, Visual Aids, Invisible Elements menu option to display them on the page. To create a comment, select the Common category on the Insert panel, click Comment, type a comment in the Comment dialog box, and then click OK. Comments are not visible in browser windows. Comments are also not visible in Design view unless you turn them on as a preference. To do this, click View, Visual Aids, Invisible elements.

Modify and Test
WEB PAGES

What You'll Do

In this lesson, you will preview the home page in the browser to check for typographical errors, grammatical errors, broken links, and overall appearance. After previewing, you will make slight formatting adjustments to the page to improve its appearance.

Testing and Modifying Web Pages

Testing web pages is a continuous process. You never really finish a website, because there are always additions and corrections to make. As you add and modify pages, you must test each page as part of the development process. The best way to test a web page is to preview it in Live view or in a browser window to make sure that all text and image elements appear the way you expect them to. You should also test your links to make sure they work properly. You need to proofread your text to make sure it contains all the necessary information for the page with no typographical or grammatical errors.

Designers typically view a page in a browser, return to Dreamweaver to make necessary changes, and then view the page in a browser again. They repeat this process many times before the page is ready for publishing. In fact, it is sometimes difficult to stop making improvements to a page and move on to another project. You need to strike a balance among quality, creativity, and productivity.

Testing a Web Page Using Different Browsers and Screen Sizes

Because users access the Internet using a wide variety of computer systems, it is important to design your pages so that

---

DESIGN TIP

Using "Under Construction" Or "Come Back Later" Pages

Many people are tempted to insert an unfinished page as a placeholder for a page that they intend to finish later. Rather than have real content, these pages usually contain text or an image that indicates the page is not finished, or "under construction." You should not publish a web page that has a link to an unfinished page. It is frustrating to click a link for a page you want to open only to find an "under construction" note or image displayed. You want to make the best possible impression on your viewing audience. If you cannot complete a page before publishing it, at least provide enough information on it to make it "worth the trip."

all browsers and screen sizes can display them well. You should test your pages using different browsers and a wide variety of screen sizes to ensure the best view of your page by the most people possible. Although the most common screen size that designers use today is 1024 × 768, some viewers restore down (reduce) individual program windows to a size comparable to 800 × 600 to be able to have more windows open simultaneously on their screen. In other words, people use their "screen real estate" according to their personal work style. To view your page using different screen sizes, click the Window Size

pop-up menu on the status bar, then choose the setting you want to use. Table 2 lists the Dreamweaver default window screen sizes. To view your pages using several different browsers, click the Preview/Debug in Browser button on the Application bar (Win) Menu bar (Mac), click Edit Browser List, then use the Add icon to add additional browsers of your choice to the list. You can also designate which browser to use as the default browser, the browser which opens when the F12 key is pressed. Remember also to check your pages using Windows and Macintosh platforms. Some page elements

such as fonts, colors, table borders, layers, and horizontal rules might not appear consistently in both.

Testing a Web Page as Rendered in a Mobile Device

Dreamweaver has another preview feature that allows you to see what a page would look like if it were viewed on a mobile hand-held device, such as a BlackBerry or iPhone. To use this feature, click the Preview/Debug in Browser button on the Document toolbar, then click Preview in Device Central.

TABLE 2: DREAMWEAVER DEFAULT WINDOW SCREEN SIZES	
Window Size (Inside Dimensions of the Browser Window Without Borders)	Monitor Size
592W	
536 × 196	640 × 480, default
600 × 300	640 × 480, maximized
760 × 420	800 × 600, maximized
795 × 470	832 × 624, maximized
955 × 600	1024 × 768, maximized

Modify a web page

1. Click the **Restore Down button** 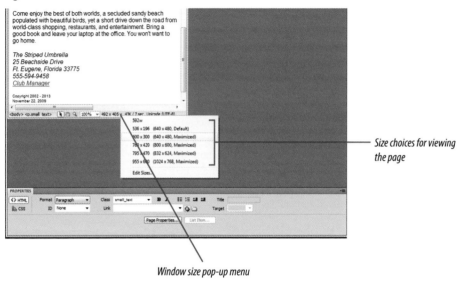 on the index.html title bar to decrease the size of the home page window (Win) or skip to Step 2 (Mac).

   TIP You cannot use the Window Size options if your Document window is maximized (Win).

2. Click the current window size on the status bar, as shown in Figure 35, then click **600 × 300 (640 × 480, Maximized)**, if necessary.

   A viewer using this setting will be forced to use the horizontal scroll bar to view the entire page.

3. Click the current window size on the status bar, then click **955 × 600 (1024 × 768, Maximized)**.

4. Replace the period after the last sentence, "You won't want to go home." with an exclamation point.

5. Click the **Maximize button** ☐ on the index.html title bar to maximize the home page window.

   TIP If you don't see the Maximize button, collapse your panels temporarily.

6. Save your work.

You viewed the home page using two different window sizes and you made simple formatting changes to the page.

Figure 35 *Window screen sizes*

Size choices for viewing the page

Window size pop-up menu

Using Smart Design Principles in Web Page Layout

As you view your pages in the browser, take a critical look at the symmetry of the page. Is it balanced? Are there too many images compared to text, or vice versa? Does everything "heavy" seem to be on the top or bottom of the page, or do the page elements seem to balance with the weight evenly distributed between the top, bottom, and sides? Use design principles to create a site-wide consistency for your pages. Horizontal symmetry means that the elements are balanced across the page. Vertical symmetry means that they are balanced down the page. Diagonal symmetry balances page elements along the invisible diagonal line of the page. Radial symmetry runs from the center of the page outward, like the petals of a flower. These principles all deal with balance; however, too much balance is not good, either. Sometimes it adds interest to place page elements a little off center or to have an asymmetric layout. Color, white space, text, and images should all complement each other and provide a natural flow across and down the page. The **rule of thirds**—dividing a page into nine squares like a tic-tac-toe grid—states that interest is increased when your focus is on one of the intersections in the grid. The most important information should be at the top of the page where it is visible without scrolling, or "above the fold," as they say in the newspaper business.

Figure 36 *Viewing The Striped Umbrella home page in the Firefox browser*

Visited links

Edited text

1. Click the **Preview/Debug in browser button** 🌐 on the Document toolbar, then choose your browser from the menu that opens.

   The Striped Umbrella home page opens in your default browser.

   TIP If previewing the page in Internet Explorer 7, click the Information bar when prompted, click Allow Blocked Content, then click Yes to close the Security Warning dialog box.

2. Click each link on the menu bar, then after each click, use the Back button on the browser toolbar to return to the home page.

   Pages with no content at this point will appear as blank pages. Compare your screen to Figure 36.

3. Close your browser window, then close all open pages in Dreamweaver.

You viewed The Striped Umbrella home page in your browser and tested each link on the menu bar.

DESIGNTIP

Choosing a Window Size

Today, the majority of viewers use a screen resolution of 1024 × 768 or higher. Because of this, more content can be displayed at one time on a computer monitor. Some people might use their whole screen to view pages on the Internet. Others might choose to allocate a smaller area of their screen to the browser window. In other words, people tend to use their "screen real estate" in different ways. The ideal web page will not be so small that it tries to spread out over a larger screen size or so large that the viewer has to use horizontal scroll bars to read the page content. The WCAG guideline 1.4.8 states that " … Text can be resized without assistive technology up to 200 percent in a way that does not require the user to scroll horizontally to read a line of text on a full-screen window." Achieving the best balance and meeting accessibility guidelines is one of the design decisions that you must make during the planning process.

Create head content and set page properties.

1. Open the Blooms & Bulbs website.
2. Open the index page and view the head content.
3. Edit the page title so it reads **Blooms & Bulbs - your complete garden center**.
4. Insert the following keywords: **garden, plants, nursery, flowers, landscape, bulbs, Blooms & Bulbs, Alvin, Texas**.
5. Insert the following description: **Blooms & Bulbs is a premier supplier of plants, trees, and shrubs for both professional and home gardeners**.
6. Switch to Code view to view the HTML code for the head content, then switch back to Design view.
7. Open the Page Properties dialog box to view the current page properties.
8. Change the background color to a color of your choice.
9. Change the background color to white, then save your work.

Create, import, and format text.

1. Create a new paragraph after the second paragraph of text and type the following text, inserting a line break after each line.
   Blooms & Bulbs
   Highway 43 South
   Alvin, Texas 77511
   555-248-0806
2. Verify that the HTML button is selected in the Property inspector, and select it if it is not.
3. Italicize the address and phone number lines.
4. Change to Code view to view the formatting code for the italicized text.

5. Return to Design view, save your work, hide the head content, then close the home page.
6. Open dw2_2.html and save it as **tips.html** in the Blooms & Bulbs website, overwriting the existing file, but not updating links.
7. Click the broken image link below the Blooms & Bulbs banner, use the Property inspector to browse to the chapter_2 assets folder where you store your Data Files, select the file butterfly.jpg in the assets folder, then click OK to save a copy of it in the Blooms & Bulbs website.
8. Place the insertion point to the right of the butterfly image, then insert a paragraph break.
9. Import gardening_tips.doc from where you store your Data Files, using the Import Word Document command (Win) or copy and paste the text (Mac).
10. Use the Clean Up Word HTML command to correct or remove any unnecessary code.
11. Click inside the Seasonal Gardening Checklist heading, then use the Property inspector to apply a Heading 3 format.
12. Click inside the Basic Gardening Tips heading, then use the Property inspector to format the selected text with a Heading 3 format.
13. Place the insertion point at the top of the document, then check the page for spelling errors by using the Check Spelling command, and make any necessary corrections.
14. Save your work and close the tips page and the data file.

Add links to web pages.

1. Open the index page, then select the current menu bar and replace it with **Home - Featured Plants -**

Garden Tips - Workshops - Newsletter. Use a hyphen with a space on either side to separate the items.
2. Add a horizontal rule between the menu bar and the first paragraph of text.
3. Use the Property inspector to link Home on the menu bar to the index.html page in the Blooms & Bulbs website.
4. Link Featured Plants on the menu bar to the plants.html page.
5. Link Garden Tips on the menu bar to the tips.html page.
6. Link Workshops on the menu bar to the workshops.html page.
7. Link Newsletter on the menu bar to the newsletter.html page.
8. Create a line break after the telephone number and then use the Insert panel to create an email link, with **Customer Service** as the text and **mailbox@ blooms.com** as the email address.
9. Save your work.
10. View the email link in the Assets panel, refreshing it if necessary, then view the Files panel.

Use the History panel and edit code.

1. Open the History panel, then clear its contents.
2. Select the horizontal rule under the menu bar, then change the width to 900 pixels and the alignment to Left.
3. Change the width to 70% and the alignment to Center.
4. Use the History panel to restore the horizontal rule settings to 900 pixels wide, left aligned.

5. Close the History panel.
6. Open the Code Inspector and verify that Word Wrap is selected.
7. Edit the code in the Code Inspector to change the width of the horizontal rule to 950 pixels.
8. Open the Reference panel and scan the information about horizontal rules.
9. Close the Code Inspector and close the Reference panel tab group.
10. Delete the current date in the Last updated on statement on the home page and replace it with a date using the March 7, 1974 format that will update automatically when the file is saved.
11. Examine the code for the date at the bottom of the page to verify that the code that forces it to update on save is included in the code. (*Hint*: The code should be highlighted with a light yellow background.)
12. Return to Design view, then save your work.

Modify and test web pages.

1. Restore down the document window if necessary, use the Window Size pop-up menu to view the home page at 600 × 300 (640 × 480, Maximized) and 760 × 420 (800 × 600, Maximized), then maximize the Document window.
2. View the page in your browser. (*Hint*: If previewing the page in Internet Explorer 7, click the Information bar when prompted to allow blocked content.)

3. Verify that all links work correctly, then close the browser.
4. On the home page, add the text "We are happy to deliver or ship your purchases." to the end of the first paragraph.

5. Save your work, then view the pages in your browser, comparing your pages to Figure 37 and Figure 38.
6. Close your browser, then save and close all open pages.

Figures 37 & 38 *Completed Skills Review, home page and tips page*

You have been hired to create a website for TripSmart, a travel outfitter. You have created the basic framework for the website and are now ready to format and edit the home page to improve the content and appearance.

1. Open the TripSmart website, then open the home page.
2. Enter the following keywords: **TripSmart, travel, trips, vacations,** and **tours**.
3. Enter the following description: **TripSmart is a comprehensive travel store. We can help you plan trips, make travel arrangements, and supply you with travel gear**.
4. Change the page title to **TripSmart - serving all your travel needs**.
5. Replace the existing menu bar with the following text: **Home**, **Catalog**, **Services**, **Tours**, and **Newsletter**. Between each item, use a hyphen with a space on either side to separate the items.
6. Replace the date in the last updated statement with a date that will update automatically on save.
7. Add a paragraph break after the last paragraph, then type the following address, using line breaks after each line:
   TripSmart
   1106 Beechwood
   Fayetteville, AR 72704
   555-848-0807

8. Insert an email link in the line below the telephone number, using **Contact Us** for the text and **mailbox@tripsmart.com** for the email link.
9. Italicize TripSmart, the address, phone number, and email link.
10. Link the menu bar entries to index.html, catalog.html, services.html, tours.html, and newsletter.html.
11. View the HTML code for the page, then return to Design view.
12. Insert a horizontal rule above the address.

13. Change the horizontal rule width to 950 pixels and align it to the left side of the page.
14. Save your work.
15. View the page using two different window sizes, then test the links in your browser window.
16. Compare your page to Figure 39, close the browser, then close all open pages.

Figure 39 *Completed Project Builder 1*

Home - Catalog - Services - Tours - Newsletter

Welcome to TripSmart — the smart choice for the savvy traveler. We're here to help you with all your travel needs. Choose customized trips to any location or one of our Five-Star Tours, recently rated first in customer satisfaction by *Traveler* magazine. We are happy to arrange travel for small groups, large groups, or individuals. Our specialty is custom itineraries for independent travelers who enjoy travel at their own pace and on their own schedule. With over 30 years of experience, we can provide knowledgeable guides, comfortable and convenient hotels, and dining recommendations for every size budget.

Call 555-848-0807 today to speak with one of our friendly staff.

TripSmart
1106 Beechwood
Fayetteville, AR 72704
555-848-0807
Contact Us

Copyright 2002 - 2013
Last updated on December 10, 2009

Your company has been selected to design a website for a catering business named Carolyne's Creations. You are now ready to add content to the home page and apply formatting options to improve the page's appearance, using Figure 40 as a guide.

1. Open the Carolyne's Creations website, then open the home page.
2. Edit the page title to read **Carolyne's Creations - Premier Gourmet Food Shop**.
3. Add the description **Carolyne's Creations is a full-service gourmet food shop. We offer cooking classes, take-out meals, and catering services. We also have a retail shop that stocks gourmet items and kitchen accessories.**
4. Add the keywords **Carolyne's Creations, gourmet, catering, cooking classes, kitchen accessories, take-out.**
5. Place the insertion point in front of the sentence in the second paragraph beginning "Give us a call" and type **We also have a pick-up window on the right side of the building for take-out orders.**
6. Add the following address below the second paragraph using line breaks after each line:
   Carolyne's Creations
   496 Maple Avenue
   Seven Falls, Virginia 52404
   555-963-8271
7. Enter another line break after the telephone number and type **Email**, add a space, then add an email link using Carolyne Kate for the text and carolyne@carolynescreations.com for the email address.

8. Create links from each menu bar element to its corresponding web page.
9. Replace the date that follows the text "Last updated on" with a date object that will automatically update on save, then save your work.
10. Insert a horizontal rule between the menu bar and the Welcome heading.
11. Set the width of the horizontal rule to 400 pixels, then left-align the horizontal rule.

12. Save your work, view the completed page in your default browser, then test each link. (*Hint*: If previewing the page in Internet Explorer 7, click the Information bar when prompted to allow blocked content.)
13. Close your browser.
14. Close all open pages.

Figure 40 *Completed Project Builder 2*

Home | Shop | Classes | Catering | Recipes

Welcome

Let Carolyne's Creations be your personal chef, your one-stop shop for the latest in kitchen items and fresh ingredients, and your source for new and innovative recipes. We enjoy planning and presenting special events for all occasions — from children's birthday parties to corporate retreats. Pick-up and drop-off options are also available. We also offer beautiful baskets overflowing with delicious assortments of casseroles, salads, homemade breads, and desserts; trays of vegetables and cheeses or cookies; or coffee cakes and pastries with fresh ground coffee or specialty teas as perfect gifts for family and friends. We offer seasonal cooking classes in our newly redesigned kitchen for aspiring chefs of all ages.

How to find us

We are located in the Plaza Shopping Center at 496 Maple Avenue in Seven Falls, Virginia. We are the second building on the left side of the complex when entering from the Main Street entrance. We also have a pick-up window on the right side of the building for take-out orders. Give us a call at 555-963-8271 or stop by our shop to browse through our selections.

Carolyne's Creations
496 Maple Avenue
Seven Falls, Virginia 52404
555-963-8271
Email Carolyne Kate

Copyright 2001 - 2013
Last updated on December 10, 2009

Albert Iris is looking for a durable laptop case that he can use for the frequent trips he takes with his laptop computer. He is searching the Internet looking for one that is attractive, strong, and that provides quick access for removing the laptop for airport security. He knows that websites use keywords and descriptions in order to receive "hits" with search engines. He is curious about how they work. Follow the steps below and write your answers to the questions.

1. Connect to the Internet, then go to **www.sfbags.com** to view the Waterfield Designs website's home page, as shown in Figure 41.
2. View the page source by clicking View on the Application bar, then clicking Source (Internet Explorer) or Page Source (Mozilla Firefox).
3. Can you locate a description and keywords? If so, what are they?

4. How many keyword terms do you find?
5. Is the description appropriate for the website? Why or why not?
6. Look at the numbers of keyword terms and words in the description. Is there an appropriate number?

7. Use a search engine such as Google at www.google.com, then type the words **laptop bag** in the Search text box.
8. Click a link in the list of results and view the source code for that page. Do you see keywords and a description? Do any of them match the words you used in the search?

Figure 41 *Design Project*

Waterfield Designs website used with permission from Waterfield Designs – www.sfbags.com

In this assignment, you will continue to work on the website you defined in Chapter 1. In Chapter 1, you created a wireframe for your website with at least four pages. You also created a local site folder for your site and an assets folder to store the site asset files. You set the assets folder as the default storage location for your images. You began to collect information and resources for your site and started working on the home page.

1. Think about the head content for the home page. Add the title, keywords, and a description.

2. Create the main page content for the home page.
3. Add the address and other contact information to the home page, including an email address.
4. Consult your wireframe and design the menu bar.
5. Link the menu bar items to the appropriate pages.
6. Add a last updated on statement to the home page with a date that will automatically update when the page is saved.
7. Edit the page content until you are satisfied with the results. You will format the content after you have learned to use Cascading Style Sheets in the next chapter.

8. Verify that all links, including the email link, work correctly.
9. When you are satisfied with the home page, review the checklist questions shown in Figure 42, then make any necessary changes.
10. Save your work.

Figure 42 *Portfolio Project*

> ### Website Checklist
> 1. Does the home page have a page title?
> 2. Does the home page have a description and keywords?
> 3. Does the home page contain contact information, including an email address?
> 4. Does the home page have a menu bar that includes a link to itself?
> 5. Does the home page have a "last updated on" statement that will automatically update when the page is saved?
> 6. Do all paths for links and images work correctly?
> 7. Does the home page look good using at least two different browsers and screen resolutions?

CHAPTER 3 **WORKING WITH TEXT AND**
CASCADING STYLE SHEETS

1. Create unordered and ordered lists

2. Create, apply, and edit Cascading Style Sheets

3. Add rules and attach Cascading Style Sheets

4. Use coding tools to view and edit rules

CHAPTER **3** WORKING WITH TEXT AND
CASCADING STYLE SHEETS

Introduction

Most web pages depend largely on text to convey information. Dreamweaver provides many tools for working with text that you can use to make your web pages attractive and easy to read. These tools can help you format text quickly and make sure your text has a consistent look across all your web pages.

Formatting Text as Lists

If a web page contains a large amount of text, it can be difficult for viewers to digest it all. You can break up the monotony of large blocks of text by dividing them into smaller paragraphs or by organizing them as lists. You can create three types of lists in Dreamweaver: unordered lists, ordered lists, and definition lists.

Using Cascading Style Sheets

You can save time and ensure that all your page elements have a consistent appearance by using **Cascading Style Sheets (CSS)**. CSS are sets of formatting instructions, usually stored in a separate file, that control the appearance and position of text and graphics on a web page or throughout a website. CSS are a great way to define consistent formatting attributes for page elements such as paragraph text, lists, and table data throughout your website. You can then apply the formatting attributes to any element in a single document or to all of the pages in a website. This chapter will focus on using Cascading Style Sheets to format text.

Create Unordered
AND ORDERED LISTS

What You'll Do

> - Salt Glow
>   Imported sea salts are massaged into the skin, exfoliating and cleansing the pores
> - Herbal Wrap
>   Organic lavender blooms create a detoxifying and calming treatment to relieve aches and pains
> - Seaweed Body Wrap
>   Seaweed is a natural detoxifying agent that also helps improve circulation.
>
> Call The Sea Spa desk for prices and reservations. Any of our services can be personalized according to your needs. Our desk is open from 7:00 a.m. until 9:00 p.m. Call 555-594-9458, extension 39.
>
> Questions you may have
>
> 1. How do I schedule Spa services?
>   Please make appointments by calling The Club desk at least 24 hours in advance. Please arrive 15 minutes before your appointment to allow enough time to shower or use the sauna.
> 2. Will I be charged if I cancel my appointment?
>   Please cancel 24 hours before your service to avoid a cancellation charge. No-shows and cancellations without adequate notice will be charged for the full service.
> 3. Are there any health safeguards I should know about?
>   Please advise us of medical conditions or allergies you have. Heat treatments like hydrotherapy and body wraps should be avoided if you are pregnant, have high blood pressure, or any type of heart condition or diabetes.
> 4. What about tipping?
>   Gratuities are at your sole discretion, but are certainly appreciated.

In this lesson, you will create an unordered list of spa services on the spa page. You will also import text with questions and format them as an ordered list.

Creating Unordered Lists

Unordered lists are lists of items that do not need to appear in a specific sequence, such as a grocery list, which often lists items in a random order. Items in unordered lists are usually preceded by a **bullet**, a small dot or similar icon. Unordered lists that contain bullets are sometimes called **bulleted lists**. Although you can use paragraph indentations to create an unordered list, bullets can often make lists easier to read. To create an unordered list, first select the text you want to format as an unordered list, then use the Unordered List button in the HTML Property inspector to insert bullets at the beginning of each paragraph of the selected text.

Formatting Unordered Lists

In Dreamweaver, the default bullet style is a round dot. To change the bullet style to a square, click inside a bulleted item, expand the HTML Property inspector to its full size, as shown in Figure 1, click the List Item button in the Property inspector to open the List Properties dialog box, as shown in Figure 2, then set the style for bulleted lists to Square. Be aware, however, that not all browsers display square bullets correctly, in which case the bullets will appear differently.

Creating Ordered Lists

Ordered lists, which are sometimes called **numbered lists**, are lists of items that are presented in a specific sequence and that are preceded by sequential numbers or letters. An ordered list is appropriate for a list in which each item must be executed according to its specified order. A list that provides numbered directions for driving from Point A to Point B or a list that provides instructions for assembling a bicycle are both examples of ordered lists.

Formatting Ordered Lists

You can format an ordered list to show different styles of numbers or letters by using the List Properties dialog box, as shown in Figure 3. You can apply numbers, Roman numerals, lowercase letters, or uppercase letters to an ordered list.

Creating Definition Lists

Definition lists are similar to unordered lists but are displayed with a hanging indent and are not preceded by bullets. They are often used with terms and definitions, such as in a dictionary or glossary. To create a definition list, select the text to use for the list, click Format on the Application bar (Win) or Menu bar (Mac), point to List, and then click Definition List.

Figure 1 *Expanded HTML Property inspector*

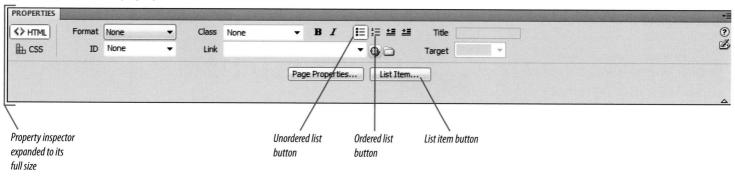

Property inspector
expanded to its
full size

Unordered list
button

Ordered list
button

List item button

Figure 2 *Choosing a bulleted list style in the List Properties dialog box*

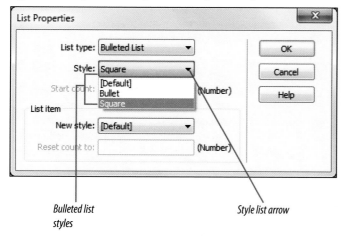

Bulleted list
styles

Style list arrow

Figure 3 *Choosing a numbered list style in the List Properties dialog box*

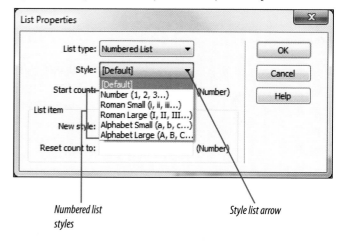

Numbered list
styles

Style list arrow

Create an unordered list

1. Open the spa page in The Striped Umbrella website.

2. Select the three items and their descriptions under the Massages heading.

3. Click the **HTML button** <> HTML in the Property inspector to switch to the HTML Property inspector if necessary, click the **Unordered List button** to format the selected text as an unordered list, click anywhere to deselect the text, then compare your screen to Figure 4.

   Each spa service item and its description are separated by a line break. That is why each description is indented under its corresponding item, rather than formatted as a new list item. You must enter a paragraph break to create a new list item.

4. Repeat Step 3 to create unordered lists of the three items under the Facials and Body Treatments headings, being careful not to include the contact information in the last paragraph on the page as part of your last list.

TIP Pressing [Enter] (Win) or [return] (Mac) once at the end of an unordered list creates another bulleted item. To end an unordered list, press [Enter] (Win) or [return] (Mac) twice.

You opened the spa page in Design view and formatted three spa services lists as unordered lists.

Figure 4 *Creating an unordered list*

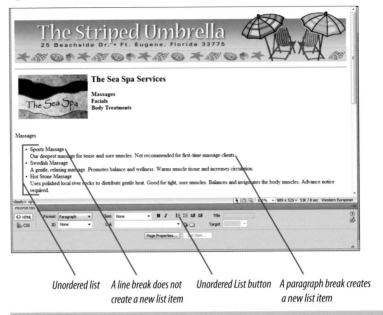

Unordered list   A line break does not   Unordered List button   A paragraph break creates
create a new list item   a new list item

DESIGN TIP

Coding for the Semantic Web

You may have heard the term "semantic web." The word "semantics" refers to the study of meanings of words or sentences. So the term "semantic web" refers to the way page content can be coded to convey meaning to other computer programs such as search engines. One example is to use the <em> tag which means "emphasis" rather than the <i> tag which means "italic" to show emphasis. Another example would be to use font size attributes such as <small> or <medium> rather than using font size attributes expressed in pixels. Cascading Style Sheets are used to define the appearance of semantic tags. For instance, you can specify the attributes of the <h1> heading tag by choosing the Selector Type: Tag (redefines an HTML element) rules in the New CSS Rules dialog box. CSS and semantic coding work together to enhance the meaning of the page content and provide well-designed pages that are attractive and consistent throughout the site. An ideal website would incorporate semantic coding with external style sheets to format all website content. This approach will enable "Semantic Web" programs to interpret the content presented, make it easier for web designers to write and edit, and enhance the overall experience for site visitors.

Working with Text and Cascading Style Sheets

Figure 5 *List Properties dialog box*

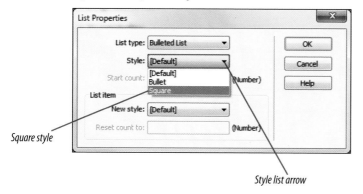

Square style

Style list arrow

Figure 6 *HTML tags in Code view for unordered list*

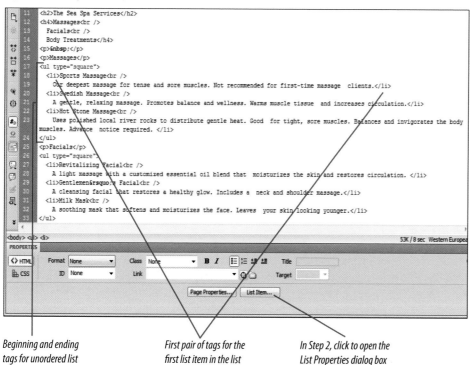

Beginning and ending
tags for unordered list

First pair of tags for the
first list item in the list

In Step 2, click to open the
List Properties dialog box

Format an unordered list

1. Click any of the items in the first unordered list to place the insertion point in the list.

2. Expand the Property inspector if necessary, click **List Item** in the HTML Property inspector to open the List Properties dialog box, click the **Style list arrow**, click **Square**, as shown in Figure 5, then click **OK**.

   The bullets in the unordered list now have a square shape.

3. Repeat Step 2 to format the next two unordered lists.

4. Position the insertion point to the left of the first item in the first unordered list, then click the **Show Code view button** Code on the Document toolbar to view the code for the unordered list, as shown in Figure 6.

   A pair of HTML tags surrounds each type of element on the page. The first tag in each pair begins the code for a particular element, and the last tag ends the code for the element. For instance, the tag <ul>begins the unordered list, and the</ul>tag ends it. The tags <li>and</li> surround each item in the list.

5. Click the **Show Design view button** Design on the Document toolbar.

6. Save your work.

You used the List Properties dialog box to apply the Square bullet style to the unordered lists. You then viewed the HTML code for the unordered lists in Code view.

Create an ordered list

1. Place the insertion point at the end of the page, after the words "extension 39."

2. Use the File, Import, Word Document command to import **questions.doc** from where you store your Data Files (Win) or open **questions.doc** from where you store your Data Files, select all, copy, then paste the copied text on the page (Mac).

   The inserted text appears on the same line as the existing text.

3. Use the Clean Up Word HTML command, place the insertion point to the left of the text "Questions you may have," then click **Horizontal Rule** in the Common category on the Insert panel.

   A horizontal rule appears and separates the unordered list from the text you just imported.

4. Select the text beginning with "How do I schedule" and ending with the last sentence on the page.

5. Click the **Ordered List button** ≔ in the HTML Property inspector to format the selected text as an ordered list.

6. Deselect the text, then compare your screen to Figure 7.

You imported text on the spa page. You also added a horizontal rule to help organize the page. Finally, you formatted selected text as an ordered list.

Figure 7 *Creating an ordered list*

- Salt Glow
  Imported sea salts are massaged into the skin, exfoliating and cleansing the pores.
- Herbal Wrap
  Organic lavender blooms create a detoxifying and calming treatment to relieve aches and pains.
- Seaweed Body Wrap
  Seaweed is a natural detoxifying agent that also helps improve circulation.

Call The Sea Spa desk for prices and reservations. Any of our services can be personalized according to your needs. Our desk is open from 7:00 a.m. until 9:00 p.m. Call 555-594-9458, extension 39.

Questions you may have

1. How do I schedule Spa services?
   Please make appointments by calling The Club desk at least 24 hours in advance. Please arrive 15 minutes before your appointment to allow enough time to shower or use the sauna.
2. Will I be charged if I cancel my appointment?
   Please cancel 24 hours before your service to avoid a cancellation charge. No-shows and cancellations without adequate notice will be charged for the full service.
3. Are there any health safeguards I should know about?
   Please advise us of medical conditions or allergies you have. Heat treatments like hydrotherapy and body wraps should be avoided if you are pregnant, have high blood pressure, or any type of heart condition or diabetes.
4. What about tipping?
   Gratuities are at your sole discretion, but are certainly appreciated.

*Ordered
list items*

Figure 8 *Spa page with ordered list*

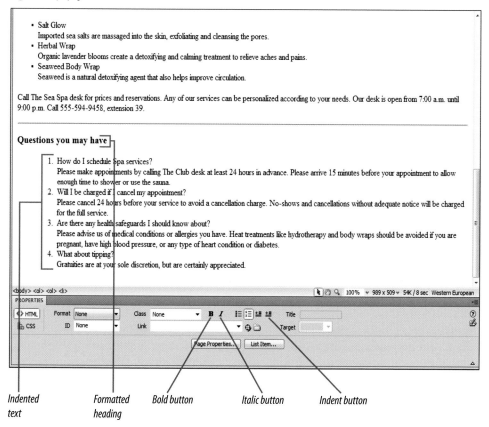

Indented text

Formatted heading

Bold button

Italic button

Indent button

Format an ordered list

1. Click to place the insertion point in the heading "Questions you may have," then use the HTML Property inspector to apply the **Heading 3** format.

   TIP You could show emphasis by using the Bold button **B** or the Italic button *I* on the HTML Property inspector, as shown in Figure 8, but the heading code shows the significance (semantics) of the phrase more clearly. It shows that the phrase is a heading related to the text that follows it.

2. Select the four questions and answers, click the **Indent button** in the HTML Property inspector, deselect the text, then compare your screen to Figure 8.

   When a list item is selected, the Blockquote and Remove Blockquote button names change to Indent and Outdent. The Indent and Outdent buttons are used to indent selected text or remove an indent from selected text.

   TIP If you want to see more of your web page in the Document window, you can collapse the Property inspector.

3. Save your work.

You formatted the "Questions you may have" heading. You also indented the four questions and answers text.

Create, Apply, and
EDIT CASCADING STYLE SHEETS

What You'll Do

In this lesson, you will create a Cascading Style Sheet file for The Striped Umbrella website. You will also create a rule named list_headings and apply it to the list item headings on the spa page.

Understanding Cascading Style Sheets

Cascading Style Sheets (CSS) are made up of sets of formatting attributes called **rules**, which define the formatting attributes for page content. Rules are also referred to as styles. Style sheets are classified by where the code is stored. The code can be saved in a separate file (**external style sheet**), as part of the head content of an individual web page (**internal or embedded styles**), or as part of the body of the HTML code (**inline styles**). External CSS are saved as files with the .css extension and are stored in the website's directory structure. Figure 9 shows an external style sheet named su_styles.css listed in the Files panel. External style sheets are the preferred method for creating and using styles.

CSS are also classified by their type. A **Class type** can be used to format any page element. An **ID type** and a **Tag type** are used to redefine an HTML tag. A **Compound** type is used to format a selection. In this chapter, we will use the class type stored in an external style sheet file.

Using the CSS Styles Panel

You use buttons on the CSS Styles panel to create, edit, and apply rules. To add a rule, use the New CSS Rule dialog box to name the rule and specify whether to add it to a new or existing style sheet. You then use the CSS Rule definition dialog box to set the formatting attributes for the rule. Once you add a new rule to a style sheet, it appears in a list in the CSS Styles panel. To apply a rule, you select the text to which you want to apply the rule, and then choose a rule from the Targeted Rule list in the CSS Property inspector. You can apply CSS rules to elements on a single web page or to all of the pages in a website. When you edit a rule, such as changing the font size it specifies, all page elements formatted with that rule are automatically updated. Once you create an external CSS, you can attach it to the remaining pages in your website.

Use the CSS Styles panel to manage your styles. The Properties pane displays properties for a selected rule at the bottom of the panel. You can easily change a property's value by clicking an option from a drop-down menu.

Comparing the Advantages of Using Style Sheets

You can use CSS styles to save an enormous amount of time. Being able to define a rule and then apply it to page elements on all the pages of your website means that you can make hundreds of formatting changes in a few minutes. In addition, style sheets create a more uniform look from page to page and they generate cleaner code. Using style sheets separates the development of content from the way the content is presented. Pages formatted with CSS styles are much more compliant with current accessibility standards than those with manual formatting.

QUICK TIP

For more information about Cascading Style Sheets, visit www.w3.org/Style.

Understanding CSS Code

You can see the properties for a CSS rule by looking at the style sheet code. A CSS rule consists of two parts: the selector and the declaration. The **selector** is the name of the tag to which the style declarations have been assigned. The **declaration** consists of a property (such as font-size or font-weight) and a value (such as 14 px or bold). For example, Figure 10 shows the code for an internal style that sets the background color for a page. In this example, the selector is the body tag. The only property assigned to this selector is background-color. The value for this property is #FFF, or white. The property and value together comprise the declaration. When there is more than one property, each additional property and value are separated by a semicolon.

When you create a new CSS external file, you will see it as a related files document in the Document window. Save this file as you make changes to it.

Figure 9 *Cascading Style Sheet file created in striped_umbrella site root folder*

Cascading Style Sheet file

Figure 10 *Viewing CSS code*

Selector — Declaration

Property   Value

Create a Cascading Style Sheet and add a rule

1. Click the **CSS button** 🔳 CSS in the Property inspector to switch to the CSS Property inspector, as shown in Figure 11.

2. If the CSS Styles panel is not open, click **Window** on the Application bar (Win) or Menu bar (Mac), then click **CSS Styles** to open the CSS Styles panel.

3. Click the **Switch to All (Document) Mode button** All on the CSS Styles panel if it's not already active, then click the **New CSS Rule button** 🔳 in the CSS Styles panel to open the New CSS Rule dialog box.

4. Verify that Class (can apply to any HTML element) is selected under Selector Type, then type **list_headings** in the Selector Name text box.

TIP Class selector names are preceded by a period in the code and in the CSS panel. If you don't enter a period when you type the name, Dreamweaver will add the period for you when the rule is created.

5. Click the **Rule Definition list arrow**, click **(New Style Sheet File)**, compare your screen with Figure 12, then click **OK**.

   This indicates that you want to create a new style sheet file, which will contain your list_headings rule and any other rules you may create for this site. The Save Style Sheet Files As dialog box opens.

   (continued)

Figure 11 *CSS Property inspector*

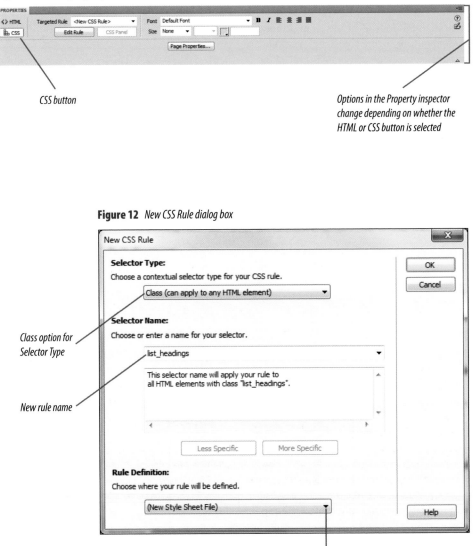

CSS button

Options in the Property inspector change depending on whether the HTML or CSS button is selected

Figure 12 *New CSS Rule dialog box*

Class option for Selector Type

New rule name

Rule Definition list arrow

Figure 13 *CSS Rule Definition for .list_headings in su_styles.css dialog box*

Type category selected

Figure 14 *CSS Styles panel with list_headings rule added*

list_headings rule

Properties for list_headings rule

Choosing Fonts

There are two classifications of fonts: sans-serif and serif. **Sans-serif** fonts are block-style characters that are often used for headings and subheadings. The headings in this book and the text you are reading now use a sans-serif font. Examples of sans-serif fonts include Arial, Verdana, and Helvetica. **Serif** fonts are more ornate and contain small extra strokes at the beginning and end of the characters. Serif fonts are considered easier to read in printed material, because the extra strokes lead your eye from one character to the next. Examples of serif fonts include Times New Roman, Times, and Georgia. The paragraph text on the first page of each chapter is in a serif font. Many designers feel that a sans-serif font is preferable when the content of a website is primarily intended to be read on the screen, but that a serif font is preferable if the content will be printed. When you choose fonts, you need to keep in mind the amount of text each page will contain and whether most viewers will read the text on-screen or print it. A good rule of thumb is to limit each website to no more than three font variations.

6. Type **su_styles** in the File name text box (Win) or the Save As text box (Mac), verify that the striped_umbrella folder appears in the Save in box, then click **Save** to open the CSS Rule Definition for .list_headings in su_styles.css dialog box.

   The .list_headings rule will be stored within the su_styles.css file in the Striped Umbrella local site folder. Next, you define the formatting properties of the rule.

7. Verify that Type is selected in the Category list, set the Font-family to **Arial**, **Helvetica**, **sans-serif**, set the Font-size to **12 px**, set the Font-weight to **bold**, set the Font-style to **normal**, set the Color to **#006**, compare your screen to Figure 13, then click **OK**.

TIP You can modify the font combinations in the Font-family list by clicking Format on the Application bar (Win) or Menu bar (Mac), pointing to Font, then clicking Edit Font List.

   Other interesting type options that are available in the CSS Rule Definition dialog box are Line-height, which changes the height of each line measured in pixels; Text-decoration, which adds text effects, Font-variant, which allows you to change the text to small caps, and Text-transform, which has options to change text to all upper-case or all lower-case.

8. Click the **plus sign** (Win) or the **expander arrow** (Mac) next to su_styles.css in the CSS Styles panel and expand the panel, if necessary, to see the list_headings rule displayed, then select the **list_headings rule**.

   The CSS rule named .list_headings and its properties appear in the CSS Styles panel, as shown in Figure 14.

You created a Cascading Style Sheet file named su_styles.css and a rule called .list_heading within the style sheet.

Apply a rule in a Cascading Style Sheet

1. Click **View** on the Application bar (Win) or Menu bar (Mac), point to **Toolbars**, then click **Style Rendering**.

TIP You can also right-click on an empty area on an open toolbar to see the displayed and hidden toolbars listed in a drop-down menu. The displayed toolbars have a check next to them. To display or hide a toolbar, click its name on the menu.

2. Verify that the Toggle Displaying of CSS Styles button on the Style Rendering toolbar is active, as shown in Figure 15.

TIP You can determine if the Toggle Displaying of CSS Styles button is active if it has a dark outline around the button. As long as this button is active, you do not have to display the toolbar on the screen.

You use the Toggle Displaying of CSS Styles button to see how styles affect your page. If it is not active, you will not see the effects of your styles and the default browser settings will be used to display the content.

3. Select the paragraph heading "Massages," click the **Targeted Rule list arrow** in the Property inspector, then click **list_headings**, as shown in Figure 16.

4. Repeat Step 3 to apply the list_headings rule to each of the spa services unordered list headings, click anywhere in the document to deselect the text, then compare your screen to Figure 17.

TIP You can use the keyboard shortcut [Ctrl][Y] (Win) or [Command][Y] (Mac) to repeat the previous action.

You applied the list_headings rule to each of the Spa Services category headings.

Figure 15 *Style Rendering toolbar*

Toggle Displaying of CSS Styles button

Figure 16 *Applying a CSS rule to selected text*

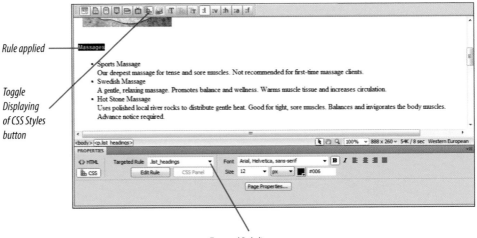

Rule applied

Toggle Displaying of CSS Styles button

Targeted Rule list arrow

Figure 17 *Unordered list with list_headings rule applied*

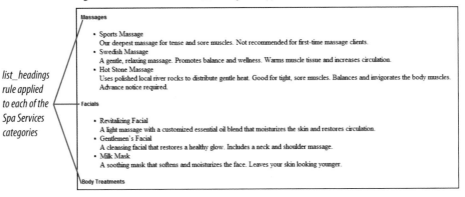

list_headings rule applied to each of the Spa Services categories

Figure 18 *Editing a rule*

Properties of the list_headings rule

font-size list arrow

Click 14 on this menu

Figure 19 *Viewing the changes made to the list_headings rule*

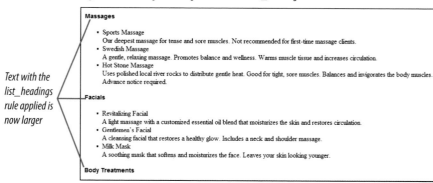

Text with the list_headings rule applied is now larger

1. Click **.list_headings** in the CSS Styles panel.

   The rule's properties and values appear in the Properties pane, the bottom part of the CSS Styles panel.

   TIP Click the plus sign (Win) or expander arrow (Mac) to the left of su_styles.css in the CSS Styles panel if you do not see .list_headings. Click the plus sign (Win) or expander arrow (Mac) to the left of <style> if you do not see su_styles.css.

2. Click **12 px** in the CSS Styles panel, click the **font-size list arrow**, click **14** as shown in Figure 18, then compare your screen to Figure 19.

   All of the text to which you applied the list_headings rule is larger, reflecting the changes you made to the list_headings rule. You can also click the **Edit Rule button** ✏ in the CSS Styles panel to open the CSS Rule Definition for .list_headings dialog box.

   TIP If you position the insertion point in text that has a CSS rule applied to it, that rule is displayed in the Targeted Rule text box in the CSS Property inspector or the Class text box in the HTML Property inspector.

3. Use the File, Save All command to save the spa page and the style sheet file.

4. Hide the Style Rendering toolbar.

You edited the list_headings rule to change the font size to 14 pixels. You then viewed the results of the edited rule in the unordered list.

View code with the Code Navigator

1. Click in the paragraph heading "Massages" and hover until the **Click indicator to bring up the Code Navigator** icon ☀ appears, as shown in Figure 20.

2. Click the **Click indicator to bring up the Code Navigator icon** ☀ .

   A window opens, as shown in Figure 21, with the name of the style sheet that is linked to this page (su_styles.css) and the name of the rule in the style sheet that has been applied to this text (list_headings).

   (continued)

Figure 20 *Viewing the Click indicator to bring up the Code Navigator icon*

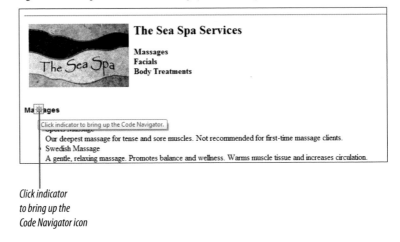

Click indicator
to bring up the
Code Navigator icon

Figure 21 *Viewing the Code Navigator*

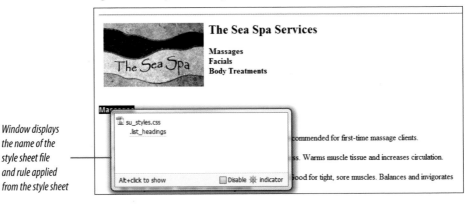

Window displays
the name of the
style sheet file
and rule applied
from the style sheet

Figure 22 *Viewing the Code Navigator*

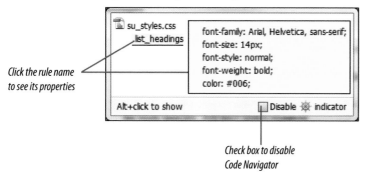

Click the rule name to see its properties

Check box to disable Code Navigator

TIP You can also [Alt]-click (Win) or [Command] [Option]-click (Mac) the text on the page to display the Code Navigator.

3. Position your cursor over the list_headings rule name until you see a box with the rule's properties, as shown in Figure 22.

TIP You can disable the Code Navigator by clicking the Disable check box as shown in Figure 22.

You displayed the Code Navigator to view the properties of the list_headings rule.

Using the Style Rendering Toolbar

The Style Rendering toolbar allows you to display your page as it would appear for different media types, such as print, TV, or handheld. To display it when a page is open, click View on the Application bar (Win); or Menu bar (Mac), point to Toolbars, and then click Style Rendering. The buttons on the Style Rendering toolbar allow you to see how your page will look as you select different media types. The seventh button on the toolbar is the Toggle Displaying of CSS Styles button, which you can use to view how a page looks with styles applied. It works independently of the other buttons. The next button to the right is the Design-time Style Sheets button, which you can use to show or hide particular combinations of styles while you are working in the Document window.

NEW The Style Rendering toolbar in Dreamweaver CS5 has several additional buttons on the right side of the toolbar that can be used to change the text size or show the link properties for links in the active document.

Use the Code Navigator to edit a rule

1. Click **.list_headings** in the Code Navigator.

   The document window splits into two panes. The left pane displays the code for the CSS file and the right section displays the HTML page in Design view, as shown in Figure 23.

TIP The default setting for Show Code and Design views in Dreamweaver CS5 splits the two windows vertically, rather than horizontally. To view the two windows split horizontally on the screen, click View on the Application bar (Win) or Menu bar (Mac), then click Split Vertically to uncheck the option and split the screens horizontally.

(continued)

Figure 23 *Using Code and Design views to view rule properties*

```
1   .list_headings {
2       font-family: Arial, Helvetica, sans-serif;
3       font-size: 14px;
4       font-style: normal;
5       font-weight: bold;
6       color: #006;
7   }
8
```

Massages

- Sports Massage
  Our deepest massage for tense and sore muscles. Not recommended for first-time massage clients.
- Swedish Massage
  A gentle, relaxing massage. Promotes balance and wellness. Warms muscle tissue and increases circulation.
- Hot Stone Massage
  Uses polished local river rocks to distribute gentle heat. Good for tight, sore muscles. Balances and invigorates the body muscles. Advance notice required.

Facials

Transitioning to a Real-World Work Process

As you learn Dreamweaver throughout the chapters in this book, you practice its many features in a logical learning sequence. You will develop an understanding of both current concepts like CSS and older, but still used, features such as HTML formatting and embedded styles. Once you learn Dreamweaver and start using it to create your own websites, you would ideally format all pages with rules from one external style sheet. You would move all of the embedded styles in the predesigned CSS layouts to the external style sheet because the embedded styles on each page would be redundant. After you have worked through this book, you should have the skills and understanding to design sites built entirely and efficiently with CSS.

Figure 24 *Using Code and Design views to edit a rule*

Replace color "006"
with "003"

The headings will
not appear correctly
with the split
window

You can also edit
the color in the CSS
Styles panel

2. Type directly in the code to replace the color "006" with the color "**003**" as shown in Figure 24. The page subheadings to the right of the logo will not wrap correctly in Split view if the document window is too small. When you return to Design view, they will wrap correctly.

TIP You can also edit the rule properties in the CSS Styles panel.

3. Save all files.

4. Click the **Show Design view button** Design .
   The font color has changed in Design view to reflect the new shade of blue in the rule.

You changed the color property in the .list_headings rule.

Add Rules and Attach
CASCADING STYLE SHEETS

What You'll Do

In this lesson, you will add a rule to a Cascading Style Sheet. You will then attach the style sheet file to the index page and apply one of the rules to text on the page.

Understanding External and Embedded Style Sheets

When you are first learning about CSS, the terminology can be confusing. In the last lesson, you learned that external style sheets are separate files in a website, saved with the .css file extension. You also learned that CSS can be part of an HTML file, rather than a separate file. These are called internal, or embedded, style sheets. External CSS files are created by the web designer. Embedded style sheets are created automatically in Dreamweaver if the designer does not create them, using default names for the rules. The code for these rules resides in the head content for that page. These rules are automatically named style1, style2, and so on. You can rename the rules as they are created to make them more recognizable for you to use, for example, paragraph_text, subheading, or address. Embedded style sheets apply only to a single page, although you can copy them into the code in other pages or move them to an external style sheet. Remember that style sheets can be used to format much more than text objects. They can be used to set the page background, link properties, or determine the appearance of almost any object on the page. Figure 25 shows the code for some embedded rules and a link to an external style sheet. The code resides in the head content of the web page.

When you have several pages in a website, you will probably want to use the same CSS for each page to ensure that all your elements have a consistent appearance. To attach a style sheet to another document, click the Attach Style Sheet button on the CSS Styles panel to open the Attach External Style Sheet dialog box, make sure the Add as Link option is selected, browse to locate the file you want to attach, and then click OK. The rules contained in the attached style sheet will appear in the CSS Styles panel, and you can use them to apply rules to text on the page. External style sheets can be attached, or linked, to any page. This is an extremely powerful tool. If you decide to edit a rule, the changes will automatically be made to every object that it formats.

Understanding Related Page Files

When an HTML file is linked to other files necessary to display the page content, these files are called **related files.** When a file that has related files is open in the Document window, each related file name is displayed in the Related Files toolbar above the Document window. A Cascading Style Sheet file is an example of a related file. When an HTML document has an attached CSS file, the page file will display in the browser without the CSS file, but will not be formatted correctly. It takes both the HTML file and the CSS file working together to display the content properly. When HTML files are uploaded, it is important to remember to upload all related page files. Other examples of related page files are Flash player, video files and JavaScript files.

When an HTML file with a linked CSS file is open in Dreamweaver, the name of the CSS filename appears below the page tab. When you click on the CSS filename, the screen changes to Split view, with the right side displaying the open HTML page in Design view and the left side displaying the CSS file. If you click Source Code next to the related page filename, the code for the top level document (open HTML file) will appear on the left side. You can edit both Code view windows by typing directly in the code.

Figure 25 *Code for embedded rules and a link to an external style sheet*

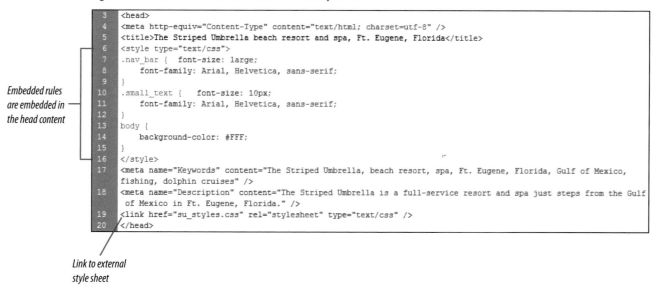

Embedded rules are embedded in the head content

Link to external style sheet

Add a rule to a Cascading Style Sheet

1. Click the **New CSS Rule button** 🗗 in the CSS Styles panel.

2. Type **body_text** in the Selector Name text box, verify that su_styles.css appears in the Rule Definition text box, as shown in Figure 26, then click **OK**.

   The new rule will be saved in the su_styles.css file as an external style.

3. Set the Font-family to **Arial**, **Helvetica**, **sans-serif**, set the Font-size to **12**, set the set the Color to **#000**, compare your screen to Figure 27, then click **OK**.

4. Select the three list items and their descriptions under the Massages heading, click the **Targeted Rule list arrow** in the CSS Property inspector, then click **body_text** to apply it to the three massage names and descriptions.

   The rule is applied to the text, but the text would be easier to read if it were a little larger.

5. Click the **Edit Rule button** ✏ in the CSS Styles panel.

6. Change the font size to **14** in the Type category of the CSS Rule Definition for body_text in su_styles.css dialog box, as shown in Figure 28, then click **OK**.

(continued)

Figure 26 *Adding a rule to a CSS*

New rule name

su_styles.css is displayed in the Rule Definition text box

Figure 27 *Formatting options for body_text rule*

Figure 28 *Editing the body_text rule*

Change the Font-size to 14

Working with Text and Cascading Style Sheets

Figure 29 *Spa page with style sheet applied to rest of text on page*

Text formatted with the
body_text rule

7. Repeat Step 4 to apply the body_text rule to the rest of the text on the page except for the text that has already been formatted with the list_headings rule or heading tags, as shown in Figure 29.

8. Click **File** on the Application bar (Win) or Menu bar (Mac), then click **Save All**, to save both the spa page and the su_styles.css file.

The rule is saved in the style sheet file and applied to the text in the HTML file.

TIP You must save the open su_styles.css file after editing it, or you will lose your changes.

You added a new rule called body_text to the su_styles.css file. You then applied the rule to selected text.

Attach a style sheet

1. Close the spa page and open the index page.
2. Click the **Attach Style Sheet button** 🔗 on the CSS Styles panel.
3. Click **Browse** then navigate to the file su_styles.css, if necessary, click the **su_styles.css** file, click **OK** (Win) or click **Choose** (Mac), verify that the **Link option button** is selected, as shown in Figure 30, then click **OK**.

   There are now two rules named body_text. One is an internal style that was in the data file when we brought it into the website and one is in the external style sheet. Since these rules have duplicate names, it would be better to delete the internal style and let the external style format the text.

4. Select the **body_text rule** under the <style> section of the CSS Styles panel, as shown in Figure 31, then click the **Delete CSS Rule button** 🗑 on the CSS Styles panel.
5. Click the **Show Code view button** `Code` and view the code that links the su_styles.css file to the index page, as shown in Figure 32.
6. Click the **Show Design view button** `Design`, then save your work.

You attached the su_styles.css file to the index.html page and deleted the body_text internal style, allowing the body_text external style to format the page text.

Figure 30 *Attaching a style sheet to a file*

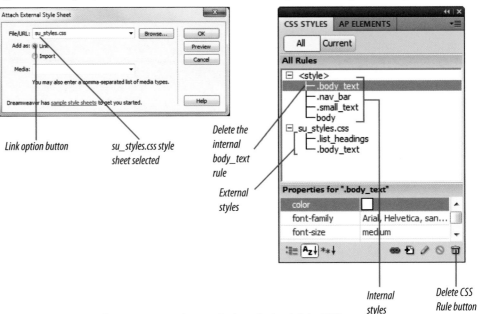

Link option button

su_styles.css style sheet selected

Figure 31 *Deleting an internal style*

Delete the internal body_text rule

External styles

Internal styles

Delete CSS Rule button

Figure 32 *Viewing the internal styles and code to link the CSS file*

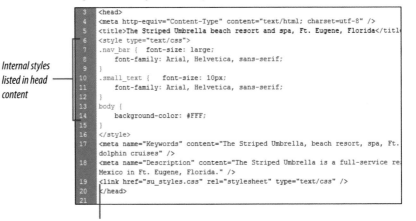

Internal styles listed in head content

Code linking external style sheet file to the index page in head content

Working with Text and Cascading Style Sheets

Figure 33 *Using the Related Files toolbar to view an external style sheet file*

Click su_styles.css to view external style sheet file

Left pane displays code for external style sheet

1. Click **su_styles.css** on the Related Files toolbar.

   The document window changes to Show Code and Design views with the external CSS file in the left pane and the HTML page in Design view in the right pane, as shown in Figure 33.

2. Click **Source Code** on the Related Files toolbar.

   The code for the HTML file appears on the left with the code for the embedded styles as shown in Figure 34.

3. Click the **Show Design view button** to return to Design view.

You viewed the external and embedded styles using the Related Files toolbar.

Figure 34 *Using the Related Files toolbar to view embedded styles*

Click Source Code to view embedded styles

Left pane displays code for embedded styles

Use Coding Tools to
VIEW AND EDIT RULES

What You'll Do

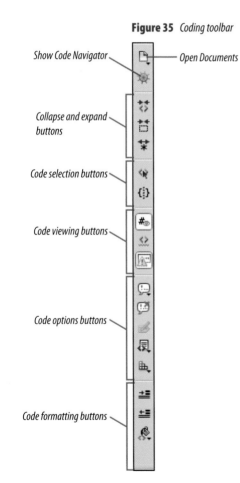

In this lesson, you will collapse, then expand the code for the index page to view the code for the embedded and external styles. You will then move embedded styles to the external style sheet file.

Coding Tools in Dreamweaver

In Code view, you can see the Coding toolbar, shown in Figure 35. It contains a number of handy tools that help you navigate your code and let you view your code in different ways. It has buttons that expand or collapse code, buttons for changing the way the code is displayed, and buttons for inserting and removing comments. The Coding toolbar appears on the left side of the Document window. Although you cannot move it, you can hide it, using the Toolbars command on the View menu in Code view.

As you learned in Chapter 2, you can customize the way your page code appears in Code view. You can wrap the lines of code, display or hide line numbers and hidden characters, or highlight invalid code so you can fix it. You can also have different code types appear in different colors, indent lines of code, and display syntax error alerts. In Chapter 2, you viewed these options using the View Options button on the Code Inspector toolbar. You can also view and change them on the Code View options menu under the View menu on the Document toolbar.

Figure 35 *Coding toolbar*

Show Code Navigator — Open Documents

Collapse and expand buttons

Code selection buttons

Code viewing buttons

Code options buttons

Code formatting buttons

Using Coding Tools to Navigate Code

As your pages get longer and the code more complex, it is helpful to collapse sections of code, much as you can collapse and expand panels, folders, and styles. Collapsing code lets you temporarily hide code between two different sections of code that you would like to read together. To collapse selected lines of code, you can click the minus sign (Win) or the triangle (Mac) next to the line number. You can also use the Collapse Full Tag or Collapse Selection buttons on the Coding toolbar. This will allow you to look at two different sections of code that are not adjacent to each other.

Adding comments is an easy way to add documentation to your code, which is especially helpful when you are working in a team environment and other team members will be working on pages with you. For example, you might use comments to communicate instructions like "Do not alter code below this line." or "Add final schedule here when it becomes available." Comments are not visible in the browser.

Using Code Hints to Streamline Coding

If you are typing code directly into Code view, Dreamweaver can speed your work by offering you code hints. **Code hints** are lists of tags that appear as you type, similar to other auto-complete features that you have probably used in other software applications. As you are typing code, Dreamweaver will recognize the tag name and offer you choices to complete the tag simply by double-clicking a tag choice in the menu, as shown in Figure 36. You can also add your own code hints to the list using JavaScript. Code hints are stored in the file CodeHints.xml.

Converting Styles

You can also convert one type of style to another. For instance, you can move an embedded style to an external style sheet or an inline style to either an embedded style or a style in an external style sheet. To do this, select the style in Code view, right-click the code, point to CSS Styles, then click Move CSS Rules. You can also move styles in the CSS Styles panel by selecting the style, right-clicking the style, and choosing the action you want from the shortcut menu.

Figure 36 *Using code hints*

As you begin typing code, the shortcut menu appears when Dreamweaver recognizes the code

Double-click from the list to complete your tag

Collapse code

1. Verify that the index page is open, then change to Code view.

2. Scroll up the page, if necessary, to display the code that ends the embedded styles (</style>).

   The code will probably be on or close to line 16 in the head section.

3. Select the line of code under the line ending the embedded style code (it begins with <meta name = "Keywords"), then drag down to select all of the code above the line of code that links the external style sheet, as shown in Figure 37.

   TIP   If your code is in a slightly different order, scroll to find the meta data code to select it.

4. Click the **minus sign** (Win) or **vertical triangle** (Mac) in the last line of selected code to collapse all of the selected code.

   You can now see both code fragments—before and after the collapsed code section—as shown in Figure 38. The plus sign (Win) or horizontal triangle (Mac) next to the line of code indicates that there is hidden code. You also see a gap in the line numbers where the hidden code resides.

   You collapsed a block of code in Code view to be able to see two non-adjacent sections of the code at the same time.

Figure 37 *Selecting lines of code on the index page to collapse*

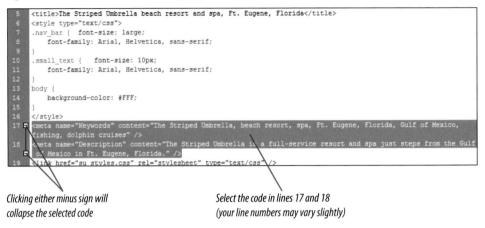

Clicking either minus sign will collapse the selected code

Select the code in lines 17 and 18 (your line numbers may vary slightly)

Figure 38 *Collapsed code in Code view*

Line 18 is hidden

Plus sign shows that there is collapsed code

Figure 39 *Expanded code for index page*

```
5   <title>The Striped Umbrella beach resort and spa, Ft. Eugene, Florida</title>
6   <style type="text/css">
7   .nav_bar {  font-size: large;
8       font-family: Arial, Helvetica, sans-serif;
9   }
10  .small_text {  font-size: 10px;
11      font-family: Arial, Helvetica, sans-serif;
12  }
13  body {
14      background-color: #FFF;
15  }
16  </style>
17  <meta name="Keywords" content="The Striped Umbrella, beach resort, spa, Ft. Eugene, Florida, Gulf of Mexico,
    fishing, dolphin cruises" />
18  <meta name="Description" content="The Striped Umbrella is a full-service resort and spa just steps from the Gulf
    of Mexico in Ft. Eugene, Florida." />
19  <link href="su_styles.css" rel="stylesheet" type="text/css" />
```

Code is expanded again

Expand code

1. Click the **plus sign** (Win) or **horizontal triangle** (Mac) on line 17 to expand the code.
2. Compare your screen to Figure 39, then click in the page to deselect the code.

   All line numbers are visible again.

You expanded the code to display all lines of the code again.

POWER USER SHORTCUTS	
To do this:	**Use this shortcut:**
Switch views	[Ctrl][`] (Win) or [control][`] (Mac)
Indent text	[Ctrl][Alt][]] (Win) or ⌘ [option][]] (Mac)
Outdent text	[Ctrl][Alt][[] (Win) or ⌘ [option][[] (Mac)
Align Left	[Ctrl][Alt][Shift][L] (Win) or ⌘ [option][shift][L] (Mac)
Align Center	[Ctrl][Alt][Shift][C] (Win) or ⌘ [option][shift][C] (Mac)
Align Right	[Ctrl][Alt][Shift][R] (Win) or ⌘ [option][shift][R] (Mac)
Align Justify	[Ctrl][Alt][Shift][J] (Win) or ⌘ [option][shift][J] (Mac)
Bold	[Ctrl][B] (Win) or ⌘ [B] (Mac)
Italic	[Ctrl][I] (Win) or ⌘ [I] (Mac)
Refresh	[F5]

Move an embedded style to an external CSS

1. Select the lines of code in the head section with the properties of the small_text rule (including the closing bracket) on the index page.

   The code will be on or close to lines 10 and 12.

2. Right-click (Win) or control-click (Mac) the **selected code**, point to **CSS Styles**, then click **Move CSS Rules**, as shown in Figure 40.

   TIP You can also convert a rule in the CSS Styles panel. To do this, right-click the rule name, then click Move CSS Rules.

3. In the Move to External Style Sheet dialog box, verify that su_styles.css appears in the Style Sheet text box, as shown in Figure 41, then click **OK**.

   (continued)

Figure 40 *Moving the embedded small_text rule to the external style sheet file*

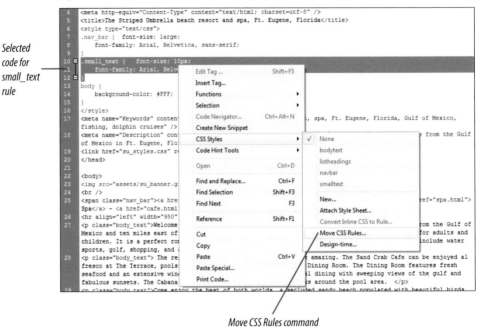

Selected code for small_text rule

Move CSS Rules command

Figure 41 *Moving the embedded style to the external style sheet file*

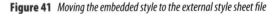

The embedded small_text rule will move to the su_styles file

Working with Text and Cascading Style Sheets

Figure 42 *Viewing the small_text rule in the external style sheet*

small_text rule is now in the su_styles.css file

4. Expand the su_styles.css style in the CSS Styles panel, if necessary, to display its rules, then compare your panel with Figure 42 to verify that the style has been moved to the external style sheet file.

5. Return to Design view, then save and close all open files.

You moved an embedded style for the small_text rule to an external CSS.

Create unordered and ordered lists.

1. Open the Blooms & Bulbs website.
2. Open the tips page.
3. Select the text items below the Seasonal Gardening Checklist heading and format them as an unordered list. (*Hint*: There are no paragraph breaks between each item. To correct this, enter a paragraph break between each line, then remove any extra spaces.)
4. Select the lines of text below the Basic Gardening Tips heading and format them as an ordered list. (Refer to the Step 3 hint if each line does not become a separate list item.)
5. Indent the unordered list items one stop, then change the bullet format to square.
6. Add a line break before the Seasonal Gardening checklist heading, then save your work.

Create, apply, and edit Cascading Style Sheets.

1. Create a new CSS rule named **bullet_term**, making sure that the Class option button is selected in the Selector Type section and that the (New Style Sheet File) option button is selected in the Rule Definition section of the New CSS Rule dialog box.
2. Click OK, name the style sheet file **blooms_styles** in the Save Style Sheet File As dialog box, then click Save.

3. Choose the following settings for the bullet_term rule: Font-family = Arial, Helvetica, sans-serif; Font-size = large; Font-style = normal; Font-weight = bold; and Color = #333.
4. Apply the bullet_term rule to the names of the seasons in the Seasonal Gardening Checklist: Fall, Winter, Spring, and Summer.
5. Edit the bullet_term rule by changing the font size to 16 pixels.

Add rules and attach Cascading Style Sheets.

1. Create a new class rule named **paragraph_text** in the blooms_styles.css file with the Arial, Helvetica, sans-serif, size 14 px.
2. Apply the paragraph_text rule to the rest of the text on the page that has not been previously formatted with either an HTML heading or a rule, then save the page. (*Hint*: If the Seasonal Gardening Checklist heading is not under the picture, verify that there's a line break before it, and add one if necessary.)
3. Open the index page and attach the blooms_styles.css file.
4. Select the paragraphs and the contact information and apply the paragraph_text rule.
5. Delete the body_text embedded style.

6. Use the Save All command on the File menu to save both the page and the style sheet, then view both pages in the browser. (*Hint*: If previewing the page in Internet Explorer 7, click the Information bar when prompted to allow blocked content.)
7. Close the browser.

Use coding tools to view and edit rules.

1. Verify that the index page is open, then change to Code view.
2. Display the code that ends the embedded styles.
3. Select the lines of code under the line ending the embedded style code (it begins with <meta name = "Keywords"), then drag down to select all of the code above the line of code that links the external style sheet.
4. Collapse all of the selected code.
5. Expand the code.
6. Select the lines of code that define the small_text rule properties in the head section (including the closing bracket), then move the rule to the blooms_styles external style sheet.
7. Return to Design view, save all open files, compare your pages to Figures 43 and 44, then close all open files.

Figure 43 & 44 *Completed Skills Review*

Use Figure 45 as a guide to continue your work on the TripSmart website that you began in Project Builder 1 in Chapter 1, and continued to work on in Chapter 2. You are now ready to create some rules to use for the text on the newsletter and index pages.

1. Open the TripSmart website.
2. Open dw3_1.html from where you store your Data Files and save it in the tripsmart site folder as **newsletter.html**, overwriting the existing newsletter.html file and not updating the links.
3. Verify that the path for the banner is correctly set to the assets folder of the TripSmart website, then type the title **Travel Tidbits** in the Title text box on the Document toolbar.
4. Create an unordered list from the text beginning "Be organized." to the end of the page.
5. Create a new CSS rule called **paragraph_text** making sure that the Class option is selected in the Selector Type section and that the (New Style Sheet File) option is selected in the Rule Definition section of the New CSS Rule dialog box.
6. Save the style sheet file as **tripsmart_styles.css** in the TripSmart website site folder.
7. Choose a font family, size, style, weight, and color of your choice for the paragraph_text style.
8. Apply the paragraph_text rule to all of the text on the page except the "Ten Tips for Stress-Free Travel" heading.
9. Create another class rule in the tripsmart_styles.css file called **list_heading** with a font, size, style, color, and weight of your choice and apply it to the "Ten Tips for Stress-Free Travel" heading.

10. Create another rule in the external style sheet called **list_term** with a font, size, style, color, and weight of your choice and apply it to each of the item names in the list such as "Be organized."
11. Save the newsletter page and the style sheet, then close the dw3_1.html page.
12. Open the index page, then attach the tripsmart_styles style sheet.
13. Select the two paragraphs and contact information, then apply the paragraph_text rule.
14. Delete the body_text embedded rule, then save the index page.
15. Preview the index and newsletter pages in your browser. (*Hint*: If previewing the page in Internet Explorer 7, click the Information bar when prompted to allow blocked content.)
16. Close your browser, then close all open files.

Figure 45 *Sample Project Builder 1*

In this exercise, you continue your work on the Carolyne's Creations website that you started in Project Builder 2 in Chapter 1, and continued to build in Chapter 2. You are now ready to add a page to the website that will showcase a recipe. Figure 46 shows a possible solution for this one page in this exercise. Your finished page will look different if you choose different formatting options.

1. Open the Carolyne's Creations website
2. Open dw3_2.html from where you store your Data Files, save it to the website site folder as **recipes. html**, overwriting the existing file and not updating the links. Close the dw3_2.html file.
3. Select the pie image broken link placeholder, then use the Property inspector to browse for the pie.jpg image in the assets folder where you store your Data Files.
4. Format the list of ingredients on the recipes page as an unordered list.
5. Create a CSS rule named **body_text** and save it in a style sheet file named **cc_styles.css** in the website root folder. Use any formatting options that you like, then apply the body_text rule to all text except the menu bar and the text "Caramel Coconut Pie," "Ingredients," and "Directions."
6. Create another rule in the external style sheet called **headings** using appropriate formatting options and apply it to the text "Caramel Coconut Pie," "Ingredients," and "Directions."
7. Save the page.
8. Open the index page, then attach the cc_styles.css to the file.

9. Delete the embedded body_text rule, allowing the body_text rule in the external style sheet to format the text.
10. Convert the nav_bar rule to an external rule in the cc_styles style sheet, then switch back to the recipes page and format the menu bar with the nav_bar rule.

11. Save all open files, then preview both pages in the browser. (*Hint*: If previewing the page in Internet Explorer 7, click the Information bar when prompted to allow blocked content.)
12. Close your browser, then close all open pages.

Figure 46 *Sample Project Builder 2*

Charles Chappell is a new sixth-grade history teacher. He is reviewing educational websites for information he can use in his classroom.

1. Connect to the Internet, then navigate to the Library of Congress website at www.loc.gov. The Library of Congress website is shown in Figure 47.
2. Which fonts are used for the main content on the home page—serif or sans-serif? Are the same fonts used consistently on the other pages in the site?
3. Do you see ordered or unordered lists on any pages in the site? If so, how are they used?
4. Use the Source command on the View menu to view the source code to see if a style sheet was used.
5. Do you see the use of Cascading Style Sheets noted in the source code?

Figure 47 *Design Project*

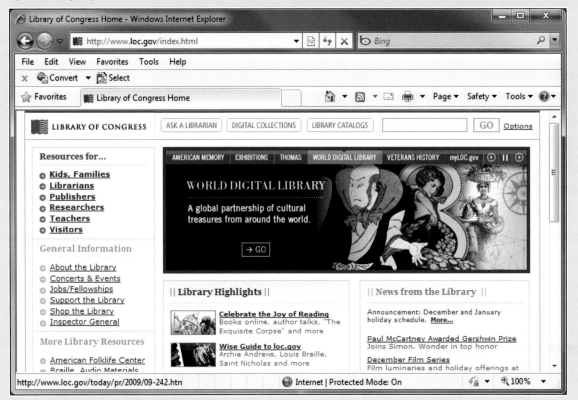

The Library of congress website – www.loc.gov

In this assignment, you will continue to work on the website that you started in Chapter 1, and continued to build in Chapter 2. No Data Files are supplied. You are building this site from chapter to chapter, so you must do each Portfolio Project assignment in each chapter to complete your website.

You continue building your website by designing and completing a page that contains a list, headings, and paragraph text. During this process, you will develop a style sheet and add several rules to it

1. Consult your wireframe and decide which page to create and develop for this chapter.

2. Plan the page content for the page and make a sketch of the layout. Your sketch should include at least one ordered or unordered list, appropriate headings, and paragraph text. Your sketch should also show where the paragraph text and headings should be placed on the page and what rules should be used for each type of text. You should plan on creating at least two CSS rules.

3. Create the page using your sketch for guidance.

4. Create a Cascading Style Sheet for the site and add to it the rules you decided to use. Apply the rules to the appropriate content.

5. Attach the style sheet to the index page you developed in Chapter 2 and consider converting any existing embedded styles to the external style sheet.

6. Preview the new page in a browser, then check for page layout problems and broken links. Make any necessary corrections in Dreamweaver, then preview the page again in the browser. Repeat this process until you are satisfied with the way the page looks in the browser. (*Hint*: If previewing the page in Internet Explorer 7, click the Information bar when prompted to allow blocked content.)

7. Use the checklist in Figure 48 to check all the pages in your site.

8. Close the browser, then close all open pages.

Figure 48 *Design Project*

> ### Website Checklist
>
> 1. Does each page have a page title?
> 2. Does the home page have a description and keywords?
> 3. Does the home page contain contact information?
> 4. Does every completed page in the site have consistent navigation links?
> 5. Does the home page have a last updated statement that will automatically update when the page is saved?
> 6. Do all paths for links and images work correctly?
> 7. Is there a style sheet with at least two rules?
> 8. Did you apply the rules to all text blocks?
> 9. Do all pages look good using at least two different browsers?

CHAPTER **4** ADDING IMAGES

1. Insert and align images
2. Enhance an image and use alternate text
3. Insert a background image and perform site maintenance
4. Add graphic enhancements

ADDING IMAGES

Introduction

Most web pages contain a combination of text and images. The majority of web page information appears in the form of text. But pages are much more interesting if they also contain images that enhance or illustrate the information. A well-designed web page usually includes a balanced combination of text and images. Dreamweaver provides many tools for working with images that you can use to make your web pages attractive and easy to understand.

Using Images to Enhance Web Pages

Images make web pages visually stimulating and more exciting than pages that contain only text. However, you should use images sparingly. You should add images to a page just as you would add seasoning to food. A little seasoning enhances the flavor and brings out the quality of the dish. Too much seasoning overwhelms the dish and masks the flavor of the main ingredients. Too little seasoning results in a bland dish. There are many ways to work with images

so that they complement the content of pages in a website. You can use specific file formats used to save images for websites to ensure maximum quality with minimum file size.

Graphics Versus Images

Two terms that designers sometimes use interchangeably are graphics and images. For the purposes of discussion in this text, we will use the term **graphics** to refer to the appearance of most non-text items on a web page, such as photographs, logos, menu bars, Flash animations, charts, background images, and drawings. Files for items such as these are called graphic files. They are referred to by their file type, or graphic file format, such as JPEG (Joint Photographic Experts Group), GIF (Graphics Interchange Format), or PNG (Portable Network Graphics). We will refer to the actual pictures that you see on the pages as images. But don't worry about which term to use. Many people use one term or the other according to habit or region, or use them interchangeably.

Alt text box

H space text box *V space text box* *Border text box* *Align text box*

Insert and
ALIGN IMAGES

What You'll Do

In this lesson, you will insert three images on the about_us page in The Striped Umbrella website. You will then adjust the alignment of the images on the page to make the page more visually appealing.

Understanding Graphic File Formats

When you choose graphics to add to a web page, it's important to use graphic files in the appropriate file format. The three primary graphic file formats used in web pages are **GIF** (Graphics Interchange Format), **JPEG** or **JPG** (Joint Photographic Experts Group), and **PNG** (Portable Network Graphics). GIF files download very quickly, making them ideal to use on web pages. Though limited in the number of colors they can represent, GIF files have the ability to show transparent areas. JPEG files can display many colors. Because they often contain many shades of the same color, photographs are often saved in JPEG format. Files saved with the PNG format can display many colors and use various degrees of transparency, called **opacity**. However, not all older browsers support the PNG format.

> **QUICK TIP**
>
> The Dreamweaver status bar shows the total download time for the open web page. Each time you add a new graphic to the page, you can see how much additional download time that graphic has added to the total.

Understanding the Assets Panel

When you add a graphic to a website, Dreamweaver automatically adds it to the Assets panel. The **Assets panel**, located in the Files panel group, displays all the assets in a website. The Assets panel contains nine category buttons that you use to view your assets by category. These include Images, Colors, URLs, SWF, Shockwave, Movies, Scripts, Templates, and Library. To view a particular type of asset, click the appropriate category button.

The Assets panel is divided into two panes. When you click the Images button, as shown in Figure 1, the lower pane displays a list of all the images in your site and is divided into five columns. You might need to resize the Assets panel to see all five columns. To resize the Assets panel, undock the Files tab group and drag a side or corner of the panel border.

The top pane displays a thumbnail of the selected image in the list. You can view assets in each category in two ways. You can use the Site option button to view all the assets in a website, or you can use the Favorites option button to view those assets that you have designated as **favorites**, or assets that you expect to use repeatedly while you work on the site.

You can use the Assets panel to add an asset to a web page by dragging the asset from the Assets panel to the page or by using the Insert button on the Assets panel. If you are working on a page layout without final images ready to place, you can insert an image placeholder to hold the image position on the page. An **image placeholder** is a graphic the size of an image you plan to use. You can place it on a page until the actual image is finalized and ready to place on the page. To insert an image placeholder, use the Insert, Image Objects, Image Placeholder command. When the final image is ready, simply replace the image placeholder with the final image.

Inserting Files with Adobe Bridge

You can manage project files, including video and Camera Raw files, with a file-management tool called Adobe Bridge. **Camera Raw** file formats are files that contain unprocessed data and are not yet ready to be printed, similar to a negative from a film camera. **Adobe Bridge** is an image file management program that is used across the Adobe suite applications. Bridge is an easy way to view files in their original locations before bringing them into the website. Bridge is an integrated application, which means you can use it to manage files among other Adobe programs such as Photoshop and Illustrator. You can also use Bridge to add meta tags and search text to your files. To open Bridge, click the Browse in Bridge command on the File menu or click the Browse In Bridge button on the Standard toolbar.

Aligning Images

When you insert an image on a web page, you need to position it in relation to other page elements such as text or other images. Positioning an image is also called **aligning** an image. By default, when you insert an image in a paragraph, its bottom edge aligns with the baseline of the first line of text or any other element in the same paragraph. When you select an image, the Align button in the Property inspector shows the alignment setting for the image. You can change the alignment setting using the options in the Align menu in the Property inspector.

QUICK TIP

The Align menu options function differently from the Align buttons in the Property inspector. You use the Align buttons to center, left-align, or right-align an element without regard to how the element is aligned in relation to other elements. The Align menu options align an image in relation to other elements on the page.

Figure 1 *The Assets panel*

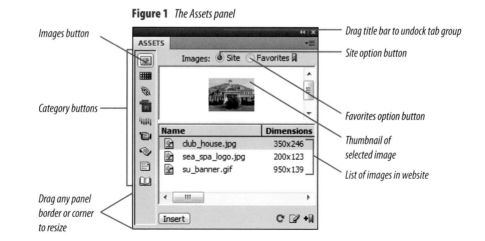

Images button

Category buttons

Drag any panel
border or corner
to resize

Drag title bar to undock tab group

Site option button

Favorites option button

Thumbnail of
selected image

List of images in website

Insert an image

1. Open The Striped Umbrella website, open dw4_1.html from the drive and folder where you store your Data Files, then save it as **about_us.html** in the striped_umbrella site root folder.

2. Click **Yes** (Win) or **Replace** (Mac) to overwrite the existing file, click **No** to Update Links, then close dw4_1.html.

3. Click the **Attach Style Sheet button** 🔗 in the CSS Styles panel, then attach the su_styles.css style sheet to the page.

4. Select the two large paragraphs of text on the page, click the **HTML button** <> HTML on the Property inspector, verify that the Format is set to Paragraph, click the **CSS button** 🔓 CSS, then apply the **body_text** rule to the selected text.

5. Click the **HTML button** <> HTML, then apply the Heading 3 tag to the text "Welcome guests!"

6. Place the insertion point before "When" in the first paragraph, click the **Images list arrow** in the Common category in the Insert panel, then click **Image** to open the Select Image Source dialog box.

7. Navigate to the assets folder in the drive and folder where you store your Data Files, double-click **club_house.jpg**, type the alternate text **Club House** if prompted, click **OK**, open the Files panel if necessary, then verify that the file was copied to your assets folder in the striped_umbrella site root folder.

   Compare your screen to Figure 2.

   (continued)

Figure 2 *The Striped Umbrella about_us page with the inserted image*

club_house.jpg file inserted

Path should begin with the word "assets"

Click Image to insert an image

Style sheet is attached

Inserted file listed in the assets folder

Figure 3 *Image files for The Striped Umbrella website listed in Assets panel*

Images button
Thumbnail of selected image
List of images in The Striped Umbrella website

Refresh Site List button

8. Click the **Assets panel tab** in the Files tab group, click the **Images button** in the Assets panel (if necessary), then click the **Refresh Site List button** in the Assets panel to update the list of images in The Striped Umbrella website.

The Assets panel displays a list of all the images in The Striped Umbrella website, as shown in Figure 3. If you don't see the new image listed, press and hold [CTRL] (Win) or ⌘ (Mac) before you click the Refresh Site List button.

You inserted one image on the about_us page and copied it to the assets folder of the website.

Organizing Assets for Quick Access

Your can organize the assets in the Assets panel in two ways, using the Site and Favorites options buttons. The Site option lists all of the assets in the website in the selected category in alphabetical order. But in a complex site, your asset list can grow quite large. To avoid having to scroll to search for frequently used items, you can designate them as Favorites. To add an asset to the Favorites list, right-click (Win) or [control]-click (Mac) the asset name in the Site list, and then click Add to Favorites. When you place an asset in the Favorites list, it still appears in the Site list. To delete an asset from the Favorites list, click the Favorites option button in the Assets panel, select the asset you want to delete, and then press [Delete] or the Remove from Favorites button on the Assets panel. If you delete an asset from the Favorites list, it still remains in the Site list. You can further organize your Favorites list by creating folders for similar assets and grouping them inside the folders.

Insert an image placeholder

1. Click to place the insertion point before the word "After" at the beginning of the second paragraph.

2. Click the **Images list arrow** in the Common category in the Insert panel, then click **Image Placeholder** to open the Image Placeholder dialog box.

3. Type **boardwalk** in the Name text box, **350** in the Width text box, **218** in the Height text box, and **Boardwalk to the beach** in the Alternate text text box, as shown in Figure 4.

4. Click **OK** to accept these settings, then compare your screen to Figure 5.

You inserted an image placeholder on the about_us page to hold the location on the page until the final image is ready to insert.

Figure 4 *Image Placeholder dialog box*

Figure 5 *Image placeholder on the about_us page*

Image placeholder

Click to insert an
image placeholder

Adding Images

Figure 6 *The about_us page with the boardwalk image inserted*

Settings remain
from the image
placeholder settings

boardwalk image
replaces placeholder
image

Src Browse
for File icon

1. Click to select the **image placeholder** on the about_us page.

2. Click the **Browse for File icon** next to the Src text box on the Property inspector and browse to the assets folder where you store your Data Files if necessary.

TIP You can also double-click an image placeholder to open the Select Image Source dialog box.

3. Double-click **boardwalk.png** to replace the image placeholder with the boardwalk image.

   The alternate text and the height and width settings on the Property inspector are the same that you entered in the Image Placeholder dialog box, as shown in Figure 6.

4. Save your work.

You replaced an image placeholder on the about_us page with a final image.

Use Adobe Bridge

1. Click to place the insertion point at the end of the last sentence on the page, then enter a paragraph break.

2. Click **File** on the Application bar (Win) or Menu bar (Mac), click **Browse in Bridge**, close the dialog box asking if you want Bridge to start at login by answering Yes or No, (if necessary), click the **Folders tab**, navigate to where you store your Data Files, then click the thumbnail image **su_logo.gif** in the assets folder, as shown in Figure 7.

   The Bridge window is divided into several panels; files and folders are listed in the Folders panel. The files in the selected folder appear in the Content panel. A picture of the file appears in the Preview panel. The Metadata and Keywords panels list any tags that have been added to the file.

3. Click **File** on the Application bar (Win) or Menu bar (Mac), point to **Place**, then click **In Dreamweaver**.

4. Type the alternate text **The Striped Umbrella logo**, if prompted, then click **OK**.

   The image appears on the page.

   TIP You can also click the Browse in Bridge button ⬚ on the Standard toolbar to open Bridge.

   After refreshing, your Assets panel should resemble Figure 8.

   You inserted an image on the about_us page using Adobe Bridge.

Figure 7 *Using Adobe Bridge*

Your path may differ — Folders tab — Folders panel — su_logo.gif image is selected in Content panel — Preview panel — Metadata and Keywords panels

Figure 8 *Assets panel with five images*

Five image files saved in The Striped Umbrella website

Click Refresh Site List button to refresh file list

Figure 9 *Left-aligned club house image*

Left-aligned
club house
image

Text wrapped
around club
house image

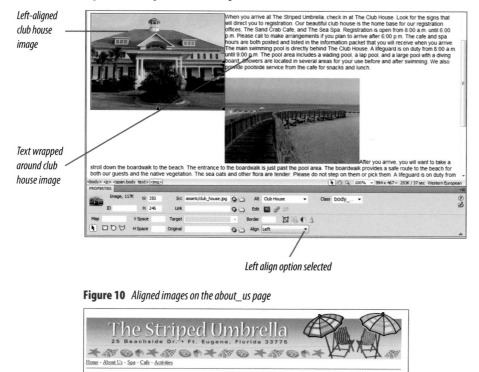

Left align option selected

Figure 10 *Aligned images on the about_us page*

Align an image

1. Scroll to the top of the page, then click the **club house image**.

   Because an image is selected, the Property inspector displays tools for setting the properties of an image.

2. Click the **Align list arrow** in the Property inspector, then click **Left**.

   The club house photo is now left-aligned with the text and the paragraph text flows around its right edge, as shown in Figure 9.

3. Select the boardwalk image, click the **Align list arrow** in the Property inspector, then click **Right**.

   You do not need to set the alignment for the logo because it does not have another object next to it.

4. Save your work.

5. Preview the web page in your browser, compare your screen to Figure 10, then close your browser.

   TIP If you are previewing the page in Internet Explorer 7, click the Information bar when prompted to allow blocked content.

6. Close Adobe Bridge.

You used the Property inspector to set the alignment for two of the images. You then previewed the page in your browser.

Enhance an Image and
USE ALTERNATE TEXT

What You'll Do

In this lesson, you will add borders to images, add horizontal and vertical space to set them apart from the text, and then add or edit alternate text to each image on the page.

Enhancing an Image

After you place an image on a web page, you have several options for enhancing it, or improving its appearance. To make changes to the image itself, such as removing scratches from it, or erasing parts of it, you need to use an image editor such as Adobe Fireworks or Adobe Photoshop.

QUICK TIP

You can copy a Photoshop PSD file and paste it directly into Dreamweaver. After inserting the image, Dreamweaver will prompt you to optimize the image for the web.

You can use Dreamweaver to enhance how images appear on a page. For example, you can modify the brightness and contrast, add borders around an image or add horizontal and vertical space. **Borders** are frames that surround an image. Horizontal and vertical space is blank space above, below, and on the sides of an image that separates the image from text or other elements on the page. Adding horizontal or vertical space is the same as adding white space, and helps images stand out on a page. In the web page from the First Federal Bank website shown in Figure 11, the horizontal and vertical space around the images helps make these images more

DESIGNTIP

Resizing Graphics Using an External Editor

Each image on a web page takes a specific number of seconds to download, depending on the size of the file. Larger files (in kilobytes, not width and height) take longer to download than smaller files. It's important to determine the smallest acceptable size for an image on a page. Then, if you need to resize an image to reduce the file size, use an external image editor to do so, instead of resizing it in Dreamweaver. Decreasing the size of an image using the H (height) and W (width) settings in the Property inspector does not reduce the file size or the time it will take the file to download. Ideally you should use images that have the smallest file size and the highest quality possible, so that each page downloads as quickly as possible.

prominent. Adding horizontal or vertical space does not affect the width or height of the image. Spacing around web page objects can also be created by using "spacer" images, or transparent images that act as placeholders.

Using Alternate Text

One of the easiest ways to make your web page viewer-friendly and accessible to people of all abilities is to use alternate text. Alternate text is descriptive text that appears in place of an image while the image is downloading or not displayed. Screen readers, devices used by persons with visual impairments to convert written text on a computer monitor to spoken words, can "read" alternate text and make it possible for viewers to have an image described to them in detail. You should also use alternate text when inserting form objects, text displayed as graphics, buttons, frames, and media files. Without alternate text assigned to these objects, screen readers will not be able to read them.

One of the default preferences in Dreamweaver is to prompt you to enter alternate text whenever you insert an image on a page. You can set alternate text options in the Accessibility category of the Preferences dialog box. You can program some browsers to display only alternate text and to download images manually. Earlier versions of some browsers used to show alternate text when the mouse was placed over an image, such as Internet Explorer versions before version 8.0.

The use of alternate text is the first checkpoint listed in the Web Content

Accessibility Guidelines (WCAG), Version 2.0, from the World Wide Web Consortium (W3C). It states that a website should "Provide text alternatives for any non-text content so that it can be changed into other forms people need, such as large print, Braille, speech, symbols, or simpler language." To view the complete set of accessibility guidelines, go to the Web Accessibility Initiative page at www.w3.org/WAI/. You should always strive to meet these criteria for all web pages.

Figure 11 *First Federal Bank website*

First Federal Bank website used with permission from First Federal Bank – www.ffbh.com

Add a border

1. Select the club house image.

2. Type **1** in the Border text box, press **[Tab]** to apply the border to the club house image, then compare your screen to Figure 12.

   The border setting is not visible until you preview the page in a browser.

3. Repeat Step 2 to add a border to the boardwalk image.

You added a 1-pixel border to two images on the about_us page.

Add horizontal and vertical space

1. Select the club house image, type **10** in the V Space text box in the Property inspector, press **[Tab]**, type **10** in the H Space text box, press **[Tab]**, deselect the image, then compare your screen to Figure 13.

   The text is more evenly wrapped around the image and is easier to read, because it is not so close to the edge of the image.

2. Repeat Step 1 to set the V Space and H Space to 10 for the boardwalk image.

   The spacing under each picture differs because of the difference in the lengths of the paragraphs.

You added horizontal spacing and vertical spacing around two images on the about_us page.

Figure 12 *Using the Property inspector to add a border*

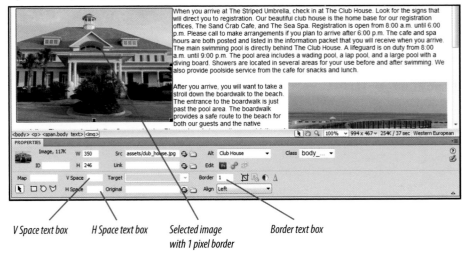

V Space text box   H Space text box   Selected image with 1 pixel border   Border text box

Figure 13 *Comparing images with and without horizontal and vertical space*

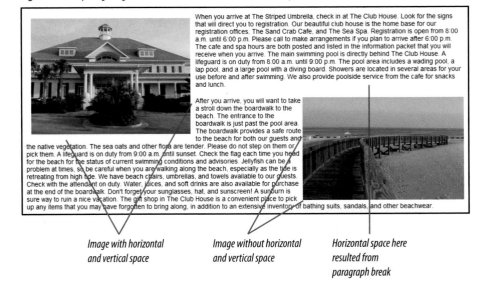

Image with horizontal and vertical space   Image without horizontal and vertical space   Horizontal space here resulted from paragraph break

Adding Images

Figure 14 *Viewing the Image Preview dialog box*

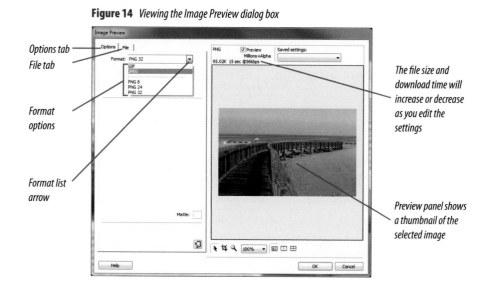

Options tab
File tab

Format options

Format list arrow

The file size and download time will increase or decrease as you edit the settings

Preview panel shows a thumbnail of the selected image

Edit image settings

1. Select the **boardwalk image** if necessary.

2. Click the **Edit Image Settings button** ⚓ in the Property inspector, then click the **Format list arrow** on the Options tab, as shown in Figure 14.

   You can use the Image Preview dialog box to save a copy of the image in a different file format. File property options vary depending on which graphics format you choose. When you choose a different file format, then edit and save it, the program creates a copy and does not alter the original file.

3. Choose the JPEG format, then notice that the file size that appears in the Preview panel is much smaller than the PNG image.

4. Click **OK** to save the changes and close the Image Preview dialog box.

   TIP In addition to being able to save an image using different file formats on the Options tab, you can also use the File tab to scale or resize an image.

   The Save Web Image dialog box opens. Here you choose the location where you want to save the image with the new file format.

5. Navigate to the website assets folder in the Save Web Image dialog box, then click **Save** to save the boardwalk.jpg image.

   There are now two copies of this image in the assets folder. One is a PNG and one is a JPG. If you don't see the new image, refresh the Files panel.

You experimented with file format settings in the Image Preview dialog box, then saved the image as a JPG file.

Integrating Photoshop CS5 with Dreamweaver

Dreamweaver has many functions integrated with Photoshop CS5. For example, you can copy and paste a Photoshop PSD file directly from Photoshop into Dreamweaver. Dreamweaver will prompt you to optimize the image by choosing a file format and settings for the web. Then it will paste the image on the page. If you want to edit the image later, select the image, then click the Edit button in the Property inspector to open the image in Photoshop. (The appearance of the Edit button will change according to the default image editor you have specified.) Photoshop users can set Photoshop as the default image editor in Dreamweaver for specific image file formats. Click Edit on the Application bar, click Preferences (Win), or click Dreamweaver, click Preferences (Mac), click File Types/Editors, click the Extensions plus sign button, select a file format from the list, click the Editors plus sign button, then use the Select External Editor dialog box to browse to Photoshop (if you don't see it listed already), and then click Make Primary. You can also edit an image in Photoshop and export an updated Smart Object instantly in Dreamweaver. A **Smart Object** is an image layer that stores image data from raster or vector images. Search the Adobe website for a tutorial on Photoshop and Dreamweaver integration. Fireworks is another commonly used default image editor. Use the same steps to select it rather than Photoshop.

Edit alternate text

1. Select the club house image, select **Club House** in the Alt text box in the Property inspector (if necessary), type **The Striped Umbrella Club House** as shown in Figure 15, then press **[Enter]** (Win) or **[return]** (Mac).

2. Select the boardwalk image, type **The boardwalk to the beach** in the Alt text box, then press **[Enter]** (Win) or **[return]** (Mac).

3. Save your work.

4. Preview the page in your browser, compare your screen to Figure 16, then close your browser.

You edited the alternate text for three images on the page.

Figure 15 *Alternate text setting in the Property inspector*

Alt text box

Figure 16 *about_us page viewed in browser*

Adding Images

Figure 17 *Preferences dialog box with Accessibility category selected*

Accessibility category

Check boxes for Form objects, Frames, Media, and Images

These options are not available in Mac OS X

Preferences	
Category	**Accessibility**
General	
Accessibility	Show attributes when inserting:
AP Elements	
Code Coloring	☑ Form objects
Code Format	☑ Frames
Code Hints	
Code Rewriting	☑ Media
Copy/Paste	☑ Images
CSS Styles	
File Compare	
File Types / Editors	
Fonts	☐ Keep focus in the panel when opening
Highlighting	☑ Offscreen rendering (need to disable when using screen readers)
Invisible Elements	
New Document	

POWER USER SHORTCUTS	
To do this:	**Use this shortcut:**
Switch views	[Ctrl][`] (Win) or ⌘ [`] (Mac)
Insert image	[Ctrl][Alt][I] (Win) or ⌘ [option][I] (Mac)
Refresh	[F5]
Browse in Bridge	[Ctrl][Alt][O] (Win) or ⌘ [option][O] (Mac)

Displaying Alternate Text in a Browser

There is a simple method you can use to force alternate text to display in a browser when a mouse is held over an image. To do this, add a title tag to the image properties using the same text as the alt tag. Example: <img src="assets/club_house.jpg" alt="The Striped Umbrella Club House" title="The Striped Umbrella Club House" width="350" height="246" hspace="10" vspace="10" border="1" align="left" /> This method will work in Internet Explorer 8 and later versions and Mozilla Firefox.

Set the alternate text accessibility option

1. Click **Edit** on the Application bar (Win) or **Dreamweaver** on the Menu bar (Mac), click **Preferences** to open the Preferences dialog box, then click the **Accessibility category**.

2. Verify that the four attributes check boxes are checked, as shown in Figure 17, check them if they are not checked, then click **OK**.

TIP Once you set the Accessibility preferences, they will be in effect for all websites that you develop, not just the one that's open when you set them.

You set the Accessibility preferences to prompt you to enter alternate text each time you insert a form object, frame, media, image, or object on a web page.

Insert a Background Image and
PERFORM SITE MAINTENANCE

What You'll Do

In this lesson, you will insert two types of background images. You will then use the Assets panel to delete them both from the website, along with the boardwalk.png file. You will also check for non-web-safe colors in the Assets panel.

Inserting a Background Image

You can insert a background image on a web page to provide depth and visual interest to the page, or to communicate a message or mood. **Background images** are image files used in place of background colors. Although you can use background images to create a dramatic effect, you should avoid inserting them on web pages where they would not provide the contrast necessary for reading page text. Even though they might seem too plain, standard white backgrounds are usually the best choice for web pages. If you choose to use a background image on a web page, it should be small in file size. You can choose a single image that fills the page background, or you can choose a tiled image. A **tiled image** is a small image that repeats across and down a web page, appearing as individual squares or rectangles. A tiled image will download much faster than a large image.

When you create a web page, you can use either a background color or a background image, unless you want the background color to appear while the background image

finishes downloading. The background in the web page shown in Figure 18 uses an ocean-wave graphic, which ties to the restaurant name "Mermaids" and the ocean theme for the restaurant decor. This image background does not compete with the text on the page, however, because a solid black background is placed behind the text and in front of the image background. This can be done using tables or divs.

Managing Images

As you work on a website, you might find that you accumulate files in your assets folder that you don't use in the website. To avoid accumulating unnecessary files, it's a good idea to look at an image first, before you place it on the page, and copy it to the assets folder. If you inadvertently copy an unwanted file to the assets folder, you should delete it or move it to another location. This is a good website management practice that will prevent the assets folder from filling up with unwanted image files.

Removing an image from a web page does not remove it from the assets folder in the local site root folder of the website. To remove an asset from a website, if you have a lot of files, it is faster to locate the file you want to remove in the Assets panel. You then use the Locate in Site command to open the Files panel with the unwanted file selected. If you don't have many images in your site, it is faster to locate them in the Files panel. You can then use the Delete command to remove the file from the site.

QUICK TIP

You cannot use the Assets panel to delete a file. You must use the Files panel to delete files and perform all file-management tasks.

Removing Colors from a Website

You can use the Assets panel to locate non-web-safe colors in a website. **Non-web-safe** colors are colors that may not appear uniformly across computer platforms. After you replace a non-web-safe color with another color, you should use the Refresh Site List button on the Assets panel to verify that the color has been removed. Sometimes it's necessary to press [Ctrl] (Win) or ⌘ (Mac) while you click the Refresh Site List button. If refreshing the Assets panel does not work, try re-creating the site cache, and then refreshing the Assets panel.

QUICK TIP

To re-create the site cache, click Site on the Application bar (Win) or Menu bar (Mac), point to Advanced, then click Recreate Site Cache.

Figure 18 *Mermaids website*

Mermaids website used with permission from Mermaids Restaurant and Catering – www.mermaids.ws

Insert a background image

1. Click **Modify** on the Application bar (Win) or Menu bar (Mac), then click **Page Properties** to open the Page Properties dialog box.

2. Click the **Appearance (CSS) category**, if necessary.

3. Click **Browse** next to the Background image text box, navigate to the assets folder in the drive and folder where you store your Data Files, then double-click **umbrella_back.gif**.

4. Click **OK** to close the Page Properties dialog box, then click the **Refresh Site List button** ⟳ to refresh the file list in the Assets panel. The umbrella_back.gif file is automatically copied to The Striped Umbrella assets folder.

   A file with a single umbrella forms a background made up of individual squares, replacing the white background, as shown in Figure 19. It is much too busy and makes it difficult to read the page.

5. Repeat Steps 1–4 to replace the umbrella_back.gif background image with stripes_back.gif, located in the chapter_4 assets folder.

   As shown in Figure 20, the striped background is also tiled, but with vertical stripes, so you aren't aware of the small squares making up the pattern. Although it is an improvement, it is still too busy.

You applied a tiled background to the about_us page. Then you replaced the tiled background with another tiled background that was not as busy.

Figure 19 *The about_us page with a busy tiled background*

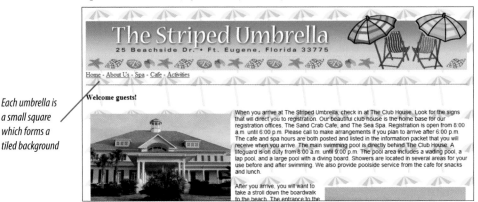

Each umbrella is a small square which forms a tiled background

Figure 20 *The about_us page with a more subtle tiled background*

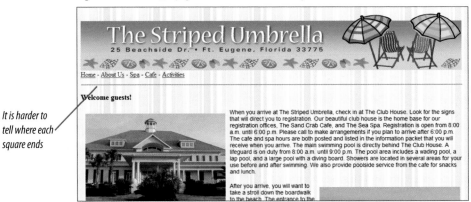

It is harder to tell where each square ends

Adding Images

Figure 21 *Removing a background image*

Selected filename

Remove a background image from a page

1. Click **Modify** on the Application bar (Win) or Menu bar (Mac), click **Page Properties**, then click **Appearance (CSS)**.

2. Select the text in the Background image text box, as shown in Figure 21, press **[Delete]**, then click **OK**.

   The background of the about_us page is white again.

3. Save your work.

You deleted the link to the background image file to change the about_us page background back to white.

Understanding HTML Body Tags

When you set page preferences, it is helpful to understand the HTML tags that are being generated. Sometimes it's easier to make changes to the code, rather than use menus and dialog boxes. The code for the page background color is located in the head section. If you want to change the page properties, you add additional codes to the body tag. Adding a color to the background will add a style to the page; for example, "body { background-color: #000; }". If you insert an image for a background, the code will read "body { background-image: url assets/stripes.gif); }".

Delete files from a website

1. Click the **Assets panel tab** if necessary, then click the **Images button** 🔳 if necessary.

2. With the Site option selected, refresh the Assets panel, right-click (Win) or [control]-click (Mac) **stripes_back.gif** in the Assets panel, click **Locate in Site** to open the Files panel, select **stripes_back.gif** on the Files panel, if necessary, press **[Delete]**, then click **Yes** in the dialog box that appears.

   TIP Refresh the Files panel if you don't see the highlighted file; then refresh the Assets panel if you still see the file listed.

3. Click the **Assets panel tab**, then repeat Step 2 to remove umbrella_back.gif and boardwalk.png from the website, open the Assets panel, then refresh the Assets panel.

   TIP If you delete a file on the Files panel that has an active link to it, you will receive a warning message. If you rename a file on the Files panel that has a link to it, the Files panel will update the links to correctly link to the renamed file. To rename a file, right-click (Win) or [control]-click (Mac) the file you want to rename, point to Edit, click Rename, then type the new name.

   Your Assets panel should resemble Figure 22.

   You removed three image files from The Striped Umbrella website, then refreshed the Assets panel.

Figure 22 *Images listed in Assets panel*

Images button

Images file list after removing umbrella_back.gif and stripes_back.gif

Managing Image Files

It is a good idea to store original unedited copies of your website image files in a separate folder, outside the assets folder of your website. If you edit the original files, resave them using different names. Doing this ensures that you will be able to find a file in its original, unaltered state. You may have files on your computer that you are currently not using at all; however, you may need to use them in the future. Storing currently unused files also helps keep your assets folder free of clutter. Storing copies of original website image files in a separate location also ensures that you have back-up copies in the event that you accidentally delete a file from the website.

Adding Images

Figure 23 *Colors listed in Assets panel*

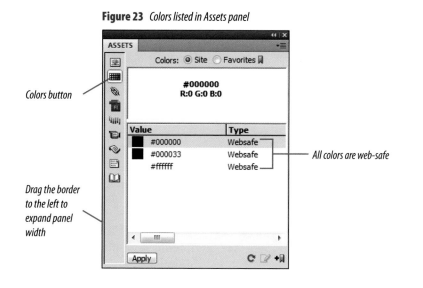

Colors button

Drag the border
to the left to
expand panel
width

All colors are web-safe

Check for non-web-safe colors

1. Click the **Colors button** ⊞ in the Assets panel to display the colors used in the website, then drag the left border of the Assets panel to display the second column, if necessary, as shown in Figure 23.

    Colors listed may either be on pages or in style sheet files. The Assets panel does not list any non-web-safe colors for The Striped Umbrella website.

    TIP If you see a non-web-safe color listed, click Site on the Application bar (Win) or Menu bar (Mac), point to Advanced, then click Recreate Site Cache. The non-web-safe color should then be removed from the Assets panel. This should also remove any colors you have experimented with, unless you have saved a page with a color left on it. If you see an extra color, use the Find and Replace command to locate it, then remove it from the page and refresh the Assets panel again.

2. Save your work, preview the page in your browser, then close your browser.

You checked for non-web-safe colors in the Assets panel list of colors.

Using Color in Compliance with Accessibility Guidelines

Web Content Accessibility Guidelines (WCAG), Version 2.0, from the World Wide Web Consortium (W3C), states that a website should not rely on the use of color alone. This means that if your website content depends on your viewer correctly seeing a color, then you are not providing for those people who cannot distinguish between certain colors or do not have monitors that display color. Be especially careful when choosing color used with text, so you provide a good contrast between the text and the background.

If you are typing in the code or in a text box, it is better to reference colors as numbers, rather than names. For example, use "#FFF" instead of "white." Using style sheets for specifying color formats is the preferred method for coding. For more information, see the complete list of accessibility guidelines listed on the W3C website, www.w3.org.

Add Graphic ENHANCEMENTS

What You'll Do

In this lesson, you will use a small image to link to a larger image and add a favicon to a page.

Adding a Link to a Larger Image

Sometimes designers want to display a small image on a page with an option for the viewer to click on the image to display a larger image. You frequently see this practice on retail sites with multiple items for sale. It is done both to conserve space and to keep the page size as small as possible. These sites will display a **thumbnail image**, or small version of a larger image, so that more images will fit on the page. Another technique is to link from one image to a second image that incorporates the first image. For example, a furniture site may create a link from an image of a chair to an image of the chair in a furnished room. An additional enhancement is often added to allow viewers to click on the larger image to magnify it even more.

To accomplish this, you need two versions of the same image using an image editor such as Photoshop: one that is small (in dimensions and in file size) and one that is large (in dimensions and in file size.) After you have both images ready, place the small image on your page, select it, then link it to the large image. When a user clicks the small image in a browser, the large image will open. Another option is to place the large image on a new web page so you can also include additional descriptive text about the image or a link back to the previous page.

Adding Favicons

In most browsers today, when you add a web page to your favorites list or bookmarks, the page title will appear with a small icon that represents your site, similar to a logo, called a **favicon** (short for favorites icon). This feature was introduced in Microsoft Internet Explorer 5. Most browsers will now also display favicons in the browser address bar. Favicons are a nice way to add branding, or recognition, for your site. To create a favicon, first create an icon that is 16 pixels by 16 pixels. Second, save the file as an icon file with the .ico file extension in your site root folder. Do not save it in a subfolder such as an assets or images folder.

QUICK TIP

There are plug-ins available for Photoshop that will save files with an icon file format, or you can search the Internet for programs that will generate icons.

Third, add HTML code to the head section of your page to link the icon file. The browser will then find the icon and load it in the address bar when the page loads.

Figure 24 shows a favicon in the Snapfish by HP website. Notice that the favicon is displayed both on the address bar and on the page tab. The design of the favicon ties in with the name of the company and other images of fish that are used in the page content. This is a nice touch to complete a well-designed site.

Adding a No Right-Click Script

On most websites, viewers are able to save an image on a page by right-clicking an image, then clicking Save on the shortcut menu. If you would like to prevent viewers from having this option, you can add a **no right-click script**, or JavaScript code that will not allow users to display the shortcut menu by right-clicking an image. To do this, locate JavaScript code that will add this option and copy and paste it into the head content of your page. To locate JavaScript code, use a search engine to search the Internet with a term such as "no right-click script." You will find scripts that prevent viewers from saving any image on the page, or all content of any kind on the page. Some scripts return a message in the browser such as "This function is disabled," and some do not return a message at all. These scripts will keep many viewers from saving your images, but they will not stop the most serious and knowledgeable perpetrators.

You can also protect website images by inserting the image as a table, cell, or CSS block background and then placing a transparent image on top of it. When a viewer attempts to save it with the shortcut menu, they will only save the transparent image.

Figure 24 *Snapfish website*

Favicon displayed in the address bar and on the page tab

Favicon is similar in appearance to other images on the page

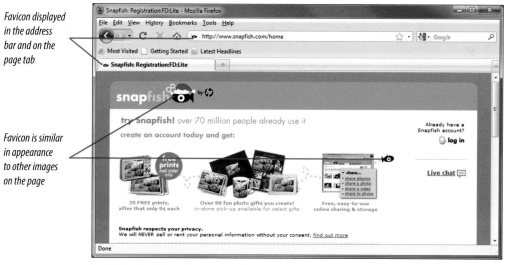

© 2009 The Snapfish by HP website used with permission from Snapfish by HP – www.snapfish.com

Use an image to link to another image

1. Click to place the insertion point to the right of the su_logo image, insert the image **map_small.jpg** from the assets folder where you store your Data Files, type **Map to The Striped Umbrella** in the Image Tag Accessibility Attributes dialog box, then click **OK**.

2. Select the **map_small image**, then type **30** in the H Space text box, then press **[Tab]**.

3. With the map_small image selected, click the **Browse for File icon** next to the Link text box, navigate to the assets folder in the drive and folder where you store your Data Files, click **map_large.jpg**, then click **OK**.

   The small map image now links to the large map image, so viewers can click the small version to view the large version.

4. Click to place the insertion point after the last paragraph, insert a paragraph break, type **Click the map below to view a larger size image**, then compare your screen to Figure 25.

5. Save your work, then preview the page in your browser.

6. Click the **small map image** to view the large map image in a separate window, use the Back button to return to the about_us page, then close the browser.

You inserted a small image on the page and linked it to a larger image.

Figure 25 *The about_us page with an image linking to a larger image*

Link text box

Small map image links to large map image

Figure 26 *Copying the favicon.ico file to the site root folder*

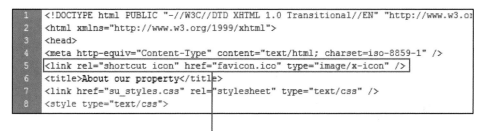

Copy the favicon.ico file
to the striped_umbrella
site root folder

Figure 27 *Adding code to link the favicon*

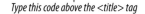

```
1  <!DOCTYPE html PUBLIC "-//W3C//DTD XHTML 1.0 Transitional//EN" "http://www.w3.or
2  <html xmlns="http://www.w3.org/1999/xhtml">
3  <head>
4  <meta http-equiv="Content-Type" content="text/html; charset=iso-8859-1" />
5  <link rel="shortcut icon" href="favicon.ico" type="image/x-icon" />
6  <title>About our property</title>
7  <link href="su_styles.css" rel="stylesheet" type="text/css" />
8  <style type="text/css">
```

Type this code above the <title> tag

Figure 28 *Viewing a favicon in the Firefox browser*

Starfish favicon

Insert a favicon on a page

1. Open Windows Explorer (Win) or Finder (Mac), then browse to the chapter_4 folder in the drive and folder where your Data Files are stored.

2. Right-click the file **favicon.ico**, copy it, browse to your site root folder, then paste the **favicon.ico** file into the site root folder, as shown in Figure 26, then close Windows Explorer (Win) or Finder (Mac).

3. Switch to Code view in Dreamweaver, insert a blank line above the line of code for the page title, then insert this code directly above the <title> tag: **<link rel = "shortcut icon" href = "favicon.ico" type = "image/x-icon" />** as shown in Figure 27.

4. Save your work, then preview the about_us page in the browser.

   The favicon will appear in the address bar right before the page title and on the page tab in browsers that use tabbed pages, as shown in Figure 28.

   TIP Internet Explorer may not display the favicon until the website is published to a server.

5. Copy the code for the favicon link, then paste it into the code for the index and spa pages.

6. Save your work, close all open pages, then exit Dreamweaver.

You copied a favicon to the site root folder, then added code to the About Us page to direct browsers to display the favicon in the title bar when the page is viewed in a browser.

Insert and align images.

1. Open the Blooms & Bulbs website, open dw4_2.html from the drive and folder where you store your Data Files, then save it as **plants.html** in the Blooms & Bulbs website, overwriting the existing plants.html file. Do not update links.
2. Verify that the path of the Blooms & Bulbs banner is set correctly to the assets folder in the blooms site root folder.
3. Verify that the Accessibility preferences will prompt you to add alternate text to images is set.
4. Insert an image placeholder to the left of the words "Who can resist" with the following settings: Name: **rose_bud**; Width: **300 pixels**; Height: **207 pixels**; Alternate text: **Rose bud on bird bath**.
5. Use the Browse for file button next to the Src text box on the Property inspector to replace the image placeholder with the rose_bud.jpg file from the assets folder in the drive and folder where you store your Data Files
6. Use Bridge to insert the rose_bloom.jpg file, from the assets folder in the drive and folder where you store your Data Files, in front of the words "For ease of growing" and add **Rose bloom** as alternate text.
7. Insert the two_roses.jpg file from the assets folder in the drive and folder where you store your Data Files in front of the words "The Candy Cane" and add **Candy Cane Floribunda** as alternate text.
8. Refresh the Files panel to verify that all three images were copied to the assets folder.
9. Left-align the rose_bud image.
10. Right-align the rose_bloom image.
11. Left-align the two_roses image.
12. Save your work.

Enhance an image and use alternate text.

1. Apply a 1-pixel border, vertical spacing of 10 pixels, and horizontal spacing of 20 pixels around the rose_bud image.
2. Apply a 1-pixel border, vertical spacing of 10 pixels, and horizontal spacing of 20 pixels around the rose_bloom image.
3. Apply a 1-pixel border, vertical spacing of 10 pixels, and horizontal spacing of 20 pixels around the two_roses image.
4. Attach the blooms_styles.css file to the page, then use the HTML Property inspector to apply the Heading 3 format to the heading at the top of the page and the paragraph_text rule to the rest of the text on the page. (*Hint*: Use the Class text box to select the paragraph_text rule from the list.)
5. Save your work, preview it in the browser, then compare your screen to Figure 29. (*Hint*: If previewing the page in Internet Explorer 7, click the Information bar when prompted to allow blocked content.)

Figure 29 *Completed Skills Review*

Featured Spring Plant: Roses!

Who can resist the romance of roses? Poets have waxed poetically over them throughout the years. Many persons consider the beauty and fragrance of roses to be unmatched in nature. The varieties are endless, ranging from floribunda to hybrid teas to shrub roses to climbing roses. Each variety has its own personality and preference in the garden setting. Pictured on the left is a Summer Breeze Hybrid Tea bud. This variety is fast growing and produces spectacular blooms that are beautiful as cut flowers in arrangements. The enchanting fragrance will fill your home with summer sweetness. They require full sun. Hybrid teas need regular spraying and pruning, but will reward you with classic blooms that will be a focal point in your landscaping and provide you with beautiful arrangements in your home. They are well worth the effort!

For ease of growing, Knock Out® roses are some of our all-time favorites. Even beginners will not fail with these garden delights. They are shrub roses and prefer full sun, but can take partial shade. They are disease resistant and drought tolerant. You do not have to be concerned with either black spot or dead-heading with roses such as the Knock out®, making them an extremely low-maintenance plant. They are also repeat bloomers, blooming into late fall. The shrub can grow quite large, but can be pruned to any size. The one you see on the right is Southern Belle. Check out all our varieties as you will not fail to have great color with these plants.

The Candy Cane Floribunda shown on the left is a beautiful rose with cream, pink, and red stripes and swirls. They have a heavy scent that will remind you of the roses you received on your most special occasions. These blooms are approximately four inches in diameter. They bloom continuously from early summer to early fall. The plants grow up to four feet tall and three feet wide. They are shipped bare root in February.

Insert a background image and perform site maintenance.

1. Insert the daisies.jpg file as a background image from the assets folder where you store your Data Files.
2. Save your work.
3. Preview the web page in your browser, then close your browser.
4. Remove the daisies.jpg file from the background.
5. Open the Assets panel, then refresh the Files list.
6. Use the Files panel to delete the daisies.jpg file from the list of images.
7. Refresh the Assets panel, then verify that the daisies.jpg file has been removed from the website.
8. View the colors used in the site in the Assets panel, then verify that all are web-safe.
9. Save your work.

Add graphic enhancements.

1. Select the two_roses image on the plants page.
2. Use the Link text box on the Property inspector to link the two_roses image to the two_roses_large.jpg file in the assets folder where you store your Data Files.
3. Add the sentences **You must see a close-up of these beauties! Click the image on the left to enlarge them**. at the end of the last paragraph.
4. Save your work, preview the page in the browser, then click the two_roses image to view the larger version of the image.
5. Use the Back button to return to the plants page, then close the dw4_2.html data file.

6. Open Windows Explorer (Win) or Finder (Mac), browse to the folder where you store your Data Files, then copy the file flower.ico.
7. Paste the file flower.ico in the blooms site root folder, then rename it **favicon.ico.**
8. Close Windows Explorer (Win) or Finder (Mac), then switch to Code view for the plants page.
9. Insert a blank line above the title tag, then type this code directly above the <title> tag:
   <link rel = "shortcut icon" href = "favicon.ico" type = "image/x-icon" />

10. Verify that you entered the code correctly, copy the new line of code, then switch back to Design view.
11. Copy the same code you typed in step 9 to the index and tips pages, then save all files.
12. Preview the page in the browser, compare your screen to Figure 30, then close all open page.

Figure 30 *Completed Skills Review*

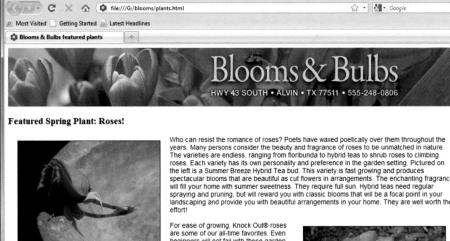

Use Figure 31 as a guide to continue your work on the TripSmart website that you began in Project Builder 1 in Chapter 1, and continued to work on in Chapters 2 and 3. You are now ready to begin work on the destinations page that showcases one of the featured tours to Spain. You want to include some colorful pictures on the page.

1. Open the TripSmart website.
2. Open dw4_3.html from the drive and folder where you store your Data Files and save it in the tripsmart site root folder as **tours.html**, overwriting the existing tours.html file and not updating the links.
3. Verify that the path for the banner is correctly set to the assets folder of the TripSmart website.
4. Attach the tripsmart_styles.css file, then apply the paragraph_text rule to all of the text on the page except the "Destination: Spain" heading.
5. Apply the Heading 2 format to the "Destination: Spain" heading.
6. Insert bull_fighter.jpg from the assets folder in the drive and folder where you store your Data Files to the left of the sentence beginning "Our next trip to Spain", then add appropriate alternate text.
7. Insert stallion.jpg from the assets folder in the drive and folder where you store your Data Files to the left of the sentence beginning "We will also visit Jerez", then add appropriate alternate text.
8. Align both images using the Align button in the Property inspector with alignments of your choice, then add horizontal spacing, vertical spacing, or borders if desired.

9. Apply any additional formatting to enhance the page appearance if you would like to, then add the page title **Destination: Spain**.
10. Check the site for non-web-safe colors and remove them if you find any.
11. Copy the file airplane.ico from the folder where you store your data files to your site root folder, then rename it **favicon.ico**.
12. Add appropriate code to the head content to link the favicon to the page, then copy the code to the index and newsletter pages.
13. Save your work, then preview the tours, index, and newsletter pages in your browser. (*Hint:* If previewing the page in Internet Explorer 7, click the Information bar when prompted to allow blocked content.)
14. Close your browser, then close all open files.

Figure 31 *Sample Project Builder 1*

In this exercise, you continue your work on the Carolyne's Creations website that you started in Project Builder 2 in Chapter 1, and continued to build in Chapters 2 and 3. You are now ready to add a new page to the website that will display featured items in the kitchen shop. Figure 32 shows a possible solution for this exercise. Your finished page will look different if you choose different formatting options.

1. Open the Carolyne's Creations website.
2. Open dw4_4.html from the drive and folder where you store your Data Files, save it to the site root folder as **shop.html**, overwriting the existing file and not updating the links.
3. Insert paella_pan.jpg from the assets folder in the drive and folder where you store your Data Files, on the page, add alternate text and your choice of alignment, horizontal space, and vertical space settings. (*Hint*: In Figure 32 the align setting is set to right, and the H space is set to 30.)
4. Attach the cc_styles.css file to the page.
5. Apply the nav_bar rule to the navigation links, the headings rule to the page heading "January Special: Paella Pans" and the body_text rule to the paragraphs of text.
6. Link the paella_pan image to the file paella.jpg from the assets folder where you store your Data Files, then enter some descriptive text on the page to prompt viewers to click on the paella_pan image.

7. Save the shop page, then preview it in the browser. (*Hint*: If previewing the page in Internet Explorer 7, click the Information bar when prompted to allow blocked content.)
8. Close your browser, then close all open pages.

Figure 32 *Sample Project Builder 2*

Home | Shop | Classes | Catering | Recipes

January Special: Paella Pans

We try to feature special items each month and love to promote local foods. This month features paella pans in three sizes: 12 inches, 18 inches, and 24 inches.

This pan is made of polished stainless steel with red baked enamel handles for easy transfer from stove top to table. Paella is a traditional Spanish dish with rice as the basic ingredient. Caroline found these wonderful pans during a recent trip to Valencia, Spain. Although it looks a little similar in appearance to a wok, you do not stir paella while it is cooking! The secret to the perfect paella is to cook it until it is almost burned, forming a crunchy crust on the bottom, called soccarat. To view some of Chef Carolyne's tempting paella, click on the image on the right.

Patsy Broers is working on a team project to design a website for her high school drama department. She has been assigned the task of gathering images to add interest and color.

1. Connect to the Internet, then navigate to the William J. Clinton Presidential Center website at www.clintonpresidentialcenter.org, shown in Figure 33.
2. Do you see a favicon used on the page?
3. Are any of the images on the page used as links to other images or pages?
4. Is a background image used for any of the page objects?
5. How do the images, horizontal and vertical spacing, color, and text work together to create an attractive and interesting experience for viewers?

Figure 33 *Design Project*

The William J. Clinton Presidential Center website used with permission from the William J. Clinton Presidential Center
www.clintonpresidentialcenter.org

Adding Images

In this assignment, you will continue to work on the website that you started in Chapter 1, and continued to build in Chapters 2 and 3. No Data Files are supplied. You are building this site from chapter to chapter, so you must do each Portfolio Project assignment in each chapter to complete your website.

You continue building your website by inserting appropriate images on a page and enhancing them for maximum effect. You will also check for non-web-safe colors and remove any that you find.

1. Consult your wireframe and decide which page to create and develop for this chapter.
2. Plan the page content and make a sketch of the layout. Your sketch should include several images and a background color or image.
3. Create the page using your sketch for guidance.
4. Access the images you gathered, and place them on the page so that the page matches the sketch you created in Step 2. Add a background image if you want, and appropriate alternate text for each image.
5. Remove any non-web-safe colors.
6. Identify any files in the Assets panel that are currently not used in the site. Decide which of these assets should be removed, then delete these files.

7. Preview the new page in a browser, then check for page layout problems and broken links. (*Hint*: If previewing the page in Internet Explorer 7, click the Information bar when prompted to allow blocked content.) Make any necessary corrections in Dreamweaver, then preview the page again in the browser. Repeat this process until you are satisfied with the way the page looks in the browser.
8. Use the checklist in Figure 34 to check all the pages in your site.
9. Close the browser, then close the open pages.

Figure 34 *Portfolio Project checklist*

Website Checklist

1. Does each page have a page title?
2. Does the home page have a description and keywords?
3. Does the home page contain contact information?
4. Does the home page have a last updated statement that will automatically update when the page is saved?
5. Do all paths for links and images work correctly?
6. Do all images have alternate text?
7. Are all colors web-safe?
8. Are there any unnecessary files you can delete from the assets folder?
9. Is there a style sheet with at least two rules?
10. Did you apply the rules to all text?
11. Do all pages look good using at least two different browsers?

Adding Images

CHAPTER **5**

WORKING WITH LINKS AND NAVIGATION

1. Create external and internal links
2. Create internal links to named anchors
3. Create, modify, and copy a Spry menu bar
4. Create an image map
5. Manage website links
6. Incorporate Web 2.0 technology

5

WORKING WITH LINKS
AND NAVIGATION

Introduction

What makes websites so powerful are the links, or hyperlinks, that connect one page to another within a website or to any page on the web. Although you can enhance a website with graphics, animations, movies, and other features to make it visually attractive, the links you include are often a site's most essential components. Links that connect the pages within a site are important because they help viewers navigate between the pages of the site. If it's important to keep viewers within your site, link only to pages within your website and avoid including links to external sites. For example, most e-commerce sites only link to other pages in their own site to discourage shoppers from leaving.

In this chapter, you will create links to other pages in The Striped Umbrella website and to other sites on the web. You will insert a Spry menu bar, and check the site links to make sure they all work correctly. You will also learn about Web 2.0 and social networking, an area of the Internet that has exploded in recent years. **Social networking** refers to the grouping of individual web users who connect and interact with other users in online communities. **Online communities**, or virtual communities, are social websites you can join, such as Facebook and Twitter, where you can communicate with others by posting messages or media content such as images or videos. You will learn about how you can connect your website to these communities.

Understanding Internal and External Links

Web pages contain two types of links: internal links and external links. **Internal links** are links to web pages within the same website, and **external links** are links to web pages in other websites or to email addresses. Both internal and external links have two important parts that work together. The first part of a link is displayed on a web page, for example, text, an image, or a button that is used for a link. The second part of a link is the **path**, or the name and location of the web page or file that will open when viewers click the element. Setting and maintaining the correct paths for all of your links is essential to avoid having broken links in your site, which can cause a visitor to click away immediately.

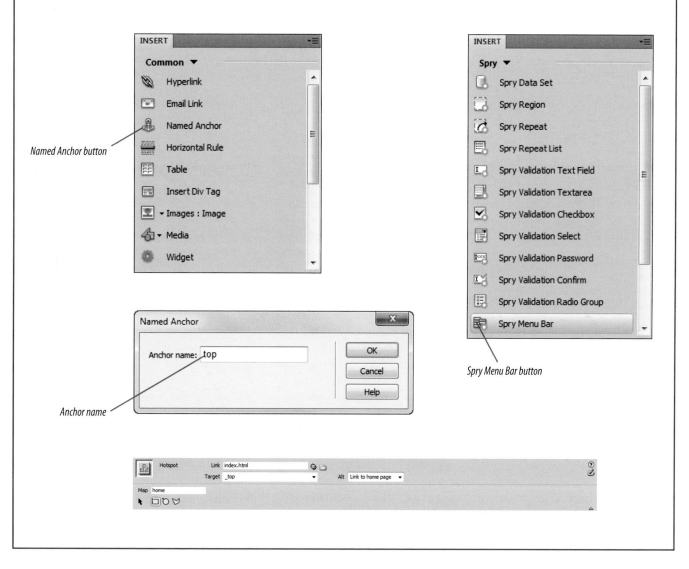

Named Anchor button

Anchor name

Spry Menu Bar button

Create External and
INTERNAL LINKS

What You'll Do

In this lesson, you will create external links on The Striped Umbrella activities page that link to websites related to area attractions. You will also create internal links to other pages within The Striped Umbrella website.

Creating External Links

A good website often includes a variety of external links to other related websites so that viewers can get more information on a particular topic. To create an external link, you first select the text or object that you want to serve as a link, then you type the absolute path to the destination web page in the Link text box in the Property inspector. An **absolute path** is a path used for external links that includes the complete address for the destination page, including the protocol (such as http://) and the complete **URL** (Uniform Resource Locator), or address, of the destination page. When necessary, the web page filename and folder hierarchy are also part of an absolute path. Figure 1 shows an example of an absolute path showing the protocol, URL, and filename. An example

for the code for an external link would be <a href="http://www.adobe.com"> Adobe website</a>.

Creating Internal Links

Each page in a website usually focuses on an individual information category or topic. You should make sure that the home page provides links to each major page in the site, and that all pages in the site contain numerous internal links so that viewers can move easily from page to page. To create an internal link, you first select the text element or image that you want to use to make a link, and then use the Browse for File icon next to the Link text box in the HTML Property inspector to specify the relative path to the destination page. A **relative path** is a type of path that

Figure 1 An example of an absolute path

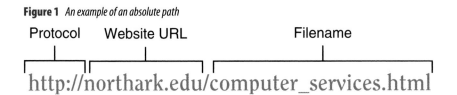

Protocol   Website URL   Filename

http://northark.edu/computer_services.html

references web pages and image files within the same website. Relative paths include the filename and folder location of a file. An example for the code for a relative internal link would be <a href="activities.html"> Activities</a>. Figure 2 shows an example of a relative path. Table 1 describes absolute and relative paths. Relative paths can either be site-root relative or document-relative. The internal links that you will create in this lesson will be document-relative. You can also use the Point to File icon in the HTML Property inspector to select the file you want to link to, or drag the file you want to use for the link from the Files panel into the Link text box in the Property inspector.

You should take great care in managing your internal links to make sure they work correctly and are timely and relevant to the page content. Design the navigation structure of your website so that viewers are never more than three or four clicks away from the page they are seeking.

Figure 2 *An example of a relative path*

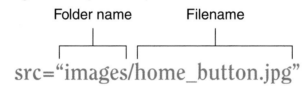

TABLE 1: DESCRIPTION OF ABSOLUTE AND RELATIVE PATHS

Type of path	Description	Examples
Absolute path	Used for external links and specifies protocol, URL, and filename of destination page	http://www.yahoo.com/recreation
Relative path	Used for internal links and specifies location of file relative to the current page	spa.html or assets/heron.gif
Root-relative path	Used for internal links when publishing to a server that contains many websites or where the website is so large it requires more than one server	/striped_umbrella/activities.html
Document- relative path	Used in most cases for internal links and specifies the location of file relative to current page	cafe.html or assets/heron.gif

Create an external link

1. Open The Striped Umbrella website, open dw5_1.html from the drive and folder where you store your Chapter 5 Data Files, then save it as **activities.html** in the striped_umbrella site root folder, overwriting the existing activities page, but not updating links.

2. Attach the **su_styles.css** file, then apply the **body_text rule** to the paragraphs of text on the page (not to the menu bar).

3. Select the first broken image link, click the **Browse for File icon** next to the Src text box, then select heron_waiting_small.jpg in the Data Files assets folder to save the image in your assets folder.

4. Click on the page next to the broken image link to see the heron_waiting_small image, then click to select the image, as shown in Figure 3.

5. Repeat Step 3 for the second image, two_dolphins_small.jpg, then refresh the Assets panel if necessary.

   The two new files are copied into the assets folder, as shown in Figure 4.

6. Scroll down, then select the text "Blue Angels" in the first line of the second to last paragraph.

   (continued)

Figure 3 *Saving an image file in assets folder*

Broken image is replaced when file is saved in the assets folder

Image is saved in assets folder

Figure 4 *Assets panel with two new images added*

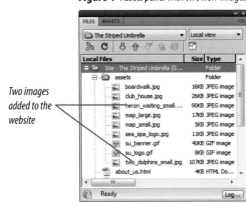

Two images added to the website

Figure 5 *Creating an external link to the Blue Angels website*

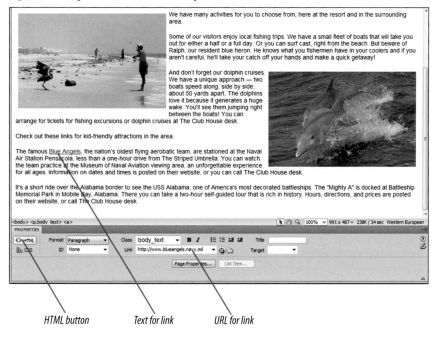

HTML button   Text for link   URL for link

7. Click the **HTML button** `<> HTML` in the Property inspector to switch to the HTML Property inspector if necessary, click in the Link text box, type **http://www.blueangels.navy.mil**, press [**Enter**] (Win) or [**return**] (Mac), click on the page to deselect the link, then compare your screen to Figure 5.

8. Repeat Steps 6 and 7 to create a link for the USS Alabama site in the next paragraph: **http://www.ussalabama.com**.

9. Save your work, preview the page in your browser, test all the links to make sure they work, then close your browser.

TIP You must have an active Internet connection to test the external links. If clicking a link does not open a page, make sure you typed the URL correctly in the Link text box.

You opened The Striped Umbrella website, replaced the existing activities page, attached the su_styles.css.file, applied the paragraph_text style to the text, then imported images into the site. You added two external links to other sites, then tested each link in your browser.

Typing URLs

Typing URLs in the Link text box in the Property inspector can be tedious. When you need to type a long and complex URL, it is easy to make mistakes and create a broken link. You can avoid such mistakes by copying and pasting the URL from the Address text box (Internet Explorer) or Location bar (Mozilla Firefox) to the Link text box in the Property inspector. Copying and pasting a URL ensures that the URL is entered correctly.

Create an internal link

1. Select the text "fishing excursions" in the third paragraph.

2. Click the **Browse for File icon** 📁 next to the Link text box in the HTML Property inspector, then double-click **fishing.html** in the Select File dialog box to set the relative path to the fishing page.

   The filename fishing.html appears in the Link text box in the Property inspector, as shown in Figure 6 (The link is deselected in the figure for readability.)

   TIP Pressing [F4] will hide or redisplay all panels, including the Property inspector and the panels on the right side of the screen.

3. Select the text "dolphin cruises" in the same sentence.

4. Click the **Browse for File icon** 📁 next to the Link text box in the HTML Property inspector, then double-click **cruises.html** in the Select File dialog box to specify the relative path to the cruises page.

   The words "dolphin cruises" are now a link to the cruises page.

5. Save your work, preview the page in your browser, verify that the internal links work correctly, then close your browser.

   The fishing and cruises pages do not have page content yet, but serve as placeholders until they do.

You created two internal links on the activities page, then tested the links in your browser.

Figure 6 *Creating an internal link on the activities page*

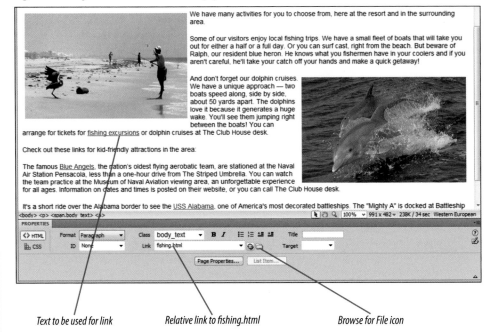

Text to be used for link   Relative link to fishing.html   Browse for File icon

---

Using Case-Sensitive Links

When you hear that text is "case sensitive," it means that the text will be treated differently when it is typed using uppercase letters rather than lowercase letters, or vice-versa. With some operating systems, such as Windows, it doesn't matter which case you use when you enter URLs. However, with other systems, such as UNIX, it does matter. To be sure that your links will work with all systems, use lowercase letters for all URLs. This is another good reason to select and copy a URL from the browser address bar, and then paste it in the Link text box or Dreamweaver code when creating an external link. You won't have to worry about missing a case change.

Figure 7 *Assets panel with three external links*

Three external
links, including
the email link.

1. Click the Assets panel tab if necessary to view the Assets panel.

2. Click the **URLs button** in the Assets panel.

3. Click the **Refresh Site List button** C.

   Three links appear in the Assets panel: one external link for the email link on the home page and two external links, to the Blue Angels and USS Alabama websites on the activities page, as shown in Figure 7. Notice that the internal links do not appear in the Assets panel. The Assets panel shows the links for the entire site, not just for the open page.

4. Click the **Files panel tab** to view the Files panel.

5. Close the activities page and the dw5_1.html page.

You viewed the external links on the activities page in the Assets panel.

Create Internal Links
TO NAMED ANCHORS

What You'll Do

 In this lesson, you will insert four named anchors on the spa page: one for the top of the page and three for each of the spa services lists. You will then create internal links to each named anchor.

Inserting Named Anchors

Some web pages have so much content that users must scroll repeatedly to get to the bottom of the page and then back up to the top of the page. To make it easier for users to navigate to specific areas of a page without scrolling, you can use a combination of internal links and named anchors. A **named anchor** is a specific location on a web page that has a descriptive name. Named anchors act as targets for internal links and make it easy for users to jump to a particular place on the same page quickly. A **target** is the location on a web page that a browser displays when users click an internal link. For example, you can insert a named anchor called "top" at the top of a web page, and then create a link to it from the bottom of the page.

You can also insert named anchors in strategic places on a web page, such as at the beginning of paragraph headings. The Ozark Arts Council website shown in Figure 8 uses named anchors on their About Us page to divide the content about the organization into separate sections on the page. Text links at the top of the page link to the respective section headers with named anchors.

You insert a named anchor using the Named Anchor button in the Common category on the Insert panel. You then enter the name of the anchor in the Named Anchor dialog box. You should choose short names that describe the named anchor location on the page. Named anchors appear on a web page as yellow anchor icons in Design view. Selected anchors appear as blue icons. You can show or hide named anchor icons by clicking View on the Application bar (Win) or Menu bar (Mac), bar, pointing to Visual Aids, and then clicking Invisible Elements.

Creating Internal Links to Named Anchors

Once you create a named anchor, you can create an internal link to it using one of two methods. You can select the text or image on the page that you want to use to make a link, and then drag the Point to File icon from the Property inspector to the named anchor icon on the page. Or, you can select the text or image to which you want to use to make a link, then type # followed by the named anchor name (such as "#top") in the Link text box in the Property inspector.

QUICK TIP

To avoid possible errors, you should create a named anchor before you create a link to it.

Figure 8 *Ozark Arts Council website with named anchors*

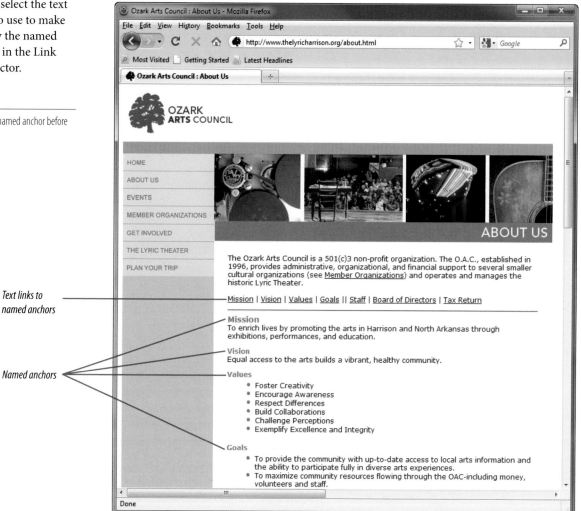

Text links to named anchors

Named anchors

Ozark Arts Council website used with permission from the Ozark Arts Council – www.thelyricharrison.org

Insert a named anchor

1. Open the spa page, click the **banner image** to select it, then press [←] to place the insertion point to the left of the banner.

2. Click **View** on the Application bar (Win) or Menu bar (Mac), point to **Visual Aids,** then verify that Invisible Elements is checked.

TIP If there is no check mark next to Invisible Elements, this feature is turned off. Click Invisible Elements to turn this feature on.

3. Select the Common category on the Insert panel if necessary.

4. Click **Named Anchor** on the Insert panel to open the Named Anchor dialog box, type **top** in the Anchor name text box, compare your screen with Figure 9, then click **OK**.

   An anchor icon now appears before The Striped Umbrella banner. Depending on your window size, the anchor icon might appear above the banner or to the left of the banner.

TIP Use lowercase letters, no spaces, and no special characters in named anchor names. You should also avoid using a number as the first character in a named anchor name.

(continued)

Figure 9 *Named Anchor dialog box*

Name of new anchor

Using Visual Aids

The Visual Aids submenu on the View menu gives you several choices for displaying page elements in Design View, such as named anchor icons. Named anchor icons are considered invisible elements. When you check the Invisible Elements option, you will see the named anchor icons on the page. The icons do not appear when the page is viewed in a browser. Turning on visual aids makes it easier to edit the page. Other options in the Visual Aids menu are CSS Layout Backgrounds, CSS Layout Box Model, CSS Layout Outlines, AP Element Outlines, Table Widths, Table Borders, Frame Borders, and Image Maps. The Hide All option hides all of these page elements. In later chapters, as you work with each page object that these refer to, you will see the advantages of displaying them. The CSS options allow you to see the formatting properties for CSS layout blocks such as the outline, background color, and margins.

Figure 10 *Named anchors on the spa page*

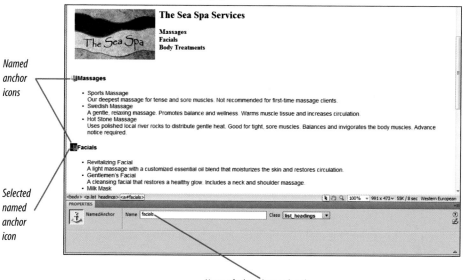

Named anchor icons

Selected named anchor icon

Name of selected named anchor

5. Scroll down to the list of massages, click to the left of the Massages heading, then insert a named anchor named **massages**.

6. Insert named anchors to the left of the Facials and Body Treatments headings using the following names: **facials** and **body_treatments**.

Your screen should resemble Figure 10.

You created four named anchors on the activities page, one at top of the page, and three that will help viewers quickly access the Spa Services headings on the page.

Create an internal link to a named anchor

1. Select the word "Massages" to the right of The Sea Spa logo, then drag the **Point to File icon** ⊕ from the Property inspector to the anchor next to the massages heading, as shown in Figure 11.

   The word "Massages" is now linked to the Massages named anchor. When viewers click the word "Massages" at the top of the page, the browser will display the Massages heading at the top of the browser window. The Link text box on the Property inspector now reads #massages.

TIP The name of a named anchor is always preceded by a pound (#) sign in the Link text box in the Property inspector.

2. Create internal links for Facials and Body Treatments to the right of The Sea Spa logo by first selecting each of these words or phrases, then dragging the **Point to File icon** ⊕ to the appropriate named anchor icon.

   The words "Facials" and "Body Treatments" are now links that connect to the Facials and Body Treatments headings.

TIP Once you select the text on the page you want to link, you might need to scroll down to view the named anchor on the screen. Once you see the named anchor on your screen, you can drag the Point to File icon on top of it. You can also move the pointer to the edge of the page window (still in the white area of the page) to scroll the page.

(continued)

Figure 11 *Dragging the Point to File icon to a named anchor*

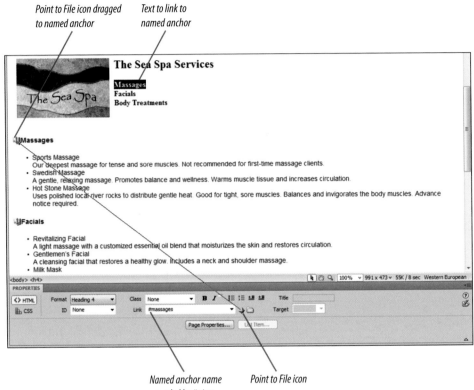

Point to File icon dragged to named anchor

Text to link to named anchor

Named anchor name preceded by # sign

Point to File icon

Figure 12 *Spa page with internal links to named anchors*

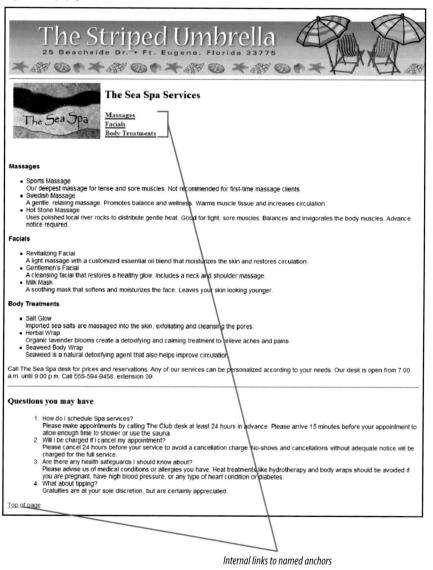

Internal links to named anchors

3. Scroll down to the bottom of the page, then place the insertion point at the end of the last sentence on the page.

4. Press **[Enter]** (Win) or **[return]** (Mac) twice to insert two paragraph breaks, then type **Top of page**.

5. Place the insertion point to the left of the text "Top of page," then click the **Remove Blockquote button** ≤≡ to move the text to the left margin.

6. Apply the body_text rule to "Top of page" if necessary.

7. Select the text "Top of page", scroll to the top of the page, then use the Point to File icon on the HTML Property inspector to link the text to the anchor named top.

8. Save your work, preview the page in your browser, as shown in Figure 12, then test the links to each named anchor, using the Back button to return to the links.

   When you click the spa packages link in the browser, the associated named anchor may appear in the middle of the page instead of at the top. This happens because the spa page is not long enough to position this named anchor at the top of the page.

9. Close your browser.

You created internal links to the named anchors next to the Spa Services headings and to the top of the spa page. You then previewed the page in your browser and tested each link.

Create, Modify, and
COPY A SPRY MENU BAR

What You'll Do

In this lesson, you will create a menu bar on the spa page that can be used to link to each main page in the website. The menu bar will have five elements: Home, About Us, Cafe, Spa, and Activities. You will also copy the new menu bar to other pages in the website. On each page you will modify the appropriate element state to reflect the current page.

Creating a Spry Menu Bar

To make your website more visually appealing, you can add special effects. For example, you can create a menu bar with rollover images rather than plain text links. One way to do this is to insert a Spry menu bar. A **Spry menu bar** is one of the pre-set widgets available in Dreamweaver that creates a dynamic, user-friendly menu bar that is easy to insert and customize. A **widget** is a piece of code that allows a user to interact with a program, such as clicking a menu item to open a page. Other examples of widgets are interactive buttons, pop-up windows, and progress indicators. **Spry**, or **Spry framework**, is open source code developed by Adobe Systems to help designers quickly incorporate dynamic content on their web pages. To insert a Spry menu bar, click Insert on the Application bar (Win) or Menu bar (Mac), point to Layout Objects, then click Spry Menu Bar. The Insert Spry Menu Bar dialog box appears. You use this dialog box to specify the appearance of the menu bar and each link, called an **item**. When you first insert a Spry menu bar, Dreamweaver automatically assigns it four menu items, some of which have submenu items. It you want your menu

bar to display a different number of menu items and submenu items, you can add new ones and delete the ones you do not need.

You can add special effects for menu bar items by changing the characteristics for each item's state. A **state** is the condition of the item relative to the mouse pointer. You can create a rollover effect for each menu item by using different background and text colors for each state, to represent how the menu item appears when the users move their mouse over it or away from it. You can also create special effects for web page links. The NASA website shown in Figure 13 contains a menu bar that uses rollovers and also contains images that link to featured items in the website.

When you insert a menu bar on a web page using the Insert Spry Menu Bar command, Dreamweaver automatically adds JavaScript code and CSS styles to the page to make the interaction work with the menu bar items. Dreamweaver also creates a SpryAssets folder and adds it to the site root folder. The SpryAssets folder stores the newly created files that make the menu function correctly in the browser. When a viewer views a web page with one of these menu bars, the files that run the menu functions are stored on the user's, or client's, computer.

There are other methods that you can use to create a menu bar with images, such as an image map. You will learn about image maps in Lesson 4.

Copying and Modifying a Menu Bar

After you create a menu bar, you can save time by copying and pasting it to the other main pages in your site. Make sure you place the menu bar in the same position on each page. This practice ensures that the menu bar will look the same on each page, making it much easier for viewers to navigate to all the pages in your website. If you are even one line or one pixel off, the menu bar will appear to "jump" as it changes position from page to page.

Figure 13 *NASA website*

Menu bar with rollovers

Navigation links with rollovers

Images serving as links

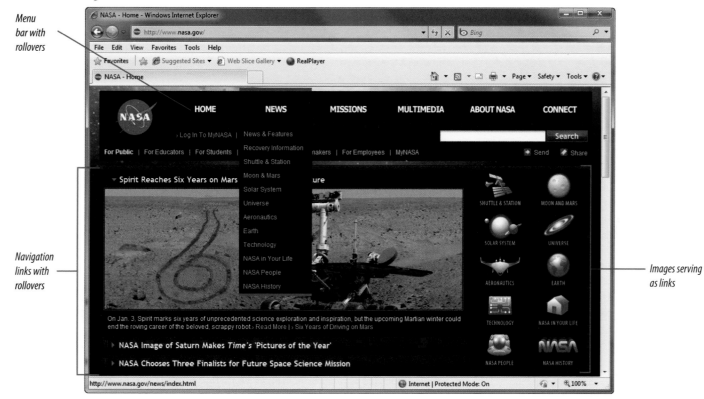

NASA website – www.nasa.gov

Create a Spry menu bar

1. Select the banner on the spa page, press the **right arrow key,** then press **[Shift][Enter]** (Win) or **[Shift][return]** (Mac) to enter a line break after the banner.

   The insertion point is now positioned between the banner and the horizontal rule.

2. Click the **Spry** category on the Insert panel, then click **Spry Menu Bar**.

   TIP The Spry Menu Bar button is also in the Layout category on the Insert panel.

3. Click to select the **Horizontal** layout on the Spry Menu Bar dialog box to specify that the menu bar be placed horizontally on the page, if necessary, as shown in Figure 14, then click **OK**.

   Your new menu bar containing four items appears under the banner. The menu bar is selected and the Property inspector shows its properties. Each button contains placeholder text, such as Item 1.

   TIP If your horizontal rule is not below the menu bar, click to the right of the menu bar, then press [Shift] [Enter] (Win) or [Shift] [return] (Mac) to create another line break, then point to the menu bar and click its Spry MenuBar: MenuBar1 label to select it again. If your menu bar wraps to two lines, this will correct itself when viewed in the browser. Your screen size may not be quite large enough to see all page elements in the Dreamweaver workspace.

4. Type **Menu** in the Menu Bar text box on the Property inspector, then notice that Item 1 is selected in the Item column (first column on the left) in the Property inspector.

   (continued)

Figure 14 *Spry Menu Bar dialog box*

Horizontal
layout option

Inserting a Fireworks Menu Bar

Another option for adding a menu bar to your page is to create a menu bar in Fireworks and import it onto an open page in Dreamweaver. To do this you first create a menu bar in Fireworks and export the file to a Dreamweaver site folder. This file contains the HTML code that defines the menu bar properties. Next, open the page you want to insert it on in Dreamweaver, then use the Insert, Image objects, Fireworks HTML command to place the HTML code on the page. You can also use Dreamweaver to import rollover images and buttons created in Fireworks.

Figure 15 *Property inspector with Menu Bar properties*

Menu Bar   Home menu   Item 1.1   Click Remove menu item   Text text box
text box   item   button to delete submenu
                              Item 1.1

Figure 16 *Home item on the Menu Bar*

Submenu items have   Click Browse for File button
been deleted   to select index.html

Figure 17 *The Spry Menu Bar on the spa page*

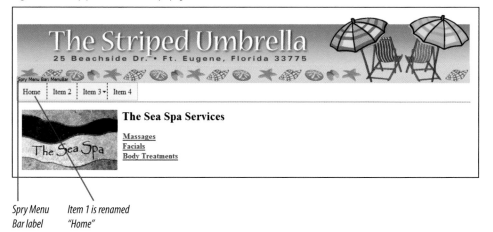

Spry Menu   Item 1 is renamed
Bar label   "Home"

Now you are ready to rename the first item, delete its submenu items, and choose the file you want this item to link to.

5. Select Item 1 in the Text text box on the right side of the Property inspector, type **Home**, select Item 1.1 in the first submenu column (second column) in the Property inspector, as shown in Figure 15, then click the **Remove menu item** button — above the first submenu column to delete the submenu item 1.1.

6. Click the **Remove menu item button** — two more times to delete the submenu Item 1.2 and Item 1.3.

   The three submenu items would have appeared as a drop-down menu under the Home menu, but the Home link does not require a submenu, so they can be deleted.

   TIP You can add submenu items by clicking the Add menu item button ✚.

7. Click the **Browse for File** button 🗁 next to the Link text box on the Property inspector, then double-click the file **index.html**.

   The Home item is now linked to the index page.

8. Click to place the insertion point to the right of the menu bar, enter a line break, compare your screen to Figures 16 and 17, save your file, then click **OK** to close the Copy Dependent Files dialog box.

   A SpryAssets folder and six files are copied to the site root folder. These are dependent files necessary for the SpryMenu bar. If you don't see them listed, refresh the Files panel.

You used the Insert Spry Menu Bar dialog box to create a menu bar for the spa page and renamed the first item "Home." You deleted the placeholder submenu items under the Home menu item.

Add items to a menu bar

1. Click the Spry Menu Bar tab to select it, click **Item 2** in the first column under the Home item in the Property inspector, then replace the text "Item 2" in the Text text box with **About Us**.

2. Click the **Browse for File button** 📁 next to the Link text box, then double-click **about_us.html** in the site folder to link the About Us menu item to the about_us page.

3. Repeat Steps 1 and 2 to rename Item 3 **Sand Crab Cafe** and link it to the cafe.html page.

4. Delete each submenu item under the Sand Crab Cafe item, clicking **OK** to close the warning box that asks if you want to also remove the submenus, or children menus, under the submenu item.

5. Repeat Steps 1 and 2 to rename Item 4 **The Sea Spa** and link it to the spa.html page.

6. With The Sea Spa menu item selected in the Property inspector, click the **Add menu item button** ➕ above the first column to add an additional menu item, then name it **Activities** and link it to the activities.html page.

7. With the Activities menu item selected, click the **Add menu item button** ➕ above the *second* column to add a submenu item named **Cruises** and link it to the cruises.html page.

8. Repeat Step 7 to add another submenu item named **Fishing** that is linked to the fishing.html page.

9. Save your work, then compare your screen to Figure 18.

TIP If you accidentally created menus, instead of submenus, for Cruises and Fishing, delete them and try again, selecting Activities and adding the items to the second column.

You completed The Striped Umbrella menu bar by adding four more elements to it, each of which contains links to four pages in the site. You then added two submenus under the Activities menu item.

Figure 18 *Menu bar with all menu and submenu items in place*

Menu item names

Submenu item names

Link to fishing page

Submenu items

Figure 19 *Settings for .ulMenuBarHorizontal rule*

Font-size = 14   Font-family = Trebuchet MS,   Apply button   Select ul.MenuBarHorizontal rule
                         Arial, Helvetica, sans-serif

Use CSS to format a menu bar

1. Click the **All button** [All] in the CSS Styles panel if necessary, click the **plus sign** next to SpryMenuBarHorizontal.css in the CSS Styles panel, select the rule ul.MenuBarHorizontal, then click the **Edit Rule** button ✎ to open the CSS Rule Definition for ul.MenuBarHorizontal in SpryMenuBarHorizontal.css dialog box.

   The SpryMenuBarHorizontal.css style sheet, which was automatically created when you inserted the Spry menu bar, contains properties for the way the menu items will appear in the browser. In that style sheet, the ul.MenuBarHorizontal rule determines the global settings, including the font family, font size, and font alignment, for all the menu and submenu items, regardless of whether the mouse is placed over them.

   TIP You can also use the Properties pane in the CSS Styles panel to modify style properties.

2. Click the **Type** Category, click the **Font-family** list arrow, then click **Trebuchet MS, Arial, Helvetica, sans-serif.**

3. Click the **Font-size** list arrow, click **14**, click the **Font size unit of measure list arrow**, then click **px** as shown in Figure 19, then click **OK**.

   Next, you set the width and height for each menu item button by modifying the ul.MenuBarHorizontal li rule. Recall that the <li> tag is HTML code for list item. The Spry menu bar is built using unordered list items for each menu item. This rule sets the properties that determine the appearance of the menu items.

(continued)

4. Select the rule **ul.MenuBarHorizontal li** in the CSS Styles panel, then click the **Edit Rule** button ✎ to open the CSS Rule Definition for ul.MenuBarHorizontal li in SpryMenuBarHorizontal.css dialog box

5. Click the **Box** Category, click the **Width** text box, replace the current value with **190**, click the **Width unit of measure list arrow,** then click **px** if necessary.

TIP To calculate the width for each menu item, divide the number of pixels of the banner width by the number of menu items.

6. Click the **Height** text box, type **25**, click the **Height unit of measure list arrow**, click **px** if necessary, then compare your screen to Figure 20.

   The menu bar items are now spread across the page to equal the width of the banner. Next, you'll edit the rule that defines the properties, and therefore the appearance, of each menu item button when the mouse is not positioned over them.

7. In the Block category, change the Text-align value to **center**, then click **OK**.

8. Click the **ul.MenuBarHorizontal a** rule in the CSS Styles panel, then click the **Edit Rule** button ✎ to open the CSS Rule Definition for ul.MenuBarHorizontal a in SpryMenuBarHorizontal.css dialog box

TIP If you want to understand the function of each rule in the SpryMenuBarHorizontal.css style sheet, click the SpryMenuBarHorizontal.css button in the Related files toolbar and take a few minutes to read the comments for each rule. Click the Show Design View button to return to Design view.

(continued)

Figure 20 *Add properties to the ul.MenuBarHorizontal li rule*

Box Category   Height = 25 px   Width = 190 px

Figure 21 *Setting the menu item appearance when the mouse will not be over them*

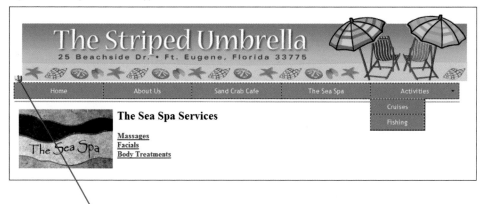

The named anchor icon may keep the menu bar from lining up right under the banner, but will appear correctly in the browser

9. Click the **Type** Category, type **#FFF** in the Color text box, click the **Background** Category, type **#09C** in the Background-color text box, then click **OK**

   The menu items will have a blue background with white text when the mouse is not positioned over them, as shown in Figure 21. Now you are ready to set the colors the menu bar items will be when users point to (hover their mouse over) a menu item that has submenus (in this case, the Activities button). This rule is the longest one in the style sheet, because it includes properties that determine the appearance of menu items with submenus open. It determines their appearance when the mouse is hovering over them and when the mouse is not hovering over them.

10. Click the longest rule name,
   ul.MenuBarHorizontal a.MenuBarItemHover,
   ul.MenuBarHorizontal a.MenuBarItemSubmenuHover,
   ul.MenuBarHorizontal a.MenuBarSubmenuVisible in the CSS Styles panel, then click the **Edit Rule** button ✎ to open the rule definition dialog box, click the **Type** Category, type **#630** in the Color text box, click the **Background** category, type **#FC9** in the Background-color text box, then click **OK**.

   The menu and submenu items will have a sand background with brown text when the mouse is positioned over them in the browser.

   TIP To locate the longest rule, place your mouse over each rule name to see the extended names. You will quickly spot the longest name!

   (continued)

11. Save all files, preview your page in the browser, compare your screen to Figure 22, test each link to ensure that each works correctly, then close the browser.

The cafe, cruises, and fishing pages are still blank. You will have to use your Back button after you click these links to return to pages with content.

TIP If you see a message asking if you want to allow blocked content, click yes. The code from the Spry menu bar is being flagged by your Internet security settings.

As you roll the mouse over each menu and submenu item, the background and text colors change.

You edited the properties of four rules in the style sheet that sets the appearance of the menu bar on the page. The appearance of each menu and submenu item changes when the mouse is placed over it.

Figure 22 *Spa page in the browser with the mouse over the About Us item*

Menu item appearance when the mouse is placed over it

Figure 23 *Selecting the menu bar on the spa page*

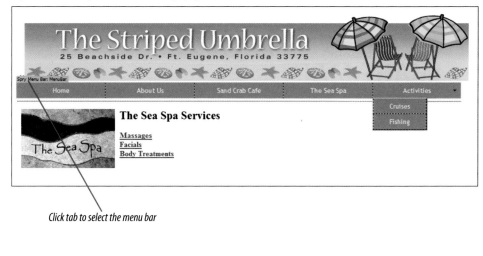

Click tab to select the menu bar

Figure 24 *The activities page with the completed menu bar*

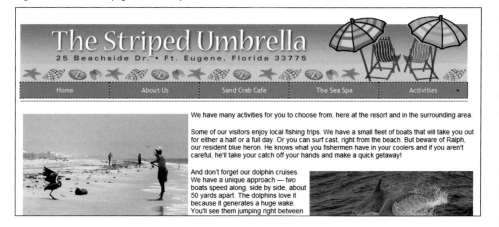

Copy and paste a menu bar

1. Click the **Spry Menu Bar: Menu tab** above the top left corner of the menu bar, as shown in Figure 23.

2. Click **Edit** on the Application bar (Win) or Menu bar (Mac), then click **Copy**.

3. Double-click **activities.html** on the Files panel to open the activities page.

4. Select the original menu bar on the page, click **Edit** on the Application bar (Win) or Menu bar (Mac), click **Paste**, click to the right of the menu bar, enter a line break, compare your screen to Figure 24, then save the page.

5. Open the index page, delete the existing menu bar, paste the new menu bar, add 2 line breaks between the menu bar and horizontal rule if necessary, then save and close the index page.

6. Open the about_us page, replace the existing menu bar with the new menu bar, add 2 line breaks between the menu bar and horizontal rule if necessary, then save your work.

7. Preview the about_us page in your browser, test the menu bar on the home, about_us, spa, and activities pages, then close your browser.

   The cafe, cruises, and fishing pages are blank at this point, so use the Back button when you test those links to return to the page you were viewing previously.

8. Close all open pages except the activities page.

You copied the menu bar on the spa page to three additional pages in The Striped Umbrella website.

Create an
IMAGE MAP

What You'll Do

In this lesson, you will create an image map by placing a hotspot on The Striped Umbrella banner on the activities page that will link to the home page.

Another way to create links for web pages is to combine them with images by creating an image map. An **image map** is an image that has one or more hotspots placed on top of it. A **hotspot** is a clickable area on an image that, when the user clicks it, links to a different location on the page or to another web page. For example, see the National Park Service website shown in Figure 25. When you click a state, you link to information about national parks in that state. You can create hotspots by first selecting the image on which you want to place a hotspot, and then using one of the hotspot tools in the Property inspector to define its shape.

There are several ways to create image maps to make them user-friendly and accessible. One way is to be sure to include alternate text for each hotspot. Another is to draw the hotspot boundaries a little larger than they need to be to cover the area you want to set as a link. This allows viewers a little leeway when they place their mouse over the hotspot by creating a larger target area for them. Always assign a unique name for each image map.

Dreamweaver hotspot tools make creating image maps a snap. In addition to the Rectangle Hotspot Tool, you can create any shape you need using the Circle Hotspot Tool and the Polygon Hotspot Tool. For instance, on a map of the United States, you can draw an outline around each state with the Polygon Hotspot Tool and then make each state "clickable." You can easily change and rearrange hotspots on the image. Use the Pointer Hotspot Tool to select the hotspot you would like to edit. You can drag one of the hotspot selector handles to change its size or shape. You can also move the hotspot by dragging it to a new position on the image. It is a good idea to limit the number of complex hotspots in an image because the code can become too lengthy for the page to download in a reasonable length of time.

Figure 25 *Viewing an image map on the National Park Service website*

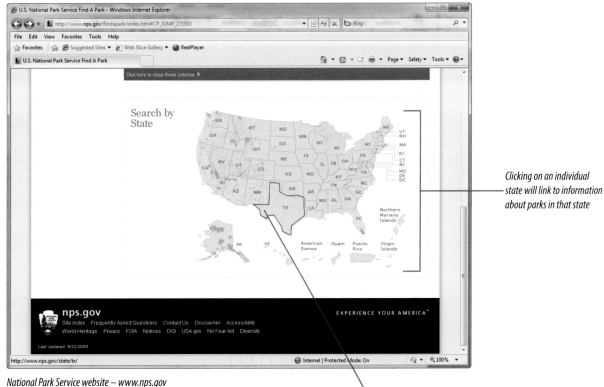

Clicking on an individual state will link to information about parks in that state

National Park Service website – www.nps.gov

Pointing to the Texas image and holding down the mouse button causes the hotspot border to be visible.

Create an image map

1. Select the banner on the activities page, then click the **Rectangle Hotspot Tool** □ in the Property inspector.

2. Drag the **pointer** to create a rectangle over the text "The Striped Umbrella" in the banner, as shown in Figure 26, then click **OK** to close the dialog box that reminds you to supply alternate text for the hotspot.

TIP To adjust the shape of a hotspot, click the Pointer Hotspot Tool ▲ in the Property inspector, then drag a sizing handle on the hotspot.

3. Drag the **Point to File icon** ⊕ next to the Link text box in the Property inspector to the index.html file on the Files panel to link the hotspot to the index page.

4. Replace the default text "Map" with **home** in the Map text box in the Property inspector to give the image map a unique name.

5. Click the **Target list arrow** in the Property inspector, then click **_top**.

   When the hotspot is clicked, the _top option causes the home page to open in the same window. See Table 2 for an explanation of the four target options.

   (continued)

Figure 26 *Properties of the hotspot on the banner*

Hotspot

Rectangle Hotspot Tool

TABLE 2: OPTIONS IN THE TARGET LIST	
Target	**Result**
_blank	Displays the destination page in a separate browser window
_parent	Displays the destination page in the parent frameset (replaces the frameset)
_self	Displays the destination page in the same frame or window
_top	Displays the destination page in the whole browser window

Working with Links and Navigation

Figure 27 *Hotspot properties*

Image map name   Target for hotspot   Link to index page   Alternate text for the hotspot

Figure 28 *Preview of the image map on the activities page in the browser*

Pointing finger indicates pointer is over the link hotspot

6. Type **Link to home page** in the Alt text box in the Property inspector, as shown in Figure 27, then press **[Enter]** (Win) or **[return]** (Mac).

    You may see a small space between the banner and the menu bar, but it will display correctly in the browser.

7. Save your work, preview the page in your browser, then place the pointer over the image map.

    As you place the pointer over the hotspot, the pointer turns to a pointing finger, indicating that it is a link, as shown in Figure 28.

8. Click the link to test it, close the browser, then close all open pages.

You created an image map on the banner of the activities page using the Rectangle Hotspot Tool. You then linked the hotspot to the home page.

Manage
WEBSITE LINKS

What You'll Do

In this lesson, you will use some Dreamweaver reporting features to check The Striped Umbrella website for broken links and orphaned files.

Managing Website Links

Because the World Wide Web changes constantly, websites might be up one day and down the next. If a website changes server locations or goes down due to technical difficulties or a power failure, the links to it become broken. Broken links, like misspelled words on a web page, indicate that a website is not being maintained diligently.

Checking links to make sure they work is an ongoing and crucial task you need to perform on a regular basis. You must check external links manually by reviewing your website in a browser and clicking each link to make sure it works correctly. The Check Links Sitewide feature is a helpful tool for managing internal links. You can use it to check your entire website for the total number of links and the number of links that are broken, external, or orphaned, and then view the results in the Link Checker panel. **Orphaned files** are files that are not linked to any pages in the website.

DESIGNTIP

Using Good Navigation Design

As you work on the navigation structure for a website, you should try to limit the number of links on each page to no more than is necessary. Too many links may confuse visitors to your website. You should also design links so that viewers can reach the information they want within a few clicks. If finding information takes more than three or four clicks, the viewer may become discouraged or "lost" in the site. It's a good idea to provide visual clues on each page to let viewers know where they are, much like a "You are here" marker on a store directory at the mall, or a breadcrumbs trail. A **breadcrumbs trail** is a list of links that provides a path from the initial page you opened in a website to the page that you are currently viewing. Many websites provide a list of all the site's pages, called a **site map**. A site map is similar to an index. It lets viewers see how the information is divided between the pages and helps them locate the information they need quickly.

Figure 29 *Link Checker panel displaying external links*

List of external links   *Show list arrow*

Figure 30 *Link Checker panel displaying no orphaned files*

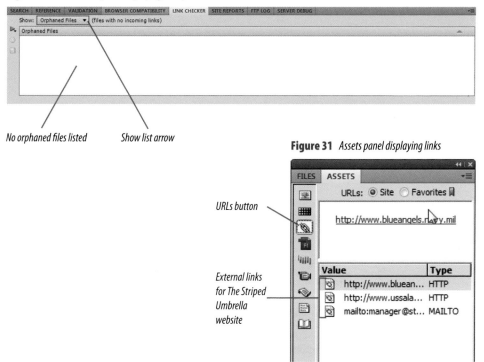

No orphaned files listed   *Show list arrow*

Figure 31 *Assets panel displaying links*

URLs button

External links for The Striped Umbrella website

Manage website links

1. Click **Site** on the Application bar (Win) or Menu bar (Mac), point to **Advanced**, then click **Recreate Site Cache**.

2. Click **Site** on the Application bar (Win) or Menu bar (Mac), then click **Check Links Sitewide**.

   The Results tab group opens, with the Link Checker panel in front. By default, the Link Checker panel initially lists any broken internal links found in the website. The Striped Umbrella website has no broken links.

3. Click the **Show list arrow** in the Link Checker panel, click **External Links**, then compare your screen to Figure 29.

4. Click the **Show list arrow**, then click **Orphaned Files** to view the orphaned files in the Link Checker panel, as shown in Figure 30.

   The Striped Umbrella website has no orphaned files.

5. Right-click (Win) or Control-click (Mac) in an empty area of the Results tab group title bar, then click **Close tab group**.

6. Display the Assets panel if necessary, then click the **URLs button** 🐌 in the Assets panel if necessary to display the list of links in the website.

   The Assets panel displays the external links used in the website, as shown in Figure 31.

You used the Link Checker panel to check for broken links, external links, and orphaned files in The Striped Umbrella website. You also viewed the external links in the Assets panel.

Update a page

1. Open dw5_2.html from the drive and folder where you store your Data Files, then save it as **fishing.html** in the striped_umbrella site root folder, overwriting the existing fishing page, but not updating the links.

2. Click the broken link image placeholder, click the **Browse for File icon** next to the Src text box in the Property inspector, then browse to the drive and folder where you store your Data Files, open the assets folder, then select the file heron_small.jpg to copy the file to the striped_umbrella assets folder.

3. Deselect the image placeholder and the image appears, as shown in Figure 32.

   The text is automatically updated with the body_text style. The code was already in place on the page linking su_styles.css to the file. The Spry menu bar was also updated with the internal styles already in place for the menu bar.

4. Save and close the fishing page, then close the dw5_2.html page.

5. Open dw5_3.html from the drive and folder where you store your Data Files, then save it as **cruises.html** in the striped_umbrella site root folder, overwriting the existing cruises page, but not updating the links.

6. Click the broken link graphic placeholder, click the **Browse for File icon** next to the Src text box in the Property inspector, then browse to the drive and folder where you store your Data Files, open the assets folder, then select the file boats.jpg to copy the file to the striped_umbrella assets folder.

(continued)

Figure 32 *Fishing page updated*

As you can see, Ralph scores occasionally. We certainly don't encourage you to feed Ralph. We feel it is important to intrude as little as possible with our wild friends and their diets. Just don't be surprised if you see him roaming the beach trying to blend in with the other fishermen.

Testing Your Website Against the Wireframe

Another test you should be running regularly is a comparison of how your developing website pages are meeting the specifications of your wireframe prototype. Compare each completed page against its corresponding wireframe to make sure that all page elements have been placed in their proper locations on the page. Verify that all specified links have been included and test them to make sure that they work correctly. You might also consider hiring site-usability testers to test your site navigation. A site usability test provides impartial feedback on how intuitive and user-friendly your site is to use.

Figure 33 *Cruises page updated*

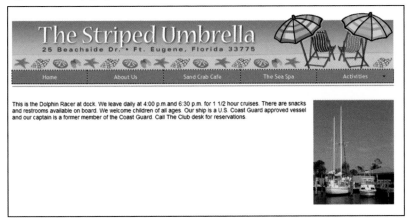

Deselect the image placeholder and the image will appear as shown in Figure 33.

The text is automatically updated with the body_text style. The code was already in place on the page linking su_styles.css to the file. The Spry menu bar was also updated as the internal styles were applied.

8. Save your work if necessary.

9. Preview each page in the browser, close the browser, then close all open pages.

You added content to two previously blank pages in the website and previewed each page to check for consistent layout.

POWER USER SHORTCUTS	
To do this:	**Use this shortcut:**
Close a file	[Ctrl][W] (Win) or ⌘ [W] (Mac)
Close all files	[Ctrl][Shift][W] (Win) (Win) or ⌘ [Shift][W] (Mac)
Print code	[Ctrl][P] (Win) or ⌘ [P] (Mac)
Check page links	[Shift][F8] (Win) or [fn][shift][F8] (Mac)
Undo	[Ctrl][Z], [Alt][BkSp] (Win) or ⌘ [Z], [option][delete] (Mac)
Redo	[Ctrl][Y], [Ctrl][Shift][Z] (Win) or ⌘ [Y], ⌘ [Shift][Z] (Mac)
Refresh Design view	[F5]
Hide all visual aids	[Ctrl][Shift][I] (Win) or ⌘ [Shift][I] (Mac)
Insert a named anchor	[Ctrl][Alt][A] (Win) or ⌘ [option][A] (Mac)
Make a link	[Ctrl][L] (Win) or ⌘ [L] (Mac)
Remove a link	[Ctrl][Shift][L] (Win) or ⌘ [Shift][L] (Mac)
Check links sitewide	[Ctrl][F8] (Win) or [fn] ⌘ [F8] (Mac)
Show Files tab group	[F8] (Win) or ⌘ [Shift][F] (Mac)

Incorporate Web 2.0
TECHNOLOGY

What You'll Do

In this lesson, you will explore some of the Web 2.0 applications that can be used to engage website viewers.

What Exactly is Web 2.0?

The term **Web 2.0** describes the recent evolution of web applications that facilitate and promote information sharing among Internet users. These applications not only reside on computers, but on cell phones, in cars, on portable GPS devices, and in game devices. **GPS (Global Positioning System)** devices are used to track your position through a global satellite navigation system, and are popular to use for driving directions, hiking, and map making. Web 2.0 applications do not simply display information for viewers to read passively; they allow viewers to actively contribute to the content.

RSS feeds are another easy way to share information with viewers. **RSS** stands for **Really Simple Syndication**. Websites use **RSS feeds** to distribute news stories, information about upcoming events, and announcements. Web users can subscribe to RSS feeds to receive regular releases of information from a site. Users can download and play these digitally broadcasted files called **podcasts (Programming On Demand)** using devices such as computers or MP3 players. Many news organizations and educational institutions publish both audio

and video podcasts. Video podcasts are referred to as **vodcasts** or **vidcasts**.

Web 2.0 also includes the ever-increasing use of social networking. **Social networking** refers to any web-based service that facilitates social interaction among users. Examples of social networking sites include **Facebook** and **MySpace**. These sites allow users to set up profile pages and post information on them for others to view. Facebook and MySpace pages often contain lots of text, images, and videos. To fully view and post to an individual's page, you must be accepted by that person as a "friend," which lets you control who has access to your page content.

A wiki is another example of a Web 2.0 application. The term **wiki** (named for the Hawaiian word for "quick") refers to a site where a user can use simple editing tools to contribute and edit the page content in a site. A good example is **Wikipedia**, an online encyclopedia. Wikipedia allows viewers to post new information and edit existing information on any topic. Although people have different opinions about the academic integrity of the information on Wikipedia, Wikipedia is still a rich source of information. Proponents argue that its many active and vigilant users maintain its information integrity.

Blogs (web logs) are another example of a Web 2.0 application. **Blogs** are websites where the website owner regularly posts commentaries and opinions on various topics. Content can consist of text, video, or images. Viewers can respond to the postings and read postings by other viewers. **Twitter** is a website where viewers can post short messages, called **tweets**. Twitter is considered a blog or a micro blog, because you cannot enter more than 140 characters in each post. To use Twitter, you must first join by creating a free account. Then you can post messages about yourself, "follow" other people's tweets, and invite others to "follow" you. It is a quick and easy way to exchange short bits of information and keep in touch with friends.

There are many video sharing applications such as Skype, Google Video Chat, and YouTube. **Skype** and **Google Video Chat** are free applications that you use to communicate live with other people through video conferencing, using a high-speed Internet connection and a web camera, called a **web cam**. You can also use Skype or Google Chat to make regular telephone calls over the Internet. **YouTube** is a website where you can upload and share videos. To upload videos, you need to register with the site. But you don't need to register if you only want to view videos others have posted.

So how do these various Web 2.0 components relate to the process of creating websites? Most websites today engage their viewers or "users" of their site in one or more of these applications. The Peace Corps website, shown in Figure 34, has links to Facebook, Twitter, YouTube, and RSS Feeds. When you are designing a site, one of the decisions you must make is not if, but how you will incorporate Web 2.0 technology to fully engage your viewers. To incorporate one of these applications into your website, first register to set up an account on the social networking site, then place a link on one of your site's web pages (usually the home page) that links to the social networking site and opens your page. For example, if your Twitter account is located at www.twitter.com/your_name, add this link to your home page using the Twitter logo as a graphic link. You can download social networking sites' logos from their websites. You can also enter plain text links if you prefer. Some applications specify how you should refer to and link to their site.

Using the applications that are a part of Web 2.0 with your website can bring your site from simply presenting information on pages for viewers to read to facilitating a compelling dialog with your viewers. They will no longer be just "viewers," but active participants.

Figure 34 *Viewing social networking links on the Peace Corps website*

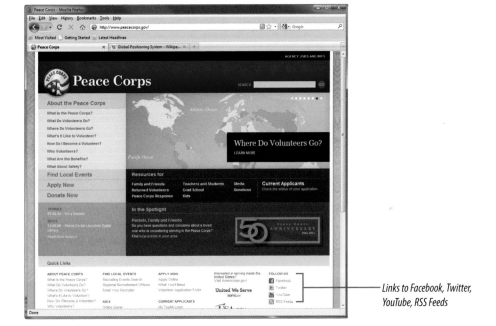

Links to Facebook, Twitter, YouTube, RSS Feeds

Peace Corps website – www.peacecorps.gov

Create external and internal links.

1. Open the Blooms & Bulbs website.
2. Open dw5_4.html from the drive and folder where you store your Data Files, then save it as **newsletter.html** in the Blooms & Bulbs website, overwriting the existing file without updating the links. Close dw5_4.html.
3. Verify that the banner path is set correctly to the assets folder in the website and correct it, if it is not, then browse to the drive and folder where you store your Chapter 5 Data Files assets folder and copy the grass, trees, and plants broken images to the site assets folder.
4. Scroll to the bottom of the page, then link the National Gardening Association text to http://www.garden.org.
5. Link the Organic Gardening text to http://www.organicgardening.com.
6. Link the Southern Living text to http://www.southernliving.com/southern.
7. Save the file, then preview the page in your browser, verifying that each link works correctly.
8. Close your browser, then return to the newsletter page in Dreamweaver.
9. Scroll to the paragraph about gardening issues, select the gardening tips text in the last sentence, then link the selected text to the tips.html file in the blooms site root folder.
10. Enter the page title **Gardening Matters,** then save your work.
11. Open the plants page and add a new paragraph to the bottom of the page: **In addition to these marvelous roses, we have many annuals, perennials, and water plants that have just arrived**.

12. Apply the paragraph_text rule to the new paragraph if necessary.
13. Link the "annuals" text to the annuals.html file, link the "perennials" text to the perennials.html file, and the "water plants" text to the water_plants.html file.
14. Save your work, test the links in your browser, then close your browser. (*Hint*: These pages do not have content yet, but are serving as placeholders.)

Create internal links to named anchors.

1. Show Invisible Elements, if necessary.
2. Click the Common category in the Insert panel.
3. Switch to the newsletter page, then insert a named anchor in front of the Grass heading named **grass**.
4. Insert a named anchor in front of the Trees heading named **trees**.
5. Insert a named anchor in front of the Plants heading named **plants**.
6. Use the Point to File icon in the Property inspector to create a link from the word "grass" in the Gardening Issues paragraph to the anchor named "grass."
7. Create a link from the word "trees" in the Gardening Issues paragraph to the anchor named "trees."
8. Create a link from the word "plants" in the Gardening Issues paragraph to the anchor named "plants."
9. Save your work, view the page in your browser, test all the links to make sure they work, then close your browser.

Create, modify, and copy a Spry menu bar.

1. Select the banner, press the right arrow key, enter a line break, click the Spry category on the Insert panel, then click Spry Menu Bar to insert a horizontal Spry menu bar at the top of the newsletter page below the banner and

above the horizontal rule. Add two paragraph breaks to separate the menu bar from the horizontal rule.
2. Select Item 1 in the Property inspector if necessary, remove the three submenu items under Item 1, type **Home** in the Text text box, then browse to link the Home menu item to the **index.html** file.
3. Select Item 2, then replace the text name with **Newsletter** and link it to the **newsletter.html** file.
4. Repeat Step 3 to rename Item 3 **Plants** and link it to the **plants.html** file.
5. Select the submenu Item 3.1, rename it **Annuals**, link it to the **annuals.html** file, then delete the submenu items under the Annuals submenu item.
6. Repeat Step 5 to rename Item 3.2 **Perennials**, then link it to the **perennials.html** file.
7. Repeat Step 5 to rename Item 3.3 **Water Plants**, then link it to the **water_plants.html** file.
8. Select the Item 4 menu item, rename it **Tips**, then link it to the **tips.html** file.
9. Add a new menu item named **Workshops**, then link it to the **workshops.html** file.
10. Edit the ul.MenuBarHorizontal rule to change the Font-family to **Verdana, Geneva, sans-serif**, and the Font-size to **14 px**.
11. Edit the u.MenuBarHorizontal li to set the Text-align to **Center**, the Box width to **190 px** and the Box height to **25 px**.
12. Edit the ul.MenuBarHorizontal a rule to change the Type color to **#030** and the background color to **#99F**.
13. Edit the ul.MenuBarHorizontal a.MenuBarItemHover, ul.MenuBarHorizontal a.MenuBarItemSubmenuHover, ul.MenuBarHorizontal a.MenuBarSubmenuVisible

rule to change the Type color to **#FFC** and the background color to **#030**.

14. Save all files, copying dependent files, test each link in the browser to make sure the links work correctly, then close the browser.

15. Select and copy the menu bar, then open the home page.

16 Delete the current menu bar on the home page, and paste the new menu bar under the banner, but above the horizontal rule. Remove any space between the banner and menu bar if necessary. (*Hint*: If you see space between the banner and the menu bar, go to Code view and check to make sure that you used a <br /> tag between the banner and the menu bar.)

17. Save and close the page, switch to the plants page, then copy the menu bar to the page in the same position under the banner.

18. Add a horizontal rule under the banner, then save and close the page. (*Hint*: Make sure the spacing between the banner and the horizontal rule is the same as on the index and newsletter pages. Use Code view to check for any differences and correct them.)

19. Open the tips page and repeat Steps 17 and 18 to add the menu bar and horizontal rule to the page.

20. Save and close the tips page.

21. Save your work, preview all the pages in your browser, compare your newsletter page to Figure 35, test all the links, then close your browser.

Figure 35 *Completed Skills Review*

Gardening Matters

Welcome, fellow gardeners. My name is Cosie Simmons, the owner of blooms & bulbs. My passion has always been my gardens. Ever since I was a small child, I was drawn to my back yard where all varieties of beautiful plants flourished. A lush carpet of thick grass bordered with graceful beds is truly a haven for all living creatures. With proper planning and care, your gardens will draw a variety of birds and butterflies and become a great pleasure to you.

Gardening Issues

There are several areas to concentrate on when formulating your landscaping plans. One is your grass. Another is the number and variety of trees you plant. The third is the combination of plants you select. All of these decisions should be considered in relation to the climate in your area. Be sure and check out our gardening tips before you begin work.

Grass

Lawn experts classify grass into two categories: cool-climate and warm-climate. The northern half of the United States would be considered cool-climate. Examples of cool-climate grass are Kentucky bluegrass and ryegrass. Bermuda grass is a warm-climate grass. Before planting grass, whether by seeding, sodding, sprigging, or plugging, the ground must be properly prepared. The soil should be tested for any nutritional deficiencies and cultivated. Come by or call to make arrangements to have your soil tested. When selecting a lawn, avoid letting personal preferences and the cost of establishment be the overriding factors. Ask yourself these questions: What type of lawn are you expecting? What level of maintenance are you willing to provide? What are the site limitations?

Trees

Before you plant trees, you should evaluate your purpose. Are you interested in shade, privacy, or color? Do you want to attract wildlife? Attract birds? Create a shady play area? Your purpose will determine what variety of tree you should plant. Of course, you also need to consider your climate and available space. Shape is especially important in selecting trees for ornamental and shade purposes. Abundant shade comes from tall trees with long spreading or weeping branches. Ornamental trees will not provide abundant shade. We carry many varieties of trees and are happy to help you make your selections to fit your purpose.

Plants

There are so many types of plants available that it can become overwhelming. Do you want border plants, shrubs, ground covers, annuals, perennials, vegetables, fruits, vines, or bulbs? In reality, a combination of several of these works well. Design aspects such as balance, flow, definition of space and focalization should be considered. Annuals provide brilliant bursts of color in the garden. By selecting flowers carefully to fit the conditions of the site, it is possible to have a beautiful display without an unnecessary amount of work. Annuals are also great as fresh and dry cut flowers. Perennials can greatly improve the quality of your landscape. Perennials have come and gone in popularity, but today are as popular as ever. Water plants are also quite popular now. We will be happy to help you sort out your preferences and select a harmonious combination of plants for you.

Further Research

These are some of my favorite gardening links. Take the time to browse through some of the information they offer, then give me a call at (555) 248-0806 or e-mail me at cosie@blooms&bulbs.com.

National Gardening Association
Organic Gardening
Southern Living

Create an image map.

1. Use the Rectangle Hotspot Tool to draw an image map across the name "Blooms & Bulbs", on the banner on the newsletter page that will link to the home page.

2. Name the image map **home** and set the target to _top.

3. Add the alternate text **Link to home page**, save the page, then preview it in the browser to test the link. (*Hint*: You might see a small space between the banner and menu bar, but it will display correctly in the browser.)

4. Close the page.

Manage website links.

1. Use the Link Checker panel to view and fix broken links and orphaned files in the blooms & bulbs website. (*Hint*: Remember to recreate your site cache if you see any. That usually fixes them.)

2. Open dw5_5.html from the drive and folder where you store your Data Files, then save it as **annuals. html**, replacing the original file. Do not update links, but save the file coleus.jpg from the Chapter 5 Data Files assets folder in the assets folder of the website. Close dw5_5.html.

3. Repeat Step 2 using dw5_6.html to replace perennials.html, saving the ruby_grass.jpg file in the assets folder and using dw5_7.html to replace water_plants.html, saving the water_lily.jpg file in the assets folder.

4. Save your work, then close all open pages.

Use Figure 36 as a guide to continue your work on the TripSmart website, which you began in Project Builder 1 in Chapter 1 and developed in the previous chapters. You have been asked to create a new page for the website that lists helpful links for customers. You will also add content to the destinations, china, and spain pages.

1. Open the TripSmart website.
2. Open dw5_8.html from the drive and folder where you store your Data Files, then save it as **services.html** in the TripSmart website root folder, replacing the existing file and not updating links. Close dw5_8.html.
3. Verify that the TripSmart banner is in the assets folder of the site root folder.
4. Apply the paragraph_text rule to the paragraphs of text and the list_heading rule to the four main paragraph headings.

5. Create named anchors named **reservations**, **outfitters**, **tours**, and **links** in front of the respective headings on the page, then link each named anchor to "Reservations," "Travel Outfitters," "Escorted Tours," and "Helpful Links in Travel Planning" in the first paragraph.
6. Link the text "on-line catalog" in the Travel Outfitters paragraph to the catalog.html page.
7. Link the text "CNN Travel Channel" under the heading Helpful Links in Travel Planning to http://www.cnn.com/TRAVEL.
8. Repeat Step 7 to create links for the rest of the websites listed:
   U.S. Department of State: http://travel.state.gov
   Yahoo! Currency Converter:
   http://finance.yahoo.com/currency-converter
   The Weather Channel: http://www.weather.com

9. Save the services page, preview the page in the browser to test each link, then open the index page.
10. Replace the menu bar on the home page with a horizontal Spry menu bar, using formatting of your choice. The menu bar should contain the following elements: **Home**, **Catalog**, **Services**, **Tours**, and **Newsletter**. Figure 36 shows one example of a possible menu bar. Create two submenu items for the china and spain pages under the tours menu item, then delete all other submenu items.
11. Test the menu bar links in the browser, then close the browser and correct any errors you find.
12. Copy the menu bar, then place it on each completed page of the website.
13. Save each page, then check for broken links and orphaned files.

14. Open the tours.html file in your site root folder and save it as **spain.html**, overwriting the existing file, then close the file.

15. Open dw5_9.html from the drive and folder where you store your Data Files, then save it as **china.html**, overwriting the existing file. Do not update links, but save the warriors.jpg and great_wall.jpg files from the data files folder in the assets folder of the website, then save and close the file. Close dw5_9.html.

16. Open dw5_10.html from the driver and folder where you store your Data Files, then save the file as **tours.html**, overwriting the existing file. Do not update links, but save the panda.jpg and gaudi_dragon.jpg files from the data files folder in the assets folder of the website. Close dw5_10.html.

17. Link the text "Spain" in the second sentence of the first paragraph on the tours page to the spain.html file.

18. Link the text "China" in the first sentence in the second paragraph on the tours page to the china.html file.

19. Save all files and preview them in the browser, checking to see that all links work and all pages have a consistent look.

20. Compare your tours page to Figure 36, close your browser, then close all open pages.

Figure 36 *Sample Project Builder 1*

You are continuing your work on the Carolyne's Creations website, which you started in Project Builder 2 in Chapter 1 and developed in the previous chapters. Chef Carolyne has asked you to create a page describing her cooking classes offered every month. You will create the content for that page and individual pages describing the children's classes and the adult classes. Refer to Figures 37, 38, and 39 for possible solutions.

1. Open the Carolyne's Creations website.
2. Open dw5_11.html from the drive and folder where you store your Data Files, save it as **classes.html** in the site root folder of the Carolyne's Creations website, overwriting the existing file and not updating the links. Close dw5_11.html.
3. Select the broken banner image, browse to the data files folder, then select the new banner, cc_banner_with_text.jpg, then verify that it was saved to the site assets folder. Notice that styles have already been applied to the page text, the data file included a relative link to the style sheet.
4. Select the text "adults' class" in the last paragraph, then link it to the adults.html page. (*Hint*: This page has not been developed yet.)
5. Select the text "children's class" in the last paragraph and link it to the children.html page. (*Hint*: This page has not been developed yet.)
6. Create an e-mail link from the text "Sign me up!" that links to **carolyne@carolynescreations.com**
7. Insert the image file fish.jpg from the assets folder where you store your Data Files at the beginning of

the second paragraph, add appropriate alternate text, then choose your own alignment and formatting settings.
8. Add the image file children_cooking.jpg from the assets folder where you store your Data Files at the beginning of the third paragraph, then choose your own alignment and formatting settings.
9. Create hot spots on the black bar at the bottom of the new banner that was imported with the data file, cc_banner_with_text.jpg, that link each menu

item with its corresponding page. (*Hint*: Remember to include alternate text and a target for each menu item.)
10. Compare your work to Figure 37 for a possible solution, copy the new banner, then save and close the file.
11. Open dw5_12.html from the drive and folder where you store your Data Files, then save it as **children.html**, overwriting the existing file and not updating links. Save the image cookies_oven.jpg from the assets folder where you store your Data Files to the website assets folder. Close dw5_12.html.

Figure 37 *Completed Project Builder 2*

Cooking Classes are fun!

Chef Carolyne loves to offer a fun and relaxing cooking school each month in her newly refurbished kitchen. She teaches an **adult class** on the fourth Saturday of each month from 6:00 to 8:00 pm. Each class will learn to cook a complete dinner and then enjoy the meal at the end of the class with a wonderful wine pairing. This is a great chance to get together with friends for a fun evening.

 Chef Caroline also teaches a **children's class** on the second Tuesday of each month from 4:00 to 5:30 pm. Our young chefs will learn to cook two dishes that will accompany a full meal served at 5:30 pm. Kids aged 5–8 years accompanied by an adult are welcome. We also host small birthday parties where we put the guests to work baking and decorating the cake! Call for times and prices.

We offer several special adult classes throughout the year. The **Valentine Chocolate Extravaganza** is a particular favorite. You will learn to dip strawberries, make truffles, and bake a sinful Triple Chocolate Dare You Torte. We also host the **Not So Traditional Thanksgiving** class and the **Super Bowl Snacks** class each year with rave reviews. Watch the Web site for details!

Prices are $40.00 for each adults' class and $15.00 for each children's class. Sign up for classes by calling 555-963-8271 or by emailing us: Sign me up!

See what's cooking this month for the adults' class and children's class.

12. Paste your new banner on the children.html page, replacing the previous banner, compare your work to Figure 38 for a possible solution, then save and close the file.

13. Repeat Steps 11 and 12 to open the dw5_13.html file and save it as **adults.html**, overwriting the existing file and saving the files dumplings1.jpg, dumplings2.jpg, and dumplings3.jpg from the folder where you save your data files in the assets folder, then use alignment settings of your choice. Replace the banner with your new banner, compare your work to Figure 39 for a possible solution, then save and close the files.

14. Open the index page and delete the menu bar and horizontal rule.

15. Replace the banner with your new banner.

16. Copy the new banner with the menu bar to each completed page, deleting existing menu bars and banners.

17. Save all the pages, then check for broken links and orphaned files. You will see one orphaned file, the original version of the banner. Delete this file.

18. Apply a rule from the style sheet to any text that is not formatted with a style.

19. Preview all the pages in your browser, check to make sure the links work correctly, close your browser, then close all open pages.

Figure 38 *Completed Project Builder 2*

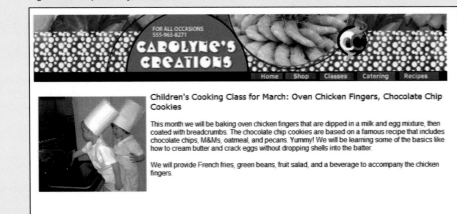

Figure 39 *Completed Project Builder 2*

Sherrill Simmons is a university English instructor. She would like to find new ways to engage her students through her university website. She decided to explore incorporating podcasts, FaceBook, and Twitter. She spends several hours looking at other websites to help her get started.

1. Connect to the Internet, then navigate to the Shiloh Museum website pictured in Figure 40 at www.springdalear.gov/shiloh. This site won the Media & Technology Committee of the American Association of Museums 2008 Bronze MUSE Award for one of their vodcasts. There have been over 25,000 downloads since they began offering podcasting in May of 2006. Their iTunes U content has been downloaded over 14,000 times since June of 2008.
2. How do you think podcasting has enhanced the museum website?

Figure 40 *Design Project*

Shiloh Museum website used with permission from the Shiloh Museum of Ozark History, Springdale, Arkansas – www.springdalear.gov/shiloh

3. Navigate to the U.S. Navy website at
   www.navy.mil, as shown in Figure 41.
4. Describe how the Navy is using Web 2.0 technology.
   What do you think their purpose might be for
   incorporating each application?
5. Which Web 2.0 applications would you include on
   your website if you were Sherrill?
6. Describe how you would use each one of them to
   engage her students.

Figure 41 *Design Project*

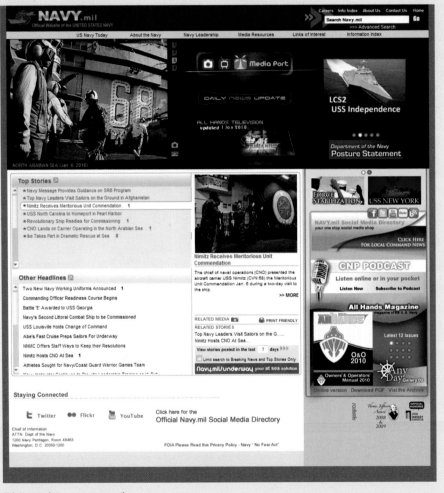

U.S. Navy website – www.navy.mil

In this assignment, you will continue to work on the website that you started in Chapter 1 and developed in the previous chapters.

You will continue building your website by designing and completing a page with a menu bar. After creating the menu bar, you will copy it to each completed page in the website. In addition to the menu bar, you will add several external links and several internal links to other pages as well as to named anchors. You will also link text to a named anchor. After you complete this work, you will check for broken links and orphaned files.

1. Consult your wireframe to decide which page or pages you would like to develop in this chapter. Decide how to design and where to place the menu bar, named anchors, and any additional page elements you decide to use. Decide which reports should be run on the website to check for accuracy.

2. Research websites that could be included on one or more of your pages as external links of interest to your viewers. Create a list of the external links you want to use. Using your wireframe as a guide, decide where each external link should be placed in the site.

3. Add the external links to existing pages or create any additional pages that contain external links.

4. Create named anchors for key locations on the page, such as the top of the page, then link appropriate text on the page to them.

5. Decide on a design for a menu bar that will be used on all pages of the website.

6. Create the menu bar and copy it to all finished pages on the website.

7. Think of a good place to incorporate an image map, then add it to a page.

8. Decide on at least one Web 2.0 application that you might like to incorporate and determine how and on what page they would be included.

9. Use the Link Checker panel to check for broken links and orphaned files.

10. Use the checklist in Figure 42 to make sure your website is complete, save your work, then close all open pages.

Figure 42 *Portfilio Project checklist*

> **Website Checklist**
> 1. Do all pages have a page title?
> 2. Does the home page have a description and keywords?
> 3. Does the home page contain contact information?
> 4. Does every page in the website have consistent navigation links?
> 5. Does the home page have a last updated statement that will automatically update when the page is saved?
> 6. Do all paths for links and images work correctly?
> 7. Do all images have alternate text?
> 8. Are all colors web-safe?
> 9. Are there any unnecessary files that you can delete from the assets folder?
> 10. Is there a style sheet with at least two styles?
> 11. Did you apply the style sheet to all page content?
> 12. Does at least one page contain links to one or more named anchors?
> 13. Does at least one page contain either a named anchor or an internal link?
> 14. Do all pages look good using at least two different browsers?
> 15. Did you incorporate at least one Web 2.0 technology?

CHAPTER **6** POSITIONING OBJECTS
WITH CSS AND TABLES

1. Create a page using CSS layouts
2. Add content to CSS layout blocks
3. Edit content in CSS layout blocks
4. Create a table
5. Resize, split, and merge cells
6. Insert and align images in table cells
7. Insert text and format cell content

CHAPTER 6 POSITIONING OBJECTS
WITH CSS AND TABLES

Introduction

To create an organized, attractive web page, you need precise control of the position of page elements. CSS page layouts can provide this control. **CSS page layouts** consist of containers formatted with CSS into which you place web page content. These containers can accommodate images, blocks of text, Flash movies, or any other page element. The appearance and position of the containers are set through the use of HTML tags known as **div tags**. Using div tags, you can position elements next to each other as well as on top of each other.

Another option for controlling the placement of page elements is through the use of tables. **Tables** are placeholders made up of small boxes called **cells**, into which you can insert text and graphics. Cells in a table are arranged horizontally in **rows** and vertically in **columns**. Using tables on a web page gives you control over the placement of each object on the page, similar to the way CSS blocks control placement. In this chapter, you use a predesigned CSS page layout with div tags to place text and graphics on a page. You then add a table to one of the CSS blocks on the page.

Using Div Tags Versus Tables for Page Layout

Div tags and tables both enable you to control the appearance of content in your web pages. Unlike tables, div tags allow you to stack your information, allowing for one piece of information to be visible at a time. Tables are static, which makes it difficult to change them quickly as need arises. Div tags can be dynamic, changing in response to variables such as a mouse click. You can create dynamic div tags using JavaScript **behaviors**, simple action scripts that let you incorporate interactivity by modifying content based on variables like user actions. For example, you could add a JavaScript behavior to text in a div tag to make it become larger or smaller when the pointer is over it.

There has been much discussion since the inception of CSS about which tool is better—CSS layouts or table layouts. Both have advantages and disadvantages, but designers tend to prefer CSS layouts for page design and tables for placing lists of data. In practice, many designers use a combination of both tools, choosing the tool that is the better suited to the current design challenge.

Create a Page
USING CSS LAYOUTS

What You'll Do

Insert_logo (100 x 90)	
Link one	**Instructions**
Link two	
Link three	Be aware that the CSS for these layouts is heavily commented. If you do most of your
Link four	work in Design view, have a peek at the code to get tips on working with the CSS for the fixed layouts.
The above links demonstrate a basic navigational structure using an unordered list styled with CSS. Use this as a starting point and modify the properties to produce your own unique look. If	**Clearing Method**
	Because all the columns are floated, this layout uses a clear:both declaration in the .footer rule. This clearing technique forces the .container to understand where the columns end in order to show any borders or background colors you place on the .container. If your design requires you to remove the .footer from the .container, you'll need to use a different clearing method. The most reliable will be to add a <br class="clearfloat" /> or <div class="clearfloat"></div> after your final floated column (but before the .container closes). This will have the same clearing effect.
	Logo Replacement

In this lesson, you will create a new page based on a predesigned CSS layout to become the new cafe page for the website.

Understanding Div Tags

Div tags are HTML tags that define how areas of content are formatted or positioned on a web page. For example, when you center an image on a page or inside a table cell, Dreamweaver automatically inserts a div tag in the HTML code. In addition to using div tags to align page elements, designers also use them to assign background colors or borders to content blocks, CSS styles to text, and many other properties to page elements. One type of div tag is an AP div tag. AP stands for absolutely positioned, so an **AP div tag** creates a container that has a specified, fixed position on a web page. The resulting container that an AP div tag creates on a page is called an **AP element**.

NEW Using CSS Page Layouts

Because building a web page using div tags can be tedious for beginning designers, Dreamweaver CS5 provides 16 predesigned layouts that are available in the New Document dialog box, as shown in Figure 1. This is a change from CS4, which offered 32 predesigned layouts. Although there are fewer choices, the layouts are better designed with more helpful information for the designer in the placeholder text. You can use these layouts to create web pages with attractive and consistent layouts. There are two types of CSS layouts: fixed and liquid. A **fixed layout** expresses all widths in pixels and remains the same size regardless of the size of the browser window. A **liquid layout** expresses all widths in percents and changes size depending on the size of the browser window.

Predesigned CSS layouts contain div tags that control the placement of page content using placeholders. Each div tag container has placeholder text that appears until you replace it with your own content. Because div tags use CSS for formatting and positioning, designers prefer them for building web page content. When you use the Dreamweaver predesigned layouts, you can be sure that your pages will appear with a consistent design when viewed in all browsers. Once you become more comfortable using the predesigned layouts, you will begin to build your own CSS-based pages from scratch.

QUICK TIP

The Browser Compatibility Check feature flags code that might present a CSS rendering issue in some browsers by underlining code in green. To see this feature, switch to Code view and browse through the code.

Viewing CSS Layout Blocks

As you design your page layouts using div tags, you can use Design view to see and adjust CSS content blocks. In Design view, text or images that have been aligned or positioned using div tags have a dotted border, as shown in Figure 2. In the Visual Aids list on the View menu, you can display selected features of div tag elements, such as CSS Layout Backgrounds, CSS Layout Box Model, CSS Layout Outlines, and AP Element Outlines. The CSS Layout Box Model displays the padding and margins of a block element.

Figure 1 *New Document dialog box*

Preview of selected layout

Predesigned div tag layouts

Figure 2 *CSS blocks defined by dotted borders*

Dotted-line borders surround the CSS content blocks

Using Tracing Images for Page Design

Another design option for creating a page layout is the use of a tracing image. A **tracing image** is an image that is placed in the background of a document. By adjusting the transparency (opacity) of the image, you can then use it to create page elements on top of it, similar to the way you would place a piece of tracing paper on top of a drawing and trace over it. To insert a tracing image, Use the Modify, Page Properties, Tracing Image dialog box or the View, Tracing Image, Load command. Browse to select the image you want to use for the tracing image, then adjust the transparency as desired. The tracing image serves as a guide or pattern, and is not needed after you complete your design.

Create a page with a CSS layout

1. Open The Striped Umbrella website.

2. Click **File** on the Application bar (Win) or Menu bar (Mac), click **New**, verify that Blank Page is highlighted in the first column of the New Document dialog box, click **HTML** in the Page Type column if necessary, then click **2 column fixed, left sidebar, header and footer** in the Layout column, as shown in Figure 3.

   A fixed layout remains the same size regardless of the size of the browser window.

3. Click the **Attach Style Sheet button** in the bottom-right corner of the dialog box, then click **Browse** in the Attach External Style Sheet dialog box.

   The Select Style Sheet File dialog box opens.

4. Select the su_styles.css external style sheet in the Select Style Sheet File dialog box, then click **OK** to close the Select Style Sheet File dialog box.

   If a dialog box opens reminding you to save your file before a document-relative path can be created, click OK to close the dialog box.

   NEW Dreamweaver CS5 also has a new option in the New Document dialog box to enable **InContext Editing**, or **ICE**. This feature sets up editable regions on web pages that users can make changes to while the page is being viewed in a browser.

5. Verify that the Link option is selected in the Attach External Style Sheet dialog box, then click **OK** to close the Attach External Style Sheet dialog box.

   (continued)

Figure 3 *Predesigned CSS layout selected for new page*

Blank Page option selected

HTML page type

2 column fixed, left sidebar, header and footer Layout

Attach Style Sheet button

Using XML and XSL to Create and Format Web Page Content

You can also create information containers on your web pages using XML, Extensible Markup Language, and XSL, Extensible Stylesheet Language. **XML** is a language that you use to structure blocks of information, similar to HTML. It uses similar opening and closing tags and the nested tag structure that HTML documents use. However, XML tags do not determine how the information is formatted, which is handled using XSL. **XSL** is similar to CSS; the XSL stylesheet information formats the containers created by XML. Once the XML structure and XSL styles are in place, **XSLT, Extensible Stylesheet Language Transformations**, interprets the code in the XSL file to transform an XML document, much like style sheet files transform HTML files from an unformatted file to a formatted file. XSL transformations can be written as client-side or server-side transformations. To create XML documents, use the XML page type in the New Document dialog box.

Figure 4 *The su_styles.css file is attached to the new page*

Enable InContext   Create button   su_styles.css
Editing option   file is attached

Figure 5 *New page based on CSS layout*

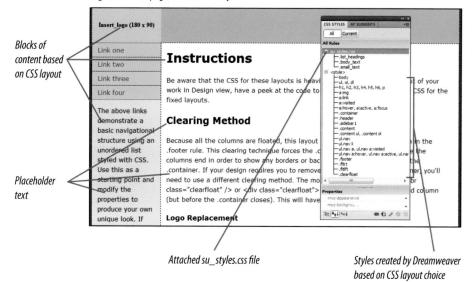

Blocks of
content based
on CSS layout

Placeholder
text

Attached su_styles.css file   Styles created by Dreamweaver
                                      based on CSS layout choice

The su_styles.css file is attached to the new page, as shown in Figure 4. The next time you create a new page, the style sheet will be selected automatically.

6. Click **Create** in the New Document dialog box, open the CSS Styles panel if necessary, then expand the style sheets if necessary.

A new two-column HTML page opens based on the predesigned CSS layout you chose. It has CSS content blocks arranged in two columns, one as a sidebar on the left side, as well as a header and footer. Placeholder text appears in each of the blocks, as shown in Figure 5. You will replace the text with content for The Striped Umbrella website. The CSS blocks each have a different color background to help you see how the blocks are arranged on the page. This new page will replace the blank cafe page.

Notice that you have two sets of styles now: the external style sheet su_styles.css; and the internal style sheet <style> containing the styles that define the CSS blocks on the page.

You created a new page based on a predesigned CSS layout with the attached style sheet for The Striped Umbrella website.

Add Content to CSS
LAYOUT BLOCKS

What You'll Do

In this lesson, you will copy the menu bar and banner from the index page and paste it into the new page. You will then overwrite the old cafe page with this new one.

Understanding Div Tag Content

As you learned in Lesson 1, a div tag is a container that formats blocks of information on a web page, such as background colors, images, links, tables, and text. Once you have created a layout using div tags, you are ready to insert and format text. As with formatting text on a web page, you should use CSS styles to format text in div tags. You can also add all other properties such as text indents, padding, margins, and background color using CSS styles.

In this lesson, you use a CSS layout to create a new cafe page that arranges the content into defined areas on the page.

Using Dreamweaver New Page Options

You can use either the Welcome Screen or the New command on the File menu to create several different types of pages. The predesigned CSS page layouts make it easy to design accessible web pages based on Cascading Style Sheets, without an advanced level of expertise in writing HTML code. Predesigned templates are another time-saving feature that promotes consistency across a website. Framesets, CSS Style Sheets, and Sample Pages are a few of the other options. It is worth the time to explore each category to understand what is available to you as a designer. Once you have selected a page layout, you can customize it to suit your client's content and design needs.

Understanding CSS Code

When you view a page based on a predesigned CSS layout in Code view, you see helpful comments that explain sections of the code, as shown in Figure 6. The comments are in gray to differentiate them from the rest of the code. The CSS rules reside in the Head section. The code for a CSS container begins with the class, or name of the rule, and is followed by rule properties. For example, in Figure 6, the container described on line 45 begins with the class name .container, which is followed by three properties and values: width: 960 px; background: #FFF; and margin: 0 auto. The code that links the rules to the content is located in the body section.

Figure 6 *Code view for CSS in head content*

Comments in gray text

Class name preceded by period

Rule properties

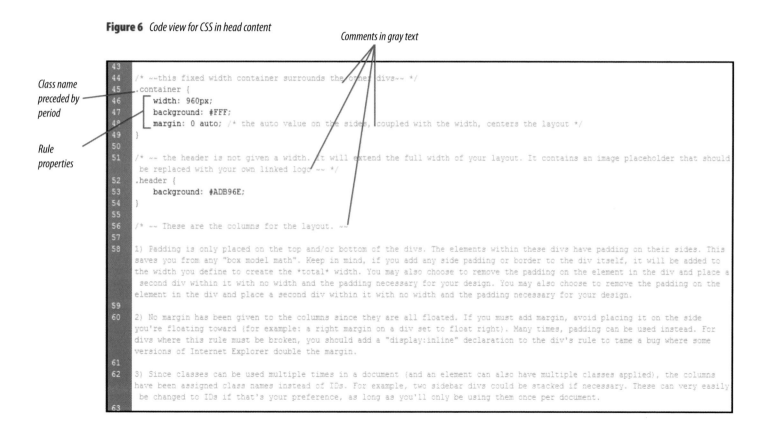

```
43
44   /* ~~this fixed width container surrounds the other divs~~ */
45   .container {
46       width: 960px;
47       background: #FFF;
48       margin: 0 auto; /* the auto value on the sides, coupled with the width, centers the layout */
49   }
50
51   /* ~~ the header is not given a width. It will extend the full width of your layout. It contains an image placeholder that should
     be replaced with your own linked logo ~~ */
52   .header {
53       background: #ADB96E;
54   }
55
56   /* ~~ These are the columns for the layout. ~~
57
58   1) Padding is only placed on the top and/or bottom of the divs. The elements within these divs have padding on their sides. This
     saves you from any "box model math". Keep in mind, if you add any side padding or border to the div itself, it will be added to
     the width you define to create the *total* width. You may also choose to remove the padding on the element in the div and place a
     second div within it with no width and the padding necessary for your design. You may also choose to remove the padding on the
     element in the div and place a second div within it with no width and the padding necessary for your design.
59
60   2) No margin has been given to the columns since they are all floated. If you must add margin, avoid placing it on the side
     you're floating toward (for example: a right margin on a div set to float right). Many times, padding can be used instead. For
     divs where this rule must be broken, you should add a "display:inline" declaration to the div's rule to tame a bug where some
     versions of Internet Explorer double the margin.
61
62   3) Since classes can be used multiple times in a document (and an element can also have multiple classes applied), the columns
     have been assigned class names instead of IDs. For example, two sidebar divs could be stacked if necessary. These can very easily
     be changed to IDs if that's your preference, as long as you'll only be using them once per document.
63
```

Add text to a CSS container

1. Select all content between the Header and Footer in the main section (content block) of the page through the last paragraph describing the backgrounds, as shown in Figure 7, then press **[Delete]**.

TIP Before you delete placeholder text, it is a good idea to read it. The placeholder text has helpful information that helps you to understand the way the page is designed. It gives you pointers for the best way to replace the placeholder text with your text.

2. Change to the HTML Property inspector, click the **Format list arrow**, then click **Paragraph** if necessary.

   If you had a remaining H1 tag in the block, this removes it.

3. Import the file cafe.doc from the drive and folder where you store your Data Files (Win) or copy and paste it (Mac) in the blank container, then delete any extra space after the paragraph.

(continued)

Figure 7 *Text selected in content block of new page*

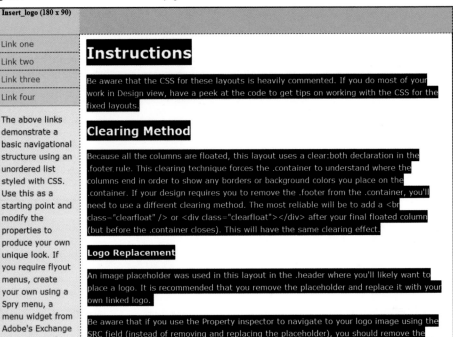

Figure 8 *Text selected in sidebar1 block in Code view*

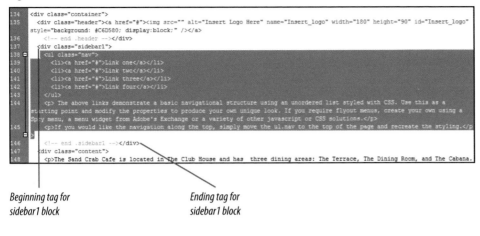

```
134  <div class="container">
135    <div class="header"><a href="#"><img src="" alt="Insert Logo Here" name="Insert_logo" width="180" height="90" id="Insert_logo"
       style="background: #C6D580; display:block;" /></a>
136    <!-- end .header --></div>
137    <div class="sidebar1">
138      <ul class="nav">
139        <li><a href="#">Link one</a></li>
140        <li><a href="#">Link two</a></li>
141        <li><a href="#">Link three</a></li>
142        <li><a href="#">Link four</a></li>
143      </ul>
144      <p> The above links demonstrate a basic navigational structure using an unordered list styled with CSS. Use this as a
       starting point and modify the properties to produce your own unique look. If you require flyout menus, create your own using a
       Spry menu, a menu widget from Adobe's Exchange or a variety of other javascript or CSS solutions.</p>
145      <p>If you would like the navigation along the top, simply move the ul.nav to the top of the page and recreate the styling.</p
146      <!-- end .sidebar1 --></div>
147    <div class="content">
148      <p>The Sand Crab Cafe is located in The Club House and has  three dining areas: The Terrace, The Dining Room, and The Cabana.
```

Beginning tag for sidebar1 block

Ending tag for sidebar1 block

Figure 9 *Text pasted into Content block and typed into sidebar1 block and footer block of new page*

Insert_logo (180 x 90)	
Reservations are recommended for The Dining Room during the peak summer season.	The Sand Crab Cafe is located in The Club House and has three dining areas: The Terrace, The Dining Room, and The Cabana. The Terrace is outdoor dining with a breathtaking view of the Gulf, especially at sunset. The Dining Room is casual, indoor dining on the second floor. The Cabana is poolside.
Copyright 2002 - 2013 The Striped Umbrella	

4. Switch to Code view, select the code between the beginning and end of the <div class="sidebar1"> tag, as shown in Figure 8, then press **[Delete]** to delete the placeholder text.

   Be careful not to delete the beginning and ending div tags.

5. Return to Design view, then type **Reservations are recommended for The Dining Room during the peak summer season.** at the insertion point.

6. Delete all of the text in the footer block, then type **Copyright 2002 - 2013 The Striped Umbrella** as shown in Figure 9.

7. Save the page as **cafe.html** in The Striped Umbrella website, overwriting the existing file.

You imported text and typed text in the CSS blocks, replacing the placeholder text, then saved the page as the new cafe.html page.

Add images to a CSS block

1. Open the Striped Umbrella index page and copy both the banner and the menu bar.

TIP You might find it easier to copy the banner and menu bar separately. If you copy them together, you can use Code view to make sure you have selected all the necessary code.

2. Switch back to the cafe page, click the **placeholder logo image**, then paste the banner and menu bar into the header section of the page.

TIP Press [Ctrl][Tab] (Win) or ⌘ ['] (Mac) to switch between two open pages.

3. Close the index page.

4. Place the insertion point immediately in front of the word "Reservations", insert a paragraph break, press [↑], insert **cafe_logo.gif** from the drive and folder where you store your Data Files, then type **Sand Crab Cafe logo** as the alternate text in the Image Tag Accessibility Attributes dialog box.

5. Select the **crab logo** if necessary, press [←], then enter a line break in front of the logo.

6. Place the insertion point after the period after the word "poolside", insert a paragraph break, insert **cafe_photo.jpg** from the drive and folder where you store your Data Files, as shown in Figure 10, then type **Sand Crab Cafe photo** as the alternate text.

(continued)

Figure 10 *Images added to header, sidebar 1, and content blocks*

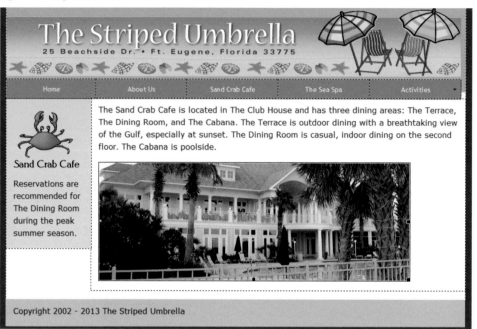

Figure 11 *Images placed on page*

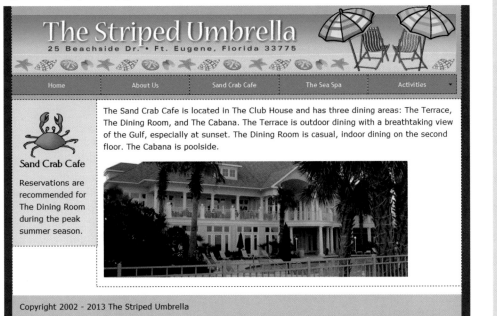

7. Deselect the image, click the **HTML Property inspector button** <> HTML if necessary to switch to the HTML Property inspector, then click to place the insertion point in the content CSS block above the cafe_photo image.

   Notice that the Class text box in the HTML Property inspector shows the class to be "content."

8. Click to place the insertion point in the sidebar1 and header blocks.

   The Property inspector displays the class rule assigned to each block.

TIP If you have difficulty placing the insertion point in the header block, select the banner, then press [←].

9. Select the menu bar, press [→], then enter two line breaks.

10. Save your file, not updating links if prompted, then compare your screen to Figure 11.

You copied the banner and menu bar from the index page, pasted it onto the new cafe page, then added the cafe logo and photo to the page.

Edit Content in CSS
LAYOUT BLOCKS

What You'll Do

In this lesson, you will center the two images you have added to the page. You will then view the div tag properties and edit the background colors. You will also change the body background color.

Editing Content in CSS Layout Blocks

It is unlikely that you will find a predesigned CSS page layout that is exactly what you have in mind for your website. However, once you have created a page with a predesigned CSS layout, it is easy to modify the individual style properties to change content formatting or placement to better fit your needs. For example, you can easily change the properties to fit the color scheme of your website.

If your CSS layout has both external and internal style sheets, you can change the rule properties the same way. Click the plus sign next to the style sheet name, if necessary, to see the rules listed in each section, as shown in Figure 12, and then select the rule you want to modify. The properties and values for the selected rule appear in the Properties pane, where you can modify them. You can use either style sheet or a combination of both style sheets to format the page content.

Figure 12 *Viewing the CSS Styles panel*

Styles for external style sheet

Styles for predesigned CSS layout

SpryMenuBarHorizontal.css styles

Figure 13 *Centering content in layout blocks*

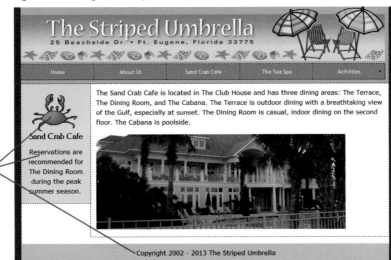

Logo and text
are centered
within CSS blocks

Edit block properties to center content

1. Place the insertion point in front of the cafe logo.

   Notice that the class rule for this block is named .sidebar1.

2. Click the **.sidebar1 rule** in the CSS Styles panel, click the **Edit Rule button** ✏, click the **Block category** in the CSS Rule definition for .sidebar1 dialog box, click the **Text-align list arrow**, click **center**, then click **OK**.

   The logo and text are now centered in the left sidebar.

3. Click to place the insertion point in the footer block at the bottom of the page.

   The class rule for this block is .footer.

4. Click the **.footer rule** in the CSS Styles panel, click the **Edit Rule button** ✏, click the **Block category** in the CSS Rule definition for .footer dialog box, click the **Text-align list arrow**, click **center**, then click **OK**.

5. Compare your screen to Figure 13. The content in both blocks should be centered within each block.

(continued)

Using the Adobe CSS Advisor for Cross-Browser Rendering Issues

You can use the **Browser Compatibility Check (BCC)** feature to check for problems in the HTML code for CSS features that may render differently in multiple browsers. It flags and rates code on three levels: an error that could cause a serious display problem; an error that probably won't cause a serious display problem; or a warning that it has found code that is unsupported, but won't cause a serious display problem. Each bug is linked to the CSS Advisor, a part of the Adobe website, that offers solutions for that particular bug and other helpful information for resolving any issues with your pages. To check for browser compatibility, click File, point to Check Page, and then click Browser Compatibility or click the Check browser compatibility button on the Document toolbar.

6. Move the pointer over the top of the content block (the block containing the cafe description and picture), click the **red border** to select the block (the border turns blue after it is selected), then move the pointer inside the block and hover until the floating window shown in Figure 14 appears.

The properties of the div tag are displayed in a floating window. The Property inspector displays the div tag class name.

TIP You can change the border color of div tags when the mouse is positioned over them in the Preferences dialog box. Select the Highlighting category, then click the Mouse-Over color box and select a different color. You can also disable highlighting by deselecting the Show check box for Mouse-Over.

7. Save your work.

You centered the logo, reservations text, and copyright statement. You also viewed the properties of the div tag.

Figure 14 *Viewing the class properties*

Border for div block

Properties of class

Class rule assigned to div tag

Viewing Options for CSS Layout Blocks

You can view your layout blocks in Design view in several ways. You can choose to show or hide outlines, temporarily assign different background colors to each individual layout block, or view the **CSS Layout Box Model** (padding, margins, borders, etc.) of a selected layout. To change these options, use the View/Visual Aids menu, and then select or deselect the CSS Layout Backgrounds, CSS Layout Box Model, or CSS Layout Outlines menu choice. You can also use the Visual Aids button on the Document toolbar.

Figure 15 *Setting the body Font-family value*

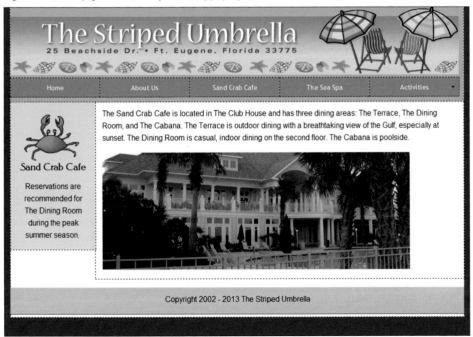

Figure 16 *The cafe page with edited body Font-family property*

Edit type properties in CSS layout blocks

1. Select the **body rule** in the CSS Styles panel, click the **Edit Rule button** , then click the **Type category** in the CSS Rule definition for body dialog box.

2. Click the **Font-family list arrow** in the CSS Rule definition for body dialog box, then click **Arial, Helvetica, sans-serif,** as shown in Figure 15.

3. Click **OK** to close the dialog box, compare your screen to Figure 16, then save your work.

The new font family property is applied to the text on the page. The Font-family property in the body rule determines the font family for all text on the page unless another one is specified for a different container, such as the footer, with an external style or a different internal style. The body is a **parent container**, a container with other tags falling between its opening and closing tags. **Child containers** are containers whose code resides inside a parent container. All HTML tags for page content are inside the body tags. So unless a different font is specified in a different container, each child container inherits the properties from the parent container.

You leave the rest of the type properties with the default CSS settings.

You changed the font-family property in the body that determines the font family for all text on the page.

Edit CSS layout block properties

1. Click the **header rule** in the CSS Styles panel to select it, then click the **Show only set properties button** ✱✱↓.

   The value for the background property is displayed in the Properties pane. The header block has background color of #ADB96E, a muted green color.

2. Click the **background text box** to place the insertion point, replace #ADB96E with **#FFF**, press **[Enter]** (Win) or **[return]** (Mac) and compare your screen to Figure 17.

   TIP You may have to adjust the size of your CSS Styles panel to view both panes.

   The header background color changes to white.

3. With the header rule still selected, click the **Edit Rule button** ✎, click the **Box category**, type **5** in the Top Margin text box, verify that the Same for all check box is checked, as shown in Figure 18, then click **OK**.

   You can edit rule properties in either the CSS Styles Properties pane or by opening the CSS Rule definition dialog box. With block margins set, the banner now appears more centered on the page.

   (continued)

Figure 17 *Editing the properties of the header rule*

Select the header rule

Change the background color to #FFF

Show only set properties button

Figure 18 *Editing the properties of the header rule*

Box category

Same for all check box

Change the Top Margin value to 5 px

Figure 19 *The four layout blocks now have a white background*

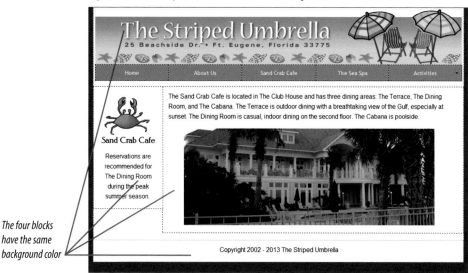

The four blocks have the same background color

4. Select the cafe photo image, click the **H space text box** in the Property inspector, type **40** to indent the image in the block, then press **[Tab]**.

5. Repeat Step 2 to change the background color in the footer rule to #FFF and the background color in the sidebar1 rule to #FFF.

   The header, footer, and sidebar1 background colors are now white.

TIP You only need to use the abbreviated hexadecimal color code, such as #FFF, when specifying colors. However, in the Dreamweaver predesigned CSS layouts, the color codes are shown with the full 6-character codes. Either code works. You can also specify colors by their names. For example, the color magenta can be specified as "magenta", #FF00FF or #F0F

6. Save your work, then compare your screen to Figure 19.

You changed the margin width of a CSS layout block, indented the cafe photo, then changed the background color of three CSS layout blocks to white.

Edit page properties

1. Select the **container rule** in the CSS Styles panel.

2. Open the CSS Rule definition for .container dialog box, then click the **Border category**.

   A border around the page sets it off from the extra space around it when it is viewed in a browser.

3. Click the **Top list arrow** in the Style column, then click **solid**.

4. Click the **Width list arrow** in the first text box in the Width column, then click **thin**.

5. Click the first **Color text box** in the Color column, type **#033**, press **Tab**, compare your screen to Figure 20, then click **OK**.

6. Click the **body rule** in the CSS Styles panel, then open the CSS Rule definition for body dialog box.

7. Click the **Background category**, change the Background-color text box to **#FFF**, then click **OK**.

(continued)

Figure 20 *Adding a border to the container*

Select the Border category

Border settings

Positioning Objects with CSS and Tables

Figure 21 *Viewing the cafe page in the browser*

Border appears around
page in browser

8. Use the Document toolbar to add the page title **The Striped Umbrella Sand Crab Cafe** to the page.

9. Save your work, preview the page in your browser, compare your screen to Figure 21, then close the browser.

TIP If you are using Internet Explorer and receive a warning message about the page being restricted from running scripts, click the yellow bar above the page, click Allow Blocked Content, then click Yes to close the dialog box.

You added a border to the page.

Create
A TABLE

What You'll Do

In this lesson, you will create a table for the cafe page in The Striped Umbrella website to provide a grid for the cafe hours.

Understanding Table Modes

Now that you have learned how CSS can act as containers to hold information in place on web pages, let's look at tables as another layout tool. Tables are great when you need a grid layout on a page, such as a list of items and prices. Some web pages are based entirely on tables for their page layouts and some pages contain tables inside CSS layout blocks. To create a table, click the Table button on the Insert panel. When the Layout category of the Insert panel is displayed, you can choose between two modes that give you different ways to view your table: Standard mode or Expanded Tables mode. Expanded Tables mode adds extra space between cells, which makes it easier to select small cells. Click the appropriate button on the Insert panel after selecting a table on the page.

Creating a Table

To create a table in Standard mode, click the Table button on the Insert panel to open the Table dialog box. Enter values for the number of rows and columns, the border thickness, table width, cell padding, and cell spacing. The **border** is the outline or frame around the table and the individual cells

and is measured in pixels. The table width can be specified in pixels or as a percentage. When the table width is specified as a percentage, the table width expands to fill up its container (the browser window, a CSS container, or another table). A table placed inside another table is called a **nested table**. Figure 22 shows a table set to 100% width of a CSS container. The content spreads across the entire width of the container. When the table width is specified in pixels, the table width stays the same, regardless of the size of the container. The table in Figure 23 is an example of the same table with a fixed width. Regardless of the size of the container, the table width remains constant. **Cell padding** is the distance between the cell content and the **cell walls**, the lines inside the cell borders. **Cell spacing** is the distance between cells.

Before you create a table, you should include in your wireframe a plan for it that shows its location on the page and the placement of text and graphics in its cells. You should also decide whether to include borders around the tables and cells. Setting the border value to 0 causes the table borders to appear invisible. Viewers will not realize that you used a table for the layout unless they look at the code. Figure 24 shows a sketch of the table you will create on The Striped Umbrella cafe page to organize the cafe hours.

Using Expanded Tables Mode

Expanded Tables mode is a feature that allows you to change to a table view with expanded table borders and temporary cell padding and cell spacing. This mode makes it easier to actually see how many rows and columns you have in your table. Often, especially after splitting empty cells, it is difficult to place the insertion point precisely in a table cell. Expanded Tables mode allows you to see each cell clearly. However, most of the time, you will want to work in Standard mode to maintain the WYSIWYG environment. **WYSIWYG** is the acronym for What You See Is What You Get, and means that your page should look the same in the browser as it does in the web editor.

Setting Table Accessibility Preferences

You can make a table more accessible to visually disabled viewers by adding a table caption and a table summary that screen readers can read. The table caption appears on the screen; the table summary does not. The table summary is added to the page code and is used by screen readers. Captions and summaries are especially useful for tables that are used for tabular data, rather than for page layout. **Table headers** are another way to provide accessibility. Table headers can be placed at the top or sides of a table containing data. They are automatically centered and bold and are used by screen readers to help viewers identify the table content. Table captions, summaries, and headers are all created in the Table dialog box.

Figure 22 *Table based on a 100% width spreads across the page*

Content spreads across
the available space

Figure 23 *Same table shown with a fixed-width*

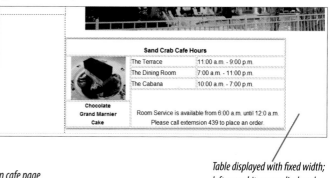

Table displayed with fixed width;
leftover white space displayed
outside table borders

Figure 24 *Sketch of table on cafe page*

Create a table

1. Click to place the insertion point to the right of the cafe photo.
2. Click **Table** in the Common category on the Insert panel.

   The Table dialog box opens.
3. Type **5** in the Rows text box, type **3** in the Columns text box, type **600** in the Table width text box, click the **Table width list arrow**, click **pixels** if necessary, type **0** in the Border thickness text box, then click the **Top** Header.

   TIP It is better to add more rows than you think you need when you create your table. After they are filled with content, it is easier to delete rows than to add rows if you decide later to split or merge cells in the table.

4. In the Summary text box, type **This table contains the cafe hours for each dining room.**, then compare your screen to Figure 25.
5. Click **OK**.

   The table appears on the page, but the table summary is not visible. The summary does not appear in the browser, but is read by screen readers.

   TIP To edit accessibility preferences for a table, switch to Code view to edit the code directly.

   (continued)

Figure 25 *Table dialog box*

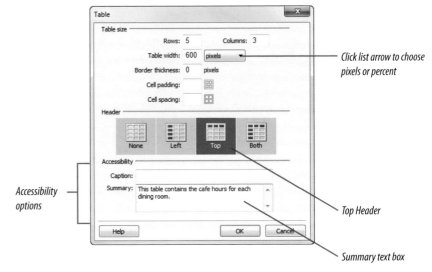

Click list arrow to choose pixels or percent

Accessibility options

Top Header

Summary text box

DESIGNTIP

Setting Table and Cell Widths when Using Tables for Page Layout

If you use a table to place all the text and graphics on a web page, it is wise to set the width of the table in pixels. This ensures that the table will remain one size and not resize itself proportionately if the browser window size is changed. For example, if the width of a table is set to slightly less than 800, the table will stretch across the whole width of a browser window set at a resolution of 800 x 600. The same table would be the same size on a screen set at 1024 x 768 and therefore would not stretch across the entire screen. Most designers use a resolution of 800 x 600 or higher. Be aware, however, that if you set the width of your table at 800 pixels, your table will be too wide to print the entire width of the page, and part of the right side of the page will be cut off. If you are designing a table layout for a page that you expect viewers to print, you should make your table narrower to fit on a printed page. If you set a table width as a percentage, however, the table would resize itself proportionately in any browser window, regardless of the resolution. Many designers prefer this option. You can also set each cell width as either a percentage of the table or as fixed pixels.

Figure 26 *Expanded Tables mode*

— *Expanded Tables mode button*

— *Standard mode button*

— *Click "exit" to return to Standard mode*

Expanded Tables mode displays more space between cells for easier editing

Figure 27 *Property inspector showing properties of selected table*

Selected table

Align list arrow

6. Click the **Insert panel list arrow**, click **Layout**, click the **Expanded Tables mode button** `Expanded`, click **OK** in the Getting Started in Expanded Tables Mode dialog box if necessary, then compare your screen to Figure 26.

   The Expanded Tables mode makes it easier to select and edit tables.

7. Click the **Standard mode button** `Standard` to return to Standard mode.

   TIP You can also return to Standard mode by clicking [exit] in the blue bar below the Document toolbar.

You created a table on the cafe page that will display the cafe hours with five rows and three columns and a width of 600 pixels. You used a top header and added a table summary that will be read by screen readers.

Set table properties

1. Select the table by clicking the **<table> tag** on the tag selector.

   TIP You can also select a table by moving the pointer slowly to the top or bottom edge of the table until you see the pointer change to a Table pointer ⊞, then clicking the table border.

2. Expand the Property inspector (if necessary) to display the current properties of the new table.

   The Property inspector displays information about the table only when the table is selected.

3. Click the **Align list arrow** in the Property inspector, then click **Left** to left-align the table in the content block on the page, as shown in Figure 27.

   The left-alignment formatting left-aligns the table inside the CSS container.

You selected and left-aligned the table.

Resize, Split,
AND MERGE CELLS

What You'll Do

In this lesson, you will set the width of the table cells to be split across the table in predetermined widths. You will then split one cell. You will also merge some cells to provide space for the table header.

Resizing Table Elements

You can resize the rows or columns of a table by dragging. To resize a table, row, or column, you must first select the table, then drag one of the table's three selection handles. To change all the columns in a table so that they are the same size, drag the middle-right selection handle. To resize the height of all rows simultaneously, drag the middle-bottom selection handle. To resize the entire table, drag the right-corner selection handle. To resize a row or column individually, drag the interior cell borders up, down, to the left, or to the right. You can also resize selected columns, rows, or individual cells by entering specific measurements in the W and H text boxes in the Property inspector specified either in pixels or as a percentage. Cells whose width or height is specified as a percentage maintain that percentage in relation to the width or height of the entire table if the table is resized.

Adding or Deleting a Row

As you add new content to your table, you might find that you have too many or too few rows or columns. You can add or delete one row or column at a time or several at once. You use commands on the Modify menu to add and delete table rows and columns. When you add a new column or row, you must first select the existing column or row to which the new column or row will be adjacent. The Insert Rows or Columns dialog box lets you choose how many rows or columns you want to insert or delete, and where you want them placed in relation to the selected row or column. The new column or row will have the same formatting and number of cells as the selected column or row. After you have split and merged cells, it can be challenging to add or delete rows.

Using the Table button creates a new table with evenly-spaced columns and rows. Sometimes you want to adjust the cells in a table by splitting or merging them. To **split** a cell means to divide it into multiple rows or columns. To **merge** cells means to combine multiple cells into one cell. Using split and merged cells gives you more flexibility and control in placing page elements in a table and can help you create a more visually exciting layout. When you merge cells, the HTML tag used to describe the merged cell changes from a width size tag to a column span or row span tag. For example, <td colspan="2"> is the code for two cells that have been merged into one cell that spans two columns.

QUICK TIP

You can split merged cells and merge split cells.

DESIGNTIP

Using Nested Tables

A nested table is a table inside a table. To create a nested table, you place the insertion point in the cell where you want to insert the nested table, then click the Table button on the Insert panel. A nested table is a separate table that can be formatted differently from the table in which it is placed. Nested tables are useful when you want part of your table data to have visible borders and part to have invisible borders. For example, you can nest a table with red borders inside a table with invisible borders. You need to plan carefully when you insert nested tables. It is easy to get carried away and insert too many nested tables, which makes it more difficult to apply formatting and rearrange table elements. Before you insert a nested table, consider whether you could achieve the same result by adding rows and columns or by splitting cells.

Resize columns

1. Click inside the **first cell** in the bottom row.

2. Type **30%** in the W text box in the Property inspector, then press **[Enter]** (Win) or **[return]** (Mac) to change the width of the cell to 30 percent of the table width.

   Notice that the column width is shown as a percentage at the top of the first column in the table, along with the table width of 600 pixels.

   TIP You need to type the % sign next to the number you type in the W text box. Otherwise, the width is expressed in pixels.

3. Repeat Steps 1 and 2 for the next two cells in the last row, using **30%** for the middle cell and **40%** for the last cell, then compare your screen to Figure 28.

   The combined widths of the three cells add up to 100 percent. As you add content to the table, the columns remain in this proportion unless you insert an image that is larger than the table cell. If a larger image is inserted, the cell width expands to display it.

   TIP Changing the width of a single cell changes the width of the entire column.

You set the width of each of the three cells in the bottom row to set the column sizes for the table. This will keep the table from resizing when you add content.

Figure 28 *Setting a cell width*

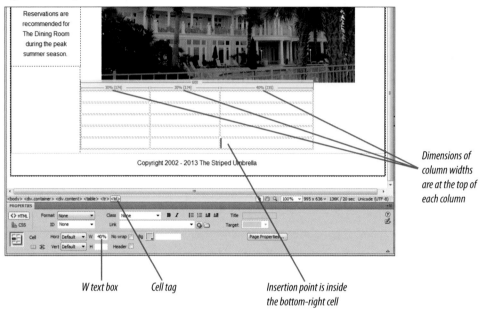

Dimensions of column widths are at the top of each column

W text box   Cell tag   Insertion point is inside the bottom-right cell

---

Resetting Table Widths and Heights

After resizing columns and rows in a table, you might want to change the sizes of the columns and rows back to their previous sizes. To reset columns and rows to their previous widths and heights, select the table, click Modify on the Application bar (Win) or Menu bar (Mac), point to Table, then click Clear Cell Heights or Clear Cell Widths. Using the Clear Cell Heights command also forces the cell border to snap to the bottom of any inserted graphics, so you can also use this command to tighten up extra white space in a cell. This menu also has choices for converting table widths and heights from pixels to percents and vice versa.

Figure 29 *Resizing the height of a row*

The Sand Crab Cafe is located in The Club House and has three dining areas: The Terrace, The Dining Room, and The Cabana. The Terrace is outdoor dining with a breathtaking view of the Gulf, especially at sunset. The Dining Room is casual, indoor dining on the second floor. The Cabana is poolside.

Sand Crab Cafe

Reservations are recommended for The Dining Room during the peak summer season.

30% (174)   30% (174)   40% (235)

Copyright 2002 - 2013 The Striped Umbrella

Resizing pointer

Resize rows

1. Place the pointer over the bottom border of the first row until it changes to a resizing pointer ⬍, as shown in Figure 29, then click and drag down about 1/4 of an inch to increase the height of the row.

   The border turns darker when you select and drag it.

2. Click **Window** on the menu bar, click **History**, then drag the **slider** in the History panel up one line to the **Set Width: 40%** mark to return the row to its original height.

3. Close the History panel.

You changed the height of the top row, then used the History panel to change it back to its original height.

Understanding HTML Table Tags

When formatting a table, it is important to understand the basic HTML table tags. The tags for creating a table are <table> </table>. The tags to create table rows are <tr></tr>. The tags used to create table cells are <td></td>. Dreamweaver places the   code into each empty table cell at the time you create it. The   code represents a nonbreaking space, or a space that a browser will display on the page. Some browsers collapse an empty cell, which can ruin the look of a table. The nonbreaking space holds the cell until you place content in it, when it is automatically removed.

Split cells

1. Click inside the first cell in the fifth row, then click the **<td>** in the tag selector.

TIP You can click the cell tag <td> (the HTML tag for that cell) on the tag selector to select the corresponding cell in the table.

2. Click the **Splits cell into rows or columns button** 🔲 in the Property inspector.

3. Click the **Split cell into Rows option button** (if necessary), type **2** in the Number of rows text box (if necessary), as shown in Figure 30, click **OK**, then click in the cell to deselect it.

   The cell is split, as shown in Figure 31.

TIP To create a new row identical to the one above it at the end of a table, place the insertion point in the last cell, then press [Tab].

You split a cell into two rows.

Figure 30 *Splitting a cell into two rows*

Splits cell into rows or columns button

Selected cell

Number of rows text box

Figure 31 *Splitting one cell into two rows*

Two cells split from one cell

Positioning Objects with CSS and Tables

Figure 32 *Merging selected cells into one cell*

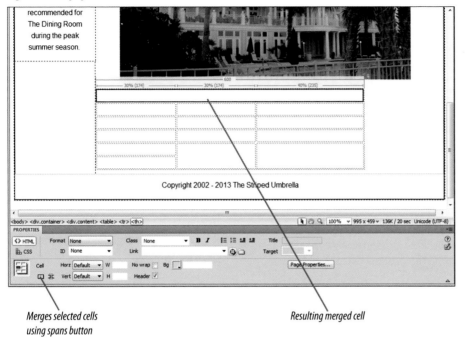

Merges selected cells
using spans button

Resulting merged cell

Figure 33 *Code for merged cells*

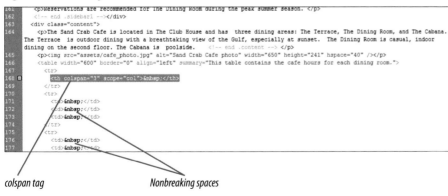

colspan tag

Nonbreaking spaces

Merge cells

1. Click to set the insertion point in the first cell in the top row, then drag to the right to select the three cells in the top row.

2. Click the **Merges selected cells using spans button** ⊡ in the Property inspector.

   The three cells are merged into one cell, as shown in Figure 32. Merged cells are good placeholders for banners or headings.

TIP You can only merge cells that are adjacent to each other.

3. Click the **Show Code view button** Code , then view the code for the merged cells, as shown in Figure 33.

   Notice the table tags denoting the column span (th colspan="3") and the nonbreaking spaces ( ) inserted in the empty cells.

4. Click the **Show Design view button** Design , select and merge the first cells in rows 2, 3, 4, and 5 in the left column, then save your work.

You merged three cells in the first row to make room for the table header. You then merged four cells in the left column to make room for an image.

Insert and Align
IMAGES IN TABLE CELLS

What You'll Do

In this lesson, you will insert an image of a chocolate cake in the left column of the table. After placing the image, you will align it within the cell.

Inserting Images in Table Cells

You can insert images in the cells of a table using the Image command in the Images menu on the Insert panel. If you already have images saved in your website that you would like to insert in a table, you can drag them from the Assets panel into the table cells. When you add a large image to a cell, the cell expands to accommodate the inserted image. If you select the Show attributes when inserting Images check box in the Accessibility category of the Preferences dialog box, the Image Tag Accessibility Attributes dialog box opens after you insert an image, prompting you to enter alternate text. Figure 34 shows the John Deere website, which uses several tables for page layout and contains images in its table cells. Notice that some images appear in cells by themselves, and some appear in cells containing text or other graphics. Some cells have a white background, and some have a green background.

Aligning Images in Table Cells

You can align images both horizontally and vertically within a cell. You can align an image horizontally using the Horz (horizontal) alignment options in the Property inspector, as shown in Figure 35. This option is used to align the entire contents of the cell, whether there is one object or several. You can also align an image vertically by the top, middle, bottom, or baseline of a cell. To align an image vertically within a cell, use the Vert (vertical) Align list arrow in the Property inspector, then choose an alignment option.

To control spacing between cells, you can use cell padding and cell spacing. **Cell padding** is the space between a cell's border and its contents. **Cell spacing** is the distance between adjacent cells.

Figure 34 *Deere & Company website*

Figure 35 *Horizontally aligning cell contents*

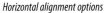

Horizontal alignment options

Insert images in table cells

1. Click in the merged cells in the left column of the table (under the merged cell in the top row) to place the insertion point.
2. Insert **chocolate_cake.jpg** from the drive and folder where you store your Data Files, then type **Chocolate Grand Marnier Cake** for the alternate text.

TIP You may have to click out of the cell if you see extra space around the image.

3. Compare your screen to Figure 36.
4. Refresh the Files panel and verify that the new image was copied to The Striped Umbrella website assets folder.
5. Save your work, then preview the page in your browser.
6. Close your browser.

You inserted an image into a table cell on the cafe page.

Figure 36 *Image inserted into table cell*

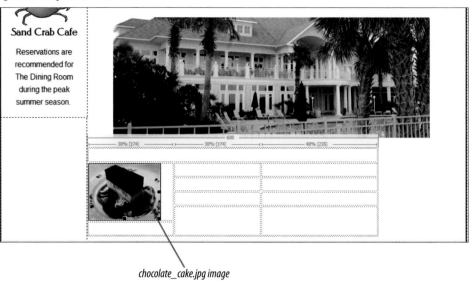

chocolate_cake.jpg image

Using Rulers, Grids, and Guides for Positioning Page Content

To help you position your page content, the View menu offers grids and guides. **Grids** provide a graph paper-like view of a page. Horizontal and vertical lines fill the page when this option is turned on. You can edit the line colors, the distance between them, whether they are composed of lines or dots, and whether or not objects "snap" to them. **Guides** are horizontal or vertical lines that you drag onto the page from the rulers. You can edit both the colors of the guides and the color of the distance, a feature that shows you the distance between two guides. You can lock the guides so you don't accidentally move them and you can set them either to snap to page elements or have page elements snap to them. To display grids or guides, click View on the Application bar (Win) or Menu bar (Mac), point to Grid, then click Show Grid or point to Guides and then click Show Guides.

Figure 37 *Aligning image in cell*

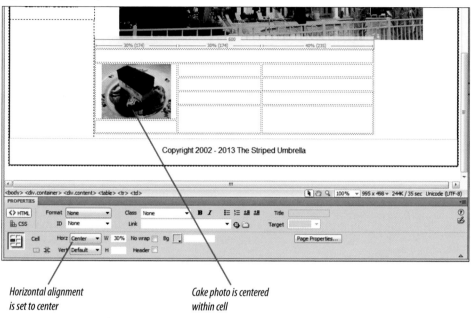

Copyright 2002 - 2013 The Striped Umbrella

Horizontal alignment is set to center

Cake photo is centered within cell

Align graphics in table cells

1. Click to the right side of the **chocolate_cake image** in the same cell to place the insertion point.

2. Click the **Horz list arrow** in the Property inspector, then click **Center**. (Both the HTML and CSS Property inspectors have the alignment options.)

   The chocolate cake image is centered in the cell. The alignment applies to all content inserted into this cell. The effect of the alignment, however, may not be apparent until you add more content to the table.

3. Compare your screen to Figure 37.

4. Save your work.

5. Preview the page in your browser, view the aligned image, then close your browser.

You center-aligned cell content.

Insert Text and Format
CELL CONTENT

What You'll Do

In this lesson, you will type the cafe hours in the table. You will also format the text to enhance its appearance on the page. Last, you will add formatting to some of the cells and cell content.

Inserting Text in a Table

You can enter text in a table either by typing it in a cell, copying it from another source and pasting it into a cell, or importing it from another program. Once you place text in a table cell, you can format it to make it more readable and more visually appealing on the page.

Formatting Cell Content

To format the contents of a cell, select the cell contents, then apply formatting to it. For example, you can select an image in a cell and center it, add a border, or add V space. Or, you can select text in a cell and apply a style or use the Blockquote or Remove Blockquote buttons in the HTML Property inspector to move the text farther away from or closer to the cell walls.

If a cell contains multiple objects of the same type, such as text, you can either format each item individually or select the entire cell and apply formatting that applies identically to all items. You can tell whether you have selected the cell contents or the cell itself by looking at the options showing in the Property inspector. Figure 38 shows a selected image in a cell. Because the image is selected, the Property inspector displays options for formatting the object, rather than options for formatting the cell.

Formatting Cells

Formatting a cell is different from formatting a cell's contents. Formatting a cell can include setting properties that visually enhance the cell's appearance, such as setting a cell width and assigning a background color.

You can also set global alignment properties for the cell content, using the Horz or Vert list arrows on the Property inspector. These options align the cell content horizontally or vertically. To format a cell, you need to either select the cell or place the insertion point inside the cell you want to format, then choose the cell formatting options you want in the Property inspector. For example, to choose a fill color for a selected cell, click the Background Color button in the Property inspector, then choose a color from the color picker. To format a cell, expand the Property inspector to display the cell formatting options.

QUICK TIP

You can also set cell and table formatting using rules in a Cascading Style Sheet. Some options, such as using an image for a cell background, cannot be set using the Property inspector and must be set using CSS.

In Figure 39, the insertion point is positioned in the chocolate cake cell, but the image is not selected. The Property inspector displays the formatting options for cells.

Figure 38 *Property inspector showing properties for selected image*

Property inspector shows properties for selected image

Image selected inside a cell

Figure 39 *Property inspector showing options for formatting a cell*

Property inspector shows cell properties, not image properties

Insertion point in cell

Insert text

1. Click in the cell below the chocolate cake photo, type **Chocolate**, press **[Shift][Enter]** (Win) or **[shift][return]** (Mac), type **Grand Marnier**, press **[Shift][Enter]** (Win) or **[shift][return]** (Mac), then type **Cake**.

   TIP If you can't see the last lines you typed, click the <div.container> tag on the Tag selector to refresh the container size on the screen, or resize your screen to refresh the screen.

2. Click in the top row of the table to place the insertion point, then type **Sand Crab Cafe Hours**.

   The text is automatically bolded because you selected the top row header when you created the table. A table's header row is bold by default.

3. Merge the two bottom-right cells in the last row, then enter the cafe dining area names, hours, and room service information as shown in Figure 40. Use a line break after the first line of text in the last cell.

   The type in the table has inherited the Font-family property from the body tag properties.

   TIP If your table cells seem to have extra space in them, click the <table> tag to tighten it up.

   You entered text in the table to provide information about the dining room hours.

Figure 40 *Typing text into cells*

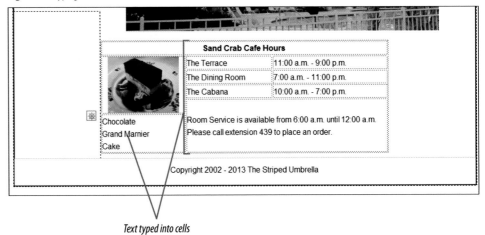

Text typed into cells

Importing and Exporting Data from Tables

You can import and export tabular data into and out of Dreamweaver. Tabular data is data that is arranged in columns and rows and separated by a **delimiter**: a comma, tab, colon, semicolon, or similar character. **Importing** means to bring data created in another software program into Dreamweaver, and **exporting** means to save data created in Dreamweaver in a special file format that can be opened by other programs. Files that are imported into Dreamweaver must be saved as delimited files. **Delimited files** are database, word processing, or spreadsheet files that have been saved as text files with delimiters such as tabs or commas separating the data. Programs such as Microsoft Access and Microsoft Excel offer many file formats for saving files. To import a delimited file, click File on the Application bar (Win) or Menu bar (Mac), point to Import, then click Tabular Data. The Import Tabular Data dialog box opens, offering you formatting options for the imported table. To export a table that you created in Dreamweaver, click File on the Application bar (Win) or Menu bar (Mac), point to Export, then click Table. The Export Table dialog box opens, letting you choose the type of delimiter you want for the delimited file.

Figure 41 *Formatting text using a Cascading Style Sheet*

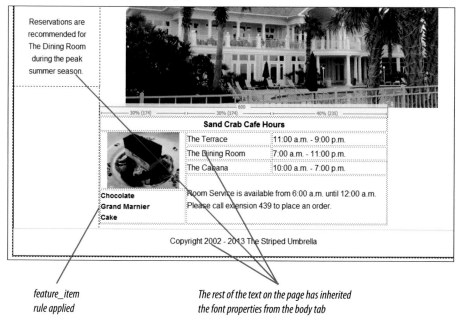

feature_item
rule applied

The rest of the text on the page has inherited the font properties from the body tab

1. Click the **New CSS Rule button** ⊡ to create a new class style called **feature_item** in the su_styles.css style sheet file.

   The CSS Rule Definition for .feature_item in su_styles.css dialog box opens.

2. In the Type category, set the Font-size to **14**, the Font-weight to **bold**, the Color to **#003**, then click **OK** to close the CSS Rule Definition for .feature_item in su_styles.css dialog box.

   You use this rule to format the name of the featured dessert.

3. Select **Chocolate Grand Marnier Cake** under the cake image, click the **CSS button** ▣ CSS on the Property inspector, then apply the **feature_item rule** to the text.

   Your screen should resemble Figure 41. Because the only property values you set for the feature_item rule were for the font size, font weight, and color, the font family value was inherited from the parent body tag and is the same as the rest of the text on the page.

You created a new rule in the su_styles.css style sheet and used it to format text in a table cell.

POWER USER SHORTCUTS	
To do this:	**Use this shortcut:**
Insert table	[Ctrl][Alt][T] (Win) or ⌘ [option][T] (Mac)
Select a cell	[Ctrl][A] (Win) or ⌘ [A] (Mac)
Merge cells	[Ctrl][Alt][M] (Win) or ⌘ [option][M] (Mac)
Split cell	[Ctrl][Alt][S] (Win) or ⌘ [option][S] (Mac)
Insert row	[Ctrl][M] (Win) or ⌘ [M] (Mac)
Insert column	[Ctrl][Shift][A] (Win) or ⌘ [Shift][A] (Mac)
Delete row	[Ctrl][Shift][M] (Win) or ⌘ [Shift][M] (Mac)
Delete column	[Ctrl][Shift][-] (Win) or ⌘ [Shift][-] (Mac)
Increase column span	[Ctrl][Shift][]] (Win) or ⌘ [Shift][]] (Mac)
Decrease column span	[Ctrl][Shift][[] (Win) or ⌘ [Shift][[] (Mac)

Format cells

1. Click to place the insertion point in the cell with the cake text.

2. Click the **Horz list arrow** in the Property inspector, then click **Center** to center the cell contents.

    You do not need to select the text because you are setting the alignment for all contents in the cell.

3. Repeat Steps 1 and 2 for the cell with the room service information.

4. With the insertion point in the room service text, click the **Vert list arrow**, then click **Bottom**, as shown in Figure 42.

5. Save your work.

You formatted table cells by adding horizontal and vertical alignment.

Modify cell content

1. Click after the word "cake" in the bottom left cell, then press **[Tab]**.

    Pressing the Tab key while the insertion point is in the last cell of the table creates a new row. Even though it looks like the cell with the room service information is the last cell, it is not because of the merged cells.

2. Merge the cells in the new row, click in the merged cells, click **Insert** on the Application bar (Win) or Menu bar (Mac), point to **HTML**, then click **Horizontal Rule**.

3. Click in front of the table header, insert another horizontal rule, then save your work.

You added two horizontal rules to the table to set the table off from the rest of the page.

Figure 42 *Formatting cells using horizontal and vertical alignment*

Vert list arrow   Horz list arrow   Insertion point inside cell with no elements selected

Using Inherited Properties to Format Cell Content

If a table is inside a CSS layout, you can simply let the properties from the existing CSS rules format the content, rather than applying additional rules. This is called **inheritance**. When a tag is placed, or **nested**, inside another tag (the parent tag), the properties from the parent tag are inherited by any tags nested within that tag. For example, if you set the Font-family property in the body tag, all content on the page inherits and displays that same font family unless you specify otherwise.

Figure 43 *Hiding visual aids*

Dotted lines showing borders are hidden

Live View button

Visual aids button

Check layout

1. Click the **Visual Aids button** 🔲 on the Document toolbar, then click **Hide All Visual Aids**.

   As shown in Figure 43, the borders around the table, table cells, and CSS blocks are all hidden, allowing you to see more clearly how the table will look in the browser. Visual aids are helpful while you are editing and formatting a page. However, turning them off is a quick way to see how the page will appear in the browser without having to open it in the browser window.

2. Repeat Step 1 to show the visual aids again.

TIP You can also click the Live View button on the Document toolbar to see how the page will look in the browser. Turn Live View off by clicking it again.

3. Save your work, preview the cafe page in the browser, close the browser, then close Dreamweaver.

You used the Hide All Visual Aids command to hide the table borders and layout block outlines, then showed them again.

Create a page using CSS layouts.

1. Open the Blooms & Bulbs website, then create a new blank HTML page with the 2 column fixed, left sidebar, header and footer style, linking the blooms_styles.css file to the page.

2. Save the file as **workshops.html**, overwriting the existing workshops page.

Add content to CSS layout blocks.

1. Open the index page, then copy the banner and menu bar. (*Hint*: Select the banner, hold down your Shift key, then click the SpryMenuBar tab to select the menu bar and the banner together.)

2. Close the index page, then on the workshops page, delete the logo placeholder in the header, then paste the banner and menu bar in the header block. (*Hint*: If you have trouble copying and pasting the banner and menu bar together, try copying and pasting them separately.)

3. Delete the footer placeholder text, then type **Copyright 2001 - 2013 Blooms & Bulbs** in the footer Block.

4. Delete the placeholder content from the content block.

5. Type **New Composting Workshop!**, enter a paragraph break, then import the text composting.doc from the drive and folder where you store you Data Files.

6. Enter a paragraph break, then insert the chives.jpg from the drive and folder where you store your Data Files. Add the alternate text **Even chives can be beautiful** to the image when prompted.

7. Select the chives image and add a 40 pixel H space.

8. Save your work.

Edit content in CSS layout blocks.

1. Select the footer rule in the Styles panel, then edit its Text-align property in the Block category to center the content.

2. Select the heading "New Composting Workshop!" and format it using the H3 tag.

3. Select the header rule in the CSS Styles panel and change its background color to **#FFF**.

4. Repeat Step 3 to change the background color of the sidebar1 rule to **#FFF**.

5. Edit the header rule so that the header has a 5-pixel margin on all sides.

6. Edit the body rule to change the Font-size to 14 pixels.

7. Save your work.

Create a table.

1. Delete the placeholder text, including the <H1> tag, in the sidebar, then insert a table with the following settings: Rows: **8**, Columns: **2**, Table width: **175 pixels**, Border thickness: **0**, Cell padding: **5**, Cell spacing: **5**, and Header: **Top**. In the Summary text box, enter the text **This table is used to list the workshop names and dates**.

2. Edit the sidebar1 rule to center-align the contents.

3. Add the page title **Blooms & Bulbs scheduled workshops** then save your work.

Resize, split, and merge cells.

1. Select the first cell in the second row of the table, then set the cell width to **60%**.

2. Select the second cell in the second row, then set the cell width to **40%**.

3. Merge the two cells in the first row.

4. Merge the two cells in the last row.

5. Save your work.

Insert and align images in table cells.

1. Use the Insert panel to insert gardening_gloves.gif in the last row of the table. You can find this image in the assets folder where you store your Data Files. Add the alternate text **Gardening gloves** to the image when prompted, then center the image in the merged cell.

2. Save your work.

Insert text and format cell content.

1. Type **Scheduled Workshops** in the merged cell in the first row.

2. Go to Code View, locate the .sidebar1 style around line 75, verify that the text alignment is set to center, then return to Design view.

3. Type the names and dates for the workshops from Figure 44 in each row of the table.

4. Save your work, preview the page in your browser, then close your browser.

5. Close all open pages.

Figure 44 *Completed Skills Review*

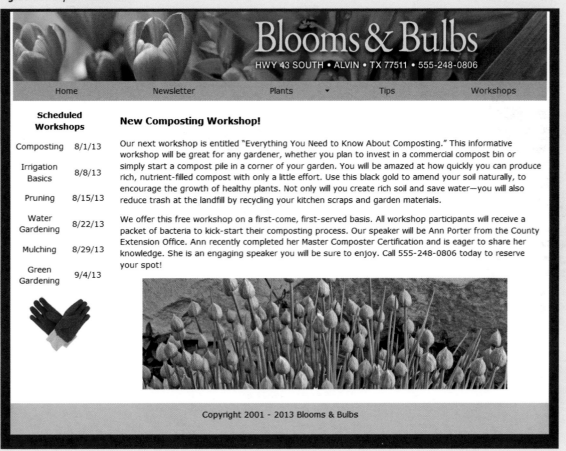

PROJECT BUILDER 1

In this exercise, you continue your work on the TripSmart website that you began in Project Builder 1 in Chapter 1 and developed in the previous chapters. You are ready to begin work on a page featuring catalog items. You plan to use a CSS layout with a table to place the information on the page.

1. Open the TripSmart website.
2. Create a new page based on the 1 column fixed, centered, header and footer CSS page layout, attaching the tripsmart_styles.css file, then save the file as **catalog.html**, replacing the placeholder catalog page in the website.
3. Open the index page, copy the banner and menu bar, then close the index page.
4. Delete the logo image placeholder in the header, then paste the banner and menu bar in the header block. (*Hint*: Check the code to make sure you did not copy any break tags after the menu bar or you will have extra space on the page after the menu bar.)
5. Edit the embedded footer rule to center align the content, remove the top and bottom padding, and set the background color to #FFF.
6. Edit the header rule so its background is #FFF and all margins to 5 px.
7. Edit the embedded body style to change the Font-family to Arial, Helvetica, sans-serif, the Font-size to 14 pixels, and the background color to white.
8. Save your work.
9. Delete the placeholder content in the content block, use the Format list arrow in the HTML Property inspector to change the formatting to Paragraph, then enter a line break after the menu bar.
10. Insert a table into the content block with the following settings: Rows: **5**, Columns: **3**, Table width: **950 pixels**, Border thickness: **0**, Header: **Top**. Delete any value, if necessary, in the cell padding text box, enter an appropriate table summary, then center-align the table.
11. Set the cell widths in the bottom row to **33%**, **33%**, and **34%**.
12. Merge the three cells in the first row, enter a line break in the merged cell, then type **Our products are backed with a 100% guarantee**.
13. In the three cells in the second row, type **Protection from UV rays; Cool, light-weight, versatile;** and **Pockets for everything** then center the text in each cell.
14. Place the files hat.jpg, pants.jpg, and vest.jpg from the assets folder where you store your Data Files in the three cells in the third row, adding the following alternate text to the images: **Safari hat**, **Kenya convertible pants**, and **Photographer's vest**; center the three images.
15. Type **Safari Hat**, **Kenya Convertible Pants**, and **Photographer's Vest** in the three cells in the fourth row, then center each label.
16. Type **Item number 50501** and **$29.00** with a line break between them in the first cell in the fifth row.
17. Repeat Step 16 to type **Item number 62495** and **$39.50** in the second cell in the fifth row.
18. Repeat Step 16 to type **Item number 52301** and **$54.95** in the third cell in the fifth row, then center each item number and price in the cells.
19. Create a new class rule in the tripsmart_styles.css style sheet named **reverse_text** with the following settings: Font-family, Arial, Helvetica, sans-serif; Font-size, 14 px; Font-style, normal; Font-weight, bold; Color, #FFF. (*Hint*: Be sure to choose Class under Selector Type.)
20. Apply the reverse_text rule to the three item names under the images, then change the cell background color to #666633.
21. Create a new class rule called **item_numbers** with the following settings: Font: Arial, Helvetica, sans-serif; Size: 12 px; Style: normal; Weight: bold.
22. Apply the item_numbers rule to the three items' numbers and prices.
23. Delete the footer placeholder text, then type **TripSmart Copyright 2002 – 2013**.
24. Edit the footer style to change the Font-size property to 12 pixels and remove any padding if necessary.
25. Edit the container style properties to include a solid, thin border, color #030.
26. Save your work, view the page in your browser, then close the browser.
27. Add the page title **TripSmart featured catalog items**.
28. Open the index page and copy the line of code that inserts the favicon on the page, then paste it in the code on the catalog page right above the code for the title.
29. Save your work, preview the page in the browser and compare your screen to Figure 45, close the browser, then close all open pages.

Figure 45 *Sample Project Builder 1*

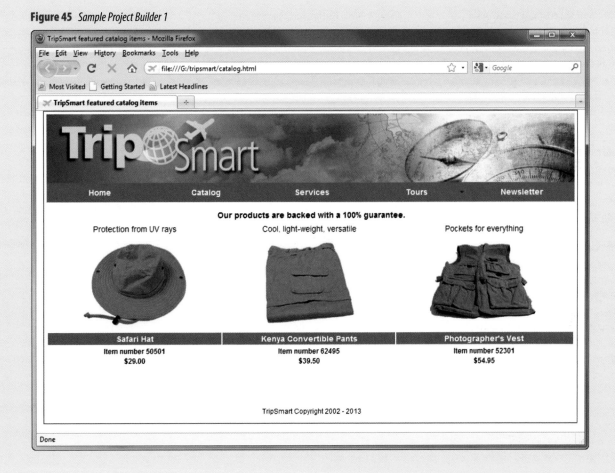

Use Figure 46 as a guide to continue your work on the Carolyne's Creations website that you started in Chapter 1 and developed in the previous chapters. You are now ready to begin work on a page showcasing the company's catering services. You decide to use CSS with a table for page layout.

1. Open the Carolyne's Creations website, then create a new page based on the 1 column fixed, centered, header and footer layout, attach the cc_styles.css file, and save the page as **catering.html**, overwriting the existing page.
2. Copy the banner that includes the menu bar from one of the other pages, then paste it on the page, replacing the logo placeholder.
3. Delete the container placeholder text, then edit the container rule properties with values of your choice to format the page to blend with the existing pages in the website.
4. Insert a table in the content block to showcase the catering services, with the following settings: Rows: 9, Columns: 3, Table width: 925 pixels, Border thickness: 0, Cell padding: 3, Cell spacing: 0, Header: Top, then add an appropriate table summary.
5. Center-align the table and set the width of the three cells to 33%, 33%, and 34%.
6. Merge the cells in the top row, then type **Catering for All Occasions** in the merged cells.
7. Merge the cells in the 5th row, type **Dinner to Go**, apply the H4 format, then center-align it.
8. Merge the cells in the 4th and 8th rows, then insert horizontal rules in the resulting merged cells. (*Hint*: Change the view to Expanded Tables mode to be able to see the cells more easily.)
9. Type **Lunch Boxes**, **Brunch Boxes**, and **Gift Baskets** in the three cells in the second row.
10. Type **Soups**, **Entrees**, and **Desserts** in the three cells in the sixth row.
11. Apply the headings rule to the text you typed in Steps 9 and 10, then center each of the labels.
12. Use a color of your choice for the background for each cell in the second and sixth rows.
13. In the first cell of the last row, enter the following text on three lines, using a line break between each sentence: **Call/fax by 9:00 a.m. for lunch orders. Call/fax by 1:00 p.m. for dinner orders. Fax number: 555-963-5938**.
14. Apply the body_text rule to the text you typed in Step 13.
15. Use your word processor to open the file **menu items.doc** from the drive and folder where you store your Data Files. Copy and paste each text block into the cells in the third and seventh rows, apply the body_text rule to each text block, then center align each text block in the cells, using Figure 46 as a guide.
16. Merge the last two cells in the last row, then insert the image muffins.jpg with alternate text and any additional formatting of your choice.
17. Edit the footer properties with values of your choice, then type **Carolyne's Creations Copyright 2001 – 2013**.
18. Add the page title **Carolyne's Creations Catering Services**.
19. Modify the properties for the header block to blend in with the page color scheme.
20. Save your work, preview the page in your browser, make any adjustments that you feel would improve the page appearance, then close all open files.

Figure 46 *Sample Project Builder 2*

Jon Bishop is opening a new restaurant and wants to launch his restaurant website two weeks before his opening. He has hired you to create the site and has asked for several design proposals. You begin by looking at some restaurant sites with pleasing designs.

1. Connect to the Internet, then go to www.jamesatthemill.com, as shown in Figure 47.

2. How are CSS styles used in this site?

3. How are CSS styles used to prevent an overload of information in one area of the screen?

4. View the source code for the page and locate the html tags that control the CSS layout on the page.

5. Use the Reference panel in Dreamweaver to look up the code used in this site to place the content on the page. (*Hint*: To do this, make note of a tag that you don't understand, then open the Reference panel and find that tag in the Tag list in the Reference panel. Select it from the list and read the description in the Reference panel.)

6. Do you see any tables on the page? If so, how are they used?

Figure 47 *Design Project*

James at the Mill website used with permission from Miles James – www.jamesatthemill.com

For this assignment, you continue to work on the portfolio project that you have been developing since Chapter 1. No Data Files are supplied. You are building this website from chapter to chapter, so you must do each Portfolio Project assignment in each chapter to complete your website.

You continue building your website by designing and completing a page that uses a CSS layout for page design.

1. Consult your wireframe to decide which page to create and develop for this chapter. Draw a sketch of the page to show how you plan to use CSS to lay out the content.
2. Create the new page for the site using one of the predesigned CSS layouts.
3. Add text, background images, and background colors to each container.
4. Create the navigation links that will allow you to add this page to your site.

5. Update the other pages of your site so that each page includes a link to this new page.
6. Add images in the containers (where appropriate), making sure to align them attractively.
7. Review the checklist in Figure 48 and make any necessary changes.
8. Save your work, preview the page in your browser, make any necessary modifications to improve the page appearance, close your browser, then close all open pages.

Figure 48 *Portfolio Project checklist*

Website Checklist

1. Do all pages have page titles?
2. Do all navigation links work correctly?
3. Are all colors in the site web-safe?
4. Did you use a predesigned CSS page layout for at least one page?
5. Do your pages look the same in at least two current browsers?
6. Does all content in your CSS containers appear correctly?

CHAPTER **7**

MANAGING A WEB
SERVER AND FILES

MANAGING A WEB
SERVER AND FILES

Once you have created all the pages of your website, finalized all the content, and performed site maintenance, you are ready to publish your site to a remote server so the rest of the world can access it. In this chapter, you start by running some reports to make sure the links in your site work properly and that any orphaned files are removed. Next, you set up a connection to the remote site for The Striped Umbrella website. You then transfer files to the remote site and learn how to keep them up to date. You also check out a file so that it is not available to other team members while you are editing it and you learn how to cloak files. When a file is **cloaked**, it is excluded from certain processes, such as being transferred to the remote site. Next, you export the site definition file from The Striped Umbrella website so that other designers can import the site. Finally, you research important copyright issues that affect all websites, and learn how to present your work to a client.

Preparing to Publish a Site

Before you publish a site, it is extremely important that you test it to make sure the content is accurate and up to date and that everything is functioning properly. When viewing pages over the Internet, users find it frustrating to click a link that doesn't work or to wait for pages that load slowly because of large graphics and animations. Remember that the typical user has a short attention span and limited patience.

Before you publish your site, be sure to use the Link Checker panel to check for broken links and orphaned files. Make sure that all image paths are correct and that all images load quickly and have alternate text. Verify that all pages have titles, and remove all non-websafe colors that could present a problem. View the pages in at least two different browsers and different versions of the same browser to ensure that everything works correctly. The more frequently you test, the better the chance that your users will have a positive experience at your site and want to return. Finally, before you publish your pages, verify that all content is original to the website, has been obtained legally, and is used properly without violating the copyright of someone else's work.

Reports

Report on: [Current Document ▼]

Current Document
Entire Current Local Site
Selected Files in Site
Folder...

[Run]
[Cancel]

Select repor

☐ 📁 Workflow
 ☐ Checked Out By
 ☐ Design Notes
 ☐ Recently Modified
☐ 📁 HTML Reports
 ☐ Combinable Nested Font Tags
 ☐ Missing Alt Text
 ☐ Redundant Nested Tags
 ☐ Removable Empty Tags
 ☐ Untitled Documents

[Report Settings...]

[Help]

[Basic] [Advanced]

Server Name: [Server 1]

Connect using: [FTP ▼]

FTP Address: [www.webhost.com]   Port: [21]

Username: [student]

Password: [•••••••]   ☑ Save

[Test]

Root Directory: [/home]

Web URL: [http://www.webhost.com/]

▶ More Options

[Help]   [Save]   [Cancel]

Perform WEBSITE MAINTENANCE

What You'll Do

In this lesson, you will use some Dreamweaver site management tools to check for broken links, orphaned files, and missing alternate text. You will also verify that all colors are websafe. You will then evaluate and correct any problems that you find.

Maintaining a Website

As you add pages, links, and content to a website, it can quickly become difficult to manage. It's easier to find and correct errors as you go, rather than waiting until the end of the design phase. It's important to perform maintenance tasks frequently to make sure your website operates smoothly and remains "clean." You have already learned about some of the tools described in the following paragraphs. Although it is important to use them as you create and modify your pages, it is also important to run them at periodic intervals after publishing your website to make sure it is always error-free.

Using the Assets Panel

You should use the Assets panel to check the list of images and colors used in your website. If you see images listed that are not being used, you should move them to a storage folder outside the website until you need them. You should also make note of any non-websafe colors. This is much less of an issue today than in the past, but it doesn't hurt to evaluate any non-websafe colors you find to evaluate whether slight variations in the way the colors are rendered could cause contrast problems.

Checking Links Sitewide

Before and after you publish your website, you should use the Link Checker panel to make sure all internal links are working. If the Link Checker panel displays any broken links, you should repair them. If the Link Checker panel displays any orphaned files, you should evaluate whether to delete them or link them with existing pages. To delete a file that you decide not to use, select it in the Files panel, then press [Delete] or right-click the file, click Edit, then click Delete. You should also check all external links by testing them in a browser to make sure that all links find the intended website.

Using Site Reports

You can use the Reports command in the Site menu to generate five different HTML reports that can help you maintain your website. You choose the type of report you want to run in the Reports dialog box, shown in Figure 1. You can specify whether to generate the report for the current document, the entire current local site, selected files in the site, or a selected folder. You can also generate workflow reports to see files that have been checked out by others or recently modified or you can view the Design Notes attached to files.

Design Notes are separate files in a website that contain additional information about a page file or a graphic file. If several designers are working collaboratively to design a site, they can record notes to exchange information with other design team members about the status of a file. Design Notes are also a good place to store information about the source files for graphics, such as Flash or Fireworks files.

Validating Markup

Because web development can now use multiple languages, it's important to ensure that the various language versions are compatible. To address this need, Dreamweaver can validate markup. To **validate markup**, Dreamweaver searches through the code to look for errors that

could occur with different language versions, such as XHTML or XML. To validate code for a page, click File on the Application bar (Win) or Menu bar (Mac) point to Validate, and then click ColdFusion or As XML. The Results tab group displaying the Validation panel opens and lists any pages with errors, the line numbers where the errors occur, and an explanation of the errors.

Testing Pages

Finally, you should test your website using many different types and versions of browsers, platforms, and screen resolutions. You can use the Check browser compatibility button on the Document toolbar to check for issues with your site pages that might cause problems when they are viewed using

certain browsers. Examples can include the rendering of square bullets, table borders, horizontal rules, or CSS AP elements. If you find such issues, you can choose to change your pages to eliminate the problems. The Results Tab group's Browser Compatibility panel includes a URL that you can visit to find the solutions to identified problems. You should test every link to make sure it connects to a valid, active website.

NEW Adobe has an application called **Adobe BrowserLab** that is a useful tool for cross-browser and cross-platform compatibility testing. Adobe BrowserLab is an online service, so you can access it from any computer with an Internet connection. There are two MXP extensions that you can download to enable this service to be used with Dreamweaver. Go to http://browserlab.adobe.com to learn more about using Adobe BrowserLab.

If, in your testing, you find any pages that download slowly, reduce their size to improve performance. Consider optimizing graphics by cropping or resizing images, reducing the number of Flash files, or streamlining the page code.

As part of your ongoing site testing, you should present the web pages at strategic times in the development process to your team members and to your clients for feedback and evaluation. Analyze all feedback on the website objectively, incorporating both the positive and the negative comments to help you make improvements to the site and meet the clients' expectations and goals.

Figure 1 *Reports dialog box*

Check for broken links

1. Open The Striped Umbrella website.

2. Show the Files panel, if necessary.

3. Click **Site** on the Application bar (Win) or Menu bar (Mac), point to **Advanced**, then click **Recreate Site Cache**.

   It is a good idea to recreate the site cache to force Dreamweaver to refresh the file listing before running reports.

4. Click **Site** on the Application bar (Win) or Menu bar (Mac), then click **Check Links Sitewide**.

   No broken links are listed in the Link Checker panel of the Results Tab Group, as shown in Figure 2.

You verified that there are no broken links in the website.

Check for orphaned files

1. On the Link Checker panel, click the **Show list arrow**, then click **Orphaned Files**.

   There are no orphaned files, as shown in Figure 3.

2. Close the Results Tab Group.

You verified that there are no orphaned files in the website.

Figure 2 *Link Checker panel displaying no broken links*

No broken links listed

Figure 3 *Link Checker panel displaying no orphaned files*

Summary

No orphaned files listed

Managing a Web Server and Files

Figure 4 *Assets panel displaying websafe and non-websafe colors*

Several colors are listed
as non-websafe

Figure 5 *Locating a non-websafe color*

Find Next
button

Color 42413c is
located in code

Search for "42413c"
in code

Search list
arrow

Find in list
arrow

Search for non-websafe colors

1. Click the **Assets panel tab**, then click the **Colors button** ⊞ to view the website colors, as shown in Figure 4.

   The Assets panel shows that all but four colors listed are websafe. It is a good idea to look at any non-websafe colors listed and decide whether they could affect the appearance of any page elements. If they do, you might consider replacing them with websafe colors.

2. Open the **cafe page**, switch to Code view, click **Edit** on the Application bar (Win) or Menu bar (Mac), click **Find and Replace**, verify that Current Document is selected next to Find in, verify that Source Code is selected next to Search, type **42413c** in the Find text box, then click **Find Next**.

   The text "42413c" is a search string. A **string** is a series of characters or words. You use strings each time you enter terms in a search text box. The string "42413c" is located and selected in the cafe page code, as shown in Figure 5. This color is in one of the styles from the predesigned page layout and is not used on this page, so it is not a problem.

3. Click **Find Next**.

   There are no more occurrences of this search string. The bottom of the Find and Replace dialog box shows that the search is done, with one item found in the current document.

4. Close the Find and Replace dialog box, then close the cafe page.

(continued)

5. Click **Edit** on the Application bar (Win) or Menu bar (Mac), click **Find and Replace**, click the **Find in list arrow**, click **Entire Current Local Site**, click the **Search list arrow**, click **Source Code**, type **6e6c64** in the Find text box, then click **Find Next**.

The cafe page opens in Code view with the non-websafe color selected. This color is in another style from the predesigned page layout that is not used on this page, so it is not a problem. Any unopened page with this code will be opened in Code view with the code selected after you click Find Next.

6. Search for the rest of the non-websafe colors, then close the Find and Replace dialog box.

None of these colors affect the page elements on the cafe page, so no changes need to be made at this time.

You viewed the websafe and non-websafe colors in the website and decided that the non-websafe colors were not a problem.

Check for untitled documents

1. Click **Site** on the Application bar (Win) or Menu bar (Mac), then click **Reports** to open the Reports dialog box.

2. Click the **Report on list arrow**, click **Entire Current Local Site**, click the **Untitled Documents check box**, as shown in Figure 6, then click **Run**.

The Site Reports panel opens in the Results Tab Group, and shows that all pages have page titles, as shown in Figure 7.

You ran a report for untitled documents, and verified that all pages have page titles.

Figure 6 *Reports dialog box with Untitled Documents option selected*

Report on list arrow

Untitled Documents check box

Figure 7 *Reports dialog box showing no pages without page titles*

No pages are listed without page titles

Using Find and Replace to Locate Non-Websafe Colors

As with many software applications, Dreamweaver has a Find and Replace feature on the Edit menu that you can use both in Design view and in Code view. Use this command to search the current document, selected files, or the entire current local site. If you are looking for a particular non-websafe color, you can save time by using the Find and Replace feature to locate the hexadecimal color code in Code view. If a site has many pages, this is the fastest way to locate it. The Find and Replace feature can also be used to locate other character strings, such as a phrase that begins or ends with a particular word or tag. These patterns of character strings are referred to as **regular expressions**. To find out more, search for "regular expressions" in Dreamweaver Help.

Figure 8 *Reports dialog box with Missing Alt Text option selected*

Missing Alt Text check box

Check for missing alternate text

1. Using Figure 8 as a guide, run another report that checks the entire current local site for missing alternate text.

   There are no images with missing alternate text, as shown in Figure 9.

2. Close the Results Tab Group, then close all open pages.

You ran a report to check for missing alternate text in the entire site.

Figure 9 *Site Reports panel displaying missing "alt" tag*

No missing Alt Text found

Validating Accessibility Standards

There are many accessibility issues to consider to ensure that your website conforms to current accessibility standards. HTML Reports provide an easy way to check for missing alternate text, missing page titles, and improper markup. You can run HTML Reports on the current document, selected files, or the entire local site.

Enable Design Notes

1. Click **Site** on the Application bar (Win) or Menu bar (Mac), click **Manage Sites**, verify that The Striped Umbrella site is selected, click **Edit**, click **Advanced Settings**, then click **Design Notes**.

2. Click the **Maintain Design Notes check box**, to select it, if necessary, as shown in Figure 10.

   When this option is selected, designers can record notes about a page in a separate file linked to the page. For instance, a Design Note for the index.html file would be saved in a file named index.html.mno. Dreamweaver creates a folder named _notes and saves all Design Notes in that folder. This folder does not appear in the Files panel, but it is visible in the site root folder in Windows Explorer (Win) or Finder (Mac).

3. Click **File View Columns**, then click **Notes** in the Name column.

4. Click the **Edit existing Column button** 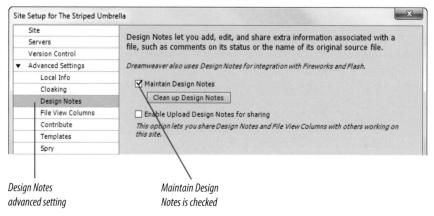, click the **Options: Show check box** to select it, if necessary, then click **Save**.

   The Notes column now displays the word "Show" in the Show column, as shown in Figure 11, indicating that the Notes column will be visible in the Files panel.

5. Click **Save** to close the Site Setup for The Striped Umbrella dialog box, then click **Done** in the Manage Sites dialog box.

You set the preference to use Design Notes in the website. You also set the option to display the Notes column in the Files panel.

Figure 10 *Design Notes setting in the Site Setup for The Striped Umbrella*

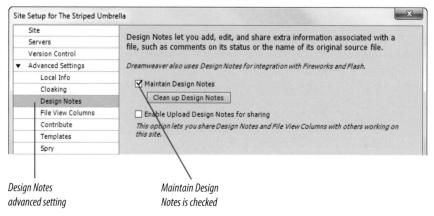

Design Notes
advanced setting

Maintain Design
Notes is checked

Figure 11 *Site Setup for The Striped Umbrella*

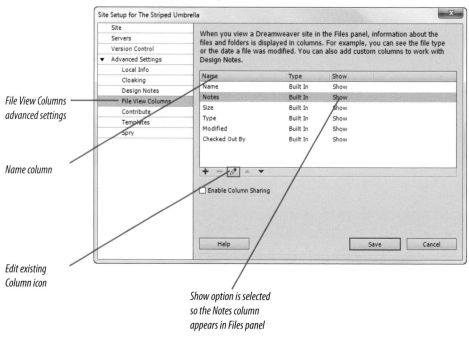

File View Columns
advanced settings

Name column

Edit existing
Column icon

Show option is selected
so the Notes column
appears in Files panel

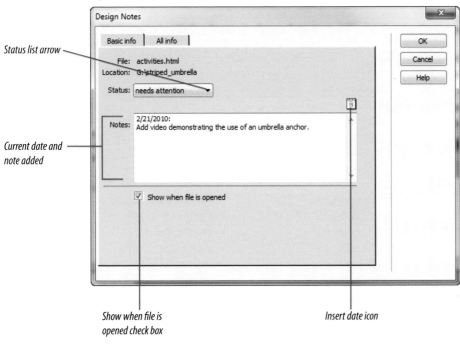

Figure 12 *Design Notes dialog box*

Status list arrow

Current date and note added

Show when file is opened check box

Insert date icon

Associate a Design Note with a file

1. Open the activities page, click **File** on the Application bar (Win) or Menu bar (Mac), click **Design Notes**, then click the **Basic info tab**, if necessary.

   The Design Notes dialog box opens. You can enter a note related to the open file in the text box. You can also assign the note a status, insert today's date, and indicate if the note appears whenever the file is opened.

2. Click the **Insert date icon** above the Notes text box on the right.

   The current date is added to the Notes text box.

3. Click under the date, then type **Add video demonstrating the use of an umbrella anchor**. in the Notes text box.

4. Click the **Status list arrow**, then click **needs attention**.

5. Click the **Show when file is opened** check box to select it, as shown in Figure 12, then click **OK**.

6. Click the **Refresh button** on the Files panel.

   An icon appears next to the activities page in the Notes column in the Files panel, indicating that there is a Design Note attached to the file.

You added a design note to the activities page with the current date and a status indicator. The note opens each time the file is opened.

Using Version Cue to Manage Assets

Another way to collaborate with team members is through Adobe Version Cue, a workgroup collaboration system that is included in Adobe Creative Suite 5. You can manage security, back up data, and use metadata to search files. **Metadata** includes information about a file such as keywords, descriptions, and copyright information. Adobe Bridge also organizes files with metadata.

Edit a Design Note

1. Click **File** on the Application bar (Win) or Menu bar (Mac), then click **Design Notes** to open the Design Note associated with the activities page.

   TIP You can also right-click (Win) or [control]-click (Mac) the filename in the Files panel, as shown in Figure 13, then click Design Notes to open the Design Note.

2. Edit the note by adding the sentence **Ask Sue Geren to send the file**. after the existing text in the Notes section, then click **OK** to close it.

   Dreamweaver created a file named activities.html.mno in a new folder called _notes in the site root folder. This folder and file do not appear in the Files panel unless you have selected the option to show hidden files and folders. To show hidden files, click the Files Panel options button, then click View, Show hidden files. However, you can switch to Windows Explorer (Win) or Finder (Mac) to see them without selecting this option. When you select the option to Enable Upload Design Notes for sharing, you can share the notes with team members working with you on the site.

3. Right-click (Win) or [control]-click (Mac) **activities.html** in the Files panel, then click **Explore** (Win) or **Reveal in Finder** (Mac).

   (continued)

Figure 13 *Files panel with Notes icon displayed*

Notes icon for activities file

Deleting a Design Note

There are two steps to deleting a Design Note that you don't need anymore. The first step is to delete the Design Note file. To delete a Design Note, right-click the filename in the Files panel that is associated with the Design Note you want to delete, and then click Explore (Win) or Reveal in Finder (Mac) to open your file management system. Open the _notes folder, delete the .mno file in the files list, and then close Explorer (Win) or Finder (Mac). The second step is done in Dreamweaver. Leave Maintain Design Notes selected in the Site Setup dialog box, then click Site on the Application bar (Win) or Menu bar (Mac), click Manage Sites, click Edit, click Advanced Settings, then select the Design Notes category. Click the Clean Up button. (*Note*: Don't do this if you deselect Maintain Design Notes first or it will delete all of your Design Notes!) The Design Notes icon will be removed from the Notes column in the Files panel.

Figure 14 *Windows Explorer displaying the _notes file and folder*

Notes file in _notes folder

4. Double-click the **_notes** folder to open it, then double-click the file **activities.html.mno**, shown in Figure 14, to open the file in Dreamweaver.

   The notes file opens in Code view in Dreamweaver, as shown in Figure 15.

5. Read the file, close it, close Explorer (Win) or Finder (Mac), then close the activities page.

You opened the Design Notes dialog box and edited the note in the Notes text box. Next, you viewed the .mno file that Dreamweaver created when you added the Design Note.

Figure 15 *Code for the activities.html.mno file*

```
1  <?xml version="1.0" encoding="utf-8" ?>
2  <info>
3      <infoitem key="notes" value="1/29/2010: &#xD;Add video demonstrating the use of an umbrella anchor. Ask Sue Geren to send
   the file." />
4      <infoitem key="status" value="needs attention" />
5      <infoitem key="showOnOpen" value="true" />
6  </info>
7
```

Publish a Website
AND TRANSFER FILES

What You'll Do

In this lesson, you will set up remote access to either an FTP folder or a local/network folder for The Striped Umbrella website. You will also view a website on a remote server, upload files to it, and synchronize the files.

Defining a Remote Site

As you learned in Chapter 1, publishing a site means transferring a copy of all the site's files to a web server. A **web server** is a computer with software that enables it to host websites and is connected to the Internet with an IP (Internet Protocol) address so that it is available on the Internet. Before you can publish a site to a web server, you must first define the remote site by specifying the Servers settings in the

Site Setup dialog box as shown in Figure 16. You can specify remote settings when you first create a new site and define the site root folder (as you did in Chapter 1 when you defined the remote access settings for The Striped Umbrella website). Or you can do it after you have completed all of your pages and are confident that your site is ready for public viewing. To specify the remote settings for a site, click the Add new Server button in the Site Setup

Figure 16 *Accessing the server settings in the Site Setup dialog box*

Servers tab

Add new Server
button

dialog box, then add your server name, and choose a connection setting, which specifies the type of server you will use.

NEW Dreamweaver CS5 allows you to set up multiple servers. You can set up a server for testing purposes only and a server for the live website. The most common connection setting is FTP (File Transfer Protocol). If you choose FTP, you need to specify a server address and folder name on the FTP site where you want to store your site root folder. You can also use **Secure FTP (SFTP)**, an FTP option, which lets you encrypt file transfers to protect your files, user names, and passwords. To use SFTP, check the Use Secure FTP (SFTP) check box in the Site Setup dialog box. You also need to enter login and password information. Figure 17 shows an example of FTP settings in the Add new server dialog box.

QUICK TIP

If you do not have access to an FTP site, you can publish a site to a local/network folder. This is referred to as a **LAN**, or a Local Area Network. Use the alternate steps provided in this lesson to publish your site to a local/network folder.

Viewing a Remote Site

Once you have set up a remote server, you can then view the remote folder in the Files panel by choosing Remote view from the View list. If your remote site is located on an FTP server, Dreamweaver will connect to it. You will see the File Activity dialog box showing the progress of the connection. You can also use the Connects to remote host button on the Files panel toolbar to connect to the remote site. If you defined your site on a local/network folder, then you don't need to use the Connects to remote host button; the site root folder and any files and folders it contains appear in the Files panel when you switch to Remote view.

Transferring Files to and from a Remote Site

After you set up a remote site, you need to **upload**, or copy, your files from the local version of your site to the remote host. To do this, view the site in Local view, select the files you want to upload, and then click the Put File(s) button on the Files panel toolbar.

NEW In Dreamweaver CS5, the Put File(s) button now includes the name of the server in the tooltip. Once you click this button, a copy of the files is transferred to the remote site. To view the uploaded files, switch to Remote server in the Files panel. Or, you can expand the Files panel to view both the Remote Site and the Local Site panes by clicking the Expand to show local and remote sites button in the Files panel.

If a file you select for uploading requires additional files, such as graphics, a dialog box opens after you click the Put File(s) button and asks if you want those files (known as **dependent files**) to be uploaded. By clicking Yes, all dependent files for the selected page will be uploaded to the appropriate folder in the remote site. If a file that you want to upload is located in a folder in the local site, the folder will automatically be transferred to the remote site.

QUICK TIP

To upload an entire site to a remote host, select the site root folder, then click the Put File(s) button.

Figure 17 *Viewing remote server settings in the Add new server dialog box*

User login and password to access remote server

Folder on FTP site where site will be published

Server name

Connection method

FTP site location

If you are developing or maintaining a website in a group environment, there might be times when you want to transfer or **download** files that other team members have created from the remote site to your local site. To do this, switch to Remote Server in the Files panel, select the files you want to download, then click the Get File(s) button on the Files panel toolbar.

NEW In Dreamweaver CS5, the Get File(s) button now includes the name of the server in the tooltip.

Synchronizing Files

To keep a website up to date—especially one that contains several pages and involves several team members—you need to update and replace files. Team members might make changes to pages on the local version of the site or make additions to the remote site. If many people are involved in maintaining a site, or if you are constantly making changes to the pages, ensuring that both the local and remote sites have the most up-to-date files could get confusing. Luckily, you can use the Synchronize command to keep things straight. The **Synchronize command** instructs Dreamweaver to compare the dates of the saved files in both versions of the site, then transfers only copies of files that have changed. To synchronize files, use the Synchronize Files dialog box, shown in Figure 18. You can synchronize an entire site or only selected files. You can also specify whether to upload newer files to the remote site, download newer files from the remote site, or both.

Figure 18 *Synchronize Files dialog box*

Instructs Dreamweaver to synchronize all files in the site

Understanding Dreamweaver Connection Options for Transferring Files

The connection types with which you are probably the most familiar are FTP and Local/Network. Other connection types that you can use with Dreamweaver include Microsoft Visual SafeSource (VSS), WebDav, and RDS. **VSS** is used only with the Windows operating system with Microsoft Visual SafeSource Client version 6. **WebDav** stands for Web-based Distributed Authoring and Versioning. This type of connection is used with the WebDav protocol. An example would be a website residing on an Apache web server. The **Apache web server** is a public domain, open source web server that is available using several different operating systems including UNIX and Windows. **RDS** stands for Remote Development Services, and is used with web servers using Cold Fusion.

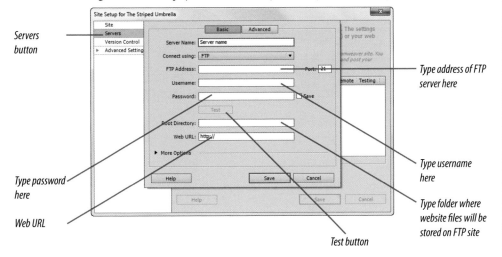

Servers button

Type password here

Web URL

Type address of FTP server here

Type username here

Type folder where website files will be stored on FTP site

Test button

Comparing Two Files for Differences in Content

There are situations where it would be helpful to be able to compare the contents of two files, such as a local file and the remote version of the same file; or an original file and the same file that has been saved with a different name. Once the two files are compared and differences are detected, you can merge the information in the files. A good time to compare files is before you upload them to a remote server to prevent accidentally writing over a file with more recent information. To compare files, you must first locate and install a third-party file comparison utility, or "dif" tool, such as Araxis Merge or Beyond Compare. (Dreamweaver does not have a file comparison tool included as part of the software, so you need to download one. If you are not familiar with these tools, find one using your favorite search engine.)

After installing the file comparison utility, use the Preferences command on the Edit menu to open the Preferences dialog box, then select the File Compare category. Next, browse to select the application you want to use to compare files. After you have set your Preferences, click the Compare with Remote Server command on the File menu to compare an open file with the remote version.

Set up a web server connection on an FTP site

NOTE: Complete these steps only if you know you can store The Striped Umbrella files on an FTP site and you know the login and password information. If you do not have access to an FTP site, complete the exercise called Set up web server access on a local or network folder on Page 7-18.

1. Click **Site** on the Application bar (Win) or Menu bar (Mac), then click **Manage Sites**.

2. Click **The Striped Umbrella** in the Manage Sites dialog box, if necessary, then click **Edit**.

3. Click **Servers** in the Site Setup dialog box, click the **Add new Server** button ✚, type your server name, click the **Connect using list arrow**, click **FTP** if necessary, then compare your screen to Figure 19.

4. Enter the FTP Address, Username, Password, Root Directory, and Web URL information in the dialog box.

TIP You must have file and folder permissions to use FTP. The server administrator can give you this and also tell you the folder name and location you should use to publish your files.

5. Click the **Test button** to test the connection to the remote site.

6. If the connection is successful, click **Save** to close the dialog box; if it is not successful, verify that you have the correct settings, then repeat Step 5.

7. Click **Save** to close the open dialog box, click **Save** to close the Site Setup dialog box, then click **Done** to close the Manage Sites dialog box.

You set up remote access information for The Striped Umbrella website using FTP settings.

Set up a web server connection to a local or network folder

NOTE: Complete these steps if you do not have the ability to post files to an FTP site and could not complete the previous lesson.

1. Using Windows Explorer (Win) or Finder (Mac), create a new folder on your hard drive or on a shared drive named **su_yourlastname** (e.g., if your last name is Jones, name the folder **su_jones**).

2. Switch back to Dreamweaver, open The Striped Umbrella website, then open the Manage Sites dialog box.

3. Click **The Striped Umbrella**, then click **Edit** to open the Site Setup for The Striped Umbrella dialog box.

TIP You can also double-click the site name in the Site Name box in the Files panel to open the Site Setup dialog box.

4. Click **Servers**, then click the **Add new Server button ➕**.

5. Type **SU Remote** for the Server Name, click the **Connect using list arrow**, then click **Local/Network**.

6. Click the **Browse icon 🗁** next to the Server Folder text box to open the Browse For Folder dialog box, navigate to and double-click the folder you created in Step 1, then click **Select**.

7. Compare your screen to Figure 20, click **Save**, click **Save** to close the Site Setup dialog box, then click **Done**.

You created a new folder and specified it as the remote location for The Striped Umbrella website, then set up remote access to a local or network folder.

Figure 20 *Local/Network settings in the Site Setup for The Striped Umbrella dialog box*

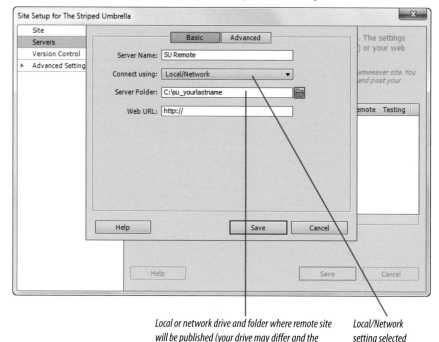

Local or network drive and folder where remote site will be published (your drive may differ and the folder name should end with your last name)

Local/Network setting selected

Testing Your Site's Usability

Once you have at least a prototype of the website ready to evaluate, it is a good idea to conduct a site usability test. This is a process that involves asking unbiased people, who are not connected to the design process, to use and evaluate the site. A comprehensive usability test includes pre-test questions, participant tasks, a post-test interview, and a post-test survey. This provides much-needed information as to how usable the site is to those unfamiliar with it. Typical questions include: "What are your overall impressions?"; "What do you like the best and the least about the site?"; and "How easy is it to navigate inside the site?" For more information, go to www.w3.org and search for "site usability test."

Figure 21 *Connecting to the remote site*

Connects to remote host button

Remote folder name

Remote server selected

Expand to show local and remote sites button

Figure 22 *Viewing the local and remote site folders*

Remote folder

Disconnects to remote host button

Local site folder

Collapse to show only local or remote site button

View a website on a remote server

1. Click the **View list arrow** in the Files panel, then click **Remote Server**, then compare your screen to Figure 21.

   If you set your remote access to be a local or network folder, then the su_yourlastname folder appears in the Files panel. If your remote access is set to an FTP site, Dreamweaver connects to the host server and displays the remote folders and file.

2. Click the **Expand to show local and remote sites button** on the Files panel to view both the Remote Site and Local Files panes. The su_yourlastname folder appears in the Remote Site portion of the expanded Files panel, as shown in Figure 22.

TIP If you don't see your remote site files, click the Connects to remote host button or the Refresh button. If you don't see two panes, one with the remote site files and one with the local files, drag the panel border to enlarge the panel.

When the Files panel is expanded to show both the local and remote sites, the Expand to show local and remote sites button becomes the Collapse to show only local or remote site button. and the Connects to remote host button becomes the Disconnects from remote host button.

You used the Files panel to set the view for The Striped Umbrella site to Remote view. You then connected to the remote server to view the remote folder you created earlier.

Upload files to a remote server

1. Click the **about_us.html file**, then click the **Put file(s) button** ⬆ on the Files panel toolbar.

   Notice that the Put File(s) button tooltip includes the name of the remote server you are using. The Dependent Files dialog box opens, asking if you want to include dependent files.

2. Click **Yes**.

   The about_us file, the style sheet files, the Spry assets files, and the image files used in the about_us page are copied to the remote server. The Background File Activity dialog box appears and flashes the names of each file as they are uploaded.

3. Expand the assets folder and the SpryAssets folder in the remote site if necessary, then compare your screen to Figure 23.

   The remote site now contains the about_us page as well as the Spry files, the image files, and the external style sheet files, all of which are needed by the about_us page.

TIP You might need to expand the su_yourlastname folder in order to view the assets folder.

You used the Put File(s) button to upload the about_us file and all files that are dependent files of the about_us page.

Figure 23 *Remote view of the site after uploading the about_us page*

about_us page and its dependent files in remote site

Local site files

Continuing to Work While Transferring Files to a Remote Server

During the process of uploading files to a remote server, there are many Dreamweaver functions that you can continue to use while you wait. For example, you can create a new site, create a new page, edit a page, add files and folders, and run reports. However, there are some functions that you cannot use while transferring files, many of which involve accessing files on the remote server or using Check In/Check Out.

Figure 24 *Synchronize Files dialog box*

Figure 25 *Files that need to be uploaded to the remote site*

Synchronize files

1. Click the **Collapse to show only local or remote site button** ▣, change to Local view, then open each page in the website in Code view and locate those that are missing the link to the website favicon in the line above the code for the page title.

2. Open the index page, then copy the code in the head content that links the favicon to the page.

3. Copy the favicon link to each of the pages you identified in Step 1, then save each page.

4. Click the **Synchronize button** ⟳ on the Files panel toolbar to open the Synchronize Files dialog box.

5. Click the **Synchronize list arrow**, then click **Entire 'The Striped Umbrella' Site**.

6. Click the **Direction list arrow**, click **Put newer files to remote** if necessary, then compare your screen to Figure 24.

7. Click **Preview**.

   The Background File Activity dialog box might appear and flash the names of all the files from the local version of the site that need to be uploaded to the remote site. The Synchronize dialog box, shown in Figure 25, opens and lists all the files that need to be uploaded to the remote site.

8. Click **OK**.

   All the files from the local The Striped Umbrella site are copied to the remote version of the site. If you open the Files panel, you will notice that the remote folders are yellow (Win) or blue (Mac) and the local folders are green.

You synchronized The Striped Umbrella website files to copy all remaining files from the local root folder to the remote root folder.

Check Files
OUT AND IN

What You'll Do

In this lesson, you will use the Site Setup dialog box to enable the Check Out feature. You will then check out the cafe page, make a change to it, and then check it back in.

Managing a Website with a Team

When you work on a large website, chances are that many people will be involved in keeping the site up to date. Different individuals will need to make changes or additions to different pages of the site by adding or deleting content, changing graphics, updating information, and so on. If everyone had access to the pages at the same time, problems could arise. For instance, what if you and another team member both made edits to the same page at the same time? If you post your edited version of the file to the site after the other team member posts his edited version of the same file, the file that you upload will overwrite his version and none of his changes will be incorporated. Not good! Fortunately, you can avoid this scenario by using Dreamweaver's collaboration tools.

Checking Out and Checking In Files

Checking files in and out is similar to checking library books in and out or video/DVD rentals. No one else can read the same copy that you have checked out. Using Dreamweaver's Check Out feature ensures that team members cannot overwrite each other's pages. When this feature is enabled, only one person can work on a file at a time. To check out a file, click the file you want to work on in the Files panel, and then click the Check Out File(s) button on the Files panel toolbar. Files that you have checked out are marked with green check marks in the Files panel. Files that have been checked in are marked with padlock icons.

After you finish editing a checked-out file, you need to save and close the file, and then click the Check in button to check the file back in and make it available to other users. When a file is checked in, you cannot make edits to it unless you check it out again. Figure 26 shows the Check Out File(s) and Check in buttons on the Files panel toolbar.

Enabling the Check out Feature

To use the Check out feature with a team of people, you must first enable it. To turn on this feature, check the Enable file check-out check box in the Remote Info settings of the Site Setup dialog box. If you do not want to use this feature, you should turn it off so you won't have to check files out every time you open them.

Using Subversion control

Another file management tool is Subversion control. A remote SVN (Apache Subversion) repository is used to maintain current and historical versions of your website files. It is used in a team environment to move, copy, and delete shared files. You can protect files from being accessed using the svn:ignore property to create a list of files that are to be ignored in a directory.

Figure 26 *Check Out File(s) and Check in buttons on the Files Panel toolbar*

Activate the Enable file Check-out feature

1. Change to expanded view in the Files panel, click **Site** on the Application bar (Win) or Menu bar (Mac), click **Manage Sites** to open the Manage Sites dialog box, click **The Striped Umbrella** in the list, then click **Edit** to open the Site Setup for The Striped Umbrella dialog box.

2. Click **Servers**, select your remote server, click the **Edit existing Server button** ✎, click the **Advanced tab**, then click the **Enable file check-out check box** to select it.

3. Check the **Check out files when opening check box** to select it, if necessary.

4. Type your name using all lowercase letters and no spaces in the Check-out Name text box.

5. Type your email address in the Email Address text box.

6. Compare your screen to Figure 27, click **Save** to close the open dialog box, click **Save** to close the Site Setup for The Striped Umbrella dialog box, then click **Done** to close the Manage Sites dialog box. Your dialog box will differ from the figure if you are using FTP access.

You used the Site Definition for The Striped Umbrella dialog box to enable the Check out feature, which tells team members when you are working with a site file.

Figure 27 *Enabling the Check-out feature*

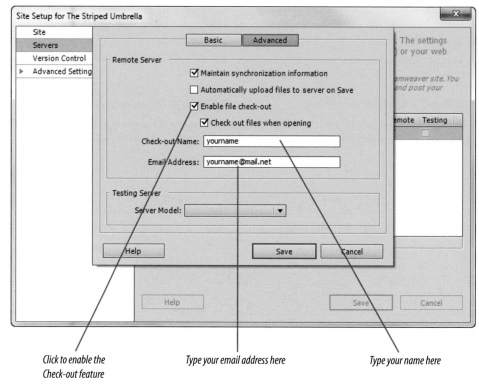

Click to enable the Check-out feature

Type your email address here

Type your name here

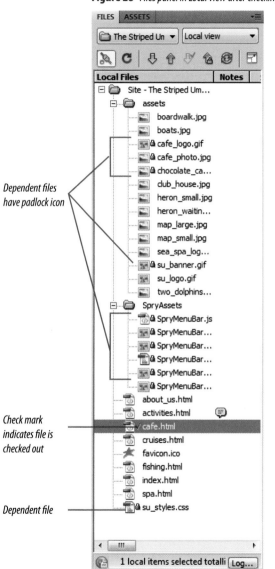

Figure 28 *Files panel in Local view after checking out cafe page*

Dependent files
have padlock icon

Check mark
indicates file is
checked out

Dependent file

Check out a file

1. Click the **cafe page** in the Local Files list in the Files panel to select it.

2. Click the **Check Out File(s) button** ⬇ on the Files panel toolbar.

   The Dependent Files dialog box appears, asking if you want to include all files that are needed for the cafe page.

3. Click **Yes**, expand the assets and SpryAssets folders if necessary in the local site files, collapse the Files panel, click the **View list arrow**, click **Local view**, then compare your screen to Figure 28.

   The cafe file has a check mark next to it indicating you have checked it out. The dependent files have a padlock icon, indicating that they cannot be changed as long as the cafe file is checked out.

You checked out the cafe page so that no one else can use it while you work on it.

Check in a file

1. Open the cafe page, change the closing hour for The Cabana in the table to **8:00 p.m.**, then save your changes.

2. Close the cafe page, then click the **cafe page** in the Files panel to select it.

3. Click the **Check In button** 🔒 on the Files panel toolbar.

   The Dependent Files dialog box opens, asking if you want to include dependent files.

4. Click **Yes**, click another file in the Files panel to deselect the cafe page, then compare your screen to Figure 29.

   A padlock icon appears instead of a green check mark next to the cafe page on the Files panel. The padlock icon indicated that the file is read-only now and cannot be edited unless it is checked out.

You made a content change on the cafe page, then checked in the cafe page, making it available for others to check it out.

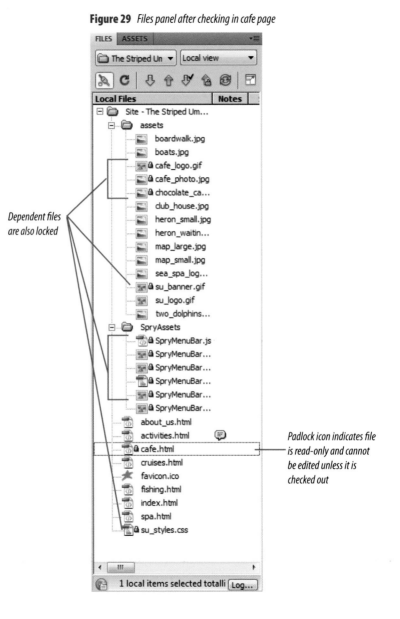

Figure 29 *Files panel after checking in cafe page*

Dependent files are also locked

Padlock icon indicates file is read-only and cannot be edited unless it is checked out

Figure 30 *Files panel after turning off the read-only feature*

All files are now — unlocked

Edit site preferences

1. Click **Site** on the Application bar (Win) or Menu bar (Mac), click **Manage Sites** to open the Manage Sites dialog box, click **The Striped Umbrella** in the list, then click **Edit** to open the Site Setup for The Striped Umbrella dialog box.

2. Click **Servers**, select your remote server, click the **Edit existing Server button** ✐, click the **Advanced tab**, then click the **Enable file check-out check box** to deselect it.

   Now that you understand how to use this feature, it will be easier to have this option turned off so that each time you open a page you will not have to check it out the next time you use it.

3. Click **Save** to close the open dialog box, click **Save** to close the Site Setup dialog box, then click **Done** to close the Manage Sites dialog box.

4. Right-click the **site root folder** in the Files panel, then click **Turn off Read Only** (Win) or **Unlock** (Mac).

   All files are writeable now and the padlock icons have disappeared, as shown in Figure 30.

You disabled the Enable file check-out feature and then turned off the Read-only feature for all site files.

Cloak
FILES

What You'll Do

In this lesson, you will cloak the assets folder so that it is excluded from various operations, such as the Put, Get, Check In, and Check Out commands. You will also use the Site Setup dialog box to cloak all .gif files in the site.

Understanding Cloaking Files

There may be times when you want to exclude a particular file or files from being uploaded to a server. For instance, suppose you have a page that is not quite finished and needs more work before it is ready to be viewed by others. You can exclude such files by **cloaking** them, which marks them for exclusion from several commands, including Put, Get, Synchronize, Check In, and Check Out. Cloaked files are also excluded from site-wide operations, such as checking for links or updating a template or library item. You can cloak a folder or specify a type of file to cloak throughout the site.

Cloaking a Folder

In addition to cloaking a file or group of files, you might also want to cloak an entire folder. For example, if you are not concerned with replacing outdated image files, you might want to cloak the assets folder of a website to save time when synchronizing files. To cloak a folder, select the folder, click the Files panel Options button, point to Site, point to Cloaking, and then click Cloak. The folder you cloaked and all the files it contains appear with red slashes across them, as shown in Figure 31. To uncloak a folder, click the Panel options button on the Files panel, point to Site, point to Cloaking, and then click Uncloak.

QUICK TIP

To uncloak all files in a site, click the Files Panel options button, point to Site, point to Cloaking, then click Uncloak All.

Cloaking Selected File Types

There may be times when you want to cloak a particular type of file, such as a .jpg file.

To cloak a particular file type, open the Site Setup dialog box, click Advanced, click Cloaking, click the Cloak files ending with check box, and then type a file extension in the text box below the check box. All files throughout the site that have the specified file extension will be cloaked.

Figure 31 *Cloaked assets folder in the Files panel*

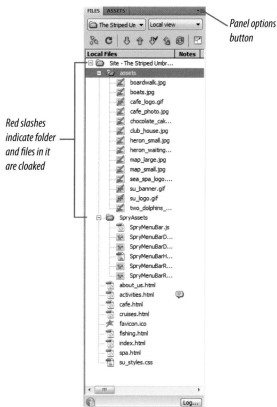

Panel options button

Red slashes indicate folder and files in it are cloaked

Cloak and uncloak a folder

1. Verify that Local view is displayed in the Files panel, then open the Manage Sites dialog box.

2. Click **The Striped Umbrella** if necessary, click **Edit** to open the Site Setup for The Striped Umbrella dialog box, click **Advanced Settings**, click **Cloaking**, verify that the Enable Cloaking check box is checked, click **Save**, then click **Done**.

3. Click the **assets folder** in the Files panel, click the **Files Panel options button** ▾≡ , point to **Site**, point to **Cloaking**, click **Cloak**, then compare your screen to Figure 32.

   A red slash now appears on top of the assets folder in the Files panel, indicating that all files in the assets folder are cloaked and will be excluded from putting, getting, checking in, checking out, and many other operations.

TIP You can also cloak a folder by right-clicking (Win) or [control]-clicking (Mac) the folder, pointing to Cloaking, then clicking Cloak.

4. Right-click (Win) or [control]-click (Mac) the **assets folder**, point to **Cloaking**, then click **Uncloak**.

   The assets folder and all the files it contains no longer appear with red slashes across them, indicating they are no longer cloaked.

You cloaked the assets folder so that this folder and all the files it contains would be excluded from many operations, including uploading and downloading files. You then uncloaked the assets folder.

Figure 32 *Assets folder after cloaking*

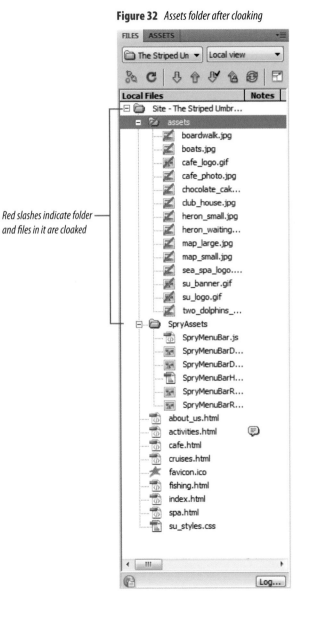

Red slashes indicate folder and files in it are cloaked

Figure 33 *Specifying a file type to cloak*

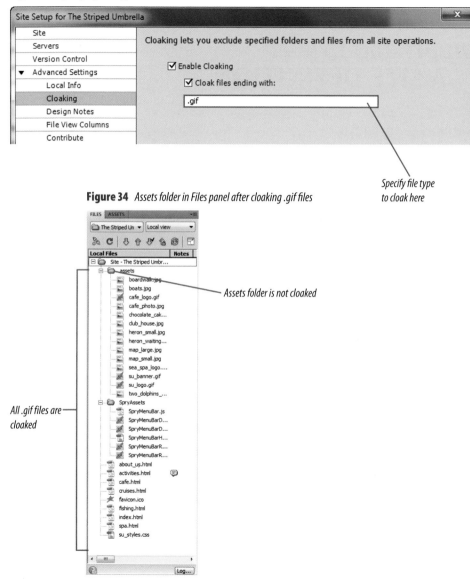

Figure 33 callout: *Specify file type to cloak here*

Figure 34 *Assets folder in Files panel after cloaking .gif files*

Figure 34 callouts: *Assets folder is not cloaked* / *All .gif files are cloaked*

Cloak selected file types

1. Right-click (Win) or [control]-click (Mac) the **assets folder** in the Files panel, point to **Cloaking**, then click **Settings** to open the Site Setup for The Striped Umbrella dialog box with the Cloaking category selected.

2. Click the **Cloak files ending with check box**, select the text in the text box that appears, type **.gif** in the text box, then compare your screen to Figure 33.

3. Click **Save**.

   A dialog box opens, indicating that the site cache will be recreated.

4. Click **OK**, expand the assets folder if necessary, then compare your screen to Figure 34.

   All of the .gif files in the assets folder appear with red slashes across them, indicating that they are cloaked. Notice that the assets folder is not cloaked.

5. Click the **site root folder** in the Files panel, right-click, point to **Cloaking**, click **Uncloak All**, then click **Yes** to close the warning message.

   All files are uncloaked now and will not be excluded from any site commands.

You cloaked all the .gif files in The Striped Umbrella website. You then uncloaked all files.

Import and Export
A SITE DEFINITION

What You'll Do

In this lesson, you will export the site definition file for The Striped Umbrella website. You will then import The Striped Umbrella website.

Exporting a Site Definition

When you work on a website for a long time, it's likely that at some point you will want to move it to another machine or share it with other collaborators who will help you maintain it. When you move a site, you need to move its site definition. The **site definition** for a website contains important information about the site, including its URL, preferences that you've specified, and other secure information, such as login and password information. You can use the Export command to export the site definition file to another location. The Export command creates a file with an .ste file extension. To do this, open the Manage Sites dialog box, click the site you want to export, and then click Export. Because the site definition file contains password information that you will want to keep secret from other site users, you should never save the site definition file in the website. Instead, save it in an external folder.

Importing a Site Definition

If you want to be able to access the site settings in a website that someone else has created, you can import the site definition file once you have the necessary .ste file. To do this, click Import in the Manage Sites dialog box to open the Import Site dialog box, navigate to the .ste file you want to import, then click Open.

Figure 35 *Saving The Striped Umbrella.ste file in the su_site_definition folder*

Export a site definition

1. Use Windows Explorer (Win) or Finder (Mac) to create two new folders on your hard drive or external drive named **su_site_definition** and **su_backup_site**

2. Switch back to Dreamweaver, open the Manage Sites dialog box, click **The Striped Umbrella**, then click **Export** to open the Export Site dialog box.

TIP If you see a message asking if you are exporting the site to back up your settings or to share your settings with other users, choose the Back up my settings option, then click **OK**.

3. Navigate to and double-click to open the **su_site_definition folder** that you created in Step 1, as shown in Figure 35, click **Save**, then click **Done**.

You used the Export command to create the site definition file and saved it in the su_site_definition folder.

Import a site definition

1. Open the Manage Sites dialog box, click **The Striped Umbrella**, then click **Import** to open the Import Site dialog box.

2. Navigate to the su_site_definition folder, compare your screen to Figure 36, select **The Striped Umbrella.ste**, then click **Open**.

   A dialog box opens and says that a site named The Striped Umbrella already exists. It will name the imported site The Striped Umbrella 2 so that it has a different name.

3. Click **OK**.

4. Click **The Striped Umbrella 2** if necessary, click **Edit**, then compare your screen to Figure 37.

   The settings show that The Striped Umbrella 2 site has the same site root folder and default images folder as The Striped Umbrella site. Both of these settings are specified in The Striped Umbrella.ste file that you imported. Importing a site in this way makes it possible for multiple users with different computers to work on the same site.

   TIP Make sure you know who is responsible for which files to keep from overwriting the wrong files when they are published. The Synchronize Files and Check In/Check Out features are good procedures to use with multiple designers.

5. Click **Save**, click **OK** to close the warning message, then click **Done**.

   TIP If a dialog box opens warning that the root folder chosen is the same as the folder for the site "The Striped Umbrella," click OK. Remember that you only import the site settings when you import a site definition. You are not importing any of the website files.

You imported The Striped Umbrella.ste file and created a new site, The Striped Umbrella 2.

Figure 36 *Import Site dialog box*

Figure 37 *Site Definition for The Striped Umbrella 2 dialog box*

Name of imported site

Figure 38 *Viewing The Striped Umbrella 2 website files*

View the imported site

1. Click the **Expand to show local and remote sites button** 🗗 on the Files panel toolbar to expand the Files panel.

2. Expand the Site root folder in the Local Files pane to view the contents, if necessary.

3. Click the **Refresh button** ⟳ to view the files in the Remote Site pane.

   As shown in Figure 38, the site is identical to the original The Striped Umbrella site, except the name has been changed to The Striped Umbrella 2.

   TIP If you don't see your remote site files, click the Connects to remote host button.

4. Click the **Collapse to show only local or remote site button** 🗗 to collapse the Files panel.

5. Open the Manage Sites dialog box, verify that The Striped Umbrella 2 site is selected, click **Remove**, click **Yes** in the warning dialog box, then click **Done** to delete The Striped Umbrella 2 website.

6. Close all open pages, then close Dreamweaver.

You viewed the expanded Files panel for The Striped Umbrella 2 website, then deleted The Striped Umbrella 2 website.

POWER USER SHORTCUTS	
To do this:	**Use this shortcut:**
Get	[Ctrl][Shift][D] (Win) or ⌘ [Shift][D] (Mac)
Check Out	[Ctrl][Alt][Shift][D] (Win) or ⌘ [opt] [Shift][D] (Mac)
Put	[Ctrl][Shift][U] (Win) or ⌘ [Shift][U] (Mac)
Check In	[Ctrl][Alt][Shift][U] (Win) or ⌘ [opt] [Shift][U] (Mac)
Check Links	[Shift][F8] (Win) or [fn][shift][F8] (Mac)
Check Links Sitewide	[Ctrl][F8] (Win) or [fn] ⌘ [F8] (Mac)

Evaluate Web Content
FOR LEGAL USE

What You'll Do

In this lesson, you will examine copyright issues in the context of using content gathered from sources such as the Internet.

Can I Use Downloaded Media?

The Internet has made it possible to locate compelling and media-rich content to use in websites. A person who has learned to craft searches can locate a multitude of interesting material, such as graphics, animations, sounds, and text. But just because you can find it easily does not mean that you can use it however you want or under any circumstance. Learning about copyright law can help you decide whether or how to use content created and published by someone other than yourself.

Understanding Intellectual Property

Intellectual property is a product resulting from human creativity. It can include inventions, movies, songs, designs, clothing, and so on.

The purpose of copyright law is to promote progress in society, not expressly to protect the rights of copyright owners. However, the vast majority of work you might want to download and use in a project is protected by either copyright or trademark law.

Copyright protects the particular and tangible *expression* of an idea, not the idea itself.

If you wrote a story using the idea of aliens crashing in Roswell, New Mexico, no one could copy or use your story without permission. However, anyone could write a story using a similar plot or characters—the *idea* of aliens crashing in Roswell is not copyright-protected. Generally, copyright lasts for the life of the author plus 70 years.

Trademark protects an image, word, slogan, symbol, or design used to identify goods or services. For example, the Nike swoosh, Disney characters, or the shape of a classic Coca-Cola bottle are works protected by trademark. Trademark protection lasts for 10 years with 10-year renewal terms, lasting indefinitely provided the trademark is in active use.

What Exactly Does the Copyright Owner Own?

Copyright attaches to a work as soon as you create it; you do not have to register it with the U.S. Copyright Office. A copyright owner has a "bundle" of six rights, consisting of:

1) reproduction (including downloading)
2) creation of **derivative works** (for example, a movie version of a book)
3) distribution to the public

4) public performance
5) public display
6) public performance by digital audio transmission of sound recordings

By default, only a copyright holder can create a derivative work of his or her original by transforming or adapting it.

Understanding Fair Use

The law builds in limitations to copyright protection. One limitation to copyright is **fair use**. Fair use allows limited use of copyright-protected work. For example, you could excerpt short passages of a film or song for a class project or parody a television show. Determining if fair use applies to a work depends on the *purpose* of its use, the *nature* of the copyrighted work, *how much* you want to copy, and the *effect* on the market or value of the work. However, there is no clear formula on what constitutes fair use. It is always decided on a case-by-case basis.

How Do I Use Work Properly?

Being a student doesn't mean you can use any amount of any work for class. On the other hand, the very nature of education means you need to be able to use or reference different work in your studies. There are many situations that allow you to use protected work.

In addition to applying a fair use argument, you can obtain permission, pay a fee, use work that does not have copyright protection, or use work that has a flexible copyright

license, where the owner has given the public permission to use the work in certain ways. For more information about open-access licensing, visit www.creativecommons.org. Work that is no longer protected by copyright is in the **public domain**; anyone can use it however they wish for any purpose. In general, the photos and other media on Federal government websites are in the public domain.

Understanding Licensing Agreements

Before you decide whether to use media you find on a website, you must decide whether you can comply with its licensing agreement.

A **licensing agreement** is the permission given by a copyright holder that conveys the right to use the copyright holder's work under certain conditions.

Websites have rules that govern how a user may use its text and media, known as **terms of use**. Figures 39, 40, and 41 are great examples of clear terms of use for the Library of Congress website.

A site's terms of use do not override your right to apply fair use. Also, someone cannot compile public domain images in a website and then claim they own them or dictate

Figure 39 *The Library of Congress home page*

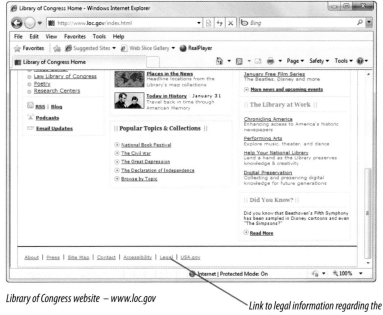

Library of Congress website – www.loc.gov

Link to legal information regarding the use of content on the website

how the images can be used. Conversely, someone can erroneously state in their terms of use that you can use work on the site freely, but they may not know the work's copyright status. The burden is on you to research the veracity of anyone claiming you can use work.

Obtaining Permission or a License

The **permissions process** is specific to what you want to use (text, photographs, music, trademarks, merchandise, and so on) and how you want to use it (school term paper, personal website, fabric pattern). How you want to use the work determines the level and scope of permissions you need to secure. The fundamentals, however, are the same. Your request should contain the following:

- Your full name, address, and complete contact information.
- A specific description of your intended use. Sometimes including a sketch, storyboard, wireframe, or link to a website is helpful.
- A signature line for the copyright holder.
- A target date when you would like the copyright holder to respond. This can be important if you're working under deadline.

Posting a Copyright Notice

The familiar © symbol or "Copyright" is no longer required to indicate copyright, nor does it automatically register your work, but it does serve a useful purpose. When you post or publish it, you are stating clearly to those who may not know anything about copyright

Figure 40 *Library of Congress website legal page*

Library of Congress website – www.loc.gov

Figure 41 *Library of Congress website copyright information*

About Copyright and the Collections

Whenever possible, the Library of Congress provides factual information about copyright owners and related matters in the catalog records, finding aids and other texts that accompany collections. As a publicly supported institution, the Library generally does not own rights in its collections. Therefore, it does not charge permission fees for use of such material and generally does not grant or deny permission to publish or otherwise distribute material in its collections. Permission and possible fees may be required from the copyright owner independently of the Library. It is the researcher's obligation to determine and satisfy copyright or other use restrictions when publishing or otherwise distributing materials found in the Library's collections. Transmission or reproduction of protected items beyond that allowed by fair use requires the written permission of the copyright owners. Researchers must make their own assessments of rights in light of their intended use.

If you have any more information about an item you've seen on our website or if you are the copyright owner and believe our website has not properly attributed your work to you or has used it without permission, we want to hear from you. Please contact OGC@loc.gov with your contact information and a link to the relevant content.

⊙ View more information about copyright law from the U.S. Copyright Office.

Library of Congress website – www.loc.gov

law that this work is claimed by you and is not in the public domain. Your case is made even stronger if someone violates your copyright and your notice is clearly visible. That way, a violator can never claim ignorance of the law as an excuse for infringing. Common notification styles include:

Copyright 2013
Delmar, Cengage Learning
or
© 2013 Delmar, Cengage Learning

Giving proper attribution for text excerpts is a must; giving attribution for media is excellent practice, but is never a substitute for applying a fair use argument, buying a license, or simply getting permission.

You must provide proper citation for materials you incorporate into your own work, such as the following:

References
Waxer, Barbara M., and Baum, Marsha L. 2006. *Internet Surf and Turf—The Essential Guide to Copyright, Fair Use, and Finding Media.* Boston: Thomson Course Technology.

This expectation applies even to unsigned material and material that does not display the copyright symbol (©). Moreover, the expectation applies just as certainly to ideas you summarize or paraphrase as to words you quote verbatim.

Guidelines have been written by the American Psychological Association (APA) to establish an editorial style to be used to present written material. These guidelines include the way citations are referenced. Here's a list of the elements that make up an APA-style citation of web-based resources:

■ Author's name (if known)
■ Date of publication or last revision (if known), in parentheses
■ Title of document
■ Title of complete work or website (if applicable), underlined
■ URL
■ Date of access, in parentheses

Following is an example of how you would reference the APA Home page on the Reference page of your paper:

APA Style.org. (Retrieved August 22, 2012), from APA Online website: http://www.apastyle.org/electext.html.

There are APA styles that are used for other sources of text such as magazines, journals, newspaper articles, blogs, and email messages. Here's a list of the elements that make up an APA-style citation of images, sounds, or video:

■ Name of the researching organization
■ Date of publication
■ Caption or description
■ Brief explanation of what type of data is there and in what form it appears (shown in brackets)
■ Project name and retrieval information.

Another set of guidelines used by many schools and university and commercial presses is the Modern Language Association (MLA) style. For more information, go to http://www.mla.org.

Present a
WEBSITE TO A CLIENT

What You'll Do

In this lesson, you will explore options for presenting a website to a client at the completion of a project.

Are You Ready to Present Your Work?

Before you present a website to a client as a finished project, you should do a final check on some important items. First, do all your final design and development decisions reflect your client's goals and requirements? Does the website not only fulfill your client's goals and requirements, but those of the intended audience as well? Second, did you follow good web development practices? Did you check your pages against your wireframes as you developed them? Did you check each page against current accessibility standards? Did you run all necessary technical tests, such as validating the code, and searching for missing alternate text or missing page titles? Did you verify that all external and internal links work correctly? Third, did your final delivery date and budget meet the timeframe and budget you originally promised the client?

If you find that you did spend more time on the site than you expected to, determine if it was because you underestimated the amount of work it would take, ran into unforeseen technical problems, or because the client changed the requirements or increased the scope of the project as it went

along. If you underestimated the project or ran into unexpected difficulties from causes other than the client, you usually cannot expect the client to make up the difference without a prior agreement. No client wants surprises at the end of a project, so it's best to communicate frequently and let the client know the status of all site elements as you go.

If the client changes the project scope, make sure you discuss the implication of this with the client. Ideally, you have made the client aware of any schedule or budget changes at the time they began to occur, and the client expects that your estimate will grow by a predictable, agreed-upon amount.

Client communication, both at the beginning of a project and throughout a project, is critical to a successful web design and a solid customer relationship. In building a house, a good architect makes an effort to get to know and understand a new client before beginning a house design. The design must be functional and meet the client's checklist of requirements, but it must also fit the client's personality and taste. The final structure must continue to meet those needs; the same is true of a website.

Some clients have a difficult time looking at architectural drawings and visualizing what the home will look like, so architects use different methods to communicate their design. Some use scale mockups, 3-D renderings, or photos of similarly styled homes to help the client visualize what their home will look like when completed. Web designers use similar strategies. You may be capable of building a great website, but you must communicate with the client from the beginning of the project to set and satisfy client expectations. Without this mutual understanding, the project's successful completion will be at risk. It is much less expensive to make changes and adjustments at the beginning of a project, and as changes occur, rather than close to completion. Communication is key.

What Is the Best Way to Present Your Work?

Ideally, you presented some form of prototype of the website at the beginning of the development process. You may have chosen to use low-fidelity wireframes such as one created in Microsoft PowerPoint or Adobe Photoshop. Or you may have used a high-fidelity wireframe that is interactive and multidimensional such as OverSight, ProtoShare, or Adobe Flash Catalyst, as shown in Figure 42. To communicate with your client and ensure a mutual understanding of the project, you could also use **BaseCamp**, a web-based project collaboration tool that many companies use. There is a monthly fee for using it, based on the number of projects you are running and your storage needs. You can use BaseCamp throughout the project cycle, not just at the end. To present the final project, consider publishing the site to a server and sending the client a link to view the completed website. Creating PDFs of the site and sending them to the client for approval is another possible method.

Another communication option is to invite the client to your office and do a full walkthrough of the site with them, which offers them a chance to ask questions. This is probably one of the best options if it is feasible. If you have taken the time to build a relationship of trust over the project, neither side should expect unpleasant surprises at the end.

Figure 42 *Adobe Flash Catalyst information on the Adobe website*

Adobe product screen shot reprinted with permission from Adobe Systems Incorporated – www.adobe.com

Perform website maintenance.

1. Open the Blooms & Bulbs website, then re-create the site cache.
2. Use the Link Checker panel to check for broken links, then fix any broken links that appear.
3. Use the Link Checker to check for orphaned files. If any orphaned files appear in the report, take steps to link them to appropriate pages or remove them.
4. Use the Assets panel to check for non-websafe colors. Evaluate any non-websafe colors you find to see if they affect your page content.
5. Run an Untitled Documents report for the entire local site. If the report lists any pages that have no titles, add page titles to the untitled pages. Run the report again to verify that all pages have page titles.
6. Run a report to look for missing alternate text. Add alternate text to any graphics that need it, then run the report again to verify that all images contain alternate text.
7. Verify that the Design Notes preference is enabled and add a Design Note to the workshops page as follows: **Shoot a video of the hanging baskets class to add to the page**. Add the status **needs attention**, add the current date, and check the Show when file is opened option.

Publish a website and transfer files.

1. Set up web server access for the Blooms & Bulbs website on an FTP server or a local/network server (whichever is available to you) using blooms_ yourlastname as the remote folder name.
2. View the Blooms & Bulbs remote site in the Files panel.
3. Upload the water_lily.jpg file to the remote site, then view the remote site.
4. Add the code that links the favicon to the head content of any pages in the site that do not have it.
5. Synchronize all files in the Blooms & Bulbs website, so that all files from the local site are uploaded to the remote site.

Check files out and in.

1. Enable the Enable file check-out feature.
2. Check out the plants page and all dependent pages.
3. Open the plants page, then change the heading to "Featured Spring Plants: Roses!" and the style to Heading 2, then save the file.
4. Check in the plants page and all dependent files.
5. Disable the Enable file check-out feature.
6. Turn off read only (Win) or Unlock (Mac) for the entire site.

Cloak files.

1. Verify that cloaking is enabled in the Blooms & Bulbs website.
2. Cloak the assets folder, then uncloak it.
3. Cloak all the .jpg files in the Blooms & Bulbs website, then expand the assets folder if necessary to view the cloaked files in the Files panel.
4. Uncloak the .jpg files.

Import and export a site definition.

1. Create a new folder named **blooms_site_ definition** on your hard drive or external drive.
2. Export the Blooms & Bulbs site definition to the blooms_site_definition folder.
3. Import the Blooms & Bulbs site definition to create a new site called **Blooms & Bulbs 2**.
4. Make sure that all files from the Blooms & Bulbs website appear in the Files panel for the imported site, then compare your screen to Figure 43.
5. Remove the Blooms & Bulbs 2 site.
6. Close all open files.

Figure 43 *Completed Skills Review*

In this Project Builder, you publish the TripSmart website that you have developed throughout this book to a local/network folder. Thomas Howard, the owner, has asked that you publish the site to a local folder as a backup location. You first run several reports on the site, specify the remote settings for the site, upload files to the remote site, check files out and in, and cloak files. Finally, you export and import the site definition.

1. Use the TripSmart website that you began in Project Builder 1 in Chapter 1 and developed in previous chapters.
2. Use the Link Checker panel to check for broken links, then fix any broken links that appear.
3. Use the Link Checker to check for orphaned files. If any orphaned files appear in the report, take steps to link them to appropriate pages or remove them.
4. Use the Assets panel to check for non-websafe colors. If you find any, evaluate whether or not they pose a problem for any of the pages.
5. Run an Untitled Documents report for the entire local site. If the report lists any pages that lack titles, add page titles to the untitled pages. Run the report again to verify that all pages have page titles.
6. Run a report to look for missing alternate text. Add alternate text to any graphics that need it, then run the report again to verify that all images contain alternate text.
7. Enable the Design Notes preference, if necessary, and add a design note to the tours page as follows: **Add content and a Flash video for the San**

Francisco tour. Add the current date, the status **needs attention** and check the Show when file is opened option.
8. If you did not do so in Project Builder 1 in Chapter 1, use the Site Definition dialog box to set up web server access for a remote site using a local or network folder.
9. Upload the index page and all dependent files to the remote site.
10. View the remote site to make sure that all files uploaded correctly.
11. Add the code that links the favicon to the head content of any pages in the site that do not have it.
12. Synchronize the files so that all other files on the local TripSmart site are uploaded to the remote site.
13. Enable the Enable file check-out feature.
14. Check out the index page in the local site and all dependent files.
15. Open the index page, close the index page, then check in the index page and all dependent pages.
16. Disable the Enable file check-out feature, then turn off the read-only status (Win) or unlock (Mac) for the entire site.
17. Cloak all .jpg files in the website.
18. Export the site definition to a new folder named **tripsmart_site_definition**.
19. Import the TripSmart.ste file to create a new site named TripSmart 2.
20. Expand the assets folder in the Files panel if necessary, then compare your screen to Figure 44.
21. Remove the TripSmart 2 site.
22. Uncloak all files in the TripSmart site, then close any open files.

Figure 44 *Sample completed Project Builder 1*

In this Project Builder, you finish your work on the Carolyne's Creations website. You are ready to publish the website to a remote server and transfer all the files from the local site to the remote site. First, you run several reports to make sure the website is in good shape. Next, you enable the Enable file check-out feature so that other staff members may collaborate on the site. Finally, you export and import the site definition file.

1. Use the Carolyne's Creations website that you began in Project Builder 1 in Chapter 1 and developed in previous chapters.
2. If you did not do so in Project Builder 2 in Chapter 1, use the Site Definition dialog box to set up web server access for a remote site using either an FTP site or a local or network folder.
3. Run reports for broken links and orphaned files, correcting any errors that you find.
4. Run reports for untitled documents and missing alt text, correcting any errors that you find.
5. Check for non-web-safe colors. If you find any, evaluate them to see whether or not they pose a problem for any of the pages.
6. Upload the classes.html page and all dependent files to the remote site.
7. View the remote site to make sure that all files uploaded correctly.
8. Synchronize the files so that all other files on the local Carolyne's Creations site are uploaded to the remote site.
9. Enable the Enable file check-out feature.

10. Check out the classes page and all its dependent files.
11. Open the classes page, then change the price of the adult class to **$45.00**.
12. Save your changes, close the page, then check in the classes page and all dependent pages.
13. Disable the Enable file check-out feature, then turn off read only for the entire site.

14. Export the site definition to a new folder named **cc_site_definition**.
15. Import the Carolyne's Creations.ste file to create a new site named Carolyne's Creations 2.
16. Expand the site root folder in the Files panel if necessary, compare your screen to Figure 45, then remove the Carolyne's Creations2 site.

Figure 45 *Sample completed Project Builder 2*

Throughout this book you have used Dreamweaver to create and develop several websites that contain different elements, many of which are found in popular commercial websites. For instance, Figure 46 shows the National Park Service website, which contains photos and information on all the national parks in the United States. This website contains many types of interactive elements, such as image maps and tables—all of which you learned to create in this book.

1. Connect to the Internet, then go to the National Park Service website at www.nps.gov.
2. Spend some time exploring the pages of this site to familiarize yourself with its elements.
3. Type a list of all the elements in this site that you have learned how to create in this book. After each item, write a short description of where and how the element is used in the site.
4. Click the link for the Site Index in the menu bar at the bottom of the page. Describe the information provided with the site index.
5. Click the Text Sizes links and describe how the page appearance changes as you click each option. How do you think this feature adds to the page accessibility?
6. Print the home page and one or two other pages that contain some of the elements you described and attach it to your list.

Figure 46 *Design Project*

National Park Service website – www.nps.gov

In this project, you will finish your work on the website that you created and developed throughout this book. You publish your site to a remote server or local or network folder.

1. Before you begin the process of publishing your website to a remote server, make sure that it is ready for public viewing. Use Figure 47 to assist you in making sure your website is complete. If you find problems, make the necessary changes to finalize the site.

2. Decide where to publish your site. The folder where you will publish your site can be either an FTP site or a local/network folder. If you are publishing to an FTP site, be sure to write down all the information you will need to publish to the site, including the URL of the FTP host, the directory on the FTP server where you will publish your site root folder, and the login and password information.

3. Use the Site Setup dialog box to specify the remote settings for the site using the information that was decided upon in Step 2.

4. Transfer one of the pages and its dependent files to the remote site, then view the remote site to make sure the appropriate files were transferred.

5. Synchronize the files so that all the remaining local pages and dependent files are uploaded to the remote site.

6. Enable the Enable file check-out feature.

7. Check out one of the pages. Open the checked-out page, make a change to it, save the change, close the page, then check the page back in.

8. Cloak a particular file type.

9. Export the site definition for the site to a new folder on your hard drive or on an external drive.

10. Close any open pages, then exit Dreamweaver.

Figure 47 *Portfolio Project*

Website Checklist
1. Are you satisfied with the content and appearance of every page?
2. Are all paths for all links and images correct?
3. Does each page have a title?
4. Are all colors web-safe?
5. Do all images have appropriate alternate text?
6. Have you eliminated any orphaned files?
7. Have you deleted any unnecessary files?
8. Have you viewed all pages using at least two different browsers?
9. Does the home page have keywords and a description?
10. Is all text based on a CSS style?

CHAPTER 1

GETTING STARTED WITH FLASH

1. Understand the Flash workspace

2. Open a document and play a movie

3. Create and save a movie

4. Work with the Timeline

5. Distribute an Adobe Flash movie

6. Plan an application or a website

CHAPTER 1

GETTING STARTED WITH FLASH

Introduction

Adobe Flash Professional CS5 is a development tool that allows you to create compelling interactive experiences, often by using animation. You can use Flash to create entire websites, including e-commerce, entertainment, education, and personal use sites. In addition, Flash is an excellent program for developing animations that are used in websites, such as product demonstrations, banner ads, online tutorials, and electronic greeting cards. Also, Flash can be used to create applications, such as games and simulations, which can be delivered over the web and on DVDs. These applications can even be scaled to be displayed on mobile devices, such as cell phones. While it is known as a tool for creating complex animations for the web, Flash also has excellent drawing tools and tools for creating interactive controls, such as navigation buttons and menus. Furthermore, Flash provides the ability to incorporate sounds and video easily into an application.

Flash has become the standard for both professional and casual application developers, as well as for web developers. Flash is popular because the program is optimized for the web. Web developers need to provide high-impact experiences for the user, which means making sites come alive and turning them from static text and pictures to dynamic, interactive experiences. The problem has been that incorporating high-quality graphics and motion into a website can dramatically increase the download time and frustrate viewers as they wait for an image to appear or for an animation to play. Flash allows developers to use vector images, which reduce the size of graphic files. Vector images appeal to designers because they are scalable, which means they can be resized and reshaped without distortion. For example, using a vector graphic, you can easily have an object, such as an airplane, become smaller as it moves across the screen without having to create the plane in different sizes.

In addition, Flash provides for streaming content over the Internet. Instead of waiting for all the content of a web page to load, the viewer sees a continuous display of images. This chapter provides an overview of Flash and presents concepts that are covered in more detail in later chapters.

Understand the
FLASH WORKSPACE

What You'll Do

In this lesson, you will learn about the development workspace in Adobe Flash and how to change Flash settings to customize your workspace.

Organizing the Flash Workspace

As a designer, one of the most important things for you to do is to organize your workspace—that is, to decide what to have displayed on the screen and how to arrange the various tools and panels. Because **Flash** is a powerful program with many tools, your workspace may become cluttered. Fortunately, it is easy to customize the workspace to display only the tools needed at any particular time.

The development process in Flash operates according to a movie metaphor: objects placed on the Stage also are incorporated in frames on a Timeline. As you work in Flash, you create a movie by arranging objects (such as graphics and text) on the Stage, and then animating the objects using the Timeline. You can play the movie on the Stage as you are working on it by using the movie controls (start, stop, rewind, and so on). Once completed, the movie can be incorporated into a website or as part of an application, such as a game.

When you start Flash, three basic parts of the workspace are displayed: a menu bar that organizes commands within menus, a Stage where objects are placed, and a Timeline

used to organize and control the objects on the Stage. In addition, one or more panels may be displayed. Panels, such as the Tools panel, are used when working with objects and features of the movie. Figure 1 shows a typical Flash workspace.

Stage

The **Stage** contains all of the objects (such as drawings, photos, animations, text, and videos) that are part of the movie that will be seen by your viewers. It shows how the objects behave within the movie and how they interact with each other. You can resize the Stage and change the background color applied to it. You can draw objects directly on the Stage or drag them from the Library panel to the Stage. You can also import objects developed in another program directly to the Stage. You can specify the size of the Stage (in pixels), which will be the size of the area that displays the movie within your browser window. The gray area surrounding the Stage is the Pasteboard. You can place objects on the Pasteboard as you are creating a movie. However, neither the Pasteboard nor the objects on it will appear when the movie is played in a browser or the Flash Player.

Timeline (Frames and Layers)

The **Timeline** is used to organize and control the movie's contents by specifying when each object appears on the Stage. The Timeline is critical to the creation of movies because a movie is merely a series of still images that appear over time. The images are contained within **frames**, which are segments of the Timeline. Frames in a Flash movie are similar to frames in a motion picture. When a Flash movie is played, a playhead moves from frame to frame on the Timeline, causing the contents of each frame to appear on the Stage in a linear sequence.

The Timeline indicates where you are at any time within the movie and allows you to insert, delete, select, copy, and move frames. The Timeline contains **layers** that help to organize the objects on the Stage. You can draw and edit objects on one layer without affecting objects on other layers. Layers are a way to stack objects so they can overlap and give a 3D appearance on the Stage.

Panels

Panels are used to view, organize, and modify objects and features in a movie. The most commonly used panels are the Tools panel, the Properties panel (also called the Property inspector), and the Library panel. The **Tools panel** contains a set of tools, such as the rectangle, oval and text tools, used to draw and edit graphics and text. The **Properties panel** is used to display and change the properties of an object, such as the size and transparency of a circle. The **Library panel** is used to store and organize the various assets of your movie such as graphics, buttons, sounds, and video.

You can control which panels are displayed individually or you can choose to display panel sets. Panel sets are groups of the

Figure 1 *A typical Flash workspace*

Title bar

Menu bar (your Title bar and Menu bar may be combined as one bar)

Movie menu bar

Object in the Library panel

Object on the Stage

Pasteboard

Playhead

Selecting frame 1 displays the object (car) on the Stage

Properties and Library panels grouped with Library panel displayed

Draw, paint, text, and selection tools on the Tools panel

View tools on the Tools panel

Color tools on the Tools panel

Options on the Tools panel

most commonly used panels. For example, the Properties and the Library panels are often grouped together to make a panel set. Although several panels open automatically when you start Flash, you may choose to close them and then display them only when they are needed. This keeps your workspace from becoming too cluttered. Panels are floating windows, meaning that you can move them around the workspace. This allows you to group (dock) panels together as a way to organize them in the workspace. In addition, you can control how a panel is displayed. That is, you can expand a panel to show all of its features or collapse it to show only the title bar. Collapsing panels reduces the clutter on your workspace, provides a

larger area for the Stage, and still provides easy access to often used panels.

If you choose to rearrange panels, first decide if you want a panel to be grouped (docked) with another panel, stacked above or below another panel, placed as a floating panel, or simply positioned as a stand-alone panel. An example of each of these is shown in Figure 2. When panels are grouped and expanded, clicking on a panel's tab makes it the active panel so that the panel features are displayed.

The key to rearranging panels is the blue drop zone that appears when a panel is being moved. The drop zone is the area to which the panel can move and is indicated by either a blue line or a rectangle with a

blue border. A single blue line indicates the position for stacking a panel above or below another panel. A rectangle with a blue border indicates the position for grouping panels. If you move a panel without using a drop zone, the panel becomes a floating panel and is neither grouped nor stacked with other panels. To move a panel, you drag the panel by its tab until the desired blue drop zone appears, then you release the mouse button. Figure 3 shows the Library panel being grouped with the Properties panel. The process is to drag the Library panel tab adjacent to the Properties panel tab. Notice the rectangle with the blue border that surrounds the Properties panel. This indicates the drop

Figure 2 *Arranging panels*

Collapsed panel sets

Grouped panels: Properties/Library

Stand-alone panel (Tools)

Stacked panels (Properties/Library and Color)

Floating panel

zone for the Library panel. (*Note*: Dragging a panel by its tab moves only that panel. To move a panel set you must drag the group by its title bar.)

Floating panels can be resized by dragging the left side, right side, or bottom of the panel. Also, you can resize a panel by dragging one of the bottom corners. In addition to resizing panels, you can collapse a panel so that only its title bar appears, and then you can expand it to display the entire panel. The Collapse to Icons button is located in the upper-right corner of each panel's title bar, as shown in Figure 3. The Collapse to Icons button is a toggle button, which means it changes or toggles between two states. When clicked,

the Collapse to Icons button changes to the Expand Panels button.

If you want to close a panel, you can click the Panel options button (shown in Figure 3) to display a drop down menu and then click the Close option. Alternately, you can right-click (Win) or [control]-click (Mac) the panel tab and choose close. If the panel is a floating panel you can click the Close button on the title bar. Finally, if the panel is expanded, you can display the Windows menu and deselect the panel (or panel group).

Arranging panels can be a bit tricky. It's easy to start moving panels around and find that the workspace is cluttered with panels arranged in unintended ways. To clean up

your workspace, you can close a panel(s) or simply display the default Essentials workspace described below.

Flash provides several preset workspace configurations that provide panels and panel sets most often used by designers, developers, and animators. The default workspace, shown in Figure 4, is named Essentials and can be displayed by clicking the ESSENTIALS button on the title bar and choosing Reset 'Essentials'. (*Note*: Your ESSENTIALS button may be on your menu bar.) Alternately, you can choose Reset 'Essentials' from the Workspace command on the Window menu. This workspace includes the Timeline panel (grouped with the Motion Editor, which is

Figure 3 *Grouping the Library panel with the Properties panel*

Toggle between Collapse to Icons and Expand Panel button

Panel options button

Library panel being dragged

Rectangle with blue border indicates drop zone

used to edit animations); the Tools panel which is expanded; the Properties and Library panels grouped and expanded; and several other panel sets that are stacked and collapsed. Your Essentials workspace may open with additional panel sets depending on user settings and previous use. These panels can be displayed by clicking the button icons which act as a toggle to expand and collapse the panels and panel sets. The Essentials workspace is a good development environment when learning Flash.

Regardless of how you decide to customize your development workspace, the Stage and the menu bar are always displayed. Usually, you display the Timeline, Tools panel, Library panel, Properties panel, and one or more other panels.

Other changes that you can make to the workspace are to change the size of the Stage, move the Stage around the Pasteboard, and change the size of the Timeline panel. To increase the size of the Stage so that the objects on the Stage can be edited more easily, you can change the magnification setting using commands on the View menu or by using the View tools on the Tools panel. The Hand tool on the Tools panel and the scroll bars at the bottom and right of the Stage can be used to reposition the Stage. The Timeline can be resized by dragging the top border. As your Flash movie gets more complex, you will use more layers on the Timeline. Increasing the size of the Timeline allows you to view more layers at one time.

QUICK TIP

When working with panels, you can collapse, move, and close them as suits your working style. Settings for an object, such as the fill color of a circle, are not lost if you close or collapse a panel. If, at any time the panels have become confusing, simply return to the Essentials workspace and open and close panels as needed.

Figure 4 *The Essentials workspace*

Your panel sets may vary; mouse over a button to see the name of a collapsed panel

Figure 5 *The Flash Welcome screen*

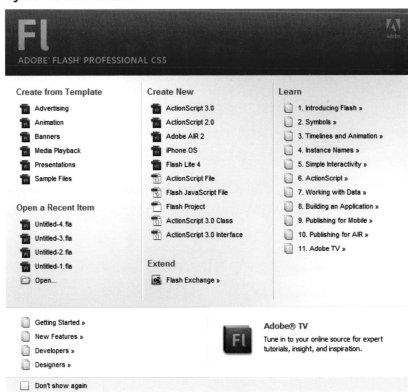

Start Adobe Flash and work with panels

1. Start the Adobe Flash Professional CS5 program ▣ .

   The Adobe Flash CS5 Welcome screen appears, as shown in Figure 5. This screen allows you to open a recent document or create a new Flash file.

2. Click **ActionScript 3.0** under Create New.

3. Click the **ESSENTIALS button** on the title bar, then click **Reset 'Essentials'**.

   Note: The ESSENTIALS button may be on the menu bar.

   TIP When you open a new file or as you are rearranging your workspace, use the Reset 'Essentials' option to display the default workspace.

4. Click **Window** on the menu bar, then note the panels with check marks.

   The check marks identify which panels and panel sets are open.

   TIP The Properties, Library, Colors, Swatches, Align, Info, Transform, and Actions panels may be grouped, stacked, and/or collapsed, depending upon the configuration of your Essentials workspace. If so, only the panel that is active will have a check mark.

5. With the Windows menu still open, click **Hide Panels**.

6. Click **Window** on the menu bar, then click **Timeline**.

7. Click **Window** on the menu bar, then click **Tools**.

8. Click **Window** on the menu bar, then click **Library**.

   The Library and Properties panels are grouped, and the Library panel is the active panel.

   (continued)

9. Click the **Properties panel tab**.

   The Properties panel is the active tab and the panel's features are displayed.

10. Click the **Library panel tab**, then drag the **Library panel** to the left side of the Stage as a floating panel.

11. Click the **Collapse to Icons button** on the Library panel title bar.

12. Click the **Expand Panels button** on the Library panel title bar.

13. Click the **Library panel tab**, drag the **Library panel tab** to the right of the Properties panel tab, then when a rectangle with a blue border appears, as shown in Figure 6, release the mouse button to group the panels.

    Note: If the panels do not appear grouped, repeat the step making sure there is a rectangle with a blue border before releasing the mouse button.

14. Click the **Collapse to Icons button** in the upper-right corner of the grouped panels, as shown in Figure 6.

15. Click the **Expand Panels button** to display the grouped panels.

16. Click the **Color panel button** 🎨.

    The Color panel is expanded and shown grouped with the Swatches panel.

17. Click the **Collapse to Icons button** for the Color panel.

18. Click **ESSENTIALS** on the title bar, then click **Reset 'Essentials'**.

You started Flash and configured the workspace by hiding, moving, and displaying panels.

Figure 6 *Library panel grouped with the Properties panel*

Click to toggle between Collapse to Icons button and Expand Panel button

Grouped panels share one title bar

Library tab placed next to Properties tab

Blue rectangle shows drop zone

Understanding Your Workspace

Organizing the Flash workspace is like organizing your desktop. You may work more efficiently if you have many of the most commonly used items in view and ready to use. Alternately, you may work better if your workspace is relatively uncluttered, giving you more free "desk space." Fortunately, Flash makes it easy for you to decide which items to display and how they are arranged while you work. You should become familiar with quickly opening, collapsing, expanding, and closing the various windows, toolbars, and panels in Flash, and experimenting with different layouts and screen resolutions to find the workspace that works best for you.

Figure 7 *Changing the size of the Timeline panel*

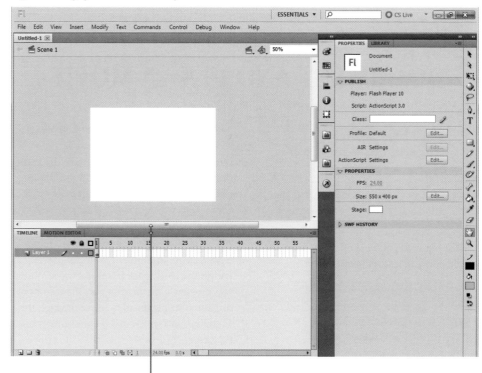

Double-headed pointer

Change the Stage view and display of the Timeline

1. Click the **Hand tool** 🖑 on the Tools panel, click the middle of the Stage, then drag the **Stage** around the Pasteboard.

2. Click **View** on the menu bar, point to **Magnification**, then click **50%**.

3. Move the pointer to the top of the Timeline title bar then, when the pointer changes to a double-headed pointer ↕, click and drag the **title bar** up to increase the height of the Timeline, as shown in Figure 7.

   Increasing the height of the Timeline panel allows you to view more layers as you add them to the Timeline.

4. Move the pointer to the top of the Timeline title bar then, when the pointer changes to a double-headed pointer ↕, click and drag the **title bar** down to decrease the height of the Timeline.

5. Double-click the word **TIMELINE** to collapse the Timeline.

6. Click the word **TIMELINE** again to expand the Timeline.

7. Click the **View list arrow** on the movie menu bar, then click **100%**.

8. Click **ESSENTIALS** on the title bar, then click **Reset 'Essentials'**.

9. Click **File** on the menu bar, then click **Save**.

10. Navigate to the drive and folder where your Data Files are stored, type **workspace** for the filename, then click **Save**.

11. Click **File** on the menu bar, then click **Close**.

You used a View command to change the magnification of the Stage; you used the Hand tool to move the Stage around the workspace; you resized, collapsed, and expanded the Timeline panel; then you saved the document.

Open a
DOCUMENT AND PLAY A MOVIE

What You'll Do

In this lesson, you will open a Flash document (movie); preview, test, and save the movie; then change the movie's Stage settings.

Opening a Movie in Flash

Flash files are called documents (or movies, interchangeably) and have an .fla file extension. If you have created a movie in Flash and saved it with the name myMovie, the filename will be myMovie.fla. Files with the .fla file extension can only be opened and edited using Flash. After they are opened, you can edit and resave them.

In order for Flash movies to be viewed on computers that do not have the Flash program installed, the movies must be changed to the Flash Player (.swf) file format. Files using the .swf file format are created from Flash movies using the Publish command. For example, when a Flash file named myMovie.fla is published using the Publish command, a new file named myMovie.swf is created. Flash .swf movies can be played in a browser without the Flash program, but the Flash Player must be installed on the computer. Flash Players are pre-installed on almost all computers. For those that do not have the player, it can be downloaded free from the Adobe website, *www.adobe.com*. Because .swf files cannot be edited in the Flash

program, you should preview the Flash .fla files on the Stage and test them before you publish them as .swf files. Be sure to keep the original .fla file so that you can make changes, if needed, at a later date.

Previewing a Movie

After creating a new Flash movie or opening a previously saved movie, you can preview it within the workspace in several ways. When you preview a movie, you play the frames by directing the playhead to move through the Timeline, and you watch the movement on the Stage.

Control Menu Commands (and Keyboard Shortcuts)

Figure 8 shows the Control menu commands and the Controller, which has buttons that resemble common DVD-type options:

- Play ([Enter] (Win) or [return] (Mac)) begins playing the movie frame by frame, from the location of the playhead to the end of the movie. For example, if the playhead is on frame 5 and the last frame is frame 40, choosing the Play command will play frames 5–40 of the movie.

- Rewind ([Shift][,]) (Win) or ([option] ⌘[R]) (Mac) moves the playhead to frame 1.
- Go To End ([Shift][.]) moves the playhead to the last frame of the movie.

- Step Forward One Frame (.) moves the playhead forward one frame at a time.
- Step Backward One Frame (,) moves the playhead backward one frame at a time.

You can turn on the Loop Playback setting to allow the movie to continue playing repeatedly. A check mark next to the Loop Playback command on the Control menu indicates that the feature is active. To turn off this feature, click the Loop Playback command.

Controller

You can also preview a movie using the Controller. To display the Controller, open the Window menu, point to Toolbars, and then click Controller.

Testing a Movie

When you play a movie within the Flash workspace, some interactive functions (such as buttons that are used to jump from one part of the movie to another) do not work. To preview the full functionality of a movie, you need to play it using a Flash Player. You can use the Test Movie command on the Control menu to test the movie using a Flash Player.

Figure 8 *Methods to control a movie*

Controller

Control menu

Documents, Movies, and Applications

As you work in Flash, you are creating a document. When you save your work as an .fla file, you are saving the document. This is consistent with other Adobe products, such as Photoshop, that use the word *document* to refer to work created in that program. In addition, because Flash uses a movie metaphor with a Stage, Timeline, frames, animations, and so on, the work done in Flash is often referred to as a movie. So, the phrase *Flash document* and the phrase *Flash movie* are synonymous. Movies can be as small and simple as a ball bouncing across the screen or as complex as a full-length interactive adventure game. Products such as games and educational software, as well as online advertisements and product demonstrations, are referred to as applications (see Figure 9). Applications usually contain multiple Flash documents or movies that are linked.

Using the Flash Player

To view a Flash movie on the web, your computer needs to have the Flash Player installed. An important feature of multimedia players, such as Flash Player, is the ability to decompress a file that has been compressed. Compressing a file gives it a small file size, which means it can be delivered more quickly over the Internet than its uncompressed counterpart. In addition to Adobe, companies such as Apple (QuickTime), Microsoft (Windows Media Player), and RealNetworks (RealPlayer) create players that allow applications, developed with their and other companies' products, to be viewed on the web. The multimedia players are distributed free and can be downloaded from the company's website. The Flash Player is created by Adobe and the latest version is available at *www.adobe.com*.

Figure 9 *Example of an application*

New York Philharmonic: Courtesy of http://www.nyphilkids.org/games/main.phtml?

Figure 10 *Playhead moving across Timeline*

Circle moves across the Stage   *Playhead moves along the Timeline*

Open and play a movie using the Control menu and the Controller

1. Open fl1_1.fla from the drive and folder where your Data Files are stored, then save it as **demoMovie.fla**.

2. Verify the view is set to 100%.

    The view setting is displayed on the movie menu bar, which is above and to the right of the Stage.

3. Click **Control** on the menu bar, then click **Play**.

    Notice how the playhead moves across the Timeline as the blue circle moves from the left of the Stage to the right, as shown in Figure 10.

4. Click **Control** on the menu bar, then click **Rewind**.

5. Press [**Enter**] (Win) or [**return**] (Mac) to play the movie, then press [**Enter**] (Win) or [**return**] (Mac) again to stop the movie before it ends.

6. Click **Window** on the menu bar, point to **Toolbars**, then click **Controller**.

7. Use all the buttons on the Controller to preview the movie, then close the Controller.

8. Point to the **playhead** on the Timeline, then click and drag the **playhead** back and forth to view the contents of the movie frame by frame.

9. Click number **1** on the Timeline to select the frame.

10. Press the **period key** several times, then press the **comma key** several times to move the playhead one frame at a time forward and backward.

You opened a Flash movie and previewed it, using various controls.

Test a movie

1. Click **Control** on the menu bar, point to **Test Movie**, then click **in Flash Professional**.

   The Flash Player window opens, as shown in Figure 11, and the movie starts playing automatically.

2. Click **Control** on the menu bar of the Flash Player window (Win) or application menu bar (Mac), then review the available commands.

3. Click **File** on the menu bar of the Flash Player window (Win) or application menu bar (Mac), then click **Close** to close the Flash Player window.

4. Use your file management program to navigate to the drive and folder where you saved the demoMovie.fla file and notice the demoMovie.swf file.

   TIP When you test a movie, Flash automatically creates a file that has an .swf extension in the folder where your movie is stored and then plays the movie in the Flash Player.

5. Return to the Flash program.

You tested a movie in the Flash Player window and viewed the .swf file created as a result of testing the movie.

Figure 11 *Flash Player window*

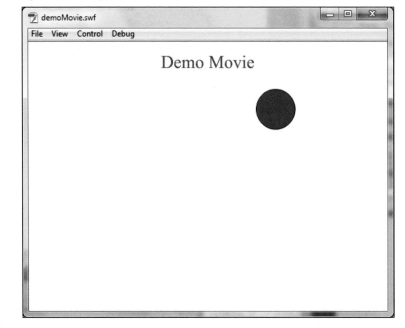

Figure 12 *Document Settings dialog box*

Document Settings

Dimensions: 550 px (width) x 160 px (height)

☑ Adjust 3D Perspective Angle to preserve current stage projection

Ruler units: Pixels ▼   Match: ⦿ Default
                                  ○ Contents
                                  ○ Printer

Background color: ▢

Frame rate: 12.00

Make Default

OK
Cancel

Background color swatch

Figure 13 *Completed changes to the document properties*

Stage resized

Gray background color

Demo Movie

Change the Document Properties

1. Click **Modify** on the menu bar, then click **Document**.

   The Document Settings dialog box opens.

2. Double-click in the **height text box** to select the number, then type **160**.

3. Click the **Background color swatch**, then click a **gray (#999999) color swatch** in the far-left column of the color palette.

   Note: The color code for a color appears next to the sample color swatch above the palette as you point to a color. The Color Swatch palette allows you to click a color to choose it or to enter a number that represents the color.

4. Review the remaining default values shown in Figure 12, then click **OK**.

   The dialog box closes.

5. Click **View** on the menu bar, point to **Magnification**, then click **100%** if it is not already selected.

   Your screen should resemble Figure 13.

6. Press **[Enter]** (Win) or **[return]** (Mac) to play the movie.

7. Click **File** on the menu bar, then click **Save As**.

8. Navigate to the drive and folder where your Data Files are stored, type **demoMovieBanner** for the filename, then click **Save**.

9. Click **File** on the menu bar, then click **Close**.

You set the document properties including the size of the Stage and the background color, then you set the magnification and saved the document.

Create and
SAVE A MOVIE

What You'll Do

In this lesson, you will create a Flash movie that will include a simple animation, you will add animation effects, and then save the movie.

Creating a Flash Movie

Flash movies are created by placing objects (graphics, text, sounds, photos, and so on) on the Stage, editing these objects (for example, changing their brightness), animating the objects, and adding interactivity with buttons and menus. You can create graphic objects in Flash using the drawing tools, or you can create them in another program, such as Adobe Illustrator, Photoshop, or Fireworks, and then import them into a Flash movie. In addition, you can acquire clip art and stock photographs and import them into a movie. When objects are placed on the Stage, they are automatically placed on a layer and in the current frame of the Timeline.

Figure 14 shows a movie that has a circle object created in Flash. Notice that the playhead is on frame 1 of the movie. The object placed on the Stage appears in frame 1 and appears on the Stage when the playhead is on frame 1. The dot in frame 1 on the Timeline indicates that this frame is a keyframe. The concept of keyframes is critical to understanding how Flash works. A **keyframe** indicates that there is a change in the movie, such as the start of an animation, or the resizing of an object on the Stage. A keyframe is automatically designated in frame 1 of every layer. In addition, you can designate any frame to be a keyframe.

The circle object in Figure 14 was created using the Oval tool. To create an oval or a rectangle, you select the desired tool and then drag the pointer over an area on the Stage. *Note:* Flash uses one button on the Tools panel to group the Oval and Rectangle tools, along with three other drawing tools. To display a menu of zthese tools, click and hold the rectangle (or oval) button on the Tools panel to display the menu and then click the tool you want to use. If you want to draw a perfect circle or square, press and hold [Shift] after the tool is selected, and then drag the pointer. If you make a mistake, you can click Edit on the menu bar, and then click Undo. To make changes to an object, such as resizing or changing its color, or to animate an object, you must first select it. You can use the Selection tool to select an entire object or group of objects. You drag the Selection tool pointer around the entire object to make a **marquee**. An object that has been selected displays a dot pattern or a blue border.

Creating an Animation

Figure 15 shows a movie that has 24 frames, as specified by the blue shading on the Timeline. The blue background color on the Timeline indicates a motion animation that starts in frame 1 and ends in frame 24. The dotted line on the Stage indicates the path the object will follow during the animation. In this case, the object will move from left to right across the Stage. The movement of the object is caused by having the object in different places on the Stage in different frames of the movie. In this case, frame 12 displays the object midway through the animation

and frame 24 displays the object at the end of the animation. A basic motion animation requires two keyframes. The first keyframe sets the starting position of the object, and the second keyframe sets the ending position of the object. The number of frames from keyframe to keyframe determines the length of the animation. If the starting keyframe is frame 1 and the ending keyframe is frame 24, the object will be animated for 24 frames. As an object is being animated, Flash automatically fills in the frames between these keyframes, with a process called **motion tweening**.

The Motion Tween Animation Process

Having an object move around the screen is one of the most common types of animations. Flash provides a process called motion tweening that makes it relatively simple to move objects. The process is to select an object on the Stage, then select the Motion Tween command from the Insert menu. If the object is not a symbol, a dialog box opens asking if you want to convert the object to a symbol. Creating a symbol allows you to reuse the object for this and other movies, as well as to apply a motion tween. Only symbols and text blocks can be motion

Figure 14 *Circle object in frame 1*

Object on the Stage is in frame 1 on the Timeline

Figure 15 *Motion animation*

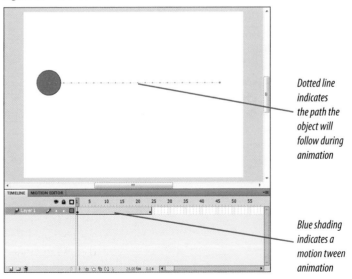

Dotted line indicates the path the object will follow during animation

Blue shading indicates a motion tween animation

tweened. The final step in the animation process is to select the ending frame for the animation and drag the object to another location on the Stage.

Two important things happen during the animation process. First, the Timeline shows the **tween span** (also called motion span), which is the number of frames in the motion tween. The tween span can be identified on the Timeline by a blue color, which, in this example, extends for 24 frames. The default tween span when starting from frame 1 of a new movie is determined by the number of frames per second setting. In this example, we used the default setting of 24 frames per second, so the initial number of frames in a tween for this movie is 24 frames. You can increase or decrease the length of the animation by pointing to either end of the span and dragging it to a new frame. The tween span will have more or fewer frames based on this action. The duration of the tween will still be based on the number of frames per second setting. For example, if we drag the tween span from frame 24 to frame 48, there are now 48 frames in the tween span. The tween span will still play at 24 frames per second because we did not change that setting. It will take two seconds to play the new tween span. If a movie has an ending frame beyond frame 1, the tween span will extend to the end of the movie. For example, if a movie has 50 frames and you insert a motion tween starting at frame 10, the tween span will extend from frames 10 through 50. The length of the motion tween is determined automatically by the last frame in the movie or manually by you if you designate a frame other than the last frame of the movie as the end of the animation.

Second, a dotted line, called the **motion path**, represents the path the object takes from the beginning frame to the ending frame. This path can be reshaped to cause the object to travel in a non-linear way, as shown in Figure 16. Reshaping a path can be done by using the Selection tool on the Tools panel. You see the tween span on the Timeline and the motion path on the Stage.

Figure 16 *A reshaped motion path*

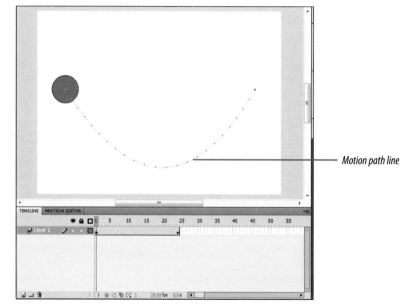

Motion path line

Motion Presets

Flash provides several preconfigured motion tweens that you can apply to an object on the Stage. These allow you to bounce an object across the Stage, fly-in an object from off the Stage, cause an object to pulsate and to spiral in place, as well as many other types of object animations. Figure 17 shows the Motion Presets panel where you choose a preset and apply it to an object. You can preview each preset before applying it and you can easily change to a different preset, if desired.

Adding Effects to an Object

In addition to animating the location of an object (or objects), you can also animate an object's appearance. Objects have properties such as color, brightness, and size. You can alter an object's properties as it is being animated using the motion tween process. For example, you could give the appearance of the object fading in by changing its transparency (alpha setting) or having it grow larger by altering its size over the course of the animation. Another useful effect is applying filters, such as drop shadows or bevels. All of these changes can be made using the Properties panel after selecting the object.

Figure 17 *Panel set with Motion Presets panel active*

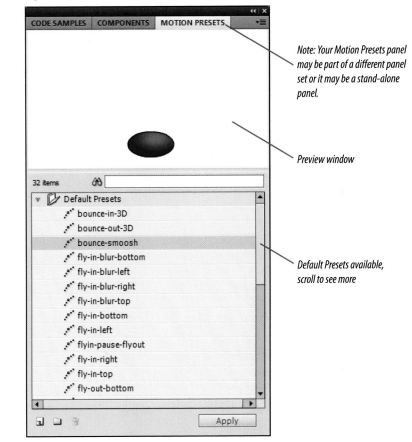

Note: Your Motion Presets panel may be part of a different panel set or it may be a stand-alone panel.

Preview window

Default Presets available, scroll to see more

Create objects using drawing tools

1. Click **ActionScript 3.0** to open a new Flash document.

2. Save the movie as **tween.fla**.

3. Verify the view is set to 100%.

4. Click and hold the **Rectangle tool** (or the Oval tool if it is displayed) on the Tools panel to display the list of tools, as shown in Figure 18, then click the **Oval tool**.

5. Verify that the Object Drawing option in the Options area of the Tools panel is not active, as shown in Figure 18.

6. Click the **Fill Color tool color swatch** on the Tools panel, then, if necessary, click the **red color swatch** in the left column of the color palette.

7. Click the **Stroke Color tool color swatch** on the Tools panel, then, if necessary, click the **black color swatch** in the left column of the color palette.

8. Press and hold **[Shift]**, drag the **pointer** on the left side of the Stage to draw the circle, as shown in Figure 19, then release the mouse button.

   Pressing and holding [Shift] creates a circle.

9. Click the **Selection tool** on the Tools panel, drag a **marquee** around the object to select it, as shown in Figure 20, then release the mouse button.

   The object appears covered with a dot pattern.

You created an object using the Oval tool, and then the object using the Selection tool.

Figure 18 *Drawing tools menu*

Rectangle tool

Rectangle Tool (R)
Oval Tool (O)
Rectangle Primitive Tool (R)
Oval Primitive Tool (O)
PolyStar Tool

Oval tool

Object Drawing option
is not active

Figure 19 *Drawing a circle*

Figure 20 *Creating a marquee selection*

Use the Selection tool
to draw a marquee,
which selects the entire
object

Figure 21 *The circle on the right side of the Stage*

Indicates the active frame,
which is frame 24

Figure 22 *Pointing to the end of the tween span*

Double-headed arrow
over end of tween span

Create a motion tween animation

1. Click **Insert** on the menu bar, then click **Motion Tween**.

   The Convert selection to symbol for tween dialog box opens.

2. Click **OK**.

   A blue border surrounds the object indicating that the object is a symbol. Notice that, in this example, the playhead automatically moved to frame 24, the last frame in the tween span. When you move the object to a new location on the Stage, the object's new location will be reflected in frame 24.

3. Click and then drag the **circle** to the right side of the Stage, as shown in Figure 21, then release the mouse button.

4. Press **[Enter]**(Win) or **[return]**(Mac) to play the movie.

   The playhead moves through frames 1–24 on the Timeline, and the circle moves across the Stage.

5. Click **frame 12** on Layer 1 on the Timeline.

   Verify the frame number on the status bar of the Timeline is 12, and notice that the object is halfway across the screen. This is the result of the tweening process in which the frames between 1 and 24 are filled in with the object in the correct location for each frame.

6. Verify the Selection tool ▶ is active, then point to the end of the tween span until the pointer changes to a double-headed arrow ↔, as shown in Figure 22.

7. Click and drag the **tween span** to frame 48, then verify the frame number on the status bar is 48, or adjust as needed.

(continued)

8. Press **[Enter]**(Win) or **[return]**(Mac) to play the movie.

Notice it now takes longer (2 seconds, not 1 second) to play the movie. Also notice that a diamond symbol appears in frame 48 indicating that it is now a Property keyframe. A Property keyframe indicates a change in the property of an object. In this case, it indicates the location of the object on the Stage has changed from frame 24 to frame 48.

9. Click **frame 24** and notice that the object is now halfway across the screen.

10. Click **File** on the menu bar, then click **Save**.

You created a motion tween animation and changed the length of the tween span.

Reshape the Motion Path

1. Click **File** on the menu bar, click **Save As**, then save the document with the filename **tweenEffects.fla**.

2. Verify the Selection tool 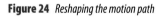 is active.

3. Click **frame 1** to select it.

   Note: When you see the direction to click a frame, click the frame on the layer not the number on the Timeline.

4. Point to just below the middle of the path until the pointer changes to a pointer with an arc as shown in Figure 23.

5. Click and drag the **path** to reshape the path, as shown in Figure 24.

6. Play the movie.

   Note: When you see the direction to play the movie, press [Enter] (Win) or [return] (Mac).

(continued)

Figure 23 *Using the Selection tool to reshape a motion path*

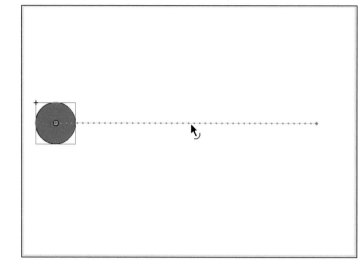

Figure 24 *Reshaping the motion path*

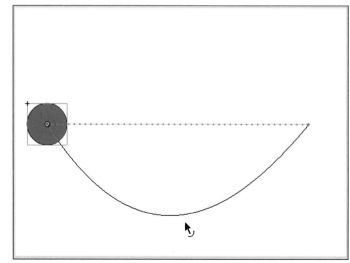

Figure 25 *The Properties panel displayed*

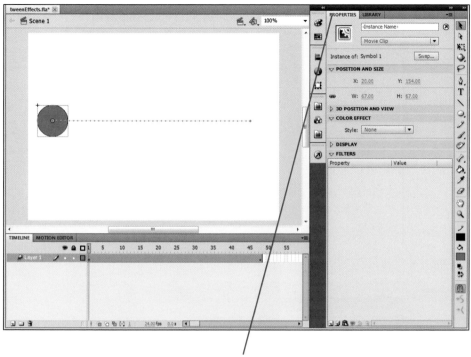

Properties panel and
its features

7. Test the movie.

    Note: When you see the direction to test the movie, click Control on the menu bar, point to Test Movie, then click in Flash Professional. Alternately, you can press [Ctrl]+[Enter] (Win) or [command]+[return](Mac).

8. View the movie, then close the Flash Player window.

9. Click **Edit** on the menu bar, then click **Undo Reshape**.

    Note: The Undo command starts with the most recent action and moves back through the actions. As a result, you may have to click Undo more than one time before you are able to click Undo Reshape.

You used the Selection tool to reshape a motion path and the Undo command to undo the reshape.

Change the transparency of an object

1. Click **frame 1** to select it, then click the **circle object** on the Stage to select it.

2. Click the **Properties panel tab** to display the Properties panel, as shown in Figure 25.

    Note: If the Properties panel is not open, click Window on the menu bar, then click Properties.

    Note: To verify the object is active, review the available settings in the Properties panel. Make sure POSITION AND SIZE is one of the options.

3. Click **COLOR EFFECT** on the Properties panel to display the Color Effect area if it is not already displayed, click the **Style list arrow**, then click **Alpha**.

    (continued)

4. Drag the **Alpha slider** ⌂ to **0**.

   The object becomes transparent.

5. Click **frame 48** on the layer to select it.

6. Click a white area inside the bounding box on the Stage to select the object and check that the object's properties are displayed in the Properties panel.

   Note: To verify the object is active, review the available settings in the Properties panel. Make sure POSITION AND SIZE is one of the options.

7. Drag the **Alpha slider** ⌂ to **100**.

8. Play the movie.

9. Test the movie, then close the Flash Player window.

You used the Color Effect option on the Properties panel to change the transparency of an object.

Resize an object

1. Click **frame 1** to select it.

2. Click a white area inside the bounding box to select the **object**.

3. Click **POSITION AND SIZE** on the Properties panel if this area is not already open.

4. Review the W (width) and H (height) settings of the object.

   The width and height are the dimensions of the bounding box around the circle.

5. Click **frame 48** to select it, then click the **circle object** to select it.

6. Verify the **Lock icon** ⊜ in the Properties panel is not broken.

   Note: If the lock is broken, click the broken lock to lock it, as shown in Figure 26, to ensure the width and height change proportionally.

   (continued)

Figure 26 *Resizing the circle*

Make sure the Lock icon is not broken

Your values may vary

Drag the number for width left to decrease the size

Figure 27 *The Add filter icon*

Filters area open   Add filter icon   Delete filter icon

7. Point to the number next to W: and when the pointer changes to a double-headed arrow ⚙, drag the ⚙ **pointer** left to decrease the width so that the circle shrinks to about half its size, as shown in Figure 26.

   Hint: You can also double-click a value in the Properties panel and type a value.

8. Click the **circle object** on the Stage.

9. Play the movie.

10. Test the movie, then close the Flash Player window.

11. Click **frame 1** to select it, then click the **object** to select it.

12. Drag the **Alpha slider** ⌂ to **100**.

You used the Position and Size option on the Properties panel to change the size of an object.

Add a filter to an object

1. Verify the object is selected by viewing the Properties panel and verifying the object's properties are displayed.

2. Click **FILTERS** on the Properties panel to display the Filters area if it is not already displayed.

3. Click the **Add filter icon** 🔲 at the bottom of the Filters area, as shown in Figure 27.

4. Click **Drop Shadow**, point to the number for the angle, then when the pointer changes to a double-headed arrow ⚙, drag the ⚙ pointer right to change the number of degrees to **100**.

5. Click **frame 1** to select it, then play the movie.

6. Click **frame 1** to select it, then click the **circle object** to select it.

(continued)

7. Click **Drop Shadow** in the Filters area, then click the **Delete Filter icon** 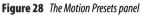 at the bottom of the Filters area.

   The drop shadow filter is removed from the circle object.

8. Click the **Add filter icon** at the bottom of the panel.

9. Click **Bevel**, test the movie, then close the Flash Player window.

You used the Filters option in the Properties panel to add and delete filters.

Add a motion preset

1. Verify the playhead is on frame 1, then click the object to select it.

2. Click **Window** on the menu bar, then click **Motion Presets**.

   The Motion Presets panel opens. It may open as a stand-alone panel or it may be grouped with other panels.

3. Drag the **Motion Presets panel or the panel set** by its title bar (not one of the tabs) to the right so that it does not obscure the Stage.

4. Click the **expand icon** ▶ for the Default Presets, then click **bounce-smoosh** and watch the animation in the preview widow, as shown in Figure 28.

5. Click **Apply**.

   A dialog box opens asking if you want to replace the current motion object with the new selection. You can only apply one motion tween or motion preset to an object at any one time.

   (continued)

Figure 28 *The Motion Presets panel*

Click to toggle between
expanding and collapsing the list

Preview window

Figure 29 *Diamond symbols indicating Property keyframes*

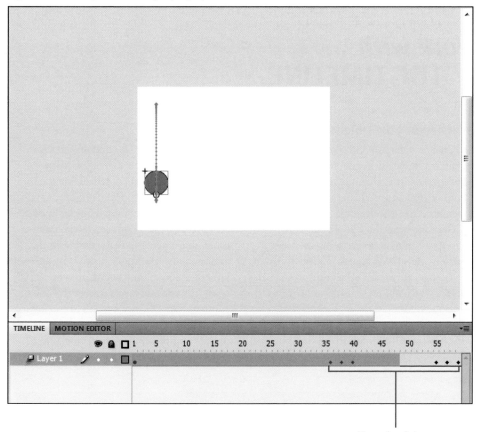

Diamond symbols appear where the ball is resized

6. Click **Yes**.

   The bevel filter is deleted and a new path is displayed.

7. Play the movie, then test the movie.

   Notice the circle object disappears from the Stage.

8. Close the Flash Player window.

9. Click **View** on the menu bar, point to **Magnification**, then click **50%**.

10. Click **frame 1**, click the **Selection tool** , draw a **marquee** around the circle object and the path to select both of them.

11. Press the **up arrow key [↑]** on the keyboard to move the circle object and the path toward the top of the Stage.

12. Play the movie.

   Notice the Timeline has several diamond symbols, as shown in Figure 29. Each one is a Property keyframe and indicates that there is a change in the object during the motion tween. In this case the change comes each time the ball is resized.

13. Click **frame 1** to select it, then drag the **playhead** from frame 1 to the last frame and notice the change that occurs at each keyframe.

14. Scroll the list of presets, click **pulse**, click **Apply**, then click **Yes**.

15. Play the movie.

16. Close the Motion Presets panel or panel set if the Motion Presets panel is part of a panel set.

17. Save and close the movie.

You applied motion presets to an object and viewed how keyframes identify changes in the motion tween.

Work with
THE TIMELINE

What You'll Do

In this lesson, you will add another layer, allowing you to create an additional animation, and you will use the Timeline to help organize the contents of your movie.

Understanding the Timeline

The Timeline organizes and controls a movie's contents over time. By learning how to read the information provided on the Timeline, you can determine and change what will be happening in a movie, frame by frame. You can determine which objects are animated, what types of animations are being used, when the various objects will appear in a movie, when changes are made to the properties of an object, which objects will appear on top of others, and how fast the movie will play. Features of the Timeline are shown in Figure 30 and explained in this lesson.

Using Layers

Each new Flash movie contains one layer, named Layer 1. **Layers** are like transparent sheets of plastic that are stacked on top of each other. This is shown in Figure 31, which also shows how the stacked objects appear on the Stage. Each layer can contain one or more objects. In Figure 31, the tree is on one layer, the heading Solitude is on another layer, and the colored backdrop is on a third layer. You can add layers using the Timeline command on the Insert menu or by clicking the New Layer icon on the Timeline. Placing objects on different layers and locking the

Figure 30 *Elements of the Timeline*

Layers   Playhead   Current frame   Frame rate   Elapsed time   Status bar   Frames   Frame View icon

layers helps avoid accidentally making changes to one object while editing another.

When you add a new layer, Flash stacks it on top of the other layer(s) on the Timeline. The stacking order of the layers on the Timeline is important because objects on the Stage appear in the same stacking order. For example, if you have two overlapping objects, and the top layer has a drawing of a tree and the bottom layer has a drawing of a house, the tree appears as though it is in front of the house. You can change the stacking order of layers simply by dragging them up or down in the list of layers. You can name layers, hide them so their contents do not appear on the Stage, and lock them so that they cannot be edited.

Using Frames and Keyframes

The Timeline is made up of individual segments called **frames**. The contents of each layer appear as the playhead moves over the frames, so any object in frame 1, no matter which layer it is on, appears on the Stage whenever frame 1 is played. Frames are numbered in increments of five for easy reference. The upper-right corner of the Timeline contains a Frame View icon. Clicking this icon displays a menu that provides different views of the Timeline, showing more frames or showing a preview (thumbnails) of the objects on a layer, for example. The status bar at the bottom of the Timeline indicates the current frame (the frame that the playhead is currently on), the frame rate (frames per second, also called fps), and the elapsed time from frame 1 to the current frame. Frames per second is the unit of measure for movies. If the frame rate is set to 24 frames per second and the movie has 48 frames, the movie will take 2 seconds to play.

Keyframes are locations on the Timeline where a new occurrence of an object appears or a change is made in the object. So, if you draw an object on the Stage, the current frame will need to be changed to a keyframe. In addition, if you create a motion tween, the first frame of the tween span will be a keyframe. One type of keyframe is a Property keyframe, which is used to specify locations on the Timeline where you want an animation to change. For example, you may have an animation of an object that moves across the Stage in frames 1 through 20. If you decide to resize the object in frame 5, a Property keyframe will appear on the Timeline in frame 5 when you make the change to that object. Another type of keyframe is a Blank keyframe, which is used to indicate that no content (objects) appears in that frame.

Interpreting the Timeline

The Timeline provides many clues to what is happening on the Stage. Interpreting these clues is essential to learning Flash. These clues are in the form of symbols and colors that appear on the Timeline. Figure 32 shows the most common symbols and colors. These are explained next. Others will be explained as they appear in subsequent chapters. The top layer on the Timeline in Figure 32 shows that frame 1 is a blank keyframe as indicated by the unfilled circle. No content will appear in frame 1 of this layer. In addition, the white background which extends to frame 24 indicates a span of blank frames. An unfilled rectangle appears at the end of the span and indicates the end of the blank frames.

Figure 31 *The concept of layers*

Layer 1   Layer 2   Layer 3

the Stage

The next layer shows a keyframe with content as indicated by the filled circle. The content in this frame also appears in frames 2-24 as indicated by the gray background. Again, an unfilled rectangle appears at the end of the span and indicates the end of the frames with the same content. The next layer shows a keyframe in frame 1 and a motion tween using the contents of frame 1 as indicated by the blue background in frames 2-24. No rectangle appears at the end of this span because the animation is not complete. Once frame 24 is selected and a change is made to the object being animated, such as moving it to a different location on the Stage, a keyframe will appear in frame 24. The bottom layer shows a keyframe in frame 1 and property keyframes (indicated by diamonds) in frames 5, 10, 15 and 20. Again, no symbol appears at the end of this span because no change has been made to the object in frame 24.

Figure 33 shows the Timeline of a movie created in Lesson 3 but now a second

object, a square at the top of the Stage, has been added to the movie. By studying the Timeline, you can learn several things about the square object and this movie. First, the darker blue color highlighting Layer 2 indicates that this layer is active. Second, the square object is placed on its own layer, Layer 2 (indicated by the darker blue color that highlights the layer name and the motion animation). Third, the layer has a motion animation (indicated by the blue background in the frames and the motion path on the Stage). Fourth, the animation runs from frame 1 to frame 48. Fifth, if the objects intersect during the animation, the square will be on top of the circle, because the layer it is placed on (Layer 2) is above the layer that the circle is placed on (Layer 1). Sixth, the frame rate is set to 24, which means that the movie will play 24 frames per second. Seventh, the playhead is at frame 1, which causes the contents of frame 1 for both layers to appear on the Stage.

QUICK TIP

You can adjust the height of the Timeline by positioning the pointer over the top edge of the Timeline title bar until a double-headed pointer appears, and then dragging the border up or down.

Using the Playhead

The **playhead** indicates which frame is playing. You can manually move the playhead by dragging it left or right. This makes it easier to locate a frame that you may want to edit. Dragging the playhead also allows you to do a quick check of the movie without having to play it.

Figure 33 *The Timeline of a movie with a second object*

Figure 32 *Common symbols and colors on the Timeline*

TIMELINE	MOTION EDITOR										
		👁	🔒	☐	1	5	10	15	20		25
Blank keyframe - no content in the frame		🖊	•	•	☐	o					☐
Same content in all frames			•	•	■	•					☐
Motion Tween animation			•	•	■	•					
Motion Tween with Property frames			•	•	■	•	◆	◆	◆	◆	

Figure 34 *Drawing a square*

Figure 35 *Positioning the square at the bottom of the Stage*

Add a layer

1. Open tween.fla, then save it as **layers.fla**.
2. Click **frame 1** on Layer 1.
3. Click **Insert** on the menu bar, point to **Timeline**, then click **Layer**.

   A new layer—Layer 2—appears at the top of the Timeline.

You added a layer to the Timeline.

Create a second animation

1. Click **frame 1** on Layer 2.
2. Click and hold the **Oval tool** on the Tools panel, then click the **Rectangle tool** on the menu that opens.
3. Click the **Fill Color tool color swatch** on the Tools panel, then click the **blue color swatch** in the left column of the color palette.
4. Press and hold [**Shift**], then draw a **square** resembling the dimensions and position of the square, as shown in Figure 34.
5. Click the **Selection tool** on the Tools panel, then drag a **marquee** around the square to select the object.
6. Click **Insert** on the menu bar, click **Motion Tween**, then click **OK** in the Convert selection to symbol for tween dialog box.
7. Click **frame 48** on Layer 2, then drag the **square** to the bottom of the Stage, as shown in Figure 35.

   When you click frame 48, the circle object moves to the right side of the Stage. Remember, when a frame is selected, all objects in that frame on every layer appear on the Stage.

   (continued)

8. Play the movie.

The square appears on top if the two objects intersect.

You drew an object and used it to create a second animation.

Work with layers and view Timeline features

1. Click **Layer 2** on the Timeline, then drag **Layer 2** below Layer 1.

   Layer 2 is now the bottom layer, as shown in Figure 36.

2. Play the movie and notice how the square appears beneath the circle if the objects intersect.

3. Click **Layer 2** on the Timeline, then drag **Layer 2** above Layer 1.

4. Play the movie and notice how the square now appears on top of the circle if they intersect.

5. Click the **Frame View icon** ▾≣ on the right corner of the Timeline title bar, as shown in Figure 37, to display the menu.

6. Click **Tiny** to display more frames.

   Notice how more frames appear on the Timeline, but each frame is smaller.

7. Click the **Frame View icon** ▾≣ , then click **Short**.

8. Click the **Frame View icon** ▾≣ , then click **Preview**.

   The object thumbnails appear on the Timeline.

9. Click the **Frame View icon** ▾≣ , then click **Normal**.

You changed the order of the layers, the display of frames, and the way the Timeline is viewed.

Figure 36 *Changing the stacking order of layers*

Figure 37 *Changing the view of the Timeline*

Frame View icon   Frame View options

Getting Started with Flash

Figure 38 *Changing the frame rate*

Pointer changes to
double-headed arrow

Figure 39 *Displaying the Properties option*

PROPERTIES option
in the Properties
panel

Drag to change
frames per second

Click to open color
palette and change
the Stage color

Modify the frame rate and change the layer names

1. Point to the **Frame Rate (fps)** on the Timeline status bar so the pointer changes to the double-headed arrow ↔, as shown in Figure 38.

2. Drag the ↔ **pointer** to change the frame rate to **3**.

TIP Alternately, you can click the frame rate number, then type a new number.

3. Play the movie and notice that the speed of the movie changed.

4. Click a blank area of the Stage, then verify the Properties panel is the active panel. If not, click **Window**, then click **Properties**.

5. If the PROPERTIES options are not displayed, as shown in Figure 39, click **PROPERTIES** on the Properties panel.

   The Properties panel provides information about the Stage, including size and background color.

6. Change the frame rate (fps) to **18** and the Stage color to **black**, then play the movie.

7. Click **frame 24** on the Timeline and notice the position of the objects on the Stage.

8. Drag the **playhead** left and right to display frames one by one.

9. Double-click **Layer 1** on the Timeline, type **circle**, then press **[Enter]**(Win) or **[return]**(Mac).

10. Double-click **Layer 2** on the Timeline, type **square**, then press **[Enter]**(Win) or **[return]** (Mac).

11. Save your work.

You changed the frame rate of the movie and named layers.

Distribute an
ADOBE FLASH MOVIE

What You'll Do

In this lesson, you will prepare a movie for distribution on the web.

Distributing Movies

When you develop Flash movies, the program saves them in a file format (.fla) that only users who have the Flash program installed on their computers can view. Usually, Flash movies are viewed on the web as part of a website or directly from a viewer's computer using the Flash Player. Flash files (.fla) cannot be viewed on the web using a web browser. They must be converted into a Flash Player file (.swf) so that the web browser knows the type of file to play (.swf) and the program needed to play the file (Flash Player). In addition, the HTML code needs to be created that instructs the web browser to play the swf file. Fortunately, Flash generates both the swf and HTML files when you use the Flash Publish command.

The process for publishing a Flash movie is to create and save a movie and then select the Publish command on the File menu. You can specify various settings, such as dimensions for the window in which the movie plays in the browser, before publishing the movie. Publishing a movie creates two files: an HTML file and a Flash Player (.swf) file. Both the HTML and swf files retain the same name as the Flash movie file, but with different file extensions:

- .html—the HTML document
- .swf—the Flash Player file

For example, publishing a movie named layers.fla generates two files–layers.html and layers.swf. The HTML document contains the code that the browser interprets to display the movie on the web. The code also specifies which Flash Player movie the browser should play. Sample HTML code referencing a Flash Player movie is shown in Figure 40. If you are familiar with HTML code, you will recognize this as a complete HTML document. Even if you are not familiar with HTML code, you might recognize some of the code that the browser uses to display the Flash movie. For example, the movie source is set to layers.swf; the display dimensions (determined by the size of the Stage) are set to 550 × 400; and the background color is set to black (#000000 is the code for black).

Specifying a Background color for a Flash document will cause the HTML document that is created when using the Publish command to fill the browser window with the color.

If you want to display a background color only for the dimensions of the Stage, you can add a layer to the Flash document and draw a rectangle the same dimensions of the Stage and with the desired fill color. Be sure this backdrop layer is the bottom layer. Then, when you publish the Flash document and view it in a browser, the movie (displayed using the dimensions of the Stage) will have the rectangle color as a background color and the rest of the browser window will be a different color. A shortcut to previewing a Flash document within an HTML document is to use the Default – (HTML) option from the Publish Preview command in the File menu or simply pressing [F12].

Flash provides another way to distribute your movies that may or may not involve delivery on the web. You can create an executable file called a **projector**. When you create a projector file, you specify the type of file you want to create, such as Windows .exe files and Macintosh .app files. Projector files maintain the movie's interactivity. So, if a movie has buttons that the user clicks to play an animation, the buttons will work in a projector file.

Projector files do not need the Flash Player to play them. You can play projector files directly from a computer, or you can incorporate them into an application, such as a game, that is downloaded or delivered on a CD or DVD. In addition, Flash provides features for creating movies specifically for mobile devices, such as cell phones.

Figure 40 *Sample HTML code*

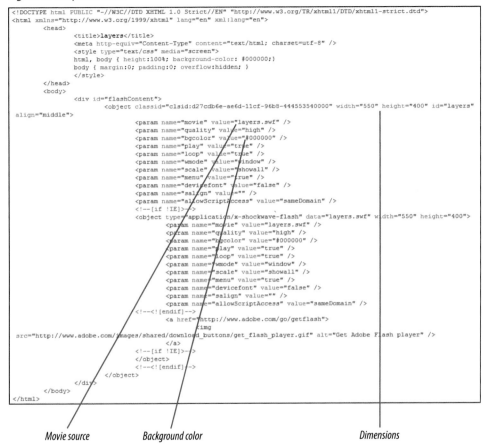

Movie source   Background color   Dimensions

Publish a movie for distribution on the web

1. Verify layers.fla is open, then save it as **layersWeb.fla**.

2. Click **File** on the menu bar, then click **Publish**.

   The files layers.html and layers.swf are automatically generated and saved in the same folder as the Flash document.

3. Use your file management program to navigate to the drive and folder where you save your work.

4. Notice the three files that begin with "layers," as shown in Figure 41.

   The three files are layersWeb.fla, the Flash movie; layersWeb.html, the HTML document; and layersWeb.swf, the Flash Player file.

5. Double-click **layersWeb.html** to play the movie in the browser.

   Note: Depending on your browser, browser settings and version, you may need to complete additional steps (such as accepting blocked content) to view the layers.html document.

TIP Click the browser button on the taskbar if the movie does not open automatically in your browser.

   Notice the animation takes up only a portion of the browser window, as shown in Figure 42. This is because the Stage size is set to 550 x 440, which is smaller than the browser window. Notice also that the entire browser window has been filled with the black background. This is because a background color was used rather than creating a backdrop layer.

6. Close the browser, and return to Flash.

You used the Publish command to create an HTML document (.html) and a Flash Player file (.swf), then you displayed the HTML document in a web browser.

Figure 41 *The three layers files after publishing the movie*

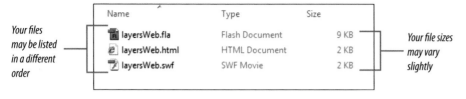

Your files may be listed in a different order

Your file sizes may vary slightly

Figure 42 *The animation played in a browser window*

Getting Started with Flash

Figure 43 *Drawing a rectangle the size of the Stage*

Rich Media Content and Accessibility

Flash provides the tools that allow you to create compelling applications and websites by incorporating rich media content, such as animations, sound, and video. Generally, incorporating rich media enhances the user's experience. However, accessibility becomes an issue for those persons who have visual, hearing, or mobility impairments, or have a cognitive disability. Designers need to utilize techniques that help ensure accessibility, such as providing consistency in navigation and layout, labeling graphics, captioning audio content throughout the applications and website, and providing keyboard access.

Draw a backdrop color for the Stage

1. Click **Modify** on the menu bar, then click **Document**.
2. Change the Background color to **white**, then click **OK**.
3. Click **square** on the Timeline to select the square layer.
4. Click **Insert** on the menu bar, point to **Timeline**, then click **Layer**.
5. Double-click **Layer 3** on the Timeline to select the name of the new layer, type **backdrop**, then press **[Enter]** (Win) or **[return]** (Mac).
6. Click **frame 1** of the backdrop layer.
7. Click the **Rectangle tool** ⬜ on the Tools menu.
8. Use the Tools panel to set the Fill Color to **black** and the Stroke Color to **black**.
9. Draw a **rectangle** that covers the Stage, as shown in Figure 43.
10. Click **backdrop** on the Timeline, then drag the **backdrop** layer below the circle layer.
11. Click **File** on the menu bar, point to **Publish Preview**, then click **Default – (HTML)**.

    Notice how the HTML document has a white background and the Flash movie plays in an area the size of the Stage.

    Note: If a warning message opens, follow the directions to allow blocked content.
12. Close the browser and return to Flash.
13. Save and close the layersWeb.fla document.

You changed the background color of a Flash document and added a backdrop color.

Plan an
APPLICATION OR A WEBSITE

What You'll Do

Purpose	"What do we want to accomplish?"
Audience	"Who will use our application or website?"
Treatment	"What is the look and feel?"
Specifications	"What does the application include and how does it work?"

 In this lesson, you will learn how to plan a Flash application. You will also learn about the guidelines for screen design and the interactive design of web pages.

Planning an Application or a Website

Flash can be used to develop animations that are part of a product, such as a game or educational tutorial, and delivered via the internet, a CD, a DVD, or a mobile device. You can use Flash to create enhancements to web pages, such as animated logos, interactive navigation buttons, and banner ads. You can also use Flash to create entire websites. No matter what the application, the first step is planning the movie. Often, the temptation is to jump right into the program and start developing movies. The problem is that this invariably results in a more time-consuming process at best; and wasted effort, resources, and money at worst. The larger and more complex the project is, the more critical the planning process becomes. Planning an application or an entire website should involve the following steps:

Step 1: Stating the Purpose (Goals). "What, specifically, do we want to accomplish?"

Determining the goals is a critical step in planning because goals guide the development process, keep the team members on track, and provide a way to evaluate the application or website, both during and after its development.

Step 2: Identifying the Target Audience. "Who will use our application or website?"

Understanding the potential viewers helps in developing an application or a website that can address their needs. For example, children respond to exploration and surprise, so having a dog wag its tail when the mouse pointer rolls over it might appeal to this audience.

Step 3: Determining the Treatment. "What is the look and feel?"

The treatment is how the application or website will be presented to the user, including the tone, approach, and emphasis.

Tone. Will the application or website be humorous, serious, light, heavy, formal, or informal? The tone of an application or a site can often be used to make a statement—projecting a progressive, high-tech, well-funded corporate image, for instance.

Approach. How much direction will be provided to the user? An interactive game might focus on exploration such as when the user points to an object on the screen and the object becomes animated. While an informational website might provide lots of direction and include lists of options in the form of drop-down menus.

Emphasis. How much emphasis will be placed on the various multimedia elements? For example, a company may want to develop an informational application or website that shows the features of its new product line, including video demonstrations and sound narrations of how each product works. The budget might not allow for the expense of creating the videos, so the emphasis would shift to still pictures with text descriptions.

Step 4: Developing the Specifications, Flowchart, and Storyboard. "What precisely does the application or website include and how does it work?"

The **specifications** state what will be included in each screen, including the arrangement of each element and the functionality of each object (for example, what happens when you click the button labeled Skip Intro). Specifications should include the following:

Playback System. The choice of what configuration to target for playback is critical, especially Internet connection speed, browser versions, screen resolution, screen size (especially when targeting mobile devices), and plug-ins.

Elements to Include. The specifications should include details about the various elements that are to be included in the site. What are the dimensions for the animations, and what is the frame rate? What are the sizes of the various objects such as photos, buttons, and so on? What fonts, font sizes,

and font formatting will be used? Should video or sound be included?

Functionality. The specifications should include the way the program reacts to an action by the user, such as a mouse click. For example, clicking a door (object) might cause a doorbell to ring (sound), the door to open (an animation), an "exit the program" message to appear (text), or an entirely new screen to be displayed.

A **flowchart** is a visual representation of how the contents in an application or a website are organized and how various screens are linked. It provides a guide for the developer and helps to identify problems with the navigation scheme before work begins. Figure 44 shows a simple flowchart illustrating the site organization and links.

Flowcharts vary based on the purpose of the site or application. For example, an informational website might include an extensive menu (navigation) system with lots of buttons that allow the user to easily navigate to the desired information.

Figure 44 *Sample flowchart*

Whereas, an online sales site might have a more controlled user experience with fewer options as the user is led through product review, selection, and purchase (checkout).

A **storyboard** shows the layout of the various screens, often in the form of thumbnail sketches. It describes the contents and illustrates how text, graphics, animation, and other screen elements will be positioned. It also indicates the navigation process, such as menus and buttons. Figure 45 shows a storyboard. The exact content (such as a specific photo) does not have to be decided, but it is important to show where text, graphics, photos, buttons,

and other elements, will be placed. Thus, the storyboard includes placeholders for the various elements. Storyboards can be created using the dimensions of the Flash Stage.

Flowcharts and storyboards make up the **user interface**, that is the appearance of objects (how each object is arranged on the screen) and the interactivity (how the user navigates through the site or application).

Using Screen Design Guidelines

The following screen design guidelines are used by application and web developers. The implementation of these guidelines is affected

by the goals of the application or website, the intended audience, and the content.

Balance in screen design refers to the distribution of optical weight in the layout. Optical weight is the ability of an object to attract the viewer's eye, as determined by the object's size, shape, color, and so on. The storyboard in Figure 45 shows a fairly well-balanced layout, especially if the logo has as much optical weight as the text description. In general, a balanced design is more appealing to a viewer. However, for a game application or an entertainment site, a balanced layout may not be desired.

Figure 45 *Sample Storyboard*

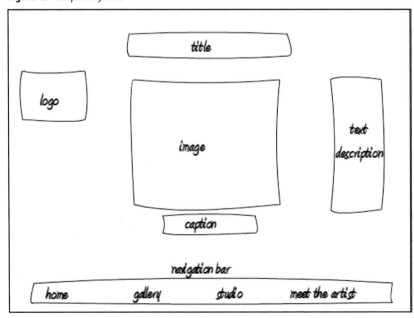

Unity helps the screen objects reinforce each other. **Intra-screen unity** has to do with how the various screen objects relate and how they all fit in. For example, a children's game might only use cartoon characterizations of animals for all the objects—including navigation buttons and sound control buttons, as well as the on-screen characters. **Inter-screen unity** refers to the design that viewers encounter as they navigate from one screen to another, and it provides consistency throughout the application or site. For example, all navigation buttons are located in the same place on each screen.

Movement refers to the way the viewer's eyes move through the objects on the screen. Different types of objects and various animation techniques can be used to draw the viewer to a location on the screen.

For example, a photo of a waterfall may cause the viewer's eyes to follow the flow of the water down, especially if the waterfall is animated. The designer could then place an object, such as a logo or a sales message, below the waterfall.

Using Interactive Design Guidelines

In addition to screen design guidelines, interactive guidelines determine the interactivity of the application. The following guidelines are not absolute rules since they are affected by the goals of the application, the intended audience, and the content:

- Make it simple, easy to understand, and easy to use so that viewers do not have to spend time learning what the application is about and what they need to do.
- Build in consistency in the navigation scheme. Help the users know where they are in the application and help them avoid getting lost.
- Provide feedback. Users need to know when an action, such as clicking a button, has been completed. Changing its color or shape, or adding a sound can indicate this.
- Give the user control. Allow the user to skip long introductions; provide controls for starting, stopping, and rewinding animations, video, and audio; and provide controls for adjusting audio.

The Flash Workflow Process

After the planning process, you are ready to start work on the Flash documents. The following steps can be used as guidelines in a general workflow process suggested by Adobe.

Step 1: Create and/or acquire the elements to be used in the application. The elements include text, photos, drawings, video, and audio. The elements become the raw material for the graphics, animations, menus, buttons, and content that populate the application and provide the interactivity. You can use the various Flash drawing and text tools to create your own images and text content; or, you can use another program, such as Adobe Photoshop, to develop the elements, and then import them into Flash. Alternately, you can acquire stock clip art and photographs. You can produce video and audio content in-house and import it into Flash or you can acquire these elements from a third party.

Step 2: Arrange the elements and create the animations. Arrange the elements (objects) on the Stage and on the Timeline to define when and how they appear in your application. Once the elements are available, you can create the various animations called for in the specifications.

Step 3: Apply special effects. Flash provides innumerable special effects that can be applied to the various media elements and animations. These include graphic and text filters, such as drop shadows, blurs, glows, and bevels. In addition, there are effects for sounds and animations such as fade-ins and fade-outs, acceleration and deceleration, morphing. and even 3D effects.

Step 4: Create the interactivity. Flash provides a scripting feature, ActionScript, which allows you to develop programming code to control how the media elements behave, including how various objects respond to user interactions, such as clicking buttons and rolling over images.

Step 5: Test and publish the application. Testing can begin before the actual development process with usability testing, which involves potential users being observed as they navigate through thumbnail sketches of the storyboard. Testing should continue throughout the development process, including using the Test Movie feature in the Control menu to test the movie using the Flash Player and to publish the movie in order to test it in a browser.

Project Management

Developing websites or any extensive application, such as a game, involves project management. A project plan needs to be developed that provides the project scope and identifies the milestones, including analyzing, designing, building, testing, and launching. Personnel and resource needs are identified, budgets built, tasks assigned, and schedules developed. Successful projects are a team effort relying on the close collaboration of designers, developers, project managers, graphic artists, programmers, testers, and others. Adobe provides various product suites, such as their Creative Suite 5 (CS5) Web Collection series, that include programs such as Flash, Dreamweaver, Photoshop, Illustrator, and Fireworks. These are the primary tools needed to develop interactive applications and websites. These programs are designed for easy integration. So, a graphic artist can use Photoshop to develop an image that can easily be imported into Flash and used by an animator. In addition, other tools in the suites, such as Adobe Bridge and Adobe Version Cue, help ensure efficient workflow when working in a team environment.

Using the Flash Help Feature

Flash provides a comprehensive Help feature that can be very useful when first learning the program. You access the Help feature from the Help menu. The Help feature is organized by categories, including Using Flash Professional CS5, which have several topics such as Workspace and Managing documents. In addition, the Help feature has a Help Search feature. You use the Help Search feature to search for topics using keywords, such as Timeline. Searching by keywords accesses the Flash Community Help feature, which displays links to content relevant to the search terms. Other resources not affiliated with Adobe are available through the web. You may find some by searching the web for Flash resources. The CS Live button on the title bar provides access to Adobe's CS Live online services, including product registration, support, and news; as well as links to Flash forums and user groups.

Figure 46 *The Flash Help categories*

Figure 47 *The Flash Help Search feature*

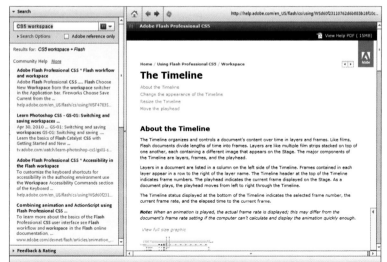

Use Flash Help

1. Start a new Flash document.

2. Click **Help** on the menu bar, then click **Flash Help**.

   Note: If you see a page not found message, be sure you are connected to the Internet.

3. Maximize the Help window, then click the **Expand button** + next to Workspace to expand the category, as shown in Figure 46.

4. Click **The Timeline**, then click **About the Timeline**.

5. Read through the text in About the Timeline.

6. Scroll to display the top of the Help window.

7. Click in the **Search text box**, type **CS5 workspace**, then verify the Flash icon is displayed to the right of the Search text box.

   Your search is refined to the Flash product when the Flash icon is displayed.

8. Press **[Enter]** (Win) or **[return]** (Mac) to access the Community Help site.

9. Study the various links provided on the site.

   Note: Figure 47 shows the results of one search using the keywords CS5 workspace. New links are added regularly because this is community-based help. Therefore, your results may differ.

10. Close the Flash Help site, then exit the Flash program.

You used the Flash Help feature to access information on the Timeline and the workspace.

Open a document and understand the Flash workspace.

1. Start Flash, open fl1_2.fla, then save it as **skillsDemo1.fla**. This movie has two layers. Layer 1 contains the heading and the line at the top of the Stage. Layer 2 contains an animation that runs for 75 frames.
2. Change the magnification to 50% using the View menu. (*Hint*: Click View, point to Magnification, then click 50%.)
3. Change the magnification to Fit in Window.
4. Change the Timeline view to Small. (*Hint*: Click the Frame View icon in the upper-right corner of the Timeline title bar.)
5. Hide all panels.
6. Display the Tools panel, Timeline panel, Properties panel, and the Library panel if it did not open with the Properties panel.
7. Group the Library and Properties panels if they are not already grouped.
8. Drag the Library panel from the Properties panel, then position it on the Stage.
9. Collapse the Library panel.
10. Close the Library panel to remove it from the screen.
11. Reset the Essentials workspace.

Play and test a movie.

1. Drag the playhead to view the contents of each frame. Use the commands on the Control menu to play and rewind the movie.
2. Press [Enter] (Win) or [return] (Mac) to play and stop the movie.
3. Use the Controller to rewind, play, and stop the movie, then close the Controller.
4. Test the movie in the Flash Player window, then close the Flash Player window.

Change the document size and background color.

1. Use the Document command on the Modify menu to display the Document Settings dialog box.
2. Change the document height to 380.
3. Change the background color to a medium gray color (#999999).
4. Click OK to close the Document Settings dialog box.
5. Play the movie.

Create and save a movie.

1. Insert a new layer above Layer 2, then select frame 1 of the new layer.
2. Draw a green ball in the middle of the left side of the Stage, approximately the same size as the red ball. (*Hint*: The green gradient color can be used to draw the ball. Several gradient colors are found in the bottom row of the color palette when you click the Fill Color tool in the Tools panel.)
3. Use the Selection tool to draw a marquee around the green ball to select it, then create a motion tween to animate the green ball so that it moves across the screen from left to right. (*Hint*: Select frame 75 on Layer 3 before repositioning the green ball.)
4. Use the Selection tool to reshape the motion path to an arc by dragging the middle of the path downward.
5. Play the movie.

6. Use the Undo command to undo the reshape. (*Note*: You may need to use the Undo feature twice.)
7. Use the Selection tool to select frame 75 of the new layer, click the green ball if it is not already selected to select it, then use the Properties panel to change the transparency (alpha) from 100% to 20%. (*Hint*: If the Properties panel COLOR EFFECT option is not displayed, make sure the Properties panel is open and click the green ball to make sure it is selected.)
8. Play the movie.
9. Click frame 75 on Layer 3 and click the green ball to select it.
10. Use the Properties panel to decrease the width of the ball to approximately half its size. (*Hint*: Make sure the lock width and height value icon in the Properties panel is unbroken. You may need to click the Stage to have the new value take effect.)
11. Play the movie.
12. Select frame 1 on Layer 3, then click the green ball to select it.
13. Use the Filters option in the Properties panel to add a drop shadow.
14. Play the movie.
15. Select frame 1 on Layer 2, then click the red ball to select it.
16. Open the Motion Presets panel, then add a bounce-smoosh preset.
17. Move Layer 3 below Layer 2.
18. Play the movie.
19. Save the movie.

Getting Started with Flash

Work with the Timeline.

1. Change the frame rate to 8 frames per second, play the movie, change the frame rate to 24, then play the movie again.
2. Change the view of the Timeline to display more frames.
3. Change the view of the Timeline to display a preview of the object thumbnails.
4. Change the view of the Timeline to display the Normal view.
5. Click frame 1 on Layer 1, use the playhead to display each frame, then compare your screens to Figure 48.
6. Save the movie.

Distribute an Adobe Flash movie.

1. Click File on the menu bar, then click Publish.
2. Open your browser, then open skillsDemo1.html.
3. View the movie, close your browser, then return to Flash.

Work with the Flash workspace.

1. Use the Document Settings dialog box to change the document background color to white.
2. Insert a new layer, then rename the layer **gray backdrop**.
3. Select frame 1 of the gray backdrop layer.
4. Select the rectangle tool, then set the Fill Color and the Stroke Color to the same shade of gray.
5. Draw a rectangle that covers the Stage.
6. Drag the gray backdrop layer to the bottom of the list of layers on the Timeline.

7. Rename the layers using these names: **heading**, **green ball**, and **red ball**. Use clues on the Timeline to help you know what to name each layer.

8. Play the movie in the browser, then close the browser window.
9. Save and close the Flash document.

Figure 48 *Completed Skills Review*

A friend cannot decide whether to sign up for a class in Flash or Dreamweaver. You help her decide by showing her what you already know about Flash. You want to show her how easy it is to create a simple animation because you think she'd enjoy a class in Flash. You decide to animate three objects. The first object is placed on the center of the Stage and pulsates throughout the movie. The second object enters the Stage from the left side and moves across the middle of the Stage and off the right side of the Stage. The third object enters the Stage from the right side and moves across the middle of the Stage and off the left side of the Stage. The motion paths for the two objects that move across the Stage are reshaped so they go above and below the pulsating object in the middle of the Stage.

1. Open a Flash document, then save it as **demonstration.fla**.
2. Verify the view is set to 100%.
3. Use the tools on the Tools panel to create a circle (or object of your choice) and color of your choice on the middle of the Stage.
4. Draw a marquee around the object to select it and apply a pulse motion preset.
5. Insert a new layer, then select frame 1 on the layer.
6. Create a simple shape or design using a color of your choice, and place it off the left side of the Stage and halfway down the Stage.
7. Select the object and insert a motion tween that moves the object directly across the screen and off the right side of the Stage. (*Hint*: Drag the object off the right side of the Stage.)
8. Reshape the motion path so that the object goes in an arc below the center pulsating object.
9. Insert a new layer, then select frame 1 on the layer.
10. Create an object using the color of your choice and place it off the right side of the Stage and halfway down the Stage.
11. Draw a marquee to select the object and insert a motion tween that moves the object directly across the screen and off the left side of the Stage.
12. Reshape the motion path so that the object goes in an arc above the center pulsating object.
13. Play the movie.
14. Add a background color.
15. Rename the layers with descriptive names.
16. Play the movie, test it , then close the Flash Player window.
17. Save the movie, then compare your movie to the sample provided in Figure 49.

Figure 49 *Sample completed Project Builder 1*

You've been asked to develop a simple movie about recycling for a day care center. For this project, you will add two animations to an existing movie. You will show three objects that appear on the screen at different times, and then move each object to a recycle bin at different times. You can create the objects using any of the Tools on the Tools panel.

1. Open fl1_3.fla, then save it as **recycle.fla**.
2. Play the movie and study the Timeline to familiarize yourself with the movie's current settings. Currently, there are no animations.

3. Insert a new layer above Layer 2, then draw a small object in the upper-left corner of the Stage.
4. Create a motion tween that moves the object to the recycle bin. (*Hint*: Be sure to select frame 40 on the new layer before moving the object to the recycle bin.)
5. Reshape the path so that the object moves in an arc to the recycle bin. (*Note*: At this time, the object will appear outside the recycle bin when it is placed in the bin.)
6. Insert a new layer above the top layer, draw a small object in the upper-center of the Stage, then

create a motion tween that moves the object to the recycle bin.
7. Insert a new layer above the top layer, draw a small object in the upper-right corner of the Stage, then create a motion tween that moves the object to the recycle bin.
8. Reshape the path so that the object moves in an arc to the recycle bin.
9. Move Layer 1 to the top of all the layers.
10. Play the movie and compare your movie to the sample provided in Figure 50.
11. Save the movie.

Figure 50 *Sample completed Project Builder 2*

This figure shows the animated objects with outlines of their positions during the animations. Your completed project will not show these outlines.

Figure 51 shows the home page of a website. Study the figure and answer the following questions. For each question, indicate how you determined your answer.

1. Connect to the Internet, then go to *www.argosycruises.com*.
2. Open a document in a word processor or open a new Flash document, save the file as **dpc1**, then answer the following questions. (*Hint*: Use the Flash Text tool if you open a Flash document.)
   - Whose website is this?
   - What is the goal(s) of the site?
   - Who is the target audience?
   - What treatment (look and feel) is used?
   - What are the design layout guidelines being used (balance, movement, etc.)?
   - How can animation enhance this page?
   - Do you think this is an effective design for the company, its products, and its target audience? Why, or why not?
   - What suggestions would you make to improve the design, and why?

Figure 51 *Design Project*

Courtesy of www.argosy-cruises.com

Getting Started with Flash

There are numerous companies in the business of developing websites for others. Many of these companies use Flash as one of their primary development tools. These companies promote themselves through their own websites and usually provide online portfolios with samples of their work. Log onto the Internet, then use your favorite search engine and keywords such as Flash developers and Flash animators to locate three of these companies, and generate the following information for each one. A sample website is shown in Figure 52.

1. Company name:
2. Contact information (address, phone, and so on):
3. Website URL:
4. Company mission:
5. Services provided:
6. Sample list of clients:
7. Describe three ways the company seems to have used Flash in its website. Were these effective? Why, or why not?
8. Describe three applications of Flash that the company includes in its portfolio (or showcases or samples). Were these effective? Why, or why not?
9. Would you want to work for this company? Why, or why not?
10. Would you recommend this company to another company that was looking to enhance its website? Why, or why not?

Figure 52 *Sample website for Portfolio Project*

Courtesy of www.bluegelmedia.com

CHAPTER **2** **DRAWING OBJECTS IN ADOBE FLASH**

1. Use the Flash drawing and alignment tools
2. Select objects and apply colors
3. Work with drawn objects
4. Work with text and text objects
5. Work with layers and objects

2

DRAWING OBJECTS IN
ADOBE FLASH

Introduction

Computers can display graphics in either a bitmap or a vector format. The difference between these formats is in how they describe an image. A bitmap graphic represents an image as an array of dots, called **pixels**, which are arranged within a grid. Each pixel in an image has an exact position on the screen and a precise color. To make a change in a bitmap graphic, you modify the pixels. When you enlarge a bitmap graphic, the number of pixels remains the same, resulting in jagged edges that decrease the quality of the image. A vector graphic represents an image using lines and curves, which you can resize without losing image quality. Also, the file size of a vector image is generally smaller than the file size of a bitmap image, which makes vector images particularly useful for a website. However, vector graphics are not as effective as bitmap graphics for representing photo-realistic images. Even so, one of the most compelling features of Flash is the ability to create and manipulate vector graphics.

Flash images are vector graphics and they are referred to as objects. Images (objects) created using Flash drawing tools have a stroke (border line), a fill, or both. In addition, the stroke of an object can be segmented into smaller lines. You can modify the size, shape, rotation, and color of each stroke, fill, and segment.

Flash provides two drawing modes, called models. In the Merge Drawing Model, when you draw two shapes and one overlaps the other, a change in the top object may affect the object it overlaps. For example, if you draw a circle on top of a rectangle and then move the circle off the rectangle, the portion of the rectangle covered by the circle is removed. The Object Drawing Model allows you to overlap shapes which are then kept separate, so that changes in one object do not affect another object. Another way to avoid having changes in one object affect another is to place the objects on separate layers on the Timeline as you did in Chapter 1.

PROPERTIES LIBRARY

Rectangle Tool

▽ **FILL AND STROKE**

Stroke: ▭ 2.00

Style: Solid ▾ ✏

Scale: Normal ▾ ☐ Hinting

Cap: ⬭ | ▾

Join: ⟨⟨ | ▾   Miter: 3.00

▽ **RECTANGLE OPTIONS**

10.00   10.00

10.00   10.00

⬭ —●—   Reset

PROPERTIES LIBRARY

T ⟨Instance Name⟩

TLF Text ▾

Read Only ▾ | ▾

▽ **CHARACTER**

Family: Arial ▾

Style: Bold ▾ | Embed...

Size: 14.0 pt   Leading: 126 % ▾

Color: ▭   Tracking: 0

Highlight: ▱   Kerning: Auto ▾

Anti-alias: Readability ▾

Rotation: Auto ▾   T F T T,

▷ **ADVANCED CHARACTER**

▽ **PARAGRAPH**

Align: ☰ ☰ ☰   ☰ ☰ ☰ ☰

Margins: →☰ 0.0 px   ☰← 0.0 px

Indent: →☰ 0.0 px

Spacing: →☰ 0.0 px   ☰ 0.0 px

Text Justify: Word spacing ▾

Direction: Left to Right ▾

▷ **ADVANCED PARAGRAPH**

▽ **CONTAINER AND FLOW**

Behavior: Multiline no wrap ▾

Max chars: -   ☐ ☐ ☐ ☐

Columns: ▥ -   ▤ - px

Padding: L: 2.0 px   R: 2.0 px

#000000 ▱ ◉

TIMELINE   MOTION EDITOR

👁 🔒 ☐ 1

Heading ✏ · · ☐

Labels · · ☐

Ovals · · ☐

Guide · 🔒 ☐

Heading Background · 🔒 ☐

ALIGN   INFO   TRANSFORM

Align:

⊫ ⊹ ⊨   ⊓ ⊪ ⊔

Distribute:

⊼ ⊹ ⊥   ⊪ ⊹ ⊩

Match size: Space:

⊡ ⊡ ⊞   ⊐⊏ ⊐⊏

☐ Align to stage

Use the Flash Drawing
AND ALIGNMENT TOOLS

What You'll Do

▶ *In this lesson, you will use several drawing tools to create various vector graphics.*

Using Flash Drawing and Editing Tools

When you point to a tool on the Tools panel, its name appears next to the tool. Figure 1 identifies the tools described in the following paragraphs. Several of the tools have options that modify their use. These options are available in the Options area of the Tools panel when the tool is selected.

Selection—Used to select an object or parts of an object, such as the stroke or fill; and to reshape and reposition objects. The options for the Selection tool are Snap to Objects (aligns objects), Smooth (smooths lines), and Straighten (straightens lines).

Subselection—Used to select, drag, and reshape an object. Vector graphics are composed of lines and curves (each of which is a segment) connected by **anchor points**. Selecting an object with this tool displays the anchor points and allows you to use them to edit the object.

Free Transform—Used to rotate, scale, skew, and distort objects.

Gradient Transform—Used to transform a gradient fill by adjusting the size, direction, or center of the fill.

The Free and Gradient Transform tools are grouped within one icon on the Tools panel.

3D Rotation—Used to create 3D effects by rotating movie clips in 3D space on the Stage.

3D Translation—Used to create 3D effects by moving movie clips in 3D space on the Stage.

The 3D Rotation and the 3D Translation tools are grouped within one icon on the Tools panel.

Lasso—Used to select objects or parts of objects. The Polygon Mode option allows you to draw straight lines when selecting an object.

Pen—Used to draw lines and curves by creating a series of dots, known as anchor points, that are automatically connected. Other tools used to add, delete, and convert the anchor points created by the Pen tool are grouped with the Pen tool. To see the menu containing these tools, click and hold the Pen tool until the menu opens.

Text—Used to create and edit text.

Line—Used to draw straight lines. You can draw vertical, horizontal, and 45° diagonal lines by pressing and holding [Shift] while drawing the line.

Rectangle—Used to draw rectangular shapes. Press and hold [Shift] to draw a perfect square.

Oval—Used to draw oval shapes. Press and hold [Shift] to draw a perfect circle.

Primitive Rectangle and Oval—Used to draw objects with properties, such as corner radius or inner radius, that can be changed using the Properties panel.

PolyStar—Used to draw polygons and stars.

The Rectangle, Oval, Primitive, and PolyStar tools are grouped within one tool on the Tools panel.

Pencil—Used to draw freehand lines and shapes. The Pencil Mode option displays a menu with the following commands: Straighten (draws straight lines), Smooth (draws smooth curved lines), and Ink (draws freehand with no modification).

Brush—Used to draw (paint) with brush-like strokes. Options allow you to set the size and shape of the brush, and to determine the area to be painted, such as inside or behind an object.

Spray Brush—Used to spray colors and patterns onto objects. Dots are the default pattern for the spray. However, you can use a graphic symbol, such as a flag, to create a pattern.

The Brush and Spray Brush tools are grouped together.

Deco—Used to turn graphic shapes into geometric patterns or create kaleidoscopic-like effects.

Bone—Used to animate objects that have joints. For example you could use a series of linked objects, such as arms and legs to create character animations.

Bind—Used to adjust the relationships among individual bones. The Bone and Bind tools are grouped together.

Paint Bucket—Used to fill enclosed areas of a drawing with color. Options allow you to fill areas that have gaps and to make adjustments in a gradient fill.

Ink Bottle—Used to apply line colors and thickness to the stroke of an object.

The Paint Bucket and Ink Bottle are grouped together.

Eyedropper—Used to select stroke, fill, and text attributes so they can be copied from one object to another.

Eraser—Used to erase lines and fills. Options allow you to choose what part of the object to erase, as well as the size and shape of the eraser.

Hand—Used to move the Stage around the Pasteboard by dragging the Stage.

Zoom—Used to change the magnification of an area of the Stage. Clicking an area of the Stage zooms in and holding down [Alt] (Win) or [option] (Mac) and clicking zooms out.

Stroke Color—Used to set the stroke color of drawn objects.

Fill Color—Used to set the fill color of drawn objects.

Figure 1 *Flash tools*

- Selection
- Subselection
- Free Transform (Gradient)
- 3D Rotation (3D Translation)
- Lasso
- Pen (Add Anchor Point, etc.)
- Text
- Line
- Rectangle (Oval, etc.)
- Pencil
- Brush (Spray)
- Deco
- Bone (Bind)
- Paint Bucket (Ink Bottle)
- Eyedropper
- Eraser
- Hand
- Zoom
- Stroke Color
- Fill Color
- Black and White
- Swap Color
- Options area (options change depending on which tool is selected)

Black and White—Used to set the stroke color to black and the fill color to white.

Swap Color—Used to swap the stroke and fill colors.

Options—Used to select an option for a tool, such as the type of rectangle (object drawing mode) or size of the brush when using the Brush tool.

Working with Grouped Tools

To display a list of grouped tools, you click the tool and hold the mouse button until the menu opens. For example, if you want to select the Oval tool and the Rectangle tool is displayed, you click and hold the Rectangle tool. Then, when the menu opens, you click the Oval tool option. You know a tool is a grouped tool if you see an arrow in the lower-right corner of the tool icon.

Working with Tool Options

Some tools have additional options that allow you to modify their use. For example, the brush tool has options to set the brush size and to set where the brush fill will be applied. If additional options for a tool are available, they appear at the bottom of the Tools panel in the Options area when the tool is selected. If the option has a menu associated with it, such as a list of brush sizes for the brush tool, then the option icon will have an arrow in the lower-right corner. Click and hold the option until the menu opens.

Tools for Creating Vector Graphics

The Oval, Rectangle, Pencil, Brush, Line, and Pen tools are used to create vector objects.

NEW Positioning Objects on the Stage

The Stage dimensions are made up of pixels (dots) matching the Stage size. So, a Stage size of 550 × 400 would be 550 pixels wide and 400 pixels high. Each pixel has a location on the Stage designated as the X (across) and Y (down) coordinates. The location of any object on the Stage is determined by its position from the upper-left corner of the Stage, which is 0,0 and the object's registration point. The registration point of an object is used to align it with the coordinates. The registration point, which is shown as a crosshair, is initially set at the upper-left corner of an object, as shown in Figure 2. So, an object having coordinates of 100,100 would be positioned at 100 pixels across and 100 pixels down the Stage, as shown in Figure 2. The Properties panel displays the X,Y values of any selected object. The most precise way to position an object on the Stage is to use the Properties panel to enter X and Y values for the object. Other ways to position objects on the Stage include using rulers, gridlines, and guides, as well as the align options. The Rulers, Grid, and Guides commands, which are found on the View menu, are used to turn on and off these features. Figure 2 shows the rulers and the ruler lines, which are used to indicate

Figure 2 *Using rulers to position an object*

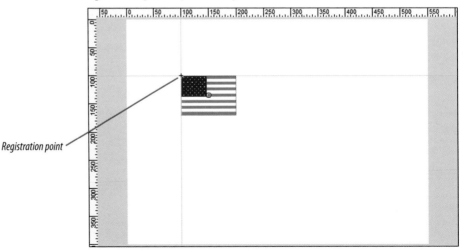

Registration point

the position of an object. (*Note:* Normally ruler lines display on top of objects on the Stage. In Figure 2, the registration point is displayed above the ruler lines to show its exact placement.)

After displaying the rulers, you can drag the lines from the top ruler or the left side ruler to the Stage. To remove a ruler line, you drag the ruler line up to the top ruler or across to the left ruler.

Figure 3 shows the Stage with gridlines displayed. The gridlines can be used to position an object. You can modify the grid size and color. In addition to using rulers and guides to help place objects, you can create a new layer as a Guide layer that you use to position objects on the Stage. When you turn gridlines and guides on, they appear on the Stage. However, they do not appear in the Flash movie when you test or publish it.

NEW Using the Align Panel

Figure 4 shows the Align panel, which allows you to position objects on the Stage either relative to the Stage or to other objects. The Align panel has four areas (Align, Distribute, Match size, Space) each with options. The Align options are used to align the edge or center of an object with the edge or center of the Stage—or, if multiple objects are selected, to align their edges and centers. The Distribute options are used to position objects across or down the Stage. The Match size options are used to resize selected objects to match the height and/or width of the largest object or to match the Stage if the Align to stage option is selected. The Space options are used to space out objects evenly across and down the Stage.

Figure 3 *Using gridlines to position an object*

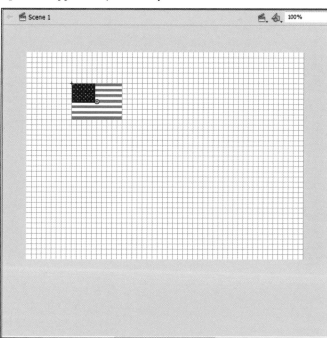

Figure 4 *The Align panel*

Show gridlines and check settings

1. Open fl2_1.fla from the drive and folder where your Data Files are stored, then save it as **tools.fla**.

2. Click **Window** on the menu bar, point to **Workspace**, then click **Reset 'Essentials'**.

3. Click **View** on the menu bar, point to **Magnification**, then click **Fit in Window**.

4. Click the **Stroke Color tool color swatch** 🖉 on the Tools panel, then click the **red color swatch** in the left column of the Color palette.

5. Click the **Fill Color tool color swatch** 🖉 on the Tools panel, then click the **blue color swatch** in the left column of the Color palette.

6. Click **View** on the menu bar, point to **Grid**, then click **Show Grid** to display the gridlines.

   A gray grid appears on the Stage.

7. Point to each tool on the Tools panel, then read its name.

8. Click the **Text tool** T , then click **CHARACTER** on the Properties panel to open the area if it is not open already.

   Notice the options in the Properties panel including the CHARACTER area, as shown in Figure 5. The Properties panel options change depending on the tool selected. For the Text tool the properties include the character family and the paragraph family.

You opened a document, saved it, set up the workspace, changed the stroke and fill colors, displayed the grid, viewed tool names on the Tools panel, then viewed the Text tool options in the Properties panel.

Figure 5 *Tool name on the Tools panel*

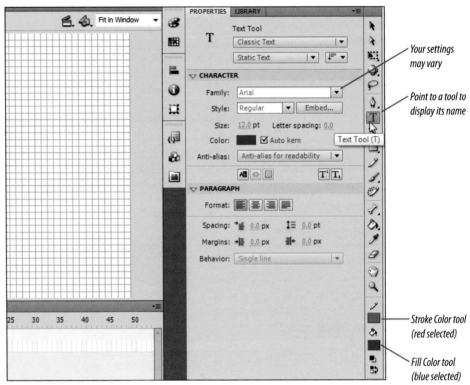

Your settings may vary

Point to a tool to display its name

Stroke Color tool (red selected)

Fill Color tool (blue selected)

Drawing Objects in Adobe Flash

Figure 6 *Objects created with drawing tools*

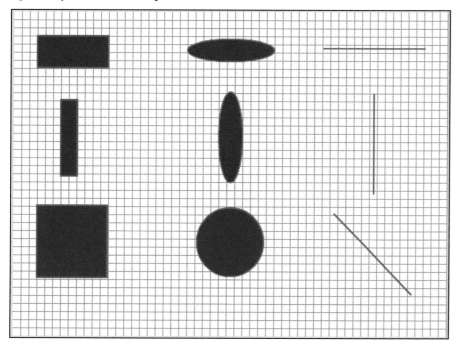

Use the Rectangle, Oval, and Line tools

1. Click the **Rectangle tool** ▢ on the Tools panel.

   Note: If the Rectangle tool is not displayed, click and hold the Oval tool to display the group of tools.

2. Verify that the Object Drawing option ◯ in the Options area of the Tools panel is not active.

   TIP When the Object Drawing option is not active, the object is drawn so that its stroke and fill can be selected separately.

3. Draw **three rectangle shapes** using Figure 6 as a guide.

   TIP Use the grid to approximate shape sizes, and press and hold [Shift] to draw a square. To undo an action, click the Undo command on the Edit menu.

   Notice the blue color for the fill and the red color for the strokes (border lines).

4. Click and hold the **Rectangle tool** ▢ on the Tools panel, then click the **Oval tool** ◯.

5. Draw **three oval shapes** using Figure 6 as a guide.

   TIP Press and hold [Shift] to draw a perfect circle.

6. Click the **Line tool** ╲ , then draw **three lines** using Figure 6 as a guide.

   TIP Press and hold [Shift] to snap the line to the nearest 45-degree increment, such as 45, 90, 180 and so on.

You used the Rectangle, Oval, and Line tools to draw objects on the Stage.

Use the Pen, Pencil, and Brush tools

1. Click **Insert** on the menu bar, point to **Timeline**, then click **Layer**.

   A new layer—Layer 2—appears above Layer 1.

2. Click **frame 5** on Layer 2.

3. Click **Insert** on the menu bar, point to **Timeline**, then click **Keyframe**.

   Since the objects were drawn in frame 1 on Layer 1, they are no longer visible when you insert a keyframe in frame 5 on Layer 2. A keyframe allows you to draw in any location on the Stage on the specified frame.

4. Click the **Zoom tool** 🔍 on the Tools panel, click near the upper-left quadrant of the Stage to zoom in, then scroll as needed to see more of the grid.

5. Click the **Pen tool** ✒ on the Tools panel, position it in the upper-left quadrant of the Stage, as shown in Figure 7, then click to set an anchor point.

6. Using Figure 8 as a guide, click the remaining anchor points to finish drawing an arrow.

TIP To close an object, be sure to re-click the first anchor point as your last action.

7. Click the **Paint Bucket tool** 🪣 , then click inside the arrow.

8. Click **View** on the menu bar, point to **Magnification**, then click **Fit in Window**.

9. Click **View** on the menu bar, point to **Grid**, then click **Show Grid** to turn off the gridlines.

10. Insert a **new layer**, Layer 3, then insert a **keyframe** in frame 10.

(continued)

Figure 7 *Positioning the Pen Tool on the Stage*

Figure 8 *Setting anchor points to draw an arrow*

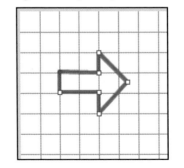

Drawing Objects in Adobe Flash

Figure 9 *Pencil Tool options*

Click the Pencil Mode Smooth icon to display the 3 options (Note: The Straighten icon might be displayed instead of the Smooth icon.)

Click the Smooth option

Figure 10 *Images drawn using drawing tools*

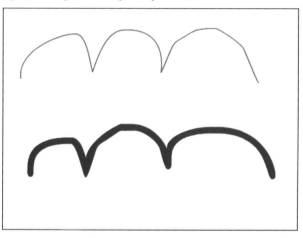

Figure 11 *The dot pattern indicating the object is selected*

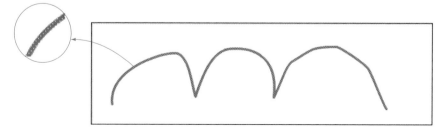

11. Click the **Pencil tool** 🖉 on the Tools panel.

12. Click **Pencil Mode** Ⓢ in the Options area of the Tools panel, then click the **Smooth** option, as shown in Figure 9.

13. Draw the **top image** shown in Figure 10.

    Note: The line may not appear until after you release the mouse button.

14. Click the **Brush tool** 🖌 on the Tools panel.

15. Click the **Brush Size Icon** ▪ in the Options area at the bottom of the Tools panel, then click the fifth option from the top.

16. Draw the **bottom image** shown in Figure 10.

    Notice the Pencil tool displays the stroke color and the Brush tool displays the fill color.

You added a layer, inserted a keyframe, then used the Pen tool to draw an arrow; you selected the Smooth option for the Pencil tool and drew an object; you selected a brush size for the Brush tool and drew an object.

Modify an object using tool options

1. Click the **Selection tool** ▸ on the Tools panel, then drag a **marquee** around the top object to select it.

   The line displays a dot pattern, as shown in Figure 11, indicating that it is selected.

2. Click the **Pencil Mode Smooth icon** Ⓢ in the Options area of the Tools panel three times. The line becomes smoother as the humps tend to flatten.

3. Click and hold the **Stroke slider** 🛆 in the FILL AND STROKE area of the Properties panel, then drag the **Stroke slider** 🛆 to change the stroke size to **20.**

   (continued)

4. Click the **Style list arrow** in the FILL AND STROKE area, then click **Dotted**.

5. Repeat Step 4 and change the line style to **Hairline**.

6. Save your work.

You smoothed objects using the tool options.

Use the Spray tool with a symbol

1. Click **Insert** on the menu bar, point to **Timeline**, then click **Layer**.

2. Click **frame 15** on Layer 4.

3. Click **Insert** on the menu bar, point to **Timeline**, then click **Keyframe**.

4. Click and hold the **Brush tool** on the Tools panel, then click the **Spray Brush tool** .

5. Display the Properties panel if it is not already displayed, then click the **Edit button** in the SYMBOL area of the Properties panel, as shown in Figure 12.

    Note: If the Properties panel does not display the options for the Spray Brush tool, click the Selection tool, then click the Spray Brush tool.

(continued)

Figure 12 *The properties for the Spray Brush tool*

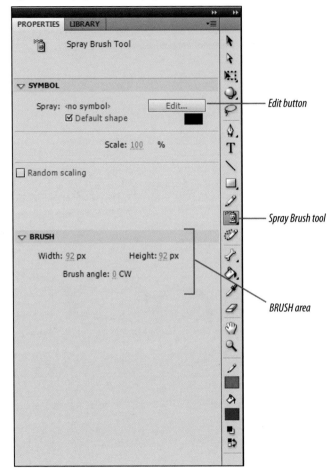

Edit button

Spray Brush tool

BRUSH area

Drawing Objects in Adobe Flash

Figure 13 *A design created using the Spray Brush tool*

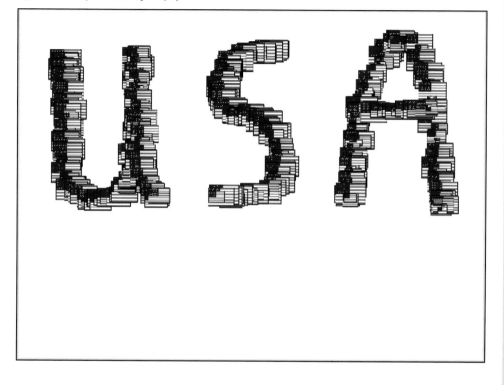

6. Click **Flag** in the Select Symbol dialog box, then click **OK**.

   The flag symbol is a graphic that was imported into this Flash document.

7. Click the **Random scaling check box** to select it, then click to deselect the **Rotate symbol check box** and the **Random rotation check box** if they are checked.

8. Display the **Brush area** on the Properties panel, then set the width and height to **9 px**.

9. Click the **Spray Brush tool** 🔲 in the Tools panel, then slowly draw the **U** in USA, as shown in Figure 13.

10. Continue to use the **Spray brush tool** 🔲 to draw the **S** and **A**.

    Hint: If you need to redo the drawing, use the Undo command on the Edit menu or use the Selection tool to draw a marquee around the drawing, then delete the selection.

11. Save your work, then close the document.

You specified a symbol as a pattern and used the Spray Brush tool to complete a drawing.

1. Open fl2_2.fla, then save it as **alignObjects.fla**.

2. Click the **Selection tool** on the Tools panel, click the **flag** on the Stage, then display the Properties panel, if it is not displayed.

   Notice the X and Y coordinates are set to 100.

3. Click **View** on the menu bar, then click **Rulers**.

4. Click and hold the **horizontal ruler** at the top of the Stage, then drag a **ruler line** down to 100 on the vertical ruler, as shown in Figure 14.

5. Click and hold the **vertical ruler** at the left of the Stage, then drag a **ruler line** across to 100 on the horizontal ruler.

   The point where the two ruler lines cross identifies the X,Y coordinates 100,100. The ruler lines meet at the registration point of the object.

6. Click the **flag**, point to the **100** next to X: on the Properties panel, then, when the pointer changes to a hand with a double-headed arrow , drag the pointer to the left to change the X value to **0**.

   This aligns the registration point of the object to the left edge of the Stage.

7. Repeat Step 6 to change the Y value to **0**.

   Note: You can click a value, type in a new value, and press [Enter] (Win) or [return] (Mac).

8. Type **550** for the X value and **400** for the Y value.

   Notice the flag is positioned off the Stage because the registration point is in the upper-left corner of the object.

   (continued)

Figure 14 *Positioning an object on the Stage using XY coordinates*

XY coordinates

Ruler line

Drawing Objects in Adobe Flash

Figure 15 *Setting the registration point*

Registration point options

9. Change the view to **50%**.
10. Point to the **flag**, then click and drag the **flag** around the Stage noticing how the values for X and Y in the Properties panel change.
11. Drag the **flag** to approximately the middle of the Stage.
12. Change the view to **Fit in Window**.
13. Use the **arrow keys** on the keyboard to move the flag one pixel at a time in all four directions, then observe the changes to the X and Y values in the Properties panel as you move the object.
14. Click the **flag** to select it, click **Modify** on the menu bar, then click **Convert to Symbol**.

    The Convert to Symbol dialog box opens allowing you to change the registration point.
15. Click the **lower-right icon** as shown in Figure 15, then click **OK**.

    Notice the registration point is now located on the lower-right corner of the flag.
16. Change the **X** and **Y** values in the Properties panel to **100** and **100**.

    Notice the flag is now positioned using the new location of the registration point.
17. Drag each **ruler line** to its respective ruler to remove it from the Stage.
18. Click **View** on the menu bar, then click **Rulers** to remove them from view.
19. Save, then close the Flash document.

You used the X and Y values of an object to position it on the Stage. You used the Convert to Symbol dialog box to change the registration point of an object.

NEW Use the Align options

1. Open fl2_3.fla, then save it as **alignOptions.fla**.

   This document has three objects (flags) of different sizes randomly placed on the Stage.

2. Click **Window** on the menu bar, then click **Align** to open the Align panel.

TIP Alternately, you can click the Align icon that is part of a collapsed panel set on your workspace.

3. Drag the **Align panel set** by its title bar and position it adjacent to the right side of the Stage, as shown in Figure 16.

4. Verify the **Align to stage check box** in the Align panel is active, then click the Align to stage check box if it is not already active.

5. Click the **largest flag** to select it, then click the **Align left edge icon** 🔲 .

6. Point to the next **Align icon** 🔲 , read the name that appears, then click the **Align horizontal center icon** 🔲 and notice the new position of the object on the Stage.

7. Click the other **Align options** on the top row of the Align panel.

8. Click the **Align horizontal center icon** 🔲 , then click the **Align vertical center icon** 🔲 .

   When you use these two align options together, they position the center of the object with the center of the Stage.

9. Click the **Match width icon** 🔲 , then click the **Match height icon** 🔲 .

10. Click **Edit** on the menu bar, then click **Undo Match Size**.

(continued)

Figure 16 *Positioning the Align panel*

Be sure Align to stage is active (checked)

Figure 17 *All three objects selected*

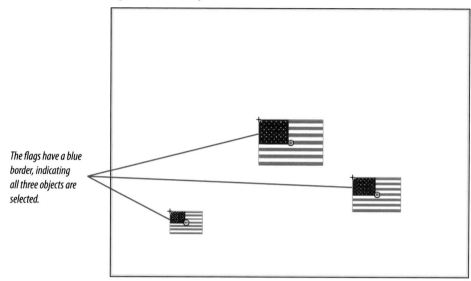

The flags have a blue border, indicating all three objects are selected.

11. Click **Edit** on the menu bar, then click **Undo Match Size**.

12. Use the **Selection tool** ▶ to draw a marquee around all three flags to select them, as shown in Figure 17.

13. Click the **Align left edge icon** ▣ , then click the **Align horizontal center icon** ▣ .

14. Click the **Space evenly vertically icon** ▤ , then click the **Align vertical center icon** ▤ .

15. Click the **Align to stage check box** to make this feature not active.

16. With all three objects selected, click each of the **Align options** on the top row of the Align panel.

    Notice that the objects align to each other instead of the Stage.

17. Click the **Match width and height icon** ▦ .

    This changes the dimension of each object to match the size of the largest object.

18. Close the Align panel, then save and close the Flash document.

You used the Align panel to position objects on the Stage relative to the Stage and to each other.

Select Objects
AND APPLY COLORS

What You'll Do

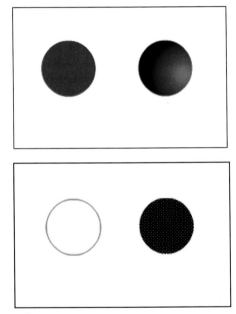

In this lesson, you will use several techniques to select objects, change the color of strokes and fills, and create a gradient fill.

Selecting Objects

Before you can edit a drawing, you must first select the object, or the part of the object, on which you want to work. Drawn objects are made up of a stroke(s) and a fill. Strokes can have several segments. For example, a rectangle has four stroke segments, one for each side of the object. These can be selected separately or as a whole. Flash highlights objects that have been selected, as shown in Figure 18. When the stroke of an object is selected, a dotted colored line appears. When the fill of an object is selected, a dot pattern appears. When the stroke and fill of an object are selected, both the stroke and the fill appear dotted. When a group of objects is selected, a bounding box appears.

Using the Selection Tool

You can use the Selection tool to select part or all of an object, and to select multiple objects. To select only the fill, click just the fill; to select only the stroke, click just the stroke. To select both the fill and the stroke, double-click the object or draw a marquee around it. To select part of an object, drag a marquee that defines the area you wish to select, as shown in Figure 18. To select

multiple objects or combinations of strokes and fills, press and hold [Shift], then click each item. To deselect an item(s), click a blank area of the Stage.

Using the Lasso Tool

The Lasso tool provides more flexibility than the Selection tool when selecting an object(s) or parts of an object on the Stage. You can use the tool in a freehand manner to draw any shape that then selects the object(s) within the shape. Alternately, you can use the Polygon Mode option to draw straight lines and connect them to form a shape that will select any object(s) within the shape.

Drawing Model Modes

Flash provides two drawing modes, called models. In the Merge Drawing Model mode, the stroke and fill of an object are separate. Thus, as you draw an object such as a circle, the stroke and fill can be selected individually as described earlier. When using the Object Drawing Model mode, the stroke and fill are combined and cannot be selected individually. However, you can use the Break Apart option from the Modify menu to separate the stroke and fill so that they can be selected individually. In addition, you can turn off either the stroke or fill when drawing an object in either mode. You can toggle between the two modes by clicking the Object Drawing option in the Options area of the Tools panel.

Working with Colors

Flash allows you to change the color of the stroke and fill of an object. Figure 19 shows the Colors area of the Tools panel. To change a color, you click the color swatch of the Stroke Color tool or the color swatch of the Fill Color tool, and then select a color swatch on the Color palette. The Color palette, as shown in Figure 20, allows you to select a color from the palette or type in a six-character code that represents the values of three colors (red, green, blue),

referred to as RGB. When these characters are combined in various ways, they can represent virtually any color. The values are in a hexadecimal format (base 16), so they include letters and digits (A–F + 0–9 = 16 options), and they are preceded by a pound sign (#). The first two characters represent the value for red, the next two for green, and the last two for blue. For example, #000000 represents black (lack of color); #FFFFFF represents white; and #FFCC33 represents a shade of gold. You do not have to memorize the codes. There are reference manuals with the codes, and many programs allow you to set the values visually by selecting a color from a palette. You can also use the Properties panel to change the stroke and fill colors.

You can set the desired colors before drawing an object, or you can change a color of a previously drawn object. You can use the Ink Bottle tool to change the stroke color, and you can use the Paint Bucket tool to change the fill color.

Working with Gradients

A gradient is a color fill that makes a gradual transition from one color to another. Gradients can be very useful for creating a 3D effect, drawing attention to an object, and generally enhancing the appearance of an object. You can apply a gradient fill by using the Paint Bucket tool. The position of the Paint Bucket tool over the object is important because it determines the direction of the gradient fill. The Color palette can be used to create and alter custom gradients.

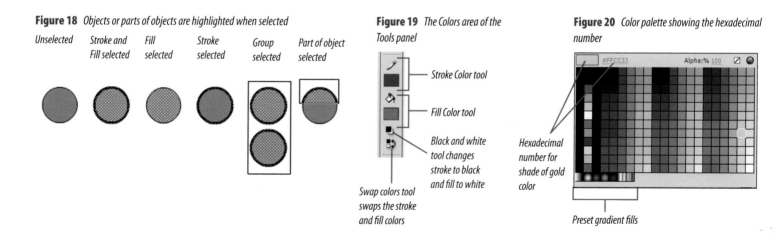

Figure 18 *Objects or parts of objects are highlighted when selected*

Unselected   Stroke and Fill selected   Fill selected   Stroke selected   Group selected   Part of object selected

Figure 19 *The Colors area of the Tools panel*

Stroke Color tool

Fill Color tool

Black and white tool changes stroke to black and fill to white

Swap colors tool swaps the stroke and fill colors

Figure 20 *Color palette showing the hexadecimal number*

#FFCC33   Alpha:% 100

Hexadecimal number for shade of gold color

Preset gradient fills

Select a drawing using the Selection tool

1. Open tools.fla, then click **frame 1** on the Timeline.

TIP   The options available to you in the Properties panel differ depending on whether you click a frame number on the Timeline or a frame on a layer.

2. Click the **Selection tool** 🡤 on the Tools panel if it is not already selected, then drag a **marquee** around the circle to select the entire object (both the stroke and the fill).

3. Click anywhere on the Stage to deselect the object.

4. Click **inside the circle** to select the fill only, then click outside the circle to deselect it.

5. Click the **stroke** of the circle to select it, as shown in Figure 21, then deselect it.

6. Double-click the **circle** to select it, press and hold **[Shift]**, double-click the **square** to select both objects, then click the **Stage** to deselect both objects.

7. Click the **right border** of the square to select it, as shown in Figure 22, then deselect it.

   Objects, such as rectangles, have border segments that can be selected individually.

8. Drag a **marquee** around the square, circle, and diagonal line to select all three objects.

9. Click a blank area of the Stage to deselect the objects.

10. Click **inside the oval** in row 2 to select the fill, then drag the **fill** outside the stroke, as shown in Figure 23.

11. Look at the Properties panel.

(continued)

Figure 21 *Using the Selection tool to select the stroke of the circle*

Figure 22 *Using the Selection tool to select a segment of the stroke of the square*

Figure 23 *Separating the stroke and fill of an object*

Drawing Objects in Adobe Flash

Figure 24 *Circles drawn with the Oval tool*

Figure 25 *Changing the stroke color*

Notice the stroke color is none and the fill color is blue. This is because only the object's fill is selected. You can use the Properties panel to verify what you have selected when working with the Selection tool.

12. Click **Edit** on the menu bar, then click **Undo Move**.

You used the Selection tool to select the stroke and fill of an object, and to select multiple objects.

Change fill and stroke colors

1. Click **Layer 4,** click **Insert** on the menu bar, point to **Timeline,** then click **Layer.**

2. Click **frame 20** of the new layer, click **Insert** on the menu bar, point to **Timeline,** then click **Keyframe.**

3. Select the **Oval tool** on the Tools panel, then draw **two circles** similar to those shown in Figure 24.

4. Click the **Fill Color tool color swatch** on the Tools panel, then click the **yellow color swatch** in the left column of the Color palette.

5. Click the **Paint Bucket tool** on the Tools panel, then click the **fill** of the right circle.

6. Click the **Stroke Color tool color swatch** on the Tools panel, then click the **yellow color swatch** in the left column of the color palette.

7. Click and hold the **Paint Bucket tool** on the Tools panel, click the **Ink Bottle tool**, point to the red stroke line of the left circle, as shown in Figure 25, then click to change the stroke color to yellow.

8. Click **Edit** on the menu bar, then click **Undo Stroke.**

You used the Paint Bucket and Ink Bottle tools to change the fill and stroke colors of an object.

Apply a gradient and make changes to the gradient

1. Click the **Fill Color tool color swatch** on the Tools panel, then click the **red gradient color swatch** in the bottom row of the Color palette, as shown in Figure 26.

2. Click and hold the **Ink Bottle tool** on the Tools panel, click the **Paint Bucket tool**, then click the **yellow circle**.

3. Click different parts of the right circle to view how the gradient changes.

4. Click the **right side** of the circle, as shown in Figure 27.

5. Click and hold the **Free Transform tool** on the Tools panel, then click the **Gradient Transform tool**.

6. Click the **gradient-filled circle**.

7. Drag each of the four handles shown in Figure 28 to determine the effect of each handle on the gradient, then click the **Stage** to deselect the circle.

8. Click the **Selection tool** on the Tools panel, then click inside the left circle.

9. Click the **Fill Color tool color swatch** in the FILL AND STROKE area of the Properties panel, click the **Hex Edit text box**, type **#006637** (two zeros), then press **[Enter]** (Win) or **[return]** (Mac).

    The Fill color swatch and the fill color for the circle change to a shade of green.

10. Save your work.

You applied a gradient fill, you used the Gradient Transform tool to alter the gradient, and you applied a new color using its Hexadecimal number.

Figure 26 *Selecting the red gradient*

Click red gradient color swatch to select it

Figure 27 *Clicking the right side of the circle*

Figure 28 *Gradient Transform handles*

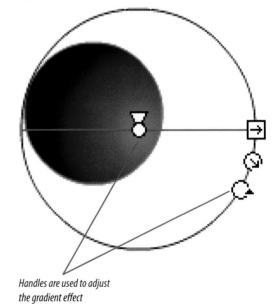

Handles are used to adjust the gradient effect

Drawing Objects in Adobe Flash

Figure 29 *Circle drawn using the Object Drawing Model mode*

Blue bounding box indicates
the object is selected

Object Drawing option
active; active mode is Object
Drawing Model

Work with Object Drawing Model mode

1. Insert a **new layer**, then insert a **keyframe** on frame 25.
2. Select the **Oval tool** 🔘, click the **Stroke Color tool color swatch** 🖍, then click the **red swatch**.
3. Click the **Fill Color tool color swatch** 🖍, then click the **black swatch**.
4. Click the **Object Drawing option** 🔘 in the Options area of the Tools panel to make the icon active.

   The icon is active and the mode changes to Object Drawing Model.
5. Draw a **circle** as shown in Figure 29.

   Notice that when you use Object Drawing Model mode, the object is selected automatically, which means both the stroke and fill areas of the circle are selected.
6. Click the **Selection tool** ▶ on the Tools panel, then click a blank area of the Stage to deselect the object.
7. Click the **circle** once, then drag the **circle** around the Stage.

   The entire object is selected, including the stroke and fill areas.
8. Click **Modify** on the menu bar, then click **Break Apart**.

   Breaking apart an object drawn in Object Drawing Model mode allows you to select the strokes and fills individually.
9. Click a blank area of the Stage, click the **fill** area of the circle, drag to the right, then save your work.

   Notice the fill moves but the stroke stays.

You used the Object Drawing Model mode to draw an object, deselect it, then break it apart to display and then separate the stroke and fill.

Work with Drawn OBJECTS

What You'll Do

In this lesson, you will copy, move, and transform (resize, rotate, and reshape) objects.

Copying and Moving Objects

To copy an object, select it, and then click the Copy command on the Edit menu. To paste the object, click the Paste command on the Edit menu. You can copy an object to another layer by selecting the frame on the layer prior to pasting the object. You can copy and paste more than one object by selecting all the objects before using the Copy or Paste commands.

You move an object by selecting it and dragging it to a new location. You can position an object more precisely by selecting it and then pressing the arrow keys, which move the selection up, down, left, and right in small increments. In addition, you can change the X and Y coordinates in the Properties panel to position an object exactly on the Stage.

Transforming Objects

You use the Free Transform tool and the Transform panel to resize, rotate, skew, and reshape objects. After selecting an object, you click the Free Transform tool to display eight square-shaped handles used to transform the object, and a circle-shaped transformation point located at the center

of the object. The transformation point is the point around which the object can be rotated. You can also change its location.

Resizing an Object

You enlarge or reduce the size of an object using the Scale option, which is available when the Free Transform tool is active. The process is to select the object and click the Free Transform tool, and then click the Scale option in the Options area of the Tools panel. Eight handles appear around the selected object. You drag the corner handles to resize the object without changing its proportions. That is, if the object starts out as a square, dragging a corner handle will change the size of the object, but it will still be a square. On the other hand, if you drag one of the middle handles, the object will be reshaped as taller, shorter, wider, or narrower. In addition, you can change the Width and Height settings in the Properties panel to resize an object in increments of one-tenth of one pixel.

Rotating and Skewing an Object

You use the Rotate and Skew option of the Free Transform tool to rotate an object and to skew it. The process is to select the object, click the Free Transform tool, and then click the Rotate and Skew option in the Options area of the Tools panel. Eight handles appear around the object. You drag the corner handles to rotate the object, or you drag the middle handles to skew the object, as shown in Figure 30. The Transform panel can be used to rotate and skew an object in a more precise way; select the object, display the Transform panel (available via the Window menu), enter the desired rotation or skew in degrees, and then press [Enter] (Win) or [return] (Mac).

Distorting an Object

You can use the Distort and Envelope options to reshape an object by dragging its handles. The Distort option allows you to reshape an object by dragging one corner without affecting the other corners of the object. The Envelope option provides more than eight handles to allow more precise distortions. These options are accessed through the Transform command on the Modify menu.

Flipping an Object

You use a Flip option on the Transform menu to flip an object either horizontally or vertically. You select the object, click the Transform command on the Modify menu, and then choose Flip Vertical or Flip Horizontal. Other Transform options allow you to rotate and scale the selected object. The Remove Transform command allows you to restore an object to its original state.

Reshaping a Segment of an Object

You use the Subselection tool to reshape a segment of an object. You click an edge of the object to display handles that can be dragged to reshape the object.

You use the Selection tool to reshape objects. When you point to the edge of an object, the pointer displays an arc symbol. Using the Arc pointer, you drag the edge of the object you want to reshape, as shown in Figure 31. If the Selection tool points to a corner of an object, the pointer changes to an L-shape. You drag the pointer to reshape the corner of the object.

Figure 30 *Using handles to manipulate an object*

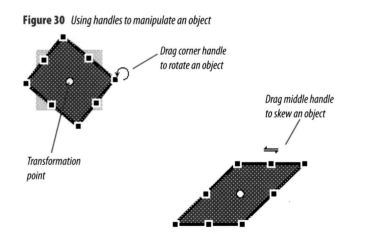

Drag corner handle
to rotate an object

Transformation
point

Drag middle handle
to skew an object

Figure 31 *Using the Selection tool to distort an object*

Copy and move an object

1. Click **frame 5** on the Timeline.

2. Click the **Selection tool** ▶ on the Tools panel, then draw a **marquee** around the arrow object to select it.

3. Click **Edit** on the menu bar, click **Copy**, click **Edit** on the menu bar, then click **Paste in Center**.

4. Drag the newly copied **arrow** to the upper-right corner of the Stage, as shown in Figure 32.

5. Verify the right arrow object is selected on the Stage, press the **down arrow key [↓]** on the keyboard.

   The object moves down in approximately one-pixel increments and the Y coordinate in the Properties panel changes each time the arrow key is pressed.

6. Press the **right arrow key [→]** on the keyboard.

   The object moves right in one-pixel increments and the X coordinate in the Properties panel changes each time the arrow key is pressed.

7. Select the number in the X coordinate box in the Properties panel, type **450**, as shown in Figure 33, then press **[Enter]** (Win) or **[return]** (Mac).

8. Select the **number** in the Y coordinate box in the Properties panel, type **30**, then press **[Enter]** (Win) or **[return]** (Mac).

9. Drag a **marquee** around the left arrow object, then set the X and Y coordinates to **36** and **30**, respectively.

10. Click a blank area of the Stage to deselect the object.

You used the Selection tool to select an object, then you copied and moved the object.

Figure 32 *Moving the copied object*

Figure 33 *Changing the X coordinate in the Properties panel*

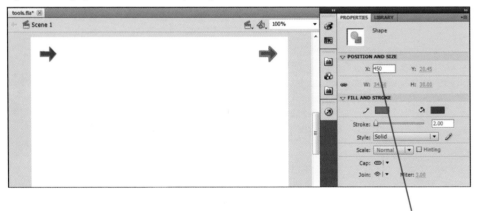

This value indicates the X coordinate position of the selected object

Figure 34 *Resizing an object using the corner handles*

Pointer used to drag
corner handle

Figure 35 *Reshaping an object using the middle handles*

Pointer used to reshape
the object

Transform Options

Different transform options, such as rotate, skew, and scale, can be accessed through the Options area on the Tools panel when the Free Transform tool is active, the Transform command on the Modify menu, and the Transform panel via the Transform command on the Window menu.

Resize and reshape an object

1. Click the **Free Transform tool** 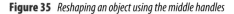 on the Tools panel.

   Note: You may need to click and hold the Gradient tool to display the Free Transform tool.

2. Draw a **marquee** around the arrow object on the right side of the Stage to select the object.

3. Click the **Scale option** in the Options area on the Tools panel to make it active.

4. Drag each **corner handle** toward and then away from the center of the object, as shown in Figure 34.

   As you drag a corner handle, the object's size is changed, but its proportions remain the same.

5. Click **Edit** on the menu bar, then click **Undo Scale**.

6. Repeat Step 5 until the arrow returns to its original size.

TIP The object is its original size when the option Undo Scale is no longer available on the Edit menu.

7. Verify the arrow is still selected and the handles are displayed, then select the **Scale option** in the Options area on the Tools panel to make it active.

8. Drag each **middle handle** toward and then away from the center of the object, as shown in Figure 35.

   As you drag the middle handles, the object's size and proportions change.

9. Click **Edit** on the menu bar, then click **Undo Scale** as needed to return the arrow to its original size.

You used the Free Transform tool and the Scale option to display an object's handles, and you used the handles to resize and reshape the object.

Skew, rotate, and flip an object

1. Verify that the Free Transform tool and the right arrow are selected (handles displayed), then click the **Rotate and Skew option** ⤵ in the Options area of the Tools panel.

2. Click and drag the **upper-middle handle** to the right.

3. Click and rotate the **upper-right corner handle** of the object clockwise.

   The arrow slants down and to the right.

4. Click **Edit** on the menu bar, click the **Undo Rotate** command, then repeat, selecting the Undo Rotate and Undo Skew commands until the arrow is in its original shape and orientation.

5. Click the **Selection tool** ▸ on the Tools panel, verify that the right arrow is selected, click **Window** on the menu bar, then click **Transform**.

6. Click the **Rotate text box**, type **45**, then press **[Enter]** (Win) or **[return]** (Mac).

   The arrow rotates 45°, as shown in Figure 36.

7. Click **Edit** on the menu bar, click **Undo Transform**, then close the Transform panel if it is still open.

8. Draw a **marquee** around the arrow in the upper-left corner of the Stage to select the object.

9. Click **Modify** on the menu bar, point to **Transform**, then click **Flip Horizontal**.

10. Save your work.

You used options on the Tools panel and the Transform panel, as well as commands on the Modify menu to skew, rotate, and flip an object.

Figure 36 *Using the Transform panel to rotate an object*

Rotate text box

Drawing Objects in Adobe Flash

Figure 37 *Using the Subselection tool to select an object*

Click the tip of the object to display the handles

Figure 38 *Using the Subselection tool to drag a handle to reshape the object*

Figure 39 *Using the Selection tool to drag an edge to reshape the object*

Click here, then drag

Use the Zoom, Subselection, and Selection tools

1. Drag a **marquee** around the arrow in the upper-right corner of the Stage, click **Edit** on the menu bar, click **Copy**, click **Edit** on the menu bar, then click **Paste in Center**.

2. Click the **Zoom tool** 🔍 on the Tools panel, then click the **middle of the arrow** in the center of the Stage to enlarge the view.

3. Click the **Subselection tool** ⊳ on the Tools panel, then click the **tip of the arrow** to display the handles, as shown in Figure 37.

   TIP The handles allow you to change any segment of the object.

4. Click the **handle** at the tip of the arrow, then drag it, as shown in Figure 38.

5. Click the **Oval tool** ⃝ on the Tools panel, then click the **Object Drawing option** ⃞ in the Options area of the Tools panel so the option is not active.

6. Verify the Fill color is set to blue, then draw a **circle** to the left of the arrow you just modified.

7. Click the **Selection tool** ▸ on the Tools panel, then point to the left edge of the circle until the Arc pointer ▸⌒ is displayed.

8. Drag the ▸⌒ **pointer** to the position shown in Figure 39.

9. Change the **View** to **100%**.

10. Save your work.

You used the Zoom tool to change the view, and you used the Subselection and Selection tools to reshape objects.

Use the Rectangle Primitive and Oval tools

1. Insert a **new layer** above Layer 6, click **frame 30** on Layer 7, then insert a **keyframe**.

2. Click and hold the **Oval tool** (or the Rectangle tool if it is displayed) to display the menu.

3. Click the **Rectangle Primitive tool**, then click the **Reset button** in the Properties panel RECTANGLE OPTIONS area to clear all of the settings.

4. Press and hold **[Shift]**, point to the **middle of the Stage**, then draw the **square** shown in Figure 40.

5. Click the **Selection tool** in the Tools panel, then drag **the upper-right corner handle** toward the center of the object.

   As you drag the corner, the radius of each of the four corners is changed.

6. Click the **Reset button** in the Properties panel to clear the setting.

7. Slowly drag the **slider** in the RECTANGLE OPTIONS area to the right until the radius changes to 100, then slowly drag the **slider** to the left until the radius changes to 100.

8. Click the **Reset Button** on the Properties panel to clear the radius settings.

9. Click the **Lock corner radius icon** in the Properties panel RECTANGLE OPTIONS area to unlock the individual controls.

10. Type **-60** in the upper-left corner radius text box, then type **-60** in the upper-right corner text box, as shown in Figure 41.

(continued)

Figure 40 *Drawing an object with the Rectangle Primitive tool*

The corner handles can be dragged to change the radius of the corners; in addition, the Properties panel can be used to make changes to the object

Figure 41 *Setting the corner radius of two corners*

Your values will differ

Type the values

Use the slider to quickly change the radius of the corners

Drawing Objects in Adobe Flash

Figure 42 *Drawing an object with the Oval Primitive tool*

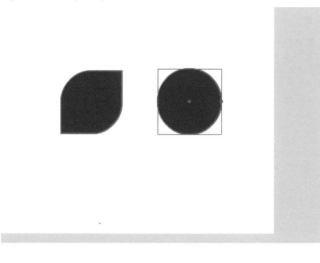

Figure 43 *Setting the stroke value to 12*

Set the stroke value to 12

11. Click the **Reset button** in the Properties panel to clear the radius settings.

12. Click the **Lock corner radius icon** ⇔ to unlock the individual controls.

13. Set the upper-left corner radius to **60** and the lower-right corner to **60**.

14. Click a blank area of the Stage to deselect the object.

15. Click and hold the **Rectangle Primitive tool** 📇 , click the **Oval Primitive tool** ⬭ on the Tools panel, then press and hold **[Shift]** and draw the **circle** shown in Figure 42.

TIP Remember some tools are grouped. Click and hold a grouped tool, such as the Oval tool, to see the menu of tools in the group.

16. Click the **Reset button** in the Properties panel OVAL OPTIONS area to clear any settings.

17. Drag the **Start angle slider** ⌂ and the **End angle slider** ⌂ to view their effect on the circle, then drag each **slider** back to 0.

18. Click the **Reset button** to clear the settings.

19. Drag the **Inner radius slider** ⌂ to see the effect on the circle, then set the inner radius to **30**.

20. Display the FILL AND STROKE area of the Properties panel, then set the Stroke value to **12**, as shown in Figure 43.

21. Save your work.

You used the Primitive tools to create objects and the Properties panel to alter them.

Work with Text
AND TEXT OBJECTS

What You'll Do

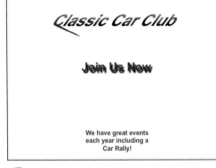

In this lesson, you will enter text using text blocks. You will also resize text blocks, change text attributes, and transform text.

Learning About Text

Flash provides a great deal of flexibility when using text. Among other settings for text, you can specify the typeface (font), size, style (bold, italic), and color (including gradients). You can transform the text by rotating, scaling, skewing, and flipping it. You can even break apart a letter and reshape its segments. There are two different text engines for working with text: Classic Text and Text Layout Framework (TLF). Classic Text mode is appropriate for many text applications and is easy to work with. Text Layout Framework mode provides advanced features and is appropriate for more text intensive applications.

Entering Text and Changing the Text Block for Classic Text

It is important to understand that text is entered into a text block, as shown in Figure 44. You use the Text tool to place a text block on the Stage and to enter and edit text. A text block expands as more text is entered and may even extend beyond the edge of the Stage. You can adjust the size of the text block so that it is a fixed width by dragging the handle in the upper-right

corner of the block. Figure 45 shows the process of using the Text tool to enter text and resize the text block. Once you select the Text tool, you click the Stage where you want the text to appear. An insertion point indicates where the next character will appear in the text block when it is typed. You can resize the text block to a fixed width by dragging the circle handle. After resizing the text block, the circle handle changes to a square, indicating that the text block now has a fixed width. Then, when you enter more text, it automatically wraps within the text block. You can resize the width of a text block at any time by selecting it with the Selection tool (either clicking on the text or drawing a marquee around it) and dragging any handle.

Changing Text Attributes

You can use the Properties panel to change the font, size, and style of a single character or an entire text block. Figure 46 shows the Properties panel when a text object is selected. You select text, display the Properties panel, and make the changes. You use the Selection tool to select the entire text block by drawing a marquee around it. You use the Text tool to select a single

Drawing Objects in Adobe Flash

character or string of characters by dragging the I-beam pointer over the text you want to select, as shown in Figure 47.

Working with Paragraphs

When working with large bodies of text, such as paragraphs, Flash provides many of the features found in a word processor. You can align paragraphs (left, right, center, justified) within a text block, set margins (space between the border of a text block and the paragraph text), set indents for the first line of a paragraph, and set line spacing (distance between paragraphs) using the Properties panel.

Transforming Text

It is important to understand that a text block is an object. Therefore, you can apply filters, such as drop shadows, and you can transform (reshape, rotate, skew, and so on) a text block in the same way you transform other objects. If you want to transform individual characters within a text block, you must first break apart the text block. To do this, you use the Selection tool to select the text block, then you click the Break Apart command on the Modify menu. Each character (or a group of characters) in the text block can now be selected and transformed.

NEW The Text Layout Framework (TLF)

Text Layout Framework (TLF) provides several advanced text features such as character color highlighting, underlining, strikethrough, and rotation. Text in the TLF format is displayed in a container, similar to a text block. Containers can be resized and linked using a Container icon. This allows you to flow text between them. The containers can have a border and background color, and the text in containers can be formatted into columns.

Figure 46 *The Properties panel when a text object is selected*

Figure 44 *A text block*

Figure 45 *Using the Text tool*

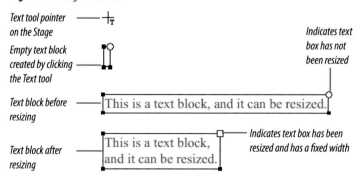

Figure 47 *Dragging the I-beam pointer to select text*

Enter text and change text attributes

1. Click **Layer 7**, insert a **new layer**, then insert a **keyframe** in frame 35 of the new layer.

2. Click the **Text tool** T , then verify the **Text engine** is set to Classic Text mode and the Text type is set to Static Text in the T area on the Properties panel.

3. Click the left-center of the Stage, then type **We have great events each year including a Rally**!

4. Click the **I-Beam pointer** ⌶ before the word "Rally," as shown in Figure 48, then type **Car** followed by a space.

5. Drag the **I-Beam pointer** ⌶ across the text to select all the text.

6. Make the following changes in the CHARACTER area of the Properties panel: Family: **Arial**; Style: **Bold**; Size: **16**; Color: **#990000**, then click the **text box**.

   Your Properties panel should resemble Figure 49.

7. Verify the text block is selected, position the **text pointer** ⊹T over the circle handle until the pointer changes to a double arrow ↔, then drag the **handle** to just before the word each, as shown in Figure 50.

8. Select the text using the I-Beam pointer ⌶, then click the **Align center icon** ≣ in the PARAGRAPH area of the Properties panel.

9. Click the **Selection tool** ⬉ on the Tools panel, click the **text object**, then drag the **object** to the lower-middle of the Stage.

TIP The Selection tool is used to select the text block, and the Text tool is used to select and edit the text within the text block.

You entered text and changed the font, type size, and text color; you also resized the text block and changed the text alignment.

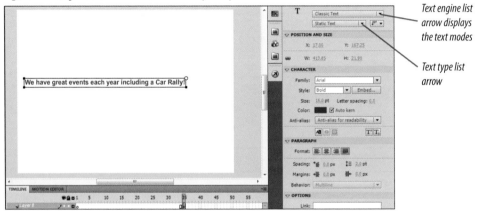

Figure 48 *Using the Text tool to enter text*

We have great events each year including a|Rally!

Figure 49 *Changes to the CHARACTER area of the Properties panel*

Text engine list arrow displays the text modes

Text type list arrow

Figure 50 *Resizing the text block*

We have great events each year including a Car Rally!

Drag handle to this position

Circle handle

Figure 51 *The Filters options in the Properties panel*

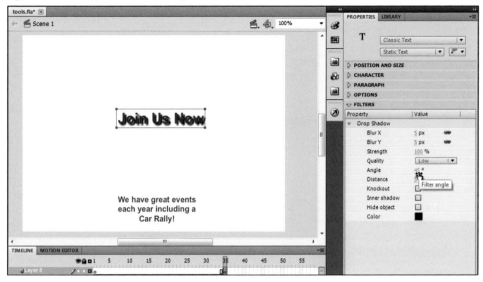

Using Filters

You can apply special effects, such as drop shadows, to text using options in the FILTERS area of the Properties panel. The process is to select the desired text, display the FILTERS area of the Properties panel, choose the desired effect, and make any adjustments, such as changing the angle of a drop shadow. You can copy and paste a filter from one object to another using the clipboard icon in the FILTERS area of the Properties panel.

Add a Filter effect to text

1. Click the **Text tool** T on the Tools panel, click the center of the Stage, then type **Join Us Now**. *Hint*: If the text box does not appear, double-click the Stage.

2. Drag the **I-Beam pointer** I across the text to select it, then use the Properties panel to change the Font size to **30** and the Text (fill) color to **#003399**.

3. Click **CHARACTER** on the Properties panel to close the CHARACTER area, then close all areas in the Properties panel except for the FILTERS area.

4. Click the **Selection tool** on the Tools panel, then verify the text block is selected.

5. Click the **Add filter icon** at the bottom of the FILTERS area, then click **Drop Shadow**.

6. Point to the **Angle value** in the FILTERS area of the Properties panel, as shown in Figure 51.

7. When the pointer changes to a double-headed arrow, drag the **pointer** to the right to view the effect on the shadow, then set the Angle to **50**.

8. Point to the **Distance value**, when the pointer changes to a double-headed arrow, drag the **pointer** to the right and notice the changes in the drop shadow.

9. Set the Distance to **6**.

10. Click the **Selection tool**, click the text box to select it, drag the **text box** as needed to match the placement shown in Figure 51, then save your work.

You used the Filter panel to create a drop shadow, then made changes to it.

Skew text and align objects

1. Click the **Text tool** T to select it, click the ┼T **pointer** near the top middle of the Stage, then type **Classic Car Club**.

2. Click **CHARACTER** in the Properties panel to display the CHARACTER area.

   The attributes of the new text reflect the most recent settings entered in the Properties panel.

3. Drag the **I-Beam pointer** I to select the text, then use the CHARACTER area of the Properties panel to change the font size to **40** and the fill color to **#990000**.

4. Click the **Selection tool** ▶ on the Tools panel, click the **text box** to select it, then click the **Free Transform tool** ▒ on the Tools panel.

5. Click the **Rotate and Skew option** 𝌆 in the Options area of the Tools panel.

6. Drag the **top middle handle** to the right, as shown in Figure 52, to skew the text.

7. Click the **Selection tool** ▶ on the Tools panel.

8. Drag a **marquee** around all of the objects on the Stage to select them.

9. Click **Modify** on the menu bar, point to **Align**, click the **Align to stage check box** to make it active, then click **Horizontal Center**.

   Note: If the Modify menu closes before you select Horizontal Center, repeat Step 9.

10. Click a blank area of the Stage to deselect the objects.

You entered a heading, changed the font size and color, and skewed text using the Free Transform tool, then you aligned the objects on the Stage.

Figure 52 *Skewing the text*

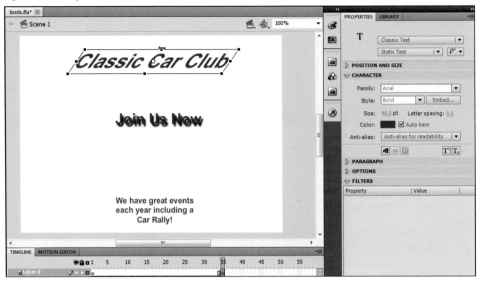

Figure 53 *Reshaping a letter*

Drag this anchor point; notice the lines are drawn from the anchor points on either side of the anchor point being dragged

Figure 54 *Applying a gradient fill to each letter*

Reshape and apply a gradient to text

1. Click the **Selection tool** ▶ , click the **Classic Car Club text block** to select it, click **Modify** on the menu bar, then click **Break Apart**.

   The letters are now individual text blocks.

2. Click **Modify** on the menu bar, then click **Break Apart**.

   The letters are filled with a dot pattern, indicating that they can now be edited.

3. Click the **Zoom tool** 🔍 on the Tools panel, then click the first **"C"** in Classic.

4. Click the **Subselection tool** ▶ on the Tools panel, then click the **edge** of the letter **"C"** to display the object's segment handles.

5. Drag a **lower anchor point** on the "C" in Classic, as shown in Figure 53.

6. Click the **Selection tool** ▶ , then click a blank area of the Stage to deselect the objects.

7. Click the **View** list arrow on the movie menu bar, then click **Fit in Window**.

8. Click the **Fill Color tool color swatch** 🎨 on the Tools panel, then click the **red gradient color swatch** in the bottom row of the Color palette.

9. Click the **Paint Bucket tool** 🪣 on the Tools panel, then click the **top** of each letter to change the fill to a red gradient, as shown in Figure 54.

   Note: Click the Ink Bottle tool if you do not see the Paint Bucket tool.

10. Use the status bar to change the movie frame rate to **3**, test the movie, watch the movie, then close the Flash Player window.

11. Save your work, then close the document.

You broke apart a text block, reshaped text, and added a gradient to the text.

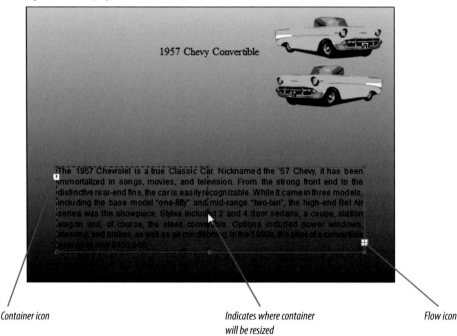 Use the Text Layout Framework

1. Open fl2_4.fla, then save it as **TLF.fla**.

2. Click the **Text tool** T on the Tools panel, then click the **text block** on the Stage.

3. Click the **Text engine list arrow** in the T area on the Properties panel, then click **TLF Text**.

   The text block on the Stage changes to a container and displays two container icons.

4. Scroll the Properties panel as needed, then click **CONTAINER AND FLOW** to display the CONTAINER AND FLOW options.

5. Click the **Behavior list arrow**, then click **Multiline**.

6. Change the Column value to **2**, change it to **3**, then change it to **1**.

7. Point to the **middle handle** on the right side of the container, when the pointer changes to a double-headed arrow ↔, click and drag the **middle handle** left to the position shown in Figure 55, then release the mouse pointer.

   (continued)

Figure 55 *Reshaping the text container*

Container icon

Indicates where container will be resized

Flow icon

Figure 56 *Positioning the Flow icon pointer*

Flow pointer

Flow icon; more text
available but not seen
in container

Figure 57 *Repostioning the text container*

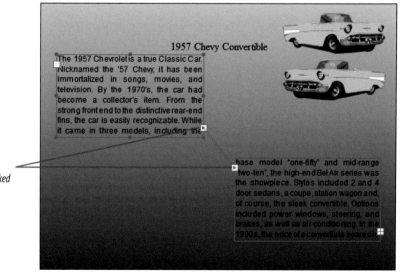

Indicates these
containers are linked

8. Click the **Container icon** on the right side
   of the container, position the **Flow pointer**
   as shown in Figure 56, then click the
   mouse button.

   Another container appears that is linked to the
   first container and with the text flowing from
   the first container.

9. Click before **From** in the first container, then
   type **By the 1970's, the car had become a
   collector's item**.

   Notice as you type in the first container that the
   text flows to the second container.

10. Click the **Selection tool** , then click and
    drag the **first container** to the position shown
    in Figure 57.

    (continued)

11. Drag the **second container** to the position shown in Figure 58.

12. Click and drag the **bottom middle handle** of the second container down to display all the text if some of the text is not visible.

13. Click the **heading**, click the **Rotation list arrow** in the CHARACTER area on the Properties Panel, then click **270°**.

    The text rotates within the container.

14. Click **Modify** on the menu bar, point to **Transform**, then click **Rotate 90° CW**.

15. Click the **heading**, then use the **arrow keys** to position the container between the two text containers.

(continued)

Figure 58 *Repositioning the second text container*

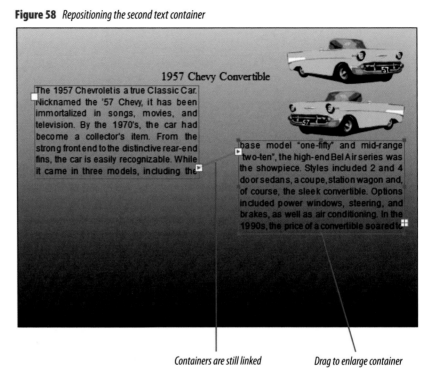

Containers are still linked   Drag to enlarge container

Figure 59 *Adding a container border*

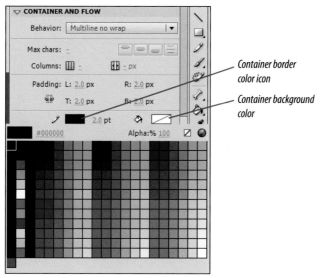

Container border color icon

Container background color

Figure 60 *The completed document*

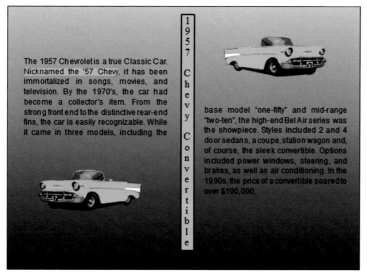

16. Click the **Container border color icon** in the CONTAINER AND FLOW area, then click **black**.

    The border color swatch changes to black, as shown in Figure 59.

17. Change the border width to **2**.

18. Click the **Container background color icon**, then click the **car** with the Eyedropper tool to select the color.

19. Click the **Text tool** T, then click and drag the pointer to select the words Nicknamed the '57 Chevy.

20. Click the **Highlight color icon** in the CHARACTER area on the Properties panel, then click the **car** to select the color.

21. Use the **Selection tool** to position the cars, as shown in Figure 60.

22. Test the movie, then save and close it.

You used the Text Layout Framework feature to display columns, create containers, add highlight color to text, add background and stroke color to a container, and rotate text.

Work with Layers
AND OBJECTS

What You'll Do

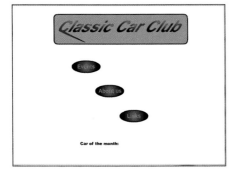

In this lesson, you will create, rename, reorder, delete, hide, and lock layers. You will also display objects as outlines on layers, use a Guide layer, distribute text to layers, and create a Folder layer.

Learning About Layers

Flash uses two types of spatial organization. First, there is the position of objects on the Stage, and then there is the stacking order of objects that overlap. An example of overlapping objects is text placed on a banner. In this case, the banner background might be placed on one layer and the banner text might be placed on a different layer. Layers are used on the Timeline as a way of organizing objects. Placing objects on their own layer makes them easier to work with, especially when reshaping them, repositioning them on the Stage, or rearranging their order in relation to other objects. In addition, layers are useful for organizing other elements such as sounds, animations, and ActionScript.

There are five types of layers, as shown in the Layer Properties dialog box displayed in Figure 61 and discussed next.

Normal—The default layer type. All objects on these layers appear in the movie.

Mask—A layer that hides and reveals portions of another layer.

Masked—A layer that contains the objects that are hidden and revealed by a Mask layer.

Folder—A layer that can contain other layers.

Guide (Standard and Motion)—You use a Standard Guide layer to set a reference point (such as a guide line) for positioning objects on the Stage. You use a Motion Guide layer to create a path for animated objects to follow.

Motion Guide, Mask, and Masked layer types are covered in a later chapter.

Working with Layers

The Layer Properties dialog box, accessed through the Timeline command on the Modify menu, allows you to specify the type of layer. It also allows you to name, show (and hide), and lock them. Naming a layer provides a clue to the objects on the layer. For example, naming a layer Logo might indicate that the object on the layer is the company's logo. Hiding a layer(s) may reduce the clutter on the Stage and make it easier to work with selected objects from the layer(s) that are not hidden. Locking a layer(s) prevents the objects from being accidentally edited. Other options in the Layer Properties dialog box allow you to view layers as outlines, change the outline color, and change layer height. Outlines can be used to help you determine which objects are on a layer. When you turn on this feature, each layer has a colored box that corresponds with the color of the objects on its layer. Icons on the Layers area of the Timeline, as shown in Figure 62, correspond to features in the Layer Properties dialog box.

Figure 61 *The Layer Properties dialog box*

Figure 62 *The Layers area of the Timeline*

Using a Guide Layer

Guide layers are useful in aligning objects on the Stage. Figure 63 shows a Guide layer that has been used to align three buttons along a diagonal path. The buttons are on one layer and the diagonal line is on another layer, the Guide layer. To create a Guide layer, you insert a new layer above the layer containing the objects to be aligned, use the Layer Properties command from the Timeline option on the Modify menu to display the Layer Properties dialog box, select Guide as the layer type, and then draw a path (such as a guide line) that will be used as the guide to align the objects.

You then verify the Snap to Guides option from the Snapping command on the View menu is active, and drag the desired objects to the guide line. Objects have a transformation point that is used when snapping to a guide. By default, this point is at the center of the object. Figure 64 shows the process.

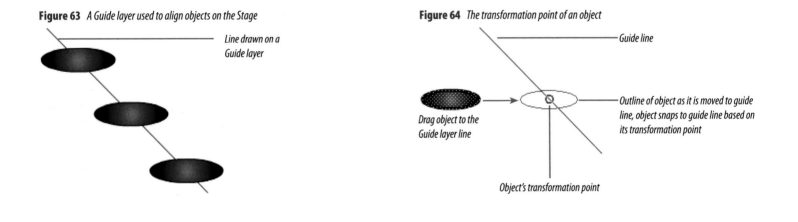

Figure 63 *A Guide layer used to align objects on the Stage*

Line drawn on a
Guide layer

Figure 64 *The transformation point of an object*

Guide line

Drag object to the
Guide layer line

Outline of object as it is moved to guide
line, object snaps to guide line based on
its transformation point

Object's transformation point

Drawing Objects in Adobe Flash

Distributing Text to Layers

Text blocks are made up of one or more characters. When you break apart a text block, each character becomes an object that can be edited independently of the other characters. You use the Distribute to Layers command from the Timeline option on the Modify menu, which causes each character to automatically be placed on its own layer.

Figure 65 shows the seven layers created after the text block containing 57 Chevy has been broken apart and distributed to layers.

Using Folder Layers

As movies become larger and more complex, the number of layers increases. Flash allows you to organize layers by creating folders and grouping other layers in the folders. Figure 66 shows a Folder layer —carName—with seven layers in it. The process is to select the layer that is to become a Folder layer, then use the Layer Properties dialog box to specify a Folder layer. To place other layers in the Folder layer, you drag them from the Timeline to the Folder layer. The Folder layer triangle next to carName is a toggle. You click the triangle to open and close the folder.

Figure 65 *Distributing text to layers*

Figure 66 *A Folder layer*

Click to expand (as seen here) or collapse a Folder layer

Create and reorder layers

1. Open fl2_5.fla from the drive and folder where your Data Files are stored, then save it as **layers2.fla**.

2. Click the **Selection tool** , click the **View list arrow** on the movie menu bar, then click **Fit in Window**.

3. Click the **New Layer icon** on the bottom of the Timeline (below the layer names) to insert a new layer, Layer 2.

4. Click **frame 1** on Layer 2.

5. Select the **Rectangle tool** on the Tools panel, then set each corner radius to **10** in the RECTANGLE OPTIONS area of the Properties panel, and set the Stroke to **2** in the FILL AND STROKE area.

6. Click the **Fill Color tool color swatch** on the Tools panel, click the **Hex Edit text box**, type **#999999**, then press **[Enter]** (Win) or **[return]** (Mac).

7. Click the **Stroke Color tool color swatch** on the Tools panel, click the **Hex Edit text box**, type **#000000**, then press **[Enter]** (Win) or **[return]** (Mac).

8. Draw the **rectangle** shown in Figure 67 so it covers the text heading.

9. Drag **Layer 1** above Layer 2 on the Timeline, as shown in Figure 68.

10. Click the **Selection tool** on the Tools panel.

11. Click a blank area of the Stage to deselect the objects.

You added a layer, drew an object on the layer, and reordered layers.

Figure 67 *Drawing a rectangle with a rounded corner*

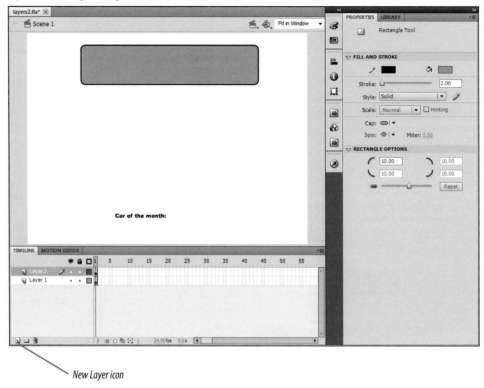

New Layer icon

Figure 68 *Dragging Layer 1 above Layer 2*

Drag Layer 1 above Layer 2

Figure 69 *Renaming layers*

Your outline colors may vary

The amount of text you see may vary   *Timeline icon*

Figure 70 *Expanding the layer name area of the Timeline*

Drag the pointer

Rename and delete layers, and expand the Timeline

1. Double-click **Layer 1** on the Timeline, type **Heading** in the Layer Name text box, then press **[Enter]** (Win) or **[return]** (Mac).

2. Rename Layer 2 as **Heading Background**.

3. Point to the **Timeline icon** ⦀ , which is below the layer names and shown in Figure 69.

4. When the pointer changes to a double arrow ⇥⇤ , drag the **pointer** ⇥⇤ to the right to display all the layer names.

   The full name of each layer is visible, as shown in Figure 70.

5. Click the **Heading layer**, then click the **Delete icon** 🗑 on the bottom of the Timeline.

6. Click **Edit** on the menu bar, then click **Undo Delete Layer**.

7. Click a blank area of the Stage to deselect all objects.

You renamed layers to associate them with objects on the layers, then deleted and restored a layer.

Hide, lock, and display layer outlines

1. Click the **Show or Hide All Layers icon** 👁 to hide all layers, then compare your image to Figure 71.

2. Click the **Show or Hide All Layers icon** 👁 to show all the layers.

3. Click the **Heading Background layer**, then click the **Show or Hide This Layer icon** ⬤ next to the layer name twice to hide and then show the layer.

4. Click the **Lock or Unlock All Layers icon** 🔒 to lock all layers.

5. With the layers locked, try to select and edit an object.

6. Click the **Lock or Unlock All Layers icon** 🔒 again to unlock the layers.

7. Click the **Heading Background layer**, then click the **Lock or Unlock This Layer** ⬤ to lock the layer.

8. Click the **Show All Layers as Outlines icon** ☐ to display the outlines of all objects.

   Notice the outlines are color-coded. For example, the two text objects are identified by their color (green) as being on the Heading layer (green).

9. Click the **Show All Layers as Outlines icon** ☐ to turn off this feature.

You hid and showed layers, you locked and unlocked layers, and you displayed the outlines of objects on a layer.

Figure 71 *Hiding all the layers*

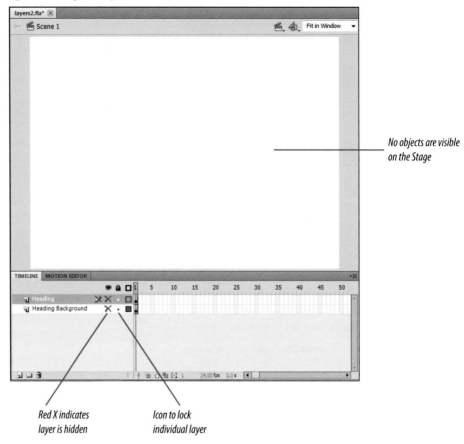

No objects are visible on the Stage

Red X indicates layer is hidden

Icon to lock individual layer

Figure 72 *A diagonal line*

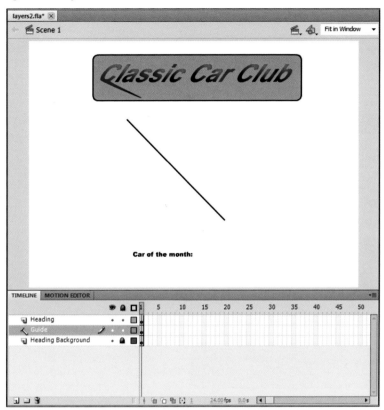

Create a guide for a Guide layer

1. Click the **Heading Background layer**, then click the **New Layer icon** 🔲 on the bottom of the Timeline to add a new layer, Layer 3.

2. Rename the layer **Guide**.

3. Verify that the Guide layer is selected.

4. Click **Modify** on the menu bar, point to **Timeline**, then click **Layer Properties** to display the Layer Properties dialog box.

5. Click the **Guide option button** in the Type area, then click **OK**.

   A symbol appears next to the word Guide indicating that this is a Guide layer.

6. Click **frame 1** of the Guide layer.

7. Click the **Line tool** ╲ on the Tools panel, press and hold **[Shift]**, then draw the diagonal line, as shown in Figure 72.

8. Click the **Lock or Unlock This Layer icon** ⚙ on the Guide layer to lock it.

9. Click **View** on the menu bar, point to **Snapping**, then verify Snap to Guides is selected.

You created a Guide layer and drew a guide line.

Add objects to a Guide layer

1. Add a new layer on the Timeline above the Guide layer, name it **Ovals**, then click **frame 1** on the Ovals layer.

2. Click the **Fill Color tool color swatch** 🎨 on the Tools panel, then click the **red gradient color swatch** in the bottom row of the Color palette.

3. Click the **Oval tool** ⬭ on the Tools panel, then verify that the **Object Drawing option** ⬭ in the Options area of the Tools panel is not active.

4. Draw the **oval**, as shown in Figure 73.

5. Click the **Selection tool** ⬐ on the Tools panel, then draw a **marquee** around the oval object to select it.

TIP Make sure the entire object (stroke and fill) is selected.

6. Point to the **center** of the oval, click and slowly drag the **oval** to the Guide layer line, as shown in Figure 74.

7. With the oval object selected, click **Edit** on the menu bar, then click **Copy**.

8. Click **Edit** on the menu bar, click **Paste in Center**, then drag the **copied object** to the Guide layer line beneath the first oval.

9. Click **Edit** on the menu bar, click **Paste in Center**, then drag the **copied object** to the bottom of the Guide layer line.

TIP When objects are pasted in the center of the Stage, one object may cover up another object. Move them as needed.

You created a Guide layer and used it to align objects on the Stage.

Figure 73 *An oval object*

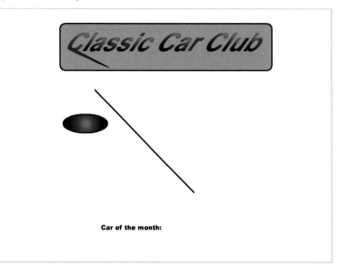

Figure 74 *Dragging an object to the Guide layer line*

The transformation point aligns with the Guide line

Drawing Objects in Adobe Flash

Figure 75 *Adding text to the oval objects*

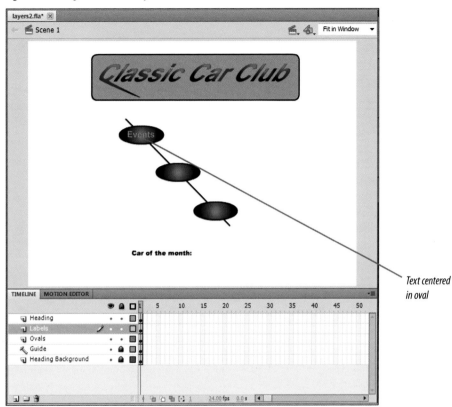

Text centered in oval

Add text on top of an object

1. Insert a **new layer** on the Timeline above the Ovals layer, then name it **Labels**.
2. Click **frame 1** of the Labels layer.
3. Click the **Text tool** T on the Tools panel, click the **top oval**, then type **Events**.
4. Drag the **I-Beam pointer** ⌶ across Events to select the text, then, using the Properties panel set the font family to **Arial**, the style to **Bold**, the font size to **14**, and the fill color to **#999999**.
5. Click the **Selection tool** ⬈ on the Tools panel, click the **text box** to select it, then drag the **text box** to center it on the oval using the Guide layer, as shown in Figure 75.

TIP You can use the arrow keys on the keyboard to nudge the text into place.

6. Repeat Steps 3 and 5, typing **About us** and **Links** for the text blocks.
7. Lock all of the layers.
8. Test the movie, then close the Flash Player window.

   Notice the guide line does not appear in the movie.
9. Save then close the document.
10. Exit Flash.

You used the Text tool to create text blocks that were placed on objects.

Use the Flash drawing and alignment tools.

1. Start Flash, open fl2_6.fla, then save it as **skillsDemo2.fla**. Refer to Figure 76 as you complete these steps. (*Note*: Figure 76 shows the objects after changes have been made to them. For example, in Step 5 you draw a rectangle in the middle of the Stage. Then, in a later step you rotate the rectangle 45 degrees.)
2. Set the view to Fit in Window, then display the Grid.
3. Set the stroke color to black (Hex: **#000000**) and the fill color to blue (Hex: **#0000FF**).
4. Use the Oval tool to draw an oval on the left side of the Stage, then draw a circle beneath the oval. (*Hint*: Use the Undo command as needed.)
5. Use the Rectangle tool to draw a rectangle in the middle of the Stage, then draw a square beneath the rectangle. (*Hint*: Reset the RECTANGLE OPTIONS as needed.)
6. Use the Line tool to draw a horizontal line on the right side of the Stage, then draw a vertical line beneath the horizontal line and a diagonal line beneath the vertical line.
7. Use the Pen tool to draw an arrow-shaped object above the rectangle. (*Hint*: Use the Zoom tool to enlarge the area of the Stage.)
8. Use the Paint Bucket tool to fill the arrow with the blue color. (*Hint*: If the arrow does not fill, be sure you closed the arrow shape by clicking the first anchor point as your last action.)
9. Use the Pencil tool to draw a freehand line above the oval, then select the line and use the Smooth option to smooth out the line.
10. Use the Rectangle Primitive tool to draw a rectangle below the square, then use the Selection tool to drag a corner to round all the corners.

11. Save your work.

Select objects and apply colors.

1. Use the Selection tool to select the stroke of the circle, then deselect the stroke.
2. Use the Selection tool to select the fill of the circle, then deselect the fill.
3. Use the Ink Bottle tool to change the stroke color of the circle to red (Hex: **#FF0000**).
4. Use the Paint Bucket tool to change the fill color of the square to a red gradient.
5. Change the fill color of the oval to a blue gradient.
6. Save your work.

Work with drawn objects.

1. Copy and paste in center the arrow object.
2. Move the copied arrow to another location on the Stage.
3. Use the Properties panel to set the height of each arrow to 30.
4. Flip the copied arrow horizontally.
5. Rotate the rectangle to a 45° angle.
6. Skew the square to the right.
7. Copy one of the arrows and use the Subselection tool to reshape it, then delete it.
8. Use the Selection tool to reshape the circle to a crescent shape.
9. Save your work.

Work with text and text objects.

1. Select the Text tool, set the text mode to Classic Text and the type to Static, then enter the following text in a text block at the top of the Stage: **Gateway to the Pacific.**
2. Select the text, then change the text to font: Tahoma, size: 24, color: red.

3. Use the Align option on the Modify menu to horizontally center the text block.
4. Use the Selection tool and the up and down arrow keys on the keyboard to align the text block with a gridline.
5. Skew the text block to the right.
6. Save your work.

Work with layers.

1. Insert a layer into the document.
2. Change the name on the new layer to **Heading Bkgnd**, then click frame 1 on the layer.
3. Use the Rectangle Primitive tool to draw a rounded corner rectangle with a blue color that covers the words Gateway to the Pacific.
4. Switch the order of the layers.
5. Lock all layers.
6. Unlock all layers.
7. Hide the Heading Bkgnd layer.
8. Show the Heading Bkgnd layer.
9. Turn on, then turn off the view of the outlines.
10. Create a new layer as a Guide layer (be sure to change the layer type to Guide), name the layer **Guide**, draw a guideline on the new layer, lock the layer, then snap the arrows to the guideline.
11. Add a layer and use the Text tool to type **Seattle** below the heading, using Tahoma, Regular, 24 pt, and the color blue.
12. Align Seattle so it is centered horizontally across the Stage.

Use the Merge Drawing Model mode.

1. Insert a new layer and name it **MergeDraw**.
2. Select the Rectangle tool and verify that the Object Drawing option is not active.

Drawing Objects in Adobe Flash

3. Draw a square in the upper-right of the Stage, then use the Oval tool to draw a circle with a different color that covers approximately half of the square.

4. Select the stroke and fill of the circle, then using the Selection tool drag the circle off the square. (*Note*: Depending on the size of the circle and where you drew it to overlap the square, your results may vary from what is shown in Figure 76.)

Use the Object Drawing Model mode.

1. Insert a new layer and name it **ObjectDraw**.
2. Select the Rectangle tool and select the Object Drawing option to make it active.
3. Draw a square with a blue fill color, then use the Oval tool to draw a circle with a different color that covers approximately half of the square.
4. Use the Selection tool to drag the circle off the square.
5. Save your work, then compare your image to the example shown in Figure 76.

Use the Spray tool with a symbol.

1. Turn off the gridlines.
2. Add a new layer to the Timeline, then add a keyframe to frame 5 of the new layer.
3. Name the layer **Aces Wild**.
4. Select the Text tool and verify the Text option is set to TLF Text, then verify rotation is set to auto and alignment is set to Align to start.
5. Drag the pointer to create a text box that covers the lower one-fourth of the Stage.
6. Type the following using Arial, 14 pt text, black:

Ace's Wild has been providing novelty items, gifts, and toys to Seattleites since 1975. Located in Seattle's Greenlake district, we provide one stop shopping for the most unusual and unique costumes, party supplies, crafts and the strangest collection of toys ever assembled. Visit Ace's Wild to have a fun time choosing that perfect present for the hard to buy for person in your life.

7. Divide the text block into two text Containers, then use the Selection tool to position them as shown in Figure 76.
8. Use the Text tool to drag the lower middle handle of the lower text block to show a blank line if there is not a blank line.
9. Use the Text tool to select the top Container, then create a **2** pt blue border (#0066FF) and a red (#FF3300) background.
10. Select the bottom Container and create a **2 pt** red (#FF3300) border and a blue (#0066FF) background.
11. Use the Text tool to select Ace's Wild in the top Container, then create a white highlight.
12. Repeat Step 10 for the lower text Container.
13. Select the Spray Brush tool.
14. Click the Edit button in the Symbol area of the Properties panel, then select the Ace symbol.
15. Set the Scale width and height to **60**, turn on Rotate symbol (*Hint*: Be sure the check box has a check mark) and turn off the other options (*Hint*: Be sure all other check boxes do not have check marks), set the Brush width and height to *5* px, then draw the ace's as shown in Figure 76.
16. Test the movie, then save and close the document. (*Note*: If the movie displays too quickly, adjust the frame rate.)
17. Exit Flash.

Figure 76 *Completed Skills Review*

A local travel company, Ultimate Tours, has asked you to design several sample home pages for its new website. The goal of the website is to inform potential customers of its services. The company specializes in exotic treks, tours, and cruises. Thus, while its target audience spans a wide age range, they are all looking for something out of the ordinary.

1. Open a new Flash document using ActionScript 2.0 and save it as **ultimateTours2.fla**. Create the Flash movie shown in Figure 77. (*Note*: ActionScript 2.0 is used because in subsequent chapters the ultimateTours project will require this version of ActionScript.)
2. Set the document properties, including the Stage size and background color. (*Note*: You can use your choice of colors.)
3. Create the following on separate layers and name the layers:
   - A text heading; select a font size and font color. Skew the heading, break it apart, then reshape one or more of the characters.
   - A subheading with a different font size and color.
   - At least three objects that will be the background for button symbols.
   - Text that will appear on the top of the button background.

   Note: You can use different colors, shapes, and placement but your project should have all the elements shown in Figure 77.

4. Use one or more of the align features (gridlines, rulers, Align command on the Modify menu, arrow keys) to align the objects on the Stage.
5. Lock all layers.
6. Compare your image to the example shown in Figure 77.
7. Save your work.
8. Test the movie, close the Flash Player window, then close the movie.

Figure 77 *Sample completed Project Builder 1*

You have been asked to create several sample designs for the home page of a new organization called The Jazz Club. The club is being organized to bring together music enthusiasts for social events and charitable fundraising activities. The club members plan to sponsor weekly jam sessions and a show once a month. Because the club is just getting started, the organizers are looking to you for help in developing a website.

1. Plan the site by specifying the goal, target audience, treatment ("look and feel"), and elements you want to include (text, graphics, sound, and so on).
2. Sketch out a storyboard that shows the layout of the objects on the various screens and how they are linked together. Be creative in your design.
3. Open a new Flash document and save it as **theJazzClub2.fla**.
4. Set the document properties, including the Stage size and background color, if desired.
5. Display the gridlines and rulers and use them to help align objects on the Stage.
6. Create a heading, text objects, and drawings (such as the lines) to be used as links to the categories of information provided on the website. (*Note*: Some of the characters are individual text blocks [e.g. the S in Sessions] allowing you to move the text block without moving the other characters. *Hint*: Use the Oval, Line, and Brush tools to create the notes. After selecting the Brush tool, experiment with the different Brush tool shapes found in the Options area at the bottom of the Tools panel.)
7. Hide the gridlines and rulers.
8. Save your work, then compare your image to the example shown in Figure 78.

Figure 78 *Sample completed Project Builder 2*

Figure 79 shows the home page of a website. Study the figure and complete the following. For each question indicate how you determined your answer.

1. Connect to the Internet, go to *www.nps.gov*, then select Explore Nature.

2. Open a document in a word processor or open a new Flash document, save the file as **dpc2**, then answer the following questions. (*Hint*: Use the Text tool in Flash.)

   - Whose website is this?
   - What is the goal(s) of the site?
   - Who is the target audience?
   - What is the treatment ("look and feel") that is used?
   - What are the design layout guidelines being used (balance, movement, and so on)?
   - What may be animated on this home page?
   - Do you think this is an effective design for the company, its products, and its target audience? Why or why not?
   - What suggestions would you make to improve the design and why?

Figure 79 *Design Project*

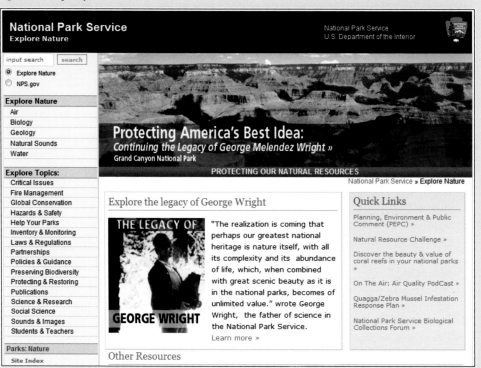

You have decided to create a personal portfolio of your work that you can use when you begin your job search. The portfolio will be a website done completely in Flash.

1. Research what should be included in a portfolio.
2. Plan the site by specifying the goal, target audience, treatment ("look and feel"), and elements you want to include (text, graphics, sound, and so on).
3. Sketch a storyboard that shows the layout of the objects on the various screens and how they are linked together. Be creative in your design.
4. Design the home page to include personal data (such as a Resume object that will link to your personal data), contact information (such as a Contact me link that will link to your contact information), previous employment (such as an Work History button that will link to your previous employment), education (such as an Education link that will link to information about your education), and samples of your work (such as an Animations link that will link to samples of your work).
5. Open a new Flash document using ActionScript 2.0 and save it as **portfolio2.fla**. (*Note*: ActionScript 2.0 is used because, in subsequent chapters, the portfolio project will require this version of ActionScript.)
6. Set the document properties, including the Stage size and background color, if desired.
7. Display the gridlines and rulers and use them to help align objects on the Stage.
8. Add a border the size of the Stage. (*Hint*: Use the Rectangle tool and set the fill color to none.)
9. Create a heading with its own background, then create other text objects and drawings to be used as links to the categories of information provided on the website. (*Hint*: In the example shown here, the Brush Script Std font is used. You can replace this font with Impact or any other appropriate font on your computer.)
10. Hide the gridlines and rulers.
11. Save your work, then compare your image to the example shown in Figure 80.

Figure 80 *Sample completed Portfolio Project*

CHAPTER **3** **WORKING WITH SYMBOLS AND INTERACTIVITY**

1. Create symbols and instances
2. Work with libraries
3. Create buttons
4. Assign actions to frames and buttons
5. Import graphics

CHAPTER 3

WORKING WITH SYMBOLS
AND INTERACTIVITY

Introduction

An important benefit of Flash is its ability to create movies with small file sizes. This allows the movies to be delivered from the web more quickly. One way to keep the file size small is to create reusable graphics, buttons, and movie clips. Flash allows you to create a graphic (drawing) and then make unlimited copies, which you can use throughout the current movie and in other movies. Flash calls the original drawing a **symbol** and the copied drawings **instances**. Flash stores symbols in the Library panel— each time you need a copy of the symbol, you can open the Library panel and drag the symbol to the Stage, which creates an instance (copy) of the symbol. Using instances reduces the movie file size because Flash stores only the symbol's information (size, shape, color), but Flash does not save the instance in the Flash movie. Rather, a link is established between the symbol and an instance so that the instance has the same properties (such as color and shape) as the symbol. There are two especially valuable editing features of this process. First, if you have created several instances of a symbol and decide to change the same property for every instance, all that is needed is to edit the symbol. For example, if a logo appears in several places in a website and you need to change the color of each instance of the logo, you simply change the color of the symbol. Because the instances are linked to the symbol they are automatically updated. Second, you can change the properties of an individual instance of a symbol. For example, if your website is to contain drawings of cars that are similar but not identical, you can create just one drawing, convert it to a symbol, insert as many instances of the car as needed, and then change the properties of each individual instance, such as its size or color. When you edit a symbol, the change made to the symbol is made to all instances of the symbol. But, when you edit an instance of a symbol, you break the link between the symbol and the instance, and any changes you make to the object are not reflected in the symbol or any instances of that symbol. Likewise, if subsequently you make changes to the symbol, the changes will not be reflected in the unlinked object.

Create Symbols
AND INSTANCES

What You'll Do

In this lesson, you will create graphic symbols, turn them into instances, and then edit the instances.

Understanding Symbol Types

There are three categories of symbols: graphic, button, and movie clip. A graphic symbol is useful because you can reuse a single image and make changes in each instance of the image. A button symbol is useful because you can create buttons for interactivity, such as starting or stopping a movie. A movie clip symbol is useful for creating complex animations because you can create a movie within a movie. For example, you could have a movie with a car moving across the screen and its wheels rotating. The wheel animation would be created as one movie clip symbol and attached to each wheel of the animated car. Symbols can be created from objects you draw using the Flash drawing tools. In addition, you can import graphics into a Flash document that can then be converted to symbols.

Creating a Graphic Symbol

You can use the New Symbol command on the Insert menu to create and then draw a symbol. You can also draw an object and then use the Convert to Symbol command on the Modify menu to convert the object to a symbol. The Convert to Symbol dialog box, shown in Figure 1, allows you to name the symbol and specify the type of symbol you want to create (Movie Clip, Button, or Graphic). When naming a symbol, it's a good idea to use a naming convention that allows you to quickly identify the type of symbol and to group like symbols together. For example, you could identify all graphic symbols by naming them g_*name* and all buttons as b_*name*. In Figure 1, the drawing on the Stage is being converted to a graphic symbol.

After you complete the Convert to Symbol dialog box, Flash places the symbol in the Library panel, as shown in Figure 2. In Figure 2, an icon identifying the symbol as a graphic symbol and the symbol name are listed in the Library panel, along with a preview of the selected symbol. To create an instance of the symbol, you simply drag a symbol from the Library panel to the Stage. To edit a symbol, you can double-click it in the Library panel or you can use the Edit Symbols command on the Edit menu. Either way displays the symbol in an edit window, where changes can be made to it. When you edit a symbol, the changes are reflected in all instances of that symbol in your movie.

For example, you can draw a car, convert the car to a symbol, and then create several instances of the car. You can uniformly change the size of all the cars by double-clicking the car symbol in the Library panel to open the edit window, and then rescaling it to the desired size.

Working with Instances

You can have as many instances as needed in your movie, and you can edit each one to make it somewhat different from the others. You can rotate, skew (slant), and resize graphic and button instances. In addition, you can change the color, brightness, and transparency. However, there are some limitations. An instance is a single object with no segments or parts, such as a stroke and a fill. You cannot select a part of an instance. Therefore, any changes to the color of the instance are made to the entire object. Of course, you can use layers to stack other objects on top of an instance to change its appearance. In addition, you can use the Break Apart command on the Modify menu to break the link between

an instance and a symbol. Once the link is broken, you can make any changes to the object, such as changing its stroke and fill color. However, because the link is broken, the object is no longer an instance of the original symbol. So, if you make any changes to the original symbol, then the unlinked object is not affected.

The process for creating an instance is to open the Library panel and drag the desired symbol to the Stage. Once the symbol is on the Stage, you select the instance by using the Selection tool to drag a marquee around it. A blue

bounding box indicates that the object is selected. Then, you can use the Free Transform tool options (such as Rotate and Skew, or Scale) to modify the entire image, or you can use the Break Apart command to break apart the instance and edit individual strokes and fills.

QUICK TIP

You need to be careful when editing an instance. Use the Selection tool to drag a marquee around the instance or click the object once to select it. Do not double-click the instance when it is on the Stage; otherwise, you will open an edit window that is used to edit the symbol, not the instance.

Figure 2 *A graphic symbol in the Library panel*

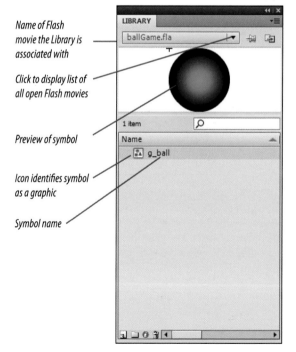

Name of Flash movie the Library is associated with

Click to display list of all open Flash movies

Preview of symbol

Icon identifies symbol as a graphic

Symbol name

Figure 1 *Using the Convert to Symbol dialog box to convert an object to a symbol*

Create a symbol

1. Open fl3_1.fla from the drive and folder where your Data Files are stored, then save it as **coolCar.fla**.

   This document has one object, a car, that was created using the Flash drawing tools.

2. Verify the Properties panel, the Library panel, and the Tools panel are displayed.

3. Set the magnification to **Fit in Window**.

4. Click the **Selection tool** ▶ on the Tools panel, then drag a **marquee** around the car to select it.

5. Click **Modify** on the menu bar, then click **Convert to Symbol**.

6. Type **g_car** in the Name text box.

7. Click the **Type list arrow** to display the symbol types, then click **Graphic**, as shown in Figure 3.

8. Set the **registration** to the upper-left corner, if necessary, as shown in Figure 3, then click **OK**.

9. Click the **Library panel tab**, then study the Library panel, as shown in Figure 4.

   The Library panel displays the symbol (red car) in the Item Preview window, an icon 🖼 indicating that this is a graphic symbol, and the name of the symbol (g_car). The symbol is contained in the library, and the car on the Stage is now an instance of the symbol.

You opened a file with an object, converted the object to a symbol, and displayed the symbol in the Library panel.

Figure 3 *Options in the Convert to Symbol dialog box*

Registration set to upper-left corner

Figure 4 *Newly created symbol in the Library panel*

Preview of g_car symbol in Item Preview window

Icon indicating a graphic symbol

Working with Symbols and Interactivity

Figure 5 *Creating an instance*

Drag the car image, the name of the symbol,
or its icon from the Library panel to below
the original instance to create a second
instance of the symbol

Figure 6 *The alpha set to 50%*

This area may not be open   Transparency set to 50%

Create and edit an instance

1. Point to the **car image** in the Item Preview window of the Library panel, then drag the **image** to the Stage beneath the first car, as shown in Figure 5.

   Both cars on the Stage are instances of the graphic symbol in the Library panel.

   TIP You can also drag the name of the symbol or its icon from the Library panel to the Stage.

2. Verify the bottom car is selected, click **Modify** on the menu bar, point to **Transform**, then click **Flip Horizontal**.

3. Display the Properties panel, then display the COLOR EFFECT area if it is not already showing.

4. Click the **Style list arrow**, then click **Alpha**.

5. Drag the **Alpha slider** left then right, then set the transparency to **50%**.

   Notice how the transparency changes. Figure 6 shows the transparency set to 50%.

6. Click a blank area of the Stage to deselect the object.

   Changing the alpha setting gives the car a more transparent look.

You created an instance of a symbol and edited the instance on the Stage.

Edit a symbol in the edit window

1. Display the Library panel, double-click the **g_car symbol icon** in the Library panel to display the edit window, then compare your screen to Figure 7.

   The g_car symbol appears in the edit window, indicating that you are editing the g_car symbol.

TIP You can also edit a symbol by selecting it, clicking Edit on the menu bar, then clicking Edit Symbols.

2. Click a blank area of the window to deselect the car.

3. Verify the Selection tool is selected, then click the **light gray hubcap** inside the front wheel to select it.

4. Press and hold **[Shift]**, then click the **hubcap** inside the back wheel so both hubcap fills are selected.

5. Set the **Fill Color** to the **blue gradient color swatch** in the bottom row of the color palette, compare your image to Figure 8, then deselect the image.

6. Click **Scene 1** at the top left of the edit window to exit the edit window and return to the main Timeline and main Stage.

   Changes you make to the symbol affect every instance of the symbol on the Stage. The hubcap fill becomes a blue gradient in the Library panel and on the Stage.

You edited a symbol in the edit window that affected all instances of the symbol.

Figure 7 *Edit window*

Graphic symbol indicates you are in the edit window

Name of symbol

Figure 8 *Edited symbol*

Hubcap fills are blue gradient

Symbol reflects changes

Figure 9 *The car with the maroon body selected*

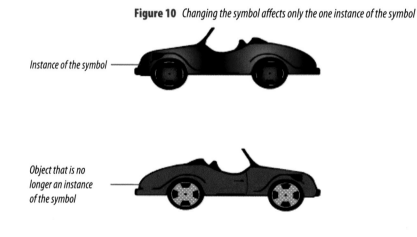

Instance of the symbol —

Object that is no longer an instance of the symbol —

Break apart an instance

1. Drag a **marquee** around the bottom car to select it if it is not selected.

2. Click **Modify** on the menu bar, then click **Break Apart**.

   The object is no longer linked to the symbol, and its parts (strokes and fills) can now be edited.

3. Click a blank area of the Stage to deselect the object.

4. Click the blue **front hubcap**, press and hold **[Shift]**, then click the **blue back hubcap** so both hubcaps are selected.

5. Set the **Fill Color** 🪣 to the **light gray color swatch (#999999)** in the left column of the color palette.

6. Double-click the **g_car symbol icon** 🖼 in the Library panel to display the edit window.

7. Click the **maroon front body** of the car to select it, press and hold **[Shift]**, then click the **maroon back body** of the car, as shown in Figure 9.

8. Set the **Fill Color** 🪣 to the **red gradient color swatch** in the bottom row of the color palette.

9. Click **Scene 1** at the top left of the edit window, then compare your images to Figure 10.

   The body color of the car in the original instance is a different color, but the body color of the car to which you applied the Break Apart command remains unchanged.

10. Save your work.

You used the Break Apart command to break the link between one instance and its symbol, you edited the object created using the Break Apart command, and then you edited the symbol, which only affected the instance still linked to the symbol.

Work with LIBRARIES

What You'll Do

In this lesson, you will use the Library panel to organize the symbols in a movie.

Understanding the Library

The library in a Flash document contains the symbols and other items such as imported graphics, movie clips, and sounds. The Library panel provides a way to view and organize the items, and allows you to change the item name, display item properties, and add and delete items. Figure 11 shows the Library panel for a document. Refer to this figure as you read the following descriptions of the parts of the library.

Tab title—Identifies the panel title, in this case, the Library panel.

Panel options menu— Labeled in Figure 11 and shown in Figure 12, the Panel options menu provides access to several features used to edit symbols (such as renaming symbols) and organize symbols (such as creating a new folder).

Display movies list arrow—Opens a menu showing all open movies. You use this menu to select an open document (movie) and display the Library panel associated with that open document. This allows you to use the items from one movie in another movie. For example, you may have developed a drawing in one Flash movie that you converted to a symbol and now you want to use that symbol in the movie you are working on. With both documents open, you simply use the Display movies list arrow to display the library with the desired symbol, and then drag the symbol to the Stage of the current movie. This will automatically place the symbol in the library for the current movie. In addition to the movie libraries, you can create permanent libraries that are available whenever you start Flash. Flash also has sample libraries that contain buttons and other objects. The permanent and sample libraries are accessed through the Common Libraries command on the Window menu. All assets in all of these libraries are available for use in any movie.

Item Preview window—Displays the selected item. If the item is animated or a sound file, a control button appears, allowing you to preview the animation or play the sound.

Name text box—Lists the folder and item names. Each item type has a different icon associated with it. Clicking an item name or icon displays the item in the Item Preview window.

Toggle Sorting Order icon—Allows you to reorder the list of folders and items within folders.

New Symbol icon—Displays the Create New Symbol dialog box, allowing you to create a new symbol.

New Folder icon—Allows you to create a new folder.

Properties icon—Displays the Properties dialog box for the selected item.

Delete icon—Deletes the selected item or folder.

To make changes to an item, you can double-click either the item icon in the Library panel, the item in the Item Preview window, or the item on the Stage to display the edit window.

Figure 11 *The Library panel*

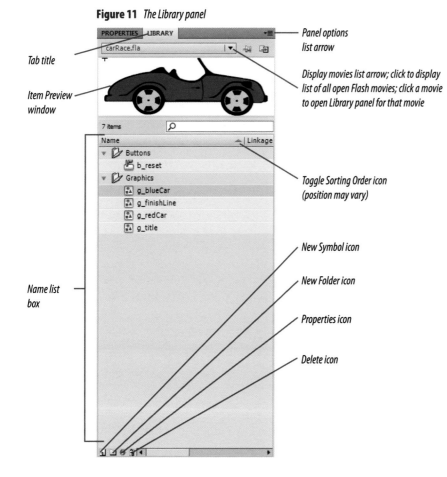

Tab title

Item Preview window

Name list box

Panel options list arrow

Display movies list arrow; click to display list of all open Flash movies; click a movie to open Library panel for that movie

Toggle Sorting Order icon (position may vary)

New Symbol icon

New Folder icon

Properties icon

Delete icon

Figure 12 *The Panel options menu*

Create folders in the Library panel

1. Open fl3_2.fla, then save it as **carRace.fla**.

2. Verify the Properties panel, the Library panel, and the Tools panel are displayed.

3. Set the magnification to **Fit in Window**.

   This movie has eight layers containing various objects such as text blocks, lines, and a backdrop. Two layers contain animations of cars.

4. Test the movie, then close the Flash Player window.

5. Click the **Show or Hide All Layers icon** 👁 on the Timeline to hide all of the layers.

6. Click each **red X** in the Show or Hide All Layers column to show the contents of each layer, click the **Show or Hide This Layer icon** ⚪ to hide the contents of that layer, then after viewing the contents of each layer, click the **Show or Hide All Layers icon** 👁 on the Timeline to show all of the layers.

   Note: The reset layer shows an empty Stage. This is because the word Reset is located in frame 65 at the end of the movie and does not appear in frame 1.

7. Click each item in the Library panel to display it in the Item Preview window.

   Notice that there is one button symbol (b_reset) and five graphic symbols.

8. Click **Name** on the Name list box title bar, as shown in Figure 13, and notice how the items are sorted.

9. Repeat Step 8 and notice how the items are sorted.

You opened a Flash movie and sorted items in the Library panel.

Figure 13 *The open Library panel*

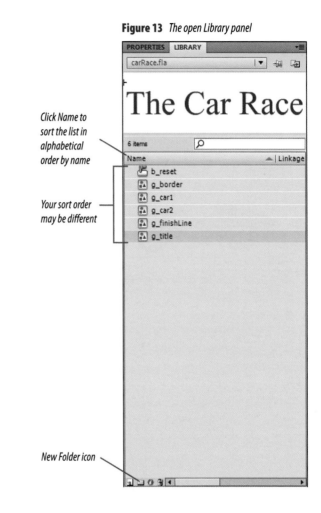

Click Name to sort the list in alphabetical order by name

Your sort order may be different

New Folder icon

Working with Symbols and Interactivity

Figure 14 *The Library panel with the folders added*

Buttons folder

Graphics folder

Figure 15 *The Library panel after moving the symbols to the folders*

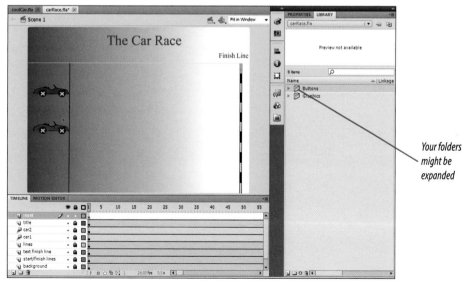

Your folders might be expanded

Organize items within Library panel folders

1. Click the **New Folder icon** in the Library panel, as shown in Figure 13.

2. Type **Graphics** in the Name text box, then press [**Enter**] (Win) or [**return**] (Mac).

3. Click the **New Folder icon** on the Library panel.

4. Type **Buttons** in the Name text box, then press [**Enter**] (Win) or [**return**] (Mac).

   Your Library panel should resemble Figure 14.

5. Drag the **g_title symbol** in the Library panel to the Graphics folder.

6. Drag the other graphic symbols to the Graphics folder.

7. Drag the **b_reset symbol** to the Buttons folder, then compare your Library panel to Figure 15.

8. Click the **Graphics folder expand icon** ▶ to open it and display the graphic symbols.

9. Click the **Buttons folder expand icon** ▶ to open it and display the button symbol.

10. Click the **Graphics folder collapse icon** ▼ to close the folder.

11. Click the **Buttons folder collapse icon** ▼ to close the folder.

    Note: To remove an item from a folder, drag the item down to a blank area of the Library panel.

You created new folders, organized the symbols within the folders, and then opened and closed the folders.

Rename symbols and delete a symbol

1. Click the **expand icon** ▶ for the Graphics folder to display the symbols.

2. Right-click (Win) or [control]-click (Mac) the **g_car1 symbol**, then click **Rename**.

3. Type **g_redCar** in the Name text box, then press **[Enter]** (Win) or **[return]** (Mac).

4. Repeat Steps 2 and 3 to rename the g_car2 symbol as **g_blueCar**.

5. Click **g_border** in the Library panel to select it.

6. Click the **Delete icon** 🗑 at the bottom of the Library panel.

   Your Library panel should resemble Figure 16.

TIP You can also select an item and press [Delete], or you can use the Panel options menu in the Library panel to remove an item from the library. The Undo command in the Edit menu can be used to undelete an item.

You used the Library panel to rename symbols and delete a symbol.

Figure 16 *Updated Library panel*

Working with Symbols and Interactivity

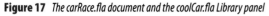
Figure 17 *The carRace.fla document and the coolCar.fla Library panel*

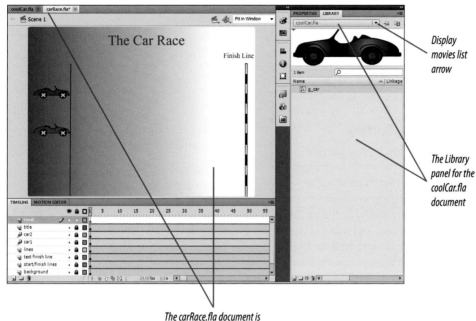

Display movies list arrow

The Library panel for the coolCar.fla document

The carRace.fla document is the active document

Use multiple Library panels

1. Click the **Display movies list arrow** near the top of the Library panel to display a list of open documents.

2. Click **coolCar.fla**, then click **g_car**.

   The Library panel for the coolCar document is displayed. However, the carRace document remains open, as shown in Figure 17.

3. Click **frame 1** on the reset layer, then drag the 🔲 **g_car symbol** from the Library panel to the center of the Stage.

   The reset layer is the only unlocked layer. Objects cannot be placed on locked layers.

4. Click the **Display movies list arrow** to display the open documents.

5. Click **carRace.fla** to view the carRace document's Library panel.

   Notice the g_car symbol is added automatically to the Library panel of the carRace document.

6. Click the **g_car symbol** in the Library panel.

7. Click the **Delete icon** 🗑 at the bottom of the Library panel.

   You deleted the g_car symbol from the carRace library but it still exists in the coolCar library. The car was also deleted from the Stage.

8. Save your work.

9. Click the **coolCar.fla tab** at the top of the workspace to display the document.

10. Close the coolCar document and save the document if asked.

You used the Library panel to display the contents of another library and added an object from that library to the current document.

Create
BUTTONS

What You'll Do

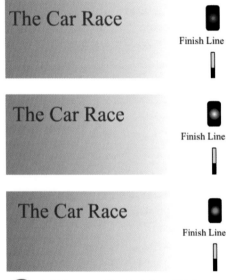

In this lesson, you will create a button, edit the four button states, and test a button.

Understanding Buttons

Button symbols are used to provide interactivity. When you click a button, an action occurs, such as starting an animation or jumping to another frame on the Timeline. Any object, including Flash drawings, text blocks, and imported graphic images, can be made into buttons. Unlike graphic symbols, buttons have four states: Up, Over, Down, and Hit. These states correspond to the use of the mouse and recognize that the user requires feedback when the mouse is pointing to a button and when the button has been clicked. This is often shown by a change in the button (such as a different color or different shape). An example of a button with different colors for the four different states is shown in Figure 18. These four states are explained in the following paragraphs.

Up—Represents how the button appears when the mouse pointer is not over it.

Over—Represents how the button appears when the mouse pointer is over it.

Down—Represents how the button appears after the user clicks the mouse.

Hit—Defines the area of the screen that will respond to the pointer. In most cases, you will want the Hit state to be the same or similar to the Up state in location and size.

When you create a button symbol, Flash automatically creates a new Timeline. The Timeline has only four frames, one for each

Figure 18 *The four button states*

Working with Symbols and Interactivity

button state. The Timeline does not play; it merely reacts to the mouse pointer by displaying the appropriate button state and performing an action, such as jumping to a specific frame on the main Timeline.

The process for creating and previewing buttons is as follows:

Create a button symbol—Draw an object or select an object that has already been created and placed on the Stage. Use the Convert to Symbol command on the Modify menu to convert the object to a button symbol and to enter a name for the button.

Edit the button symbol—Select the button and choose the Edit Symbols command on the Edit menu or double-click the button symbol in the Library panel. This displays the edit window, which includes the button Timeline, shown in Figure 19. You use the button Timeline to work with the four button states. The Up state is the original button symbol. Flash automatically places it in frame 1. You need to determine how the original object will change for the other states. To change the button for the Over state, click frame 2 and insert a keyframe. This automatically places a copy of the button that is in frame 1 into frame 2. Then, alter the button's appearance for the Over state, for instance, by changing the fill color. Use the same process for the Down state. For the Hit state, you insert a keyframe in frame 4 and then specify the area on the screen that will respond to the pointer. If you do not specify a hit area, the image for the Down state is used for the hit area. You add a keyframe to the Hit frame only if you are going to specify the hit area.

Return to the main Timeline—Once you've finished editing a button, you choose the Edit Document command on the Edit menu or click Scene 1 above the edit window to return to the main Timeline.

Preview the button—By default, Flash disables buttons so that you can manipulate them on the Stage. You can preview a button by choosing the Enable Simple Buttons command on the Control menu. You can also choose the Test Movie command on the Control menu to play the movie and test the buttons.

Figure 19 *The button Timeline*

Create a button

1. Insert a **new layer** above the top layer on the Timeline, then name the layer **signal**.

2. Select the **Rectangle Primitive tool** ⬜, click the **Stroke Color tool** on the Tools panel, then click the **No Stroke icon** ⬜ in the upper-right corner of the color palette.

3. Set the **Fill Color** to the **red gradient color swatch** in the bottom row of the color palette.

4. Display the Properties panel, click the **Reset button** in the RECTANGLE OPTIONS area, then set the corner radius to **5**.

5. Draw the **rectangle** shown in Figure 20.

6. Click the **Zoom tool** 🔍 on the Tools panel, then click the **rectangle** to enlarge it.

7. Select the **Gradient Transform tool** 🗔 on the Tools panel, then click the **rectangle**.

   You may need to click and hold the Free Transform tool first.

8. Drag the **diagonal arrow** toward the center of the rectangle as shown in Figure 21 to make the red area more round.

9. Click the **Selection tool** 🔺 on the Tools panel, then drag a **marquee** around the rectangle to select it.

10. Click **Modify** on the menu bar, then click **Convert to Symbol**.

11. Type **b_signal** in the Name text box, click the **Type list arrow**, click **Button**, then click **OK**.

12. Display the Library panel, then drag the **b_signal symbol** to the Buttons folder.

You created a button symbol on the Stage and dragged it to the Buttons folder in the Library panel.

Figure 20 *The rectangle object*

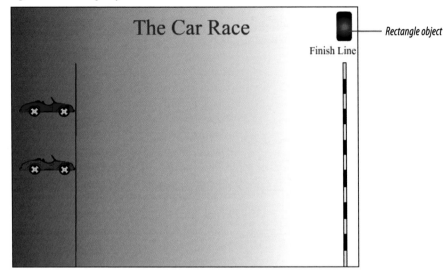

Rectangle object

The Car Race

Finish Line

Figure 21 *Adjusting the gradient*

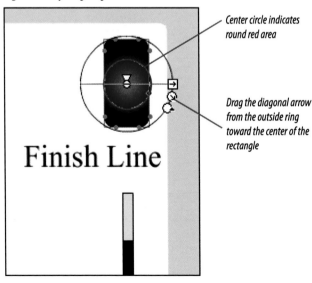

Center circle indicates round red area

Drag the diagonal arrow from the outside ring toward the center of the rectangle

Finish Line

Figure 22 *Specifying the hit area*

Blue rectangle represents hit area

Edit a button and specify a hit area

1. Open the Buttons folder, right-click (Win) or control-click (Mac) **b_signal** in the Library panel, then click **Edit**.

   Flash displays the edit window showing the Timeline with four button states.

2. Click the blank **Over frame** on Layer 1, then insert a **keyframe**.

TIP The [F6] key inserts a keyframe in the selected frame. The [fn] key may need to be used with some Mac keyboards.

3. Set the **Fill Color** to the **gray gradient color swatch** on the bottom of the color palette.

4. Insert a **keyframe** in the Down frame on Layer 1.

5. Set the **Fill Color** to the **green gradient color swatch** on the bottom of the color palette.

6. Insert a **keyframe** in the Hit frame on Layer 1.

7. Select the **Rectangle tool** on the Tools panel then set the **Fill Color** to the **blue color swatch** in the left column of the color palette.

8. Draw a **rectangle** slightly larger than the button, as shown in Figure 22, then release the mouse button.

TIP The Hit area will not be visible on the Stage.

9. Click **Scene 1** above the edit window to return to the main Timeline.

You edited a button by changing the color of its Over and Down states, and you specified the Hit area.

Test a button

1. Click the **Selection tool** ➤, then click a blank area of the Stage.

2. Click **Control** on the menu bar to display the Control menu, then click **Enable Simple Buttons**.

   This command allows you to test buttons on the Stage without viewing the movie in the Flash Player window.

3. Point to the **signal button** on the Stage, then compare your image to Figure 23.

   The pointer changes to a hand 🖑, indicating that the object is clickable, and the button changes to a gray gradient, the color you selected for the Over state.

4. Press and hold the **mouse button**, then notice that the button changes to a green gradient, the color you selected for the Down state, as shown in Figure 24.

5. Release the mouse and notice that the button changes to a gray gradient, the color you selected for the Over state.

(continued)

Figure 23 *The button's Over state*

Figure 24 *The button's Down state*

The Button Hit Area

All buttons have an area that responds to the mouse pointer, including rolling over the button and clicking it. This hit area is usually the same size and shape as the button itself. However, you can specify any area of the button to be the hit area. For example, you could have a button symbol that looks like a target with just the bulls-eye center being the hit area.

Working with Symbols and Interactivity

Figure 25 *The button's Up state*

Figure 26 *View options from the View list*

View options
for the Stage

6. Move the mouse away from the signal button, and notice that the button returns to a red gradient, the Up state color, as shown in Figure 25.

7. Click **Control** on the menu bar, then click **Enable Simple Buttons** to turn off the command.

8. Click the **View list arrow** above the Stage, then click **Fit in Window**, as shown in Figure 26.

   This shortcut allows you to change the magnification view without using the Magnification command on the View menu or the Zoom tool in the Tools panel.

9. Save your work.

You used the mouse to test a button and view the button states.

Assign Actions
TO FRAMES AND BUTTONS

What You'll Do

In this lesson, you will use ActionScript to assign actions to frames and buttons.

Understanding Actions

In a basic movie, Flash plays the frames sequentially without stopping for user input. However, you often want to provide users with the ability to interact with the movie by allowing them to perform actions, such as starting and stopping the movie or jumping to a specific frame in the movie. One way to provide user interaction is to assign an action to the Down state of a button. Then, whenever the user clicks the button, the action occurs. Flash provides a scripting language, called ActionScript, that allows you to add actions to buttons and frames within a movie. For example, you can place a stop action in a frame that pauses the movie, and then you can assign a play action to a button that starts the movie when the user clicks the button.

Analyzing ActionScript

ActionScript is a powerful scripting language that allows those with even limited programming experience to create complex actions. For example, you can create order forms that capture user input or volume controls that display when sounds are played. A basic ActionScript involves an event (such as a mouse click) that causes some action to occur by triggering the script. The following is an example of a basic ActionScript:

```
on (release) {
gotoAndPlay(10);
}
```

In this example, the event is a mouse click (indicated by the word release) that causes the movie's playback head to go to frame 10 and play the frame. This is a simple example of ActionScript code and it is easy to follow. Other ActionScript code can be quite complex and may require programming expertise to understand.

ActionScript 2.0 and 3.0

Adobe has identified two types of Flash CS5 users, designers and developers. Designers focus more on the visual features of a Flash movie, including the user interface design, drawing objects, and acquiring and editing additional assets (such as graphic images). Whereas, developers focus more on the programming aspects of a Flash movie, including creation of complex animations and writing the code that specifies how the movie responds to user interactions. In many cases, designers and developers work together to create sophisticated Flash applications. In other cases, designers work without the benefit of a developer's programming expertise. In order to accommodate the varying needs of these two types of users, Flash CS5 provides two versions of ActionScript, 2.0 and 3.0, called AS2 and AS3. ActionScript 3.0 is used by developers because it provides a programming environment that is more familiar to them and can be used to create movies that download more quickly.

However, the differences between AS2 and AS3 are transparent to designers who do not have programming expertise. AS2 allows new Flash users to create compelling applications even if they do not have a background in programming. At the same time, AS2 provides an introduction to ActionScript that can be the basis for learning ActionScript 3.0. ActionScript 2.0 will be used in this chapter. You can specify ActionScript 2.0 when creating a new document or you can use the Flash tab in the Publish Settings dialog box, which can be opened using the Publish Settings command found on the File menu, to specify AS2.

An advantage of using AS2 is a feature called Script Assist, which provides an easy way to use ActionScript without having to learn the scripting language. The Script Assist feature within the Actions panel allows you to assign basic actions to frames and objects, such as buttons. Figure 27 shows the Actions panel displaying an ActionScript indicating that when the user clicks the selected object (a button, in this example, b_signal), the movie goes to and plays frame 2.

Figure 27 *The Actions panel displaying an ActionScript*

The process for assigning actions to buttons, shown in Figure 28, is as follows:

1. Select the button on the Stage that you want to assign an action to.
2. Display the Actions panel, using the Window menu.
3. Click the Script Assist button to display the Script Assist panel within the ActionScript panel.
4. Click the Add a new item to the script button to display a list of Action categories and associated menus.
5. Click the appropriate category from a menu. Flash provides several Action categories. The Timeline Control category accessed via the Global Functions menu allows you to create scripts for controlling

movies and navigating within movies. You can use the actions available via the Timeline Control menu to start and stop movies, as well as jump to specific frames. These can be in response to user mouse movements and keystrokes.

- Select the desired action, such as goto.
- Specify the event that triggers the action, such as on (release). This step in the process is not shown in Figure 28.

Button actions respond to one or more mouse events, including:

Release—With the pointer inside the button Hit area, the user presses and releases (clicks) the mouse button. This is the default event.

Key Press—With the button displayed, the user presses a predetermined key on the keyboard.

Roll Over—The user moves the pointer into the button Hit area.

Drag Over—The user holds down the mouse button, moves the pointer out of the button Hit area, and then back into the Hit area.

Using Frame Actions

In addition to assigning actions to buttons, you can assign actions to frames. Actions assigned to frames are executed when the playhead reaches the frame. A common frame action is stop, which is often assigned to the first and last frame of a layer on the Timeline.

Figure 28 *The process for assigning actions to buttons*

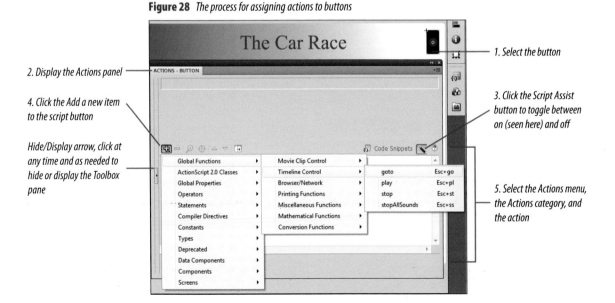

Working with Symbols and Interactivity

Understanding the Actions panel

The Actions panel has two panes. The left pane (also called the Toolbox pane) uses folders to display the Action categories. The right pane, called the Script pane, is used with the Script Assist feature and it displays the ActionScript code as the code is being generated. When using the Script Assist feature, it is best to close the left pane. This is done by clicking the Hide/Display arrow, which is shown in Figure 28 and Figure 29. In Figure 28, the Toolbox pane is collapsed, and in Figure 29, the Toolbox pane is expanded.

The lower-left corner of the Script pane displays the symbol name or the frame to which the action(s) will apply. Always verify that the desired symbol or frame is displayed. When the Script Assist feature is turned off (not active), you can type ActionScript code directly into the Script pane.

Using Frame Labels

Buttons are often used to move the playhead to a specific location on the Timeline. For example, clicking a Start button might cause the playhead to jump from frame 1 to frame 10 to start an animation. In addition to referencing frame numbers, like 10, you can reference frame labels in the ActionScript code. Frame labels have an advantage over frame numbers, especially in large and complex applications, because adding or deleting frames will not disrupt the navigation to a frame reference you already have in actions, since the label remains attached to the frame even if the frame moves. The process is to select a frame and use the Properties panel to specify a name. Then use the frame name in the ActionScript code instead of the frame number. Figure 30 shows the Timeline with a frame label and the Actions panel with the code that references the label.

Figure 29 *The Actions panel*

Script Assist off

Toolbox pane

Hide/Display arrow for the Toolbox pane

Button that the code will be applied to

Figure 30 *The Timeline with a frame label*

Frame label "StartRace" in frame 2

Code that references the frame label

Script Assist on

Assign a stop action to frames

1. Click **Control** on the menu bar, point to **Test Movie**, then click **in Flash Professional**.

   The movie plays and continues to loop.

2. Close the Flash Player window.

3. Insert a **new layer**, name it **stopMovie**, then click **frame 1** on the layer to select the frame.

4. Click **Window** on the menu bar, then click **Actions** to display the Actions panel.

5. Study the Actions panel. If the Toolbox pane is displayed as shown in Figure 31, then click the **Hide/Display arrow** to hide the pane.

6. Click the **Script Assist button** to turn on the Script Assist feature if Script Assist is not active.

7. Verify stopMovie:1 (indicating the layer and frame to which the action will be applied) is displayed in the lower-left corner of the Script pane.

8. Click the **Add a new item to the script button** to display the Script categories, point to **Global Functions**, point to **Timeline Control**, then click **stop**, as shown in Figure 32.

9. Click the **Frame view icon**, click **Small**, then click **frame 65** on the stopMovie layer.

10. Insert a **keyframe** in frame 65 on the stopMovie layer, then open the Actions panel if it is no longer open.

TIP You can collapse the Actions panel to view more of the Stage, then expand the Actions panel when needed. Alternately, you can drag the bottom or sides of the Actions panel up to make the panel smaller.

(continued)

Figure 31 *The Actions panel Toolbox pane*

Hide/Display arrow for the Toolbox pane

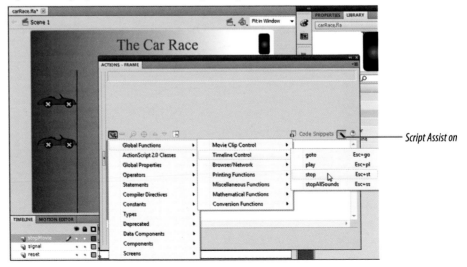

Figure 32 *Assigning an action to frame 1 on the stopMovie layer*

Script Assist on

Figure 33 *Script for the stopMovie layer*

Action *stop()*

Action assigned to frame 65 of the stopMovie layer

Figure 34 *Assigning an event and an action to a button*

Action assigned to
the button named
b_signal

11. Verify stopMovie: 65 is displayed in the lower-left corner of the Script pane, then repeat Step 8. Compare your screen to Figure 33.

12. Test the movie.

The movie does not play because there is a stop action assigned to frame 1.

13. Close the Flash Player window.

You inserted a layer and assigned a stop action to the first and last frames on the layer.

Assign a play action to a button

1. Click **frame 1** on the signal layer.

2. Move the **Actions panel** to view the signal button on the Stage, if necessary.

3. Click the **Selection tool** on the Tools panel, then click the **button** on the Stage.

4. Verify b_signal is displayed in the lower left of the Actions panel.

This ensures that the actions specified in the Actions panel will apply to the b_signal button.

5. Click ⬚ to display the Script categories, point to **Global Functions,** point to **Timeline Control,** then click **play.**

Release is the default event for a button, as shown in Figure 34.

6. Click **Control** on the menu bar, point to **Test Movie,** then click **in Flash Professional.**

7. Click the **signal button** to play the animation.

8. Close the Flash Player window.

You used the Actions panel to assign a play action to a button.

Assign a goto frame action to a button

1. Click **Control** on the menu bar, point to **Test Movie**, then click **in Flash Professional**.

2. Click the **signal button**.

   The movie plays and stops, and the word Reset, which is actually a button, appears.

3. Click the **Reset button** and notice nothing happens because it does not have an action assigned to it.

4. Close the Flash Player window.

5. Click **frame 65** on the reset layer to display the Reset button on the Stage.

   Note: You many need to close and/or move the Actions panel to view the Reset button on the Stage.

6. Click the **Reset button** on the Stage to select it.

7. Verify b_reset is displayed in the lower left of the Actions panel.

8. Verify Script Assist in the Actions panel is active , click , point to **Global Functions**, point to **Timeline Control**, click **goto**, then verify Frame 1 is specified, as shown in Figure 35.

9. Click **Control** on the menu bar, point to **Test Movie**, then click **in Flash Professional**.

10. Click the **signal button** to start the movie, then when the movie stops, click the **Reset button**.

11. Close the Flash Player window.

You used the Actions panel to assign an action to a button.

Figure 35 *Assigning a goto action to a button*

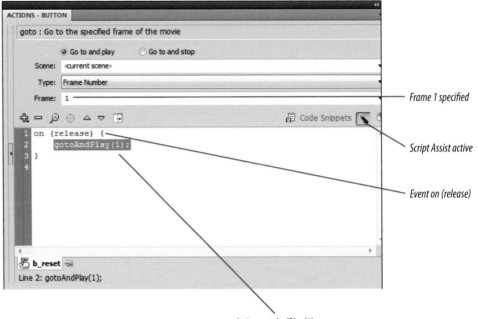

Frame 1 specified

Script Assist active

Event on (release)

Action gotoAndPlay(1)

Figure 36 *Assigning a keyPress action to a button*

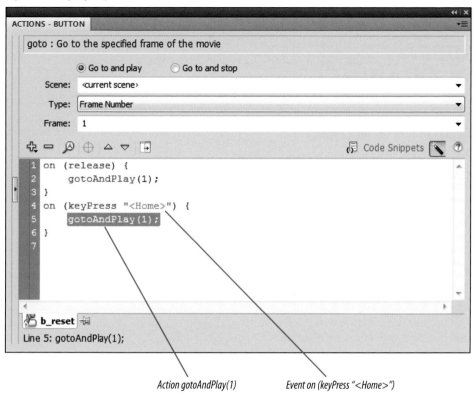

Action gotoAndPlay(1)   Event on (keyPress "<Home>")

Global Functions: Timeline Control and Movie Clip Control

The most common actions for including interactivity in a movie when using ActionScript 2.0 are added using the Global Functions categories Timeline Control and Movie Clip Control. Timeline Control actions focus on controlling the playhead (play, stop), jumping to a specific frame (goto), and stopping sounds (stopAllSounds). These actions are generally assigned to buttons. Movie Clip Control actions focus on manipulating movie clips (startDrag, stopDrag, removeMovieClip, and so on). They also provide mouse (on Release) and keyboard (Key Press) actions that can be assigned to buttons.

Assign a second event to a button

1. Click the **right curly brace** (}) in the Actions panel to highlight the brace in line 3 of the ActionScript.

2. Click ⚏ , point to **Global Functions**, point to **Movie Clip Control**, then click **on**.

   The Script Assist window displays several event options. Release is selected.

3. Click the **Release check box** to deselect the option.

4. Click the **Key Press check box** to select it, then press the **[Home] key** on the keyboard.

TIP If your keyboard does not have a [Home] key, use [fn]+[←] (Mac) or one of the function keys (Win) to complete the steps.

5. Click ⚏ , point to **Global Functions**, point to **Timeline Control**, then click **goto**.

   The ActionScript now indicates that pressing the [Home] key will cause the playhead to go to frame 1, as shown in Figure 36.

   The Reset button can now be activated by clicking it or by pressing the [Home] key.

6. Click **File** on the menu bar, point to **Publish Preview**, then click **Default – (HTML)**.

   The movie opens in your default browser.

   Note: If a warning message opens, follow the messages to allow blocked content.

7. Click the **signal button** to start the movie, then when the movie stops, press the **[Home] key**.

8. Close the browser window, close the Actions panel, then save and close the movie.

You added a keypress event that triggers a goto frame action.

Import GRAPHICS

What You'll Do

In this lesson, you will import and work with bitmap and vector graphics.

Understanding Graphic Types

Flash provides excellent drawing tools, which allow you to create various objects that can be changed into symbols. In addition, you can import graphics and other assets, such as photographs and sounds. There are two types of graphic files, bitmap graphics and vector graphics. They are distinguished by the way in which the image is represented.

Bitmap images are made up of a group of tiny dots of color called **pixels** (picture elements). Bitmap graphics are often used with photographic images because they can represent subtle gradients in color. However, one disadvantage of bitmap graphics is the inability to enlarge the graphic without distorting the image. This is because both the computer screen's resolution (pixels per inch) and the number of pixels making up the image are a fixed number. So, when you enlarge an image each pixel must increase in size to fill the larger image dimensions. This causes the pixels to display jagged edges, as shown in Figure 37.

Vector graphics represent an image as a geometric shape made up of lines and arcs that are combined to create various shapes, such as circles and rectangles. This is similar to Flash drawings that include strokes and fills. Flash drawing tools create vector graphics. One advantage of vector graphics is that they can be resized without distorting the image. The reason is that the geometric shapes are based on mathematical models that are recalculated when the image is resized. Figure 38 shows an example of a vector graphic before and after resizing. Vector graphics are best used for drawings rather than for images requiring photographic quality.

There are several programs that allow you to create and edit graphics including Adobe Illustrator, Fireworks, and Photoshop. There are also clip art and stock photograph collections that are available online. Filename extensions identify the file type. For example, .jpg, .tif, .bmp, and .gif are file formats for bitmap graphics; while .ai is a vector file format.

Importing and Editing Graphics

Once you have identified the graphic you would like to include in a Flash document, you can use the Import feature to bring the graphic into Flash. The process for importing is to select the Import command from the File menu and specify where to import (Stage or Library). Then you navigate to the location where the file is stored and select it. After importing a vector graphic you can work with it as you would any graphic. Because bitmap graphics are not easy to edit in Flash, you may want to use another program, like Photoshop, to obtain the desired size, color, and other enhancements before importing the graphic.

Figure 37 *Bitmap graphic enlarged*

Figure 38 *Vector graphic enlarged*

Import graphics

1. Start a new Flash document, then save it as **sailing.fla**.

2. Click **File** on the menu bar, point to **Import**, then click **Import to Library**.

3. Navigate to the folder where your Data Files are stored, click **islandview.jpg**, then click **Open**.

   Islandview.jpg is a digital photo that was edited in Photoshop and saved as a .jpg file.

4. Display the Library panel and notice the icon used for bitmap graphics.

5. Drag the **islandview icon** to the Stage, then lock the layer.

6. Click **File** on the menu bar, point to **Import**, then click **Import to Library**.

7. Navigate to the folder where your Data Files are stored, then click **sailboat.ai**.

   This graphic was created using Adobe Illustrator and is made up of several layers.

8. Click **Open**.

   A dialog box appears asking you to choose the layers to import. All layers are selected by default.

9. Click **OK**.

   The graphic is added to the Library panel as a symbol.

10. Add a new layer to the Timeline, click **frame 1** on the layer, then drag the **sailboat icon** to the Stage, as shown in Figure 39.

    (continued)

Figure 39 *Positioning the sailboat image on the Stage*

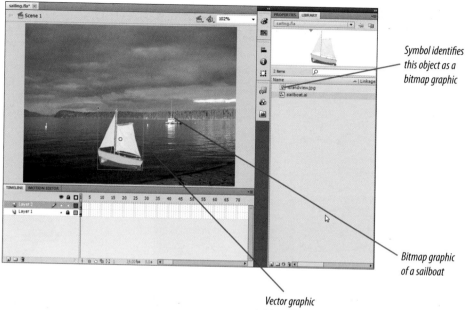

Symbol identifies this object as a bitmap graphic

Bitmap graphic of a sailboat

Vector graphic of a sailboat

Working with Symbols and Interactivity

Figure 40 *Changing the color of the sail*

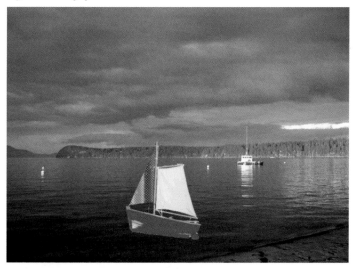

Figure 41 *Rotating and skewing the sailboat image*

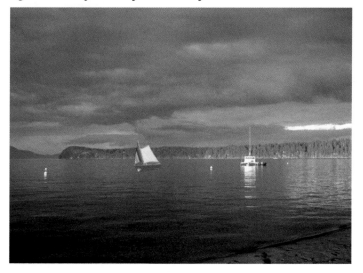

11. Click **Modify** on the menu bar, click **Break apart**, then repeat this step until the dotted pattern that indicates the image is no longer a symbol appears.

12. Click the **Selection tool** ▸ , then click a blank area of the Pasteboard.

13. Click the **left sail**, set the **Fill color icon** to the **rainbow pattern** to change the sail color, as shown in Figure 40.

    Hint: The rainbow color is found at the bottom of the palette for the Fill Color tool.

14. Use the **Selection tool** ▸ to drag a **marquee** around the entire sailboat to select it, then convert the image to a graphic symbol named **rainbowSail**.

15. Display the Properties panel, verify the Lock icon ⊕ is not broken, then change the width of the boat to **60**.

16. Click the **Zoom tool** 🔍 on the Tools panel, click the **sailboat** twice, then scroll as needed to view each sailboat.

    Notice how the bitmap photograph becomes distorted, while the vector sailboat does not.

17. Change the view to **Fit in Window**.

18. Click the **Free Transform tool** ▚, click the **Rotate and Skew option** ⟳ skew the sailboat slightly to the left, verify the Lock icon ⊕ is not broken, change the width of the boat to **60**, then position the sailboat as shown in Figure 41.

19. Test the movie, close the Flash Player window, then save your work and exit Flash.

You imported a bitmap and a vector graphic, and edited the vector graphic.

Create a symbol.

1. Start Flash, open fl3_3.fla, then save it as **skillsDemo3.fla**. This document consists of a single object that was created using the Flash drawing tools.
2. Use the Selection tool to drag a marquee around the ball to select it.
3. Convert the ball to a graphic symbol with the name **g_beachBall**.
4. Double-click the g_beachBall symbol on the Library panel to open the edit window, change the fill color to a rainbow gradient, add a text block that sits on top of the ball with the words **BEACH BALL** (see Figure 42), formated with white, Times New Roman, 12-pt, bold, then click Scene 1 to return to the main Timeline.
5. With the ball selected, create a motion tween animation that moves the ball from the left edge of the Stage to the right edge of the Stage.
6. Use the Selection tool to drag the middle of the motion path up to near the middle of the Stage to create an arc.
7. Select the last frame of the animation on the Timeline and set Rotate to 1 time in the Rotation area of the Properties panel.
8. Play the movie.
   The ball should move across the Stage in an arc and spin at the same time.
9. Lock the beachBall spin layer.

Create and edit an instance.

1. Insert a new layer and name it **redBall**.
2. Click frame 1 on the redBall layer, then drag the g_beachBall symbol from the Library panel so it is on top of the ball on the Stage.

3. Use the arrow keys as needed to align the ball so that it covers the ball on the Stage.
4. With the ball selected, break apart the object.
5. Change the fill color of the ball to a red gradient and change the text to **RED BALL**.
6. Insert a new layer and name it **greenBall**.
7. Click frame 12 on the greenBall layer, then insert a keyframe.
8. Drag the g_beachBall symbol from the Library panel so it is on top of the ball that is near the middle of the Stage. (*Note*: Align only the balls, not the text.)
9. With the ball selected, break apart the object and change the fill color of the ball to a green gradient and the text to **GREEN BALL**.
10. Move the beachBall spin layer to above the other layers.
11. Insert a new layer and name it **title.**
12. Click frame 1 on the title layer, create a text block at the top middle of the Stage with the words **BeachBall Spin** using Arial as the font, blue as the color, and 20-pt as the font size.
13. Insert a new layer above the title layer and name it **titleBkgnd**.
14. Draw a primitive rectangle with a corner radius of 10, a medium gray fill (#999999) and no stroke that covers the BeachBall Spin title text.
15. Verify the rectangle is selected, convert it to a graphic symbol, then name it **g_Bkgnd**.
16. Move the title layer so it is above the titleBkgnd layer.
17. Play the movie, then save your work.

Create a folder in the Library panel.

1. Click the New Folder button at the bottom of the Library panel to create a new folder.
2. Name the folder **Graphics**, then move the two graphic symbols to the Graphics folder.
3. Expand the Graphics folder.
4. Rename the g_Bkgnd symbol to **g_titleBkgnd** in the Library panel.
5. Save your work.

Create a button.

1. Insert a new layer above the title layer and name it **startButton**.
2. Click frame 1 of the new layer, then drag the g_titleBkgnd symbol from the Library panel to the bottom center of the Stage.
3. Create a text block with the word **Start** formatted with white, bold, 20-pt Arial, then center the text block on top of the g_titleBkgnd object.
4. Select the rectangle and the text. (*Hint*: Drag a marquee around both objects or click the Selection tool, press and hold [Shift], then click each object.)
5. Convert the selected objects to a button symbol and name it **b_start**.
6. Create a new folder named **Buttons** in the Library panel and move the b_start button symbol to the folder.
7. Open the Buttons folder, then display the edit window for the b_start button.
8. Insert a keyframe in the Over frame.
9. Select the text and change the color to a lighter shade of gray than the background rectangle.
10. Insert a keyframe in the Down frame.

Working with Symbols and Interactivity

11. Select the text and change the color to blue.
12. Insert a keyframe in the Hit frame.
13. Draw a rectangular object that covers the button area for the Hit state.
14. Click Scene 1 to exit the edit window and return to the main Timeline.
15. Save your work.

Test a button.

1. Turn on Enable Simple Buttons.
2. Point to the button and notice the color change.
3. Click the button and notice the other color change.

Stop a movie.

1. Insert a new layer and name it **stopMovie.**
2. Insert a keyframe in frame 24 on the new layer.
3. With frame 24 selected, display the Actions panel.
4. Assign a stop action to the frame.
5. Click frame 1 on the stopMovie layer.
6. Assign a stop action to frame 1.
7. Save your work.

Assign a goto action to a button.

1. Click Control on the menu bar, then click Enable Simple Buttons to turn off this feature.
2. Use the Selection tool to select the Start button on the Stage.
3. Use Script Assist in the Actions panel to assign an event and a goto action to the button. (*Hint*: Refer to the section on assigning a goto action as needed.)
4. Test the movie.

Import a graphic.

1. Import BeachScene.jpg from the drive and folder where your Data Files are stored to the Library panel.
2. Insert a new layer and name the layer **backDrop.**
3. Select frame 1 on the backDrop layer, then drag the BeachScene image to the Stage.
4. Convert the BeachScene image to a graphic symbol with the name **g_beachScene.**

5. Move the backDrop layer to the bottom of the Timeline.
6. Move the graphic symbols to the Graphics folder in the Library panel.
7. Test the movie.
8. Save your work, then compare your image to Figure 42.
9. Exit Flash.

Figure 42 *Completed Skills Review*

The Ultimate Tours travel company has asked you to design a sample navigation scheme for its website. The company wants to see how its home page will link with one of its main categories (Treks). Figure 43 shows a sample home page and Treks screen. Using the figures or the home page you created in Chapter 2 as a guide, you will add a Treks screen and link it to the home page. (*Hint*: Assume that all of the drawings on the home page are on frame 1, unless noted.)

1. Open ultimateTours2.fla (the file you created in Chapter 2 Project Builder 1), then save it as **ultimateTours3.fla**. (*Note*: If you create a new file, you must create an ActionScript 2.0 file.)
2. Insert a layer above the Subheading layer and name it **logo**.
3. Import the UTLogo.jpg file from the drive and folder where your Data Files are stored to the Library panel.
4. Select frame 1 on the logo layer and drag the logo image to the upper-left corner of the Stage.
5. Select the logo and convert it to a graphic symbol with the name **g_UTLogo**.

6. Set the last frame of the movie by inserting a keyframe on a frame on the Logo layer at least five frames farther along the Timeline, then lock the logo layer. (*Note*: You see the logo because the keyframe inserted on the last frame of the movie ensures everything on this layer appears on this last frame.)
7. Select the layer that the Ultimate Tours text block is on, then insert a keyframe on the last frame of the movie. (*Hint*: This should be the same frame number as the frame you set as the last frame of the movie in Step 6. *Note*: You see the logo and the heading Ultimate Tours because the keyframe you inserted on the last frame of the movie ensures everything on this layer appears on this last frame.)
8. Insert a new layer, name it **treks headings**, insert a keyframe on the last frame of the movie, then create the Treks screen shown in Figure 43, except for the home button. (*Note*: The underline was created using the Line tool.)
9. Convert the Treks graphic on the home page to a button symbol named **b_treks**, then edit the symbol so that different colors appear for the different states and be sure to set a hit area.

10. Assign a goto action to the Treks button that jumps the playhead to the Treks screen when the Treks button is clicked. (*Hint*: You need to use ActionScript 2.0 to complete the steps that follow. You can check the ActionScript version by selecting Publish Settings from the File menu and clicking the Flash tab.)
11. Insert a new layer and name it **stopMovie**. Add stop actions that cause the movie to stop after displaying the home page and after displaying the Treks page. Make sure there is a keyframe in the last frame of the stopMovie layer.
12. Insert a new layer and name it **homeButton**, insert a keyframe on the last frame of the movie, then draw the home button image with the Home text.
13. Convert the image to a button symbol named **b_home**, then edit the symbol so that different colors appear for the different states. Assign a goto action for the Home button that jumps the movie to frame 1.
14. Test the movie.
15. Save your work, then compare your web pages to the samples shown in Figure 43.

Figure 43 *Sample completed Project Builder 1*

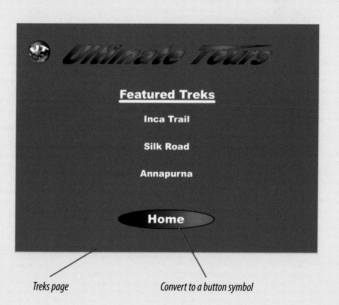

Home page

Convert to a button
symbol

Treks page

Convert to a button symbol

You have been asked to assist the International Student Association (ISA). The association sponsors a series of monthly events, each focusing on a different culture from around the world. The events are led by a guest speaker who makes a presentation, followed by a discussion. The events are free and they are open to everyone. ISA would like you to design a Flash movie that will be used with its website. The movie starts by providing information about the series, and then provides a link to the upcoming event. Refer to Figure 44 as you create the Flash movie.

1. Open a new Flash ActionScript 2.0 document and save it as **isa3.fla**.
2. Create an initial Information screen with general information about the association's series, then insert a keyframe on the last frame of the movie so that the title and subtitle appear on all screens. The title and subtitle should appear together on one layer. Be sure to add a keyframe on this layer in the last frame of this movie so that the title and subtitle appear on every frame of the movie. (*Hint*: This movie will use a minimum of three screens so consider setting the last frame of the movie on frame 5 in case you find you need more than three frames.)
3. On a new layer, assign an action to frame 1 that stops the movie.
4. Create two more screens: a next event screen starting in frame 2 on a new layer that presents information about the next event and a series screen starting in frame 3 on a new layer that lists the series (all nine events for the school year—September through May). (*Hint*: Be sure to insert keyframes in frames 2 and 3 of the new layers when adding these screens.)
5. Create a button on the general information screen that jumps the movie to the next event screen, and create a second button on the information screen that jumps the movie to the series screen. For each button you create, specify different colors for each state of each button.
6. On the next event screen, create a Return button that jumps the movie back to the general information screen. Be sure to specify different colors for each state when you create the Return button.
7. Copy an instance of the button you created in Step 6 to the series screen. (*Hint*: You can select the button, select Copy from the Edit menu, display the series screen and select Copy in Place from the Edit menu. Alternately, you can drag an instance of the button from the Library panel to the series screen.)
8. On the next event screen, copy an instance of the button you created in Step 5 that jumps the movie to the series screen.
9. On the series screen, copy an instance of the button you created in Step 5 that jumps the movie to the next event screen.
10. Add an action that stops the movie on the next event screen, and another action that stops the movie on the series screen. (*Hint*: Place the stop actions on the same layer as the stop action created in Step 3.)
11. Test the movie.
12. Save your work, then compare your movie to the sample shown in Figure 44.

Figure 44 *Sample completed Project Builder 2*

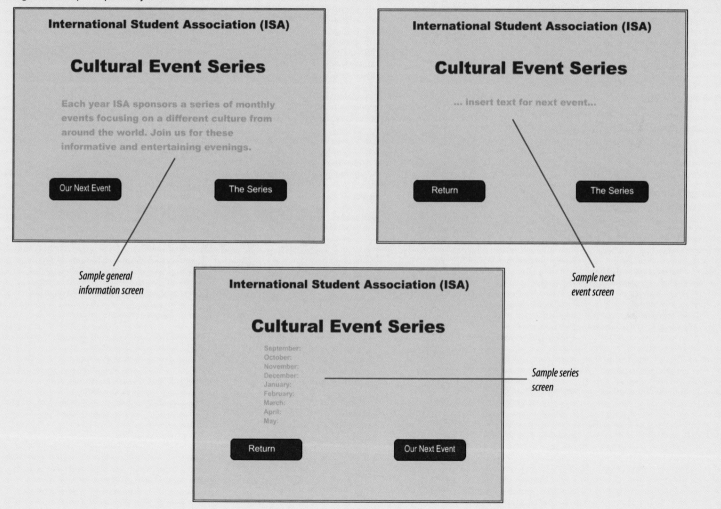

Figure 45 shows the home page of a website. Study the figure and complete the following questions. For each question, indicate how you determined your answer.

1. Connect to the Internet and go to *www.zoo.org*. Notice that this website has images that change as you visit the website.
2. Open a document in a word processor or open a new Flash document, save the file as **dpc3**, then answer the following questions. (*Hint*: Use the Text tool in Flash.)
   - Whose website is this?
   - What is the goal(s) of the site?
   - Who is the target audience?
   - What treatment ("look and feel") is used?
   - What are the design layout guidelines being used (balance, movement, and so on)?
   - What may be animated in this home page?
   - Do you think this is an effective design for the company, its products, and its target audience? Why or why not?
   - What suggestions would you make to improve the design, and why?

Figure 45 *Design Project*

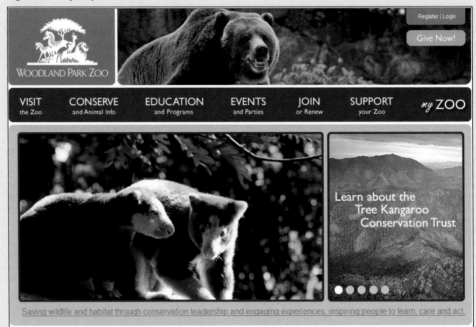

Courtesy of www.zoo.org

Working with Symbols and Interactivity

This is a continuation of the Chapter 2 Portfolio Project, which is the development of a personal portfolio. The home page has several categories, including the following:

- Personal data
- Contact information
- Previous employment
- Education
- Samples of your work

In this project, you will create a button that will be used to link the home page of your portfolio to the animations page. Next, you will create another button to start the animation.

1. Open portfolio2.fla (the file you created in Portfolio Project, Chapter 2), then save it as **portfolio3.fla**.
2. Unlock the layers as needed.
3. Insert a new layer, name it **sampleAnimations**, then insert a keyframe in frame 2.
4. Create a Sample Animations screen that has a text block with an oval background and the words **Sample Animations** at the top of the Stage, then add another text block and oval background with the word **Tweened**. *(Note: This screen will have several animation samples added to it later.)*
5. Insert a new layer, name it **home button**, then insert a keyframe in frame 2.
6. Add a text block that says **Home** and has an oval background at the bottom of the Stage.
7. Insert a new layer, name it **tweenedAnimation**, then insert a keyframe in frame 3.

8. Create an animation(s) of your choice using objects you draw or import, or objects from the Library panel of another document. (*Note*: To create a motion tween animation when starting in a frame other than frame 1, you need to specify the beginning frame of the animation by inserting a keyframe in the starting frame and you need to specify the ending frame of the animation by inserting a keyframe before repositioning the object on the Stage. *Hint*: To create more than one animation that plays at the same time, put each animation on its own layer, such as tweenedAnimationRedCar and tweenedAnimationBlueCar.)
9. Insert a new layer, name it **animationHeading**, then insert a keyframe in frame 3.
10. Add a heading to the screen used for the animation(s) that describes the animation(s).
11. On the Sample Animations screen, convert the Tweened and Home text blocks into button symbols, then edit each symbol so that different colors appear

for the different states. For the Tweened button, assign an action that jumps to the frame that plays an animation. For the Home button, assign an action to the Home button that jumps to the frame that displays My Portfolio. (*Hint*: You need to use ActionScript 2.0. You can set the ActionsScript version by selecting Publish Settings from the File menu, clicking the Flash tab and specifying ActionScript 2.0.)
12. Change the Animations graphic on the home page to a button, then edit the symbol so that different colors appear for the different states. Assign an action to the Animations button that jumps to the Sample Animations screen.
13. Insert a new layer, then name it **stopMovie**. Insert keyframes and assign stop actions to the appropriate frames.
14. Test the movie.
15. Save your work, then compare your movie to the sample shown in Figure 46.

Figure 46 *Sample completed Portfolio Project*

Click to return to main page Home Click to run the animation

CHAPTER 4 CREATING ANIMATIONS

CHAPTER 4 · CREATING ANIMATIONS

Introduction

Animation can be an important part of your application or website, whether the focus is on e-commerce (attracts attention and provides product demonstrations), education (simulates complex processes such as DNA replication), or entertainment (provides interactive games).

How Does Animation Work?

The perception of motion in an animation is actually an illusion. Animation is like a motion picture in that it is made up of a series of still images. Research has found that our eye captures and holds an image for one-tenth of a second before processing another image. By retaining each impression for one-tenth of a second, we perceive a series of rapidly displayed still images as a single, moving image. This phenomenon is known as **persistence of vision** and it provides the basis for the frame rate in animations. Frame rates of 10–12 frames-per-second (fps) generally provide an acceptably smooth computer-based animation. Lower frame rates result in a jerky image, while frame rates over 30 fps may result in a blurred image. In addition, higher frame rates may increase file size because more frames are needed for a 5 second animation running at 30 fps than at 10 fps. After creating an animation you can experiment with various frame rates to obtain the desired effect. Flash uses a default frame rate of 24 fps.

Flash Animation

Creating animation is one of the most powerful features of Flash, yet developing basic animations is a simple process. Flash allows you to create animations that can move and rotate an object around the Stage, as well as change its size, shape, or color. You can also use the animation features in Flash to create special effects, such as an object zooming or fading in and out. You can combine animation effects so that an object changes shape and color as it moves across the Stage. Animations are created by changing the content of successive frames. Flash provides two animation methods: frame-by-frame animation and tweened animation. Tweened animations can be motion, classic, or shape tweens.

Create Motion Tween
ANIMATIONS

What You'll Do

▶ *In this lesson, you will create and edit motion tween animations.*

Understanding Motion Tween Animations

An animation implies some sort of movement in an object. However, the concept of animation is much broader. Objects have specific properties such as position, size, color, and shape. Any change in a property of an object over time (i.e., across frames on the Timeline) can be considered an animation. So, having an object start at the left of the screen in frame 1 and then having it move across the screen and end up at the right side in frame 10 would be a change in the position property of the object. Each of the in-between frames (2-9) would show the position of the object as it moves across the screen. In a motion tween animation, you specify the position of the object in the beginning and ending frames and Flash fills in the in-between frames, a process known as tweening. Fortunately, you can change several properties with one motion tween.

For example, you could have a car move across the screen and, at the same time, you could have the size of the car change to give the impression of the car moving away from the viewer. The process for creating a motion tween animation is to select the frame and layer where the animation will start. If necessary, insert a keyframe (by default, frame 1 of each layer has a keyframe). Select the object on the Stage, then select the Motion Tween command from the Insert menu. If the object is not already a symbol, you will be asked if you want to convert it to a symbol. You must convert the object to a symbol if prompted because only symbols and text fields can have a motion tween applied. Then you select the ending frame and make any changes to the object, such as moving it to another location or resizing it. After you make the change, a keyframe automatically appears in the ending frame you selected. When you create a motion tween, a tween span appears on the Timeline.

Tween Spans

Figure 1 shows a motion tween animation of a car that starts in frame 1 and ends in frame 24. The Onion Skin feature is enabled so that outlines of the car are displayed for each frame of the animation in the figure. Notice a blue highlight appears on the Timeline for the frames of the animation.

The blue highlighted area is called the tween or motion span. The length of the motion tween is determined by the last frame in the movie or by other keyframes on the layer. (*Note*: The default tween span when starting from frame 1 of a new movie is determined by the number of frames in one second of the movie. So, if the frame rate is 24 frames per second, then the span is 24 frames.) You can increase or decrease the number of frames in the span by dragging the end of the span. In addition, you can move the span to a different location on the Timeline, and you can copy the span to have it apply to another object.

Figure 1 *Sample motion tween animation*

Outline of the car position in each of the selected frames

Onion Skin feature turned on   Tween span

Motion Path

The animation shown in Figure 2 includes a position change (from frame 1 to frame 24); a motion path showing the position change is displayed on the Stage. Each dot on the path corresponds to a frame on the Timeline and indicates the location of the object (in this example, the car) when the frame is played. A motion path can be altered by dragging a point on the path using the Selection tool or by using the Subselection tool to manipulate Bezier handles as shown in Figure 3. In addition, an entire path can be moved around the Stage and reshaped using the Free Transform tool.

Property Keyframes

A keyframe indicates a change in a Flash movie, such as the start or ending of an animation. Motion tween animations use property keyframes that are specific to each property such as a position keyframe, color keyframe, or rotation keyframe. In most cases these are automatically placed on the Timeline as the motion tween animation is created.

Keep in mind:

- Only one object on the Stage can be animated in each tween span.
- You can have multiple motion tween animations playing at the same time if they are on different layers.

- A motion tween is, in essence, an object animation because, while several changes can be made to an object's properties, only one object is animated for each motion tween.
- The types of objects that can be tweened include graphic, button, and movie clip symbols, as well as text fields.
- You can remove a motion tween animation by clicking the tween span on the Timeline and choosing Remove Tween from the Insert menu.

Figure 2 *The motion path*

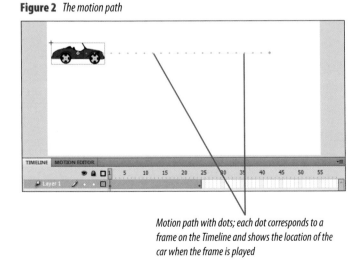

Motion path with dots; each dot corresponds to a frame on the Timeline and shows the location of the car when the frame is played

Figure 3 *Bezier handles used to alter the path*

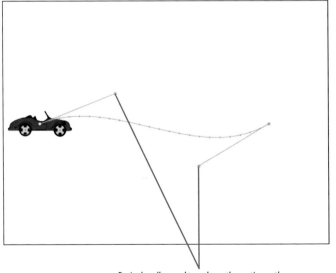

Bezier handles used to reshape the motion path

Creating Animations

Figure 4 *Positioning the car object*

Figure 5 *Changing the end of the tween span*

Drag pointer
to here

Create a motion tween animation

1. Open fl4_1.fla from the drive and folder where your Data Files are stored, then save it as **motionTw.fla**.

   This document has one drawn object—a car that has been converted to a symbol.

2. Click the **Selection tool** ![cursor] on the Tools panel, then click the **car** to select it.

3. Click **Insert** on the menu bar, then click **Motion Tween**.

   Notice the tween span appears on the Timeline. Because you started in frame 1, the number of frames in the span equals the frames per second for the movie.

4. Verify the playhead is on the last frame of the tween span, then drag the **car** to the right side of the Stage, as shown in Figure 4.

   A motion path appears on the Stage with dots indicating the position of the object for each frame. A diamond symbol appears in frame 24, which is the end of the tween span. The diamond symbol is a position keyframe and it is automatically inserted at the end of the tween path.

   Note: The end of this tween span is determined by the document frame rate, which is 24 fps. To see the diamond symbol more clearly, move the playhead.

5. Point to the end of the tween span, when the pointer changes to a double arrow ←→, drag the **tween span** to frame 40, as shown in Figure 5.

   (continued)

6. Click **frame 1** on the Timeline, then press the **period key** to move the playhead one frame at a time and notice the position of the car for each frame.

7. Play the movie, then save your work.

You created a motion tween animation, extended the length of the animation, and viewed the position of the animated object in each frame of the animation.

Edit a motion path

1. Click the **Selection tool** ⬆ on the Tools panel, then click a blank area of the Stage.

2. Click **frame 1** on Layer 1.

3. Point to the middle of the motion path, as shown in Figure 6.

4. When the pointer changes to a pointer with an arc ⬆, drag the ⬆ **pointer** down, as shown in Figure 7.

(continued)

Figure 6 *Pointing to the middle of the path*

Figure 7 *Dragging the motion path down*

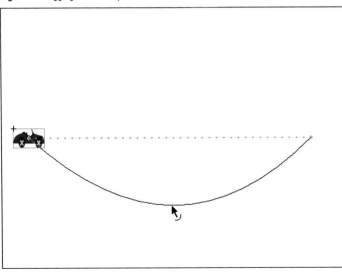

Figure 8 *Displaying the Bezier handles*

Point here

Figure 9 *Using the handles to alter the shape of the path*

Drag pointer to here

Point here to start

5. Play the movie, then click **frame 1** on Layer 1.

6. Click the **Subselection tool** ⬚ on the Tools panel, point to the end of the motion path, then, when the pointer changes into an arrow with a small square ⬚, click the end of path to display Bezier handles, as shown in Figure 8.

TIP Before using the Subselection tool to display the Bezier handles, you must use the Selection tool to drag the motion path, even if only slightly.

7. Point to the **lower-right handle**, then when the pointer changes to a delta symbol ▶, drag the **handle** up and toward the center of the Stage to form a horizontal S shape, as shown in Figure 9.

8. Play the movie, then save your work.

You edited a motion path by using the Selection tool to drag the path and by using the Subselection tool to display and reposition Bezier handles.

Change the ease value of an animation

1. Play the movie and notice that the car moves at a constant speed.

2. Display the **Properties panel**, then click **frame 1** on Layer 1.

3. Point to the **Ease value**, when the pointer changes to a hand with a double arrow 🖑, drag the 🖑 **pointer** to the right to set the value at **100**, as shown in Figure 10.

4. Click **frame 1** on Layer 1, then play the movie.

   The car starts moving fast and slows down near the end of the animation. Notice the word "out" is displayed next to the ease value on the Properties panel indicating that the object will ease out, slow down, at the end of the animation.

5. Click **frame 1** on Layer 1.

6. Point to the Ease value on the Properties panel, then drag the 🖑 **pointer** to the left to set the value to **−100**.

7. Click **frame 1** on Layer 1, then play the movie.

   The car starts moving slowly and speeds up near the end of the animation. Notice the word "in" is displayed next to the ease value on the Properties panel. Also, notice the dots are grouped closer together at the beginning of the motion path indicating that the object does not move very far in that section of the path.

8. Click **frame 1** on Layer 1, then set the ease value to **0**.

9. Save your work.

You changed the ease out and ease in values of the animation.

Figure 10 *Changing the ease value*

Drag the pointer to the right

Figure 11 *Changing the width of the object*

Drag the pointer to change the width

Lock icon

Figure 12 *Using the Free Transform tool to skew the object*

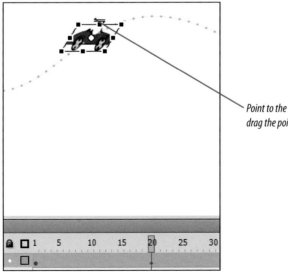

Point to the middle handle and drag the pointer to the right

Resize and reshape an object

1. Verify frame 1 is selected, click the **Selection tool** , then click the **car**.
2. Display the Properties panel, verify the lock icon is unbroken, point to the **W: value**, then, when the pointer changes to a hand with a double arrow , drag the **pointer** to the right to set the value to **80**, as shown in Figure 11.
3. Click the **car**, then play the movie.
4. Click **frame 40** on Layer 1, then click the **car**.
5. Point to the **W: value** on the Properties panel, then, when the pointer changes to a hand with a double arrow , drag the **pointer** to the left to set the value to **30**.
6. Click the **car**, then play the movie.

   The car starts out large and ends up small.
7. Click **frame 20** on Layer 1.
8. Click the **Free Transform tool** on the Tools panel, then click the **Rotate and Skew option** if it is not active.
9. Point to the **top middle handle**, then, when the pointer changes to a double line , drag the **pointer** to the right to skew the object, as shown in Figure 12.

   A keyframe indicating a change in the property (skew) of the object appears in frame 20.
10. Play the movie, use the Undo command on the Edit menu to undo the skew, then save the movie.

    The skew keyframe is removed from frame 20.

    Note: You may have to click the Undo command more than one time to undo the skew.

You resized and skewed a motion tween object.

Create a color effect

1. Click the **Selection tool** on the Tools panel.
2. Click **frame 40** on Layer 1.
3. Click the **car** to select it.
4. Click **COLOR EFFECT** to display that area if it is not open, then click **Style list arrow** in the COLOR EFFECT area of the Properties panel.
5. Click **Alpha**, then drag the **slider** to set the value to **0%**, as shown in Figure 13.
6. Play the movie.

   Notice the car slowly becomes transparent.
7. Reset the Alpha to **100%**.
8. Click **frame 40** on Layer 1.
9. Click the **car** to select it.
10. Click the **Style list arrow** in the COLOR EFFECT area of the Properties panel.
11. Click **Advanced**, then set the x R + value for Red to **100**, as shown in Figure 14.
12. Click the **car**, then play the movie.

    Notice the car slowly changes to a new shade of red. Because the car is a symbol, it is one part (not a composite of pieces). As a result, changes made to the color value affect the entire car.
13. Set the x R + value back to **0**, then save your work.

You changed the alpha and advanced color option for an object.

Figure 13 *Setting the Alpha (transparency) value*

Click to collapse or expand the COLOR EFFECT area   Drag the slider to the left   Alpha set to 0

Figure 14 *Changing a color value for the object*

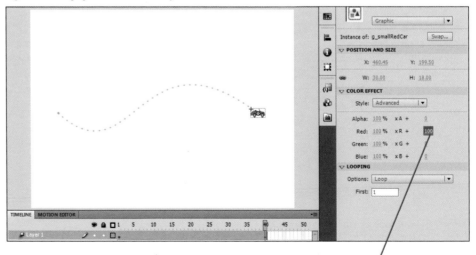

Setting the red value

Figure 15 *Aligning the car to the path*

Rotate the car to align with the path

Figure 16 *Aligning the car to the end of the motion path*

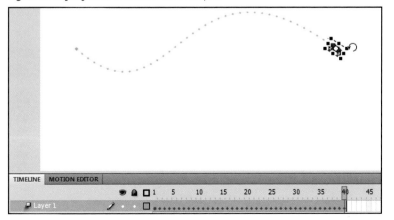

Orient an object to a path

1. Play the movie.

   Notice the car follows the path but it is not oriented to the path.

2. Click **frame 1** on Layer 1.

3. Click the **Orient to path check box** in the ROTATION area of the Properties panel.

4. Click the **Free Transform tool** on the Tools panel, then click the **Rotate and Skew option** near the bottom of the Tools panel if it is not active.

5. Point to the upper-right corner of the car, then, when the pointer changes into a circular arrow, rotate the front of the car so that it aligns with the path, as shown in Figure 15.

6. Click **frame 40** on Layer 1, then rotate the car so that its back end aligns with the path, as shown in Figure 16.

7. Play the movie.

   The car is oriented to the path.

   Notice the diamond symbols in the frames on Layer 1. These are rotation keyframes that indicate the object will change in each frame as it rotates to stay oriented to the path.

8. Test the movie, then close the Flash Player window.

9. Save your work, then close the document.

You oriented an object to a motion path and aligned the object with the path in the first and last frames of the motion tween.

Copy a motion path

1. Open fl4_2.fla, save it as **tweenEdits.fla**, then play the movie.

2. Insert a **new layer** and name it **biker2**, then click **frame 1** on the biker2 layer.

3. Click the Selection tool on the Tools panel, then drag the **g_biker symbol** from the Library panel to the Stage, as shown in Figure 17.

4. Click any frame on the tween span on the biker layer.

5. Click **Edit** on the menu bar, point to **Timeline**, then click **Copy Motion**.

6. Click the new instance of the biker, click **Edit** on the menu bar, point to **Timeline**, then click **Paste Motion**.

7. Play the movie, then hide the biker layer.

8. Click **frame 1** on the biker2 layer, click the **Free Transform tool** on the Tools panel, then click the **path** to select it, as shown in Figure 18.

9. Click **Modify** on the menu bar, point to **Transform**, then click **Flip Horizontal**.

(continued)

Figure 17 *Dragging the biker symbol to the Stage*

Drag g_biker symbol from the Library panel and position it on the Stage

Figure 18 *Selecting the path to display the handles*

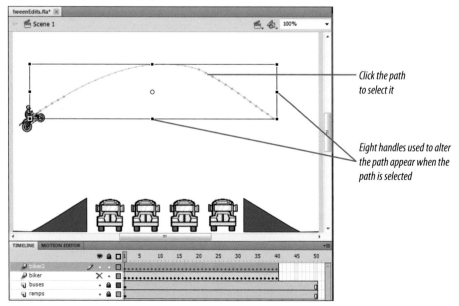

Click the path to select it

Eight handles used to alter the path appear when the path is selected

Figure 19 *Positioning the path*

10. Use the arrow keys on the keyboard to position the path, as shown in Figure 19.

11. Click the **biker object**, click **Modify** on the menu bar, point to **Transform**, then click **Flip Horizontal**.

12. Use the Free Transform tool and the arrow keys to align the biker, as shown in Figure 20.

13. Play the movie, then save your work.

You copied a motion path to another object.

Figure 20 *Aligning the biker to the path*

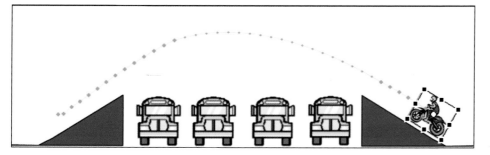

Rotate an object

1. Click **frame 1** on the biker2 layer, then display the Properties panel.

2. Point to the **Rotate times value** in the ROTATION area of the Properties panel, then, when the pointer changes to a hand with a double arrow 🖑, drag the 🖑 **pointer** to the right to set the count to **1**, as shown in Figure 21.

3. Click the **Direction list arrow**, click **CW** (Clockwise), click **frame 1** on the biker2 layer, then play the movie.

   The biker object rotates one time in a clockwise direction. Look at the Timeline. Notice some of the keyframes have been removed from the motion tween span. This is because, as the biker rotates, he is no longer oriented to the path. Motion tweens do not allow an object to be rotated and oriented to a path simultaneously because orienting an object to a path rotates the object in each frame along the path. You can use a classic tween to rotate and orient an object to a path at the same time. The remaining keyframes at the beginning and ending of the tween span are used to align the biker to the ramp.

4. Click **frame 1** on the biker2 layer, set the rotation count to **2**, set the Direction to **CCW** (Counter Clockwise), then play the movie.

5. Click **Orient to path** to select it.

   The rotate value is automatically set to no times (indicated by a 0), as shown in Figure 22.

6. Play the movie, then save your work.

You caused an object to rotate by setting the rotate value and specifying a rotation direction.

Figure 21 *Changing the rotate value*

Drag the pointer to change the rotate value

Direction list arrow

Figure 22 *The Properties panel showing that the rotate value is set to 0 times*

When Orient to path is active, Rotate value is automatically set to 0

Figure 23 *Timeline showing the motion tween removed*

Removal of motion tween in the biker2 layer
removes the blue highlight on the Timeline

Remove a motion tween

1. Unhide the **biker layer**, then play the movie.

2. Click **frame 1** on the biker2 layer to select the tween span on the Timeline.

    Note: You can click any frame on the tween span to select it.

3. Click **Insert** on the menu bar, then click **Remove Tween**.

4. Click **frame 1** on the buses layer, then notice that the blue highlight on the biker2 layer is gone, as shown in Figure 23.

5. Play the movie and notice that the biker on the biker2 layer is visible but it does not move.

6. Use the Undo command in the Edit menu to undo the Remove Tween process.

    Note: You may need to select the Undo command more than one time.

7. Click **biker2** on the Timeline to select the layer.

8. Click the **Delete icon** 🗑 at the bottom of the Timeline to delete the biker2 layer that includes the motion tween.

9. Test the movie, then close the Flash Player window.

10. Save your work.

You removed an object's motion tween, undid the action, then deleted a layer containing a motion tween.

Work with multiple motion tweens

1. Click frame **40** on the biker layer, then click the **biker** on the Stage.

2. Lock the **biker layer**, then insert a **new layer** above the biker layer and name it **bikeOffStage**.

3. Click frame **40** on the bikeOffStage layer.

4. Click **Insert** on the menu bar, point to **Timeline**, then click **Keyframe**.

5. Drag an instance of the **g_biker symbol** from the Library panel so it is on top of the biker on the Stage, as shown in Figure 24.

6. Use the Free Transform tool and the arrow keys on the keyboard to align the two biker objects.

7. Click frame **41** on the **bikeOffStage** layer, then insert a **keyframe**.

8. Use the **arrow keys** on the keyboard and the **Free Transform tool** to align the biker with the bottom of the ramp, as shown in Figure 25.

9. Click the **Selection tool**, then click the **biker**.

(continued)

Figure 24 *Placing an instance of the g_biker symbol on top of the object on the Stage*

Figure 25 *Aligning the biker with the ramp*

Creating Animations

Figure 26 *Dragging the biker object off the Stage*

Drag the object off the Stage

10. Click the **View list arrow**, then click **50%**.

11. Click **Insert** on the menu bar, then click **Motion Tween**.

12. Click **frame 45** on the bikeOffStage layer, then drag the **biker** off the Stage, as shown in Figure 26.

13. Test the movie, close the Flash Player window, save your work, then close the document.

You created a second motion tween for the movie.

Create Classic Tween
ANIMATIONS

What You'll Do

In this lesson, you will create a motion guide and attach an animation to it.

Understanding Classic Tweens

Classic tweens are similar to motion tweens in that you can create animations that change the properties of an object over time. Motion tweens are easier to use and allow the greatest degree of control over tweened animations. Classic tweens are a bit more complex to create, however, they provide certain capabilities that some developers desire. For example, with a motion tween (which consists of one object over the tween span), you can alter the ease value so that an object starts out fast and ends slow. But, with a classic tween, you can alter the ease value so that an object starts out fast, slows down, and then speeds up again. The process for creating a classic tween animation that moves an object is to select the starting frame and, if necessary, insert a keyframe. Next, insert a keyframe at the ending frame, and click anywhere on the layer between the keyframes. Then select classic tween from the Insert menu, select the ending frame, and move the object to the position you want it to be in the ending frame.

Understanding Motion Guides

When you use motion tweening to generate an animation that moves an object, a motion path that shows the movement is automatically created on the Stage. When you use classic tweening, the object moves in a straight line from the beginning location to the ending location on the Stage. There is no path displayed. You can draw a path, called a **motion guide**, that can be used to alter the path of a classic tween animation, as shown in Figure 27. A motion guide is drawn on the motion guide layer with the classic tween animation placed on its own layer beneath a motion guide layer, as shown in Figure 28. The process for creating a motion guide and attaching a classic tween animation to it is:

- Create a classic tween animation.
- Insert a new layer above the classic tween animation layer and change the layer properties to a Guide layer. Drag the classic tween animation layer to the guide layer so that it indents, as shown in Figure 28. This indicates that the classic tween animation layer is associated with the motion guide layer.
- Click the Guide layer and draw a path using the Pen, Pencil, Line, Circle, Rectangle, or Brush tools.
- Attach the object to the path by clicking the first keyframe of the layer that

contains the animation, and then dragging the object by its transformation point to the beginning of the path. Click the end keyframe and then repeat the steps to attach the object to the end of the path.

Depending on the type of object you are animating and the path, you may need to orient the object to the path.

The advantages of using a motion guide are that you can have an object move along any path, including a path that intersects itself, and you can easily change the shape of the path, allowing you to experiment with different motions. A consideration when using a motion guide is that, in some instances,

orienting the object along the path may result in an unnatural-looking animation. You can fix this by stepping through the animation one frame at a time until you reach the frame where the object is positioned poorly. You can then insert a keyframe and adjust the object as desired.

Transformation Point and Registration Point

Each symbol has a transformation point in the form of a circle (O) that is used to orient the object when it is being animated. For example, when you rotate a symbol, the transformation point is the pivot point around which the object rotates.

The transformation point is also the point that snaps to a motion guide, as shown in Figure 27. When attaching an object to a path, you can drag the transformation point to the path. The default position for a transformation point is the center of the object. You can reposition the transformation point while in the symbol edit mode by dragging the transformation point to a different location on the object. Objects also have a registration point (+) that determines the X and Y coordinates of an object on the Stage. The transformation and registration points can overlap—this is displayed as a plus sign within a circle ⊕.

Figure 27 *A motion guide with an object (motorbike) attached*

Transformation point ⊕

Figure 28 *A motion guide layer with a classic tween on the layer beneath it*

Motion guide layer containing the path

Indented layer containing the classic tween animation that will follow the path created on the motion guide layer

Create a classic tween animation

1. Open fl4_3.fla, then save it as **cTween.fla**.
2. Insert a **new layer**, then name it **biker**.
3. Click **frame 1** on the biker layer, then drag the **biker symbol** from the Library panel to the Stage, as shown in Figure 29.
4. Click **frame 30** on the biker layer, click **Insert** on the menu bar, point to **Timeline**, then click **Keyframe**.
5. Drag the **biker** to the position shown in Figure 30.
6. Click **frame 2** on the biker layer, click **Insert** on the menu bar, then click **Classic Tween**.

   An arrow appears on the Timeline indicating that this is a classic tween.
7. Play the movie.

You created an animation using a classic tween.

Add a motion guide and orient the object to the guide

1. Insert a **new layer**, then name it **Guide**.
2. Click **Modify** on the menu bar, point to **Timeline**, then click **Layer Properties**.
3. Click the **Guide option button**, click **OK**, then drag the **biker layer** up to the Guide layer, as shown in Figure 31.

   The biker layer indents below the Guide layer.
4. Click **frame 1** on the Guide layer, click the **Pencil tool** on the Tools panel, select **Smooth** in the Options area at the bottom of the Tools panel, then set the stroke color to **black**.
5. Point to the middle of the biker, then draw a **line** with a loop similar to the one shown in Figure 32.

(continued)

Figure 29 *Positioning the biker symbol on the Stage*

Drag g_biker symbol from the Library panel and position it on the Stage

Figure 30 *Repositioning the biker*

Figure 31 *Dragging the biker layer up to the Guide layer*

Drag biker layer up to but not above the Guide layer

Figure 32 *Drawing a guide path on a Guide layer*

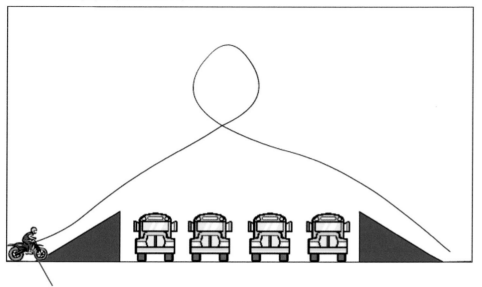

Point to the middle of the biker object

Figure 33 *Aligning the object with the guide path*

Figure 34 *Aligning the object with the end of the guide path*

Note: You may not see the line you are drawing until you are done drawing it.

6. Click **frame 30** on the biker layer, click the **Selection tool**, then drag the **biker** so that it snaps to the end of the line.

   Hint: Use the Zoom tool to zoom in on the biker to make it easier to see you have placed the transformation point on the path.

7. Play the movie.

   The biker should follow the path. If not, make sure the biker is attached to the beginning and end of the path.

8. Click **frame 1** on the biker layer, then click the **biker** to select the object.

9. Click the **Free Transform tool** on the Tools panel, then rotate the **biker,** as shown in Figure 33.

10. Click **frame 30** on the biker layer, then rotate the **biker**, as shown in Figure 34.

11. Click the **Selection tool**, then click **frame 1** on the biker layer.

12. Display the Properties panel, then click the **Orient to path check box**.

13. Play the movie.

14. Click **frame 1** on the biker layer, set the Ease value on the Properties panel to **100**, then click **frame 1** on the biker layer to accept the value.

15. Insert a **keyframe** on the frame on the biker layer that displays the highest point in the animation, set the ease value to **100**, then click **frame 1** on the biker layer to accept the value.

16. Test the movie, save your work, then close the document.

You added a motion guide, oriented the animated object to the guide, and set ease values.

Create Frame-by-Frame
ANIMATIONS

What You'll Do

In this lesson, you will create frame-by-frame animations.

Understanding Frame-by-Frame Animations

A frame-by-frame animation (also called a frame animation) is created by specifying the object that is to appear in each frame of a sequence of frames. Figure 35 shows three images that are variations of a cartoon character. In this example, the head and body remain the same, but the arms and legs change to represent a walking motion. If these individual images are placed into succeeding frames (with keyframes), an animation is created.

Frame-by-frame animations are useful when you want to change individual parts of an image. The images in Figure 35 are simple—only three images are needed for the animation. However, depending on the complexity of the image and the desired movements, the time needed to display each change can be substantial. When creating a frame-by-frame animation, you need to consider the following points:

- The number of different images. The more images there are, the more effort is needed to create them. However, the greater the number of images, the less

change you need to make in each image and the more realistic the movement in the animation may seem.

- The number of frames in which each image will appear. Changing the number of frames in which the object appears may change the effect of the animation. If each image appears in only one frame, the animation may appear rather jerky, since the frames change very rapidly. However, in some cases, you may want to give the impression of a rapid change in an object, such as rapidly blinking colors. If so, you could make changes in the color of an object from one frame to another.
- The movie frame rate. Frame rates below 10 may appear jerky, while those above 30 may appear blurred. The frame rate is easy to change, and you should experiment with different rates until you get the desired effect.

Keyframes are critical to the development of frame animations because they signify a change in the object. Because frame animations are created by changing the object, each frame in a frame animation may need to be a keyframe. The exception is when you want an object displayed in several frames before it changes.

Creating a Frame-by-Frame Animation

To create a frame animation, select the frame on the layer where you want the animation to begin, insert a keyframe, and then place the object on the Stage. Next, select the frame where you want the change to occur, insert a keyframe, and then change the object. You can also add a new object in place of the original one. Figure 36 shows the first three frames of an animation in which three different objects are placed one on top of the other in succeeding frames. In the figure, the movement is shown as shadows. These shadows are visible because the Onion Skin feature is turned on. In this movie, the objects stay in place during the animation. However, a frame animation can also involve movement of the object around the Stage.

Using the Onion Skin Feature

Normally, Flash displays one frame of an animation sequence at a time on the Stage. Turning on the Onion Skin feature allows you to view an outline of the object(s) in any number of frames. This can help in positioning animated objects on the Stage.

Figure 35 *Three images used in an animation*

Figure 36 *A frame-by-frame animation of three figures appearing to walk in place*

Onion Skin feature is turned on so that all of the objects in frames 1-3 are viewable even though the playhead is on frame 1

The 3 objects placed on top of each other on the Stage, each in its own frame on the Timeline

Create an in-place frame-by-frame animation

1. Open fl4_4.fla, then save it as **frameAn.fla**.

2. Set the view to **Fit in Window**.

3. Insert a **new layer**, name it **stickfigs**, click **frame 1** of the stickfigs layer, then drag **stickfig1** from the Library panel to the center of the Stage so it touches the white walkway.

   Note: You can use the Align panel to center the object horizontally across the Stage.

4. Click **frame 2** of the stickfigs layer to select it, click **Insert** on the menu bar, point to **Timeline**, then click **Keyframe**.

5. Drag **stickfig2** so it is on top of stickfig1, as shown in Figure 37, use the arrow keys on the keyboard to align the heads, then click a blank area of the Stage to deselect stickfig2.

6. Select **stickfig1** by clicking the foot that points up, as shown in Figure 38, then press **[Delete]**.

7. Click **frame 3** on the stickfigs layer to select it, insert a **keyframe,** drag **stickfig3** so it is on top of stickfig2, then use the **arrow keys** on the keyboard to align the heads.

8. Click a blank area of the Stage to deselect stickfig3.

9. Select stickfig2 by clicking the foot that points down, as shown in Figure 39, then press **[Delete]**.

10. Change the frame rate to **12**.

11. Play the movie.

You created a frame-by-frame animation.

Figure 37 *Dragging stickfig2 on top of stickfig1*

Figure 38 *Selecting stickfig1*

Click foot that points up

Figure 39 *Selecting stickfig2*

Click foot that points down

Figure 40 *Moving the houses layer below the stickfigs layer*

Figure 41 *Positioning the houses symbol on the Stage*

Figure 42 *Repositioning the houses object*

Copy frames and add a moving background

1. Click **frame 1** of the stickfigs layer, press and hold **[Shift]**, then click **frame 3**.

2. Click **Edit** on the menu bar, point to **Timeline**, click **Copy Frames**, then click **frame 4** of the stickfigs layer.

3. Click **Edit** on the menu bar, point to **Timeline**, then click **Paste Frames**.

4. Click **frame 7**, then repeat step 3.

5. Click **frame 10** of the stickfigs layer, press and hold **[Shift]**, then click **frame 13**.

6. Click **Edit** on the menu bar, point to **Timeline**, then click **Remove Frames**.

7. Insert a **new layer**, name the layer **houses**, then drag the **houses layer** below the stickfigs layer, as shown in Figure 40.

8. Click **frame 1** of the houses layer, drag the **houses symbol** from the Library panel to the Stage, then position the houses, as shown in Figure 41.

9. Play the movie.

10. Click **frame 1** of the houses layer, click **Insert** on the menu bar, then click **Motion Tween**.

11. Click **frame 9** on the houses layer, then drag the **houses object** to the left, as shown in Figure 42.

12. Test the movie, close the Flash Player window, save your work, then close the document.

You copied frames and added a motion tween to a movie with an in-place frame-by-frame animation.

Create a frame-by-frame animation of a moving object

1. Open fl4_5.fla, then save it as **frameM.fla**.

   This document has a backdrop layer that contains a row of houses and clouds.

2. Insert a **new layer**, then name it **stickFigs**.

3. Click **View** on the menu bar, point to **Magnification**, then click **50%**.

4. Click **frame 5** on the stickFigs layer, then insert a **keyframe**.

5. Drag **stickfig1** from the Library panel to the left edge of the Stage, as shown in Figure 43.

6. Click **frame 6** on the stickFigs layer, click **Insert** on the menu bar, point to **Timeline**, then click **Blank Keyframe**.

   A blank keyframe keeps the object in the previous frame from appearing in the current frame.

7. Click the **Edit Multiple Frames button** on the Timeline status bar to turn it on.

   This allows you to view the contents of more than one frame at a time.

8. Drag **stickfig2** to the right of stickfig1, as shown in Figure 44.

9. Click **frame 7** on the stickFigs layer, then insert a **Blank Keyframe**.

10. Drag **stickfig3** to the right of stickfig2, as shown in Figure 45.

(continued)

Figure 43 *Positioning stickfig1 on the Stage*

Edit Multiple Frames button

Figure 44 *Positioning stickfig2 on the Stage*

Figure 45 *Positioning stickfig3 on the Stage*

Creating Animations

Figure 46 *Adding stickfig3 as the final object*

Working with Frames

Selecting frames
To select one frame: click the frame.
To select a range of contiguous frames: Shift-click additional frames.
To select non-contiguous frames: Control-click (Win) or ⌘ -click (Mac).
To select a span of frames: double-click between keyframes.
To select all frames on the Timeline: choose Select All Frames from the Timeline option on the Edit menu.

Removing frames
Select the frame(s), then choose Remove Frames from the Timeline option on the Edit menu.
This removes frames from the timeline and moves the contents of succeeding frames left based on the number of frames removed.

Copy and paste
Select the frame(s), choose Copy Frames from the Timeline option on the Edit menu, select the frame(s) to copy to, then choose Paste Frames from the Timeline option on the Edit menu. (*Note*: Use Cut Frames instead of Copy Frames to move frames).

Clear contents
Select the frame(s), then choose Clear Frames from the Timeline option on the Edit menu.
This leaves the frame(s) on the Timeline but the content is cleared and not available for pasting.

---

11. Click **frame 8** on the stickFigs layer, insert a **Blank Keyframe**, then drag **stickfig1** from the Library panel to the right of stickfig3.

12. Click **frame 9** on the stickFigs layer, insert a **Blank Keyframe**, then drag **stickfig2** to the right of stickfig1.

13. Click **frame 10** on the stickFigs layer, insert a **Blank Keyframe**, then drag **stickfig3** to the right of stickfig2.

    Your screen should resemble Figure 46.

14. Click **frame 11** on the stickFigs layer, then insert a **Blank Keyframe**.

15. Click the **Edit Multiple Frames button** 🔲 on the Timeline status bar to turn it off.

16. Test the movie, then close the Flash Player window.

17. Change the frame rate to **6 fps**.

18. Test the movie, then close the Flash Player window.

19. Save the movie, then close the document.

You created a frame-by-frame animation that causes objects to appear to move across the screen.

Create Shape Tween
ANIMATIONS

What You'll Do

In this lesson, you will create a shape tween animation and specify shape hints.

Understanding Shape Tweening

In previous lessons, you learned that you can use motion tweening to change the shape of an object. You accomplish this by selecting the Free Transform tool and then dragging the handles to resize and skew the object. While this is easy and allows you to include motion along with the change in shape, there are two drawbacks. First, you are limited in the type of changes (resizing and skewing) that can be made to the shape of an object. Second, you must work with the same object throughout the animation. When you use **shape tweening**, however, you can have an animation change the shape of an object to any form you desire, and you can include two objects in the animation with two different shapes. As with motion tweening, you can use shape tweening to change other properties of an object, such as its color, location, and size.

Using Shape Tweening to Create a Morphing Effect

Morphing involves changing one object into another, sometimes unrelated, object. For example, you could turn a robot into a man, or turn a football into a basketball. The viewer sees the transformation as a series of incremental changes. In Flash, the first object appears on the Stage and changes into the second object as the movie plays. The number of frames included from the beginning to the end of this shape tween animation determines how quickly the morphing effect takes place. The first frame in the animation displays the first object and the last frame displays the second object. The in-between frames display the different shapes that are created as the first object changes into the second object.

When working with shape tweening, you need to keep the following points in mind:

- Shape tweening can be applied only to editable graphics. To apply shape tweening to instances, groups, symbols, text blocks, or bitmaps, you must break apart the object to make it editable. To do this, you use the Break Apart command on the Modify menu. When you break apart an instance of a symbol, it is no longer linked to the original symbol.
- You can shape tween more than one object at a time as long as all the objects

are on the same layer. However, if the shapes are complex and/or if they involve movement in which the objects cross paths, the results may be unpredictable.

■ You can use shape tweening to move an object in a straight line, but other options, such as rotating an object, are not available.

■ You can use the settings in the Properties panel to set options (such as the ease value, which causes acceleration or deceleration) for a shape tween.

■ Shape hints can be used to control more complex shape changes.

Properties Panel Options

Figure 47 shows the Properties panel options for a shape tween. The options allow you to adjust several aspects of the animation, as described in the following:

■ Adjust the rate of change between frames to create a more natural appearance during the transition by setting an ease value. Setting the value between –1 and –100 will begin the shape tween gradually and accelerate it toward the end of the animation. Setting the value between 1 and 100 will begin the shape tween rapidly and decelerate it toward the end of the animation. By default, the rate of change is set to 0, which causes a constant rate of change between frames.

■ Choose a blend option. The Distributive option creates an animation in which the in-between shapes are smoother and more irregular. The Angular option preserves the corners and straight lines and works only with objects that have these features. If the objects do not have corners, Flash defaults to the Distributive option.

Shape Hints

You can use shape hints to control the shape's transition appearance during animation. Shape hints allow you to specify a location on the beginning object that corresponds to a location on the ending object. Figure 48 shows two shape animations of the same objects, one using shape hints and the other not using shape hints. The figure also shows how the object being reshaped appears in one of the in-between frames. Notice that with the shape hints, the object in the in-between frame is more recognizable.

Figure 47 *The Properties panel options for a shape tween*

Figure 48 *Two shape animations (A morphing into B) with and without shape hints*

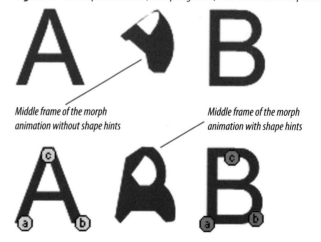

Middle frame of the morph animation without shape hints

Middle frame of the morph animation with shape hints

Create a shape tween animation

1. Open fl4_6.fla, then save it as **antiqueCar.fla**.

2. Set the view to **Fit in Window**.

3. Click **frame 30** on the shape layer, then insert a **keyframe**.

4. Click the **Selection tool** on the Tools panel, then click a blank area of the pasteboard to deselect the car.

5. Move the pointer over the top of the car near the right side until it changes to an arc pointer, then use the arc pointer to drag the **car top** to create the shape shown in Figure 49.

6. Click anywhere on the shape layer between frames 1 and 30.

7. Click **Insert** on the menu bar, then click **Shape Tween**.

8. Click **frame 1** on the shape layer, then play the movie.

9. Click **frame 30** on the shape layer.

10. Click the **Selection tool** on the Tools panel, then drag a **marquee** around the car to select it if it is not already selected.

11. Drag the **car** to the right side of the Stage.

12. Play the movie, then save and close it.

You created a shape tween animation, causing an object to change shape as it moves over several frames.

Figure 49 *The reshaped object*

Drag up from here

Figure 50 *Positioning the car instance on the Stage*

Transformation point appears when the mouse is released

Line up both cars so it appears that there is only one car; use the spokes on the wheels to help you know when the two objects are aligned

Create a morphing effect

1. Open fl4_7.fla, then save it as **morphCar.fla**.
2. Click **frame 40** on the morph layer.
3. Click **Insert** on the menu bar, point to **Timeline**, then click **Blank Keyframe**.

TIP Inserting a blank keyframe prevents the object in the preceding keyframe from automatically being inserted into the frame with the blank keyframe.

4. Click the **Edit Multiple Frames button** on the Timeline.

   Turning on the Edit Multiple Frames feature allows you to align the two objects to be morphed.

5. Display the Library panel.
6. Drag the **g_antiqueCarTopDown graphic** symbol from the Library panel directly on top of the car on the Stage, as shown in Figure 50.

TIP Use the arrow keys to move the object in small increments as needed.

7. Make sure the g_antiqueCarTopDown object is selected, click **Modify** on the menu bar, then click **Break Apart**.
8. Click the **Edit Multiple Frames button** to turn off the feature.
9. Click anywhere between frames 1 and 40 on the morph layer, click **Insert** on the menu bar, then click **Shape Tween**.
10. Click **frame 1** on the Timeline, then play the movie.

    The first car morphs into the second car.
11. Save the movie.

You created a morphing effect, causing one object to change into another.

Adjust the rate of change in a shape tween animation

1. Click **frame 40** on the morph layer.
2. Click the **Selection tool** ![cursor] on the Tools panel, then drag a **marquee** around the car to select it, if it is not already selected.
3. Drag the **car** to the right side of the Stage.
4. Click **frame 1** on the morph layer.
5. Set the ease value on the Properties panel to **−100**, as shown in Figure 51.
6. Click the **Stage**, then play the movie.

   The car starts out slow and speeds up as the morphing process is completed.
7. Repeat Steps 4 and 5, but change the ease value to **100**.
8. Click **frame 1** on the Timeline, then play the movie.

   The car starts out fast and slows down as the morphing process is completed.
9. Save your work, then close the movie.

You added motion to a shape tween animation and changed the ease value.

Figure 51 *Setting the ease value of the morph*

Creating Animations

Figure 52 *Positioning a shape hint*

Figure 53 *Adding shape hints*

Figure 54 *Matching shape hints*

Use shape hints

1. Open fl4_8.fla, then save it as **shapeHints.fla**.
2. Play the movie and notice how the L morphs into a Z.
3. Click **frame 15** on the Timeline, the midpoint of the animation, then notice the shape.
4. Click **frame 1** on the hints layer to display the first object.
5. Make sure the object is selected, click **Modify** on the menu bar, point to **Shape**, then click **Add Shape Hint**.
6. Drag the **Shape Hint icon** to the location shown in Figure 52.
7. Repeat Steps 5 and 6 to set a second and third Shape Hint icon, as shown in Figure 53.
8. Click **frame 30** on the hints layer.

    The shape hints are stacked on top of each other.
9. Drag the **Shape Hint icons** to match Figure 54.
10. Click **frame 15** on the hints layer, then notice how the object is more recognizable now that the shape hints have been added.
11. Click **frame 1** on the Timeline, then play the movie.
12. Save your work, then close the movie.

You added shape hints to a morph animation.

Create Movie
CLIPS

What You'll Do

In this lesson, you will create, edit, and animate a movie clip.

Understanding Movie Clip Symbols

Until now you have been working with two kinds of symbols, graphic and button. A third type is a **movie clip symbol**, which provides a way to create more complex types of animations. A movie clip is essentially a movie within a movie. Each movie clip has its own Timeline, which is independent of the main Timeline. This allows you to nest a movie clip that is running one animation within another animation or in a scene on the main Timeline. Because a movie clip retains its own Timeline, when you insert an instance of the movie clip symbol into a Flash document, the movie clip continues in an endless loop even if the main Timeline stops.

The wheels on a car rotating while the car is moving across the screen is an example of a movie (the moving car) with a nested animation (the rotating wheels). The nested animation is a movie clip. To create the animated movie clip, a drawing of a wheel separate from the car is converted into a movie clip symbol. Then the movie clip symbol is opened in the edit window, which includes a Timeline that is unique to the movie clip. In the edit window, an animation is created that causes the wheel to rotate. After exiting the edit window and returning to the main Timeline, an instance of the movie clip symbol is placed on each wheel of the car. Finally, the car, including the wheels, is animated on the main Timeline. As the car is moving across the screen, each wheel is rotating according to the movie clip Timeline. This process is shown in Figure 55.

In addition to allowing you to create more complex animations, movie clips help to organize the different reusable pieces of a movie and provide for smaller movie file sizes. This is because only one movie clip symbol needs to be stored in the Library panel while an unlimited number of instances of the symbol can be used in the Flash document.

An animated movie clip can be viewed in the edit window that is displayed when you double-click the movie clip symbol in the Library panel; and it can be viewed when you test or publish the movie that contains the movie clip. It is important to note that an animated movie clip cannot be viewed simply by playing the movie on the main Timeline. In this lesson, you will learn how to create a movie clip symbol from a drawn object, edit the movie clip to create an animation, and nest the movie clip in another animation.

Figure 55 *The process of nesting a movie clip within an animation*

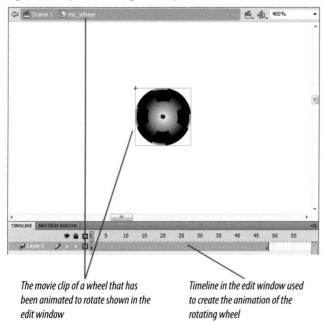

The movie clip of a wheel that has been animated to rotate shown in the edit window

Timeline in the edit window used to create the animation of the rotating wheel

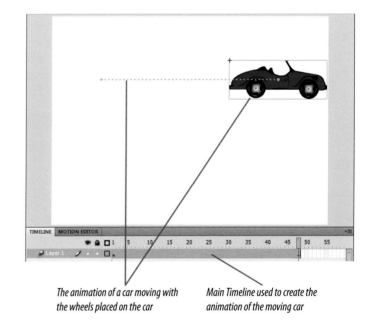

The animation of a car moving with the wheels placed on the car

Main Timeline used to create the animation of the moving car

Break apart a graphic symbol and select parts of the object to separate from the graphic

1. Open fl4_9.fla, then save it as **mClip.fla**.

   This document has one graphic symbol—a car that has been placed on the Stage.

2. Click the **Selection tool** on the Tools panel, then click the **car** to select it.

3. Click **Modify** on the menu bar, then click **Break Apart**.

4. Click a blank area of the Stage to deselect the object.

5. Click the **Zoom tool** on the Tools panel, then click the **front wheel** two times to zoom in on the wheel.

6. Click the **Selection tool** on the Tools panel.

7. Click the **gray hubcap**, press and hold **[Shift]**, then click the rest of the wheel, as shown in Figure 56.

   Hint: There are several small parts to the wheel, so click until a dot pattern covers the entire wheel, but do not select the tire. Use the Undo command if you select the tire.

8. Drag the **selected area** down below the car, as shown in Figure 57.

9. Compare your selected wheel to Figure 57, if your wheel does not match the figure, use the Undo command to move the wheel back to its original position, and repeat step 7.

You broke apart a graphic symbol and selected parts of the object to separate from the graphic.

Figure 56 *Selecting the wheel*

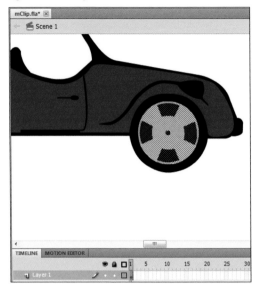

Figure 57 *Separating the wheel from the car*

Creating Animations

Figure 58 *Selecting the gray area of the wheel*

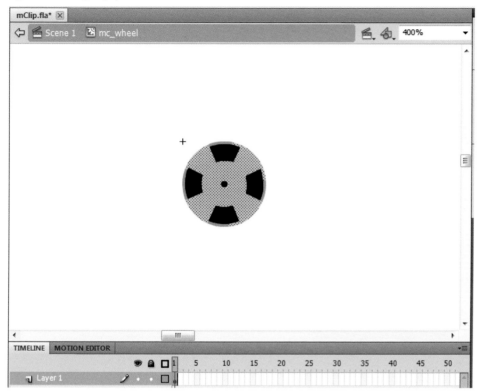

Create and edit a movie clip

1. Verify the wheel is selected, click **Modify** on the menu bar, then click **Convert to Symbol**.

2. Type **mc_wheel** for the name, select **Movie Clip** for the Type, then click **OK**.

   The mc_wheel movie clip appears in the Library panel.

3. Double-click the **mc_wheel icon** on the Library panel to display the edit window.

4. Click the **Zoom tool** 🔍 on the Tools panel, then click the **wheel** twice to zoom in on the wheel.

   The movie clip has been broken apart as indicated by the dot pattern.

5. Click the **Selection tool** , click a blank area of the Stage to deselect the object, then click the **gray area** of the wheel to select it, as shown in Figure 58.

6. Click the **Fill color tool color swatch** on the Tools panel, then click the **gray gradient color swatch** in the bottom row of the palette.

You created a movie clip symbol and edited it to change the color of the object.

Animate a movie clip

1. Click the **Selection tool** 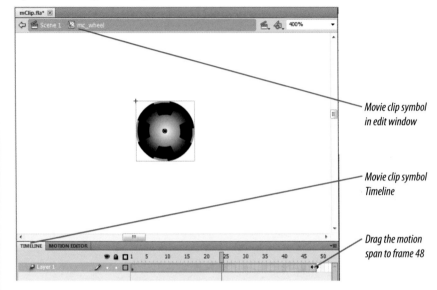, then drag a marquee around the entire wheel to select it.

2. Click **Insert** on the menu bar, click **Motion Tween**, then click **OK** for the Convert selection to symbol for tween dialog box.

3. Point to the end of the tween span on Layer 1 of the Timeline, then, when the pointer changes to a double-headed arrow ↔, drag the **span** to frame 48, as shown in Figure 59.

4. Click **frame 1** on Layer 1.

5. Display the Properties panel.

6. Change the rotate value to **4** times and verify the Direction is CW (Clockwise), as shown in Figure 60.

   Hint: If you don't see the Rotate option, click the Selection tool, then drag a marquee around the object.

7. Set the frame rate on the Timeline status bar to **12**, test the movie, then close the Flash Player window.

8. Click **Scene 1** near the top left side of the edit widow to exit the edit window.

9. Drag the **wheel** on the Stage up and position it so it is back inside the front tire of the car.

(continued)

Figure 59 *Increasing the motion span on the Timeline*

Movie clip symbol in edit window

Movie clip symbol Timeline

Drag the motion span to frame 48

Figure 60 *Changing the rotate value*

Creating Animations

Figure 61 *Repositioning the car*

10. Drag the **mc_wheel movie clip** from the Library panel and position it using the arrow keys as needed so it is on the back wheel.

11. Click **View** on the menu bar, point to **Magnification**, then click **Fit in Window**.

12. Test the movie and notice how the wheels turn, then close the Flash Player window.

13. Click the **Selection tool** ▶, then drag a **marquee** around the car to select it and the wheels.

14. Click **Insert** on the menu bar, click **Motion Tween**, then click **OK**.

15. Drag the **tween span** on Layer 1 to frame 48.

16. Click **frame 48** on Layer 1, then drag the **car** to the right side of the Stage, as shown in Figure 61.

17. Test the movie, then close the Flash Player window.

18. Save your work, then close the document.

You edited a movie clip to create an animation, then nested the movie clip in an animation on the main Timeline.

Animate TEXT

What You'll Do

In this lesson, you will animate text by scrolling, rotating, zooming, and resizing it.

Animating Text

You can motion tween text block objects just as you do graphic objects. You can resize, rotate, reposition, and change the colors of text blocks. Figure 62 shows three examples of animated text with the Onion Skin feature turned on. When the movie starts, each of the following occurs one after the other:

■ The Classic Car Club text block scrolls in from the left side to the top center of the Stage. This is done by creating the text block, positioning it off the Stage, and creating a motion-tweened animation that moves it to the Stage.

■ The Annual text block appears and rotates five times. This occurs after you create the Annual text block, position it in the middle of the Stage under the heading, and use the Properties panel to specify a clockwise rotation that repeats five times.

■ The ROAD RALLY text block slowly zooms out and appears in the middle of the Stage. This occurs after you create the text block and use the Free Transform tool handles to resize it to a small block at the beginning of the animation. Then, you resize the text block to a larger size at the end of the animation.

Once you create a motion animation using a text block, the text block becomes a symbol and you are unable to edit individual characters within the text block. You can, however, edit the symbol as a whole.

Figure 62 *Three examples of animated text*

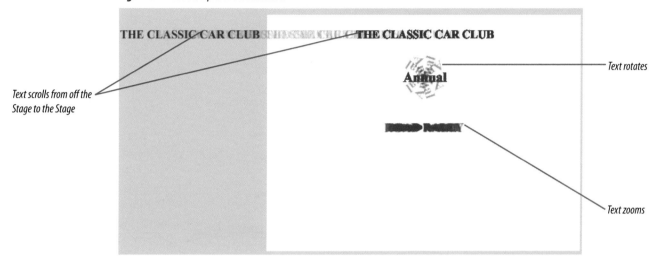

Text scrolls from off the
Stage to the Stage

Text rotates

Text zooms

Select, copy, and paste frames

1. Open fl4_10.fla, then save the movie as **textAn.fla**.

   This document has a heading and a frame-by-frame animation of a car where the front end rotates up and down, and then the car moves off the screen.

2. Play the movie, then click **frame 1** on the Timeline.

3. Press the **period key** to move through the animation one frame at a time and notice the changes to the object in each frame.

4. Change the view to **Fit in Window**.

5. Click the **Frame View icon** near the upper right of the Timeline, then click **Small**.

6. Point to the **vertical line** on the Timeline until the ┿║┿ pointer appears, then drag the ┿║┿ **pointer** to the left until frame 80 appears on the Timeline, as shown in Figure 63, if you do not see frame 80.

7. Click **frame 1** on the carGo layer, press and hold **[Shift]**, then click **frame 9** to select all the frames, as shown in Figure 64.

8. Click **Edit** on the menu bar, point to **Timeline**, then click **Cut Frames**.

9. Click **frame 72** on the carGo layer.

10. Click **Edit** on the menu bar, point to **Timeline**, then click **Paste Frames**.

11. Click **frame 1** on the carGo layer.

12. Play the movie, then save your work.

You selected frames and moved them from one location on the Timeline to another location on the Timeline.

Figure 63 *Expanding the view of the Timeline*

Drag pointer to the left

Figure 64 *Selecting a range of frames*

Click frame 1 first

Hold [Shift] and click frame 9
to select the range of frames

Figure 65 *Positioning the text block outside the Stage*

Figure 66 *Centering the text block*

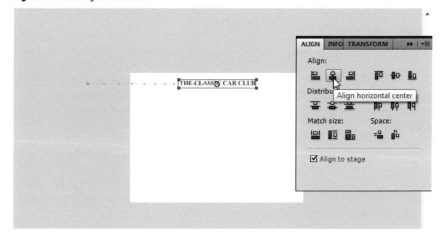

1. Change the view to **50%**.
2. Click **frame 1** on the flyInText layer.
3. Open the Motion Presets panel, display the **Default Presets**, then click **fly-in-left**.
4. Click **Apply**, read the information box, then click **OK**.

   A motion tween is applied to the text block and a motion path appears.
5. Click the **Selection tool** , then draw a **marquee** around the text and the path.
6. Use the **left arrow key** to position the object and path, as shown in Figure 65.

   Alternately, you can drag the object and path to reposition it. Using the arrow key prevents any vertical movement when repositioning the object and path.
7. Click **frame 24** on the flyInText layer.
8. Click a **blank area** of the Stage to deselect the object and the path.
9. Click the **text object** to select it, then use the align panel to **center** the text horizontally across the Stage, as shown in Figure 66.
10. Click **frame 80** on the flyInText layer, then insert a **keyframe**.
11. Change the view to **Fit in Window**.
12. Test the movie, then close the Flash Player window.

You used a motion preset to animate an object by having it fly in from the left side of the Stage.

Create rotating text

1. Insert a **new layer**, then name it **rotateText**.

2. Insert a **keyframe** in frame 24 on the rotateText layer.

3. Click the **Text tool** T on the Tools panel, position the pointer beneath the "A" in "CLASSIC," then click to display a blank text block.

4. Change the Character properties in the Properties panel to **Times New Roman**, size **24**, style **bold** and color **blue** (#0000FF).

5. Type **Annual**, then compare your image to Figure 67.

6. Click the **Selection tool** ✎ on the Tools panel, then use the Align panel to center the text block horizontally across the Stage.

7. Verify Annual is selected, click **Insert** on the menu bar, then click **Motion Tween**.

8. Click **frame 24** on the rotateText layer, then set the Rotate value on the Properties panel to **2** times with a **CW** (clockwise) direction.

9. Point to the end of the tween span (frame 80) until the pointer changes to ↔, then drag the ↔ **pointer** to frame 34, as shown in Figure 68.

10. Click **frame 80** on the rotateText layer, then insert a **keyframe**.

11. Click **frame 1** on the Timeline, then play the movie.

    The Annual text rotates clockwise two times.

You inserted a new layer, created a rotating text block, applied a motion tween to text, and used the Properties panel to rotate the text block.

Figure 67 *Adding the Annual text block*

20 point text

24 point text

Figure 68 *Resizing the motion span from frame 80 to frame 34*

Drag to here

Start here

Figure 69 *Using the Text tool to type ROAD RALLY*

THE CLASSIC CAR CLUB

Annual

ROAD RALLY

TIMELINE   MOTION EDITOR

		1	5	10	15	20	25	30	35	40	45	50	55	60	65	70	75	80
zoom...																		
rotate...																		
flyInT...																		
carGo																		

Figure 70 *Resizing the Text block*

THE CLASSIC CAR CLUB

Annual

ROAD RALLY

Resize and fade in text

1. Insert a **new layer**, name it **zoomText**, then insert a **keyframe** in frame 44 on the layer.

2. Click the **Text tool** T , position the pointer beneath the Annual text block, then type **ROAD RALLY**, as shown in Figure 69.

3. Click the **Selection tool** ▲ , then use the Align panel to center the text block horizontally across the Stage.

4. Click **frame 44** on the zoomText layer, click **Insert** on the menu bar, then click **Motion Tween**.

5. Click **frame 44** on the zoomText layer, click the **Free Transform tool** ▨ , then click the **Scale button** ▨ in the Options area of the Tools panel.

6. Drag the **upper-left corner handle** inward to resize the text block, as shown in Figure 70.

7. Click **frame 80** on the zoomText layer, verify the Scale option ▨ in the Options area of the Tools panel is selected, then drag the **upper-left corner handle** outward to resize the text block to approximately its original size.

8. Test the movie, then close the Flash Player window.

You created a motion animation that caused a text block to zoom out.

Make a text block into a button

1. Insert a **new layer**, then name it **continueBTN**.

2. Insert a **keyframe** in frame 72 on the continueBTN layer.

3. Click the **Text** tool **T** on the Tools panel, position the **Text tool pointer** beneath the car, then type **Click to continue**.

4. Drag the **pointer** over the text to select it, then change the character size on the Properties panel to **12**.

5. Click the **Selection tool** on the Tools panel, center the text block horizontally across the Stage, then compare your image to Figure 71.

6. Verify that the text block is selected, click **Modify** on the menu bar, click **Convert to Symbol**, type **b_continue** in the Name text block, set the Type to **Button**, then click **OK**.

7. Double-click the **text block** to edit the button.

8. Insert a **keyframe** in the Over frame, then set the fill color to the **black color swatch** in the left column of the color palette.

9. Insert a **keyframe** in the Down frame, set the fill color to the **bright green color swatch** in the left column of the color palette.

10. Insert a **keyframe** in the Hit frame, click the **Rectangle tool** on the Tools panel, then draw a **rectangle** that covers the text block, as shown in Figure 72.

11. Click **Scene 1** at the top left of the edit window to return to the main Timeline.

You made the text block into a button.

Figure 71 *Adding a button*

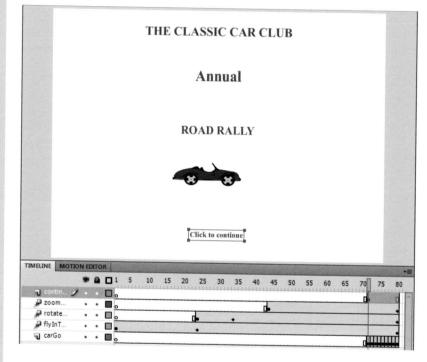

Figure 72 *The rectangle that defines the hit area*

Figure 73 *Adding a play action*

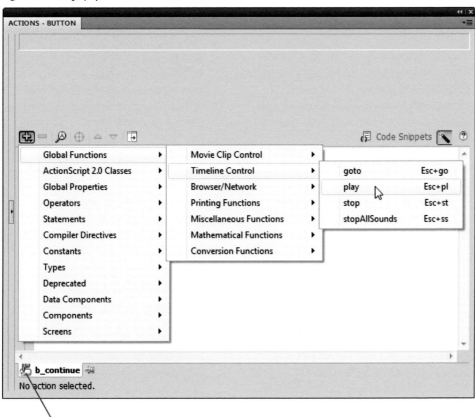

Action will be applied
to this button

Add an action to the button

1. Display the Actions panel.
2. Click the **Selection tool** on the Tools panel, then click the **Click to continue button** on the Stage.
3. Verify the Script Assist button is turned on, then verify the button symbol and b_continue are displayed in the lower-left corner of the Actions panel.

   Note: You need to have ActionScript 2.0 active. You can check your ActionScript version by choosing Publish Settings on the File menu, then selecting the Flash tab.
4. Click the **Add a new item to the script button** in the Script Assist window, point to **Global Functions**, point to **Timeline Control**, then click **play**, as shown in Figure 73.
5. Insert a **new layer**, name it **stopMovie**, then insert a **keyframe** in frame 72 on that layer.
6. Verify that stopmovie:72 is displayed in the lower-left corner of the Actions panel.
7. Click the **Add a new item to the script button** in the Script Assist window, point to **Global Functions**, point to **Timeline Control**, then click **stop**.
8. Click **Control** on the menu bar, point to **Test Movie**, click **in Flash Professional**, then click the **Click to continue button** when it appears.

   The movie begins by playing the animated text blocks. When you click the Click to continue button the movie plays the animated car and then the movie loops back to frame 1.
9. Close the Flash Player movie window, save and close the movie, then exit Flash.

You inserted a play button and added a play action to it, then inserted a stop action on another layer.

Create a motion tween animation.

1. Start Flash, open fl4_11.fla, then save it as **skillsDemo4.fla**.
2. Insert a keyframe in frame 20 on the ballAn layer.
3. Display the Library panel, then drag the g_vball graphic symbol to the lower-left corner of the Stage.
4. Click frame 20 on the ballAn layer, then insert a motion tween.
5. Point to the end of frame 20, when the pointer changes to a double-headed arrow, drag the pointer to frame 40 to set the tween span from frames 20 to 40.
6. With frame 40 selected, drag the object to the lower-right corner of the Stage.
7. Change the view of the Timeline to Small so more frames are in view.
8. Insert a blank keyframe in frame 41.
9. Play the movie, then save your work.

Edit a motion tween.

1. Click frame 20 on the ballAn layer, then use the Selection tool to alter the motion path to form an arc.
2. Use the Subsection tool to display the Bezier handles, use them to form a curved path, then play the movie.
3. Select frame 20, use the Properties panel to change the ease value to **100**, then play the movie.
4. Select frame 20, change the ease value to **−100**, then play the movie.
5. Select frame 40, select the object, use the Properties panel to change the width of the object to **30**, then play the movie. (*Hint*: Verify the Lock width and height values together chain is not broken. This will ensure that when one value is changed, the other value changes proportionally.)
6. Select frame 35, select the object, use the Free transform tool to skew the object, then play the movie.
7. Select frame 40, select the object, use the Properties panel to change the alpha setting to **0**, then play the movie.
8. Change the alpha setting back to **100**.
9. Select frame 40, select the object, then use the Advanced Style option in the COLOR EFFECT area of the Properties panel to create a red color.
10. Lock the ballAn layer.
11. Play the movie, then save your work.

Create a classic tween.

1. Insert a new layer and name it **v-ball**.
2. Insert a keyframe in frame 76 on the v-ball layer.
3. Insert a keyframe in frame 41 on the v-ball layer.
4. Drag an instance of the g_vball symbol from the Library panel to the lower-left corner of the Stage.
5. Insert a keyframe in frame 50 on the v-ball layer and drag the ball to the lower-right corner of the Stage.
6. Click any frame between 41 and 50 on the v-ball layer and insert a Classic tween.
7. Insert a blank keyframe at frame 51 on the v-ball layer.
8. Play the movie, then save your work.

Create a motion guide.

1. Insert a new layer above the v-ball layer and name it **path**.
2. Insert a keyframe in frame 76 on the path layer.
3. Change the path layer to a Guide layer.
4. Insert a keyframe at frame 41 on the path layer.
5. Select the pencil tool, point to the middle of the ball and draw a path with a loop.
6. Insert a keyframe in frame 50 on the path layer.
7. Drag the v-ball layer up to the path layer so that it indents below the path layer.
8. Click frame 41 on the v-ball layer and attach the ball to the path.
9. Click frame 50 on the v-ball layer and attach the ball to the path.
10. Click frame 41 on the v-ball layer and use the Properties panel to orient the ball to the path.
11. Lock the v-ball and path layers.
12. Hide the path layer.
13. Play the movie, then save the movie.

Create a frame-by-frame animation.

1. Insert a new layer above the path layer and name it **corner-ball**.
2. Insert a keyframe in frame 76 on the corner-ball layer.
3. Insert a keyframe in frame 51 on the corner-ball layer, then drag the g_vball graphic from the Library panel to the lower-left corner of the Stage.
4. Insert a blank keyframe in frame 55 on the corner-ball layer, then drag g_vball graphic from the Library panel to the upper-left corner of the Stage.
5. Insert a blank keyframe in frame 59 on the corner-ball layer, then drag the g_vball graphic from the Library panel to the upper-right corner of the Stage.
6. Insert a blank keyframe in the frame 63 on the corner-ball layer, then drag the g_vball graphic from the Library panel to the lower-right corner of the Stage.

Creating Animations

7. Insert a blank keyframe in frame 67 on the corner-ball layer.
8. Lock the corner-ball layer.
9. Change the movie frame rate to 3 frames per second, then play the movie.
10. Change the movie frame rate to 12 frames per second, play the movie, then save your work.

Create a movie clip.

1. Insert a new layer and name it **spin-ball**.
2. Insert a keyframe at frame 76 on the spin-ball layer.
3. Insert a keyframe at frame 51 on the spin-ball layer.
4. Drag an instance of the g_vball symbol from the Library panel to the center of the Stage.
5. Select the ball and convert it to a movie clip with the name **mc_ball**.
6. Display the edit window for the mc_ball movie clip.
7. Create a motion tween that rotates the ball 6 times counterclockwise in 12 frames.
8. Exit the edit window.
9. Insert a blank keyframe in frame 67 of the spin-ball layer.
10. Lock the spin-ball layer.
11. Test the movie, close the Flash Player window, then save your work.

Animate text.

1. Insert a new layer above the spin-ball layer and name it **heading**.
2. Click frame 1 on the heading layer.
3. Use the Text tool to click at the top-center of the Stage, then type **Having fun with a**.
4. Change the text to Arial, 20 point, light gray (#CCCCCC), and bold.
5. Select frame 1 on the heading layer and create a pulse motion using the Motion Presets panel.
6. Drag the motion span to frame 76.
7. Play the movie and save your work.
8. Lock the heading layer.
9. Insert a new layer and name it **zoom**.
10. Insert a keyframe in frame 76 on the zoom layer.
11. Insert a keyframe in frame 11 on the zoom layer.
12. Use the Text tool to type **Volleyball** below the heading, then center it as needed.
13. Select frame 11 on the zoom layer and create a motion tween.
14. Insert a keyframe in frame 20 on the zoom layer.
15. Click frame 11 on the zoom layer and select the text block.
16. Use the Free Transform tool to resize the text block to approximately one-fourth its original size.

17. Select frame 20 on the zoom layer, and resize the text block to approximately the size shown in Figure 74.
18. Lock the zoom layer.
19. Test the movie, close the Flash Player window, save your work.

Create a Shape Tween Animation.

1. Insert a new layer above the zoom layer and name it **morph**.
2. Insert a keyframe in frame 66 on the morph layer.
3. Drag the g_vball symbol to the center of the Stage so it covers the other ball (mc_ball movie clip) in the center of the Stage. Because the mc_ball movie clip (spinning ball) ends in frame 66 and the morph begins in frame 66, this will give the impression of the spinning ball morphing.
4. Use the Properties panel to resize the width to **60 px**. (*Hint*: Verify the Lock width and height values together chain is unbroken. This will ensure that when one value is changed, the other value changes proportionally.)
5. Reposition the smaller ball so it is over the center of the larger ball, then break apart the object.
6. Insert a blank keyframe in frame 76 on the morph layer.

7. Turn on the Edit Multiple Frames feature.
8. Drag the g_fball symbol to the Stage and use the Properties panel to resize the width to 60 px. (*Hint*: Verify the Lock width and height values together chain is not broken. This will ensure that when one value is changed, the other value changes proportionally.)
9. Center the football on top of the volleyball.
10. Break apart the football object.
11. Turn off the Edit Multiple Frames feature.
12. Click frame 66 on the morph layer and insert a shape tween.
13. Test the movie, then close the Flash Player window.
14. Add shape hints to the volleyball and the football.
15. Lock the morph layer.
16. Test the movie, close the Flash Player window, then save your work.
17. Exit Flash.

Figure 74 *Completed Skills Review*

The Ultimate Tours travel company has asked you to design several sample animations for its website. Figure 75 shows a sample home page and the Cruises screen. Using these (or one of the home pages you created in Chapter 3) as a guide, complete the following:

(*Hints*: If you need to insert frames, select the frame where the inserted frame is to go and press [F5] or use the Frame command via the Timeline option on the Insert menu. To insert several frames, select a range of frames and press [F5] or use the Frame command via the Timeline option from the Insert menu. To move the contents of a frame(s), you can select the frame(s) you want to move, then use the Cut and Paste commands via the Timeline option on the Edit menu.)

1. Open ultimateTours3.fla (the file you created in Chapter 3 Project Builder 1) and save it as **ultimateTours4.fla**. (*Hint*: Read through all of the steps and determine how many frames you will need to create the animation before taking any action.)
2. Animate the heading Ultimate Tours on the home page so that it zooms out from a transparent text block.
3. Have the logo appear next.
4. After the heading and logo appear, make the subheading We Specialize in Exotic Adventures appear.
5. Create motion tweens that cause each of the button shapes (Treks, Tours, Cruises) to scroll from the bottom of the Stage to its position on the Stage. Stagger the buttons on the Timeline so they scroll onto the Stage one after the other.
6. Assign a stop action after the home page appears.
7. Add a new layer, name it **cruises headings**, then add the text blocks shown in Figure 75 (Featured Cruises, Panama Canal, Caribbean, Galapagos).
8. Insert keyframes in the ending frames for the Ultimate Tours title, logo, and home button so that they appear on the cruises screen.
9. Import the graphic file ship.gif from the drive and folder where your Data Files are stored to the Library panel. (*Hint*: To import a graphic to the Library panel, click File on the menu bar, point to Import, then click Import to Library. Navigate to the drive and folder where your Data Files are stored, then select the desired file and click Open.)
10. Add a new layer and drag the ship.gif from the Library panel to the stage.
11. Convert the ship graphic to a graphic symbol named **g_ship**, create a motion tween animation that moves the ship across the screen, then alter the motion path to cause a dip in it, similar to the path shown in Figure 75. (*Hint*: Use the Selection tool to create an arc in the path. Then use the Subselection tool to display the Bezier handles and further alter the path.)
12. Orient the boat to the motion path.
13. Assign a goto action to the Cruises button so it jumps to the frame that has the Cruises screen.
14. Test the movie, then compare your movie to the example shown in Figure 75.

PROJECT BUILDER 1
(CONTINUED)

Figure 75   *Sample completed Project Builder 1*

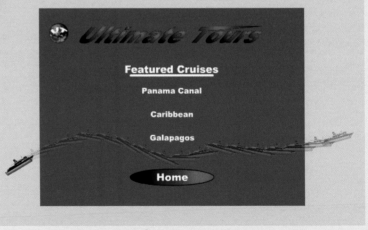

Home page

Featured Cruises Page

You have been asked to demonstrate some of the animation features of Flash. You have decided to create a movie clip that includes a frame-by-frame animation and then use the movie clip in a motion tween animation. Figure 76 shows the stick figure that will walk across the screen and jump up at each line on the sidewalk. The movement across the screen is created using a motion tween. The jumping up is created using a movie clip, as shown in Figure 76.

To complete this project, do the following:

1. Start a new Flash document and name it **jumper4.fla**.

2. Add a background color, sidewalk with lines, and houses or other graphics of your choice, adding layers as needed and naming them appropriately. (*Note*: You can open a previous movie that used the stick figures, such as frameAn, then with your movie open, click the Display movies list arrow under the Library panel tab. This displays a list of all open documents. Click the name of the file that has the stick figures to display its Library panel, then drag the symbols you need to the Pasteboard of your movie. Verify the objects are in the jumper4 Library panel, then delete them from the Pasteboard.)

3. Create a new movie clip. (*Note*: You can create a new movie clip by selecting New Symbol from the Insert menu, then you can drag objects from the Library panel to the movie clip edit window.)

4. Edit the clip to create a frame-by-frame animation of the stick figures walking in place. In the movie clip, place the stick figures one after the other but have one of the stick figures in the sequence placed above the others to create a jumping effect. You will use each stick figure two times in the sequence.

5. Exit the edit window and place the movie clip on the Stage, then create a motion tween that moves the movie clip from the left side to the right side of the Stage.

6. Test the movie. Change the fps setting as needed to create a more realistic effect, then retest the movie. (*Note*: Movie clips do not play from the Stage, you must use the Test Movie command.)

7. Close the Flash Player movie, then save the movie.

Figure 76 *Sample completed Project Builder 2*

Jumper4 movie

mc_stickfigs symbol in edit window

Figure 77 shows a website for kids. Study the figure and complete the following. For each question, indicate how you determined your answer.

1. Connect to the Internet, then go to *www.smokeybear.com/kids*.
2. Open a document in a word processor or open a new Flash document, save the file as **dpc4**, then answer the following questions. (*Hint*: Use the Text tool in Flash.)
   - What seems to be the purpose of this site?
   - Who would be the target audience?
   - How might a frame animation be used in this site?
   - How might a motion tween animation be used?
   - How might a motion guide be used?
   - How might motion animation effects be used?
   - How might the text be animated?

Figure 77 *Design Project*

Smokey Bear image used with the permission of the USDA Forest Service.

Creating Animations

This is a continuation of the Portfolio Project in Chapter 3, which is the development of a personal portfolio. The home page has several categories, including the following:

- Personal data
- Contact information
- Previous employment
- Education
- Samples of your work

In this project, you will create several buttons for the sample animations screen and link them to the animations.

1. Open portfolio3.fla (the file you created in Portfolio Project, Chapter 3) and save it as **portfolio4.fla**.
2. Display the Sample Animation screen and change the heading to Sample Animations.
3. Add layers and create buttons with labels, as shown in Figure 78, for the tweened animation, frame-by-frame animation, motion path animation, and animated text.
4. Create a tween animation or use the passing cars animation from Chapter 3, and link it to the appropriate button on the Sample Animations screen by assigning a goto action to the button.
5. Create a frame-by-frame animation, and link it to the appropriate button on the Sample Animations screen.
6. Create a motion path animation, and link it to the appropriate button on the Sample Animations screen.
7. Create several text animations, using scrolling, rotating, and zooming; then link them to the appropriate button on the Sample Animations screen.
8. Create a shape tween animation, and link it to the appropriate button on the Sample Animations screen.
9. Create a shape tween animation that produces a morphing effect, and link it to the appropriate button on the Sample Animations screen.
10. Create a shape tween animation that produces a morphing effect using shape hints, and link it to the appropriate button on the Sample Animations screen.
11. Add a layer and create a Home button that links the Sample Animations screen to the Home screen.
12. Create frame actions that cause the movie to return to the Sample Animations screen after each animation has been played.
13. Test the movie.
14. Save your work, then compare sample pages from your movie to the example shown for two of the screens in Figure 78.

Figure 78 *Sample completed Portfolio Project*

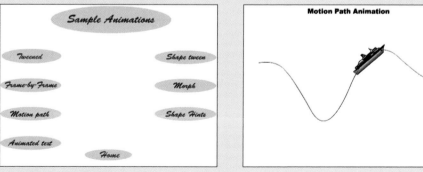

Sample Animations page   A sample animation

CHAPTER 5 CREATING SPECIAL EFFECTS

5

CREATING SPECIAL
EFFECTS

Introduction

Now that you are familiar with the basics of Flash, you can begin to apply some of the special features, such as special effects and sound effects, that can enhance a movie. Special effects can provide variety and add interest to a movie, as well as draw the viewer's attention to a location or event in the movie. One type of special effect is a spotlight that highlights an area(s) of the movie or reveals selected content on the Stage. You can use sound effects to enhance a movie by creating moods and dramatizing events. In addition, you can add sound to a button to provide feedback to the viewer when the button is clicked. Video can be incorporated into a Flash movie and effects, such as fading in and out, can be applied to the display of the video.

Another type of special effect is an animated navigation bar, for example, one that causes a drop-down menu to open when the user rolls over a button. This effect can be created using masks and invisible buttons.

Additional features of Adobe Flash CS5 are Inverse Kinematics, 3D Effects, and the Deco tool. Inverse Kinematics allows you to easily create character animations and even allows users to interact with the character when viewing the Flash movie. The 3D tools allow you to create 3D effects such as objects moving and rotating through 3D space. The Deco tool provides a variety of drawing effects that can be used to create environments and decorative patterns.

Create A
MASK EFFECT

What You'll Do

Classic Car lub

In this lesson, you will apply a mask effect.

Understanding Mask Layers

A **mask layer** allows you to cover up the objects on one or more layers and, at the same time, create a window through which you can view objects on those layer(s). You can determine the size and shape of the window and specify whether it moves around the Stage. Moving the window around the Stage can create effects such as a spotlight that highlights certain content on the Stage, drawing the viewer's attention to a specific location. Because the window can move around the Stage, you can use a mask layer to reveal only the area of the Stage and the objects you want the viewer to see.

You need at least two layers on the Timeline when you are working with a mask layer. One layer, called the mask layer, contains the window object through which you view the objects, which are on a second layer below the mask layer. The second layer, called the masked layer, contains the object(s) that are viewed through the window. Figure 1 shows how a mask layer works: The top part of the figure shows the mask layer with the window in the shape of a circle. The next part of the figure shows the layer to be masked. The last part of the figure shows the result of applying the mask. Figure 1 illustrates the simplest use of a mask layer. In most cases, you want to have other objects appear on the Stage and have the mask layer affect only a certain portion of the Stage.

The process for using a mask layer follows:

- Select an original layer that will become the masked layer—it contains the objects that you want to display through the mask layer window.
- Insert a new layer above the masked layer that will become the mask layer. A mask layer always masks the layer(s) immediately below it.
- Draw a filled shape, such as a circle, or create an instance of a symbol that will become the window on the mask layer. Flash ignores bitmaps, gradients, transparency colors, and line styles on a mask layer. On a mask layer, filled areas become transparent and non-filled areas become opaque when viewed over a masked layer.

Creating Special Effects

- Select the new layer and open the Layer Properties dialog box. To open the Layer Properties dialog box, click Modify on the menu bar, point to the Timeline, then click Layer Properties. In the Layer Properties dialog box, select Mask as the layer type. Flash converts the layer to the mask layer.

- Select the original layer and open the Layer Properties dialog box, then select Masked as the layer type. Flash converts the layer to the masked layer.
- Lock both the mask and masked layers.
- To mask additional layers: Drag an existing layer beneath the mask layer, or create a new layer beneath the mask layer

and use the Layer Properties dialog box to convert it to a masked layer.
- To unlink a masked layer: Drag it above the mask layer, or select it and select Normal from the Layer Properties dialog box.

Figure 1 *A mask layer with a window*

Mask layer with window (the filled circle, which becomes transparent when viewed over a masked layer)

Masked layer before applying mask

Masked layer after applying mask; you only see what appears through the window

Create a mask layer

1. Open fl5_1.fla, then save it as **classicCC.fla**.

2. Insert a **new layer**, name it **mask**, then click **frame 1** on the mask layer.

3. Select the **Oval tool** on the Tools panel, set the **Stroke Color** to **No Stroke** on the top row of the color palette.

4. Set the Fill Color to the **black color swatch** in the left column of the color palette.

5. Draw the circle shown in Figure 2, click the **Selection tool** on the Tools panel, then drag a **marquee** around the circle to select it.

6. Click **Insert** on the menu bar, click **Motion Tween**, then click **OK** to convert the drawing into a symbol so that it can be tweened.

   Note: Flash converts the object to a movie symbol as the default symbol type. To convert the object to a different symbol type, you must convert the symbol manually.

7. Click **frame 40** on the mask layer, then drag the **circle** to the position shown in Figure 3.

8. Click **mask** on the Timeline to select the mask layer, click **Modify** on the menu bar, point to **Timeline**, then click **Layer Properties**.

9. Verify that the Show check box is selected in the Name area, click the **Lock check box** to select it, click the **Mask option button** in the Type area, then click **OK**.

   The mask layer has a shaded mask icon next to it on the Timeline.

   Hint: Alternately, you can lock the layer using the Lock This Layer icon on the Timeline.

   (continued)

Figure 2 *Object to be used as the window on a mask layer*

Figure 3 *Repositioning the circle*

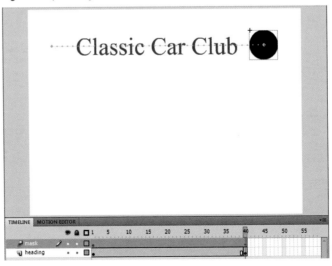

Creating Special Effects

Figure 4 *The completed Layer Properties dialog box*

*Your color
may vary*

*Lock
selected*

10. Play the movie from frame 1 and notice how the circle object covers the text on the heading layer as it moves across the Stage.

    Note: The circle object will not become transparent until a masked layer is created beneath it.

You created a mask layer containing a circle object that moves across the Stage.

Create a masked layer

1. Click **heading** on the Timeline to select the heading layer, click **Modify** on the menu bar, point to **Timeline,** then click **Layer Properties** to open the Layer Properties dialog box.

2. Verify that the Show check box is selected in the Name area, click the **Lock check box** to select it, click the **Masked option button** in the Type area, compare your dialog box to Figure 4, then click **OK.**

   The text on the Stage seems to disappear. The heading layer is indented and has a shaded masked icon next to it on the Timeline.

3. Play the movie and notice how the circle object acts as a window to display the text on the heading layer.

4. Click **Control** on the menu bar, point to **Test Movie,** then click **in Flash Professional.**

5. View the movie, then close the Flash Player window.

6. Save your work, then close the movie.

You used the Layer Properties dialog box to create a masked layer.

Add SOUND

What You'll Do

In this lesson, you will add sound to an animation and to a button click event.

Incorporating Animation and Sound

Sound can be extremely useful in a Flash movie. Sounds are often the only effective way to convey an idea, elicit an emotion, dramatize a point, and provide feedback to a user's action, such as clicking a button. How would you describe in words or show in an animation the sound a whale makes? Think about how chilling it is to hear the footsteps on the stairway of a haunted house. Consider how useful it is to hear the pronunciation of "buenos dias" as you are studying Spanish. All types of sounds can be incorporated into a Flash movie: for example, CD-quality music that might be used as background for a movie; narrations that help explain what the user is seeing; various sound effects, such as a car horn beeping; and recordings of special events, such as a presidential speech or a rock concert.

The process for adding a sound to a movie follows:

- Import a sound file into a Flash movie; Flash places the sound file in the movie's library.
- Create a new layer.
- Select the desired frame on the new layer where you want the sound to play and drag the sound symbol to the Stage.

You can place more than one sound file on a layer, and you can place sounds on layers that have other objects. However, it is recommended that you place each sound on a separate layer so that it is easier to identify and edit. In Figure 5, the sound layer shows a wave pattern that extends from frame 1 to frame 24. The wave pattern gives some indication of the volume of the sound at any particular frame. The higher spikes in the pattern indicate a louder sound. The wave pattern also gives some indication of the pitch. The denser the wave pattern, the lower the pitch. You can alter the sound by adding or removing frames. However, removing frames may create undesired effects. It is best to make changes to a sound file using a sound-editing program.

You can use options in the Properties panel, as shown in Figure 6, to specify special effects (such as fade in and fade out) and to synchronize a sound to an event (such as clicking a button). You can import the following sound file formats into Flash:

- ASND (Windows or Macintosh)
- WAV (Windows only)
- AIFF (Macintosh only)
- MP3 (Windows or Macintosh)

If you have QuickTime 4 or later installed on your computer, you can import these additional sound file formats:

- AIFF (Windows or Macintosh)
- Sound Designer II (Macintosh only)
- Sound Only QuickTime Movies (Windows or Macintosh)
- Sun AU (Windows or Macintosh)
- System 7 Sounds (Macintosh only)
- WAV (Windows or Macintosh)

Figure 5 *A wave pattern displayed on a sound layer*

Figure 6 *Sound Effect options in the Properties panel*

Click Sync button to see menu

Effect menu

Add sound to a movie

1. Open fl5_2.fla, then save it as **rallySnd.fla**.

2. Play the movie and notice that there is no sound.

3. Click the **stopMovie layer**, insert a **new layer**, then name it **carSnd**.

4. Insert a **keyframe** in frame 72 on the carSnd layer.

5. Click **File** on the menu bar, point to **Import**, then click **Import to Library**.

6. Use the Import to Library dialog box to navigate to the drive and folder where your Data Files are stored, click the **CarSnd.wav file**, then click **Open**.

7. Display the Library panel, click **CarSnd.wav**, then click the **Play button ▶** in the Preview window.

8. Click **frame 72** on the carSnd layer.

9. Drag the **CarSnd sound symbol** 🔊 to the Stage, as shown in Figure 7.

   After releasing the mouse button, notice the wave pattern that has been placed on the carSnd layer starting in frame 72.

TIP The wave pattern may not appear on the layer until the movie is played one time.

10. Change the frame rate to **12 fps**.

11. Click **Control** on the menu bar, point to **Test Movie**, then click **in Flash Professional**.

12. Click the **Click to continue button** to test the sound.

13. Close the Flash Player window.

You imported a sound and added it to a movie.

Figure 7 *Dragging the CarSnd symbol to the Stage*

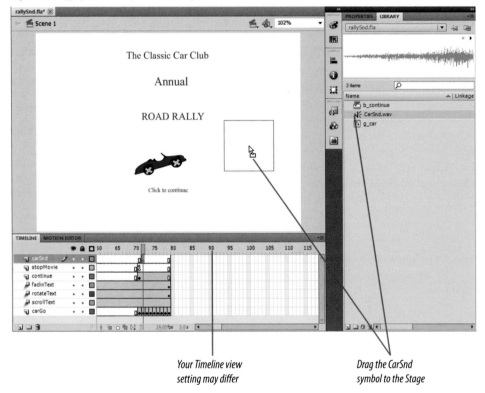

Your Timeline view setting may differ

Drag the CarSnd symbol to the Stage

Figure 8 *The Timeline for the button with the sound layer*

Sound wave pattern appears in the selected frame

Add sound to a button

1. Click **frame 71** on the carSnd layer.

2. Click the **Selection tool** ▶ on the Tools panel, drag a **marquee** around "Click to continue" to select the button, then double-click the **button** to display the button's Timeline.

3. Insert a **new layer** above Layer 1, then name it **sound**.

4. Click the **Down frame** on the sound layer, click **Insert** on the menu bar, point to **Timeline**, then click **Blank Keyframe**.

5. Click **File** on the menu bar, point to **Import**, then click **Import to Library**.

6. Use the Import to Library dialog box to navigate to the drive and folder where your Data Files are stored, click the **beep.wav file**, then click **Open**.

7. Display the Properties panel, click the **Name list arrow** in the SOUND area, then click **beep.wav**.

8. Click the **Sync list arrow** in the Properties panel, click **Event**, then compare your screen to Figure 8.

9. Click **Scene 1** on the upper left of the edit window title bar to display the main Timeline.

10. Test the movie.

11. Click the **Click to continue button** and listen to the sounds, then close the Flash Player window.

12. Save your work, then close the movie.

You added a sound layer to a button, imported a sound, then attached the sound to the button.

Add
VIDEO

What You'll Do

A FIREWORKS CELEBRATION

In this lesson, you will import a video, add actions to video control buttons, and then synchronize sound to a video clip.

Incorporating Video

Adobe Flash allows you to import FLV (Flash video) files that then can be used in a Flash document. Flash provides several ways to add video to a movie, depending on the application and, especially, the file size. Video content can be embedded directly into a Flash document, progressively downloaded, or streamed.

Embedded video becomes part of the SWF file similar to other objects, such as sound and graphics. A placeholder appears on the Stage and is used to display the video during playback. If the video is imported as a movie clip symbol, then the placeholder can be edited, including rotating, resizing, and even animating it. Because embedded video becomes part of the SWF file, the technique of embedding video is best used for small video clips in order to keep the document file size small. The process for embedding video is to import a video file using the Import Video Wizard. Then, you place the video on the Stage and add controls as desired. Figure 9 shows a video placeholder

for an embedded video. The video file (fireworks.flv) is in the Library panel and the video layer on the Timeline contains the video object. The embedded video plays when the Play button is clicked.

Progressive downloading allows you to use ActionScript to load an external FLV file into a SWF file; the video then plays when the SWF file is played. With progressive downloading, the FLV file resides outside the SWF file. As a result, the SWF file size can be kept smaller than when the video is embedded in the Flash document. The video begins playing soon after the first part of the file has been downloaded.

Streaming video provides a constant connection between the user and the video delivery. Streaming has several advantages over the other methods of delivering video, including starting the video more quickly and allowing for live video delivery. However, streaming video requires the Flash Media Server, an Adobe software product designed specifically for streaming video content.

Using the Import Video Wizard

The Import Video Wizard is used to import FLV files into Flash documents. The wizard, in a step-by-step process, leads you through a series of windows that allow you to select the file to be imported and the deployment method (embedded, progressive, streaming). In addition, you can specify whether or not to have the video converted to a movie clip symbol which allows you to animate the placeholder. The wizard appears when you choose the Import Video command from the Import option on the File menu.

Using the Adobe Media Encoder

The Adobe Media Encoder is an application used by Flash to convert various video file formats, such as .mov, .avi, and .mpeg, to the FLV (Flash Video) format so the videos can be used with Flash. The Encoder allows you to, among other things, choose the size of the placeholder the video will play in, edit the video, and insert cue points that can be used to synchronize the video with animations and sound. Figure 10 shows the Encoder ready to convert the fireworks.mov video (Source Name) to fireworks.flv (Output File). The Start Queue button is used to start the process. When the conversion is complete, a green check mark is displayed in the Status column. The Adobe Media Encoder can be accessed through the Import Video Wizard.

Figure 9 *An embedded video*

Play button   Pause button   Video placeholder

Figure 10 *The Adobe Media Encoder*

Import a video

1. Open fl5_3.fla, then save it as **fireworks.fla**.

   Note: If the Missing Font Warning message appears, click Use Default.

   The movie has four layers and 85 frames. The actions layer has a stop action in frame 1. The heading layer contains the text object. The controls layer contains start and pause buttons that will be used to control the video. The backdrop layer contains a blue gradient backdrop object. The Library panel contains the two button symbols and a sound file as well as graphics and movie clip files.

2. Set the view to **Fit in Window**.

3. Insert a **new layer** above the controls layer, name it **video**, then click **frame 1** on the video layer.

4. Click **File** on the menu bar, point to **Import**, then click **Import Video**.

   The Import Video Wizard begins by asking for the path to the video file and the desired method for importing the file, as shown in Figure 11.

5. Click the **Embed FLV in SWF and play in timeline option button**.

6. Click **Browse**, navigate to the drive and folder where your Data Files are stored, click **fireworks.mov**, then click **Open**.

   A message appears indicating that the video format is not valid for embedding video. You must convert the file to the FLV format.

7. Click **OK**, then click the **Launch Adobe Media Encoder button**.

   (continued)

Figure 11 *The Import Video Wizard*

Creating Special Effects

Figure 12 *The completed Select Video window*

Your path may vary

After several moments the encoder opens.

Note: Click the Adobe Media Encoder button on the taskbar if the encoder does not open automatically in its own window.

8. Click **Start Queue**, then, when the process is done as indicated by a green check mark, close the encoder window.

9. Click **OK** to close the message window if one opens, then click the **Browse button**.

10. Click **fireworks.flv**, then click **Open**.

    Note: If you do not see fireworks.flv, navigate to the drive and folder where you saved your solution file.

    The Select Video screen now displays the path to the fireworks.flv file, as shown in Figure 12.

11. Click **Next** (Win) or **Continue** (Mac) in the wizard.

    The Embedding window opens, which allows you to specify how you would like to embed the video.

12. Read the screen and verify all the options have a check mark.

13. Click **Next** (Win) or **Continue** (Mac).

14. Read the Finish Video Import screen, then click **Finish**.

    The video is encoded and placed on the Stage and in the Library panel.

You imported a video then specified the encoding and embed type.

Attach actions to video control buttons

1. Test the movie, then click the **control buttons**.

   Nothing happens because there is a stop action in frame 1 and no actions have been assigned to the buttons.

2. Close the Flash Player window.

3. Open the Actions panel.

4. Click the **play button** on the Stage, then verify the btn_play button symbol appears in the lower-left corner of the Script pane.

5. Turn on Script Assist if it is off.

6. Click the **Add a new item to the script button** ⚓, point to **Global Functions**, point to **Timeline Control**, then click **play** as shown in Figure 13.

7. Click the **Pause button** on the Stage, then verify the btn_pause button symbol appears in the lower-left corner of the Script pane.

8. Click the **Add a new item to the script button** ⚓, point to **Global Functions**, point to **Timeline Control**, then click **stop**.

9. Close the Actions panel.

10. Test the movie, click the **play button**, then click the **pause button**.

    The video plays, however there is no sound.

11. Close the Flash Player window.

You assigned play and stop actions to video control buttons.

Figure 13 *Using Script Assist to assign a play action to a button*

Play button selected

Figure 14 *The completed Properties panel*

Synchronize sound to a video clip

1. Insert a **new layer** above the video layer, then name it **sound**.

2. Click **frame 1** on the sound layer.

3. Display the Properties panel, then display the SOUND area options.

4. Click the **Name list arrow** in the SOUND area, then click **fireworks.wav**.

5. Click the **Sync sound list arrow** in the SOUND area, then click **Stream**.

6. Click the **Repeat list arrow**, click **Loop**, then compare your Properties panel to Figure 14.

7. Test the movie, click the **play button**, then click the **pause button**.

8. Close the Flash Player window.

9. Lock all layers.

10. Save your work, then close the file.

You inserted a layer, then you synchronized a sound to the video clip.

Create an Animated
NAVIGATION BAR

What You'll Do

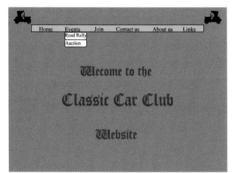

In this lesson, you will work through the process to create one drop-down menu. A navigation bar has been provided, as well as the necessary buttons.

Understanding Animated Navigation Bars

A common navigation scheme for a website is a navigation bar with drop-down menus, such as the one shown in Figure 15. Using a navigation bar has several advantages. First, it allows the developer to provide several menu options to the user without cluttering the screen, thereby providing more screen space for the website content. Second, it allows the user to go quickly to a location on the site without having to navigate several screens to find the desired content. Third, it provides consistency in function and appearance, making it easy for users to learn and work with the navigation scheme.

There are various ways to create drop-down menus using the animation capabilities of Flash and ActionScript. One common technique allows you to give the illusion of a drop-down menu by using masks that

Figure 15 *Navigation bar with drop-down menus*

reveal the menu. When the user points to (rolls over) a menu item on the navigation bar, a list or "menu" of buttons is displayed ("drops down"). Then the user can click a button, which might go to another location in the website or trigger some other action, depending on the action assigned to the button. The dropping down of the list is actually an illusion created by using a mask to "uncover" the menu options.

The process for creating a drop-down menu follows:

- **Create a navigation bar.** This could be as basic as a background graphic in the shape of a rectangle with buttons that represent the navigation bar menu items.
- **Position the drop-down buttons.** Add a drop-down buttons layer beneath the navigation bar layer. Next, select an empty frame adjacent to the first frame containing the navigation bar. Place the buttons that will be used to create the drop down list on the Stage below their respective menu items on the navigation bar. For example, if the navigation bar has an Events button with two choices, Road Rally and Auction, that you want

to appear as buttons on a drop-down menu, position these two buttons below the Events button on the drop-down buttons layer.

- **Create an animated mask.** Add a mask layer above the drop-down buttons layer and create an animation of an object that starts above the drop-down buttons and moves down to reveal them. Then change the layer to a mask layer and the drop-down buttons layer to a masked layer.
- **Assign actions to the drop-down buttons.** Select each drop-down button and assign an action, such as "on (release) gotoAndPlay."
- **Assign a roll over action to the navigation bar menu item button.** The desired effect is to have the drop-down buttons appear when the user points to a navigation bar button. Therefore, you need to assign an "on rollOver" action to the navigation bar button that causes the playhead to go to the frame that plays the animation on the mask layer. This can be done using the Script Assist feature.
- **Create an invisible button.** When the user points to a navigation bar button, the drop-down menu appears showing the drop-down buttons. There needs to be a way to have the menu disappear when the user points away from the navigation bar button. This can be done by creating a button on a layer below the masked layer. This button is slightly larger than the drop-down buttons and their navigation bar button, as shown in Figure 16. A rollOver action is assigned to this

button so that when the user rolls off the drop-down or navigation bar buttons, he or she rolls onto this button and the action is carried out. This button should be made transparent so the user does not see it.

Using Frame Labels

Until now, you have worked with frame numbers in ActionScript code when creating a goto action. Frame labels can also be used in the code. You can assign a label to a frame as an identifier. For example, you could assign the label home to frame 10 and then create a goto home action that will cause the playhead to jump to frame 10. One advantage of using frame labels is that if you insert frames on the Timeline, the label adjusts for the added frames. So, you do not have to change the ActionScript that uses the frame label. Another advantage is that the descriptive labels help you identify parts

of the movie as you work with the Timeline. You assign a frame label by selecting the desired frame and typing a label in the Frame text box in the Properties panel.

Understanding Scenes

When you create a movie, the phrase Scene 1 appears above the Stage. You can add scenes to a movie at any time. Scenes are one way to organize long movies. For example, a movie created for a website could be divided into several scenes: an introduction, a home page, and content pages. Each scene has its own Timeline. You can insert new scenes by using the Insert menu and view them using the Other Panels option on the Windows menu. Scenes can be given descriptive names, which will help you find them easily if you need to edit a particular scene. One drawback to using scenes is potentially larger file sizes.

Figure 16 *A button that will be assigned a rollOver action*

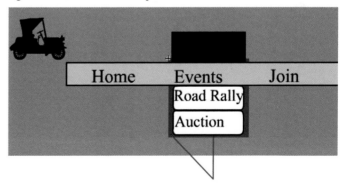

When the user rolls over any part of the blue button with the pointer, a script is executed that causes the drop-down menu to disappear

Position the drop-down buttons

1. Open fl5_4.fla, then save it as **navBar.fla**.

2. Click the **homeBkgrnd layer**, insert a **new layer**, then name it **roadRally**.

3. Click **frame 2** on the roadRally layer, then insert a **keyframe**.

4. Display the Library panel, open the Buttons folder, then drag the **b_roadRally button** to the position just below the Events button on the Navigation bar, as shown in Figure 17.

5. Insert a **new layer** above the homeBkgrnd layer, then name it **auction**.

6. Click **frame 2** on the auction layer, then insert a **keyframe**.

7. Drag the **b_auction button** from the Library panel and position it below the b_roadRally button.

8. Click the **Zoom tool** 🔍 on the Tools panel, then click the **Events button** on the navigation bar to enlarge the view.

9. Click the **Selection tool** ⭤ on the Tools panel, then click each button and use the arrow keys to position each button, as shown in Figure 18.

    The bottom border of the navigation bar must overlap the top line of the Road Rally button, and the bottom border of the Road Rally button must overlap the top border of the Auction button.

You placed the drop-down buttons on the Stage and repositioned them.

Figure 17 *Positioning the b_roadRally button*

The expand icon indicates that this is a folder layer. In this case, all of navigation bar buttons are within this folder. Clicking the arrow reveals the contents of the folder.

Drag from the library to here

Figure 18 *Positioning the buttons*

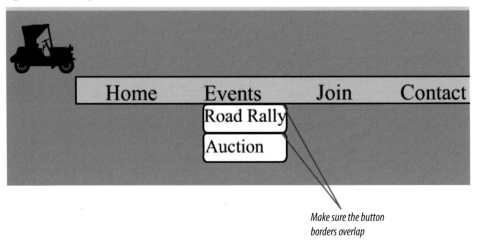

Make sure the button borders overlap

Figure 19 *The drawn rectangle that covers the buttons*

Home   Events   Join

Figure 20 *Dragging the rectangle above the buttons*

Home   Events   Join

Align bottom of
rectangle with bottom
of navigation bar

Selected object may
have a dot pattern

Figure 21 *Positioning the rectangle over the buttons*

Home   Events   Join   Contact

Add a mask layer

1. Click the **roadRally layer**, insert a **new layer** above the roadRally layer, then name it **mask**.

2. Click **frame 2** on the mask layer, then insert a **keyframe**.

3. Select the **Rectangle tool** ▢ on the Tools panel, set the Stroke Color to **none** ◹ , then set the Fill Color to **black**.

4. Draw a **rectangle** that covers the buttons, as shown in Figure 19.

5. Click the **Selection tool** ▶ on the Tools panel, then drag the **rectangle** to above the buttons, as shown in Figure 20.

6. Verify the rectangle is selected, click **Insert** on the menu bar, click **Motion Tween**, then click **OK**.

   Note: Flash automatically converts the object to a movie symbol, which can have a motion tween applied to it. If you want the object to be a different type of symbol, you need to convert the object to the symbol type of your choice before inserting the motion tween.

7. Click **frame 5** on the mask layer, then insert a **keyframe**.

8. Use the **Selection tool** ▶ to move the **rectangle**, as shown in Figure 21.

9. Click **mask** on the Timeline, click **Modify** on the menu bar, point to **Timeline**, click **Layer Properties**, click the **Mask option button**, then click **OK**.

10. Click **roadRally** on the Timeline.

(continued)

11. Click **Modify** on the menu bar, point to **Timeline**, click **Layer Properties**, click the **Masked option button**, then click **OK**.

12. Click **auction** on the Timeline, then repeat step 11.

13. Drag the **playhead** along the Timeline, noticing how the mask hides and reveals the buttons.

You added a mask that animates to hide and reveal the menu buttons.

Assign an action to a drop-down button

1. Change the view to **Fit in Window.**

2. Click **frame 2** on the roadRally layer, then click the **Road Rally button** to select it.

3. Open the **Actions panel** and verify the Script Assist button is active and b_roadRally is displayed in the lower-left corner of the Script pane, as shown in Figure 22.

   b_roadRally in the lower-left corner of the Script pane tells you that the b_roadRally button symbol is selected on the Stage and that the ActionScript you create will apply to this object.

4. Click the **Add a new item to the script icon** , point to **Global Functions**, point to **Timeline Control**, then click **goto.**

5. Click the **Scene list arrow**, point to **Scene 2** as shown in Figure 23, then click.

6. Verify the Type is set to Frame Number and the Frame is set to 1.

7. Collapse the Actions panel.

You used the Script Assist window to assign a goto action to a menu button.

Figure 22 *The Actions panel with the b_roadRally button selected*

b_roadRally button indicating the action to be created will be assigned to the button

Script Assist is active

Figure 23 *Selecting the scene to go to*

Scenes, which have their own Timeline, are a way to organize large movies. In this case, Scene 2 contains the Road Rally screen for the website.

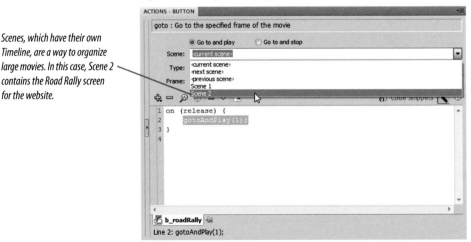

Creating Special Effects

Figure 24 *Specifying a frame label*

Figure 25 *The completed Actions panel*

Frame label

b_events button symbol
indicating the action will
be assigned to this button

Frame label used in the
gotoAndPlay command

1. Insert a **new layer** at the top of the Timeline, name it **labels**, then insert a **keyframe** in frame 2 on the labels layer.

2. Display the Properties panel, click inside the **Name text box** in the LABEL area, then type **eventsMenu**, as shown in Figure 24.

3. Click the **Events button** on the Stage to select it.

4. Expand the Actions panel, then verify b_events is displayed in the lower-left corner of the Script pane.

5. Click the **Add a new item to the script icon** 🕂 , point to **Global Functions**, point to **Movie Clip Control**, then click **on**.

6. Click the **Release check box** to deselect it, then click the **Roll Over check box** to select it.

7. Click the **Add a new item to the script icon** 🕂 , point to **Global Functions**, point to **Timeline Control**, then click **goto**.

8. Click the **Type list arrow**, then click **Frame Label**.

9. Click the **Frame list arrow**, then click **eventsMenu**.

   Your screen should resemble Figure 25.

10. Click **Control** on the menu bar, point to **Test Movie**, then click **in Flash Professional**.

11. Point to **Events**, then click **Road Rally**.

12. Close the Flash Player window, collapse the Actions panel, then save your work.

You added a frame label and assigned a rollOver action using the frame label.

Add an invisible button

1. Click **Control** on the menu bar, point to **Test Movie**, then click **in Flash Professional**.

2. Move the pointer over Events on the navigation bar, then move the pointer away from Events.

   Notice that when you point to Events, the drop-down menu appears. However, when you move the pointer away from the menu, it does not disappear.

3. Close the Flash Player window.

4. Insert a **new layer** above the homeBkgrnd layer, then name it **rollOver**.

5. Insert a **keyframe** in frame 2 on the rollOver layer.

6. Click the **Zoom tool** 🔍 on the Tools panel, then click the **Events button** on the navigation bar to enlarge the view.

7. Select the **Rectangle tool** 🔲, on the Tools panel, verify that the Stroke Color is set to **none**, then set the Fill Color to **blue**.

8. Draw a **rectangle**, as shown in Figure 26.

9. Click the **Selection tool** ▶ on the Tools panel, then click the **blue rectangle** to select it.

10. Click **Modify** on the menu bar, then click **Convert to Symbol**.

11. Type **b_rollOver** for the name, click the **Type list arrow**, click **Button**, then click **OK**.

12. Expand the Actions panel.

(continued)

Figure 26 *Drawing the rectangle*

Figure 27 *The Actions panel displaying ActionScript assigned to the b_rollOver button symbol*

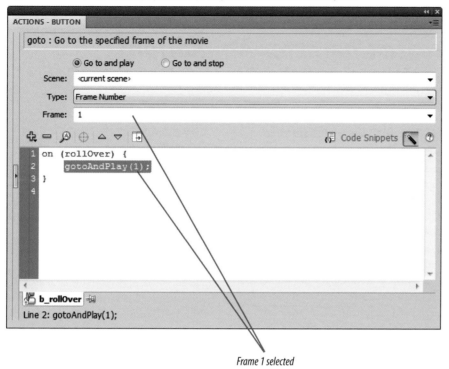

Frame 1 selected

13. Verify the rollOver button is selected and b_rollOver is displayed in the lower-left corner of the Script pane.

14. Click the **Add a new item to the script icon** 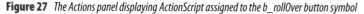, point to **Global Functions**, point to **Movie Clip Control**, then click **on**.

15. Click the **Release check box** to deselect it, then click the **Roll Over check box** to select it.

16. Click the **Add a new item to the script icon**, point to **Global Functions**, point to **Timeline Control**, then click **goto**.

17. Verify Frame 1 is specified, as shown in Figure 27.

18. Close the Actions panel.

19. Click the **Style list arrow** in the COLOR EFFECT area of the Properties panel, click **Alpha**, then set the percentage to **0**.

20. Click **Control** on the menu bar, point to **Test Movie**, then click **in Flash Professional**.

21. Point to **Events** to display the drop-down menu, then slowly move the pointer away from Events.

    The drop-down menu disappears.

22. Close the Flash Player window, then save and close the movie.

You added a button and assigned a rollOver action to it, then made the button transparent.

Create Character Animations
USING INVERSE KINEMATICS

What You'll Do

In this lesson, you will use the bone tool to create a character animation and create a movie clip that can be manipulated by the viewer.

Understanding Inverse Kinematics

One way to create character animations is to use the frame-by-frame process in which you place individually drawn objects into a series of successive frames. You did this with the stick figure graphics in an earlier chapter. Those graphics were simple to draw. However, if you have more complex drawings, such as fill shapes that are more realistic, and if you want to create animations that show an unlimited number of poses, the time required to develop all of the necessary drawings would be considerable.

Flash provides a process that allows you to create a single image and add a structure to the image that can be used to animate the various parts of the image. The process is called **Inverse Kinematics (IK)** and involves creating an articulated structure of bones that allow you to link the parts of an image. Once the bone structure is created, you can animate the image by changing the position of any of its parts. The bone structure causes the related parts to animate in a natural way. For example, if you draw an image of a person, create the bone structure, and then move the person's right foot, then all parts of the leg (lower leg, knee, upper leg) respond. This makes it easy to animate various movements.

Figure 28 shows a drawing of a character before and after the bone structure is added. Figure 29 shows how moving the right foot moves the entire leg. The image is made up of several small drawings, each one converted to a graphic symbol. These include a head, torso, upper and lower arms, upper and lower legs, hips, and feet. Together these form the IK object.

Creating the Bone Structure

The bone structure can be applied to a single drawn shape, such as an oval created with the Flash drawing tools. More often it is applied to an image, such as a character, made up of several drawings. When this is the case, each drawing is converted to a graphic symbol or a movie clip symbol and then assembled to form the desired image. If you import a graphic, it needs to be broken apart using the Modify menu and the individual parts of the imported graphic converted to graphic symbols or movie clip symbols. However, if the imported graphic

Creating Special Effects

has only one part (such as a bitmap), it needs to be broken apart and treated as a single drawn shape.

Once the image is ready, you use the Bone tool to create the bone structure, called the armature, by clicking and dragging the Bone tool pointer to link one part of the image to another. You continue adding bones to the structure until all parts of the image are linked. For a human form you would link the head to the torso and the torso to the upper left arm and the upper left arm to the lower left arm, and so on. The bones in an armature are connected to each other in a parent-child hierarchy, so that adjusting the child adjusts the parent.

Animating the IK Object

As you are creating the bone structure, a layer named Armature is added to the Timeline, and the image with the bone structure is placed in frame 1 on that layer. This new layer is called a **pose layer**. Each pose layer can contain only one armature and its associated image. Animating the image is done on this layer by inserting a keyframe in any frame after frame 1 on the Armature layer and then changing the position of one or more of the bones. This is referred to as creating a pose. Once you specify the start and end positions of the image, Flash interpolates the position of the parts of the image for the in-between frames. So, when one bone moves, the other connected bones move in relation to it. Additional poses can be set along the Timeline by inserting keyframes and adjusting the bone structure. Animations of IK objects, other than those within movie clips, only allow you to change the shape, position, and ease in the animation.

Figure 28 *Drawings showing before and after the bone structure is added*

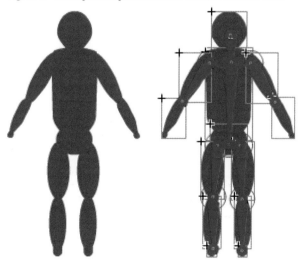

Figure 29 *Moving the foot moves the other parts of the leg*

Creating a Movie Clip with an IK Object

Movie clips provide a great deal of flexibility when animating IK objects. You can change properties such as the color effect and you can nest one movie clip within another. So, you could have a movie clip of a character walking and nest another movie clip within it to have its mouth move. In addition, you can apply a motion tween to a movie clip.

So, you could have a movie clip of a character walking and have it play within a motion tween which causes the character (movie clip) to jump over an obstacle.

Runtime Feature

Flash provides a runtime feature for manipulation of an IK object. That is, you can allow the user to click the object and adjust the image. This is useful if you are creating a game or just wanting to provide some interaction on a website. The process is to click a frame on the Armature layer, then use the Properties panel to set the Type to Runtime. The runtime feature only works with IK structures connected to drawn shapes or movie clip symbols, not graphic or button symbols. In addition, only one pose can used.

IK Objects

As you are working with IK objects, keep in mind the following:

- The Undo feature can be used to undo a series of actions such as undoing a mistake made when creating the bone structure.
- The bone structure may disappear as you are working on it. This could be caused by going outside the image as you are connecting the parts of the image. If the bone structure disappears, use the Undo feature to Undo your last action.
- To delete an individual bone and all of its children, click the bone and press [Delete]. You can select multiple bones to delete by holding down [Shift] and clicking each bone.
- To delete all bones, select the image and choose the Break Apart command from the Modify menu.
- To create IK animations, ActionScript 3.0 and Flash Player 10 need to be specified in the Publish Settings dialog box, which is displayed by choosing Publish Settings from the File menu.

Creating Special Effects

Figure 30 *Connecting the head and torso*

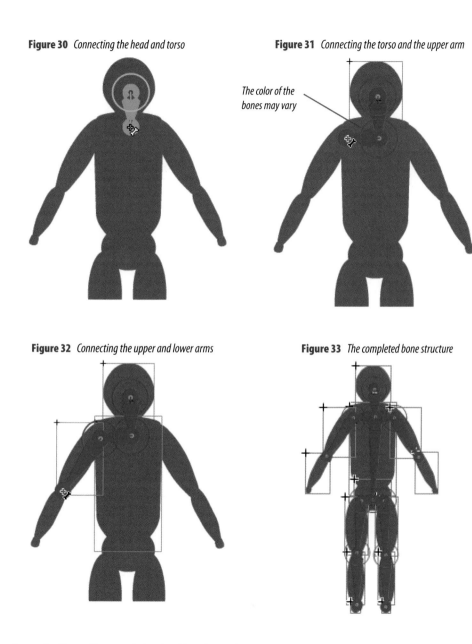

Figure 31 *Connecting the torso and the upper arm*

The color of the bones may vary

Figure 32 *Connecting the upper and lower arms*

Figure 33 *The completed bone structure*

Create the bone structure

1. Open fl5_5.fla, then save it as **kicker.fla**.

   This document has a graphic symbol made up of 13 individual drawings to form a character shape.

2. Click the **Selection tool** ➤ , then drag a **marquee** around the image to select it.

   Notice the separate objects.

3. Click a blank area of the Stage to deselect the image.

4. Click the **Zoom tool** 🔍 , then click the **image** to zoom in on it.

5. Scroll the Stage to view the head, then click the **Bone tool** 🖋 on the Tools panel.

6. Point to the middle of the head, when the pointer changes to a bone with a cross 🖋, drag the 🖋 **pointer** down to the torso as shown in Figure 30, then release the mouse button.

7. Point to the bottom of the bone, then drag the 🖋 **pointer** to the left as shown in Figure 31.

8. Point to the left end of the bone, then drag the 🖋 **pointer** down as shown in Figure 32.

   Notice that a bone connects two overlapping objects, such as the bone used to connect the upper arm and lower arm.

9. Using Figure 33 as a guide, complete the drawing of the other bones.

   Hint: Use the Undo command as needed if your connections do not match Figure 33.

10. Save your work.

You created a bone structure by connecting objects on the Stage with the Bone tool.

Animate the character

1. Change the view to **Fit in Window**.
2. Click **frame 10** on the Armature layer, then insert a **keyframe**.

   Note: The name of your Armature layer will include a number.
3. Click the **Selection tool** , then click a blank area of the Stage to deselect the object if it is selected.
4. Point to the **right foot**, then, when the pointer changes to a bone with a delta symbol , drag the **pointer** to position the foot as shown in Figure 34.
5. Point to the **right arm**, then use the pointer to position it as shown in Figure 35.
6. Use the pointer to position the left arm and left foot as shown in Figure 36.

   Hint: To position the left foot, move the left knee first, then move the left foot.
7. Click **frame 20** on the Armature layer, then insert a **keyframe**.
8. Adjust the arms and legs as shown in Figure 37.

   Hint: Move the right leg to the position shown to create a kicking motion.
9. Click the **Free Transform tool** on the Tools panel, then drag a **marquee** around the image to select it if it is not already selected.
10. Point to the **upper-right handle**, then, when the pointer changes to an arc , drag the **pointer** to the left as shown in Figure 38.
11. Test the movie, close the Flash Player window, then save the movie.

You animated the character by adjusting the armatures of the various bones.

Figure 34 *Positioning the right foot*

Figure 35 *Positioning the right arm*

Figure 36 *Positioning the left arm and left foot*

right leg

Figure 37 *Positioning the arms and legs*

right leg

Figure 38 *Rotating the object*

Figure 39 *Increasing the length of the motion span*

Create a movie clip of the IK object and animate the movie clip

1. Click **File** on the menu bar, click **Save as**, type **kickerMC**, then click **Save**.

2. Click **frame 1** on the Armature layer.

3. Click the **Selection tool** ▸ , then drag a **marquee** around the entire image to select it.

4. Click **Modify** on the menu bar, then click **Convert to Symbol**.

5. Type **mc_kicker** for the name, select **Movie Clip** for the Type, then click **OK**.

6. Click **Armature** on the Timeline, then click the **Delete icon** 🗑 to delete the layer.

7. Click **frame 1** on the kicker layer, display the Library panel, then drag the **mc_kicker symbol** to the Stage.

8. Insert a **motion tween**.

9. Drag the **tween span** on the Timeline to **frame 20**, as shown in Figure 39.

10. Click **frame 10** on the kicker layer.

11. Verify the object is selected, then press the **up arrow [↑]** on the keyboard 10 times.

12. Click **frame 20**, then press the **down arrow [↓]** on the keyboard 10 times.

    Steps 11 and 12 will give the impression of the character jumping up then coming down during the kicking motion.

13. Test the movie, close the Flash Player window, then save your work.

You created a movie clip and applied a motion tween to it.

Apply an ease value

1. Double-click the **mc_kicker symbol** in the Library panel to display the edit window, then scroll as needed to see the entire object.

2. Display the Properties panel.

3. Click **frame 10** on the Armature layer.

4. Set the Ease Strength to **-100**.

5. Click the **Type list arrow** in the EASE area, then click **Simple (Fastest)**

   The EASE type is set to Simple (Fastest), as shown in Figure 40. Frame 10 is the start of the motion tween where the right leg begins to kick downward. Setting the ease value to -100 will cause the leg motion to start out slow and accelerate as the leg follows through to the end of the kicking motion. This is a more natural way to represent the kick than to have the leg speed constant throughout the downward motion and follow through.

6. Click **Scene 1** on the edit window title bar to return to the main Timeline.

7. Test the movie, close the Flash Player window, save your work, then close the file.

You added an ease value to the movie clip.

Figure 40 *Setting the ease value*

Figure 41 *The completed armature structure*

Set the play to runtime

1. Open fl5_6.fla, then save it as **kickerRT.fla**.

   This character is similar to the one used in the kicker movie, however it has been created using movie clips instead of graphic symbols. Also, only one pose is used.

2. Use the **Bone tool** to create the armature structure as shown in Figure 41.

   Hint: Each bone should connect two body parts.

3. Click **frame 1** on the Armature layer.

   Hint: If you have trouble clicking a frame, select a larger frame view setting and try again.

4. Display the Properties panel, click the **Type list arrow** in the OPTIONS area of the Properties panel, then click **Runtime**.

5. Click **File**, point to **Publish Preview**, then click **Default - (HTML)** to display the movie in a browser.

   Hint: Press [F12] (Win) or [command][F12] (Mac) to display the movie in a browser.

6. Drag each part of the character, such as an arm or a leg.

7. Close your browser.

8. Save your work, then close the document.

You created an animated character, set the play to runtime and manipulated the character in a browser.

Create 3D
EFFECTS

What You'll Do

In this lesson, you will create a movie with 3D effects.

Understanding 3D Effects

Flash allows you to create 3D effects by manipulating objects in 3D space on the Stage. Until now you have been working in two dimensions, width and height. The default settings for the Stage are 550 pixels wide and 400 pixels high. These are represented by an x axis (across) and a y axis (down). Any position on the Stage can be specified by x and y coordinates. The upper-left corner of the Stage has an x value of 0 and a y value of 0, and the lower-right corner has an x value of 550 and a y value of 400, as shown in Figure 42. In 3D space there is also a z axis that represents depth. Flash provides two tools, 3D Translation and 3D Rotation that can be used to move and rotate objects using all three axes. In addition, Flash provides two other properties that can be adjusted to control the view of an object. The Perspective Angle property controls the angle of the object and can be used to create a zooming in and out effect. The Vanishing Point property more precisely controls the direction of an object as it moves away from the viewer. The Perspective Angle and the Vanishing Point settings are found in the Properties panel.

The 3D Tools

The 3D tools are available on the Tools panel. By default the 3D Rotation tool is displayed on the Tools panel. To access the 3D Translation tool, click and hold the 3D Rotation tool to open the menu. Toggle between these two 3D tools as needed.

The process for creating 3D effects is to create a movie clip (only movie clips can have 3D effects applied to them), place the movie clip on the Stage, create a motion tween and then click the object with either of the 3D tools. When you click an object with the 3D Translation tool, the three axes X, Y, and Z appear on top of the object, as shown in Figure 43. Each has its own color: red (X), green (Y), and blue (Z), which you see only when the 3D Rotation tool is active. The X and Y axes have arrows and the Z axis is represented by a black dot when the 3D Translation tool is active. You point to an arrow or the black dot and drag it to reposition the object. Dragging the X axis arrow moves the object horizontally. Dragging the Y axis arrow moves the object vertically. Dragging the Z axis dot zooms the object in and out.

When you click the object with the 3D Rotation tool, the three axes X, Y, and Z appear on top of the object, as shown in Figure 44. Dragging the X axis (red) will flip the object horizontally. Dragging the Y axis (green) will flip the object vertically. Dragging the Z axis (blue) will spin the object. A fourth option, the orange circle, rotates the object around the X and Y axes at the same time.

Using a Motion Tween with a 3D Effect

Creating 3D effects requires a change in the position of an object. A motion tween is used to specify where on the Timeline the effect will take place. This allows you to create more than one effect by selecting various frames in the tween span and making adjustments as desired. If you are animating more than one object, each object should be on its own layer.

Figure 42 *The x and y coordinates on the Stage*

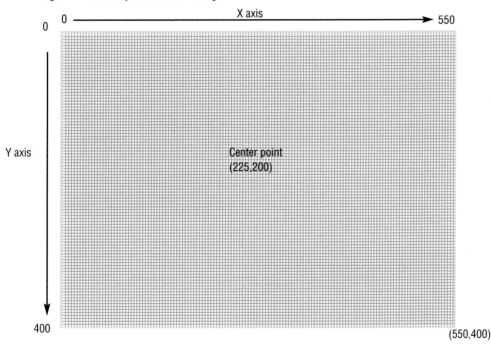

Figure 43 *The 3D Translation tool*

Figure 44 *The 3D Rotation tool*

Create a 3D animation

1. Open fl5_7.fla, then save it as **puzzle.fla**.

   Note: The document opens with the ruler feature turned on and showing the vertical and horizontal lines that intersect at the center of the Stage.

2. Change the view to **Fit in Window**.

3. Click **frame 1** on the Image 1 layer, insert a **motion tween**, then drag the **tween span** to frame 40.

4. Click **frame 20** on the Image 1 layer, then select the **3D Translation tool** ⚒ from the Tools panel.

   Note: You may need to click the 3D Rotation tool on the Tools panel to display the 3D Translation tool.

5. Click the **image** in the upper-right corner of the Stage, point to the **green arrow tip**, then use the ▶_Y pointer to drag the image down to the horizontal ruler line, as shown in Figure 45.

6. Click the **red arrow tip**, then use the ▶_X pointer to drag the image to the left, as shown in Figure 46.

7. Select the **3D Rotation tool** ⚒ from the Tools panel, point to the **green line Y axis** on the right side of the object, then, when the pointer changes to a delta symbol with a Y, drag the ▶_Y **pointer** down and to the left, as shown in Figure 47, to flip the image horizontally.

8. Click **frame 40** on the Image 1 layer, then select the **3D Translation tool** ⚒ from the Tools panel.

(continued)

Figure 45 *Using the 3D Translation tool to position the image vertically*

Point here

Drag pointer down

Figure 46 *Using the 3D Translation tool to position the image horizontally*

Figure 47 *Using the 3D Rotation tool to flip the image horizontally*

Point here

Drag left to here

Creating Special Effects

Figure 48 *Using the 3D Translation tool to position the image again*

Figure 49 *Using the 3D Translation tool to position a second image*

Figure 50 *Using the 3D Rotation tool to flip the image vertically*

Drag pointer left and up   Point here

Figure 51 *Using the 3D Translation tool to reposition the second image*

9. Click the **red arrow tip**, then use the ▶ₓ pointer to move the image to the position shown in Figure 48.

10. Select the **3D Rotation tool** 🔄 , point to the **green line Y axis** on the left side of the object, then drag the ▶ᵧ **pointer** down and to the right to flip the image horizontally again.

11. Click **frame 1** on the Image 2 layer, insert a **motion tween**, then drag the **tween span** to frame 40.

12. Click **frame 20** on the Image 2 layer, then select the **3D Translation tool** ⟁.

13. Point to the **red and green arrow tips** and use the ▶ₓ pointer and the ▶ᵧ pointer respectively to drag the image to the position shown in Figure 49.

14. Select the **3D Rotation tool** 🔄 , then point to the **bottom red line X axis**.

15. When the pointer changes to a delta symbol with an X, use the ▶ₓ pointer to drag the line to the left and up to flip the image vertically, as shown in Figure 50.

16. Click **frame 40** on the Image 2 layer, then select the **3D Translation tool** ⟁.

17. Point to the **red and green arrow tips** and use the ▶ₓ pointer and the ▶ᵧ pointer respectively to position the image as shown in Figure 51.

18. Select the **3D Rotation tool** 🔄 , then point to the bottom red line X axis.

19. When the pointer changes to a ▶ₓ, drag the **line** to the left and up to flip the image vertically again.

(continued)

20. Click **frame 1** on the Image 3 layer, insert a **motion tween**, then drag the **tween span** to frame 40.

21. Click **frame 20** on the Image 3 layer, then select the **3D Translation tool** ⚒.

22. Point to the **red and green arrow tips** and use the ▶x pointer and the ▶Y pointer respectively to drag the image to the position shown in Figure 52.

23. Select the **3D Rotation tool** ⚬, then point to the **blue circle Z axis**, as shown in Figure 53.

24. When the pointer changes to ▶z, drag the circle to rotate the image clockwise 180 degrees, as shown in Figure 54.

25. Click **frame 40** on the Image 3 layer, then select the **3D Translation tool** ⚒.

26. Point to the **red and green arrow tips** and use the ▶x pointer and the ▶Y pointer respectively to position the image as shown in Figure 55.

27. Select the **3D Rotation tool** ⚬, point to the **blue circle Z axis**, then use the ▶z pointer to drag the circle and to rotate the image clockwise 180 degrees again.

28. Click **frame 1** on the Image 4 layer, insert a motion tween, then drag the **tween span** to frame 40.

29. Click **frame 20** on the Image 4 layer, then select the **3D Translation tool** ⚒.

(continued)

Figure 52 *Using the 3D Translation tool to position the third image*

Figure 53 *Pointing to the blue circle Z axis on the 3D Rotation tool*

Point here

Figure 54 *Using the 3D Rotation tool to rotate the image*

Rotate the pointer clockwise to here

Figure 55 *Using the 3D Translation tool to reposition the third image*

Creating Special Effects

Figure 56 *Using the 3D Translation tool to position the fourth image*

Figure 57 *Using the 3D Rotation tool to rotate the image*

Drag pointer left to here　　　*Point here*

Figure 58 *Using the 3D Translation tool to reposition the fourth image*

Figure 59 *The completed 3D effects movie*

30. Point to the **red and green arrow tips** and use the ▶x pointer and the ▶y pointer respectively to position the image as shown in Figure 56.

31. Select the **3D Rotation tool** ⊙, then point to the right side of the **orange circle**.

32. When the pointer changes to a Delta symbol, drag the ▶ **pointer** to the middle of the image as shown in Figure 57.

33. Click **frame 40** on the Image 4 layer, point to the left side of the orange circle, then drag the ▶ **pointer** to the center of the image.

34. Use the **3D Translation tool** ⚒ to position the image as shown in Figure 58.

35. Click the **Selection tool** ▶, drag the **ruler lines** to remove them, then use the 3D tools and the red and green arrow tips to make adjustments as needed so your screen resembles Figure 59.

    Hint: Use the arrow keys on the keyboard to make minor adjustments to the position of an object.

36. Test the movie, then close the Flash Player window.

37. Save your work, then close the document.

You created a movie with 3D effects.

Use the
DECO TOOL

What You'll Do

In this lesson, you will use the Deco tool to create and animate a cityscape.

Understanding the Deco Tool

The Deco tool provides a variety of drawing effects that can be used to quickly create environments, such as city landscapes, and to create various animations. In addition, the Deco tool can be used to create decorative patterns that incorporate imported graphics and those drawn in Flash. These patterns can be animated and added to a movie to create special effects. Flash has a number of Deco tool brushes and effects. In addition, Adobe has designed the Deco tool so that other brushes and effects can be added by developers. This allows users to develop tools for their specific needs. Because the Deco tool is easy to use and can be used to quickly create a design and add animation, it is a valuable tool for creating prototypes in the early stages of developing an application. One drawback of using the Deco tool is that animations created with the Deco tool often result in movie file sizes that are large. This is because the images created with the brush tools are made up of small segments and the animations are frame-by-frame animations.

Basic Types of Deco Effects

There are 13 drawing effects available with the Deco tool, as shown in Figure 60.

Figure 60 The Deco drawing tools

These drawing effects are available in the Properties panel when the Deco tool is selected from the Tools panel. They are grouped into three basic types, although there is some overlap in the groups.

■ Fills—the Vine Fill, Grid Fill, and Symmetry Brush create patterns that can be used as fill for graphics or a backdrop for a movie. Figure 61 shows a vine and a grid fill. Flash allows you to create your own fill using an image of your choice, such as a logo. In addition, you can set various properties such as the pattern scale.

■ **NEW** Brushes—several brushes including the building, lightning, tree, and flower brushes can be used to create drawings that can be combined to construct environments, like the one shown in Figure 62. The Decorated Brush has 20 variations, including those shown in Figure 63.

■ **NEW** Animations—a few brushes, such as the Lightning Brush, Fire Animation, Smoke Animation, and Particle System, create animations as they are used. However, any effect created using the Deco tool can be selected, converted to a graphic or movie clip symbol, and animated by inserting a motion tween or using another animation process in Flash.

Hint: Select a keyframe before selecting the Deco tool and use different layers for each Deco tool effect.

Figure 61 *A vine fill and a grid fill*

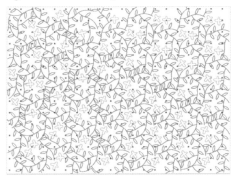

Figure 62 *Cityscape created using Deco tools*

Figure 63 *Patterns created using selected Decorative Brushes*

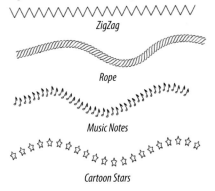

ZigZag

Rope

Music Notes

Cartoon Stars

Create screen design and animations with the Deco tool

1. Open fl5_8 .fla, then save it as **decoLand.fla**.

   This movie has six layers, dimensions of 400 x 400 pxs, a length of 65 frames, and a dark blue backdrop.

2. Change the view for the Timeline to **Small** if necessary to see all 65 frames, then set the view to **Fit in Window**.

3. Click **frame 1** on the buildings layer, click the **Deco tool** on the Tools panel, then display the Properties panel.

4. **NEW** Click the **DRAWING EFFECT list arrow**, then click **Building Brush**.

5. Verify your Properties panel displays DRAWING EFFECT: Building Brush; ADVANCED OPTIONS: Random Building and Building Size **1**.

6. Point to the Stage, then click and drag the **pointer** to the position shown in Figure 64.

   Note: The Random Building option may cause your building to display differently.

   Hint: You can use the undo command in the Edit menu to undo an action(s).

7. Continue to create four more buildings similar to Figure 65.

8. Click **frame 1** on the trees layer.

9. Click the **Deco tool** on the Tools panel, then use the Properties panel to change the DRAWING EFFECT to **Tree Brush** and the type to **Gingko Tree**.

10. Use the **pointer** to draw trees similar to the ones shown in Figure 66.

(continued)

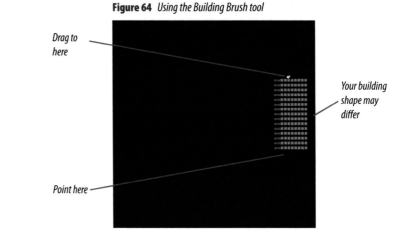

Figure 64 *Using the Building Brush tool*

Drag to here

Point here

Your building shape may differ

Figure 65 *The completed buildings*

Figure 66 *The completed trees*

Creating Special Effects

Figure 67 *Using the Lightning Brush*

Point here

Figure 68 *Inserting a blank keyframe*

Blank keyframe inserted after the
keyframes of the animation.
*Note: There may be a different number
of keyframes in your animation.*

Figure 69 *Positioning the pointer*

Point here

11. Insert a **keyframe** in frame 10 on the lightning layer.

12. Click the **Deco tool** on the Tools panel, change the DRAWING EFFECT to **Lightning Brush** and the color to **white**, then verify animation is checked.

13. Point off the Stage as shown in Figure 67, then drag the **pointer** toward the trees and release the mouse button.

14. Insert a **blank keyframe** in the frame following the last keyframe in the lightning animation, as shown in Figure 68.

15. Click **frame 20** on the fire layer, then insert a **keyframe**.

16. Click the **Deco tool** on the Tools panel, then change the DRAWING EFFECT to **Fire Animation** and the Fire duration to **30 frames**.

17. Click the **tree top** on the far left of the Stage, click **frame 50** on the fire layer, then insert a **blank keyframe**.

18. Click **frame 35** on the snow layer, then insert a **keyframe**.

19. Click the **Deco tool** on the Tools panel, change the DRAWING EFFECT to **Particle System**, verify Particle 1 and Particle 2 have a check mark, and set the particle color to **white** for each particle.

20. Point to the sky, as shown in Figure 69, then click the **pointer**.

21. Click **frame 35**, repeat Steps 19 and 20 **three times** placing the **pointer** in different areas across the sky.

22. Test the movie, close the Flash Player window, save your work, then close the document.

You created a cityscape environment, including animations, with the Deco tool.

Create a mask effect.

1. Start Flash, open fl5_9.fla, then save it as **skillsDemo5.fla**. (*Hint*: When you open the file, you may receive a missing font message, meaning a font used in this document is not available on your computer. You can choose a substitute font or use a default font.)
2. Verify the frame rate is set to 12 and the Flash Publish Settings (accessed from the File menu) are set to Flash Player 10 and ActionScript 3.0.
3. Insert a new layer above the table layer, then name it **heading**.
4. Select frame 1 on the heading layer, then use the Text tool to create the Aces Wild heading with the following characteristics: size 48, color #006633 (a dark green), and Byington (or similar) font. (*Hint*: Look at Figure 70 and find a font that matches the heading text. Use the samples provided to find a similar font, such as Constania.)
5. Use the Selection tool to select the heading, then use the Align command in the Modify menu to center the heading across the Stage.
6. With the heading still selected, convert it to a graphic symbol with the name **g_heading**.
7. Insert a keyframe in frame 40 on the heading layer.
8. Insert a new layer above the heading layer, then name it **ending-heading**.
9. Insert a keyframe in frame 40 on the ending-heading layer.
10. Drag the g_heading symbol from the Library panel and position it on top of the heading on the Stage, then use the keyboard arrow keys as needed to position the g_heading symbol.
11. Lock the ending-heading layer.
12. Insert a new layer above the heading layer, then name it **circle**.
13. Select frame 1 on the circle layer, then use the Oval tool to create a black-filled circle that is slightly larger in height than the heading text.
14. Place the circle to the left of the heading.
15. Convert the circle to a graphic symbol with the name **g_mask**.
16. Create a motion tween that moves the circle across and to the right side of the heading.
17. Verify the tween span on the Timeline extends to frame 40.
18. Change the circle layer to a mask layer and lock the layer.
19. Change the heading layer to a masked layer and lock the layer.
20. Insert keyframes in frame 40 on the table, arms, and the head and body layers.
21. Insert a new layer above the table layer, name it **stopMovie**, move the stopmovie layer below the table layer, then insert a keyframe in frame 40.
22. Open the Actions panel, verify Script Assist is turned off and stopMovie: 40 is displayed in the lower-left corner of the Script pane, then type **stop( );** for the code. (*Note*: Because ActionScript 3.0 is needed when working with Inverse Kinematics and with the 3D feature, both of which you will do shortly, you cannot use the Script Assist feature of Flash, which is why you typed the code directly into the Actions pane.)
23. Close the Actions panel.
24. Test the movie, then save your work.

Create a character animation using inverse kinematics.

1. Select frame 1 on the Timeline, then use the Zoom tool to enlarge the view of the character.
2. Use the Bone tool to join the head to the body, then to join the body with the upper and lower left arm, and with the upper and lower right arm. (*Note*: The bone structure stops at the elbow on each arm.)
3. Click the Selection tool on the Tools panel, click frame 40 on the Armature layer, then insert a keyframe.
4. Select frame 6 on the Armature layer.
5. Use the Selection tool to move the ends of the arms so that the lower left and lower right arms are horizontal and touch at the chest. This will cause the elbows to point out away from the body.
6. Select frame 12 on the Armature layer.
7. Use the Selection tool to move the end of the right arm so that it is straight and pointing to the upper-left corner of the Stage.
8. Change the view to Fit in Window.
9. Test the movie, then save your work.

Create a frame-by-frame animation.

1. Select frame 4 on the card layer, then insert a keyframe.
2. Use the Zoom tool and the keyboard arrow keys as needed to reposition the card so that it is at the end of the right arm.
3. Select frame 5 on the card layer, then insert a keyframe.
4. Use the arrow keys on the keyboard to reposition the card so that it is at the end of the right arm.

Creating Special Effects

5. Repeat steps 3 and 4 in frame 6 through frame 12 on the card layer. (*Note*: The hand moves a small increment in each frame, which is why you must reposition the card so it stays connected to the hand.)
6. Select frame 13 on the card layer, then insert a blank keyframe.
7. Test the movie, close the Flash Player window, then save your work.

Create a 3D effect.

1. Insert a new layer above the card layer, then name it **ace3D**.
2. Select frame 12 on the ace3D layer, then insert a keyframe.
3. Drag the mc_aceD movie clip from the Library panel to the Stage, display the Properties panel, verify the Lock width and height values together icon is not a broken link, then resize the width to 10.6.
4. Reposition the ace to on top of the card held by the character.
5. Verify frame 12 on the ace3D layer is selected, then create a motion tween.
6. Verify the tween span on the Timeline extends from frame 12 through frame 40.
7. Select frame 40 on the ace3D layer.
8. Use the 3D Translation tool to reposition the card to the upper-left corner of the Stage in a diagonal line that extends from the character's right shoulder. (*Hint*: Use both the red and green arrow tips to move the card to create a diagonal line.)
9. Use the Free Transform tool and the Scale option at the bottom of the Tools panel to resize the card to a width of between 80 and 90.

10. Select frame 26 on the ace3D layer.
11. Use the 3D Rotation tool to add a 3D effect.
12. Select frame 40 on the ace3D layer.
13. Use the 3D Rotation tool to add a 3D effect that causes the card to display right side up, as seen in Figure 70.
14. Test the movie, close the Flash Player window, then save your work.

Add sound to a movie.

1. Insert a new layer at the top of the Timeline, then name it **sound**.
2. Insert a keyframe in frame 5 on the sound layer.
3. Drag introSound.wav from the Library panel to the Stage.
4. Insert a keyframe in frame 40 on the sound layer.
5. Test the movie, if a warning box opens, read the message then click OK, compare your movie to the images in Figure 70, close the Flash Player window, save your work, then close the file.

Add video.

1. Open fl5_10.fla, then save it as **skillsDemo5-video.fla**.

Figure 70 *Completed Skills Review-IK 3D Animation*

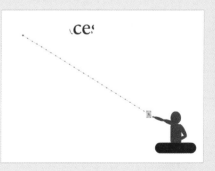

2. Add a new layer above the headings layer, then name it **video**.
3. Import the file tour-video.mov as an embedded video from the drive and folder where you store your Data Files to the Library using the Import Video command. (*Note*: You will need to use the Adobe Media Encoder to convert the file to the flv format, then you will need to browse to the drive and folder where you save your Solution Files to open the converted file.)
4. Verify that the video is in the Library panel and on the center of the Stage, note the number of frames needed to display the entire video. (*Note*: You may need to drag the video from the Library panel to the Stage. If a message appears asking if you want frames inserted into the Timeline, click Yes. *Hint*: Be sure to position the video placeholder, if necessary, to prevent overlapping the text subheading.)
5. Add a new layer, name it **controls**, then select frame 1 on the layer.
6. Use the Text tool to create a text box with the word **Play** beneath and to the left side of the video. Set the text

characteristics to the following: family Arial, style Narrow (Win) or Regular (Mac), size 20 pt, and color White.

7. Convert the text to a button symbol with the name **b_play**.

8. Edit the over and down states of the button symbol, for example, make the color of the letters change when the mouse pointer is over the word Play and when the user clicks the button.

9. Use the Actions panel and Script Assist to assign a play action to the button that plays the movie when the mouse is released.

10. Use the Text tool to create a text box with the word **Pause** beneath and to the right side of the video. Use the same text characteristics used for the Play button.

11. Convert the text to a button symbol with the name **b_pause**.

12. Edit the button symbol to match what you did in step 8.

13. Use the Actions panel to assign a stop action to the button when it is released.

14. Add a new layer, then name it **stopMovie**.

15. Add a stop action to frame 1 on the stopMovie layer.

16. Add a keyframe at the end of the movie on the headings layer. (*Note*: If a message appears asking if you want frames inserted into the timeline, click No because the frames are already inserted.)

17. Test the movie, compare your screen to Figure 71, close the Flash Player window, then save your work.

18. Close the Flash document.

Work with TLF text and create an animated navigation bar.

1. Open fl5_11.fla, then save it as **skillsDemo5-TLF.fla**.

2. Add a new layer and name it **photo**.

3. Select frame 1 of the photo layer and drag the g_birchBay graphic symbol from the Library panel to the center of the Stage.

4. Use the Align panel to center the graphic on the Stage.

5. Lock the heading and photo layers.

6. Add a new layer at the top of the Timeline and name it **text**.

7. Select frame 1 of the text layer and drag the g_text graphic from the Library panel to the middle of the Stage.

8. Verify the text image is selected, then click Modify on the menu bar and select Break Apart. (*Note*: The original text block was changed to a graphic symbol and placed in the Library panel. In order to edit the text, the symbol must be broken apart.)

9. Display the Properties panel and change the text from Classic Text to TLF Text.

10. Change the Size in the CHARACTER area to 13 pt.

11. Change the Behavior in the CONTAINER AND FLOW area of the Properties panel to Multiline.

12. Using Figure 72 as a guide complete the following:
    - Use the Selection tool to resize the Container and create a second linked Container.
    - Use the Text tool to type in the words "in the majestic Pacific Northwest" at the end of the first sentence.
    - Use the Selection tool to select the containers.
    - Justify the text using the "Justify with last line aligned to start" button in the PARAGRAPH area of the Properties panel, and adjust the text box widths as needed to closely match the line wrap shown in Figure 72.

13. Lock the text layer.

14. Test the movie, then close the Flash Player window.

15. Save your work.

Figure 71 *Completed Skills Review - video*

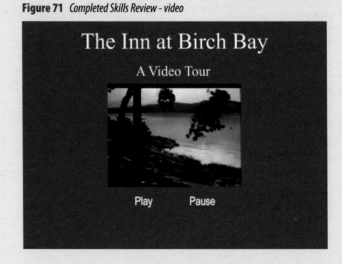

Create the drop-down buttons

1. Save the Flash document as **skillsDemo5-navBar.fla**.
2. Insert a new layer, name it **navBar Background**, create the white horizontal bar shown in Figure 72, then lock the layer.
3. Insert a new layer, name it navBar Buttons, then create the three text headings using Classic text and a black color.
4. Convert the Take a Tour heading to a button, then edit the button symbol to add a hit area around it. (*Note:* Be sure to make the hit area long enough so that it will fall below the navBar Background rectangle when the Take a Tour button is positioned on the navBar.)
5. Position the Take a Tour button so that its hit area falls below the navBar Background rectangle.
6. Insert keyframes in frame 10 of all the layers.
7. Insert a layer above the navBar Buttons layer, name it **videoBtn**, then insert a keyframe in frame 2 of the layer.
8. Create the video button, edit the button symbol to add a hit area to the button, then position it below Take a Tour.
9. Insert a layer, name it **slidesBtn**, then insert a keyframe in frame 2 of the layer.
10. Create the slides button, then position it below the video button.

Add a mask layer

1. Insert a layer, name it **cover**, then insert a keyframe in frame 2 of the layer.
2. Draw a rectangle that covers the video and slide buttons and move it above Take a Tour.
3. Verify the rectangle is selected and Insert a motion tween.

4. Insert a keyframe in frame 5 of the cover layer, then move the rectangle down to cover the buttons.
5. Change the layer properties for the cover layer to mask.
6. Select the slidesBtn layer and change it to a masked layer, if it has not changed to a masked layer.
7. Select the videoBtn layer and change it to a masked layer.

Assign actions to buttons and frames

1. Click File on the menu bar, click Publish Settings, click the Flash tab, then change the Script to ActionScript 2.0. (*Note:* ActionScript 2.0 is needed when assigning actions to buttons.)
2. When the warning message appears, click OK, then click OK to close the Publish Settings dialog box.
3. Select frame 2 on the videoBtn layer, click to select the Video button, then use ScriptAssist to add the on(release) code that causes the playhead to go to the next scene. (*Note:* The next scene will contain the video, although the scene has not been created yet.)
4. Insert a layer above the cover layer, name it **labels**, then insert a keyframe in frame 2 of the layer.
5. Add a frame label named **tourMenu**.
6. Select the Take a Tour button, then use ScriptAssist to add the code so the playhead goes to and plays the frame labeled tourMenu when the mouse pointer rolls over the button.
7. Insert a layer above the labels layer, name it **actions**, then, in frames 1 and 5 (be sure to add a keyframe) on the actions layer, use the Script pane (ScriptAssist turned off) to type **stop();**.
8. Insert a layer above the heading layer, name it **rollOver**, then insert a keyframe in frame 2 of the layer.

Figure 72 *Completed Skills Review - TLF and Animated Navigation Bar*

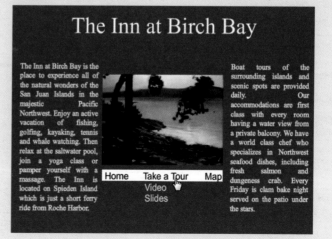

Add an invisible button

1. Draw a rectangle that covers the Take a Tour, Video and Slides buttons, then convert the rectangle to a button with the name **rollOverBtn**.
2. Use ScriptAssist to add ActionScript code that causes the playhead to go to frame 1 when the mouse pointer rolls over the button.
3. Select the rollOverBtn button and use the Properties panel to change the alpha setting to 0.
4. Test the movie, then save and close it.
   Note: If your text columns do not display as justified, unlock the text layer if it is locked, select a text block and set the Anti-alias option in the CHARACTER area of the Properties panel to Anti-alias for readability.

Work with the Deco tool.

This is a continuation of the Deco tool exercise you completed in this chapter. Figure 73 shows the changes you will make to the decoLand.fla document as you complete the following steps.

(*Hint*: Use the Undo command in the Edit menu to undo drawings as necessary.)

1. Open decoLand.fla and save it as **skillsDemo5-deco.fla**.
2. Change the view to Fit in Window.
3. Lock all the layers.
4. Insert a new layer above the backdrop layer, name it **road**, then select frame 1 on the road layer.
5. Select the Deco tool and display the Properties panel.
6. Change the DRAWING EFFECT to Decorated Brush, the ADVANCED OPTIONS to 18: Bumps, and the color to white.

7. Use the Deco pointer to draw the road below the buildings.
8. Lock the road layer.
9. Insert a new layer above the snow layer and name it **stars**.
10. Select frame 1 of the stars layer.
11. Select the Deco tool and display the Properties panel.
12. Change the ADVANCED OPTIONS to 16: Shiny Stars, then set the color to white, the pattern size to 30, and the pattern width to 20.
13. Use the Deco pointer to create the stars at the top of the Stage. (*Hint*: You can click and drag the pointer, and you can move the pointer to a new location then click and drag again to create a more scattered effect.)

14. Lock the stars layer.
15. Insert a new layer above the stars layer and name it **flowers**.
16. Select frame 1 of the flowers layer.
17. Select the Deco tool and display the Properties panel.
18. Change the DRAWING EFFECT to Flower Brush, then change the ADVANCED OPTIONS to Rose, and the flower and leaf size to 50%.
19. Click and drag to create the row of flowers at the bottom of the Stage.
20. Lock the flowers layer.
21. Save the movie.
22. Test the movie, then close the Flash Player window.
23. Exit Flash.

Figure 73 *Completed Skills Review - deco*

The Ultimate Tours travel company has asked you to design several sample animations for its website. Figure 74 shows a sample Cruises screen with a mask effect, as the spotlight rotates across the screen and highlights different ships. Complete the following for the Cruises screen of the Ultimate Tours website:

1. Open fl5_12.fla, then save it as **assets.fla**.
2. Open ultimateTours4.fla (the file you created in Chapter 4 Project Builder 1), and save it as **ultimateTours5.fla**.
3. Insert a new layer at the top of the Timeline and select frame 1 on the layer.
4. Display the Library panel, then click the Display movies list arrow below the Library tab to display the list of open documents.

5. Select assets.fla and drag each of the symbols in the Library panel to the Stage, delete the layer from the Timeline, click the assets.fla tab above the Stage, then close the assets file. (*Note*: You added the objects from the assets file to the ultimateTours5 Library panel, and then closed the assets.fla file.)
6. Display the Library panel for ultimateTours5.
7. Insert a new layer at the top of the Timeline, then name it **backdrop**.
8. Insert a keyframe in a frame that is higher than the last frame in the current movie (such as frame 100) on the backdrop layer, then draw a dark gray rectangle (#333333) that covers the Stage.
9. Insert a keyframe that is at least 30 frames higher on the backdrop layer (such as frame 130), then lock the layer. (*Note*: All of the subsequent layers you add will use the same starting frame, such as 100.)

10. Insert a new layer, name it **heading**, insert a keyframe in frame 100 (or the frame specified in Step 8), and create the Mystery Ships heading.
11. Insert a new layer, name it **lighthouse**, insert a keyframe in frame 100 (or the frame specified in Step 8), and place the g_lighthouse symbol on the Stage.
12. Insert a new layer, name it **searchlight**, insert a keyframe in frame 100 (or the frame specified in Step 8), and place the g_searchlight symbol to the left of the lighthouse.
13. Use the Free Transform tool to create a motion tween that causes the searchlight to rotate from the left to the right of the lighthouse.
    (*Hint*: The searchlight will rotate (pivot) around the transformation point (small circle) of the graphic.)

Figure 74 *Sample completed Project Builder 1*

14. Create a new layer for each of the three ships, name each layer appropriately (**ship1**, **ship2**, and **ship3**), and insert keyframes in frame 100 (or the frame specified in Step 8) of each layer.

15. Using frame 100 (or the frame specified in Step 8), place the ships on the Stage so that the searchlight highlights them as it moves from left to right across the Stage.

16. Insert a new layer above the ship layers, name it **searchlight mask**, insert a keyframe in frame 100 (or the frame specified in Step 8), add an instance of the g_searchlight symbol from the Library panel to on top of the searchlight on the stage, then add a motion tween that duplicates the one created in Step 13.

17. Create a mask effect that has a searchlight as the mask and reveals the ships when the searchlight is over them. (*Note*: The two searchlight motion tweens are needed on different layers because one will become a mask and will not be visible in the movie.)

18. Insert a new layer, name it **sound**, insert a keyframe in frame 100 (or the appropriate frame) on the layer, then drag the foghorn.wav sound file to the Stage.

19. Insert a new layer, name it **homeBTN**, insert a keyframe in the last frame of the movie, then add the b_home button to the bottom center of the Stage. (*Note*: This button does not appear on the MYSTERY SHIPS screen in Figure 74 because the last frame of the movie has not been reached.)

20. Add an action to the home button to have the playhead go to frame 1 of the movie when the button is clicked.

21. Insert a new layer, name it **stopAction**, then add a keyframe and a stop action at the end of the movie.

22. Add a new layer, name it **labels**, insert a keyframe in frame 100 (or the appropriate frame), then create a frame label named **mystery**.

23. Click frame 1 on the Timeline, drag (scrub) the playhead on the Timeline to locate the first frame that shows the Galapagos text (cruises headings layer for example), then unlock the cruise heading layer (or layer that has the Galapagos text).

24. Change the Galapagos text to **Mystery Ships**, then create a button that changes the text color for the different button states.

25. Add an action to the mystery ship button to have the playhead go to the frame labeled mystery.

26. Test the movie, then compare your image to the example shown in Figure 74.

27. Close the Flash Player window.

28. Lock all layers, save your work, then close the document.

You have been asked to develop a website illustrating the signs of the zodiac. The introductory screen should have a heading with a mask effect and 12 zodiac signs, each of which could become a button. Clicking a zodiac sign button displays an information screen with a different graphic to represent the sign and information about the sign, as well as special effects such as sound, mask effect, and character animation (inverse kinematics). Each information screen would be linked to the introductory screen. (*Note:* Using the inverse kinematics feature requires ActionScript 3.0, therefore, you will start with a movie that has the ActionScript for the buttons and stop actions already developed.)

1. Open fl5_13.fla, save it as **zodiac5.fla**, then change the frame rate to **12 fps**. (*Hint:* When you open the file, you may receive a missing font message, meaning a font used in this document is not available on your computer. You can choose a substitute font or use a default font.)

2. Test the movie, then study the Timeline to understand how the movie works.

3. Refer to Figure 75 as you complete the introductory screen with the following:
   - A new layer above the signs layer named **heading** with the heading, **Signs of the** that appears from frame 1 through frame 31
   - A new layer named **masked** that contains the word **Zodiac** and that appears from frame 1 through frame 31
   - A mask layer that passes across the heading Zodiac (*Notes:* Use a fill color that can be seen on the black background. After creating the motion tween, drag the end of the tween span on the Timeline to frame 31. Be sure to set the Layer Properties for the mask and masked layers.)
   - A new layer that displays the word **Zodiac** in frame 31 only (*Note:* Remove frames 32–80 from the layer by using the Remove Frames option from the Timeline command of the Edit menu.)
   - A new layer with a sound that plays from frame 1 through frame 31 as the mask is revealing the contents of the masked layer

4. Refer to Figure 75 as you complete the scorpio screen with the following: (*Notes:* The scorpio screen starts in frame 51. Remove frames in other layers containing content that you do not want displayed after frame 31, such as the Zodiac heading.)
   - A new layer with the three-line heading
   - An inverse kinematics animation that moves the tail (*Note:* Be sure to connect the head to the tail.)
5. Test the movie.
6. Save the movie as **zodiac5-mc.fla**.
7. Select frame 51 on the Armature layer and convert the IK animation to a movie clip.
8. Edit the movie clip and add a stop action on a separate layer at the end of the movie clip, then return to the main Timeline.
9. Delete the Armature layer, then select frame 51 on the scorpio layer and drag the movie clip to the Stage.
10. Create a motion tween to animate the movie clip so the scorpion moves across the screen.
11. Test the movie, compare your screens to Figure 75, close the Flash Player window, then save the movie.

Figure 75 *Sample completed Project Builder 2*

Tail moves while scorpion moves across the screen

Figure 76 shows the home page of a website. Study the figure and complete the following questions. For each question, indicate how you determined your answer.

1. Connect to the Internet, then go to *www.nikeid.com*, and display the women's basketball shoes. Go to the site and explore several links to get a feeling for how the site is constructed. Use Figure 76 to answer the questions.

2. Open a document in a word processor or open a new Flash document, save the file as **dpc5**, then answer the following questions. (*Hint*: Use the Text tool in Flash.)
   - Whose site is this and what seems to be the purpose of this site?
   - Who would be the target audience?
   - How might a character animation using inverse kinematics be used?
   - How might video be used?
   - How might a mask effect be used?
   - How might sound be used?
   - How might 3D be used?
   - What suggestions would you make to improve the design and why?

Figure 76 *Design Project*

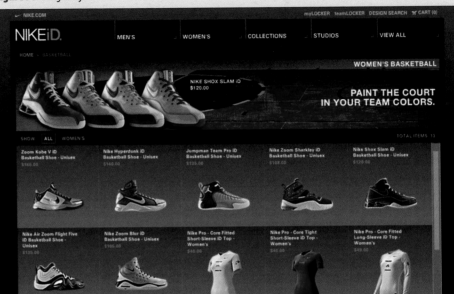

Creating Special Effects

This is a continuation of the Portfolio Project in Chapter 4, which is the development of a personal portfolio. The home page has several categories, including the following:

- Personal data
- Contact information
- Previous employment
- Education
- Samples of your work

In this project, you will create several buttons for the Sample Animations screen and link them to their respective animations.

1. Open portfolio4.fla (the file you created in Portfolio Project, Chapter 4) and save it as **portfolio5.fla**.
2. Display the Sample Animations screen. You will be adding buttons to this screen. Each of these new buttons links to a screen that plays its corresponding animation. In each case, have the animation return to the Sample Animations screen at the end of the animation.
3. Add a button for a character animation so it appears on the Sample Animations screen, add a new layer and create a character animation (inverse kinematics) on that layer, then link the character animation button to the character animation.
4. Add a button for a mask effect so it appears on the Sample Animations screen, add new layers to create a mask effect (such as to the words My Portfolio) on that layer, add a sound that plays as the mask is revealing the contents of the masked layer, then link the mask effect button to the mask effect animation.

5. Add a button for an animated navigation bar so it appears on the Sample Animations screen, add a new layer and create an animated navigation bar on that layer, then link the navigation bar button to the animated navigation bar.

6. Test the movie, then compare your Sample Animation screen to the example shown in Figure 77.
7. Close the Flash Player window, then save your work.

Figure 77 *Sample completed Portfolio Project*

CHAPTER **1**

GETTING STARTED WITH
ADOBE FIREWORKS

1. Understand the Fireworks work environment
2. Work with new and existing documents
3. Work with layers and images
4. Create shapes
5. Create and modify text

CHAPTER 1

GETTING STARTED WITH
ADOBE FIREWORKS

Understand Fireworks

Fireworks is a graphics program intended specifically for creating Web images and media for other devices. Both Web enthusiasts and professionals can create, edit, and optimize files, and then add animation and JavaScript-enabled interactivity to those optimized files. Fireworks is perfectly suited to prototyping a web site and optimizing graphics and designs created in other applications. Many Fireworks tasks are compartmentalized so that graphic artists can enhance or create designs without disturbing the programming added by developers, and vice versa.

Fireworks is an integral component of many Adobe Creative Suite 5 collections. It integrates seamlessly with other Adobe programs, including Flash, Dreamweaver, InDesign, Photoshop, and Illustrator. Fireworks is the default image editor for some file types and you can edit images using the Fireworks interface from within the host application. You can also open native Photoshop and Illustrator files in Fireworks; layers and filters are preserved and editable.

In this chapter, you will learn about the interface and learn to use the tools and apply the concepts that make Fireworks a comprehensive graphics program.

Property inspector

Color pop-up window

Align panel

Pointer tool

Pen tool

Rectangle tool

Text tool

Layers panel

Eye icon

Understand the
FIREWORKS WORK ENVIRONMENT

What You'll Do

In this lesson, you will start Fireworks, open a file, and adjust panels, including undocking and collapsing them.

Viewing the Fireworks Window

The Fireworks window, shown in Figures 1 and 2, contains the space where you work with documents, tools, and panels. The main area of the **Document window** contains the canvas, which is where you work with all the elements in your document. When you open or create a document, the Document window contains four display buttons: Original, Preview, 2-Up, and 4-Up. You can work in your document when you click the Original button; the other three are

Figure 1 *Fireworks window (Windows)*

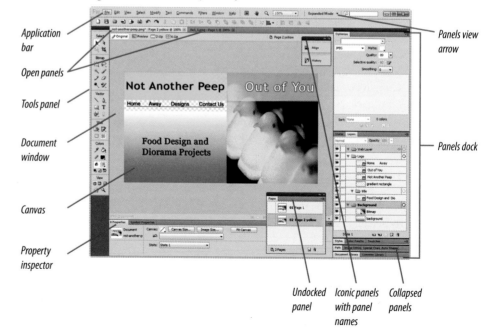

Application bar

Open panels

Tools panel

Document window

Canvas

Property inspector

Panels view arrow

Panels dock

Undocked panel

Iconic panels with panel names

Collapsed panels

Getting Started with Adobe Fireworks

document preview buttons. The 2-Up and 4-Up buttons allow you to select different optimization settings and evaluate them side by side. When you open multiple documents and the Document window is maximized, each open document's title appears on a separate tab.

QUICK TIP

The bottom of each Document window contains frame control buttons for playing animation.

Tools are housed in the **Tools panel**. The Tools panel is organized into **tool groups**: Select, Bitmap, Vector, Web, Colors, and View, so you can easily locate the tool you need. You can modify selected objects and set tool properties and other options using the **Property inspector**. Depending on the action you are performing, information in the Property inspector changes. For example, when you select a tool or an object, or click the canvas, properties specific to the selection appear in the Property inspector.

You can rearrange panels in the Fireworks window using the **panels dock** to maximize your onscreen real estate based on your work preferences. You can modify your workspace panel view by clicking an option on the **Application bar**. By default, Expanded Mode appears, but you can also select Iconic Mode, Iconic Mode With Panel Names, or Netbook Mode. Fireworks allows you to dock, undock, regroup, collapse, expand, and close panels or panel groups. To open or close a panel, click the panel name on the Window

menu on the Application bar. To expand or collapse a panel or panel group, click the gray title bar. To undock a panel group, drag the gray bar, and to undock a single panel, drag the panel name in the title bar.

QUICK TIP

You can quickly hide or show all open panels by pressing [Tab] or [F4].

Figure 2 *Fireworks window (Mac)*

Opening Windows-Specific Toolbars

If you are using Windows, you can open the Main toolbar from the Toolbars command on the Window menu. The Main toolbar includes buttons for common tasks.

Start Fireworks and open a Fireworks document

1. Windows users, click the **Start button** on the taskbar, point to **All Programs**, then click **Adobe Fireworks CS5**.

2. Mac users, click **Finder** on the Dock, click **Applications**, click the **Adobe Fireworks CS5 folder**, then double-click the **Fireworks CS5 application**. After Fireworks is running, [control]-click the **Fireworks icon**, click **Options**, then click **Keep In Dock** to add it to the Dock permanently.

   The application opens with the Start page displayed. Previously opened documents appear on the left, the button to open a new document appears on the left, along with other options for training and obtaining plug-ins.

   TIP The name of some panels differ on a Mac.

3. Click **File** on the Application bar, then click **Open**.

   TIP You can also press [Ctrl][O] (Win) or [O] (Mac) to open a file, or you can click Open on the Start page. To disable the Start page, click the Don't show again check box.

4. Navigate to where you store your Data Files, click **fw1_1.png**, then click **Open**.

5. Compare your Fireworks window to Figure 3.

   You started Fireworks and opened a file.

Figure 3 *Newly opened document*

Your open or collapsed panels might differ

Getting Started with Adobe Fireworks

Figure 4 *Changing panels to Icon view with panel names*

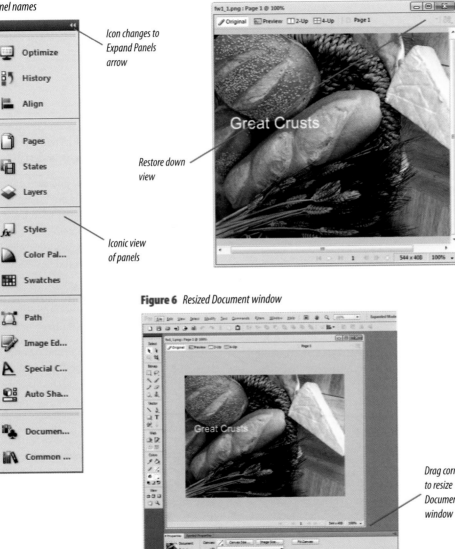

Icon changes to
Expand Panels
arrow

Restore down
view

Iconic view
of panels

Figure 5 *Changing the view of the Document window*

Figure 6 *Resized Document window*

Drag corner
to resize
Document
window

Open and adjust panels in the Fireworks window

1. Click the **Collapse to Icons arrow** ▸▸ at the top of the panels dock to collapse the panels.

   The panels are collapsed to Icon view with panel names, as shown in Figure 4. You can also open panels by clicking Window on the Application bar and then clicking a panel name, or by double-clicking a panel name in a collapsed group.

2. Click the **Expand Panels arrow** ◂◂ at the top of the panels dock.

   The Main toolbar may appear beneath the Application bar (Win). Here you can perform common actions, such as creating, saving, importing, exporting, printing a document, as well as adjusting objects on the canvas.

   TIP To increase the size of a panel, place the cursor in between panels, then drag ↕ up or down.

3. Drag the **gray title bar** on the Document window next to the name tab down, then compare your screen to Figure 5.

   The Document window is in Restore Down view.

4. Drag the **bottom-right corner** of the Document window to approximate the size shown in Figure 6.

5. Click **File** on the Application bar, then click **Close**.

   TIP You can also press [Ctrl][W] (Win) or ⌘[W] (Mac) to close a file.

You adjusted panels in the Fireworks window, and closed a document.

Work with New
AND EXISTING DOCUMENTS

What You'll Do

In this lesson, you will set document properties, use Help, add a layer, and copy an object between documents.

Working with Files

Fireworks files are known as **documents**. When you create a new document, you can set properties such as the document's size, resolution, and canvas color. Fireworks will retain the changes you make to document properties as the default settings for new documents. A Fireworks document consists of many **layers**, which you can use to organize the elements of your document. A layer can contain multiple objects, all of which are managed in the Layers panel. By default, the **Layers panel** has the Web layer, which stores HTML objects such as slices and hotspots, for use in Dreamweaver. You can also create a **sub layer**, which helps you better organize related objects in a layer in the Layers panel. A layer group can contain multiple sub layers.

Working with Pages

By default, each Fireworks document contains one page, but you can create several different pages. A **page** stores all the layers in a document, and you can create multiple pages, each containing its own layers and unique settings, which is useful when you want to view different versions of a design or of a Web page. You can also create a **Master Page**

containing repetitive elements, and share pages across layers. Using a Master Page can serve as a design template for your design.

NEW When you create a new document from a template, open, or import a document with multiple pages, you can preview each page in the respective New From Template, Open, or Import dialog boxes. You can use controls in the preview pane beneath the thumbnail to move between pages. The page visible in preview becomes active when you create, open, or import the document. Figure 7 shows page previews for a template.

To create a new page from an existing one, or create a new one, show the Pages panel, right-click the selected page, then click New Page or Duplicate Page, respectively. You can manage pages using other commands on the context menu.

Although you can open or import a wide range of file formats, the files you create in Fireworks are PNG files and have a .png extension. PNG files have unique characteristics that afford you considerable flexibility in working with images. Different file formats support images differently. You can divide a document or image into parts and then individually optimize and export them in the format that best supports the image. For example, you can save a photograph in your document as a JPEG and a cartoon illustration as a GIF. The JPEG format compresses color efficiently and is thus best suited for photographs, whereas GIF format is suitable for line art.

You can also open an existing file or import a file into a Fireworks document. You can copy and paste or drag and drop images, graphics, or text into a Fireworks document from other documents or applications, or from a scanner or digital camera. Figure 7 shows an image copied from a document to be part of the design in another document.

Accessing Help

In Windows, you access the Fireworks Help system by clicking Help on the Application bar, and then clicking Fireworks Help. You can find what you need by exploring a topic in a category or by typing a word or phrase in the Search text box on the Application bar.

You can search the extended Adobe Community, Adobe.com only, or help topics installed with your program. You can also click the Getting Started, New Features and Resources links on the Start page to access materials such as tutorials, articles, and blogs about Fireworks.

Commands on the Help menu link you to online support, such as Fireworks Exchange, where you can download useful and creative add-ins for Fireworks and other Adobe applications. You can also link to the Fireworks Support Center and Adobe Online Forums.

Figure 7 *Previewing pages in the New From Template dialog box*

Figure 8 *Object copied between documents*

Open documents

Page preview

Preview controls

Copied image

Create and save a new document

1. Click **File** on the Application bar, then click **New** to open the New Document dialog box.

   TIP You can also press [Ctrl][N] (Win) or ⌘[N] (Mac) to open a new file, or you can click Fireworks Document (PNG) on the Start page.

2. Type **325** in the Width text box, double-click the value in the Height text box, type **275**, then verify that the resolution is **72**.

3. Click the **Custom canvas option** in the Canvas color section of the New Document dialog box, then click the **Canvas Color box** ☐.

4. Select the value in the Swap colors text box, type **#0099FF**, as shown in Figure 9, press [**Enter**] (Win) or [**return**] (Mac), then click **OK**.

   A new Document window appears in the Fireworks window.

   TIP You can also select a canvas color by clicking a color swatch in the color pop-up window. The canvas color appears in the Default colors box.

5. Click **File** on the Application bar, click **Save As**, type **my_blue_heaven** in the File name text box (Win) or Save As text box (Mac), click the **Save in list arrow** (Win) or **Where box list arrow** (Mac) to choose your destination drive and folder, then click **Save**.

6. Compare your screen to Figure 10.

You set the size and color of the canvas for a new document, and then saved it.

Figure 9 *Selecting a canvas color in the New Document dialog box*

Default colors box

Swap colors text box

Custom color box

Figure 10 *Newly created document with custom canvas*

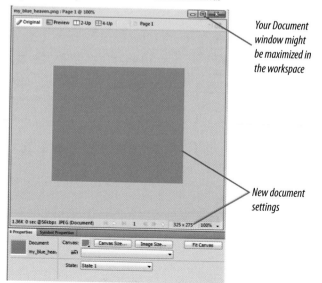

Your Document window might be maximized in the workspace

New document settings

Getting Started with Adobe Fireworks

Figure 11 *Using Help in Fireworks*

Type keywords here

Click to select search location and filter

Click to change program

Click to expand topic

Figure 12 *Help search results*

Click this search result

Search results

Figure 13 *Layer added to Layers panel*

New layer

New/Duplicate layer button

Get Help and add a layer

1. Click **Help** on the Application bar, click **Fireworks Help** (Mac), then click **Fireworks Help** (Win).

   The Adobe Fireworks CS5 help window opens, as shown in Figure 11. Because web sites are updated constantly, your page might differ.

   TIP Press Update if prompted to update local content.

2. Type **add and remove layers** in the Search text box at the top of the Help window, then press [**Enter**] (Win) or [**return**] (Mac).

   Search results appear in the left pane.

   TIP You can also open the Help system by pressing [F1].

3. Click **Adobe Fireworks CS5 * Add and remove layers** in the left pane, read the instructions on adding a layer in the right pane, as shown in Figure 12, then click the **Help window Close button**.

4. Click **Layers** in the Panels dock to open the Layers panel (if necessary), click the **New/Duplicate Layer button** in the Layers panel, then compare your Layers panel to Figure 13.

   A new layer, Layer 2, appears in the Layers panel above the active layer.

   TIP Expand the Layers panel (if necessary) to see all the layers.

You used Help to get instructions for adding a layer in Fireworks, and then used that information to add a layer in the Layers panel.

Drag and drop an object

1. Click **File** on the Application bar, navigate to where you store your Data Files, click **pool.png**, click **Open**, drag the **pool.png tab** in the Document window until it appears as a separate Document window, then resize both windows as shown in Figure 14.

   The documents first appear on separate tabs in the same Document window, and then appear side by side.

2. Make sure that the **Pointer tool** is selected in the Tools panel.

3. Click the mouse anywhere on the pool image, drag it to the my_blue_heaven document, then compare your image to Figure 15.

   TIP You can also select the object, click Edit on the Application bar, click Copy, position the pointer in the target document, click Edit on the Application bar, then click Paste.

4. Close pool.png without saving changes.

5. Click the **Align panel** at the top of the panels dock.

6. Click the **Arrange button** so it is darkened and Relative To Canvas appears on the Align panel, click the **Align horizontal center icon**, then click the **Align vertical center icon** in the Align section.

   The image is centered on the canvas horizontally and vertically, as shown in Figure 16.

7. Collapse the Align panel, click **File** on the Application bar, then click **Save**.

You copied an object from one document to another, and then aligned the object on the canvas.

Figure 14 *Viewing open documents in separate Document windows*

Figure 15 *Copying an object from one document to another*

Copied object

Figure 16 *Object aligned to canvas*

Relative To Canvas button

Align vertical center icon

Align horizontal center icon

Figure 17 *Applying an Inner Shadow filter*

Filter applied
to image

Inner Shadow
pop-up window

Figure 18 *Photoshop Live Effects dialog box*

Bevel and Emboss
check box

Effect settings

Figure 19 *Filters applied to image*

Lesson 2   Work with New and Existing Documents

Apply filters to an image

1. Verify that the **Pointer tool** and bitmap image are selected.

2. Click the **Add Live Filters button** in the Property inspector, point to **Shadow and Glow**, click **Inner Shadow**, then compare your screen to Figure 17.

   The Inner Shadow pop-up window opens, where you can adjust settings for the filter. Filters enhance the appearance of objects by transforming pixels in the image.

   TIP You can apply a filter to any Fireworks object, although not all filters can be applied to bitmap images. You'll learn more about filters in the next chapter.

3. Press **[Enter]** (Win) or **[return]** (Mac) to close the pop-up window and apply the filter.

4. Click the **Add Live Filters button** in the Property inspector, click **Photoshop Live Effects**, click the **Bevel and Emboss check box**, then click **Bevel and Emboss** (Mac).

   The Photoshop Live Effects dialog box opens to Bevel and Emboss options, as shown in Figure 18.

   TIP You can only apply one Photoshop Live Effect to an object.

5. Click the **Style list arrow**, click **Outer Bevel**, then click **OK** to apply the effect.

6. Click a blank part of the Document window, then compare your screen to Figure 19.

7. Save your work, then close my_blue_heaven.png.

You applied native Fireworks and Photoshop filters to an image.

Work with
LAYERS AND IMAGES

What You'll Do

In this lesson, you will modify a bitmap image and create and lock a layer.

Understanding the Layers Panel

Although *layer* is a common term in graphic design applications, a layer's function varies depending on the program. In other applications, such as Adobe Photoshop, you use layers to manipulate **pixels**, discrete squares of color values that are the smallest elements in a photograph. In Fireworks, you use layers to position **objects**, which are the individual elements in your document. You can arrange the elements in your document in a logical design order. For example, you can place related elements on the same layer, such as the design elements of a logo, or all the buttons for a Web page. The position of objects/layers in the Layers panel affects their appearance in your document. Each object is akin to an image on a clear piece of plastic—you can stack them on top of each other. The artwork on the bottom may be obscured by the layers above it but you can adjust visibility by making some pieces more transparent.

You can place as many objects as you want on a layer, arrange them in any order, and select one or more of them at a time. A document can easily accumulate numerous layers and objects, which can make it difficult to quickly find the ones you want. Figure 20 shows components of the Layers panel. You can collapse layers, lock layers to prevent any inadvertent editing, duplicate layers, create sub layers, and hide or show layers.

QUICK TIP

An object in Fireworks corresponds to a layer in Photoshop.

Customizing your View of the Layers Panel

You can select the size of the thumbnails that are displayed in the Layers panel or choose not to display them at all. To change thumbnail size, click the Options menu button in the Layers panel, click Thumbnail Options, then select the size you want.

Understanding Bitmap Images and Vector Objects

Fireworks allows you to work with both bitmap and vector graphic images in your document. A **bitmap graphic** represents a picture image as a matrix of dots, or pixels, on a grid. Bitmaps allow your computer screen to realistically depict the pixel colors in a photographic image. In contrast, **vector graphics** are mathematically calculated objects composed of anchor points and straight or curved line segments, which you can fill with color or a pattern and outline with a stroke.

Because a bitmap image is defined pixel by pixel, when you scale a bitmap graphic, you lose the sharpness of the original image. **Resolution** refers to the number of pixels in an image, which affects an image's clarity and fineness of detail. On-screen resolution is usually 72 or 96 pixels per inch (ppi). (Print graphics require much higher resolution.) Bitmap images are resolution-dependent—resizing results in a loss of image quality. The most visible evidence is the all-too-familiar jagged appearance in the edges of a resized image.

Because they retain their appearance regardless of how you resize or skew them, vector graphics offer far more flexibility than bitmap images. They are resolution-independent—enlarging retains a crisp edge. Figure 21 compares the image quality of enlarged vector and bitmap images.

Figure 20 *Layers panel components*

Collapsed layer

Eye icon (indicates layer is visible)

Square (indicates layer is hidden)

Sub layer

Lock/Unlock Layer icon

Delete Selection button

New/Duplicate Layer button

New Sub Layer button

Figure 21 *Comparing vector and bitmap images*

Vector image remains sharp when enlarged

Bitmap image becomes blurry and jagged when enlarged

Open a document and display the Layers panel

1. Open fw1_1.png, then save it as **breads**.

2. Make sure that the Layers panel is visible and expanded to show all the layers.

3. Click the **eye icon** 👁 next to the Great_Crusts object in Layer 1 in the Layers panel to hide the layer.

   Notice that this icon toggles between an eye icon and a blank box, depending on whether the layer is hidden or visible.

4. Compare your image to Figure 22, then click the **gray square** □ next to the Great_Crusts object in Layer 1.

5. Click the **Great_Crusts object** in Layer 1 in the Layers panel, then drag it beneath the Loaves&Brie object in the Background layer until a flashing double line (Win) or dark black line (Mac) appears beneath the Loaves&Brie object, as shown in Figure 23.

   The Great_Crusts object is now beneath or behind the Loaves&Brie object in the Background layer, so it is no longer visible, although you can still see its blue selection line.

6. Verify that the Great_Crusts object is still selected, then click the **Delete Selection button** 🗑 in the Layers panel.

You hid and displayed an object in a layer in the Layers panel and moved and deleted an object. Moving an object in the Layers panel affects its visibility in the document.

Figure 22 *Hiding a layer in the Layers panel*

Text is no longer visible
on the canvas

Blank square indicates
layer is hidden

Figure 23 *Moving an object to a different layer*

Thick double line indicates
location of layer when you
release the mouse

Object being moved to
the Background layer

Figure 24 *Brightness/Contrast dialog box*

Drag slider to
desired setting

Click check box to compare
changes to original

Figure 25 *Layer locked in Layers panel*

Click square in
lock column to
lock layer

Lock layer icon

Edit a bitmap image and lock a layer

1. Click the **Loaves&Brie object** on the Background layer to select it (if necessary).

2. Click **Filters** on the Application bar, point to **Adjust Color**, then click **Brightness/Contrast**.

   Brightness adjusts the relative lightness or darkness of an image. Contrast adjusts the relative differences in intensity between the darkest and brightest parts of an image.

3. Drag the Brightness slider to **−3**, then drag the Contrast slider to **8**.

   You cannot delete or modify a filter you apply from the Application bar. You can, however, undo the action in the current editing session.

   TIP You can also enter values in the text boxes.

4. Compare your Brightness/Contrast dialog box to Figure 24, then click **OK**.

   The colors in the image appear richer.

5. Click the **gray square** [ ] in the column in between the eye icon 👁 and the Background folder icon to lock the layer.

   The Lock layer icon 🔒 replaces [ ] in the column. You can lock entire layers or individual objects.

   TIP While it is locked, you cannot edit a layer or its objects.

6. Compare your Layers panel to Figure 25.

7. Click **File** on the Application bar, then click **Save**.

You adjusted the brightness and contrast of the Loaves&Brie object, locked the layer, and saved the file.

Create
SHAPES

What You'll Do

In this lesson, you will display rulers and guides, and create and modify a vector object.

Using Rulers, Guides, and the Grid

Rulers, guides, and the grid are design aids that help you precisely align and position objects in your document. Because Fireworks graphics are Web-oriented, where the rule of measurement is in pixels, ruler units are always in pixels. You insert guides from the rulers by dragging them onto your canvas. Guides do not print or export, although you can save them in the original PNG document. If you want to specify an exact location, you can double-click a guide and then enter a position in the Move Guide dialog box. You can adjust the grid to snap objects directly to guides and the grid.

QUICK TIP

To change guide and grid settings, click Edit on the Application bar, click Preferences, click Guides and Grids, then make desired changes.

Sizing and Repositioning Objects

You can use the Property inspector to view information about the position of the pointer on the canvas and selected objects. When an object is selected, its position on the canvas is shown in the left corner of the Property inspector. The W and H values show the object's size, while the X and Y values show the object's position on the canvas. You can use the coordinate values to create, resize, or move an object to a precise location. You can also resize and move objects by dragging their sizing handles and moving them on the canvas.

Using the Tools Panel

The Tools panel contains selection, drawing, and editing tools. Although you can use many tools on both bitmap and vector graphics, graphic mode-specific tools are housed in separate sections of the Tools panel. You can also select a tool by pressing its keyboard shortcut, shown in Figure 26.

Some tools have multiple tools associated with them. A small arrow in the lower-right corner of a tool button indicates that more tools are available in that tool group. To select additional tools, click and hold the tool, then click the tool you want from the list, as shown in Figure 26. The properties associated with a selected tool are displayed in the Property inspector, although not all tools have properties associated with them.

For example, when you select any of the basic tools or Auto Shapes, such as the Ellipse tool or the Arrow Auto Shape, you can adjust the object's fill and stroke settings in the Property inspector.

Based on the object, layer, or tool, Fireworks automatically determines whether you are editing a bitmap or a vector graphic, and activates or nullifies the tool appropriately. Figure 27 shows the Blur tool (a bitmap tool) actively blurring the floral bitmap image, but the tool can't blur the text because text is a vector object. Bitmap selection tools modify the pixels in a bitmap image, which makes them useful for retouching photographic images.

You can create vector shapes using the tools in the Vector portion of the Tools panel. The shape tool group is divided into two groups: basic shape tools (Ellipse, Rectangle, and Polygon tools) and Auto Shapes. You can adjust the height, width, and overall size of basic shapes by dragging their sizing handles. You can also use the Subselection tool to adjust individual points in any shape or path.

Understanding Auto Shapes

You can create basic shapes or Auto Shapes by selecting the shape and then dragging the mouse pointer on the canvas. For Auto Shapes, you can also click the canvas to create a presized Auto Shape. Auto Shapes are complex vector shapes that you can manipulate by dragging control points. A **control point** is the yellow diamond that appears when you select an Auto Shape on

Figure 26 *Selecting tools in the Tools panel*

Figure 27 *Using a bitmap tool on different graphic types*

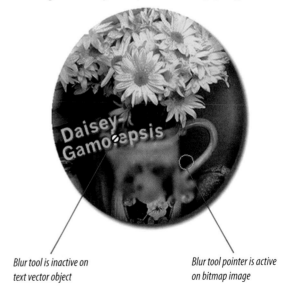

Blur tool is inactive on text vector object

Blur tool pointer is active on bitmap image

the canvas. When you roll the mouse pointer over a control point, a tool tip appears, giving you information on how to adjust the Auto Shape. You can adjust individual aspects specific to each shape, such as tips, corners, roundness, the number of points or sectors, and so on. Figure 28 shows the control points for an Auto Chamfer Rectangle and for a Smart Polygon. You can modify an Auto Shape by dragging the control point or by pressing a keyboard shortcut key, such as [Shift], [Alt], and [Ctrl] (Win); or [Shift], [option], and [⌘] (Mac). Figure 29 shows how you can radically alter the appearance of an Auto Shape by dragging control points and using the Pointer tool or the Subselection tool.

QUICK TIP

To access additional Auto Shapes in Fireworks, open the Shapes panel, and then drag one of the displayed Auto Shapes to the canvas. To download Auto Shapes from the Adobe Exchange web site, click the Panel options button in the Shapes panel, and then click Get More Auto Shapes.

Applying Fills and Strokes

You can fill an object with a solid color, texture, or pattern. When you apply a **fill**, you can adjust the following attributes: its color and category (such as solid, gradient, or pattern), and the type and amount of edge of the fill. You can apply a border, known as a **stroke**, to an object's edge. You can set several stroke attributes, including color, tip size (the size of the stroke), softness, and texture.

Anti-aliasing blends the edges of a stroke or text with surrounding pixels so that the edges appear to smooth into the background. Anti-aliasing reduces the contrast between the edge and the background by adding pixels of intermediate color.

QUICK TIP

Aliasing can occur when an analog image is represented in a digital mode, such as a graphic image viewed on a computer. The edges of the graphic are rectangles and squares, which do not always illustrate a curve well.

Figure 28 *Control points for Auto Shapes*

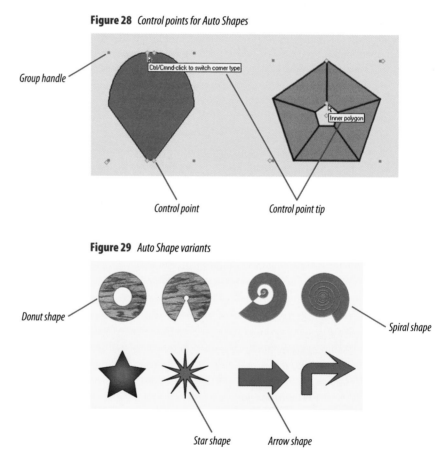

Group handle

Ctrl/Cmnd-click to switch corner type

Inner polygon

Control point

Control point tip

Figure 29 *Auto Shape variants*

Donut shape

Spiral shape

Star shape

Arrow shape

Figure 30 *Guides displayed in Document window*

Renamed layers

Guides

Rename layers and display the guides

1. Double-click **Layer 1**, type **Logo** in the Layer name text box, then press [**Enter**] (Win) or [**return**] (Mac).

   The layer is renamed.

2. Click the **New/Duplicate Layer button** on the Layers panel to create a new layer, Layer 1.

3. Double-click **Layer 1**, type **AdCopy** in the Layer name text box, then press [**Enter**] (Win) or [**return**] (Mac).

4. Click **View** on the Application bar, point to **Guides**, then click **Show Guides** (if necessary).

   Horizontal and vertical guides appear in the Document window, as shown in Figure 30.

You created and named a layer, and displayed guides in the Document window.

Create a vector object

1. Click and hold the **Rectangle tool** in the Tools panel, then click the **Rounded Rectangle tool** .

TIP The basic Rectangle shape has a Rectangle roundness setting on the Property inspector, which you can use to create a rounded rectangle basic shape.

2. Click the **Fill category list arrow** in the Property inspector, click **Solid** (if necessary), then click the **Fill Color box** to open the color pop-up window.

(continued)

3. When the pointer changes to 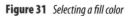, click the **last swatch** in the second row from the bottom (#FFFFCC) in the color pop-up window, as shown in Figure 31.

4. Click the **Edge of fills list arrow** in the Property inspector, click **Anti-Alias** (if necessary), click the **Texture name list arrow**, click **Grain** (if necessary), click the **Amount of texture list arrow**, then drag the slider to **10**, then click the **Transparent check box**.

TIP Fireworks automatically applies the last selected stroke and fill to a shape.

5. Use the guides to position the **pointer ┼** at the start coordinates shown in Figure 32, click, then drag the pointer until **220** appears in the Selection width box in the Property inspector and **110** appears in the Selection height box.

6. Click **Edit** on the Application bar, then click the **Undo Shape Tool** (Win) or **Undo Auto Shape Tool** (Mac).

The rectangle disappears.

TIP You can also press [Ctrl][Z] (Win) or ⌘ [Z] (Mac) to undo a command.

7. Click **Edit** on the Application bar, click **Redo Shape Tool** (Win) or **Redo Auto Shape Tool** (Mac), then compare your image to Figure 32.

TIP You can also press [Ctrl][Y] (Win) or ⌘ [Y] (Mac) to redo a command.

You set properties for the Rounded Rectangle tool, created a rounded rectangle shape, and then practiced undo and redo commands.

Figure 31 *Selecting a fill color*

Your default settings might vary

Selection width text box

Selection height text box

Texture name list arrow

Edge of fills list arrow

Amount of texture list arrow

In Step 3, click this color swatch

Figure 32 *Newly created rounded rectangle shape*

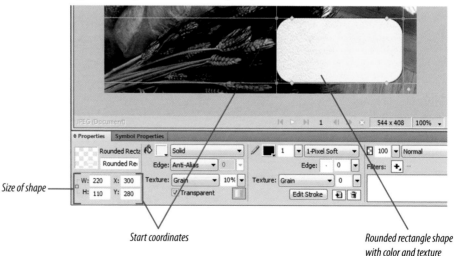

Size of shape

Start coordinates

Rounded rectangle shape with color and texture

Figure 33 *Stroke properties*

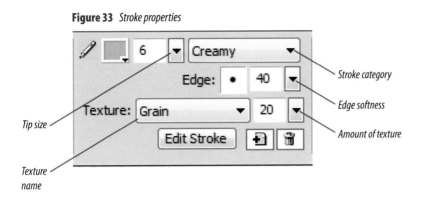

Tip size

Texture name

Stroke category

Edge softness

Amount of texture

Figure 34 *Stroke settings applied to rounded rectangle*

Apply a stroke to an object

1. Click the **Stroke Color box** ✎ ■ in the Property inspector, type **#FF9900** in the Swap colors text box, then press [**Enter**] (Win) or [**return**] (Mac).

   TIP If Grain is not selected as the Texture, click the Texture list arrow, then click Grain.

2. Click the **Stroke category list arrow**, point to **Charcoal**, then click **Creamy**.

3. Click the **Tip size list arrow**, then drag the slider to **6**.

4. Enter the remaining stroke values shown in Figure 33.

5. Click **View** on the Application bar, point to **Guides**, then click **Show Guides** to turn off guides.

6. Click **Select** on the Application bar, click **Deselect** (if necessary), then compare your image to Figure 34.

7. Save your work.

You fine-tuned stroke properties to add a border to an object that suits the style and mood you want to create. You selected stroke properties, applied a stroke to the rectangle, and turned off the guides. You used the Deselect command so that you could see the results of your work without seeing the selection bounding box.

Create and
MODIFY TEXT

What You'll Do

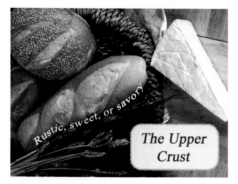

In this lesson, you will create text and a path, attach the text to the path, save your document, and then exit the program.

Using Text in a Document

The text features in Fireworks are typical of most desktop publishing programs—after you select the Text tool, you can preview the font family and modify properties, including size, color, style, kerning, leading, alignment, text flow, offset, and anti-alias properties. **Kerning** adjusts the spacing between adjacent letters, **tracking** affects the space between two letters or a block of text or a range of letters, and **leading** adjusts the amount of space between lines of text. You can set other text attributes, such as indent, alignment, the space before and after a paragraph, and baseline shift, in the Property inspector. Figure 35 shows Text tool properties in the Property inspector. You can automatically preview in your document the changes you make to Text tool properties.

After you create text, you can edit the text block as a whole, or edit just a range of text. When you create text, you can create auto-sizing or fixed-width text blocks. **Auto-sizing** means that the text block expands to accommodate the text you enter. If you delete text, the text block contracts. You can spell check text at any time, including selecting multiple text blocks to check their spelling.

QUICK TIP

You can change the orientation of any selected text block by clicking the Set text orientation button in the Property inspector, and then selecting a vertical or horizontal text orientation.

Attaching Text to a Path

You can manipulate text by creating a path, and then attaching text to it. A **path** is an open or closed vector consisting of

Using Text Blocks

Fireworks creates auto-sized text blocks by default. The text block expands or contracts as you add or delete text. To create a fixed-width text block, select the Text tool, then drag to create a text block on the canvas. As you type, the text will wrap to fit the text block.

a series of anchor points. **Anchor points** join path segments—they delineate changes in direction, whether a corner or a curve. To create a path, you use the Pen tool to define points in your document, or create a shape and then attach the text to it. You can edit text after you've attached it to a path. You can also edit the path, but only if it is not attached to text. Figure 36 shows text attached to paths.

NEW If you have a long block of text to attach to a path, it may be difficult to see if all the text fits on the path. Fireworks displays a text flow indicator (a square crosshair icon) if the text overflows the path.

QUICK TIP

You can attach text to paths created with a basic shape tool or to paths of Auto Shapes that you've modified with the Freeform tool or the Reshape Area tool.

To edit a path, you adjust the anchor points. To adjust the anchor points, select the path, select the Subselection tool in the Tools panel, and then drag points to new locations on the path as desired. You can also modify the appearance of text on a path by changing its alignment, orientation, and direction. By combining the shape of the path with the text alignment, orientation, and direction, you can create unique-looking text objects that convey the exact message you want.

Figure 36 *Text attached to a path*

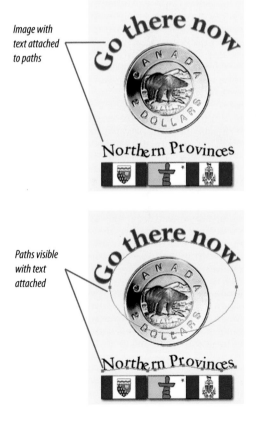

Figure 35 *Text options in the Property inspector*

Tracking

Paragraph indent

Horizontal scale

Space preceding and after a paragraph

Leading

Set text orientation

Create text using the Text tool

1. Click the **Text tool** T in the Tools panel.

2. Click the **Font Family list arrow** in the Property inspector, click **Times New Roman**, verify that Regular appears as the Font Style, double-click the **Size text box**, then type **36**.

3. Click the **Fill Color box** in the Property inspector, type **#663300** in the Swap colors text box, then press [**Enter**] (Win) or [**return**] (Mac).

4. Click the **Faux Bold button** B in the Property inspector to select it.

5. Click the **Faux Italic button** *I* to select it.

6. Click the **Auto kern check box** to select it.

7. Verify that the Center alignment button and Smooth Anti-Alias options are selected, then compare your Property inspector to Figure 37.

8. Click the top middle of the rectangle, type **The Upper**, press [**Enter**] (Win) or [**return**] (Mac), then type **Crust**.

   Text objects are automatically named with matching text in the Layers panel. Text layers are denoted by a small text icon T in the layer thumbnail.

   (continued)

Figure 37 *Setting Text tool properties*

Font Style list arrow

Font family list arrow

Fill Color box

Faux Bold button

Faux Italic button

Auto kern check box

Size text box

Figure 38 *Formatted and aligned text*

9. Expand the Align panel (if necessary), then make sure that the Relative To Object button is selected.

10. Click the **Pointer tool** in the Tools panel, press and hold [**Shift**], click the **rectangle** on the canvas, click the **Align horizontal center icon** in the Align panel, then click the **Align vertical center icon** .

    Both the rectangle and the text objects are selected and aligned to each other.

11. Click **Select** on the Application bar, then click **Deselect**.

    TIP You can also press [Ctrl][D] (Win) or ⌘ [A] (Mac) to deselect an object.

12. Compare your screen to Figure 38, then save your work.

NEW Selecting and Formatting Text

Fireworks offers a quick and useful way to select and format different words anywhere in a text block and at any time. Press and hold [Shift][Alt] (Win) or [Shift][option] (Mac), click two or more words in a text block, then format them. You can quickly reselect just those words—even if you have closed and reopened the document—by selecting the Text tool, pressing and holding [Alt] (Win) or [option] (Mac), and then clicking any of the words.

Spell check text

1. Click the **Text tool** T in the Tools panel, double-click the **Size text box** in the Property inspector, type **24**, then verify that the Faux Bold button B and Faux Italic button I are selected.

2. Click the **Fill Color box** ✎ 🔲 in the Property inspector, type **#FFFFFF** in the Swap colors text box, then press **[Enter]** (Win) or **[return]** (Mac).

3. Click the **wheat** at the bottom of the image, type **Rustic, sweet, or saviry**, then compare your screen to Figure 39.

   The word "saviry" is intentionally misspelled.

4. Click **Text** on the Application bar, click **Check Spelling**, then click **Change**, click **OK** to continue checking the document, then click **OK** to complete the spell check.

   The spell checker found "saviry" and suggests the correct spelling. The word "savory" is now spelled correctly, as shown in Figure 40.

   TIP If prompted to select a dictionary, choose an appropriate language. If you have not used the spell checker in Fireworks before now, perform Spelling Setup.

5. Save your work.

You added text and then checked the spelling of the new text.

Figure 39 *Viewing a misspelled word*

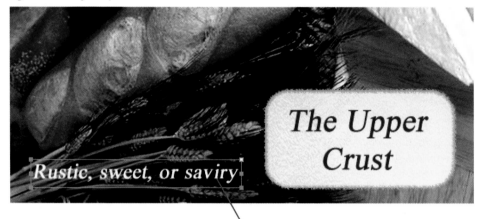

Misspelled word

Figure 40 *Results of spell checking*

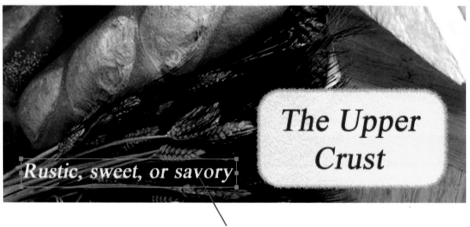

Corrected spelling

Getting Started with Adobe Fireworks

Figure 41 *Creating a path with the Pen tool*

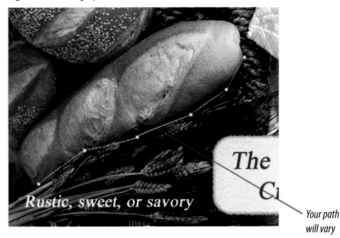

Your path
will vary

Figure 42 *Text attached to path*

1. Click the **Pen tool** in the Tools panel, then click the **AdCopy layer** in the Layers panel.
2. Click the **Fill category list arrow** in the Property inspector, click **None** (if necessary), click the **canvas** in the locations shown in Figure 41, then **double-click** when you reach the last point.

   A path appears in the document and the path is complete.
3. Click the **Pointer tool** in the Tools panel, press and hold [**Shift**], then click the **Rustic, sweet, or savory text** to select both the path and the text.

TIP To select multiple objects on the canvas at once, press and hold [Shift] while selecting each object.

4. Click **Text** on the Application bar, then click **Attach to Path**.

   The text is attached to the path, but does not fill the entire path.
5. Double-click the **Horizontal scale text box** in the Property inspector, type **125**, then press [**Enter**] (Win) or [**return**] (Mac).

   The text fills the path.
6. Click a blank part of the Document window, then compare your image to Figure 42.
7. Save your work.
8. Click **File** on the Application bar, then click **Exit** (Win); or click **Fireworks**, then click **Quit Fireworks** (Mac).

You created a path using the Pen tool, attached text to it, then saved the document and exited the program.

Start Fireworks and open a document.

1. Start Fireworks.
2. Open fw1_2.png.
3. Undock the Layers panel (Win).
4. Collapse and expand the Layers panel.
5. Close fw1_2.png without saving changes.

Create a new document and use Help.

1. Create a new document and set the Width to 200, the Height to 145, and the Canvas Color to #804A0F.
2. Save the document as **pasta_1.png**.
3. Access Help and search for "missing fonts."
4. Double-click the topic on Make missing fonts available in search results, then close the Help window.
5. Show the Pages panel, then Show the Layers panel.
6. Open the file gnocchi.png from where you store your Data Files.
7. Drag the object to pasta_1.png. (*Hint*: You might need to separate and resize the Document windows.)
8. Center the object on the canvas.
9. Close gnocchi.png without saving changes.
10. Deselect objects, then compare your image to Figure 43.
11. Save and close pasta_1.png.

Work with the Layers panel and edit a bitmap image.

1. Open fw1_2.png.
2. Save the file as **pasta_2.png**.
3. Select the Varieties object on the Background layer of the Layers panel, then apply the Auto Levels filter from the Adjust Color menu on the Filter menu.
4. Hide and display the Varieties object in the Layers panel.

5. Move the Ingredients object from Layer 1 above the Varieties object so that it is now in the Background layer.
6. Delete the Ingredients object.
7. Select the Varieties object.
8. Open the Brightness/Contrast dialog box, and set the Brightness to 5 and the Contrast to 8. (*Hint*: Use the Adjust Color command on the Filters menu.)
9. Lock the Background layer.
10. Save your work.

Create a vector object.

1. Display the guides.
2. Create a new layer above Layer 1.
3. Rename the newly created layer **Proper_Names**. (*Hint*: Double-click the layer name.)

4. Select the Smart Polygon tool in the Tools panel.
5. Enter the following fill color properties in the Property inspector: Fill Color: #66CC00, Fill category: Solid, Edge: Feather, Feather amount: 2, Texture: Crosshatch 2, and Texture amount: 30%.
6. Position the pointer at the top-left corner of the rectangle formed by the guides on the left jar.
7. Drag the pointer until the polygon is approximately W: 80 and H: 80.
8. Apply a stroke with the following properties: Color: #006600, Tip size: 2, Stroke Category: Basic Soft rounded, Edge: 100, and Texture amount: 0.
9. Hide the guides, then save your work.

Figure 43 *Completed Skills Review*

Create and modify text.

1. Select the Text tool.
2. Enter the following properties in the Property inspector: Font: Times New Roman, Size: 20 pt, Color: #000000, Bold, and Left alignment.
3. Click the pointer in the polygon, then type **Rotelie**.
4. Center the text in the rectangle (if necessary), then deselect it.
5. Make sure that the Text tool is selected, then enter the following properties: Font: Impact, Size: 40 pt, Color: #990000, and Justified alignment.
6. Click the pointer at the upper-left corner of the canvas, then type **Pasta Pasta Pasta**.
7. Deselect the Pasta Pasta Pasta text.
8. Select the L-Shape tool in the Tools panel, then create an L shape that is W: 140 and H: 200.
9. Select Subselection tool in the Tools panel, click the L-shape, then select the shape and the text. (*Hint*: The Subselection tool is next to the Pointer tool.)
10. Attach the Pasta Pasta Pasta text to the path.
11. Move the text on a path to the top and right side of the canvas.
12. Compare your document to Figure 44, then deselect the text on the path.
13. Save your work.

Figure 44 *Completed Skills Review*

You are in charge of new services at Crystal Clear Consulting. You're preparing to roll out a new Crisis Solutions division, designed to help companies that are experiencing management or financial difficulties. You plan to brief your coworkers on the services at an upcoming company lunch. Each department head—including you—is going to submit a sample introductory Web ad announcing the division. You'll use your Fireworks skills to design a simple ad.

1. Obtain images that symbolize the new consulting service. You will import and copy these images to a layer in the document. You can take your own photos, use scanned media, or obtain an image from your computer or from the Internet. When downloading from the Internet, you should always assume the work is protected by copyright. Be sure to check the web site's terms of use to determine if you can use the work for educational, personal, or noncommercial purposes. Always check the copyright information on any media you download.
2. Create a new docu ment and save it as crystal.png.
3. Import or open one of the images you obtained in Step 1 so that it serves as the background.
4. Rename Layer 1 Background.
5. Create a new layer and give it an appropriate name based on your images.
6. Open another image that you obtained in Step 1 and copy it to the document.

7. Create at least one vector object and apply a fill and stroke to it.
8. Create a new layer and name it Text Objects.
9. Create at least two text objects.
10. Attach at least one text object to a path, then rename the object in the Layers panel, if necessary.
11. Save your work, then examine the sample shown in Figure 45.

Figure 45 *Sample Completed Project Builder 1*

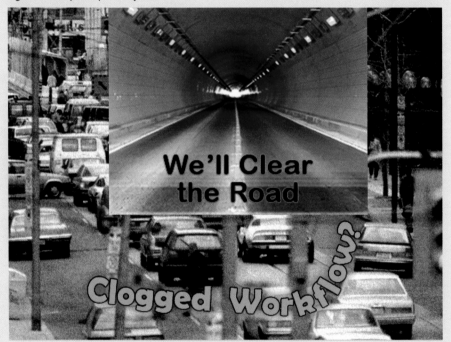

You've just completed your first class in Fireworks. Afterward, you meet with your boss to summarize some of the interesting ways you can attach text to a path. She asks you to prepare a few samples for the next staff meeting.

1. Create a new document and name it **meandering_paths.png**.
2. Create a text object that is at least 15 characters long (you can use the font of your choice and as many words as you want). (*Hint*: You can also apply Orientation commands on the Text menu to the text on the path.)
3. Duplicate the text object two times, then drag the text objects to distribute them on the canvas. (*Hint*: Drag the text layer on top of the New/Duplicate layer button in the Layers panel.)
4. Create a basic shape, then attach one of the text objects to it.
5. Create an Auto Shape, then attach a text object to it. (*Hint*: To select the path of an Auto Shape, select the Subselection tool next to the Pointer tool in the Tools panel, then click the Auto Shape.)
6. Create a simple path using the Pen tool, then attach the third text object to it.
7. Rename the layers to identify the Pen tool or the shape you used as a path.
8. Save your work, then examine the sample shown in Figure 46.

Figure 46 *Sample Completed Project Builder 2*

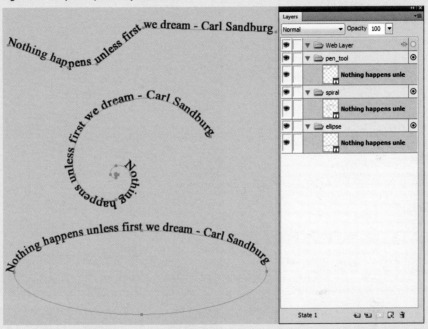

You can develop your design and planning skills by analyzing web sites. Figure 47 shows the home page of the Florida Keys National Marine Sanctuary web site. Study the image and answer the following questions. Because dynamic web sites are updated frequently to reflect current trends, this page might be different from Figure 47 when you open it online.

1. Connect to the Internet and go to *http://floridakeys.noaa.gov/*.
2. Open a document in a word processor, or open a new Fireworks document, then save the file as **floridakeys**.
3. Explore the site and answer the following questions. (*Hint*: If you work in Fireworks, use the Text tool.) For each question, indicate how you determined your answer.
   - What vector shapes does the page contain?
   - What fills or strokes have been added to vector shapes?
   - Do objects appear to have been manipulated in some manner? If so, how?
   - Do objects or text overlap? If so, list the order in which the objects could appear in the Layers panel. List from top to bottom.
   - Has text been attached to a path?
   - What is the overall effect of the text?

Figure 47 *Sample Completed Design Project*

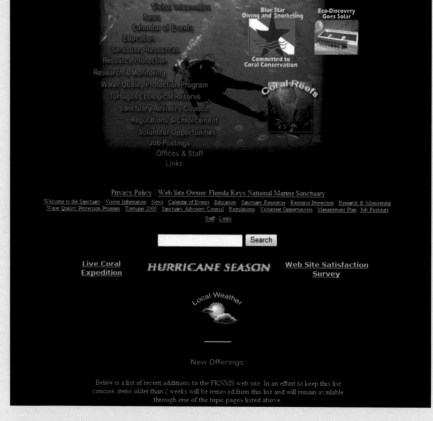

Florida Keys National Marine Sanctuary — http://floridakeys.noaa.gov/

You volunteer to help the Education Committee for Cultural Consequence, a cultural anthropology group. The group is constructing a web site that examines facial expressions and moods in people around the world. The committee is in charge of developing avatars and emoticons—a shorthand method of expressing moods—for the web site. The images will be in the style of the classic smiley face. You will draw a face and add the facial expression of your choice in developing the avatar.

1. Choose an emotion or expression you want to convey.
2. Obtain at least two images for the expression you've chosen. You can take your own photos, or obtain images from your computer or from the Internet. When downloading from the Internet, you should always assume the work is protected by copyright. Be sure to check the web site's terms of use to determine if you can use the work for educational, personal, or noncommercial purposes. Always check the copyright information on any media you download.
3. Create a new document, then save it as **avatar.png**.
4. Choose a canvas color other than white.
5. Create a new layer named Faces and copy the images you've obtained to the new layer.
6. Create a new layer and name it with the emotion you selected in Step 1.

7. Create the avatar on the layer created in Step 6 using tools in the Tools panel, and apply fills and strokes to them as desired. (*Hint*: The avatar in the sample was created with the Ellipse tool and the Pencil tool.)

8. Create a text object that identifies the expression. (*Hint*: The text in the sample is Imprint MT Shadow.)
9. Save your work, then examine the sample shown in Figure 48.

Figure 48 *Sample Completed Portfolio Project*

CHAPTER **2** WORKING
WITH OBJECTS

1. Work with vector tools
2. Modify multiple vector objects
3. Modify color
4. Apply filters to objects and text
5. Apply a style to text

CHAPTER 2 WORKING WITH OBJECTS

Understanding Vector Objects

Fireworks offers a number of vector tools you can use to create vector objects. There are many benefits to working with vector objects. For example, you can modify the properties of a vector path at any time—its shape, size, fill, and stroke—without affecting the quality of the image. This editability makes vector objects easy to work with and adds flexibility to your Web graphics.

After you create an object, you can use a variety of features to transform it into a visually interesting graphic. Many of the tools in Fireworks let you alter or enhance the object. You can combine multiple objects to create entirely new shapes using various Combine Shape tool. You can also modify a graphic's appearance by adjusting the alignment and grouping of multiple objects. You can change a path's color by filling it with a solid color, gradient color, or a texture, or by adjusting the stroke appearance.

The Stroke, Fill, and Filters sections in the Property inspector maximize your ability to experiment. You can create various combinations of strokes, fills, and filters, and turn them on or off in your document at will. An object's overall appearance varies depending on the order in which effects appear in the Filters list in the Property inspector.

TOOLS YOU'LL USE

Subselection tool

Styles panel

Edit Gradient pop-up window

Line tool
Pen tool

Text tool
Ellipse tool

Filters section

Styles section

Work with VECTOR TOOLS

What You'll Do

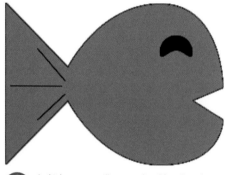

In this lesson, you will create and modify paths and objects using vector tools.

Understanding Vector Tools and Paths

A vector object can be a straight or curved path, or a group or combination of open, closed, straight, or curved paths. When you create a vector object, path segments connect the anchor points of a path. Paths can be open or closed. The points of an open path do not connect; the start and end points of a closed path do connect.

QUICK TIP

The basic Rectangle shape has a Rectangle roundness setting in the Property inspector, which you can use to create a rounded rectangle basic shape. You can choose between pixels or a percentage as your unit of measurement for the corners' curve.

You can draw free-form paths using the Vector Path and Pen tools. The Pen tool creates a path one point at a time.

Making Additional Points with the Pen Tool and Subselection Tool

To create a path with the Pen tool, you click the canvas to create corner points. You can create a curve point as you draw the path by dragging the mouse pointer as you click the canvas. If the newly created path is still selected, you can convert a corner point to a curve point by dragging the point with the Pen tool to create a curve point handle. If you want to convert a corner point that is on an existing path, select the path with the Subselection tool and then drag the point until curve point handles are visible.

Working with Objects

The Vector Path tool creates paths in one motion. Fireworks automatically inserts anchor points as you drag the pointer on the canvas. Regardless of its initial shape, a vector object's path is always editable.

If the path of an object has curves, such as a circle, ellipse, or rounded rectangle, the circular points are known as **curve points**. If the path has angles or is linear, such as a square, star, or straight line, the square points are known as **corner points**. Figure 1 shows points selected for various objects.

When you edit a vector object, you add, delete, or move points along the path; adjust the point handles; or change the shape of the path segment.

Using the Pen Tool and the Subselection Tool

You can add or delete points on a segment using the Pen tool. Modifying the number of points on a path allows you to manipulate it until you have created the exact shape you want. For example, adding points allows you to maneuver the path with greater precision, whereas deleting points simplifies the path's editability. If you want to move points on a path, you can use the **Subselection tool**. You can also use the Subselection tool to select the points of an individual object that has been grouped or to create a curved point.

QUICK TIP

To connect two unconnected paths, select the Pen tool, click the end point of one path, and then click the end point of the other path.

Figure 1 *Points on paths*

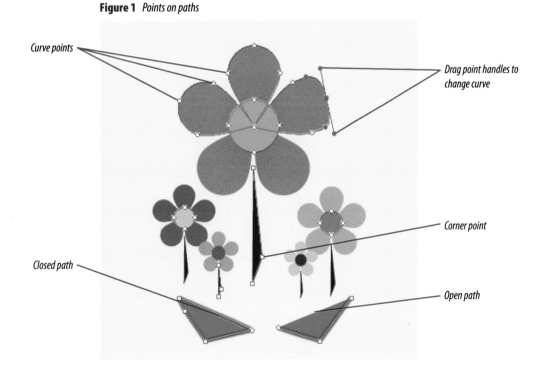

Curve points

Drag point handles to change curve

Corner point

Closed path

Open path

Each anchor point has one or more **point handle**; point handles are visible when you edit a curved path segment, but not when you edit a straight path segment. You can modify the size and angle of a curve by adjusting the length and position of the point handles. You can use both the Pen tool and the Subselection tool to create and modify point handles on curved paths, or to convert curve points into corner points and vice versa.

QUICK TIP

You can add points to an existing path by selecting the Pen tool and then clicking the path; to delete a point, double-click it. To select view and display options for the Pen tool, open the Preferences dialog box.

The two-dimensional curves in a vector object are known as **Bézier curves**, named after the French engineer who developed the mathematical formulas to represent three-dimensional (3D) automobile shapes. Figure 2 shows how you can manipulate a vector object by dragging its curve handles.

As you become more familiar with using vector objects, you can experiment with more intricate vector modifications. In the Pen tool group, you can use the Vector Path tool to draw a path with a selected stroke category and attributes; and the Redraw Path tool lets you extend or redraw a selected path. In the Freeform tool group, you can bend or reshape entire areas of a vector object by pushing and pulling the path; the Reshape Area tool distorts and stretches a path based on the size and strength of the brush tip; and, if you have created a path that has a pressure-sensitive stroke, such as Air Brush Basic or Textured, or Calligraphy Bamboo, you can alter the stroke of a path. You can use the Knife tool to slice a path into multiple objects.

QUICK TIP

You can adjust the stroke properties for all vector tools and the fill properties for many of the vector tools. You can adjust a stroke's appearance by placing it on the inside, center, or outside of the object. To do so, click a stroke alignment button beneath the Stroke color box in the Property inspector.

Figure 2 *Modifying a Bezier curve on a vector path*

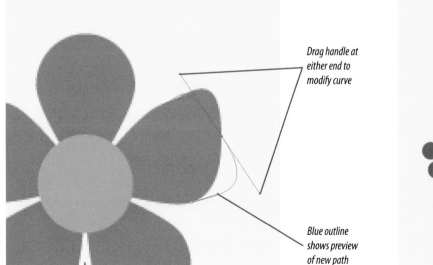

Drag handle at either end to modify curve

Blue outline shows preview of new path

Figure 3 *Modified vector path*

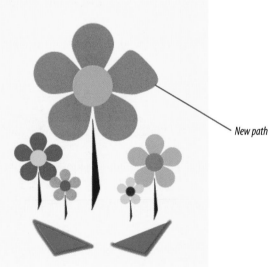

New path

Figure 4 *Selecting a stroke category*

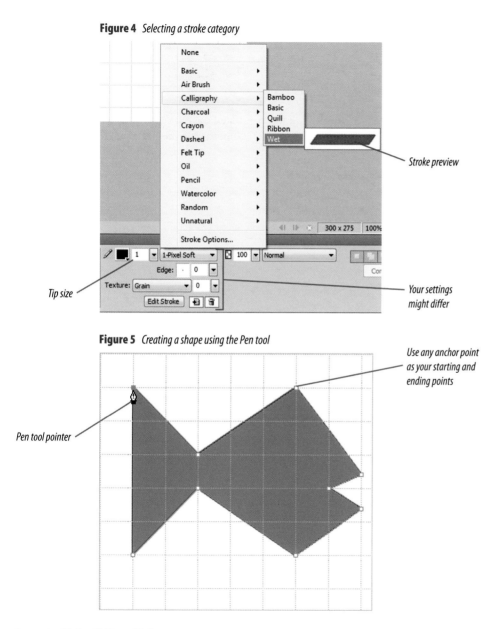

Tip size

Pen tool pointer

Stroke preview

Your settings might differ

Figure 5 *Creating a shape using the Pen tool*

Use any anchor point as your starting and ending points

Create an object using the Pen tool

1. Create a new document, set the Width to **300**, set the Height to **275**, verify that the resolution is 72, the canvas color is white, then save it as **fish.png**.

2. Click **View** on the Application bar, point to **Grid**, then click **Show Grid**.

TIP You can use the grid to help align objects on the canvas.

3. Click the **Pen tool** in the Tools panel.

4. Click the **Fill Color box** in the Property inspector, type **#3399FF** in the Swap colors text box, then press **[Enter]** (Win) or **[return]** (Mac).

5. Click the **Stroke Color box** in the Property inspector, type **#000000** in the Swap colors text box, then press **[Enter]** (Win) or **[return]** (Mac).

6. Click the **Stroke category list arrow**, point to **Calligraphy**, point to **Wet**, compare your screen to Figure 4, then click **Wet**.

TIP You can preview stroke graphics in the Stroke category list.

7. Click the **canvas** in the locations shown in Figure 5.

TIP Close the path by clicking your first anchor point.

You created a new document, set properties for the Pen tool, and created a closed path.

Use the Pen tool and the Line tool to modify a path

1. Position the **Pen tool** ![pen] over the top corner point, then click and drag the **point** to the left to create a smooth curve, as shown in Figure 6.

   The sharp point smoothes into a curve, and the curve **point** handles are visible.

   TIP Undo your changes if you're not satisfied with the results.

2. Repeat Step 1, but click and drag the **bottom corner point** to the left.

   TIP To reselect the object, click the Subselection tool ![subselection] in the Tools panel.

3. Press and hold the **Rectangle tool** ![rect] in the Tools panel, then click the **Ellipse tool** ![ellipse].

   TIP If the Rectangle tool is not visible, click the selected tool.

4. In the Property inspector, verify that the **Stroke Color box** ![stroke] is black, click the **Fill Color box** ![fill] , then click the **top-left black color swatch** in the color pop-up window.

5. Press and hold **[Shift]**, then draw the circle shown in Figure 7.

   TIP Pressing and holding [Shift] draws a perfect square or circle.

6. Click the **Line tool** ![line] in the Tools panel, then drag the **pointer** ![pointer] on the canvas to create the lines shown in Figure 8.

You modified an object using the Pen tool and the Line tool.

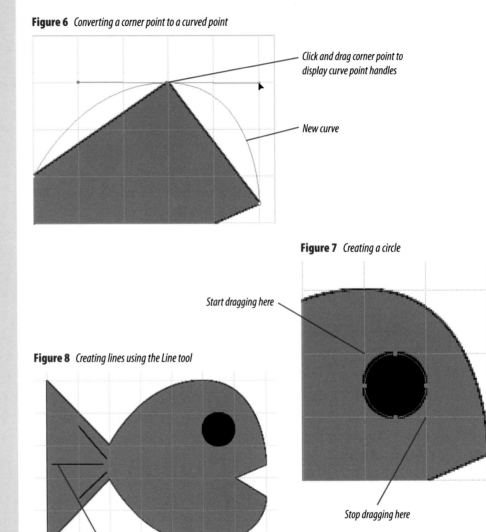

Figure 6 *Converting a corner point to a curved point*

Click and drag corner point to display curve point handles

New curve

Figure 7 *Creating a circle*

Start dragging here

Stop dragging here

Figure 8 *Creating lines using the Line tool*

Click and drag Line tool to create a line

Working with Objects

Figure 9 *Newly created document with custom canvas*

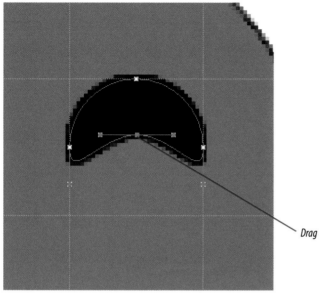

Drag curve handle up

Figure 10 *Modified vector objects*

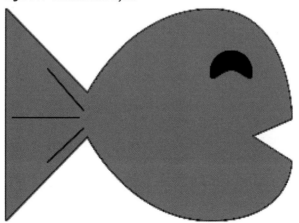

Use the Subselection tool to modify an object

1. Click the **Subselection tool** � in the Tools panel, position the **pointer** ╬ over the bottom curve handle of the black circle, then click the **point**.

TIP Click View on the Application bar, then click Zoom in if you want a larger view while you work.

2. Press and hold **[Shift]**, drag the **point** to the position shown in Figure 9, then click a blank part of the Document window to deselect the object.

   Pressing and holding [Shift] constrains the movement to a straight line.

3. Click **View** on the Application bar, point to **Grid**, then click **Show Grid** to turn off the grid.

4. Compare your image to Figure 10, then save your work.

5. Close fish.png.

You modified an object using the Subselection tool, and then closed the document.

Modify Multiple
VECTOR OBJECTS

What You'll Do

In this lesson, you will create, copy, and align objects, and combine paths of vector objects using the Punch command. You will also group objects.

Aligning and Grouping Objects

Using vector shapes allows you to work with many individual objects at the same time. The Align commands on the Modify menu allow you to align two or more objects with each other: left, centered vertically, and so on. You can open the Align panel to further align, distribute, size, and space multiple objects or to align a vector object's anchor points. You can align objects relative to each other or relative to the canvas.

You can also use the Group command on the Modify menu to configure objects on the canvas. The Group command allows you to combine two or more objects to make a single object. You can group any objects in your document: vector images, bitmap images, text, and so on. Fireworks preserves each individual object's shape and its placement in relation to the other objects. After you group objects, you can modify properties of the group as a whole; for example, by changing the fill color or by applying a stroke. If you want to modify any one of the objects, you can select it with Subselection tool. If the grouped object consists of text and another vector object or bitmap image, you can simply select the text with the Text tool.

Combining the Paths of Multiple Objects

Fireworks offers several ways for combining paths: You can use commands on the Modify, Combine Paths menu, buttons in the Combine Paths section of the Path panel, or the Compound Shape tool in the Property inspector. Many options are shared in each area, such as Join, Split, Union, Intersect, Punch, and Crop. Each command produces a different result. You must select two or more ungrouped vector objects before you can apply a combination command to them. Options for a Combine Paths command and the Compound Shape tool are described next, and illustrated in Figure 11. You can access additional path commands from the Path panel.

Working with Objects

NEW **Join**—The Join command allows you to combine the paths of two or more objects to create a single merged object that includes all the points of both paths. If the two objects are both closed, the new path is a **composite path**; if the objects are open, the new path is a **continuous path**. You can also use the Join command to join two open selected points. The first example in Figure 11 shows all three objects joined.

Add/Union—The Add/Union tool creates a path that is the sum total of all the selected paths.

If two paths overlap, the nonintersecting areas are also included. If the selected paths have different fill, stroke, or effects properties, the new path assumes the properties of the lowest object in the

stacking order, or the lowest layer on the Layers panel. The union example in Figure 11 shows all three objects combined, with the same properties as the bottom object in the Layers panel, the red rectangle.

Subtract/Punch—The outline of the top object carves through all of the lower selected images, but assumes the properties

Figure 11 *Sample Combine Path and Compound Shape features*

Shapes used in Join and Union examples

Compound Shape tool

Normal   Add/Union   Subtract/ Punch   Intersect   Crop

Join

Add/Union

of the object at the bottom of the Layers panel. In Figure 11, the *shape* of the star appears to slice through the circle and rectangle below it, but the end shape has the properties of the bottom object in the Layers panel, the red rectangle .

Intersect—The Intersect command creates an object consisting of the area where the objects' paths overlap, or the common area shared by the objects. In the intersect example shown in Figure 11, the intersection is the area shared by the star, circle, and rectangle.

Crop—The shape of the top path is used to define the areas of any paths beneath it. Crop is the opposite of Subtract/Punch. In the crop example in Figure 11, the shape of the top object, originally made up of the star, has been modified by the shapes of both selected paths beneath it, the circle and the rectangle.

Figure 11 *Sample Combine Path features (continued)*

Subtract/Punch

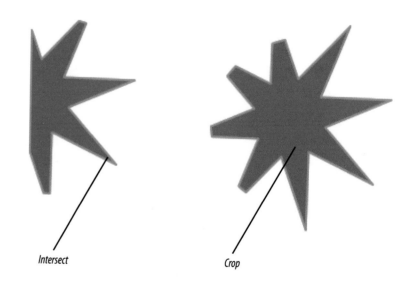

Intersect

Crop

Working with Objects

Figure 12 *New layer added to Layers panel*

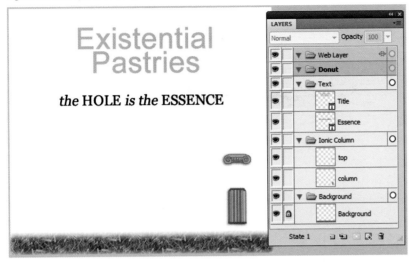

Figure 13 *Viewing fill color settings*

Lesson 2   Modify Multiple Vector Objects

Create a vector shape to an exact size

1. Open fw2_1.png from where you store your Data Files, then save it as **pastries.png**.

2. Click **Layers panel**, expand it so you can see the layers, insert a layer above the Text layer, double-click the **layer name**, type **Donut**, press [**Enter**] (Win) or [**return**] (Mac), then compare your screen to Figure 12.

3. Click the **Ellipse tool** in the Tools panel.

TIP You can modify the fill and stroke colors in the Property inspector or in the Tools panel.

4. Click the **Stroke Color tool** in the Tools panel, then click the **Transparent button** on the top of the color pop-up window, if necessary.

5. Click the **Fill Color tool** in the Tools panel, type **#E5B900** in the Swap colors text box, then press [**Enter**] (Win) or [**return**] (Mac).

TIP If Solid does not appear as the fill option, click the Fill category list arrow, then click Solid.

6. Make sure that the Property inspector is open, that the Edge and Texture values in the Fill section are 0, then compare your Property inspector to Figure 13.

7. Click **View** on the Application bar, click **Rulers**, click **View** on the Application bar, then click **Tooltips**.

Rulers appear at the top and left side of the Document window. Selecting Tooltips allows you to see measurements on the canvas as you create and edit objects.

(continued)

8. Position the pointer ┼ on the canvas at approximately 130 H/180 V on the Rulers, press and hold **[Shift]**, then drag the pointer until W and H values display **165**, as shown in Figure 14.

An orange-yellow circle appears on the canvas and in the Donut layer in the Layers panel.

TIP You can also enter 165 in the width and height text boxes in the Property inspector.

You created a new layer and a circle, and set the layer's properties and diameter.

Copy an object

1. Verify that the ellipse is selected, click **Edit** on the Application bar, then click **Copy**.

2. Click **Edit** on the Application bar, then click **Paste**.

A duplicate ellipse appears on the Layers panel and on the canvas.

TIP You can also press [Ctrl][C] and [Ctrl][V] (Win) or ⌘ [C] and ⌘ [V] (Mac) to copy and paste a selection.

3. Click the **Fill Color box** ⬧☐ in the Property inspector, then click the **top-left black color swatch** in the color pop-up window.

4. Double-click the **W text box** in the Property inspector, type **44**, repeat for the H text box, then press **[Enter]** (Win) or **[return]** (Mac).

5. Compare your image to Figure 15.

You copied an object and changed its properties.

Figure 14 *Creating a shape in a specific size and location*

Rulers

Size

Starting position

Figure 15 *Copied object*

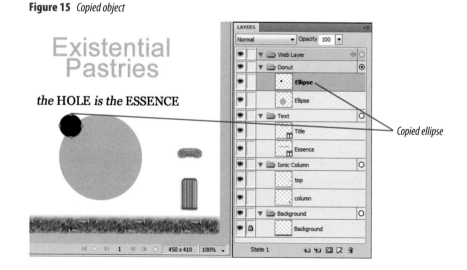

Copied ellipse

Working with Objects

Figure 16 *Aligned objects*

Objects are aligned
vertically and horizontally

Align objects and combine paths

1. Click the **Pointer tool** in the Tools panel, then verify that the black circle is selected.

2. Press and hold **[Shift]**, then click the **orange circle** to select both objects.

3. Click **Modify** on the Application bar, point to **Align**, then click **Center Vertical**.

TIP You can also press [Ctrl][Alt][2] (Win) or ⌘ [option] [2] (Mac) to center objects vertically. You can press [Ctrl][Alt][5] (Win) or ⌘ [option][5] (Mac) to center objects horizontally.

4. Click **Modify** on the Application bar, point to **Align**, click **Center Horizontal**, then compare your image to Figure 16.

   The black circle is perfectly centered on the orange-yellow circle.

(continued)

Cloning, Copying, and Duplicating

You can replicate any object using the Copy/Paste, Clone, or Duplicate commands on the Edit menu, or by pressing and holding [Alt] (Win) or [option] (Mac) and then dragging the object on the canvas. Each menu command creates an identical object and places it above the original on the Layers panel. The Copy/Paste and Clone commands replicate the object directly on top of the original object on the canvas. The Copy command places a copy of the object on the clipboard, which you can use to paste the object in other open files or in other programs. You can also use Copy/Paste commands to copy items on the Frames or Layers panels. The Duplicate command offsets the copied object 10 pixels down and to the right of the original.

5. Click **Modify** on the Application bar, point to **Combine Paths**, click **Punch**, then compare your image to Figure 17.

   The black circle appears to have punched a hole through the orange circle. Graphically, the paths combine to form a donut shape.

6. Double-click the **Composite Path layer** in the Layers panel, type **cake_donut**, press [**Enter**] (Win) or [**return**] (Mac), then compare your Layers panel to Figure 18.

   The object is renamed to a more intuitive name in the Layers panel and in the Path text box in the Property inspector.

TIP You can rename layers in the Layers panel or the Property inspector.

You aligned two objects, combined their paths, and renamed the composite object.

Figure 17 *Objects combined by the Subtract/Punch button*

the HOLE *is the* ESSENCE

Path of both objects are still visible and editable

Figure 18 *Renaming an object*

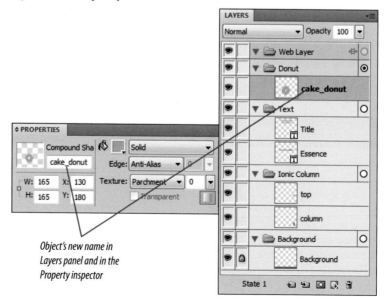

Object's new name in Layers panel and in the Property inspector

Working with Objects

Figure 19 *Moved and aligned object*

x:367 y:285

Smart guides appear to
aid in aligning objects

Figure 20 *Grouped objects*

Grouped object
has single set of
selection handles

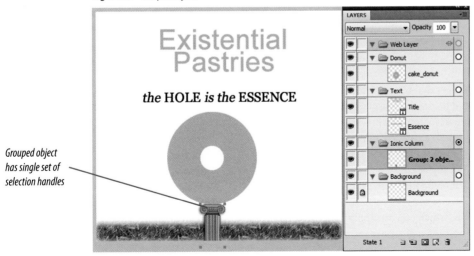

Group objects

1. Click **View** on the Application bar, point to **Smart Guides**, then make sure a check mark appears next to Smart Guides and Snap to Smart Guides.

   Smart Guides are temporary lines that appear that help align objects by snapping them relative to each other. They can also appear when transforming and editing objects.

2. Verify that the Pointer tool ▶ is selected, then click the **top object** in the Ionic Column layer on the Layers panel.

3. Drag the **top object** on top of the column object, as shown in Figure 19.

4. Press and hold [**Shift**], then click the **column object** to select both objects.

   The selection handles for both objects are visible.

5. Click **Modify** on the Application bar, click **Group**, then notice that the object on the Layers panel is renamed Group: 2 objects.

   TIP You can also press [Ctrl][G] (Win) or ⌘ [G] (Mac) to group objects.

6. Drag the **grouped object** under the circle, then when the smart guides appear, release the mouse and compare your screen to Figure 20.

   The selection handles for a single object are visible.

7. Change the name Group: 2 objects to **full_column**.

8. Save your work.

You grouped and moved objects.

Modify COLOR

What You'll Do

Existential
Pastries

the HOLE *is the* ESSENCE

 In this lesson, you will apply a gradient fill to the cake_donut object, and then modify the fill.

Understanding Fills and Gradients

After you create a vector shape, you can modify its appearance by changing its interior, or **fill**. The Property inspector provides powerful tools for enhancing fills in objects. You can apply several kinds of fills to an object, including solid, gradient, Web dither, and pattern. Some of the available fill patterns are shown in Figure 21.

A **solid fill** is the color swatch or hexadecimal value that you specify in the color pop-up window or in the Color Mixer. If you want to ensure that the colors in your document are Web-safe, you can use a **Web Dither fill.** A Web Dither fill approximates the color of a non-Web-safe color by combining two Web-safe colors. **Pattern fills** are bitmap images that have complex color schemes and textures. Fireworks offers dozens of preset patterns from which to choose, or you can create a pattern in Fireworks or another program and then add it to the list. A **gradient** consists of two or more colors that blend into each other in a fixed design. You can select from several preset gradient fills, which you can apply to an object by choosing a fill category or by selecting

the Gradient tool in the Tools panel. The Gradient tool, located as a tool option under the Paint Bucket tool, fills an object with the selected gradient, just as the Paint Bucket tool fills an object with the selected color.

NEW If you apply a linear or radial gradient, you may see a relatively coarse blend or banding in the gradient. To improve the smoothness, click the Gradient Dither button at the bottom of the Fill section of the Property inspector.

QUICK TIP

You can transform or skew a fill's pattern or gradient by adjusting the width, position, rotation, and angle of the fill handles. The gradient adjusts to the contour of the path.

Whether you select a pattern or gradient as a fill, it becomes the active fill color visible in the Tools panel and in the Property inspector. There may be times when you apply a pattern or a gradient and instantly attain the look you want. You can also experiment by modifying the pattern or gradient by adding a transparent gradient, adding an edge or texture, and adjusting the respective amounts of each.

The sophisticated styling you add to objects when you choose a pattern fill type can mimic real-world lighting, surface, and depth, and can have quite a dramatic result, as shown in Figure 22.

You can change gradient colors, including preset gradient colors, at any time without affecting the appearance of the gradient.

The Edit Gradient pop-up window allows you to modify gradient colors and the transition from one color to the next by manipulating the color swatches beneath the **color ramp**. The color ramp creates and displays the range of colors in a gradient, including their transparency.

Figure 21 *Pattern categories*

Figure 22 *Combining color or pattern and texture*

Apply a gradient to an object

1. Click the **Pointer tool** in the Tools panel, then click **cake_donut object** to select it.

2. Click the **Fill category list arrow** in the Property inspector, point to **Gradient**, point to **Ellipse**, as shown in Figure 23, then click **Ellipse**.

   An ellipse gradient is applied to the object, as shown in Figure 24. Gradient fill handles also appear on the gradient.

3. Click the **Fill Color box** in the Property inspector, click the **left color swatch** beneath the color ramp, type **#E5B900** in the Swap colors text box, then press [**Enter**] (Win) or [**return**] (Mac).

4. Repeat Step 3 for the right color swatch, but type **#FF8000** in the Swap colors text box, press [**Enter**] (Win) or [**return**] (Mac) to close the color pop-up window, then compare your color ramp to Figure 25.

5. Click the **Edge of fills list arrow**, click **Feather**, double-click the **Amount of feather text box**, then type **2**.

6. Click the **Texture name list arrow**, click **Parchment**, if necessary, click the **Amount of texture list arrow**, drag the slider to **55**, then verify that the Transparent check box is not selected.

7. Compare your image to Figure 26.

   The new gradient colors and texture are applied to the object.

You selected and modified gradient colors, and applied a texture to an object.

Figure 23 *Fill and gradient categories*

Gradient options

Selected gradient

Fill options

Figure 24 *Gradient applied to object*

Gradient preview; your second color may vary

Figure 25 *Edit Gradient pop-up window*

Click color box to open color pop-up window

Click list arrow to select preset gradient colors

Opacity swatch affects transparency

Gradient preview

Figure 26 *Gradient and texture applied to object*

Working with Objects

Figure 27 *Adjusting fill handles*

Drag round fill handle
to top of objects

Drag right square to
the object's border

Transform an object and its gradient

1. Verify that the cake_donut object is selected.
2. Click **Modify** on the Application bar, point to **Transform**, then click **Rotate 90°CW** to rotate the object.

   The gradient handles flip position.
3. Drag the **round fill handle** up to the top of the objects, then drag the **right square handle** to the position shown in Figure 27.

   The placement and shading of the gradient is altered.
4. Click a blank part of the Document window to deselect the cake_donut object, then compare your image to Figure 28.
5. Save your work.

You rotated the object and adjusted the fill handles to change the gradient.

Figure 28 *Modified gradient in an object*

Understanding Basic Colors in the Color Mixer

You can open the Color Mixer panel from the Window menu. The Color Mixer displays the color palette of the values of the active solid color, which you can also view in the Fill Color box or Stroke Color box in the Tools panel or in the Property inspector. You can edit color values to create new colors by changing the values for each color component of a color model. You can define colors in five different models: RGB (red, green, blue); Hexadecimal (Fireworks default), which has values similar to RGB; HSB (hue, saturation, and brightness); CMY (cyan, magenta, yellow); and Grayscale. The color model you choose depends on the medium in which the graphic will appear. Generally, the models Fireworks offers are geared toward screen-based and Web-based computer graphics, with the exception of the CMY or Grayscale models. If you want to use a Fireworks-created graphic in print media, you might want to export the graphic into another program that has additional print-specific color models, such as Adobe Illustrator or Adobe Photoshop. All file formats exported by Fireworks are based on the RGB color model.

Apply Filters to
OBJECTS AND TEXT

What You'll Do

In this lesson, you will add filters to objects, including text, and change the order of filters in the Filters list.

Understanding Filters

In addition to using the Fill and Stroke sections of the Property inspector, you can use the Filters section to customize the appearance of objects in your document. The Filters section includes the effects found on the Filters menu, as well as bevel, emboss, shadow, and glow effects. For example, you can sharpen, blur, and add the appearance of depth or dimension to an image.

Fireworks calls these **Live Filters** because you can always edit and preview changes to them even after you have saved, closed, and reopened the document. The Filters section lets you experiment with multiple effects. You can add, edit, delete, or hide filters in the Filters list at your convenience. Figure 29 shows the options available in the Filters section and a object with filters applied to it.

> **QUICK TIP**
>
> To edit a filter, select the object(s) to which the filter is applied, and then click the Info icon or double-click the filter name in the list to open its pop-up window or dialog box.

Using Photoshop Live Effects

In addition to Fireworks Live Filters, you can apply Photoshop Live Effects, known as layer effects in Photoshop. Some effects, such as Bevel and Emboss or Shadow, operate similar to their Fireworks equivalents, although the Photoshop Live Effects dialog box often contains additional adjustment controls. When you open a native Photoshop .psd file in Fireworks, the effects are live and editable, although not every attribute may carry over. Figure 30 shows live effects applied to an object.

Using the Filters Menu

The Filters menu on the Application bar contains commands that correspond to many of the features found in the Filters section. However, be aware that the Filters menu contains fewer effects than the Filters section of the Property inspector and you cannot alter their settings after you apply them. You can remove the effect of these filters only in the current work session—more precisely, you can *undo* these filters, not edit them. After you close the document, the Undo actions are lost, and the filter is permanently applied to your document.

Filters and File Size

Although enabled filters generally contribute to increased file size, disabling a filter instead of deleting it does not significantly add to file size. Some filters, such as the Blur, Blur More, Radial Blur, and Gaussian Blur filters, may actually decrease file size because blurring an object decreases the total number of colors in the graphic. The fewer colors used in your document, the less storage space required— hence, smaller file size.

Understanding Transparency

You can adjust the transparency of an image or effect in your document by varying its opacity settings. Fireworks adjusts transparency in terms of percentage, just as it uses percentage settings to adjust the amount of texture in strokes and fills. The **opacity setting** determines if your image is completely opaque (100%) or completely transparent (0%).

Figure 29 *Guides displayed in Document window*

Figure 30 *Viewing Photoshop Live Effects applied to objects*

Live filters

Click check mark or X to
enable or disable a filter

Click to edit
filter

Click to open Filters
pop-up menu

Apply filters to objects

1. Select the **cake_donut object**, then click the **Add Live Filters button** [+.] in the Property inspector.

2. Point to **Bevel and Emboss**, then click **Inner Bevel**.

   The Inner Bevel pop-up window opens.

3. Enter the values shown in Figure 31, then press **[Enter]** (Win) or **[return]** (Mac) to close the Inner Bevel pop-up window.

4. Click the **Add Filters button** [+.] in the Property inspector, then click **Photoshop Live Effects**.

   The Photoshop Live Effects dialog box opens.

5. Click the **Drop Shadow check box**.

6. Enter the values shown in Figure 32, click **Ok**, then click a blank area of the Document window.

   With these filters applied, the cake_donut object now appears to have depth and dimension.

7. Click the **full_column object**, then repeat Steps 4, 5, and 6.

   TIP To delete a filter, select the effect in the Filters list in the Filters section of the Property inspector, then click the Delete Filters button.

8. Deselect the full-column object, then compare your image to Figure 33.

You applied filters to the full_column and cake_donut objects to give them the illusion of three-dimensionality.

Figure 31 *Inner Bevel pop-up window*

Bevel edge shape — Smooth
Width — 35
Contrast — 75%
Softness — 9
Angle — 45
Button preset — Raised

Figure 32 *Drop Shadow properties in Photoshop Live Effects dialog box*

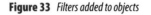

Figure 33 *Filters added to objects*

Inner Bevel

Drop Shadow

Figure 34 *Viewing filters in the Property inspector*

Filters applied to text

Reordered filters

Apply filters to text

1. Click the **Title text object**, click the **Add Filters button** ⊞ in the Property inspector, click **Photoshop Live Effects**, then click the **Bevel and Emboss check box**.

2. Change the style to **Outer Bevel**, the Technique to **Chisel Soft**, and the Depth to **50**, then click **OK** to close the Photoshop Live Effects dialog box.

3. Click the **Title text object**, click the **Add Filter button** ⊞ in the Property inspector, point to **Shadow and Glow**, then click **Inner Shadow**.

4. Double-click the **Distance text box**, type **4**, accept the remaining default settings, then deselect the object.

5. Select the **Title text object**, drag the **Inner Shadow filter** to the top of the Filters list, then notice the difference in the effect.

6. Compare your image to Figure 34, deselect the object, then save your work.

You added filters to a text object, and then rearranged the filters in the Filters list to create a more subtle visual effect.

Using the Measure Tool

The Measure tool is a calculating tool located in the vector shapes tool group in the Tools panel. Click the Rectangle tool or currently selected tool, then click Measure Tool. You can use the Measure tool to create precise measurements on the canvas, which can be very helpful when accurate distances are required. The tool does not draw a shape, but it measures distances by height, width, or on the diagonal. Simply click and drag the pointer from one location to another to create a red arrow with start and end points and the pixel dimensions.

Apply a
STYLE TO TEXT

What You'll Do

▶ In this lesson, you will align objects on the canvas, apply a style to text, and create a new custom style.

Using Live Styles and the Styles Panel

Live Styles contain preset font, color, stroke, or effects attributes that you can apply to objects and text. To access live styles, open the Styles panel from the Window menu, then select a category. Some categories are designed specifically for text, others for objects, including buttons you can use in Web pages. To apply a style, you select an object, and then click a style thumbnail. Figure 35 shows style categories in the Styles panel.

By default the Styles panel opens to the Current Document category, where you can view thumbnails of every style you've added to the current document, even if a style is not currently applied to an object.

You can use the Styles section of the Property inspector to manage styles efficiently. Click the Styles list arrow to view all the styles you've added to the current document. Figure 36 shows styles applied to different objects and text in the current document.

You can customize a style or create a new style and then save it with a unique name. To create a new style, select an object with a style attached to it, adjust the attributes as you wish in the Property inspector, click the New button in the Property inspector, enter a style name, select the attributes you want the style to affect, then click OK.

When you modify a style in the current document, the changes affect objects only in the current document. To modify a current style, select an object with a style applied to it, then change the attributes and effects as desired.

To apply the changes to other objects with that style, click the **Redefine Styles button**.

Be aware that you can permanently adjust the attributes of styles in the Styles panels, so it is best to only modify styles in the current document.

QUICK TIP

To apply the attributes of any object to another object (regardless of style), select the source object, click the Copy command on the Edit menu, select the target object, then click the Paste Attributes command on the Edit menu.

To revert to the original style before it was modified, click the **Clear Overrides button**; to remove the link to a style, click the **Break Link to Style button**; and to delete a style, click the **Delete Style button**.

Figure 35 *Styles panel*

Click to select style category

Style name

Figure 36 *Viewing objects with applied styles*

Styles used in current document

Clear Overrides button

Delete Style button

Selected style

New Style button

Redefine Style button

Break Link to Style button

Align objects and apply a style to text

1. Click **Select** on the Application bar, then click **Select All**.

2. Click **Modify** on the Application bar, point to **Align**, then click **Center Vertical**.

   The objects are centered vertically on the canvas.

3. Click the **Text layer** in the Layers panel, create a **new layer**, then name it **Tagline**.

4. Click the **Text tool** T in the Tools panel, then enter the values shown in Figure 37.

5. Click near the **bottom-left corner** of the canvas, then type **The cake is commentary**.

6. Open the **Styles panel**, click the **Category list arrow**, click **Text Corporate Styles**, then click the **Text Corporate Light Bg 010 thumbnail** at the top of the Styles panel, as shown in Figure 38.

   The style is applied to the text, overriding the settings.

   TIP To view a style's name, roll the mouse over a thumbnail; the name appears at the bottom of the styles panel.

7. Click the **Category list arrow** in the Styles panel, click **Current Document**, then compare your screen to Figure 39.

   You aligned objects, created text, and applied a style to it.

Figure 37 *Text properties*

Select these values

Figure 38 *Selecting a style in the Styles panel*

Click this style; your location may vary

Style name

Figure 39 *Style applied to text*

Selected style

Figure 40 *New Style dialog box*

Select properties to be affected by style

Figure 41 *Viewing new style*

Style name in Property inspector

New style in Styles panel

Figure 42 *New custom style applied to text*

Create a custom style

1. Select the text you just created if necessary, double-click the **Font Size text box** in the Property inspector, then type **26**.

2. Double-click the **Photoshop Live Effects filter** in the Stroke Structure section, double-click the **Size text box**, type **2**, click the **Fill color box**, double-click the **Swap Colors text box**, type **#333333**, press **[Enter]** (Win) or **[return]** (Mac), then click **OK**.

3. Verify that Current Document is selected in the Styles panel, then click the **New Style button** at the bottom of the Styles panel.

   The New Style dialog box opens.

4. Type **Tagline** in the Name text box, compare your dialog box to Figure 40, then click **OK**.

   The new style appears in the Styles panel and its name appears in the Styles sections of the Property inspector.

5. Position the mouse over the new style to view the name, then compare your Styles panel and Property inspector to Figure 41.

6. Deselect the text, align the text object to lower-left corner of the canvas, then compare your screen to Figure 42.

7. Save your work, then close the file and exit Fireworks.

You created a new style and added it to the styles available in the current document.

Create a vector object and modify its path.

1. Open fw2_2.png from where you store your Data Files, then save it as **confection.png**.
2. Select the Pen tool, then set the following properties: Fill color: #66CC99 and Stroke: #3C745C, Pencil 1-Pixel Soft, 1 px.
3. Using the large white gumdrop as a guide, draw a triangle that approximates the gumdrop's height and width.
4. Convert the corner points to curve points, using Figure 43 as a guide.
5. Use the Subselection tool to increase the height of the object, approximately half the distance to the document border.
6. Drag the object to the lower-left corner of the canvas.
7. Rename the object **gumdrop**.
8. Save your work.

Align and group objects.

1. Use the Pointer tool to drag the purple circle in back of the multicolored circle.
2. Align the two objects so that they are centered vertically and horizontally.

3. Group the two circles.
4. Move the grouped circles to the top of the stick, then group them with the stick.
5. Rename the grouped object **lollipop**.
6. Save your work.

Combine objects' paths.

1. Click the red ellipse, then move it on top of the red snowflake.
2. Align the shapes horizontally and vertically.
3. Combine the paths of the two objects, using the Intersect command.
4. Rename the combined object **insignia**.
5. Save your work.

Apply a gradient to an object and modify the gradient.

1. Select the gumdrop object and apply a Ripples gradient to it.
2. Edit the gradient, and change the left color swatch to #006600.
3. Modify the right gradient by dragging the right fill handle to the lower-right corner of the gumdrop. (*Hint*: The fill handle should resemble the hands of a clock set to 4 o'clock.)

4. Add the following fill properties: Edge: Anti-Alias and Texture: Grain, 15%.
5. Save your work.

Apply filters to objects.

1. Select the insignia object.
2. Apply a Photoshop Live Effects, Bevel and Emboss, Style: Pillow Emboss, Depth: 75, and the rest the default settings, then close the dialog box.
3. Drag the insignia object to the middle of the gumdrop object. (*Hint*: Move the insignia object on the Layers panel.)
4. Apply a Bevel and Emboss, Inset Emboss filter to the Gumdrop object with default settings.
5. Save your work.

Apply a filter to text.

1. Select the Text tool with the following properties: Font: Times New Roman, Font size: 22, Color: Red, Bold, and Italic. (*Hint*: Change the Fill type to Solid.)
2. Click the upper-left corner of the canvas, then type **Go Sugarfree**.
3. Apply a white Shadow and Glow, Glow filter to the text with a Halo Offset of 1.
4. Save your work.

Apply a style to text.

1. Open the Styles panel, then display the Text Creative Styles category.
2. Select the text.
3. Apply the Text Creative 015 style to the text.
4. Save your work.

Add a new style.

1. Change the Font size to 36.
2. Edit Photoshop Live Effects, change the Inner Shadow color #00FF00, select the Stroke effect, change the Stroke size to 1, close the dialog box, then drag the text to the left edge of the canvas.

3. Display styles for the Current Document, then create a new style named **Candy**.
4. Deselect the text object, then compare your document to Figure 43.
5. Save your work, close confection.png, then exit Fireworks.

Figure 43 *Completed Skills Review*

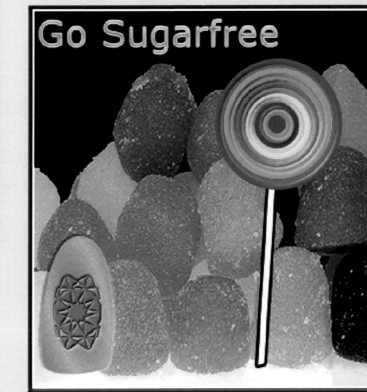

You're in charge of office security at your business. In the last four months, several employees, including the owner, have neglected to engage their screen savers when they've left their desks for lunch, meetings, and so on. So far, friendly reminders and rewards haven't done the trick, so you're going to e-mail the same obnoxious attachment to everyone. You'll develop a simple, but effective, message using Fireworks vector tools and effects.

1. Create a new document that is 504 x 246 pixels with a white background, then save it as **remember_me**.
2. Create a rounded rectangle that fills the background, and apply the following properties to it: Fill Pattern: Paint Blue; Edge: Anti-Alias; Texture: Grain, 25; and Stroke: None.
3. Add an Inner Glow filter with the following properties: Width: 8, Color: White, and Softness: 8, name the object **blue rectangle**, then lock the Background layer.
4. Create and name a new layer **ruler**, then using Figure 44 as a guide, draw a rectangle that has a Linear gradient. Adjust the swatches on the color ramp as follows: Left and Right: #CCCCCC and Middle: #FFFFFF. (*Hint*: Click beneath the color ramp to add a color swatch.)
5. Add a black 1 px Pencil, 1-Pixel-Hard stroke, and Inner Bevel filter with Width 8 and the rest default settings.

6. Use the Line tool to create evenly spaced hash marks that resemble those on a ruler, group the ruler objects, then name the object **ruler base**.
7. Create the following text in the font and filters of your choice: **don't rule out computer security**. (*Hint*: The text in the sample is bold Eras Medium ITC and has a Raised Emboss effect applied to it. It has been converted to a bitmap.)

8. Create a new layer named **Message**, then create **clean up your act** text in the font and color of your choice and apply at least one filter to it using settings of your choice. (*Hint*: The text has Glow and Photoshop Live Effects and Emboss filters applied to it.)
9. Save your work, then compare your document to Figure 44.
10. Close remember_me.png, then exit Fireworks.

Figure 44 *Sample Completed Project Builder 1*

Working with Objects

Impact Potions, a new energy drink aimed at the teen market, is sponsoring a design contest. They want you to introduce the drink by using the design in an ad window on other teen websites. They haven't decided on the container yet, so you can create the bottle or can of your choice.

1. If desired, obtain images that will reinforce your message delivery and enhance the vector shapes you will create. You can take your own photographs, or obtain an image from your computer or from the Internet. When downloading from the Internet you should always assume the work is protected by copyright. Be sure to check the website's terms of use to determine if you can use the work for educational, personal, or noncommercial purposes. Always check the copyright information on any media you download.

2. Create a new document and save it as **impact**.

3. Create a beverage container using the vector tools of your choice; apply a fill, style, or stroke; and combine paths as necessary. (*Hint*: The side grips on the can in the sample were created using Punch.)

4. Create a label for the container, applying fills, strokes, styles, transparency, and filters as necessary. (*Hint*:The label text has been attached to paths.)

5. Create text for the ad, applying fills, strokes, styles, transparency, and filters as desired.

6. Rename objects or layers on the Layers panel as appropriate.

7. Experiment with changing the order of filters in the Filters list.

8. Examine the sample shown in Figure 45, then save your work.

Figure 45 *Sample Completed Project Builder 2*

One of the many advantages to using Fireworks for your images is the ability to combine vector and bitmap images into one document. For a performance artist, such as the country musician Dwight Yoakam, an official website can reinforce both the artistic message and mood. Photographs and Fireworks-generated images combine to convey the feel of an old-time café and street scene. Many images also link the viewer to other pages within the site. Because dynamic websites are updated frequently to reflect current trends, this page might be different from Figure 46 when you open it online.

1. Connect to the Internet, go to *http://www.dwightyoakam.com/media.html* then enter the site. (*Hint*: Click Music, TV & Films from the Home page, if necessary.)
2. Open a document in a word processor, or open a new Fireworks document, then save the file as **yoakam**. (*Hint*: Use the Text tool in Fireworks to answer the questions below.)

3. Explore the site and answer the following questions:
   - When they were created in Fireworks, which objects could have been grouped?
   - Do objects appear to have been combined?
   - Which gradients, textures, styles, or other effects are applied to objects?
   - Are there objects that appear to be a combination of vector shapes, which include photographic images, objects, or that appear to have an effect applied to them? (*Hint*: Visit the site during the day and during the night and note the differences.)
4. Save your work.

Figure 46 *Sample Completed Design Project*

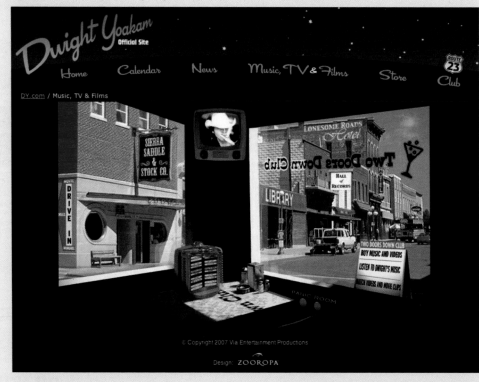

Courtesy Dwight Yoakam

Vintage Wheels, a classic car club, is known for the unusual prizes the club awards to winners of their road rallies. To promote the rallies, the prizes are shown on the group's web page. Your group has been selected to design and promote this year's grand prize: a custom belt buckle. The only requirement is that the buckle honor a classic car and be large enough to be seen from a distance. You can select the classic auto of your choice.

1. If desired, obtain an image for the buckle. You can take your own photos, or obtain an image from your computer or from the Internet. When downloading from the Internet, you should always assume the work is protected by copyright. Be sure to check the website's terms of use to determine if you can use the work for educational, personal, or noncommercial purposes. Always check the copyright information on any media you download.
2. Create a new document and save it as **classic_buckle**.
3. Create two or more vector objects for the buckle, and add fills, styles, strokes, or transparency to them. (*Hint*: The ovals in the sample have a combination of Inner Shadow, Inner Bevel, and Outer Bevel filters and a style applied to them.)

4. Apply at least one Combine Paths command or Compound Shape tool to the objects.
5. Create text as desired and apply fills, styles, and filters to them.

6. Examine the sample shown in Figure 47, then save your work.
7. Close classic_buckle.png and exit Fireworks.

Figure 47 *Sample Completed Portfolio Project*

CHAPTER **3** IMPORTING, SELECTING, AND
MODIFYING GRAPHICS

1. Work with imported files
2. Work with bitmap selection tools
3. Learn about selection areas
4. Select areas based on color

IMPORTING, SELECTING, AND MODIFYING GRAPHICS

Understanding Importing

Whether you want to create a simple image or a complex Web site, having the right graphic is crucial to the success of your project. Many times, the graphic you need may have been created in another application. Fireworks makes it easy to access such a graphic—regardless of whether it was created within Adobe CS5 in a program such as Photoshop or Illustrator, or downloaded from a digital camera or scanner.

Fireworks allows you to import several types of files, including vector and bitmap files, as well as HTML tables. Being able to work with many different file types in the same document has obvious advantages.

For example, you can edit Photoshop or Illustrator files directly in Fireworks and export them to Dreamweaver or Flash. Best of all, importing is quick allows you to resize the image and set other attributes specifically for the file you're working in.

Modifying Images

After you import a bitmap image, you can use an assortment of tools to select and modify the pixels on that image. You can select pixels based on an area or on color. After you select pixels, you can manipulate them independently. For example, you can select and edit a defined set of pixels or blend a selection into surrounding pixels.

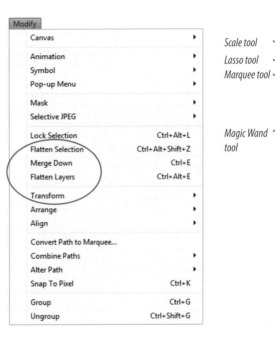

Vector File Options

Scale:	100	
Width:	612	Pixels
Height:	792	Pixels
Resolution:	72	Pixels/Inch
Anti-alias:	☑ Paths	☑ Text Smooth

File conversion

Open a page   Artboard: 1
Remember layers
☐ Include invisible layers
☑ Include background layers

Render as images
☑ Groups over   30 objects
☑ Blends over   30 steps
☑ Tiled fills over   30 objects

OK   Cancel

Edit

Undo Select Pixels	Ctrl+Z
Repeat Select Pixels	Ctrl+Y
Insert	►
Find and Replace...	Ctrl+F
Cut	Ctrl+X
Copy	Ctrl+C
Copy as Vectors	
Copy HTML Code...	Ctrl+Alt+C
Paste	Ctrl+V
Clear	Backspace
Paste as Mask	Ctrl+Alt+V
Paste Inside	Ctrl+Shift+V
Paste Attributes	Ctrl+Alt+Shift+V
Duplicate	Ctrl+Alt+D
Clone	Ctrl+Shift+D
Crop Selected Bitmap	
Crop Document	
Preferences...	Ctrl+U
Keyboard Shortcuts...	

Insert submenu:

New Button...	Ctrl+Shift+F8
New Symbol...	Ctrl+F8
Hotspot	Ctrl+Shift+U
Rectangular Slice	Alt+Shift+U
Polygon Slice	Alt+Shift+P
Empty Bitmap	
Bitmap Via Copy	
Bitmap Via Cut	
Layer	Shift+L
State	Shift+F
Page	

Modify

Canvas	►
Animation	►
Symbol	►
Pop-up Menu	►
Mask	►
Selective JPEG	►
Lock Selection	Ctrl+Alt+L
Flatten Selection	Ctrl+Alt+Shift+Z
Merge Down	Ctrl+E
Flatten Layers	Ctrl+Alt+E
Transform	►
Arrange	►
Align	►
Convert Path to Marquee...	
Combine Paths	►
Alter Path	►
Snap To Pixel	Ctrl+K
Group	Ctrl+G
Ungroup	Ctrl+Shift+G

Scale tool
Lasso tool
Marquee tool
Magic Wand tool
Zoom tool

Select
Bitmap
Vector
Web
Colors
View

Work with
IMPORTED FILES

What You'll Do

In this lesson, you will import graphics with different file formats into a Fireworks document, and group and ungroup objects.

Working with Other Adobe Creative Suite 5 Programs

Fireworks has always integrated effortlessly with Flash and Dreamweaver, through a feature known as round-trip editing. The integration features between Fireworks, Dreamweaver, and Flash are discussed at length in the Integrating Adobe CS5 Web Standard chapter. In Fireworks, you can also open and edit native Photoshop and Illustrator files, prepare them for the Web using the excellent optimization features in Fireworks, and then insert them in a Dreamweaver document, or export them in a PDF or Illustrator file. You can manage your media using Adobe Bridge, as discussed in Dreamweaver Chapter 4. Adobe Bridge is a media management and organizational tool and includes functions such as Camera Raw support and metadata editing.

Using Files Created in Other Programs

You can open and edit bitmap and vector files created in other applications such as CorelDRAW, or bitmap images created from a scanner or downloaded from a digital camera.

You can bring a Photoshop file into Fireworks in a couple different ways: you can import it or open it in Fireworks, where Fireworks retains the file's layer hierarchy, blend modes, and layer effects.

Understanding Image Resolution

For an image displayed on a computer screen—on the Web, attached to an e-mail, or viewed on a mobile phone or portable device—the unit of measurement is in PPI (pixels per inch). The standard resolution setting for Web images is 72 PPI, which is directly related to the display capability of computer monitors. The same picture that looks fabulous in a Web page often appears blurry when you enlarge it in a computer program because the same number of pixels is being spread over a larger number of inches. That picture also looks fuzzy when you print it because the on-screen resolution is too low for printing detailed tone transitions.

You can also open or import native Adobe Illustrator AI files in Fireworks. Fills, layers, masks, vector shapes, and other properties are retained and editable.

QUICK TIP

When you open a Photoshop file in Fireworks and display Guides, the guides will be used to create slices, which are Web objects that contain interactivity such as rollovers. Slicing an image also helps to optimize an image and update a Web page.

Importing and Saving Files

Figure 1 shows the import file types available in the Import dialog box (Win). You can determine how Fireworks imports a

Figure 1 *Import dialog box*

Import file types

Understanding Screen Resolution

Computer monitors also have resolution settings that refer to the number of pixels contained across the horizontal and vertical axes—that is, how densely packed the pixels are on the screen. For example, a monitor set at a resolution of 1024 × 768 can display 1024 dots on each of 768 lines, totaling around 786,400 pixels. In contrast, a resolution of 800 × 600 displays less than half that number of pixels, whereas a setting of 1600 × 1200 has nearly 2 million pixels. You can easily notice this when you change the resolution of your computer monitor: the lower the resolution, the larger the image appears, but it displays less detail than it does at a larger resolution.

Photoshop document by selecting different options for layers and text. To do so, open the Preferences dialog box from the Edit menu (Win) or the Fireworks menu (Mac), click the Photoshop Import/Open category, as shown in Figure 2, then select conversion options as desired.

When you import a vector-based file, you can select a wide range of importing options in the Vector File Options dialog box, shown in Figure 3 that allow you to ungroup and edit vector objects. In the File Conversion section, you can determine how to treat layers. The Remember layers option maintains the layer configuration of the imported file. Ignore layers places all objects on the currently selected layer. Convert layers to states places layers into individual states. You can change settings in the Render as images section to determine the number of individual objects Fireworks will import. Setting objects to render as an image is helpful if the source Illustrator file is complex.

NEW When you save or close any imported file after you've edited it, Fireworks by default will prompt you to save it as a PNG file. To save a file in another format, such as JPEG or PDF, you can click the Save As command on the File menu to open the Save As dialog box.

Figure 2 *Photoshop Import/Open options in the Preferences dialog box*   **Figure 3** *Vector File Options dialog box*

Importing, Selecting, and Modifying Graphics

Figure 4 *Imported GIF*

Info panel —

Figure 5 *Imported Fireworks PNG file*

Click here —

My alien is an honor student

Import a GIF file

1. Open **fw3_1.png**, save it as **horizons.png**, select **Expanded Mode** as the panels view, click **Window** on the Application bar, then click **Info**.
2. Show the Layers panel, then change the name of Layer 1 on the Layers panel to **Spaceships**.
3. Click **File** on the Application bar, click **Import**, then navigate to where you store your Data Files.
4. Click the **Files of type list arrow**, then click **All readable files** (if necessary) (Win).

TIP Scroll down the list.

5. Click **rocket.gif**, then click **Open**.
6. Watching coordinates on the Info panel, position the **import pointer** ⌐ on the canvas at approximately **232 X/20 Y**, then click the mouse to import the file.

TIP You can also enter precise X and Y coordinates in the Property inspector.

7. Compare your image to Figure 4.

You imported a GIF file into a Fireworks document.

Import a Fireworks PNG file

1. Click **File** on the Application bar, then click **Import**.
2. Double-click **saucer.png**, then click **Import** in the Import Page dialog box.
3. Position the **import pointer** ⌐ on the canvas at approximately **–104 X/212 Y**, then click the mouse.

   The image is imported at its original dimensions; to scale an object when you import it, click and drag on the canvas.
4. Compare your image to Figure 5, close the Info panel, then save the file.

You imported a Fireworks PNG file.

Import a vector file as editable paths

1. Click the **Background layer** on the Layers panel, click the **New/Duplicate Layer button** at the bottom of the Layers panel, then change the name of the new layer to **Book**.

2. Click **File** on the Application bar, click **Import**, navigate to where you store your Data Files, then double-click **book.eps** to import it.

   The Vector File Options dialog box opens.

   TIP You can also click the Import button on the Main toolbar (Win) to import a file.

3. Double-click **100** in the Scale text box, type **105**, compare your dialog box to Figure 6, then click **OK**.

   TIP If the imported file was created in a program that is also designed for print media, such as Illustrator or Photoshop, Fireworks converts the original color mode from print colors, such as CMYK, to RGB mode, which uses colors designed for the Web.

4. Position the **import pointer** in the upper-left corner of the canvas, click the mouse, then compare your image to Figure 7.

   The book appears on the canvas and the object appears in the Layers panel as a grouped object.

   TIP If you have a file open in Adobe Illustrator, you can copy and paste it into Fireworks.

You imported a vector file into a Fireworks document.

Figure 6 *Changing an option in the Vector File Options dialog box*

Scale text box

Your default number might vary

Figure 7 *Vector file imported as a grouped object*

Click mouse here

Objects in imported vector file are grouped

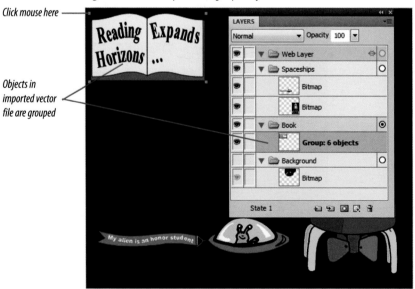

Figure 8 *Ungrouped object made up of paths and other grouped objects*

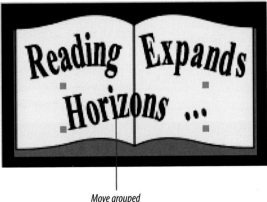

Ungrouped main object contains smaller groups

Grouped objects are grouped words

Path objects are book elements

Figure 9 *Moved grouped object*

Move grouped word here

Edit an imported vector object

1. Verify that the grouped object on the book layer is selected, click **Modify** on the Application bar, then click **Ungroup**.

    The book is initially ungrouped into smaller grouped objects and paths.

    TIP You can also ungroup objects by pressing [Ctrl][Shift][G] (Win) or ⌘ [Shift][G] (Mac).

2. Drag the **bottom border** of the Layers panel until all the layers are visible (if necessary), then compare your Layers panel to Figure 8.

    Some individual paths are ungrouped, while other objects remain grouped (the individual letters). You could ungroup all the objects if you wanted to edit them individually (for a total of 26 objects).

3. Click a blank part of the canvas to deselect the objects, click the **Group: 9 objects object** in the Layers panel to select the word **Horizons**, then drag the selected word to the location shown in Figure 9.

    TIP Resize the Layers panel, if necessary.

4. Click the **Book layer** in the Layers panel to select all the objects on the layer, click **Modify** on the Application bar, then click **Group**.

    The numerous book objects are regrouped into one object.

5. Save your work.

You ungrouped and modified an object, and then regrouped the objects.

Work with Bitmap
SELECTION TOOLS

What You'll Do

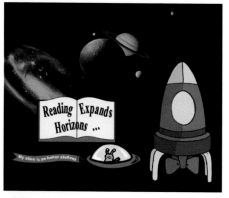

In this lesson, you will use the marquee tools to select and change pixels in an image.

Using Selection Tools

Being able to select the exact pixels you want is the crucial first step to altering or editing parts of an image. Fireworks offers several ways to select and manipulate pixels in an image. This lesson covers some of those ways. When you select pixels on an image, Fireworks creates a flashing perimeter, known as a **marquee selection**, around the pixels. (This perimeter is also referred to as "marching ants" because of the way it looks.) Marquee selections are temporary areas of selected pixels that exist until you modify the pixels themselves, for example, by cutting, copying, or recoloring them. You can save and recall a bitmap selection, but only one selection at a time. You cannot save bitmap selections in your document when you close it. You can also use the selection tools in combination to refine a selection.

After you create a marquee selection, you can transfer it to another bitmap by clicking another bitmap object on the same or on a different layer. You can copy or cut a pixel selection as a new object on the active layer in a document by using the Bitmap Via Copy or Bitmap Via Cut Insert command options on the Edit menu. For example, if you select pixels and then click the Bitmap Via Cut command, Fireworks removes the selected pixels from the original bitmap and then pastes them as a new object above the bitmap object on the active layer. Similarly, when you create a bitmap using the Bitmap Via Copy command, Fireworks copies the selected pixels and pastes them as a new object on the active layer.

Using the Marquee Tools

Marquee tools select pixels on an image in a specific shape. The properties available for

---

Moving and Copying Marquee Selections

To move a marquee selection after you have created it, click any of the bitmap selection tools and drag the marquee on the canvas. To copy a selection while a Selection tool is still selected, press [Ctrl][Alt] (Win) or ⌘ [option] (Mac), then drag the selection on the canvas.

---

the marquee tools are shown in Figure 10. You can press and hold [Shift] to constrain your rectangle or oval marquee to a square or circle. Use the Fixed Ratio style to constrain the height and width to a precise ratio and the Fixed Size style to set the marquee to an exact dimension.

Using the Transformation Tools

The transformation tool group consists of the Scale tool, Skew tool, Distort tool, and the 9-slice scaling tool. The Scale tool resizes an object, the Skew tool slants an object along the horizontal or vertical axes, and the Distort tool alters the size and proportion of an object and is useful for creating perspective in an object. The 9-slice scaling tool allows you to select part of an object and resize or scale it without distorting it in multiple areas, as often occurs when you use the Scale tool. For vector objects, the tool adds points to the shape. Figure 11 shows skew and distort samples. When you select an object with any of the transformation tools, sizing handles surround the object. You can use these handles to transform or rotate the object. The transformation tool pointer appears when you position the pointer over a sizing handle; the rotation pointer appears when you position the pointer in between the sizing handles or outside the object.

NEW Once you create an object, you can constrain its proportions when you resize it by clicking the Constrain proportions icon on the lower-left corner of the Property inspector next to the W and H text boxes.

Figure 10 *Properties for the Marquee and Oval Marquee tools*

Style options

Edge of selection list arrow

Figure 11 *Sample skew and distort images*

Original object

Skewing slants object evenly

Distorting slants points independently

Select pixels using the Marquee tool

1. Verify that horizons.png is open and that Tooltips is selected on the View menu.

2. Click the **Background layer** in the Layers panel, click the **New/Duplicate Layer button** ⟵ , then change the name of the new layer to **Galaxy**.

3. Open **galaxy.jpg** from where you store your Data Files.

4. Click the **Marquee tool** ⬚ in the Tools panel.

TIP Mac users may need to click an empty area of the canvas before performing Step 5.

5. Verify that Normal is the selected style in the Style list in the Property inspector, click the Edge of selection list arrow, then click Anti-alias.

6. Place the **pointer** ┼ on the canvas at approximately 65 X/20 Y, then drag a rectangle to 223 X/330 V that surrounds the galaxy, as shown in Figure 12.

7. Click **Edit** on the Application bar, click **Copy**, click **Edit** on the Application bar, then click **Paste**.

   The copied pixels are not noticeable because they are pasted on top of the original image on the canvas. The selection appears as the top object in the Layers panel.

8. Deselect the copied selection, click the **eye icon** 👁 next to the original bitmap in the Layers panel (the bottom one) to hide it, then compare your image to Figure 13.

You set properties for the Marquee tool, created a rectangular marquee, and copied the selection.

Figure 12 *Making a selection with the Marquee tool*

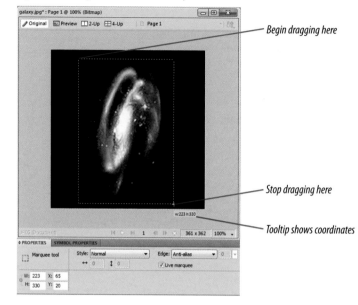

Begin dragging here

Stop dragging here

Tooltip shows coordinates

Figure 13 *Viewing copied marquee selection*

Anti-alias edge of copied selection is sharp

Importing, Selecting, and Modifying Graphics

Figure 14 *Using the Oval Marquee tool*

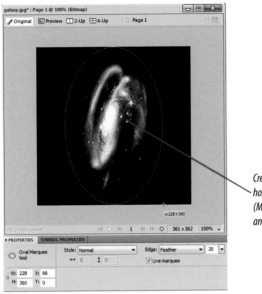

Create marquee by pressing and holding [Alt] (Win) or [option] (Mac), and then dragging down and to the right

Select pixels using the Oval Marquee tool

1. Hide the **copied selection**, then show the **original image**, respectively, in the Layers panel.

2. Click and hold the **Marquee tool** ⊡ in the Tools panel, then click the **Oval Marquee tool** ⊙.

3. Verify that **Normal** is the selected style in the Style list in the Property inspector, click the **Edge of selection list arrow**, click **Feather**, double-click the **Amount of feather text box**, then type **20**.

   The selection will have a feathered edge. When the Live marquee check box is selected, changes you make in the Property inspector affect the selection marquee.

4. Place the **pointer** ┼ in the middle of the canvas (180 X/180 Y), press and hold [**Alt**] (Win) or [**option**] (Mac), then drag down and to the right to create an oval marquee around the galaxy, as shown in Figure 14.

   Pressing and holding [Alt] (Win) or [option] (Mac) allows you to draw a marquee from the center point outward.

5. Drag the **marquee** or use the arrow keys to reposition the oval around the galaxy (if necessary).

TIP You can reselect the marquee as many times as necessary. Notice that the marquee appears to be cropped when you release the mouse button if you extend it beyond the canvas.

(continued)

6. Click **Edit** on the Application bar, point to **Insert**, then click **Bitmap Via Copy** to copy the selection.

7. Click the **eye icon** 👁 next to the original bottom galaxy bitmap on the Layers panel to hide it, then compare your image to Figure 15.

TIP Expand the Layers panel as necessary.

You set properties for the Oval Marquee tool, created an oval marquee selection, and then created a new bitmap from the original.

Transform a selection

1. Click the **feathered oval bitmap** to select it, copy the **bitmap**, click **horizons.png** in the Document window to make it active, verify that the Galaxy layer is selected, then paste the copied oval bitmap.

2. Click the **Pointer tool** ▶ in the Tools panel, then drag the selection to the location shown in Figure 16.

3. Close galaxy.jpg without saving changes.

4. Click the **Scale tool** ▦ in the Tools panel, then open the Info panel.

   Rotation handles appear around the selected object.

TIP You can press and hold [Alt] (Win) or [option] (Mac) to scale an object from its center.

(continued)

Figure 15 *Oval marquee selection*

Feathered edge

Figure 16 *Oval bitmap copied to horizons.png file*

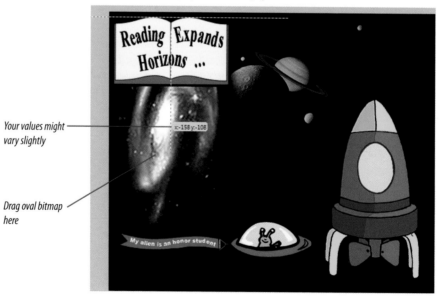

Your values might vary slightly

Drag oval bitmap here

Importing, Selecting, and Modifying Graphics

Figure 17 *Rotating an object*

Degree of rotation

Drag pointer
counterclockwise

5. Place the **pointer** ✛ above the upper-left sizing handle until the rotation pointer ↺ appears, drag the selection **counterclockwise 66.0** degrees, as shown in the Info panel, compare your image to Figure 17, then release the mouse button.

6. Click the **Opacity list arrow** in the Property inspector, drag the slider to **66**, then press [**Enter**] (Win) or [**return**] (Mac).

   TIP If the Info panel covers the right side of the Property inspector, move or close it.

7. Click the **Pointer tool** ➤ in the Tools panel, click the **Book layer** in the Layers panel, then center the **Book object** above the saucer object on the canvas.

8. Deselect the objects, compare your screen to Figure 18, then save your work.

You dragged and dropped an object, rotated it, changed its opacity, and aligned it.

Figure 18 *Moved and aligned objects*

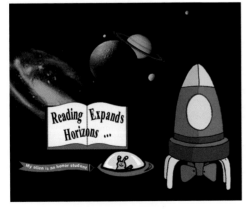

Understanding Resampling

If the bitmap selection you are copying has a print resolution that differs from the document into which you want to paste, a Resampling dialog box opens, asking if you want to resample the bitmap. Choose Resample if you want to preserve the selection's original dimensions, which will adjust the number of pixels as needed to maintain the bitmap's appearance. Choose Don't Resample to retain the number of original pixels, which may affect the size of the graphic when pasted.

Learn About
SELECTION AREAS

What You'll Do

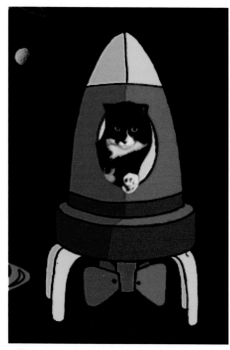

In this lesson, you will select pixels in an image using tools in the Lasso tool group.

Using the Lasso Tools

As you have seen, the marquee tools select an area of pixels in a preset, geometric shape. Using the lasso tools, you can define an exact pixel selection working freeform or following a shape on the canvas. The Lasso tool works well on images that appear to have curves, whereas the Polygon Lasso tool works well on images that have straight lines or asymmetrical outlines. You select pixels by clicking repeatedly around the perimeter of the area you want to select. With the Lasso tool, you create the marquee as you draw it on the canvas—its accuracy is linked to your tracing ability.

QUICK TIP

You can hide the marching ants selection on the screen by pressing [Ctrl][H] (Win) or [option][F9] (Mac).

Adding and Subtracting Pixels

To add pixels to an existing lasso selection, press and hold [Shift], and then drag a new marquee. The pixels you select are added to the previously selected marquee. To subtract pixels from a marquee, press and hold [Alt] (Win) or [option] (Mac). Fireworks deletes the areas where the marquees overlap. To select just the intersection of marquees, create the first marquee, press and hold [Shift][Alt] (Win) or [Shift][option] (Mac), and then create the second marquee. You can add or subtract pixels using other bitmap selection tools in much the same manner. Note that pressing [Shift] as you use the Polygon Lasso tool constrains the lines that you can draw to 45-degree angle increments.

Importing, Selecting, and Modifying Graphics

Using Select Menu Commands

Using commands on the Select menu, you can adjust a pixel selection after you create it, as shown in Figure 19. You can edit the set of selected pixels, or add pixels to or subtract pixels from the selection marquee. The Select Inverse command selects all of the pixels except the ones enclosed by the marquee.

Other commands, such as Expand Marquee or Contract Marquee, allow you to enter the number of pixels that add to or subtract from the selection's border. The Smooth Marquee command blends the pixels at the selection edge, eliminating any excess pixels that can create a jagged appearance. You can also transform a marquee to a vector path object

using the Convert Marquee to Path command. Creating a marquee can at times be a grueling process. Fortunately, after you are satisfied with a selection, you can use the Save Bitmap Selection and Restore Bitmap Selection commands to save it and recall it at any time during the current editing session or after the file has been saved, closed, and reopened.

Figure 19 *Modifying selections with commands on the Select menu*

Original selection

Select Inverse deletes initially nonselected pixels

Border Marquee

Select pixels using the Lasso tool

1. Open astrocat.jpg.

2. Click the **Zoom tool** in the Tools panel, click the **canvas** until you can view the image in detail, then drag the **borders** of the Document window until the entire image is visible.

   You might need to adjust the magnification settings a number of times before you are satisfied.

   TIP You can also increase magnification by clicking the Set magnification box on the bottom of the Document window and then clicking a magnification setting from the Set magnification pop-up menu.

3. Click the **Lasso tool** in the Tools panel, click the **Edge of selection list arrow** in the Property inspector, click **Feather**, double-click the **Amount of feather text box**, then type **1**.

4. Drag the **pointer** along the perimeter of the cat, as shown in Figure 20, then notice the areas where the marquee is off the mark.

   Because the Lasso tool is sensitive to even the slightest deviations from the path you are drawing, the exact shape of your marquee will vary.

   TIP You can change the pointer of most tools to a crosshair pointer by pressing [Caps Lock], which can make it easier to see the pixels you want to select.

5. Click **Select** on the Application bar, then click **Deselect**.

   TIP You can also remove a marquee by drawing another one, by clicking an area outside the selection with a tool in the Marquee or Lasso tool groups, or by pressing [Esc].

You selected pixels on an image using the Lasso tool.

Figure 20 *Creating a marquee with the Lasso tool*

Drag pointer along perimeter of image

Understanding Magnification and the Zoom Tool

You can increase the magnification of any area on the canvas. To change the magnification in preset increments, click the Zoom tool on the canvas or click a magnification setting in the Set magnification pop-up menu on the bottom of the Document window. To set a magnification between 6% and 6400%, use the Zoom tool to drag a zoom selection box on the canvas. The amount of magnification is based on the size of the zoom selection box. To zoom out of a selection, press and hold [Alt] (Win) or [option] (Mac), and then click the canvas.

Importing, Selecting, and Modifying Graphics

Figure 21 *Marquee created with the Polygon Lasso tool*

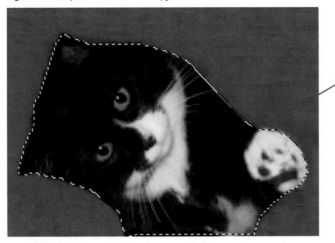

Marquee is
less erratic

Figure 22 *Save Selection dialog box*

Create a selection using the Polygon Lasso tool and save it

1. Press and hold the **Lasso tool** 🔍 in the Tools panel, then click the **Polygon Lasso tool** 📐 .

2. Create a selection by clicking the **pointer** 🔽 along the perimeter of the image, make sure you connect the start and end points, then compare your image to Figure 21.

TIP You can readjust your wrist or reposition the mouse on a flat surface in between clicks, which may ensure a more accurate selection.

3. Click **Select** on the Application bar, then click **Save Bitmap Selection**.

4. Type **Kitty** in the Name text box as shown in Figure 22, then click **OK**.

You selected pixels on an image using the Polygon Lasso tool, and then saved the selection.

Transform a selection

1. Click **Select** on the Application bar, click **Expand Marquee**, type **10** in the Expand by text box (if necessary), then click **OK**.

   The marquee expands 10 pixels in each direction.

2. Click **Select** on the Application bar, click **Contract Marquee**, type **20** in the Contract by text box, then click **OK**.

3. Click **Select** on the Application bar, click **Restore Bitmap Selection,** then click **OK** in the Restore Selection dialog box.

   The original marquee selection is restored.

4. Click **Select** on the Application bar, click **Smooth Marquee**, type **10** in the Sample radius text box (if necessary), click **OK**, then compare your image to Figure 23.

TIP Fireworks removes pixels to smooth out the jagged points on the marquee.

5. Click **Select** on the Application bar, click **Restore Bitmap Selection,** then click **OK**.

TIP You can hide the marquee display by clicking the Hide Edges command on the View menu.

6. Click **Select** on the Application bar, click **Select Inverse**, then press **[Delete]**.

7. Click **Select** on the Application bar, click **Restore Bitmap Selection,** then click **OK**.

8. Click **Edit** on the Application bar, then click **Copy**.

9. Close astrocat.jpg without saving changes.

You applied different marquee commands to transform the selection, and then restored the original marquee.

Figure 23 *Result of Smooth Marquee command*

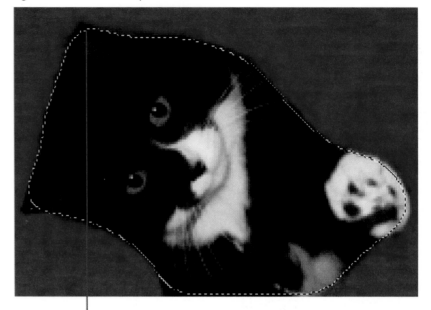

Smoothing removes pixels

Importing, Selecting, and Modifying Graphics

Figure 24 *Result of 50% numeric transform*

Figure 25 *Rotated and repositioned object*

Position cat image
in window frame

Transform a copied selection

1. Click the **Pointer tool** ▶ in the Tools panel, (if necessary), then click the **large rocket object** on the canvas.

2. Click **Edit** on the Application bar, then click **Paste**.

3. Click the **unselected Constrain proportions icon** ▫ in the Property inspector bar, then when the icon changes to the **selected Constrain proportions icon** ▯, double-click the **Selection width text box**, type **95**, then press [**Enter**] (Win) or [**return**] (Mac).

   The cat image is resized by 50 percent proportionately.

4. Drag the **cat image** on top of the rocket window, then compare your image to Figure 24.

5. Open the Info panel, click the **Scale tool** 🔲 in the Tools panel, position the **rotation pointer** ⤵ outside the object, then drag the pointer clockwise to **−73** degrees, as indicated on the Info panel.

6. Click the **Pointer tool** ▶ in the Tools panel, drag the **image** to the location shown in Figure 25, then click a blank part of the Document window.

7. Save your work.

You resized and rotated the copied selection.

Select Areas
BASED ON COLOR

What You'll Do

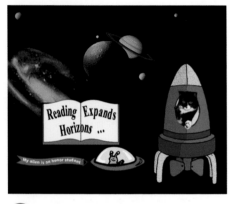

In this lesson, you will add select areas of color using the Magic Wand tool, merge layers, and then flatten objects and layers in the image.

Using the Magic Wand Tool

The Marquee and Lasso tools select pixels by enclosing them. The Magic Wand tool allows you to select similarly colored areas of a bitmap image. The Magic Wand tool includes edge and tolerance settings. **Tolerance** refers to the range of colors the tool will select. The higher the setting, the larger the selection range. The Magic Wand tool works well on areas of strongly defined or solid color, such as photographic images.

QUICK TIP

Depending on your graphic, you might find it more efficient to add pixels to a Magic Wand selection by pressing and holding [Shift], rather than increasing the tolerance setting and reclicking the bitmap.

The tolerance setting also affects the pixels selected when you click the Select Similar command on the Select menu. The Magic Wand tool selects pixels of contiguous color tone, not contiguous pixels on the image. When you use the Select Similar command, any matching pixels on the image are selected. Figure 26 shows four selections. The photo on the left shows the pixels selected with a low tolerance setting and those selected at that setting using the Select Similar command. The photo on the right demonstrates the same principle at a higher tolerance setting.

Merging and Flattening Objects and Layers

After you start creating, copying, or importing vector and bitmap objects in a document, your Layers panel can quickly fill up and appear unruly. Although creating and collapsing layers can help manage the large number of objects, you can also flatten or merge the objects you create into a single image, just as grouping objects assembles them into a single arrangement.

Flattening and merging objects and layers helps to manage objects, layers, and file size. However, you can no longer edit individual objects after you flatten or merge them.

QUICK TIP

It's a best practice to save an unflattened version of your document as a backup.

The Merge Down command on the Modify menu merges selected objects with the bitmap object that lies beneath the lowest selected object. The Flatten Selection command on the Modify menu flattens two or more objects, even if they are on different layers (the top object moves to the bottom object), converting them to bitmap objects. If you want to move all your objects to a single layer and remove all other layers, you can use the Flatten Layers command.

Figure 26 *Sample Magic Wand and Select Similar selections*

Select Similar command selects more green pixels

Select Similar command selects pixels in more colors

Tolerance 16 selects some green grape pixels

Tolerance 64 selects nearly all of grape

Select and copy pixels using the Magic Wand tool

1. Click the **bitmap object** (with the planets) on the Background layer to select it, click the **Zoom tool** in the Tools panel, then click the **canvas** until the small green moon is visible.

2. Click the **Magic Wand tool** in the Tools panel, double-click the **Tolerance text box** in the Property inspector, type **85**, click the **Edge of selection text box**, then click **Anti-alias** (if necessary).

3. Click the **center** of the small green moon, click **Edit** on the Application bar, point to **Insert**, then click **Bitmap Via Copy** to copy the selection.

   Although you cannot see the copy on the canvas (because it is directly on top of the original), notice that a new layer is created on the Layers panel.

4. Click **Select** on the Application bar, click **Deselect**, click the **Pointer tool** in the Tools panel, click the **copied bitmap** on the canvas, then drag it to the location shown in Figure 27.

5. Click the **Add Live Filters button** in the Property inspector, point to **Adjust Color**, then click **Hue/Saturation**.

6. Enter the values shown in Figure 28, then click **OK**.

   The pixels change to purple.

You selected pixels using the Magic Wand tool, and then copied, moved, and changed the color of the selection.

Figure 27 *Moving selection created with the Magic Wand tool*

Move copied bitmap here

Figure 28 *Adjusting color with the Hue/Saturation dialog box*

Preview of color

Figure 29 *Selecting pixels with Select Similar command*

All yellow pixels
are selected

Figure 30 *Noise filter applied to selection*

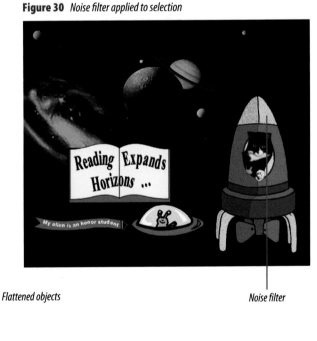

Reading Expands
Horizons ...

My alien is an honor student

Noise filter

Figure 31 *Flattened objects*

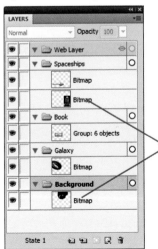

Flattened objects

Select and alter pixels

1. Click the **rocketship bitmap object**, click the **Magic Wand tool** in the Tools panel, then click the **right yellow half** of the nose cone.

2. Click **Select** on the Application bar, click **Select Similar**, then compare your image to Figure 29.

3. Click **Filters** on the Application bar, point to **Noise**, then click **Add Noise**.

4. Double-click the **Amount text box**, (if necessary), type **24**, click the **Color check box**, then click **OK**.

   Color noise is added to the yellow areas.

5. Click **Select** on the Application bar, click **Deselect**, then compare your image to Figure 30.

You applied a noise filter to a selection.

Merge and flatten objects and layers

1. Press and hold [**Ctrl**] (Win) or (Mac), then click the **cat bitmap** and the **rocket bitmap objects** on the Spaceships layer in the Layers panel.

2. Click **Modify** on the Application bar, then click **Flatten Selection** to flatten the objects into a single bitmap image.

3. Repeat Steps 1 and 2 for objects on the **Background layer**, deselect the object, then compare your Layers panel to Figure 31.

4. Save and close horizons.png, then exit Fireworks.

You flattened objects on layers.

Import files.

1. Open fw3_2.png, then save it as **sweet_essence. png**. (*Hint*: Because the canvas is narrow, readjust the size of the Document window if desired.)
2. Open the Info panel.
3. Change the name of Layer 1 to **small_bottle**.
4. Import smbottle.jpg, clicking the import cursor on the upper-left corner of the canvas.
5. Center the small bottle on the blue bottle so that it appears to be floating inside it.
6. Import sweet.png, clicking the import cursor on the upper-left corner of the canvas.
7. Move the text to the bottom of the canvas.
8. Save your work.

Edit an imported vector object.

1. Create a new layer and change the name to **Jellies**.
2. Import jelly_beans.eps, accepting the default import settings and clicking the import cursor on the upper-left corner of the canvas.
3. Regroup the objects, then resize them so they fit across the top of the canvas.
4. Save your work.

Use the marquee tools.

1. Hide the Background layer, then select the Sweet Essence bitmap object.
2. Select the Marquee tool, verify that the Style is Normal and the Edge is Anti-alias, then draw a rectangular marquee around the text part of the object.

3. Copy the selection using the Bitmap Via Copy command. (*Hint*: Use the Insert command on the Edit menu.)
4. Hide the original Sweet Essence bitmap on the Layers panel, then note the selected area.
5. Delete the copied rectangular marquee selection.
6. Save your work.

Transform a selection.

1. Show the original text bitmap, then select the Oval Marquee tool.
2. Set the Edge to Feather 2 pixels in the Property inspector, then draw an oval marquee around the text object.
3. Select the inverse of the selection, and then delete it.
4. Deselect all objects, select the Scale tool, select the oval bitmap object, then rotate the oval bitmap object −90 degrees (clockwise). (*Hint*: View the rotation angle on the Info panel or click Modify on the Application bar, point to Transform, then click Rotate 90° CW.)
5. Center the text bitmap selection on top of the small blue bottle.
6. Show the Background layer, then save your work.

Use the lasso tools.

1. Create a new layer above the small_bottle layer named **candy**.
2. Open rings.png, select the Lasso tool, then click a blank part of the canvas (Mac).
3. Set the Edge to Feather 1 pixel in the Property inspector, adjust the magnification setting as desired, then create a marquee around the pink center ring.

4. Deselect the marquee.
5. Select the Polygon Lasso tool, then create a marquee around the two vertical adjoining green rings to the left of the middle ring.
6. Save the bitmap selection and name it rings.
7. Save your work.

Transform a selection and a copied selection.

1. Expand the marquee 5 pixels.
2. Contract the marquee 15 pixels.
3. Smooth the marquee 10 pixels.
4. Restore the bitmap selection.
5. Select the inverse of the bitmap selection, then delete it.
6. Restore the bitmap selection.
7. Copy and paste the object to the sweet_essence. png document. (*Hint*: If prompted to resample the selection, click Don't Resample.)
8. Close rings.png without saving changes.
9. Position the green rings selection so it appears to be floating near the bottom of the bottle on the left.
10. Save your work.

Use the Magic Wand tool.

1. Open gumballs.tif, select the Magic Wand tool, then click a blank area of the canvas (Mac).
2. Adjust the Tolerance to 32 and the Edge to Feather 2 pixels.
3. Click the lightest part in the middle of the orange gumball, then click Select Similar.
4. Add pixels as necessary to the selection. (*Hint*: Press and hold [Shift].)

Importing, Selecting, and Modifying Graphics

5. Copy and paste the selection in the first bottle in the sweet_essence.png document. (*Hint*: If prompted to sample the selection, click Don't Resample.)
6. Repeat for the yellow, white, and pink gumballs using a combination of bitmap selection tools as needed. (*Hint*: Work with each gumball separately.)
7. Close gumballs.tif without saving changes.

Select and alter pixels.

1. Using Figure 32 as a guide, resize, rotate, and change the layer position of the gumballs.
2. Select the white gumball object, then apply a Hue/Saturation effect to it with the following settings: Colorize check box selected, Hue: 165, Saturation: 35, and Lightness: 5.
3. Save your work.

Merge objects and flatten layers.

1. Click the Jellies layer on the Layers panel, then flatten the layer. (*Hint*: Use a command on the Modify menu.)
2. Group the objects in the small_bottle layer.
3. Save your work, then compare your image to Figure 32.

Figure 32 *Completed Skills Review*

You and your friends are going to participate in a charity auction by creating a one-of-a-kind jacket. You are going to collect hundreds of different buttons and sew, staple, and glue them in solid coverage over a jean jacket. The auction has a Web site, so you will use your Fireworks skills to create the background for a Web page announcing this item.

1. Obtain images of buttons or the fastener of your choice in different file formats that will convey something unique about your jacket. You can take your own photos, or obtain images from your computer or from the Internet. When downloading from the Internet, you should always assume the material is protected by copyright. Be sure to check the Web site's terms of use to determine if you can use the work for educational, personal, or noncommercial purposes. Always check the copyright information on any media you download.
2. Create a new document and save it as **mybuttons.png**.
3. Create a background image using any of the images you've obtained or create one using vector tools and apply a fill, stroke, style, or effect to it. You can also adjust its transparency.
4. Import the following files and the files you obtained in Step 1 into your document or open and select them using the bitmap selection tools.
   - button1.ai
   - button2.gif

5. Create visual elements using the images in your document, changing their size, color, and other properties as needed. (*Hint*: Various buttons have been skewed or distorted.)
6. Flatten the layers and selections in your document, if desired.
7. Save your work, then examine the sample shown in Figure 33.

Figure 33 *Sample Completed Project Builder 1*

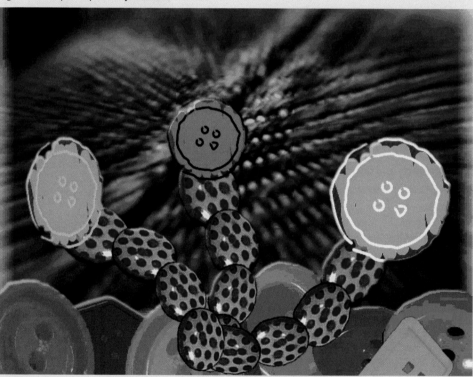

You're driving a moving truck across the country with a friend, and to occupy the time when you're not driving, you will use your new digital camera to take photographs. To memorialize this road trip, you will create a Web page dedicated to your adventure.

1. Obtain images that will fit your theme. You can obtain images from your computer or from the Internet. When downloading from the Internet, you should always assume the material is protected by copyright. Be sure to check the Web site's terms of use to determine if you can use the work for educational, personal, or noncommercial purposes. Always check the copyright information on any media you download.

2. Create a new document and save it as **roadtrip.png**.

3. Import the files into your document or open and select them using the bitmap selection tools.

4. Create an interesting arrangement of your images, changing their size, color, and other properties as needed. (*Hint*: The lights of the long building in the example were selected using the Select Inverse command.)

5. Flatten the layers and selections in your document as necessary.

6. Save your work, then examine the sample shown in Figure 34.

Figure 34 *Sample Completed Project Builder 2*

Before you can build a visual element of a Web page, you need the visuals. As a designer, you'll want to be able to access as many images as possible to create a meaningful visual experience. Because dynamic Web sites are updated frequently to reflect current trends, this page might be different from Figure 35 when you open it online.

1. Connect to the Internet and navigate to *www. hubblesite.org/gallery*.

2. Open a document in a word processor, or open a new Fireworks document, then save the file as **universe**. (*Hint*: Use the Text tool in Fireworks to answer the questions.)

3. Explore the site and answer the following questions:
   - Which techniques could have been used to isolate photographs?
   - Is a cropping technique evident? If so, identify.
   - How do the images affect the site design?
   - How are photographic images and illustrations used in the site?
   - Who is the target audience for this site, what is its goal, and how does the design reinforce that goal?

4. Save your work.

Figure 35 *Design Project*

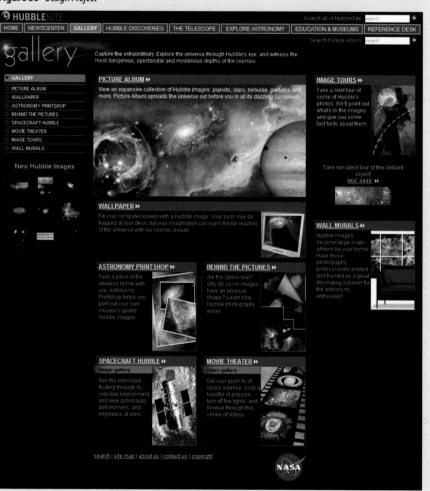

Courtesy NASA and STScI—www.hubblesite.org

Students from the entomology department at a local college are preparing an educational Web site for the reluctant public. The group, Give a Bug a Break, wants to show how beneficial insects are to the ecosystem and our lives. Your group is in charge of developing a sample template the group can show to potential sponsors.

1. Obtain images of insects, and choose an insect to feature in the document. When downloading from the Internet, you should always assume the material is protected by copyright. Be sure to check the Web site's terms of use to determine if you can use the work for educational, personal, or noncommercial purposes. Always check the copyright information on any media you download.

2. Create a new document and save it as mybug.png.

3. Import the files into your document or open and select them using the bitmap selection tools.

4. Create an interesting arrangement of your images, changing their size, color, and other properties as needed. (*Hint*: The praying mantis has a feathered edge on an oval marquee and is placed on an oval vector object with inner bevel and emboss effects.)

5. Flatten layers and selections in your document as desired.

6. Save your work, then examine the sample shown in Figure 36.

Figure 36 *Sample Completed Portfolio Project*

Kingdom - Animal
Phylum - Arthropoda
Class - Insecta
Order - Dictyoptera
Family - Mantidae
Genus - Stagomantis
Species - Carolina

CHAPTER 1

INTEGRATING ADOBE CS5
WEB STANDARD

1. Insert a Fireworks image into a
   Dreamweaver document

2. Create a Fireworks image and import it into Flash

3. Insert and edit a Flash movie in Dreamweaver

INTEGRATING ADOBE CS5
WEB STANDARD

Introduction

The Adobe CS5 Web Standard set of integrated Web development products includes Dreamweaver, Flash, and Fireworks. Used together, these tools allow you to create Web sites that include compelling graphics, animations, and interactivity. Recognizing that developing a Web site often involves team members with varying expertise (graphic designers, animators, programmers, and so on), Adobe has designed these products so that they integrate seamlessly. This integration allows you to move from one program to another as you bring together the elements of a Web site. For example, you can create a graphic image using Fireworks, import the image into Dreamweaver, and then edit the image from Dreamweaver. While each of the products can stand alone, they have a similar look and feel, with common features and interface elements, such as the Property inspector or Properties panel, that allow you to transfer your skills from one product to another. Adobe provides two other programs that you can use when working with these Web development tools. Adobe Bridge CS5 provides a quick way to organize, locate, and display the elements used to create Web sites and applications (such as Photoshop or Fireworks images, Flash movies, and Dreamweaver documents). Adobe Version Cue CS5 is used in a workgroup process where team members need access to the latest versions of a file. Using Version Cue, you set up a project, add users and assign permissions, and add files to the project. Then, users can "check out" a file and work on it. The check out process ensures that only one person is working on a file at a time. When the file is saved, a new version is created while the previous versions are maintained. Version Cue is accessed through Adobe Bridge and requires a connection to a server.

TOOLS YOU'LL USE

Insert a Fireworks Image into a
DREAMWEAVER DOCUMENT

What You'll Do

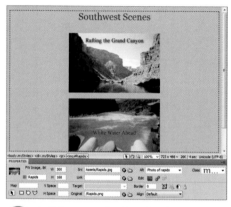

In this lesson, you will set Fireworks as the primary external image editor, set launch and edit settings in Fireworks, insert a Fireworks image into a Dreamweaver document, and edit an image in Fireworks from within Dreamweaver.

Placing a Fireworks Image into Dreamweaver

You can place PNG, JPEG, and GIF images created in Fireworks directly into a Dreamweaver document. One method is to select the position in the document where you want the image to appear, and then insert the image file. Alternately, you can export an image from Fireworks into a Dreamweaver site folder or copy and paste it from Fireworks. Exporting an image into the assets folder of the site allows you to insert the image in a document as a library item.

Using Fireworks as the Primary External Image Editor

You can easily edit a Fireworks image you've imported into Dreamweaver by launching the Fireworks program from within Dreamweaver. By default, Fireworks is the primary external image editor for GIF, JPEG, and PNG files in Dreamweaver. The round-trip editing feature between Fireworks and Dreamweaver automatically updates changes you make in Fireworks. Photoshop is the exclusive external image editor for PSD files. You can change

the external image editor using settings in the Preferences dialog box in Dreamweaver. Regardless of the selected primary image editor, you can still edit an image from Dreamweaver in any image-editing program installed on your computer. To do so, right-click (Win) or [control]-click (Mac) an image, click Edit With, and then select the image-editing program you want to use.

Using Design Notes

When you copy and paste, or export all or part of an image created in Fireworks or Flash in Dreamweaver, information about the original source file (PNG or FLA) is saved in a Design Notes file (MNO). For example, if in Dreamweaver you insert a file named lizard.jpg whose source file is lizard.png, Dreamweaver creates a Design Notes file named lizard.jpg.mno.

The Design Notes file contains references to the source PNG file. You can also add your own notes to an MNO file. Saving source image files in the Dreamweaver site folder ensures that any developer accessing the site can also edit the source PNG file, as shown in Figure 1. To share

Design Notes, be sure that the MNO file has the same site-root path. To edit a Design Notes file, you must have the file checked out.

Specifying Launch and Edit Preferences

The Fireworks launch and edit settings allow you to specify how to deal with source PNG files when editing or optimizing Fireworks images from another program, such as Dreamweaver. You use the Fireworks Preferences dialog box to specify one of the following launch and edit settings:

- Always Use Source PNG, which automatically launches the Fireworks PNG file specified in the Design Notes. Updates are made to both the source PNG file and the exported file.
- Never Use Source PNG, which automatically launches the exported Fireworks image. Updates are made to the exported image only.
- Ask When Launching allows you to specify whether or not to launch the source PNG file. This is the default setting.

Setting up the Dreamweaver Site

Figure 2 shows the structure and folders for the Web site you will use in this chapter. You will use the Southwest folder as the destination folder when you save an HTML document or SWF file. Initially, the site will contain only an Assets folder that you will use to export a Fireworks image. As you work through the chapter, you will integrate Fireworks images and a Flash movie into the Dreamweaver documents.

Figure 1 *Contents of a Fireworks Design Notes files*

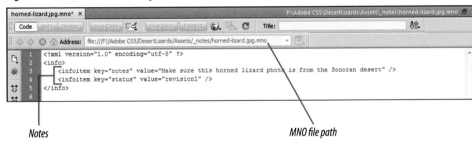

Notes

MNO file path

Figure 2 *Structure for the website*

Designate the primary external image editor

This lesson requires that you have Dreamweaver CS5 and Fireworks CS5 installed on your computer.

1. Use your operating system's file management tool to navigate to where your Data Files are stored, then create a folder named **Southwest**.

2. Create a folder named **Assets** in the Southwest folder.

3. Start Dreamweaver CS5, open **ics_1.html**, then save it to the Southwest folder as **CanyonScenes.html**.

   Your screen should resemble Figure 3.

   TIP Do not update links, if prompted, and show Design view.

4. Click **Edit** on the Application bar (Win) or **Dreamweaver** on the Menu bar (Mac), then click **Preferences**.

5. Click **File Types / Editors** to display the options shown in Figure 4.

   TIP Each file type has a default editor.

6. Make sure that .png is highlighted in the Extensions column, that Fireworks (Win) or Adobe Fireworks CS5 (Mac) appears in the Editors column, click **Fireworks** (Win) or **Adobe Fireworks CS5** (Mac) (if necessary), then click **Make Primary**.

7. Click **.gif** in the Extensions column, click **Fireworks** (Win) or **Adobe Fireworks CS5** (Mac) in the Editors column, click **Make Primary** (if necessary), then repeat for .jpg .jpe .jpeg.

(continued)

Figure 3 *The CanyonScenes.html document*

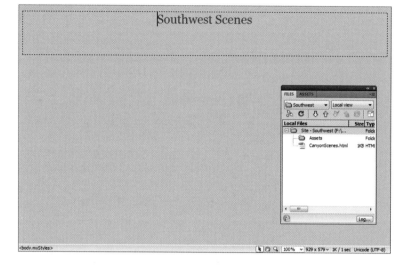

Figure 4 *Dreamweaver Preferences dialog box*

Figure 5 *Fireworks Preferences dialog box*

Select this option

8. Scroll down the Extensions column, click **.psd**, then verify that Photoshop (Primary) or Adobe Photoshop CS5 (Primary) (Mac) appears in the Editors column.

9. Click **OK** to close the Preferences dialog box.

You used the Preferences dialog box to verify that Fireworks is the primary external editor for .png .gif, and .jpg files, and that Photoshop is the only option for .psd files.

Specify launch and edit settings

This lesson requires that you have Fireworks CS5 installed on your computer.

1. Start Fireworks CS5.

2. Click **Edit** on the Application bar (Win) or Menu bar (Mac), then click **Preferences** (Win), or click the **Fireworks menu**, then click **Preferences** (Mac).

3. Click the **Launch And Edit category** to display the source file options.

4. Click the When editing from external application list arrow, then click Always Use Source PNG.

   Select this option to automatically open the source file when editing from another application.

5. Repeat Step 4 for the When optimizing from external application option, then compare your dialog box to Figure 5.

6. Click **OK** to close the Preferences dialog box.

You used the Preferences dialog box to set the Fireworks launch and edit preferences.

Edit and export an image in Fireworks

1. In Fireworks, open **ics_1.png** from where you store your Data Files, then save it as **GrandCanyon.png** in the Southwest folder.

   This document contains a single image, a photo of the Grand Canyon.

2. Click the **Text tool** T in the Tools panel, then change the font to **Times New Roman**, the size to **18**, and the color to **#0000FF** in the Property inspector.

3. Click the **top middle** of the image, type **Rafting the Grand Canyon**, then position and vertically align the text as shown in Figure 6.

TIP Make sure Tooltips is selected on the View menu.

4. Save your work, then display the Optimize panel (if necessary).

TIP When you copy a selection made from an image in Fireworks into Dreamweaver, the Image Preview dialog box opens, where you can specify optimization settings.

5. Click the Saved settings list arrow, then click **JPEG - Better Quality**.

6. Click **File** on the Application bar (Win) or Menu bar (Mac), then click **Export**.

7. In the Export dialog box, navigate to the Assets folder in the Southwest folder, then click **Save** (Win) or **Export** (Mac).

8. Save **GrandCanyon.png**, then exit Fireworks.

You opened a Fireworks PNG file, inserted text, and then optimized and exported the file as a JPG file.

Figure 6 *Aligned text in a Fireworks image*

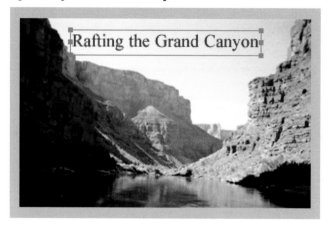

Figure 7 *Viewing source and original files*

Inserted source
Fireworks JPG file

Source and original files

Insert a Fireworks image into a Dreamweaver document

1. Display Dreamweaver, expand the assets folder in the Files panel (if necessary), then position the insertion point beneath the heading.

TIP If the images are not visible in the Files panel, right-click (Win) or [control]-click (Mac), then click Refresh Local Files.

2. Drag the **GrandCanyon.jpg** file to the insertion point in the Document window.

3. In the Image Tag Accessibility Attributes dialog box, type **A photo of the Grand Canyon** as the Alternate text, then click **OK**.

   The photo is inserted in the page, as shown in Figure 7. In the Property inspector, the path to the optimized source JPG file appears in the Src text box and the path to the original PNG file appears in the Original text box. In the Files panel, note the difference in file size between the original file and the optimized source file.

4. Save your work.

You inserted an image in an HTML document and set alternate text.

Edit a Fireworks image from Dreamweaver

1. Click the **GrandCanyon.jpg image** to select it.

2. Click the **Edit Fireworks button** in the Property inspector.

   The original PNG file opens in Fireworks.

3. If necessary, click the **Pointer tool** in the Tools panel, then click the **text** to select it.

4. Click the **Add Live Filters button** in the Property inspector, point to **Shadow and Glow**, then click **Drop Shadow**.

5. Set the Distance to **4**, accept the remaining default values, then click a blank part of the Fireworks window.

6. Click **Done** in the Editing from Dreamweaver window, as shown in Figure 8, to return to the Dreamweaver document.

   The source JPG image in Dreamweaver displays the drop shadow filter applied to the text, as shown in Figure 9.

7. Save your work.

You edited a Fireworks image from Dreamweaver.

Figure 8 *Edited image in Fireworks*

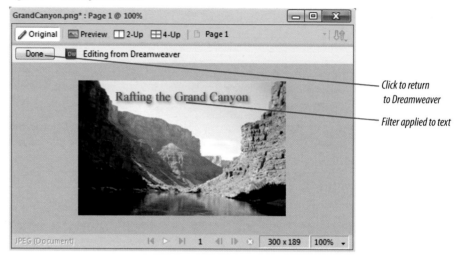

Click to return
to Dreamweaver

Filter applied to text

Figure 9 *Edited image in Dreamweaver*

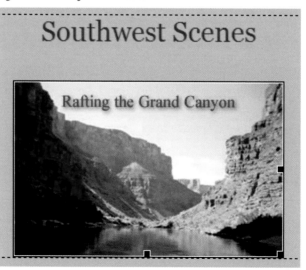

Figure 10 *Comparing quality settings in the Image Preview dialog box*

Click to
drag slider

File sizes

Copy and paste a Fireworks image in a Dreamweaver document

1. Return to Fireworks, open **ics_2.png**, then save it as **Rapids.png** in the Southwest folder.

2. Click **Select** on the Application bar (Win) or Menu bar (Mac), then click **Select All**.

3. Click **Edit** on the Application bar (Win) or Menu bar (Mac), click **Copy**, then close the document.

4. Display Dreamweaver, set an insertion point below the Grand Canyon image, click **Edit** on the Application bar (Win) or Menu bar (Mac), then click **Paste**.

5. In the Image Preview dialog box, click the **2 preview windows button** ⬜ , click the **Quality list arrow**, drag the slider to **60**, compare your dialog box to Figure 10, then click **OK**.

   The two preview windows allow you to compare file size.

   (continued)

6. In the Save Web Image dialog box, save the file as **Rapids.jpg** in the Assets folder, type **Photo of rapids** as the alternate text, then select the image.

   Figure 11 shows that the source image is placed in the document, but does not have a link to its original file in the Property inspector.

7. With the image selected, click the **Fireworks Edit button** in the Property inspector, navigate to the Southwest folder (if necessary), then double-click **Rapids.png**.

8. Click the **Text tool** T in the toolbox, type **White Water Ahead**, then position the text just in front of the raft.

   (continued)

Figure 11 *Copied and pasted source image*

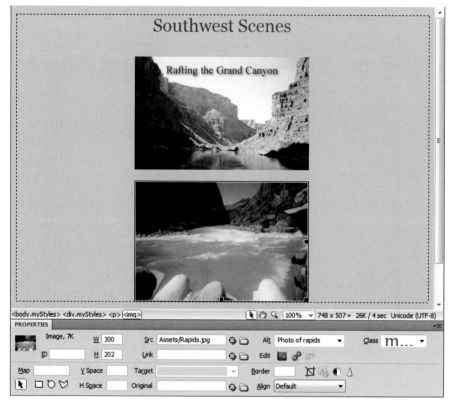

Figure 12 *Selecting part of the image*

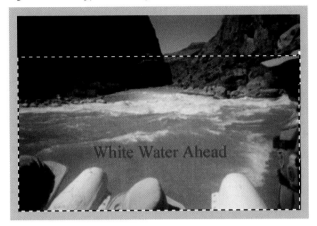

Figure 13 *Viewing edited image*

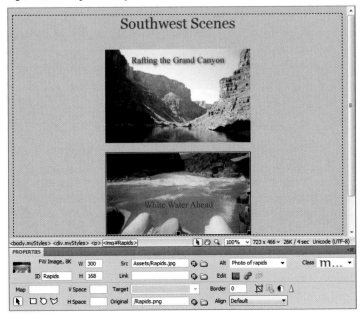

9. Use the **Rectangular Marquee tool** to select the part of the image shown in Figure 12.

10. Click **Edit** on the Application bar (Win) or Menu bar (Mac), click **Crop Document**, then click **Done** in the Editing from Dreamweaver window.

    The edited image appears in Dreamweaver, and the original file's path now appears in the Property inspector, as shown in Figure 13.

TIP Click the image if it does not update automatically.

11. Press **[F12]** to view the document in a browser, save your work, close all documents, then exit Dreamweaver and Fireworks.

You copied and pasted a Fireworks image into a Dreamweaver document, edited the image in Fireworks, then viewed the edited document in your browser.

Create a Fireworks Image
AND IMPORT IT INTO FLASH

What You'll Do

In this lesson, you will create an image in Fireworks, import it into Flash, modify layers, and then animate the object.

Importing a Fireworks Document into Flash

You can import Fireworks PNG files directly into a Flash document and then select which elements you want to be able to edit. You can import a Fireworks document as a single flattened bitmap, or retain editability for bitmap objects, including filters applied to the bitmap, or to vector objects, such as text. Depending on your selection, the document may contain the corresponding layers to the original Fireworks document. If you want to modify a flattened bitmap object, you can right-click (Win) or [control]-click (Mac) the object on the Stage or in the Library panel, and then click Edit with Fireworks, which launches Fireworks.

To import a Fireworks document into Flash, open a Flash document, make sure that the layer to which you import the file is not hidden, point to the Import command from the File menu, and then click either Import to Stage or Import to Library. Next, select the file you want to import, then in the Import Fireworks Document dialog box, select the import options you want—what remains editable—and then click OK. See Figure 14.

Figure 14 *Import Fireworks Document dialog box*

Select to import all objects and layers as a flattened bitmap

Click to select number of pages to import

Figure 15 *Resized auto shape*

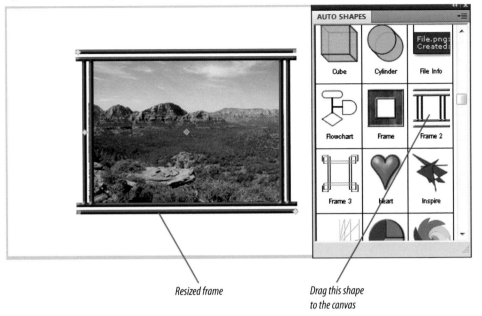

Resized frame

Drag this shape to the canvas

Create a Fireworks image with several layers

1. Start Fireworks.

2. Open **ics_3.png** from where you store your Data Files, then save it as **NorthernAZ.png**.

    This document has a bitmap layer.

3. Click the **sedona object** in the Photo layer in the Layers panel, then display the **Auto Shapes panel**.

4. Drag **Frame 2** on top of the image in the Document window, then in the Property inspector, change the following settings: W: **305**, H: **220**, X: **100**, and Y: **60** as shown in Figure 15.

    A blue frame surrounds the photo.

    TIP Your frame may differ. Mac users may need to make additional adjustments to match Figure 15.

5. Click the **Photo layer** in the Layers panel, click the **New/Duplicate Layer button** , then rename the layer **Heading**.

6. Click the **Text tool** T in the Tools panel, then change the font to **Times New Roman**, the font size to **30**, and the color to **#0000FF**.

7. Type **Northern Arizona Scenic Sites** above the photo, then vertically align the text on the canvas.

(continued)

8. Click the **Title layer** in the Layers panel, click the **New/Duplicate Layer button** , then rename the layer **Caption**.

9. Select the **Text tool** T in the Tools panel, then change the font to **Rosewood Std**, the size to **24**, and the color to **#993300**.

TIP If this font is not available, select a different font.

10. Click beneath the photo, type **SEDONA, ARIZONA**, then center it vertically, as shown in Figure 16.

11. Save your work, close the document, then exit Fireworks.

You opened and modified an image by adding a shape and text to it. You also added new layers and aligned the text.

Figure 16 *Positioned and aligned text*

Figure 17 *Setting options in the Import Fireworks Document dialog box*

Import Fireworks Document

☐ Import as a single flattened bitmap

Import: | Page 1 |

Into: | Current frame as movie clip |

Objects: ⚪ Import as bitmaps to maintain appearance
⦿ Keep all paths editable

Text: ⚪ Import as bitmaps to maintain appearance
⦿ Keep all text editable

Select to retain maximum editability

| OK | | Cancel |

Import a Fireworks document into Flash

1. Start Flash, then click **ActionScript 2.0** in the Create New section.
2. Save the new Flash document as **AZScenes.fla**.
3. Change the frame rate to **30 fps**.
4. Change the view to **Fit in Window**.
5. Click **File** on the menu bar, point to **Import**, then click **Import to Stage**.
6. Navigate to where you store your Data Files, click **NorthernAZ.png**, then click **Open** (Win) or **Import** (Mac).

   The Import Fireworks Document dialog box opens, where you can choose whether bitmaps (and any effects applied to them) and text remain editable in Flash.
7. Click the **Keep all paths editable option** for Objects, click the **Keep all text editable option** in the Text section, as shown in Figure 17, then click **OK**.

   You can edit text in Flash using Flash text tools and features.
8. Save your work.

You imported a Fireworks document and selected text to remain editable.

Edit a Fireworks image that has been imported into Flash

1. Position the pointer over the image on the Stage, double-click the **image** to display the Page 1 layers in the Flash Timeline, then click a blank part of the Stage.

   The contents of each layer are visible in the Timeline, as shown in Figure 18.

2. Double-click the **Fireworks Objects folder** in the Library panel.

   The NorthernAZ.png folder is visible.

3. Double-click the **NorthernAZ.png folder**, then double-click the **Page 1 folder** to display its contents.

4. Click **Bitmap 1** to see its thumbnail in the Preview window, repeat for **Page 1**, then click the **heading text** on the Stage.

5. Click the **Text tool** T in the Tools panel, then select the heading text.

6. Click the **Fill Color tool** in the Tools panel, then type **#336600** in the hexadecimal text box.

7. Click the **Selection tool** in the Tools panel, click a blank area of the Stage, then compare your screen to Figure 19.

8. Save your work.

You viewed the layers created from importing a Fireworks document into Flash, and changed the color of the text heading.

Figure 18 *Viewing layers in the Flash Timeline*

Imported layers

Figure 19 *Edited text*

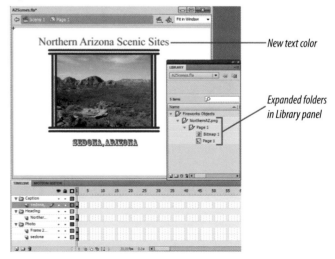

New text color

Expanded folders in Library panel

Figure 20 *Keyframes inserted in Timeline*

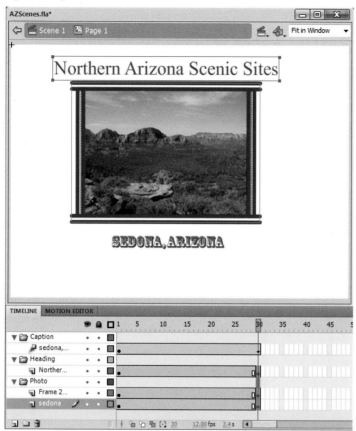

Create an animation using a Fireworks text object

1. Click the **Sedona, Arizona text** on the Stage to select it, then convert it to a Graphic symbol named **g_sedona-caption**.

2. Click **Insert** on the menu bar, then click **Motion Tween**.

3. Click **frame 1** on the sedona, arizona layer in the Timeline, then click the **text** to select it.

4. Click the **Color Effect Style list arrow** in the Properties panel, then click **Alpha**.

5. Change the alpha setting to **0**.

6. Click **frame 30** on the sedona, arizona layer, click the **blank text block** on the Stage, then change the alpha setting to **100**.

7. Set the frame rate to **12**.

8. Insert **keyframes** in frame 30 of the remaining layers, as shown in Figure 20.

9. Click **Control** on the menu bar, point to click **Test Movie**, then click **in Flash Professional**.

10. Close the test movie window.

11. Click **File** on the menu bar, click **Publish Settings**, deselect the HTML option, click **Publish**, then click **OK**.

12. Save your work, close the document, then exit Flash.

You created an animation using an imported Fireworks text object.

Insert and Edit a Flash Movie
IN DREAMWEAVER

What You'll Do

Northern Arizona Scenic Sites

SEDONA, ARIZONA

In this lesson, you will insert a Flash movie into a Dreamweaver document and edit the movie within Dreamweaver.

Inserting a Flash Movie into a Dreamweaver Document

You can easily insert a Flash movie (.swf) into a Dreamweaver document. To do this, set the insertion point where you want the movie to appear, and then use the Media command on the Insert menu to select SWF as the media to insert. If the file is not in the root folder for the Web site, Dreamweaver will ask whether you would like to copy it into the root folder. It is recommended that you copy the file to the root folder, so that it is accessible when you publish the site. When the insert process is completed, a placeholder appears at the insertion point in the document.

When you insert an SWF file into a Dreamweaver document, Dreamweaver automatically recognizes the native size of the file.

Using the Property Inspector with the Movie

When you click the placeholder to select it, the Dreamweaver Property inspector displays information about the movie, including the filename, as shown in Figure 21.

You can use the Property inspector to complete the following:

- Edit the Flash movie
- Play and stop the Flash movie
- Set width and height dimensions
- Cause the movie to loop
- Reposition the placeholder in the Document window

To edit the Flash movie, you select the placeholder, click the Edit button in the Property inspector and specify the source file (FLA). This opens Flash and the source file. After making changes to the document, you re-export it to Dreamweaver by clicking the Done button at the top of the Flash Document window or by choosing the Update for Dreamweaver command on the File menu. Choosing Done will close the document, while choosing Update to Dreamweaver will keep the document open. Both processes will automatically save the document. (*Hint*: Before starting the edit process from Dreamweaver, you should close Flash.)

Figure 21 *Flash movie placeholder selected in Dreamweaver document*

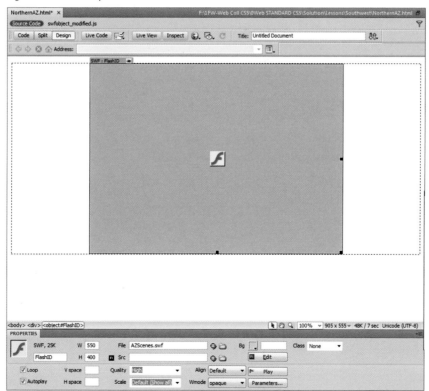

Insert a Flash movie into Dreamweaver

1. Start Dreamweaver.

2. Create a new Blank Page HTML document with no layout, then save it as **NorthernAZ.html** in the Southwest folder.

3. Click **Insert** on the Application bar (Win) or Menu bar (Mac), point to **Media**, then click **SWF**.

4. Navigate to the location where you store your Data Files, click **AZScenes.swf**, then click **OK** (Win) or **Choose** (Mac).

5. If a "This file is outside of the root folder..." message appears, click **Yes**, then click **Save** when the Copy File As dialog box appears.

6. Type **Photo of Sedona Arizona** for the title in the Object Tag Accessibility Attributes dialog box, then click **OK**.

   A Flash movie placeholder is inserted at the location of the insertion point as shown in Figure 22.

7. Verify that the placeholder is selected, click **Format** on the Application bar (Win) or Menu bar (Mac), point to **Align**, then click **Center**.

8. Save your work.

TIP If a Copy Dependent Files message box appears, click OK.

You inserted a Flash movie into a Dreamweaver document, copied the Flash movie to the root folder, and centered the movie in the document.

Figure 22 *Viewing the Flash movie placeholder*

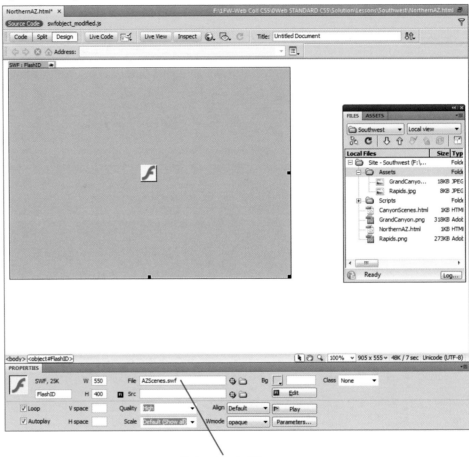

Flash movie in site folder

Figure 23 *Changing the movie height*

Height text box

Play a Flash movie and change settings from Dreamweaver

1. Click the **Flash movie placeholder** to select it (if necessary).

2. Click the **Play button** in the Property inspector.

3. Click the **Stop button** in the Property inspector.

4. Click the **Loop check box** in the Property inspector to deselect it.

5. Double-click the **height box (H)**, type **100**, then press [**Enter**] (Win) or [**return**] (Mac).

   Your screen should resemble Figure 23.

6. Click the **Play button** in the Property inspector.

7. View the resized movie, then click the **Stop button**.

8. Click the **Reset size button** ⟳ in the Property inspector to restore the previous setting.

9. Save your work.

You played a Flash movie and changed its settings in Dreamweaver by turning off the Loop option, and then changing and resetting the movie height.

Edit a Flash movie from Dreamweaver

1. Click the **Flash placeholder** to select it, then click **Edit** in the Property inspector.

   The Locate FLA File dialog box opens. If a Copy Dependent Files message box appears, click OK.

2. Navigate to where you store your Data Files, click **AZScenes.fla**, then click **Open**.

3. Double-click the **Page 1** movie clip symbol in the Library panel to display the layers in the Timeline, insert a new layer above the Caption layer, then name it **stopmovie**.

4. Click **frame 1** of the stopmovie layer.

5. Display the **Actions panel**, show the toolbox pane, if necessary, verify that ActionScript 1.0 & 2.0 is displayed above the category list, close the toolbox pane, verify that the **Script Assist button** is on, then verify that **stopmovie 1**: is displayed at the bottom of the script pane, as shown in Figure 24.

6. Click the **Add a new item to the script button**, click **Global Functions**, click **Timeline Control**, then click **stop**.

7. Click **frame 1** of the sedona layer on the Photo layer.

8. Convert the image to a button symbol named **b_sedona**, then click **OK**.

9. Display the Actions panel (if necessary), then verify that **b_sedona** is displayed at the bottom of the script pane.

10. Click the **Add a new item to the script button**, click **Global Functions**, click **Movie Clip Control**, then click **on**.

(continued)

Figure 24 *Verifying the settings in the Script pane*

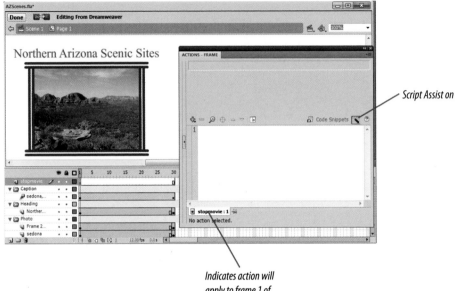

Script Assist on

Indicates action will apply to frame 1 of the stopmovie layer

Figure 25 *Specifying the frame to go to*

Northern Arizona Scenic Site

ACTIONS - BUTTON

goto : Go to the specified frame of the movie

○ Go to and play   ○ Go to and stop

Scene: <current scene>   ▼
Type: Frame Number   ▼
Frame: 2   ▼

Code Snippets

```
1  on (rollOver) {
2      gotoAndPlay(2);
3  }
4
```

b_sedona

Line 2: gotoAndPlay(2);

Frame 2 is the specified frame

11. Click the **Release check box** to deselect it, then click the **Roll Over check box** to select it.

12. Click the **Add a new item to the script button** ⊕ , click **Global Functions**, click **Timeline Control**, then click **goto**.

13. Change the Frame to **2**, as shown in Figure 25, then close the Actions panel.

14. Click **Control** on the menu bar, point to **Test Movie**, then click **in Flash Professional**.

15. Point to the image to view the animation, then close the test movie window.

    To save the FLA file and re-export it to Dreamweaver, you can click the Done button in the top-left corner of the Document window (which closes Flash), or use the Update to Dreamweaver command in the File menu.

16. Click the **Done button** in the top-left corner of the Document window to return to Dreamweaver.

17. In Dreamweaver, verify that the Flash placeholder is selected, then click **Play** in the Property inspector.

18. Point to the image to play the animation, then click **Stop**.

19. Click **File** on the Application bar (Win) or Menu bar (Mac), point to **Preview in Browser**, then click **Firefox** (Win), or **Safari** (Mac).

TIP Your default browser may vary. Allow blocked content if prompted.

20. View the movie, close the browser, save and close your work, then exit Dreamweaver and Flash.

You edited a Flash movie from Dreamweaver by creating a rollover action that plays an animation.

Designate the primary external image editor.

1. Start Dreamweaver CS5.
2. Display the Preferences dialog box and display the File Types / Editors option.
3. Verify that Fireworks is set as the default external image editor for .png, .gif, and .jpg files, and that Photoshop appears as the primary editor for .psd files.
4. Use your operating system's file management tool to navigate to where you store your Data Files, then create a folder named **Foods**.
5. Create a folder named **Assets** in the Foods folder.
6. Create a new Dreamweaver site named **Foods for Thought**, using the Foods folder as the Local Site Folder.

Specify the launch and edit settings.

1. Start Fireworks CS5.
2. Display the Preferences dialog box.
3. Set the Launch and Edit options to always use the source PNG when editing from an external application.
4. Set the Launch and Edit options to always use the source PNG when optimizing from an external application.

Edit and export a Fireworks document.

1. In Fireworks, open bread-heading.png from where you store your Data Files, then save it as **bread-headingRev.png**.
2. Add a noise filter to the text with an amount of **25**.
3. Export the file as an image-only GIF file to the Assets folder in the Foods folder.
4. Save and close bread-headingREV.png.

Insert a Fireworks image into a Dreamweaver document.

1. In Dreamweaver, create a new Blank Page HTML document and save it as **food-home.html** in the Foods folder.
2. Insert the bread-headingREV.gif file into the document and type **The Staff of Life** for the alternate text.
3. Center-align the heading across the document, make sure that bread-headingREV.png is listed as the Original in the Property inspector, then save your work.

Edit a Fireworks image from Dreamweaver.

1. Select the bread-headingREV.gif image and click Edit in the Property inspector.
2. Change the text formatting to italic.
3. Click Done to return to Dreamweaver.

Import a Fireworks document to Flash.

1. Switch to Fireworks and open bread-photo.png from where you store your Data Files.
2. Add a Bevel and Emboss filter with the following attributes: Inner Bevel, with a ring Bevel edge shape, and a width of 5.
3. Save the file as **bread-photoRev.png**, then close the file.
4. Start Flash CS5 and create a new ActionScript 2.0 document.
5. Save the document with the file name **bread-An.fla**.
6. Change the frame rate to 30 fps.
7. Import the bread-photoRev.png to the Stage, making the text editable.
8. Publish the document only as a SWF.
9. Save your work and close the document.

Insert a Flash movie into a Dreamweaver document.

1. Switch to Dreamweaver, then set an insertion point below the heading.
2. Insert the bread-An.swf file below the title and save the file to the Assets folder.
3. Enter **Animation of the word Bread** for the title.
4. Save your work.

Play a Flash movie and change the movie settings from Dreamweaver.

1. Select the Flash movie placeholder.
2. Click Play, then click Stop.
3. Deselect the Loop feature.
4. Change the movie window height to **250**, then reset the size.
5. Save your work.

Edit a Flash movie from Dreamweaver.

1. Select the movie placeholder, then click Edit. (*Hint:* Click OK if a Copy Dependent Files message box appears.)
2. Select the bread-An.fla file in the Locate FLA File dialog box, then click Open.
3. Create a motion animation that causes the word Bread on the caption layer to scroll in from off the left side of the Stage. (*Hint:* Double-click the image to display movie clip layers.)
4. Insert a keyframe into the last frame of the movie for the Bitmap layer.
5. Add a layer at the top of the Timeline named **stopmovie**, then create a stop action in frame 1 of the layer.
6. Insert a keyframe in the last frame of the stopmovie layer, then create a stop action in the frame.
7. Select the photo and convert it to a button symbol named **b_photo**.

8. Create a rollover action for the button that causes the animation to play when the pointer rolls over the photo.
9. Test the movie.
10. Click Done to return to the document in Dreamweaver.

11. Play the Flash movie in Dreamweaver, then stop the movie.
12. Save your work, display the Web page in a browser, then compare your screen to Figure 26.
13. Close the document, then exit all open programs.

Figure 26 *Completed Skills Review*

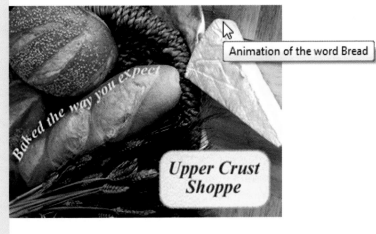

Ultimate Tours has asked you to develop a Dreamweaver Web site for their travel company. The site will include graphics exported from Fireworks and the Flash animations that were developed in Flash Chapter 5 for the Ultimate Tours Web site.

1. Create a folder on your hard drive and name it **ULTours**, then create a folder within the ULTours folder named **Assets**.
2. In Dreamweaver, create a new site named **Ultimate_Tours**, using the ULTours folder as the local root folder. Change the Background color to #069 in the Page Properties dialog box. (*Hint*: Click a color swatch in the middle of the left blue-green swatches.)
3. Open ULTours_home.html and save it to the ULTours folder as **ULTours_homeRev.html**, updating links if prompted.
4. Start Fireworks, open ULTours-heading.png, change the text formatting to italic, then save it as ULTours-headingRev.png.
5. Export the document with the filename **ULTours-headingRev.jpg** to the Assets folder in the Ultimate_Tours site folder. (*Hint*: Use the JPEG - Better Quality optimization setting.)
6. Open ULTours-photo.png, then type **The Islands** as a title and place it in the sky, then save the document as ULTours-photoRev.png.
7. Show the Layers panel, select the Background layer (Win) or Bitmap layer (Mac), show the Auto Shapes panel, insert Frame 3, then fit the image to the canvas. (*Hint*: Click Fit Canvas from the Canvas command options on the Modify menu.)

8. Create a rectangle W: 206, H: 176, fill color: #006699, move the Rectangle layer to the bottom of the Layers panel, then save and close the file.
9. Switch to Dreamweaver, insert the ULTours-headingRev.jpg image, type **The Trip of a Lifetime heading** as alternate text, then center the heading.
10. Edit ULTours-headingRev.jpg in Fireworks and change the font color to white.
11. Create a new Flash File (ActionScript 2.0) named **ULTours-photo-An.fla** and set the Document properties to 205 (width) and 175 (height).
12. Change the frame rate to 40 fps.
13. Import ULTours-photoRev.png to the Stage as a movie clip with all elements editable, then horizontally center the image.
14. Set Publish Settings to not include HTML, publish the movie, close and save the file, then exit Flash.
15. Display Dreamweaver, insert the ULTours-photo-An.swf file to the right of the heading, saving the file to the Assets folder and then adding appropriate alternate text.
16. Center the heading and photo across the page.
17. Play the Flash movie in Dreamweaver, then stop the movie.
18. Edit the movie from Dreamweaver, copy dependent files if prompted, then create an animation that zooms out the text.
19. Add keyframes to the end of the movie for each of the other layers.

20. Convert the photo to a button and add ActionScript so that the movie plays when the pointer rolls over the image.
21. Insert a new layer named **stopmovie**, then add stop actions to the first and last frames of the movie.
22. Test the movie.
23. Use the Done button to return to the Dreamweaver document.
24. Play the movie in Dreamweaver, then save your work.
25. Insert the ultimatetours5.swf file below the heading and provide a title.
26. Turn off the Loop feature.
27. Save your work, view the document in a browser, compare your image to the sample in Figure 27, then close all open files and exit open programs.

Figure 27 *Sample Completed Project Builder 1*

This project begins with the Striped Umbrella site created in Dreamweaver Chapter 5.

You have been asked to enhance the Striped Umbrella site by adding a Flash movie and changing a graphic image on the cafe page. Figure 28 shows the completed page for this part of the Web site. The idea is to replace the static crab logo image with a Flash animation that plays in the same space on the page.

1. In Fireworks, open cafe_logo.png from where you store your Data Files, save it as **cafe_logoRev.png** in the Striped Umbrella folder, then view each object in the Layers panel.
2. In Flash, in a new ActionScript 2.0 document, import the cafe_logoRev.png file as a movie clip to the Stage, specifying that all paths are editable. (*Hint*: Double-click the image on the Stage to display layers twice.)
3. In Flash, create an animation of your choice using the cafe_logoRev.png image. You decide on the type of animation, which could be a zoom or fade in; the entire crab moving; the crab claws moving; and so forth. (*Hint*: The crab image is made up of a body and left and right claws. If you want to animate these as one object, you can press and hold [Shift] to select all three, then convert them to a graphic symbol. Include a rollover effect or some other form of user interaction.)
4. Save the movie as **crab_Anim.fla** and publish the document.

5. In Dreamweaver, open the Striped Umbrella site on the Files panel.
6. Open the cafe.html page and delete the cafe_logo graphic on the page.
7. Insert the image café_logo_nameRev.gif, type **Sand Crab Café logo** as the Alt text, place the insert point above the logo, then insert the crab_Anim.swf file in the cell where the cafe_logo graphic had been. Type the Alt text of your choice.
8. Select the Flash movie placeholder and use the Property inspector to play and stop the animation.
9. Save your file as **cafeRev.html**.
10. View the Web page in your browser, then close all open files and exit open programs.

Figure 28 *Sample Completed Project Builder 2*

Figure 29 shows the home page of a Web site. Study the figure and complete the following questions. For each question, indicate how you determined your answer.

1. Connect to the Internet, and go to www.memphiszoo.org.
2. Open a document in a word processor or in Flash, save the file as **dpcIntegrationStd**.
   - What seems to be the purpose of this site?
   - Who would be the target audience?
   - Identify three elements within the Web page that could have been created or enhanced using Fireworks.
   - Identify two elements on the page and indicate how you would use Fireworks to enhance them.
   - Identify an animation that could have been developed by Flash.
   - Indicate how you would use Flash to enhance the page.
   - What would be the value of using Flash, Dreamweaver, and Fireworks to create the Web site?
   - What suggestions would you make to improve on the design, and why?

Figure 29 *Sample Completed Design Project*

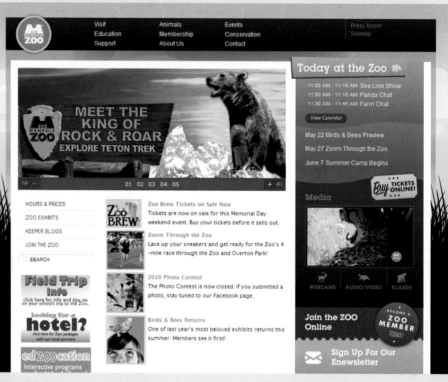

Courtesy Memphis Zoo - www.memphiszoo.org

This is a continuation of the Portfolio Project in Flash Chapter 5. You will create a Web site in Dreamweaver, import graphic files from Fireworks, and import portfolio5.swf into the site. The home page of the Web site will include a heading and photo image (of your choice), as shown in Figure 30.

1. Create a folder on your hard drive and name it **Portfoliowebsite**, then create a folder within the Portfoliowebsite folder named **Assets**.
2. In Dreamweaver, create a new site named **Portfolioweb**, using the Portfoliowebsite folder as the local root folder and Assets as the default images folder, then give it a preferred title.
3. Open portfoliohome.html and save it as **portfoliohomeRev.html** to the Portfoliowebsite site.
4. In Fireworks, open portfolio-heading.png, save it as **portfolio-headingRev.png** to the Portfoliowebsite folder, open portfolio-photo.png, then save it as **portfolio-photoRev.png** to the Portfoliowebsite folder.
5. Export both files as a JPEG - Better Quality file to the Assets folder.
6. Close both Fireworks files without saving changes, then exit Fireworks.
7. In Dreamweaver, insert the portfolio-headingRev.jpg image, and provide alternate text. (*Hint*: Refresh the Files panel, if necessary.)
8. Insert the portfolio-photoRev.jpg file from the Assets folder to the right of the heading, provide alternate text, and center the heading and photo on the page.
9. Insert portfolio5.swf below the heading and provide a title.

10. Use your file management tool to copy portfolio5.fla from where your store your Data Files to the Portfoliowebsite folder on your hard disk, then set the source file to that location.
11. Turn off the Loop and Autoplay features.
12. Select the heading and edit it in Fireworks to apply a drop shadow, then return to Dreamweaver.
13. Select the photo, edit it in Fireworks, add a blue inner glow, then return to Dreamweaver.

14. Edit the Flash movie.
15. In Fireworks, create a graphic that resembles a portfolio case and name it **portfolioCase.png**.
16. In Flash, import portfolioCase.png to the Stage.
17. Center the portfolioCase image on the Stage.
18. Return to Dreamweaver.
19. Save your work, view the page in a browser, then compare your image to the sample in Figure 30.

Figure 30 *Sample Completed Portfolio Project*

READ THE FOLLOWING INFORMATION CAREFULLY!!

Find out from your instructor the location where you will store your files.

- To complete many of the chapters in this book, you need to use the Data Files on the CD at the back of this book.
- All of the Data Files are organized in folders named after the chapter in which they are used. You should leave all the Data Files in these folders; do not move any Data File out of the folder in which it is originally stored.
- Your instructor will tell you whether you will be working from the CD or copying the files to a drive on your computer or on a server. Your instructor will also tell you where you will store the files you create and modify.

Copy and organize your Data Files.

- Use the Data Files List to organize your files to a USB storage device, network folder, hard drive, or other storage device.
- Create a subfolder for each chapter in the location where you are storing your files, and name it according to the chapter title (e.g., Flash Chapter 1).
- For each chapter you are assigned, copy the files listed in the **Data File Supplied** column into that chapter's folder.
- If you are working from the CD, you should store the files you modify or create in each chapter in the chapter folder. (Note that you cannot work from the CD for the Dreamweaver and integration chapters. The files need to be saved to a storage device.)

Find and keep track of your Data Files and completed files.

- Use the **Data File Supplied** column to make sure you have the files you need before starting the chapter or exercise indicated in the **Chapter** column.
- Use the **Student Creates File** column to determine the filename you use when saving your new file for the exercise.
- The **Used in** column tells you where a file is used in a chapter.

Use these special instructions for Dreamweaver.

- As you build each website, the exercises in this book will guide you to copy the Data Files you need from the appropriate Data Files folder to the folder where you are storing the website. Your Data Files should always remain intact because you are copying (and not moving) them to the website.

Files used in this book

ADOBE DREAMWEAVER CS5			
Chapter	**Data File Supplied**	**Student Creates File**	**Used in**
Chapter 1	dw1_1.html		Lesson 2
	assets/pool.jpg		
	assets/su_banner.gif		
	dw1_2.html	about_us.html	Lesson 4
	assets/su_banner.gif	activities.html	
		cafe.html	
		cruises.html	
		fishing.html	
		index.html	
		spa.html	
	dw1_3.html	annuals.html	Skills Review
	dw1_4.html	index.html	
	assets/blooms_banner.jpg	newsletter.html	
	assets/tulips.jpg	perennials.html	
		plants.html	
		tips.html	
		water_plants.html	
		workshops.html	
	dw1_5.html	catalog.html	Project Builder 1
	assets/tripsmart_banner.jpg	china.html	
		index.html	
		newsletter.html	

ADOBE DREAMWEAVER CS5			
Chapter	**Data File Supplied**	**Student Creates File**	**Used in**
Chapter 1, continued		services.html	
		spain.html	
		tours.html	
	dw1_6.html	adults.html	Project Builder 2
	assets/cc_banner.jpg	catering.html	
		children.html	
		classes.html	
		index.html	
		recipes.html	
		shop.html	
	none		Design Project
	none		Portfolio Project
Chapter 2	dw2_1.html		Lesson 2
	spa.doc		
	assets/su_banner.gif		
	assets/sea_spa_logo.jpg		
	dw2_2.html		Skills Review
	gardening_tips.doc		
	assets/blooms_banner.jpg		
	assets/butterfly.jpg		
	none		Project Builder 1
	none		Project Builder 2
	none		Design Project
	none		Portfolio Project

ADOBE DREAMWEAVER CS5			
Chapter	**Data File Supplied**	**Student Creates File**	**Used in**
Chapter 3	questions.doc		Lesson 1
		su_styles.css	Lesson 2
		blooms_styles.css	Skills Review
	dw3_1.html		Project Builder 1
		tripsmart_styles.css	
	assets/tripsmart_banner.jpg		
	dw3_2.html	cc_styles.css	Project Builder 2
	assets/cc_banner.jpg		
	assets/pie.jpg		
	none		Design Project
	none		Portfolio Project
Chapter 4	dw4_1.html		Lesson 1
	assets/boardwalk.png		
	assets/club_house.jpg		
	assets/su_banner.gif		
	assets/su_logo.gif		
	assets/stripes_back.gif		Lesson 3
	assets/umbrella_back.gif		
	favicon.ico		Lesson 4
	assets/map_large.jpg		
	assets/map_small.jpg		
	dw4_2.html		Skills Review
	flower.ico		

ADOBE DREAMWEAVER CS5			
Chapter	Data File Supplied	Student Creates File	Used in
Chapter 4, continued	assets/blooms_banner.jpg		
	assets/daisies.jpg		
	assets/rose_bloom.jpg		
	assets/rose_bud.jpg		
	assets/two_roses.jpg		
	assets/two_roses_large.jpg		
	dw4_3.html		Project Builder 1
	airplane.ico		
	assets/bull_fighter.jpg		
	assets/stallion.jpg		
	assets/tripsmart_banner.jpg		
	dw4_4.html		Project Builder 2
	assets/cc_banner.jpg		
	assets/paella.jpg		
	assets/paella_pan.jpg		
	none		Design Project
	none		Portfolio Project
Chapter 5	dw5_1.html		Lesson 1
	assets/su_banner.gif		
	assets/herron_waiting_small.jpg		
	assets/two_dolphins_small.jpg		
	SpryAssets/SpryMenuBar.js	SpryAssets/SpryMenuBar.js	Lesson 3
	SpryAssets/SpryMenuBarDown.gif	SpryAssets/SpryMenuBarDown.gif	
	SpryAssets/SpryMenuBarDownHover.gif	SpryAssets/SpryMenuBarDownHover.gif	

ADOBE DREAMWEAVER CS5			
Chapter	**Data File Supplied**	**Student Creates File**	**Used in**
Chapter 5, continued	SpryAssets/SpryMenuBarHorizontal.css	SpryAssets/SpryMenuBarHorizontal.css	
	SpryAssets/SpryMenuBarRight.gif	SpryAssets/SpryMenuBarRight.gif	
	SpryAssets/SpryMenuBarRightHover.gif	SpryAssets/SpryMenuBarRightHover.gif	
	dw5_2.html		Lesson 5
	dw5_3.html		
	assets/boats.jpg		
	assets/heron_small.jpg		
	dw5_4.html		Skills Review
	dw5_5.html		
	dw5_6.html		
	dw5_7.html		
	assets/blooms_banner.jpg		
	assets/coleus.jpg		
	assets/grass.jpg		
	assets/plants.jpg		
	assets/ruby_grass.jpg		
	assets/trees.jpg		
	assets/water_lily.jpg		
	SpryAssets/SpryMenuBar.js	SpryAssets/SpryMenuBar.js	
	SpryAssets/SpryMenuBarDown.gif	SpryAssets/SpryMenuBarDown.gif	
	SpryAssets/SpryMenuBarDownHover.gif	SpryAssets/SpryMenuBarDownHover.gif	
	SpryAssets/SpryMenuBarHorizontal.css	SpryAssets/SpryMenuBarHorizontal.css	
	SpryAssets/SpryMenuBarRight.gif	SpryAssets/SpryMenuBarRight.gif	

ADOBE DREAMWEAVER CS5			
Chapter	**Data File Supplied**	**Student Creates File**	**Used in**
Chapter 5, continued	SpryAssets/SpryMenuBarRightHover.gif	SpryAssets/SpryMenuBarRightHover.gif	
	dw5_8.html		Project Builder 1
	dw5_9.html		
	dw5_10.html		
	assets/gaudi_dragon.jpg		
	assets/great_wall.jpg		
	assets/panda.jpg		
	assets/tripsmart_banner.jpg		
	assets/warriors.jpg		
	SpryAssets/SpryMenuBar.js	SpryAssets/SpryMenuBar.js	
	SpryAssets/SpryMenuBarDown.gif	SpryAssets/SpryMenuBarDown.gif	
	SpryAssets/SpryMenuBarDownHover.gif	SpryAssets/SpryMenuBarDownHover.gif	
	SpryAssets/SpryMenuBarHorizontal.css	SpryAssets/SpryMenuBarHorizontal.css	
	SpryAssets/SpryMenuBarRight.gif	SpryAssets/SpryMenuBarRight.gif	
	SpryAssets/SpryMenuBarRightHover.gif	SpryAssets/SpryMenuBarRightHover.gif	
	dw5_11.html		Project Builder 2
	dw5_12.html		
	dw5_13.html		
	assets/cc_banner_with_text.jpg		
	assets/children_cooking.jpg		
	assets/cookies_oven.jpg		
	assets/dumplings1.jpg		

DATA FILES LIST

(CONTINUED)

ADOBE DREAMWEAVER CS5			
Chapter	**Data File Supplied**	**Student Creates File**	**Used in**
Chapter 5, continued	assets/dumplings2.jpg		
	assets/dumplings3.jpg		
	assets/fish.jpg		
	none		Design Project
	none		Portfolio Project
Chapter 6	cafe.doc		Lesson 2
	assets/cafe_logo.gif		
	assets/cafe_photo.jpg		
	assets/chocolate_cake.jpg		Lesson 6
	composting.doc		Skills Review
	assets/chives.jpg		
	assets/gardening_gloves.gif		
	assets/hat.jpg		Project Builder 1
	assets/pants.jpg		
	assets/vest.jpg		
	menu_items.doc		Project Builder 2
	assets/muffins.jpg		
	none		Design Project
	none		Portfolio Project
Chapter 7		The Striped Umbrella.ste	Lesson 5
		Blooms & Bulbs.ste	Skills Review
		TripSmart.ste	Project Builder 1
		Carolyne's Creations.ste	Project Builder 2
	none		Design Project
	none		Portfolio Project

ADOBE FLASH CS5			
Chapter	**Data File Supplied**	**Student Creates File**	**Used in**
Chapter 1		workspace.fla	Lesson 1
	fl1_1.fla		Lesson 2
		tween.fla	Lesson 3
		layers.fla	Lesson 4
	*layers.fla		Lesson 5
	fl1_2.fla		Skills Review
		demonstration.fla	Project Builder 1
	fl1_3.fla		Project Builder 2
		dpc1.fla	Design Project
			Portfolio Project
Chapter 2	fl2_1.fla		Lesson 1
	fl2_2.fla		
	fl2_3.fla		
	fl2_4.fla		Lesson 4
	fl2_5.fla		Lesson 5
	fl2_6.fla		Skills Review
		ultimateTours2.fla	Project Builder 1
		theJazzClub.fla	Project Builder 2
		dpc2.fla	Design Project
		portfolio2.fla	Portfolio Project
Chapter 3	fl3_1.fla		Lesson 1
	fl3_2.fla		Lessons 2–4
	islandview.jpg sailboat.ai	sailing.fla	Lesson 5

ADOBE FLASH CS5			
Chapter	**Data File Supplied**	**Student Creates File**	**Used in**
Chapter 3, continued	fl3_3.fla BeachScene.jpg		Skills Review
	**ultimateTours2.fla UTLogo.jpg		Project Builder 1
		isa3.fla	Project Builder 2
		dpc3.fla	Design Project
	**portfolio2.fla		Portfolio Project
Chapter 4	fl4_1.fla fl4_2.fla		Lesson 1
	fl4_3.fla		Lesson 2
	fl4_4.fla		Lesson 3
	fl4_5.fla		
	fl4_6.fla		Lesson 4
	fl4_7.fla		
	fl4_8.fla		
	fl4_9.fla		Lesson 5
	fl4_10.fla		Lesson 6
	fl4_11.fla		Skills Review
	**ultimateTours3.fla ship.gif		Project Builder 1
		jumper4.fla	Project Builder 2
		dpc4.fla	Design Project
	**portfolio3.fla		Portfolio Project

ADOBE FLASH CS5			
Chapter 5	fl5_1.fla		Lesson 1
	fl5_2.fla		Lesson 2
	carSnd.wav		
	beep.wav		
	fl5_3.fla		Lesson 3
	fireworks.mov		
	fl5_4.fla		Lesson 4
	fl5_5.fla		Lesson 5
	fl5_6.fla		
	fl5_7.fla		Lesson 6
	fl5_8.fla		Lesson 7
	fl5_9.fla		Skills Review
	fl5_10.fla		Skills Review
	fl5_11.fla		Skills Review
	*decoLand.fla		Skills Review
	tour-video.mov		
	fl5_12.fla		Project Builder 1
	*ultimateTours4.fla		Project Builder 1
	fl5_13.fla		Project Builder 2
		dpc5.fla	Design Project
	*portfolio4.fla		Portfolio Project

*Created in a previous Lesson or Skills Review in current chapter
**Created in a previous chapter

DATA FILES LIST

(CONTINUED)

ADOBE FIREWORKS CS5			
Chapter	**Data File Supplied**	**Student Creates File**	**Used in**
Chapter 1	fw1_1.png		Lesson 1
	pool.png	my_blue_heaven.png	Lesson 2
	fw1_1.png		Lessons 3 & 4
	fw1_2.png	pasta _1.png	Skills Review
	gnocchi.png	pasta _2.png	
	none	crystal.png	Project Builder 1
	none	meandering_paths.png	Project Builder 2
	none	floridakeys	Design Project
	none	emoticon.png	Portfolio Project
Chapter 2	none	fish.png	Lesson 1
	fw2_1.png		Lessons 2–5
	fw2_2.png		Skills Review
	none	remember_me.png	Project Builder 1
	none	impact_potions.png	Project Builder 2
	none	yoakam	Design Project
	none	classic_buckle.png	Portfolio Project

ADOBE FIREWORKS CS5			
Chapter 3	fw3_1.png		Lesson 1
	rocket.gif		
	saucer.png		
	book.eps		
	galaxy.jpg		Lesson 2
	astrocat.jpg		Lesson 3
	none		Lesson 4
	fw3_2.png		Skills Review
	smbottle.jpg sweet.png jelly_beans.eps rings.png gumballs.tif		
	button1.ai button2.gif	mybuttons.png	Project Builder 1
	none	roadtrip.png	Project Builder 2
	none	universe	Design Project
	none	mybug.png	Portfolio Project

INTEGRATION CS5			
Chapter	**Data File Supplied**	**Student Creates File**	**Used in**
Chapter 1	ics_1.html		Lesson 1
	ics_1.png		
	ics_2.png		
	ics_3.png		Lesson 2
		AZScenes.fla	
		AZScenes.swf	
	*AZScenes.swf	NorthernAZ.html	Lesson 3
	bread-heading.png	food-home.html	Skills Review
	bread-photo.png	bread-An.fla	
		bread-An.swf	
	ULTours_home.html	ULTours-PhotoAn.fla	Project Builder 1
	ULTours-photo.png	ULTours-PhotoAn.swf	
	ULTours-heading.png		
	**ultimatetours5.fla		
	**ultimatetours5.swf		
	cafe_logo.png	crab_Anim.fla	Project Builder 2
	cafe.html	crab_Anim.swf	
	Striped Umbrella site files		
	none	dpcIntegrationStdCS4	Design Project
	portfoliohome.html	portfolioCase.png	Portfolio Project
	portfolio-heading.png		
	portfolio-photo.png		
	**portfolio5.swf		
	**portfolio5.fla		

*Created in a previous Lesson or Skills Review in current chapter
**Created in a previous chapter

3D Effects
A Process in Flash that animates 2D objects through 3D space with 3D Transformation tools.

——————— **A** ———————

Absolute path
A path containing an external link that references a link on a web page outside of the current website, and includes the protocol "http" and the URL, or address, of the web page.

Acrobat.com
A management feature of the Adobe Creative Suite that can be used to organize your work.

ActionScript
The Flash scripting language used by developers to add interactivity to movies, control objects, exchange data, and create complex animations.

Actions Panel
The Flash panel used when you create and edit actions for an object or frame.

Additive colors
A color system in which, when the values of R, G, and B are 0, the result is black; when the values are all 255, the result is white.

Adobe AIR
An Adobe product used for developing content that can be delivered with a browser or as a desktop application.

Adobe Bridge
A stand-alone application that serves as the hub for the Adobe Create Suite 5. Can be used for file management tasks such as opening, viewing, sorting, and rating files.

Adobe BrowserLab
An Adobe online service for cross-browser and cross-platform compatibility testing.

Adobe Community Help
A collection of materials such as tutorials, published articles, or blogs, that is part of the Adobe Help content.

Adobe Configurator
A stand-alone program (available as a download) that lets you create your own panels.

Adobe CSS Advisor
A part of the Adobe website that offers solutions for resolving issues with your web pages.

Adobe Flash
A development tool used to create and deliver compelling interactive content, for websites, applications and mobile devices.

Adobe Flash Player
A program that must be installed on a computer to view Flash movies.

Adobe Version Cue
An asset management system that lets people work collaboratively.

Aligning an image
Positioning an image on a web page in relation to other elements on the page.

Alternate text
Descriptive text that can be set to appear in place of an image while the image is downloading. Alternate text is used by screen readers to describe images to users with visual impairment.

Altitude
A Bevel and Emboss setting that affects the amount of visible dimension.

Anchor point
Joins path segments to delineate changes in direction.

Angle
In the Layer Style dialog box, the setting that determines where a drop shadow falls relative to the text.

Animation
The perception of motion caused by the rapid display of a series of still images.

Anti-aliasing
Partially fills in pixel edges, resulting in smooth-edge type. This feature lets your type maintain its crisp appearance and is especially useful for large type.

AP div
A div that is assigned a fixed position on a page (absolute position).

AP element
The resulting container that an AP div tag creates on a page.

AP elements panel
Panel in the CSS panel group that is used to control the visibility, name, and Z-Index stacking order of AP elements on a web page.

Apache web server
A public domain, open source web server that is available using several different operating systems including UNIX and Windows.

Application bar
The toolbar located above the Document window which includes menu names (Windows only), a Workspace switcher, and other application commands.

Arrangement
How objects are positioned in space, relative to one another.

Assets
Files that are not web pages, such as images, audio files, and video clips.

Assets folder
A subfolder in the local site root folder in which you store most of the files that are not web pages, such as images, Flash files, and video clips. This folder is often named images, but can be assigned any name.

Assets panel
A panel that contains nine categories of assets, such as images, used in a website. Clicking a category button displays a list of those assets.

Asymmetrical balance
A design principle in which page elements are placed unequally on either side of an imaginary vertical line in the center of the page in order to create a feeling of tension or express a feeling or mood.

Attribution
The simplest of all Creative Commons licenses, in hich any user (commercial or non-commercial) can distribute, modify, or enhance your work, provided you are credited.

Attribution No Derivatives
Your work can be distributed by others, but not modified and in its entirety, with you being credited.

Attribution Non-Commercial
Your work can be distributed, modified, or enhanced, with credit to you, for non-commercial purposes only. Derivative works do not have to be licensed.

Attribution Non-Commercial No Derivatives
This is the most restrictive license category. Redistribution is allowed as long as credit is given. The work cannot be modified or used commercially.

Attribution Non-Commercial Share Alike
Your work can be distributed, modified, or enhanced, with credit to you, for non-commercial purposes only, but must be licensed under the identical terms. All derivative work must carry the same license, and be non-commercial.

Attribution Share Alike
The same as Attribution, except that the new owner must create their license under the same terms you used.

Auto-sizing
A text block that expands to accommodate the text you enter in Fireworks.

——————— **B** ———————

Background color
A color that fills an entire web page, frame, table, cell, or CSS layout block.

Background image
A graphic file used in place of a background color.

Balance
In screen design, balance refers to the distribution of optical weight in the layout. Optical weight is the ability of an object to attract the viewer's eye, as determined by the object's size, shape, color, and so on.

Banners
Images that generally appear across the top or down the side of a Web page and can incorporate a company's logo, contact information, and links to the other pages in the site.

Base color
The original color of an image.

Base layer
The bottom layer in a clipping group, which serves as the group's mask.

BaseCamp
A web-based project collaboration tool.

Baseline
An invisible line on which type rests.

Baseline shift
The distance type appears from its original position.

Behavior
Simple action scripts that let you incorporate interactivity by modifying content based on variables like user actions. A behavior tells a page object to respond in a specific way when an event occurs, such as when the mouse pointer is positioned over the object.

Bézier curve
Two dimensional curve in a vector object named after the French engineer who developed the mathematical formula to represent 3D automobile shapes.

Bitmap
A geometric arrangement of different color dots on a rectangular grid.

Bitmap mode
Uses black or white color values to represent image pixels; a good choice for images with subtle color gradations, such as photographs or painted images.

Bitmap type
Type that may develop jagged edges when enlarged.

Blend color
The color applied to the base color when a blending mode is applied to a layer.

Blending mode
Affects the layer's underlying pixels or base color. Used to darken or lighten colors, depending on the colors in use.

Blog
A website where the website owner regularly posts commentaries and opinions on various topics.

BMP
Bitmapped file. A file format used for images that is based on pixels.

Body
The part of a web page that appears in a browser window. It contains all of the page content that is visible to users, such as text, images, and links.

Border
An outline that surrounds a cell, a table, or a CSS layout block.

Bread crumbs trail
A list of links that provides a path from the initial page opened in a website to the page being viewed.

Break apart
The process of breaking apart text to place each character in a separate text block. Also, the process of separating groups, instances, and bitmaps into ungrouped, editable elements.

Brightness
The measurement of relative lightness or darkness of a color (measured as a percentage from 0% [black] to 100% [white]).

Broken links
Links that cannot find the intended destination file for the link.

Browser
Software used to display web pages, such as Microsoft Internet Explorer, Mozilla Firefox, Google Chrome or Apple Safari.

Browser Compatibility Check (BCC)
A Dreamweaver feature that checks for problems in the HTML code that might present a CSS rendering issue in some browsers by underlining questionable code in green.

Browser Navigation toolbar
A toolbar that contains navigation buttons you use when you are following links on your pages in Live view.

Bullet
A small dot or similar icon preceding unordered list items.

Bulleted list
An unordered list that uses bullets.

Button Symbols
Objects in Flash that appear on the Stage and that are used to provide interactivity, such as jumping to another frame on the Timeline.

C

Camera raw files
Camera raw file formats are files that contain unprocessed data and are not yet ready to be printed, similar to a negative from a film camera.

Cascading Style Sheets (CSS)
Sets of formatting attributes used to format web pages to provide a consistent presentation for content across the site.

Cell padding
The distance between the cell content and the cell walls in a table.

Cell spacing
The distance between cells in a table.

Cell walls
The edges surrounding a cell in a table.

Cells
Small boxes within a table that are used to hold text or graphics. Cells are arranged horizontally in rows and vertically in columns.

Character panel
Helps you control type properties. The Toggle the Character and Paragraph panel button is located on the options bar when you select a Type tool.

Check in files
A Dreamweaver feature that is used in a team environment to allow access to a file by team members when another team member has completed work on it.

Check out files
A Dreamweaver feature that is used in a team environment to restrict access to a file by team members when it is currently being edited by another team member.

Child container

A container created with HTML tags whose code resides inside a parent container. Its properties are inherited from its parent container unless otherwise specified.

Child page

A page at a lower level in a web hierarchy that links to a page at a higher level called a parent page.

Class type

See Custom type.

Clipboard

Temporary storage area, provided by your operating system, for cut and copied data.

Cloaked file

File that is marked to be excluded from certain processes, such as being transferred to the remote site.

Cloud computing

Allows you to share files with others in a virtual environment.

Code hints

An auto-complete feature that displays lists of tags that appear as you type in Code view.

Code Inspector

A separate floating window that displays the current page in Code view.

Code view

Code view shows the underlying HTML code for the page; use this view to read or edit the code.

Coding toolbar

A toolbar that contains buttons that are used when working in Code view.

Color management system

Keeps colors looking consistent as they move between devices.

Color mode

Used to determine how to display and print an image. Each mode is based on established models used in color reproduction. Represents the amount of color data that can be stored in a given file format, and determines the color model used to display and print an image. Determines the number and range of colors displayed.

Color Picker

A feature that lets you choose a color from a color spectrum.

Color ramp

In the Edit Gradient dialog box, the feature where you create an display the range of colors in the gradient.

Color Range command

Used to select pixels having a particular color in an existing image or layer.

Color separation

Result of converting an RGB image into a CMYK image; the commercial printing process of separating colors for use with different inks.

Columns

Table cells arranged vertically.

Comments

Helpful text describing portions of the HTML code, such as a JavaScript function. Comments are inserted in the code and are not visible in the browser window.

Composite path

A path formed by joining two open or closed paths.

Compound type

A type of style that is used to format a selection.

Continuous path

An open path formed by joining two open paths.

Control point

The yellow diamond that appears when you select an Auto Shape on the canvas in Fireworks; allows you to adust the object.

Controller

A panel that contains the playback controls for a Flash movie.

Coordinate

In Flash, the position on the Stage of a pixel as measured across (X coordinate) and down (Y coordinate) the Stage.

Copyright

A legal protection for the particular and tangible expression of an idea. The right of an author or creator of a work to copy, distribute, and modify a thing, idea, or image; a type of intellectual property.

Corner points

Path points on a vector object that has angles or lines

Crisp

Anti-aliasing setting that gives type more definition and makes it appear sharper.

Crop

To exclude part of an image. Cropping hides areas of an image without losing resolution quality.

CS Live

A management feature of the Adobe Creative Suite that can be used to organize your work whether you work in groups or by yourself; it is accessed through the CS Live list arrow on the Flash Application bar.

CSS Layout Box Model
CSS layout blocks defined as rectangular boxes of content with margins, padding, and borders.

CSS page layout
A method of positioning objects on web pages through the use of containers formatted with CSS.

CSS layout block
A section of a web page defined and formatted using a Cascading Style Sheet.

Curve points
Path points on an object with curves, such as a circle or rounded rectangle.

Custom type
A type of style that can contain a combination of formatting attributes that can be applied to a block of text or other page elements. Custom style names begin with a period (.). Also known as a class type.

—————— **D** ——————

Debug
To find and correct coding errors.

Declaration
The property and value of a style in a Cascading Style Sheet.

Deco Tool
Tool used to create drawing effects that can be used to quickly create environments, such as city landscapes, and to create various animations.

Default base font
Size 3 (Dreamweaver). The default font that is applied to any text without an assigned size that is entered on a web page.

Default font color
The color the browser uses to display text, links, and visited links if no other color is assigned.

Default link color
The color the browser uses to display links if no other color is assigned. The default link color is blue.

Defining a Website
Specifying a website's name and the location of the local site root folder using the Dreamweaver Site Setup dialog box.

Definition lists
Lists made up of terms with indented descriptions or definitions.

Delimited files
Database, word processing, or spreadsheet files that have been saved as text files with data separated with delimiters.

Delimiter
A comma, tab, colon, semicolon, or similar character that separates tabular data.

Deliverables
Products that will be provided to the client at the product completion such as pages or graphic elements created.

Dependent file
File that another file needs to be complete, such as an image or style sheet.

Derivative work
An adaptation of another work, such as a movie version of a book. A new, original product that includes content from a previously existing work.

Description
A short summary that resides in the head section of a web page and describes the website content.

Deselect
A command that removes the marquee from an area, so it is no longer selected.

Design notes
Separate files in a website that contain additional information about a file and are not displayed in a browser.

Design view
Design view shows the page as it would appear in a browser and is primarily used for creating and designing a web page.

Device Central
A program used to test Flash movies on various models of mobile devices.

Diagonal symmetry
A design principle in which page elements are balanced along the invisible diagonal line of the page.

Digital image
A picture in electronic form. It may be referred to as a file, document, picture, or image.

Distance
Determines how far a shadow falls from the text. This setting is used by the Drop Shadow and Bevel and Emboss styles.

Distort filters
Create three-dimensional or other reshaping effects. Some of the types of distortions you can produce include Glass, Pinch, Ripple, Shear, Spherize, Twirl, Wave, and ZigZag.

Div tag
An HTML tag that is used to format and position web page elements.

Dock
A collection of panels, or buttons surrounded by a dark gray bar. The arrows in the dock are used to maximize and minimize the palettes or panels.

Document
A Flash file which, by default, is given the .fla file extension; a Fireworks file whose native file type is .png.

Document toolbar
A toolbar that contains buttons and drop-down menus for changing the current work mode, checking browser compatibility, previewing web pages, debugging web pages, choosing visual aids, and viewing file management options.

Document-relative path
A path referenced in relation to the web page that is currently displayed.

Document window
The large area under the document toolbar in the Dreamweaver and Fireworks workspace where you create and edit web pages.

Documents
Flash, Photoshop, Fireworks, and Dreamweaver files.

Domain name
An IP address expressed in letters instead of numbers, usually reflecting the name of the business represented by the website. Also referred to as a URL.

Down Image state
The state of a page element when the element has been clicked with the mouse pointer.

Download
The process of transferring files from a remote site to a local site.

Download time
The time it takes to transfer a file to another computer.

Drop Shadow
A style that adds what looks like a colored layer of identical text behind the selected type. The default shadow color is black.

Drop Zone
A blue outline area that indicates where a palette or panel can be docked.

DSL
Digital Subscriber Line. A type of high-speed Internet connection.

Dual Screen layout
A layout that utilizes two monitors while working in Dreamweaver.

—————— **E** ——————

Embedded CSS
Styles that are part of an HTML page rather than comprising a separate file. Also called internal styles.

Embedded video
A video file that has been imported into a Flash document and becomes part of the SWF file.

Enable Cache
A setting to direct the computer system to use space on the hard drive as temporary memory, or cache, while you are working in Dreamweaver.

Expanded Tables Mode
A Dreamweaver mode that displays tables with temporary cell padding and spacing to make it easier to see the table cells.

Export data
To save data that was created in Dreamweaver in a special file format so that you can open it in another software program.

External CSS
Collection of styles stored in a separate file that control the formatting of content on a web page. External style sheets have a .css file extension.

External links
Links that connect to web pages in other websites or to an e-mail address.

Extract feature
Used to isolate a foreground object from its background.

—————— **F** ——————

Fair use
A concept that allows limited use of copyright-protected work.

Fair use doctrine
Allows a user to make a copy of all or part of a work, even if permission *has not* been granted.

Fastening point
An anchor within the marquee. When the marquee pointer reaches the initial fastening point, a small circle appears on the pointer, indicating that you have reached the starting point.

Favicon
Short for favorites icon. A small icon that represents your site, similar to a logo, that appears next to the title of a web page.

Favorites
Assets that are used repeatedly in a website and are included in their own category in the assets panel.

Feather
A method used to control the softness of a selection's edges by blurring the area between the selection and the surrounding pixels.

File versioning
A feature that allows you to store multiple versions of your work

Files panel
A window similar to Windows Explorer (Windows) or Finder (Macintosh), where Dreamweaver stores and manages files and folders. The Files panel contains a list of all the folders and files in a website.

Fill
A solid color, a pattern, or a gradient applied to an object.

Filters
Used to alter the look of an image and give it a special, customized appearance by applying special effects, such as distortions, changes in lighting, and blurring.

Fixed layout
A fixed page layout that expresses all container widths in pixels and remains the same size regardless of the size of the browser window.

Flash button objects
Flash graphic and text objects that you can insert onto a web page without having the Flash program installed.

Flash Lite
A program specifically developed to optimize the playing of Flash movies using mobile devices.

Flash Player
A free Adobe program that allows Flash movies (.swf and .exe formats) to be viewed on a computer.

Flash text
A vector-based graphic that contains text.

Flattening
Merges all visible layers into one layer, named the Background layer, and deletes all hidden layers, greatly reducing file size.

Floating workspace
A feature of Adobe products that allows each document and panel to appear in its own window.

Flowchart
A visual representation of how the contents in an application or a website are organized and how various screens are linked.

Focus group
A focus group is a marketing tool that asks a group of people for feedback about a product, such as the impact of a television ad or the effectiveness of a website design.

Font
Characters with a similar appearance.

Font combination
A set of three fonts that specifies which fonts a browser should use to display the text on a web page.

Font family
Represents a complete set of characters, letters, and symbols for a particular typeface. Font families are generally divided into three categories: serif, sans serif, and symbol.

Font family (Dreamweaver)
A set of font choices that specifies which fonts a browser should use to display the text on a web page.

Foreground color
Used to paint, fill, and stroke selections. The default foreground color is black.

Frame animation
An animation created by specifying the object that is to appear in each frame of a sequence of frames (also called a frame-by-frame animation).

Frame-by-frame animation
Animation that creates a new image for each frame (also called Frame animation).

Frame label
A text name for a keyframe that can be referenced within ActionScript code.

Frames
Individual cells that make up the Timeline in Flash.

Frameset
Multiple web pages displayed together using more than one frame or window.

FTP
File Transfer Protocol. The process of uploading and downloading files to and from a remote site.

Fuzziness
Similar to tolerance, in that the lower the value, the closer the color pixels must be to be selected.

G

Gamut
The range of displayed colors in a color model.

GIF file
Graphics Interchange Format file. A GIF is a type of file format used for images placed on web pages that can support both transparency and animation.

Gloss Contour
A Bevel and Emboss setting that determines the pattern with which light is reflected.

GPS
Global Positioning System. Devices are used to track your position through a global satellite navigation system.

Gradient
Two or more colors that blend into each other in a fixed design.

Gradient fill
A type of fill in which colors appear to blend into one another. A gradient's appearance is determined by its beginning and ending points.

Gradient presets
Predesigned gradient fills that are displayed in the Gradient picker.

Graphic
Picture or design element that adds visual interest to a page.

Graphic symbols
Objects in Flash, such as drawings, that are converted to symbols and stored in the Library panel. A graphic symbol is the original object. Instances (copies) of a symbol can be made by dragging the symbol from the Library to the Stage.

Grayscale image
Can contain up to 256 shades of gray. Pixels can have brightness values from 0 (black) to white (255).

Grayscale mode
Uses up to 256 shades of gray, assigning a brightness value from 0 (black) to 255 (white) to each pixel.

Grid
Horizontal and vertical lines that fill the page and are used to place page elements

Group
A command that manipulates multiple objects as a single selection.

Guide layers
Layers used to align objects on the Stage in a Flash document.

Guides
Horizontal and vertical lines that you drag from the rulers onto the page to help you align objects.

H

Handles
Small boxes that appear along the perimeter of a selected object and are used to change the size of an image.

Head content
The part of a web page that includes the page title that appears in the title bar of the browser and meta tags, which are HTML codes that include information about the page, such as keywords and descriptions, and are not visible in the browserHeadings.

Headings
Six different styles that can be applied to text: Heading 1 (the largest size) through Heading 6 (the smallest size).

Hexadecimal RGB value
A value that represents the amount of red, green, and blue in a color and is based on the Base 16 number system.

Highlight Mode
A Bevel and Emboss setting that determines how pigments are combined.

History panel
Contains a record of each action performed during an editing session. Up to 1000 levels of Undo are available through the History panel (20 levels by default).

Home page
The first page that is displayed when users go to a website.

Horizontal and vertical space
Blank space above, below, and on the sides of an image that separates the image from the text or other elements on the page.

Horizontal symmetry
A design principle in which page elements are balanced side-to-side across the page.

Hotspot
A clickable area on an image that, when clicked, links to a different location on the page or to another web page.

HTML
Hypertext Markup Language. A language web developers use to create web pages.

Hue
The color reflected from/transmitted through an object and expressed as a degree (between 0° and 360°). Each hue is identified by a color name (such as red or green).

Hyperlinks
Image or text elements on a web page that users click to display another location on the page, another web page on the same website, or a web page on a different website. Hyperlinks are also known as links.

———————— **I** ————————

Id type
A type of CSS rule that is used to redefine an HTML tag.

Image-editing program
Used to manipulate graphic images that can be reproduced by professional printers using full-color processes.

Image map
An image that has been divided up into sections, each of which serves as a link.

Image placeholder
An image placeholder is a graphic the size of an image you plan to use that holds the position on the page until the image is placed.

Import data
To bring data created in one software program into another application.

Inheritance
The CSS governing principle that allows for the properties of a parent container to be used to format the content in a child container.

Inline style
A style whose code is placed within the body tags of a web page.

Insert panel
The Insert panel includes eight categories of buttons for creating and inserting objects displayed as a drop-down menu: Common, Layout, Forms, Data, Spry, InContext Editing, Text, and Favorites.

Instances
Editable copies of symbols after you drag them from the Library panel to the canvas or Stage (in Flash).

Intellectual property
An image or idea that is owned and retained by legal control.

Interactivity
Allows visitors to your website to interact with and affect content by moving or clicking the mouse or using the keyboard.

Internal links
Links to web pages within the same website.

Inverse Kinematics
A process using a bone structure that allows objects to be animated in natural ways, such as a character running, jumping or kicking.

IP address
An assigned series of numbers, separated by periods, that designates an address on the Internet.

ISP
Internet Service Provider. A service to which you subscribe to be able to connect to the Internet with your computer.

Item
An individual link in a Spry menu bar.

———————— **J** ————————

JavaScript
A web-scripting code that interacts with HTML code to create dynamic content, such as rollovers or interactive forms on a web page.

JPEG file
Joint Photographic Experts Group file. A JPEG is a type of file format used for images that appear on web pages. Many photographs are saved with the JPEG file format.

———————— **K** ————————

Kerning
Controlling the amount of space between two characters.

Keyframe
A frame that signifies a change in the Time-line of a Flash movie, such as an object being animated.

Keywords
Words that relate to the content of a website and reside in the head section of a web page.

Kuler®
A web-hosted application that lets you create, save, share, and download color-coordinated themes for use in images. It can be accessed from a browser, the desktop, or Adobe products such as Illustrator.

———————— **L** ————————

LAN
A local area network.

Landscape orientation
An image with the long edge of the paper at the top and bottom.

Layer

An element that functions like a folder divided into sections that contain objects. A document can be made up of many layers. A section within an image on which objects can be stored. The advantage: Individual effects can be isolated and manipulated without affecting the rest of the image. The disadvantage: Layers can increase the size of your file.

Layer comp

A variation on the arrangement and visibility of existing layers within an image; an organizational tool.

Layer group

An organizing tool you use to group layers on the Layers panel.

Layer style

An effect that can be applied to a type or image layer.

Layer thumbnail

Contains a miniature picture of the layer's content, and appears to the left of the layer name on the Layers panel.

Layers (Flash)

Rows on the Timeline that are used to organize objects and that allow the stacking of objects on the Stage.

Layers panel

Displays content on all the individual layers within an active image. You can use the Layers panel to create, delete, merge, copy, or reposition layers.

Leading

An adjustment to the amount of vertical space between lines of text.

Library

A panel containing graphic symbols, button symbols, and animation symbols. You can use multiple Libraries in a document and share Libraries between documents.

Licensing agreement

The permission given by a copyright holder that conveys the right to use the copyright holder's work.

Link

See hyperlink.

Liquid layout

A page layout that expresses all container widths in percents and changes size depending on the size of the browser window.

Live filters

Filters applied to objects that remain editable.

Live styles

Preset font, color, stroke, or other effects and attributes.

Live view

Live view displays an open document as if you were viewing it in a browser, with interactive elements active and functioning.

Local site

The location of your local site root folder where your website files are stored while being developed.

Local site root folder

A folder on a hard drive, Flash drive, or floppy disk that holds all the files and folders for a website.

Logo

A distinctive image used to identify a company, project, or organization. You can create a logo by combining symbols, shapes, colors, and text.

Looping

The number of times an animation repeats.

Luminosity

The remaining light and dark values that result when a color image is converted to grayscale.

-------------------- M --------------------

Mailto: link

An e-mail address that is formatted as a link that opens the default mail program with a blank, addressed message.

Main Timeline

The primary Timeline for a Flash movie. The main Timeline is displayed when you start a new Flash document.

Marquee selection

A series of dotted lines indicating a selected area that can be edited or dragged into another image.

Mask

A feature that lets you protect or modify a particular area; created using a marquee.

Mask layer

A layer in a Flash document that is used to cover the objects on another layer(s) and, at the same time, create a window through which you can view various objects on the other layer.

Master Page

A page that contains elements common to all pages in the document.

Matte

A colorful box placed behind an object that makes the object stand out.

Menu bar
An area on a web page that contains links to the main pages of a website. Also called a navigation bar.

Merge cells
To combine multiple adjacent cells in a table into one cell.

Merge Drawing Model
A drawing mode that causes overlapping drawings (objects) to merge, so that a change in the top object, such as moving it, may affect the object beneath it.

Mesh
A series of horizontal and vertical gridlines that are superimposed in the Liquify preview window, or an object to which repoussé has been applied.

Meta data
Information about a file, such as keywords, descriptions, and copyright information.

Meta tags
HTML codes that reside in the head section of a web page and include information about the page such as keywords and descriptions.

Mode
Represents the amount of color data that can be stored in a given file format, and determines the color model used to display and print an image.

Model
Determines how pigments combine to produce resulting colors; determined by the color mode.

Mono type spacing
Spacing in which each character occupies the same amount of space.

Morphing
The animation process of changing one object into another, sometimes unrelated, object.

Motion guide layer
A path used to specify how an animated object moves around the Flash Stage.

Motion Tween Presets
Pre-built animations, such as a bouncing effect, that can be applied to objects in Flash.

Motion tweening
The process used in Flash to automatically fill in the frames between keyframes in an animation that changes the properties of an object such as the position, size, or color. Motion tweening works on groups and symbols.

Movement
In screen design, movement refers to the way the viewer's eye moves through the objects on the screen.

Movie clip symbol
An animation stored as a single, reusable symbol in the Library panel in Flash. It has its own Timeline, independent of the main Timeline.

N

Named anchor
A specific location on a web page that is used to link to that portion of the web page.

Navigation bar
A set of text or graphic links usually organized in rows or columns that viewers can use to navigate between pages of a website. See menu bar.

Navigation structure
The way that menu bars and other internal links are organized in websites for users to navigate from page to page within the website.

Nested table
A table within a table.

No right-click script
JavaScript code that will block users from displaying the shortcut menu when they right-click an image on a web page.

Non-breaking space
A space that is left on the page by a browser.

Non-Websafe colors
Colors that might not be displayed uniformly across computer platforms.

None
Anti-aliasing setting that applies no anti-aliasing, resulting in jagged edges.

Numbered lists
Lists of items that are presented in a specific order and are preceded by numbers or letters in sequence. Also called ordered lists.

O

Object Drawing Model
A drawing mode that allows you to overlap objects which are then kept separate, so that changes in one object do not affect another object. You must break apart these objects before you can select their stroke and fills.

Objects
The individual elements in a document, such as text or images. In Flash, objects are placed on the Stage and can be edited or manipulated.

Onion skin
A setting that allows you to view one or more frames before and after in the current frame.

Online communities
Online communities, or virtual communities, are social websites you can join, such as Facebook and Twitter, where you can communicate with others by posting messages or media content such as images or videos.

Opacity
Determines the percentage of transparency. Whereas a layer with 100% opacity will obstruct objects in the layers beneath it, a layer with 1% opacity will appear nearly transparent.

Optical center
The point around which objects on the page are balanced; occurs approximately 3/8ths from the top of the page.

Optical weight
The ability of an object to attract the viewer's eye, as determined by the object's size, shape, color, and so on.

Options bar
Displays the settings for the active tool. The options bar is located directly under the Application bar, but can be moved anywhere in the workspace for easier access.

Ordered lists
Lists of items that must be placed in a specific order and are preceded by numbers or letters. Sometimes called numbered lists.

Orientation
Direction an image appears on the page: portrait or landscape.

Orphaned files
Files that are not linked to any pages in the website.

Outline type
Type that is mathematically defined and can be scaled to any size without its edges losing their smooth appearance.

Over Image state
The state of a page element when the mouse pointer is over the element.

Over While Down Image state
The state of a page element when the mouse pointer is clicked and held over the element.

——————— P ———————

Page
In Fireworks, stores a unique set of layers and settings in a document.

Panels
A tabbed, floating or docked window that displays information on a particular topic or contains related commands. Used to view, organize, and modify objects. Panels contain named tabs, which can be separated and moved to another panel group. You can view a panel menu by clicking the Panel Options list arrow in its upper-right corner.

Panel groups
Sets of related panels that are grouped together and are displayed through the Window menu. Also known as Tab groups.

Panels dock
Area on the right side of the Fireworks window where panels are grouped and stacked.

Parent container
A container created with HTML tags with other containers falling between its opening and closing tags.

Parent page
A page at a higher level in a web hierarchy that links to other pages on a lower level called child pages.

Pasteboard
The gray area surrounding the Flash Stage where objects can be placed and manipulated. Neither the pasteboard, nor objects placed on it, appear in the movie unless the objects move onto the Stage during the playing of the movie.

Path (file location)
The location of an open file in relation to its place in the folder structure of the website.

Path (vector object)
An open or closed line consisting of a series of anchor points.

Pattern fill
A bitmap image with a complex color scheme and texture.

Pixels
Small squares of color used to display a digital image on a rectangular grid, such as a computer screen. Each dot in a bitmapped image that representsa color or shade.

Playhead
An indicator specifying which frame is playing in the Timeline of a Flash movie.

Plug-in
A module that adds features or enhancements to an application.

PNG file

Portable Network Graphics file. PNG is a file format used for images placed on web pages that is capable of showing millions of colors but is small in file size. The native file format in Fireworks.

Podcasts

Programming On Demand. Users can download and play digitally broadcasted files using devices such as computers or MP3 players.

Point handle

Handle extending from a point on a curved vector object used to adjust the object's shape.

Point of contact

A place on a web page that provides users with a means of contacting the company.

Points

Unit of measurement for font sizes. Traditionally, 1 inch is equivalent to 72.27 points.

Portrait orientation

An image with the short edge of the paper at the top and bottom.

PostScript

A programming language created by Adobe that optimizes printed text and graphics.

POWDER

The acronym for Protocol for Web Description Resources. This is an evaluation system for web pages developed with the World Wide Web Consortium (W3C) that provides summary information about a website.

PPI

Pixels per inch.

Preferences

Used to control the environment using your specifications.

Profile

Defines and interprets colors for a color management system.

Projector

In Flash, a standalone executable movie, such as a Windows .exe file.

Proof setup

Lets you preview your image to see how it will look when printed on a specific device.

Properties panel (also called Property Inspector)

In Flash and Fireworks, the panel that displays the properties of the selected object, such as size and color) on the Stage or the selected frame in Flash. The Properties panel can be used to edit selected properties.

Property inspector

A panel where properties and options specific to a selected tool or command appear. In Dreamweaver, a panel that displays the properties of a selected web page object. In Flash, the Property inspector displays the properties of the selected object on the Stage or the selected frame. In Firewroks, you can modify selected objects and set tool properties and other options. The contents of the Property inspector vary according to the object currently selected.

Proportional spacing

The text spacing in which each character takes up a different amount of space, based on its width.

Public domain

Work that is no longer protected by copyright. Anyone can use it for any purpose.

Publish

The process used to generate the files necessary for delivering Flash movies on the web.

Publish a Website

To make a website available for viewing on the Internet or on an intranet by transferring the files to a web server.

— Q —

QuickTime

A file format used for movies and animations that requires a QuickTime Player.

— R —

Radial symmetry

A design principle in which page elements are balanced from the center of the page outward, like the petals of a flower.

Rasterize

The process of converting a type layer to an image layer.

RDS

Remote Development Services. A connection type for transferring files used with web servers using Cold Fusion.

Reference panel

A panel used to find answers to coding questions, covering topics such as HTML, JavaScript, and Accessibility.

Refresh Local File List Automatically option

A setting that directs Dreamweaver to automatically reflect changes made in your file listings.

Registration point

The point on an object that is used to position the object on the Stage in a Flash movie.

Regular expressions

Combinations of characters, such as a phrase that begins or ends with a particular word or tag.

Related files
Files that are linked to a document and are necessary for the document to display and function correctly.

Related Files toolbar
A toolbar located below an open document's filename tab that displays the names of any related files.

Relative path
A path used with an internal link to reference a web page or graphic file within the website. In Flash, a path for an external link or to an object that is based on the location of the movie file.

Relief
The height of ridges within an object.

Remote server
A web server that hosts websites and is not directly connected to the computer housing the local site.

Remote site
A website that has been published to a remote server.

Rendering intent
The way in which a color-management system handles color conversion from one color space to another.

Resolution
The number of pixels per inch in an image. Also refers to an image's clarity and fineness of detail.

Resulting color
The outcome of the blend color applied to the base color.

Rich media content
Attractive and engaging images, interactive elements, video, or animations.

Rollover
A special effect that changes the appearance of an object when the mouse moves over it.

Root folder
See local site root folder.

Root-relative path
A path referenced from a website's root folder.

Rows
Table cells arranged horizontally.

Rule of Thirds
The rule of thirds is a design principle that entails dividing a page into nine squares and then placing the page elements of most interest on the intersections of the grid lines.

Rulers
On screen markers that help you precisely measure and position an object. Rulers can be displayed using the View menu.

Rules
Sets of formatting attributes that define styles in a Cascading Style Sheet.

─────────── S ───────────

Sampling
A method of changing foreground and background colors by copying existing colors from an image.

Sans serif fonts
Fonts that do not have tails or strokes at the end of characters. Fonts with block-style characters; commonly used for headings and subheadings.

Saturation
The strength or purity of the color, representing the amount of gray in proportion to hue (measured as a percentage from 0% [gray], to 100% [fully saturated]). Also known as chroma.

Scale
The size relationship of objects to one another.

Scene
A Timeline designated for a specific part of a Flash movie. Scenes are a way to organize long movies by dividing the movie into sections.

Scope creep
Making impromptu changes or additions to a project without corresponding increases in the schedule or budget.

Screen reader
A device used by the visually impaired to convert written text on a computer monitor to spoken words.

Script Assist
A feature found in the Actions panel that can be used to generate ActionScript without having to write programming code.

Seamless image
A tiled image that is blurred at the edges so that it appears to be all one image.

Search
The Adobe Help feature that allows you to enter a keyword to begin a search for a topic.

Selection
An area in an image that is surrounded by a selection marquee.

Selector
The name or the tag to which style declarations have been assigned.

Semantic markup
Coding to emphasize meaning.

Semantic web
Refers to the way web page content such as paragraph text or list items can be coded to emphasize their meaning to viewers.

Serif fonts
Ornate fonts that have a tail, or stroke, at the end of some characters. These tails lead the eye from one character to the next, making it easier to recognize words; therefore, serif fonts are generally used in text passages.

Shading
Bevel and Emboss setting that determines lighting effects.

Shadow Mode
Bevel and Emboss setting that determines how pigments are combined.

Shape hints
Indicators used to control the shape of an object as it changes appearance during an animation.

Shape tweening
The process of animating an object so that its shape changes. Shape tweening requires editable graphics.

Sharp
Anti-aliasing setting that displays type with the best possible resolution.

Sharpen More filter
Increases the contrast of adjacent pixels and can focus blurry images.

Sharpness
An element of composition that draws the viewer's eye to a specific area.

Show Code and Design views
A combination of Code view and Design view. The best view for correcting errors.

Site definition
The site definition for a website contains important information about the site, including its URL, preferences that you've specified, and other secure information, such as login and password information.

Site map
A graphical representation of how web pages relate to each other within a website.

Size
Determines the clarity of a drop shadow.

Slices
A web element that divides an image into different sections, which allows you to apply rollover behaviors, animation, and URLs to those areas.

Slider
The small indicator on the left side of the History panel that you can drag to undo or redo an action.

Smart Guides
A feature that displays vertical or horizontal guides that appear automatically when you draw a shape or move an object and are helpful in its positioning.

Smart object
An image layer that stores image data from raster or vector images.

Smooth
Anti-aliasing setting that gives type more rounded edges.

Social networking
Social networking refers to the grouping of individual web users who connect and interact with other users in online communities.

Soft return
A shortcut key combination that forces text to a new line without creating a new paragraph by creating a <BR> tag. Also called a line break.

Solid fill
The color value selected or hexadecimal value specified in the color pop-up window or in the Color Mixer.

Source
The image containing the color that will be matched.

Splash screen
A window that displays information about the software you are using.

Split cells
To divide cells into multiple cells.

Spread
Determines the width of drop shadow text.

Spring-loaded keyboard shortcuts
Shortcut keyboard combinations that temporarily change the active tool.

Spry
Open source code developed by Adobe Systems to help designers quickly incorporate dynamic content on their web pages. Also known as Spry framework.

Spry menu bar
One of the pre-set widgets available in Dreamweaver that creates a dynamic, user-friendly menu bar that is easy to insert and customize.

Stage
That area of the Flash workspace that contains the objects that are part of the movie and that will be seen by the viewers.

Standard Mode

A Dreamweaver mode that is used when you insert a table using the Insert Table button or command.

Standard toolbar

A toolbar that contains buttons you use to execute frequently used commands that are also available on the File and Edit menus.

State

Represents the button's appearance based on a mouse action. These include: Up, Over, Down, and Over While Down. In a browser, the condition of an item in a Spry menu bar in relation to the mouse pointer.

Status bar

The area located at the bottom of the program window (Win) or the image work area (Mac) that displays information such as the file size of the active window and a description of the active tool. In Dreamweaver, bar that appears at the bottom of the Dreamweaver document window. The left end of the status bar displays the tag selector, which shows the HTML tags being used at the insertion point location. The right end displays the window size and estimated download time for the page displayed.

Step

Each task performed in the History panel.

Storyboard

A small sketch that represents each page in a website or screen in an application. Like a flowchart, a storyboard shows the relationship of each page or screen to the other pages in the site or screens.

String

A series of characters or words.

Stroke

A border that you add to a selection

Stroking the edges

The process of making a selection or layer stand out by formatting it with a border.

Strong

Anti-aliasing setting that makes type appear heavier, much like the bold attribute.

Structure

A Bevel and Emboss setting that determines the size and physical properties of the object.

Style

Eighteen predesigned styles that can be applied to buttons.

Style Rendering toolbar

A toolbar that contains buttons to allow you to render a web page as different media types (e.g., handheld).

Sub layer

A layer stored a level below the main layer in Fireworks. Helps you organize the layers in a file.

Subselection tool

Lets you select and move points on a path to redefine the path in Fireworks.

Subtractive colors

A color system in which the full combination of cyan, magenta, and yellow absorb all color and produce black.

Swatches panel

Contains available colors that can be selected for use as a foreground or background color. You can also add your own colors to the Swatches panel.

Symbol

A graphic, animation, or button that represents an object, text, or combination group.

Symbol fonts

Used to display unique characters (such as ©, ® or ™).

Symmetrical balance

Page in which objects are placed equally on either side of an imaginary vertical line in the center of the page.

Synchronize files

A Dreamweaver command that compares the names, dates, and times on all files on a local and remote site, then transfers only the files that have changed since the last upload.

———————— T ————————

Tab groups

Sets of related panels that are grouped together. Also known as panel groups.

Table header

Text placed at the top or sides of a table on a web page that is read by screen readers to help provide accessibility for table content.

Tables

Grids of rows and columns that can be used either to hold tabular data on a web page or as a basic design tool for data placement.

Tabular data

Data arranged in columns and rows and separated by a delimiter.

Tag Selector

The left side of the status bar that displays HTML tags used at the insertion point location.

Tag type
A classification by type of style used to redefine an HTML tag.

Tags (HTML)
HTML tags are the parts of the code that specify the appearance for all page content when viewed in a browser.

Target (Dreamweaver)
The location on a web page that the browser displays when users click an internal link.

Target
When sampling a color, the image that will receive the matched color.

Templates
Web pages that contain the basic layout for each page in the site, including the location of a company logo, banner, or navigation links.

Terms of use
The rules that a copyright owner uses to establish use of his or her work.

Text Layout Format (TLF)
A text tool option in Flash that provides advanced text features such as flowing text, character coloring and column creation.

Thumbnail
A small version of a larger image.

Title bar
Displays the program name and filename of the open image. The title bar also contains buttons for minimizing, maximizing, and closing the image.

Tiled image
A small graphic that repeats across and down a web page, appearing as individual squares or rectangles.

Timeline
The component of Flash used to organize and control the movie's contents over time, by specifying when each object appears on the Stage.

Timeline Effect
Pre-built animation effects (such as rotating, fading, and wiping) that can be applied to objects using a dialog box.

Tolerance
The range of colors selected; how close a selection is to the source color.

Tone
The brightness and contrast within an image.

Tool groups
Tools grouped by function on the Tools panel.

Tools panel
A panel in Flash, Dreamweaver, and Fireworks separated into categories containing tools and their options.

Tracing image
An image that is placed in the background of a document as a guide to create page elements on top of it, similar to the way tracing paper is used.

Tracking
The insertion of a uniform amount of space between characters.

Trademark
Protects an image, word, slogan, symbol, or design used to identify goods or services.

Transformation point
The point used to orient an object as it is being animated. For example, a rotating object will rotate around its transformation point. Also, the point of an object that snaps to a motion guide.

Tweening
The process of filling the in-between frames in an animation.

Tweet
A short message posted on the Twitter website that is no more than 140 characters.

Twitter
A website where viewers can post short messages, called "tweets."

Type
Text, or a layer containing text. Each character is measured in points. In PostScript measurement, 1 inch is equivalent to 72 points. In traditional measurement, 1 inch is equivalent to 72.27 points.

Type spacing
Adjustments you can make to the space between characters and between lines of type.

———————— **U** ————————

Unity
In screen design, intra-screen unity has to do with how the various screen objects are related. Inter-screen unity refers to the design that viewers encounter as they navigate from one screen to another.

Unordered lists
Lists of items that do not need to be placed in a specific order and are usually preceded by bullets.

Unvisited links
Links that have not been clicked by the user. The default color for unvisited links is blue.

Up Image state
The state of a page element when the mouse pointer is not on the element.

Glossary

Upload

The process of transferring files from a local drive to a web server.

URL

Uniform Resource Locator. An address that determines a route on the Internet or to a web page.

—————— **V** ——————

Validate markup

A Dreamweaver command that searches through the HTML code to flag code that could cause errors to occur with different language versions, such as XHTML or XML.

Vector font

Fonts that are vector-based type outlines, which means that they are mathematically defined shapes.

Vector graphics

Mathematically calculated objects composed of anchor points and straight or curved line segments.

Version Cue

See Adobe Version Cue.

Vertical symmetry

A design principle in which page elements are balanced up and down the page.

View

A choice for displaying page content in the Document window. Dreamweaver has three working views: Design view, Code view, and Show Code and Design views.

Vignette

A feature in which the border of a picture or portrait fades into the surrounding color at its edges.

Vignette effect

A feature that uses feathering to fade a marquee shape.

Visited links

Links that have been previously clicked, or visited. The default color for visited links is purple.

Vodcasts

Video podcasts. Also referred to as vidcasts.

VSS

Microsoft Office Visual SafeSource. A connection type for transferring files with the Windows operating system.

—————— **W** ——————

Web 2.0

The evolution of web applications that facilitate and promote information sharing among Internet users.

Web browser

A program, such as Microsoft Internet Explorer, Apple Safari, or Google Chrome, Mozilla Firefox, that lets you display HTML-developed web pages.

Web cam

A camera used for video web conferencing.

Web design program

A program for creating interactive web pages containing text, images, hyperlinks, animation, sound, and video.

Web Dither fill

A fill that approximates the color of a non-web-safe color by combining two web-safe colors.

Web server

A computer dedicated to hosting websites that is connected to the Internet and configured with software to handle requests from browsers.

Website

A website is a group of related web pages that are linked together and share a common interface and design.

WebDav

Web-based Distributed Authoring and Versioning. A type of connection used with the WebDav protocol, such as a website residing on an Apache web server.

Web-safe colors

Colors that display consistently in all browsers and on Macintosh, Windows, and Unix platforms.

White space

An area on a web page that is not filled with text or graphics.

Widget

A widget is a piece of code that allows a user to interact with a program, such as clicking a menu item to open a page.

Wiki

Named for the Hawaiian word for "quick." Refers to a site where a user can use simple editing tools to contribute and edit the page content in a site.

Wireframe

A prototype that represents every page and its contents in a website. Like a flowchart or storyboard, a wireframe shows the relationship of each page in the site to all the other pages.

Workspace

The entire window, from the Application bar at the top of the window, to the status bar at the bottom border of the program window. The area in the Dreamweaver program window that includes all of the menus, panels, buttons, inspectors, and panes that you use to create and maintain websites.

Workspace switcher
A button you click to display a drop-down menu, located in the top right corner on the Application bar (Win) or Menu bar (Mac), that allows you to change the workspace layout.

WYSIWYG
An acronym for What You See Is What You Get, meaning that your web page should look the same in the browser as it does in the web editor.

—————— **X** ——————

XHTML
XHTML is the acronym for eXtensible HyperText Markup Language, the current standard language used to create web pages.

XML
XML stands for Extensible Markup Language, a type of file that is used to develop customized tags to store information.

XSL
Extensible Stylesheet Language. Similar to CSS; the XSL style sheet information formats containers created with XML.

XSLT
Extensible Stylesheet Language Transformations. XSLT interprets the code in the XSL file to transform an XML document, much like style sheet files transform HTML files

—————— **Y** ——————

YouTube
A website where you can upload and share videos.

INDEX

Note: Page numbers preceded by DW refer to Dreamweaver chapters; those preceded by FW refer to Fireworks chapters; those preceded by FL refer to Flash chapters; those preceded by INTEGRATION refer to the Integration chapter.

resizing
columns in tables, DW 6-28
graphics, DW 4-12 – 13
objects. *See* resizing objects
panels, FL 1-7
Stage, FL 1-8
table elements, DW 6-26 – 27
text, FL 4-47
Timeline, FL 1-8, FL 2-47
resizing objects, FL 1-26 – 27
drawn objects, FL 2-24, FL 2-27
tween animations, FL 4-11
resolution, FW 1-15
images, FW 3-4
screen, FW 3-5
Rewind command, FL 1-13
rich media content, DW 1-12 – 13, FL 1-39
roll over action, assigning to buttons, FL 5-19, FL 5-23
roll over event, mouse button, FL 3-24
rollover(s), DW 2-25
root folder, DW 1-20
root-relative paths, DW 5-5
Rotate and Skew option, Free Transform tool, FL 2-24 – 25, FL 2-28
rotating
drawn objects, FL 2-24 – 25, FL 2-28
objects in tween animations, FL 4-16
text, FL 4-46
rows, tables. *See* table rows
RSS (Real Simple Syndication), DW 5-34

RSS feeds, DW 5-34
rule(s), CSS. *See* CSS rule(s)
rule of thirds, DW 2-32
rulers, DW 6-34, FW 1-18
runtime feature, Inverse Kinematics, FL 5-28, FL 5-33

sans-serif fonts, DW 3-13
Save Selection dialog box, FW 3-19
saving
documents, FW 1-10
image files in assets folders, DW 1-31, DW 2-14
selections, FW 3-19
Scale option, FL 2-24
Free Transform tool, FL 2-27
scenes, animated navigation bars, FL 5-19
screen design guidelines, FL 1-42 – 43
screen resolution, FW 3-5
screen sizes, testing web pages, DW 2-31 – 32
Script pane, Actions panel, FL 3-25
Search text box, DW 1-13
Secure FTP (SFTP), DW 7-15
Select File dialog box, DW 2-21
Select Inverse command, FW 3-17
Select menu commands, FW 3-17
selecting
areas based on color, FW 3-22 – 25
frames, animating text, FL 4-44
objects, FL 2-18 – 21
pixels using Lasso tool, FW 3-16, FW 3-18

pixels using Magic Wand tool, FW 3-24, FW 3-25
Polygon Lasso tool, FW 3-19
text, FW 1-27
selection(s)
adding and subtracting pixels, FW 3-16
copied, transforming, FW 3-21
saving, FW 3-19
transforming, FW 3-20
Selection tool, FL 2-4, FL 2-5, FL 2-18, FL 2-20 – 21
reshaping objects, FL 2-29
selection tool(s), FW 3-10 – 15
Marquee tools, FW 3-10 – 14
resampling, FW 3-15
Transformation tools, FW 3-11, FW 3-14 – 15
selector, CSS rules, DW 3-11
semantic web, DW 3-6
serif fonts, DW 3-13
server(s), web. *See* web servers
setting up websites, DW 1-20, DW 1-24
SFTP (Secure FTP), DW 7-15
shape(s), FW 1-18 – 23
Auto Shapes, FW 1-19 – 20
creating vector objects, FW 1-21 – 22
fills, FW 1-20
positioning, FW 1-18
sizing, FW 1-18
strokes, FW 1-20, FW 1-23
Tools panel, FW 1-18 – 19

WEB COLLECTION STANDARD CHAPTER OPENER ART CREDITS	
Chapter	**Art credit for opening pages**
Dreamweaver	
Chapter 1	© Davthy | Dreamstime.com
	© Michael Zysman | Dreamstime.com
Chapter 2	© Dsmith123 | Dreamstime.com
	© worldswildlifewonders | Shutterstock Images
Chapter 3	© Metropoway893 | Dreamstime.com
	© Susinder | Dreamstime.com
Chapter 4	© Jay Bo | Shutterstock Images
	© 123RF LIMITED | Kitch Bain
Chapter 5	© Naluphoto | Dreamstime.com
	© Aaron Bunker | Shutterstock Images
Chapter 6	© Nilanjan Bhattacharya | Dreamstime.com
	© Clearviewstock | Dreamstime.com
Chapter 7	© Melvinlee | Dreamstime.com
	© Zozogo | Dreamstime.com
Flash	
Chapter 1	© Neal Cooper | Dreamstime.com
	© iStockphoto.com/ETIEN
Chapter 2	© Bruce Turner | Dreamstime.com
	© 123RF LIMITED\cbpix
Chapter 3	© Richard Carey | Dreamstime.com
	© iStockphoto.com/Alex Bramwell
Chapter 4	© Chris Lorenz | Dreamstime.com
	© Vladimir Sazonov | Shutterstock Images
Chapter 5	© Gkuna | Dreamstime.com
	© Tony Emmett | Shutterstock Images

ART CREDITS

(CONTINUED)

Chapter	Art credit for opening pages
Fireworks	
Chapter 1	© iStockphoto.com/Nico Smit Photography © iStockphoto.com/Freder
Chapter 2	© Jemini Joseph | Dreamstime.com © Janice Mccafferty | Dreamstime.com
Chapter 3	© Christian Bech | Dreamstime.com © iStockphoto.com/ThaiEagle
Integration	
Chapter 1	© Jay Bo | Shutterstock Images © 123RF LIMITED | Kitch Bain
Data Files/Glossary/Index	© Morten Elm | Dreamstime.com © Michael Zysman | Dreamstime.com